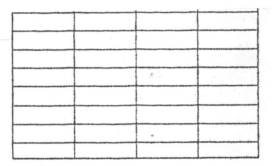

This book belongs to:

The Frances Kovacic Non-Fiction Collection
In Celebration of her Eighty-Fifth Birthday
May 27, 1996
Donated By: Robert & Carol Powers

LACKAWANNA COUNTY
LIBRARY SYSTEM
PENNSYLVANIA

DEMCO

LINCOLN'S UNKNOWN PRIVATE LIFE

LINCOLN'S UNKNOWN PRIVATE LIFE

AN ORAL HISTORY
BY HIS BLACK HOUSEKEEPER
MARIAH VANCE
1850–1860

Edited by Lloyd Ostendorf
and Walter Oleksy

Hastings House Book Publishing
Mamaroneck, New York

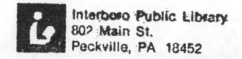

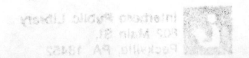

Dedication

This book is dedicated to the memory of Miss Adah Lilas Sutton, who from 1900–1904 recorded in shorthand the fascinating accounts of Abraham and Mary Todd Lincoln as told to her by Mariah Vance, who had been employed by the Lincolns from 1850 to 1860.

Miss Sutton's years of care and devotion in transcribing her shorthand notes into handwritten manuscript will be self-evident. It is preserved for history in this volume. Mariah Vance, who became her respected friend, ardently detailed her keen knowledge and observations of the Lincoln family.

Snapshot of the remarkable Adah Sutton taken by Lloyd Ostendorf in December 1956 after she had started working on the manuscript. She was 72.

ACKNOWLEDGMENTS

Thanks to all the helpful people mentioned in this acknowledgment and thanks to co-editor Walter Oleksy for all his faithful work on the book.

Heartfelt gratitude is due to my late friend, Adah Sutton, whose dedication to writing the original manuscript was a labor of love, and regretfully, she never lived to see it published.

Our thanks to historians of yesteryear for encouraging Miss Sutton to get her reminiscences of Mariah Vance published. Dr. John Wesley Hill, Chancellor of Lincoln Memorial University in 1931 expressed his keen interest in a letter. In 1937 or 1938 our late friend, Dr. Louis A. Warren, former director of the Lincoln National Life Foundation at Fort Wayne, IN, praised Adah Sutton's work for possible publication.

Among many contemporary Lincoln historians who offered assistance in the book project are Dr. Wayne C. Temple of Springfield, Dr. Wallace R. Best of California, R. Bruce Duncan of Chicago, Dr. James T. Hickey of Elkhart, IL. Dr. Joseph E. Suppiger, former Editor of the *Lincoln Herald*, Cumberland Gap, TN. Help was received by other interested professionals, Bill Satterwhite of the Danville Public Library, and Susan E Richner, Curator of the Vermillion County Museum at Danville.

Helpful references were received from members of the Church of the Brethren whose histories reveal some church connections with Abraham Lincoln. Rosalita J. Leonard of Elgin, IL, the Rev. Calvin Bright, and Don Bowman of Dayton, OH, and Karen Fildrun of Lewisburg, OH.

Generous support through the years was received from Iris Sutton, Adah Sutton's niece of Attica, IN. Miss Adah Sutton's friend during her last years, Lois Johnson of Attica, provided important information. Worth repeating is our gratitude to publisher, Hy Steirman, and his Hastings House staff.

For her endless patience and avid interest I am grateful to my wife, Rita, and my family and friends for their enthusiasm in seeing this unique Lincoln book coming to life.

—LLOYD OSTENDORF

ACKNOW-
LEDGMENTS

With thanks for their considerable help and/or encouragement to Dr. Mary Schneider, Anthony Lamberis, Stephen Delanty, John Thomas Trutter, Jerry Warshaw, Alec Rothrock, Francis O. Krupka, Dr. Wayne C. Temple, the Evanston and Wilmette (IL) Public Libraries, Ken Burns, Dr. James C. Davies of the University of Oregon, Dr. James Shenton of Columbia University, Dr. Robert M. Sutton of the University of Illinois, Dr. William Rock of Bowling Green State University, Dr. Mark Neeley Jr. of St. Louis University, Dr. Henry Louis Gates Jr. of Harvard University, Dr. John Y. Simon of Southern Illinois University, Thomas Schwartz of the Illinois Historic Preservation Agency, Kenan Heise of Chicago Historical Bookworks, Kevin Cullen of the *Lafayette* (IN) *Journal & Courier*, Doug Pokorski of the *Springfield* (IL) *State Journal Register*, Rod Harmon of the *Danville* (IL) *Commercial-News*, Marilyn Claessens of the *Evanston* (IL) *Review*, Sidney Zwick of the *Evanston* (IL) *Beacon-Forum*, Stephen Anderson of the *Illinois State Bar News*, Jack E. Horsley, John Long, Brenda Verner, Charlotte Herman, Joey Walsh, Thomas Jacobs, Rev. William D. Mannion, Rev. Donald Skiba, Deacon Richard S. Jay, the DuSable Museum of African-American History, Richard Wentworth of the University of Illinois Press, Martin Gordon, Clyde Taylor, Julian Bach, Owen Laster, David Black, Roger Scholl, Molly Friedrich, Liza Dawson, and especially to Lloyd and Rita Ostendorf, Phillip Wagner, our publisher Hy Steirman of Hastings House, my family, friends, and Max Oleksy.

—WALTER OLEKSY

The publisher wishes to thank the following for their contributions or assistance in producing this publication: Renee Roff, Harriet and Linda Ripinsky, Tom Tafuri, Beryl Robare, John Jusimo, Arthur Neuhauser, C. Linda Dingler, the Library of Congress, the Mt. Vernon Library, Byron Roff of the Scarsdale Library, The Mamaroneck Library, Albert Jerman, Historian of Robert Lincoln's Historic Home "Hildene," Millie Valentin of Staples, the American Medical Association, and the American Diabetic Association.

—HASTINGS HOUSE

CONTENTS

VOLUME ONE

Publisher's Letter 11

Foreword by Lloyd Ostendorf 15

Preface by Adah Lilas Sutton 23

Introduction: Mariah Vance and the Lincolns of Springfield
by Walter Oleksy 33

Critics and Their Comments 51

CHAPTER ONE   Mariah Meets the Lincolns 67

CHAPTER TWO   Getting Acquainted with de Missy 75

CHAPTER THREE   Mistah Abe "Cures" Billie's Lice 87

CHAPTER FOUR   De Missy Gets Confidential with Mariah 95

CHAPTER FIVE   Robert and Billie Go Fishing 107

CHAPTER SIX   A New Tantrum 115

CHAPTER SEVEN   "De Missy Pile Up the Hurts" 125

CHAPTER EIGHT   All's Well That Ends Well 133

CHAPTER NINE   The Talk of the Town 145

CHAPTER TEN   Of God and Fortune-Tellers 155

CHAPTER ELEVEN   Where There's a Will 163

CHAPTER TWELVE   Thunder at the Lincolns' 173

CHAPTER THIRTEEN   Lincoln's First Tiff with Douglas 185

CHAPTER FOURTEEN   Old Times Are Not Forgotten 197

CHAPTER FIFTEEN   The Circus Comes to Town 211

CHAPTER SIXTEEN   Pretty as a Picture 221

CHAPTER SEVETEEN   A House Divided 229

CHAPTER EIGHTEEN   Right from Wrong 239

CHAPTER NINETEEN   The Road to the Presidency   247

CHAPTER TWENTY   Mistah Abe Comes to Billie's Defense   259

CHAPTER TWENTY-ONE   Mistah Abe's Secret Baptism at Night   263

CHAPTER TWENTY-TWO   The Ann Rutledge Likeness   275

CHAPTER TWENTY-THREE The Last Time Aunt Mariah Saw Mistah Abe   283

AFTERWORD   The Way it Was—by Walter Oleksy   289

A section of photographs appears after page 304

VOLUME TWO

Facsimile Edition of Adah Sutton's Complete Handwritten Manuscript,
Transcribed from the Words of Mariah Vance

PUBLISHER'S LETTER

"That man was a man of Gawd and he was crucified every day of his life," said Mariah Vance of Abraham Lincoln.

Who was Mariah Vance and why would she make such a statement?

The fact is, Mariah Vance, a Black domestic, worked in Abraham Lincoln's Springfield, Illinois, home as laundress, maid, and housekeeper for ten years, from 1850 until 1860. She was witness to the Lincoln home life as no other person outside of the family, and her oral history reveals for the first time their often volatile private lives.

Lincoln's public life is well-documented. Until now, what little we knew of Lincoln's private life in Springfield came from Lincoln's law partner, William Herndon, who made speeches about Lincoln and wrote a biography of the President after he was assassinated. The book was strongly attacked, though Carl Sandburg relied on it as a source for his own acclaimed 1926 biography, *Abraham Lincoln, The Prairie Years*.

The question is, why wasn't Mariah Vance interviewed by journalists and historians in the years after Lincoln's death? The answer is she was Black, and Blacks were not highly regarded at the time, especially as credible witnesses to history.

In *Lincoln's Unknown Private Life,* Mariah Vance reveals many fascinating stories of incidents in the Lincoln household, among them: Mary Todd Lincoln's attack of her husband with a knife and her rages and mood swings; Abraham's spanking of his wife, Abe and Mary's prior loves, Abe's defense of Mariah's son Billie after he was arrested for disturbing the peace, and the Lincoln children's mischievous behavior and pranks.

According to the Library of Congress, 5,076 books have been written about Lincoln, yet none have been able to answer the two great controversies surrounding his life: a) whether or not Lincoln was engaged to Ann

Rutledge, and b) whether Lincoln was baptized before taking the oath as President. Mariah answers both questions.

Mariah Vance was remarkable in her own right: hardworking; extremely loyal to the Lincolns; a good wife and mother; a God-fearing, deeply devout Christian who knew her Bible thoroughly despite the fact she was barely literate; she was a wise woman who founded the Zion Baptist Church in Springfield, Illinois, in 1838. During the dark days of slavery she married Henry Vance, a runaway slave, and they lived in constant threat of his being captured and returned to the slaveholder. She ultimately bore him twelve children.

For forty years, after she last saw Abraham Lincoln in 1860, Mariah told her oft-repeated Lincoln stories to friends, family and others. No one wrote them down. In 1900, Adah Sutton, a seventeen-year-old year old White girl, not only listened but wrote down in shorthand, Mariah Vance's recollections verbatim. The "jottings" continued for four years, until Mariah's death in 1904.

Because of Adah Sutton's job and the personal burden of caring for a sick mother, she was obliged to put away her precious notes. How the project went from shorthand notes to manuscript to a published book took ninety years, and its 1995 publication is due to the determined efforts of three remarkable people: Adah Sutton, the young office worker and later antique dealer with a dedicated sense of history; Lloyd Ostendorf, a Lincoln artist and Lincoln expert who is one of the world's foremost collectors of Lincoln photos and images, who encouraged Adah to translate her shorthand into a manuscript; and Walter Oleksy, the author/journalist who prepared it for publication and persevered until it was published.

In 1993 William Morrow and Company offered $1 million for the publication rights for this book. However, comments (many not valid) from several Lincoln "experts" threw cold water on the deal and the publisher withdrew its offer. The rejection of the manuscript received world-wide attention. One of the experts said, "The book is too good to be true." If that is so, maybe it's too good *not* to be true. Another so-called expert who dismissed the manuscript altogether later admitted he hadn't read it.

The authenticity of the book is not in question. The experts who applaud it or question it, in fact, never studied the original manuscript; they read a typewritten copy or an interpretation of it. For historical integrity, Hastings House is producing a unique book of two separate volumes:

1) A facsimile edition of Adah Sutton's complete handwritten manuscript, just as Mariah Vance told it to her.

2) For easier reading, a printed version of Adah Sutton's manuscript of the words of Mariah Vance, prepared with editorial comments by co-editor Walter Oleksy, a former award-winning feature writer with the *Chicago Tribune* and author of over forty books.

This format was chosen because Mariah spoke a language called Black English, (also called Negro or Non-Standard English or Merican) and Adah transcribed Mariah's stories exactly as she heard them. Black English would make it difficult for non–African Americans to understand. (*One expert foolishly commented that the speech sounded like a minstrel show.*) The presentation of the interpolated edition and the facsimile edition will allow the reader to make his or her own interpretations and judgments.

Black English, the title of one of the best books on the subject, was written by Professor J. L. Dillard, now teaching at Northwestern State University in Louisiana (published in 1972 by Random House, currently a Vintage paperback). He wrote, "Black English, the language of about eighty percent of Americans of African ancestry, differs from other varieties of American English." He points out that though speech patterns of words and phrases are not consistent, it is not a "deficient language" as some educators would have you believe, but a separate language. *Newsweek* magazine, applauding the book, reported, "Black English is not a sloppy imitation of White English. . . .. but a precise language with a history and grammar of its own."

For centuries, West African speech patterns were gradually absorbed into mainstream American speech creating "Black English." In March 1995, in a segment called "Language Factor," *60 Minutes* focused on a growing number of U.S. high schools that arc tcaching "English as a second language" to African-Americans, their "first" language and grammar being the one brought to North America by slaves and handed down from generation to generation.

After 135 years, the long-submerged, private home life of Abraham and Mary Todd Lincoln, as seen through the eyes of Mariah Vance, a Black woman, and recorded in Black English, is now available to everyone to read and enjoy.

HY STEIRMAN
Publisher
Hastings House
April 1995

FOREWORD

by Lloyd Ostendorf

I MET ADAH SUTTON IN 1955 BECAUSE OF AN AD I PLACED IN *HOBBIES* MAGAZINE seeking authentic Abraham Lincoln and Civil War photographs. She had some, and our years of correspondence began.

Adah owned a small antique shop and wrote me about some Lincoln family photographs that she wanted authenticated, and offered to sell me those that I wanted for my collection. The photos were authentic and I purchased some of them.

Her chatty and cheerful letters continued, and they told me of her association with Mariah Vance, a Black woman who had worked from 1850 to 1860 as a laundress, maid, and then housekeeper for the Lincolns in Springfield, Illinois.

Later, when I visited Miss Sutton in Attica, Indiana, she told me Lincoln family stories that I had never read or heard before—some were humorous and some tragic. Adah Sutton then admitted that she was so fascinated that she took shorthand notes of Mariah's stories and anecdotes of the Lincoln home life.

Though I earn my living as an artist, I've been a "Lincoln addict" all my life; I own a large collection of Lincoln family photographs and memorabilia as well as a library of books about Lincoln that grew faster than I could read them. I was spellbound by Mariah's stories that Adah repeated to me and learned that she still had her shorthand notes.

As an artist and Lincoln historian, I would enjoy illustrating some of these wonderful anecdotes. More importantly, this was invaluable information that must not be allowed to disappear. I pleaded with her to translate her shorthand notes.

Miss Sutton was a spinster who earned her living from her antique shop to support herself. She was not a wealthy woman. In fact, she lived on the poor side of the tracks in Attica, 202 West Monroe Street, in an old tar-papered, medium-size Victorian house, common to the lower middle-class. Nevertheless, she agreed to take on the enormous task of her notes and to try to have them published. She would prepare a handwritten manuscript that I would type up and illustrate to enhance the story. She was as good as her word. Every few weeks or months (unless she was ill or away from home), a chapter arrived in the mail. The book correspondence spanned more than five years.

Miss Sutton retained a lifelong acquaintance with the Vance family. I encouraged her to visit her old friends to see if she could acquire any family artifacts or photographs from Mrs. Vance's descendants for use as possible photo illustrations for the book.

The urging paid off. Tintype photos and other keepsakes of the Vance and Lincoln families were given to Miss Sutton. Mariah's relatives were delighted to cooperate with Miss Sutton's venture.

For the record, Mariah Vance told her stories to Adah Sutton between 1900 and 1904. Miss Sutton proudly proclaimed to me on several occasions that she made it a rule to stick verbatim to what Mariah told her. She neither added nor deleted anything despite some words she could not understand. Her letters were usually signed "Ada," but occasionally she used her more formal name, "Adah."

I have always felt that embellishing Mariah Vance's reminiscences was not in Adah Sutton's nature. She wrote me in 1958 that she sometimes found mistakes in dates or other details in Mariah Vance stories, saying: "She got historicals mixed sometimes. I have tried very hard to straighten these errors. But as a whole, I've found very few, which to me, has made her a more remarkable person than when I first started this book."

Later, in another letter, she wrote:

> To me, this writing has been the peak of what has tried my soul. Many times I've been tempted to give up. The introduction is going to be hard for me.
>
> I feel it is so very important. It must prove how I finally came to listen to them [*Mariah's stories*]. The truth of the stories, from my point of view and viewpoint of others. They

must not be taken as fables. Or from any angle must they be doubted by real scholars. If I thought they would be, I could not face myself to go any further, regardless of financial returns.

The only reward I've had so far, outside of the fact I gave a listening ear to this poor soul, is the renewing in my mind my picturesque visits with her and the many laughs I have had.

She truly earned the title and affection given to her, "Aunt Mariah." And she proved she appreciated this title, by the love she cherished for them, by retaining in her mind each epic which, at her extreme age, left an indelible impression. Copies of which I trust will leave an indelible imprint on the mind of posterity, of proof of the truth about the Lincolns.

Adah wrote me in another letter: "I have stuff in here [*the reminiscences*] that isn't anywhere else. I could have put things in that I knew from reading about Lincoln and filled in or tied in with what Mariah told me. I'm not trying to tell what is already known. I may not have much, but I have my self respect."

She liked to collect postcards of famous and beautiful homes and wrote me in 1958 that she had asked a friend, who traveled a lot, to send her more for her collection:

"That's a little cheap hobby I've had for years. If I can't have a beautiful home, I can enjoy postal cards of homes of the highest of our nation. I came from a family of builders, so I guess my love for beautiful residences is a part of me."

With her interest in history, Adah Sutton earned a modest living selling antiques. In times of need, she sold some of her Lincoln photos and relics which she had purchased from Mariah Vance. I liked this woman. I found her to be honest, of high integrity and as good a woman as anyone would hope to meet.

It is significant that much of what Mariah Vance tells in her reminiscences of the Lincolns has been verified by historic documents. Of course, Mariah's memory was not infallible, and it is bracketed in italics where she got some dates and minor bits of information wrong. When assembling and recording Mariah's stories, Adah Sutton wrote me in 1955, "Someway down in my heart I can't believe Mariah Vance would deliberately lie."

Realizing that the Lincoln baptism story would likely be one of the most controversial elements in Mariah's reminiscences, Adah wrote me:

> I questioned at one time the wisdom of including it in my book. Perhaps it would be thoroughly convincing if I wrote it just as Mariah told it [*in her heavy Negro dialect*], especially since there were 2 other published accounts of the baptism.
>
> Mariah always said "babsized," but I changed that [*for clarity*] in that part of the dialogue. She also said "de" for "the" and "dat" for "that".
>
> I am profoundly grateful to you for your wise collaboration. When you finish with your typed copy, it does not sound like a literary masterpiece. It can't be that and be true. You please me so much better than an English teacher I had doing this work, for I was so disappointed, I simply decided to shelve the whole thing.

Another time, she wrote me: "I still could write the two other stories I sent you, using her [*Mariah's*] exact words, if you wish." I encouraged her to do this for all the Mariah Vance material and, to the best of my knowledge, she followed my advice, quoting Mariah from the handwritten manuscript. At times, when Adah Sutton came across her shorthand notes that were faded or hard to read, she might rewrite that chapter one or more times. For historical accuracy all rewrites are included in the manuscript in this book.

In 1957 she wrote me:

> Mr. and Mrs. Lincoln's voices were so different. His high pitched and hers soft, musical and cultural. However, both spoke with a Southern pronunciation. [*Mrs. Lincoln spoke with a Kentucky twang that wasn't too far from some Negro dialects.*] I wouldn't even try to distinguish the difference between colored dialect and Southern brogue. They are so much alike. So in writing my notes I followed sounds, then I interpreted meanings.

Historians over the years have suggested that, though opposite in many ways, the Lincolns managed to have a happy home life. Mariah Vance's stories reveal otherwise; what she witnessed and overheard reveal a sometimes troubled domestic condition. In addition, Mariah provides many clues to indicate the reasons for Mary's emotional instability.

However, there also was love in the Lincoln home, demonstrated by both Mr. and Mrs. Lincoln, and Mariah reveals that Mr. Lincoln sometimes openly showed his affection for Mary.

An incident I remember reading from Adah Sutton's writings that particularly stuck in my mind amid all the feuding in the Lincoln home was especially pleasing. Quoting Mariah from the handwritten manuscript: "Ah cain't zackly remember de year it war when Ah saw them carrin' on and talkin' one day when Mistah Abe war home. Yes, he war carrin' de Missy 'round de house, an dat war a sight, for a change. Just like her'n war a little girl! An dat pleasured de Missy, Ah could tell."

Mariah Vance also tells of Mary's temper tantrums and anger. Perhaps she can be forgiven for this side of her nature since she unknowingly took paregoric medication to calm her nerves. Neither she nor her doctors knew, at the time, the awful side effects of what she prescribed for herself. It occasionally caused her to lose control, and Lincoln had his own way of dealing with her. To her credit, she later regretted her outbursts and tried to make amends.

Without question, some errors in interpretation occurred between the time these events took place and the time they were finally brought to light in this book. But the sincerity expressed by Adah Sutton on Mariah's testimony which she meticulously recorded and then carefully transcribed and passed on to me, is as honest a human endeavor as possible under the circumstances. No other parties are involved.

With our mutual interest in Lincoln, Adah Sutton and I felt strongly that, historically, these stories were worth telling. Our trust in each other's integrity was expressed in numerous letters and post cards sent and received from the mid-1950's until the 1970's. This correspondence stacks several inches high, and quotes from some of her more important letters are included in this book.

Adah Sutton had kept all her shorthand notes so she could tell her family and friends the interesting stories. But while writing the manuscript she discovered some pages were too faded to read and was obliged to leave them out.

It was only in her mature years that Miss Sutton considered writing a book from her notes, which is why she finally agreed to the painstaking task of writing the Lincoln episodes in longhand. I agreed to collaborate on the book by contributing the artwork. At first I typed early chapters of the manuscript, then Adah Sutton's niece, Iris Sutton, completed it. The hope now was to get the material published.

This, unfortunately, never happened during Adah's lifetime. Her health failed in her later years. She fell and broke her hip and was confined to a hospital, then to a nursing home.

I am indebted to her friend and caretaker, Mrs. Lois Johnson, for some final facts about Adah's notes. Mrs. Johnson was awarded power of attorney for Adah Sutton, paid all her bills, and made regular visits to her in her last days. She told me she had to sell Miss Sutton's home and help clean out the house for the new owners.

Mrs. Johnson wrote me on July 5, 1993: "Adah entered Covington Nursing Home September, 1975 after breaking a hip. I sold her property October 1, 1975. Also the little [few] contents. Am told there were letters, papers, pictures, etc. in a cabinet. Sorry to say they all got thrown away!"

I was upset that the surviving letters, notes, and whatever were cleared out and thrown away as worthless.

For a number of years, I made attempts to get the manuscript published, but it seemed that the climate was not yet right for a publisher to take on a Black American's reminiscences, especially one written in a heavy Negro dialect.

In her later years, Adah Sutton let it be known in her letters that if our book could not be published in her lifetime, the original manuscript was to go to her niece, Iris Sutton, who had helped her through the years.

In 1976, at the age of ninety-two, Adah passed away peacefully. I was determined to keep faith with her and the book project and continued to work toward getting her manuscript in print. I kept in touch with Iris Sutton, who made her aunt's original manuscript available to me in the hope that we would still find a publisher.

After seeing the number of publisher rejection slips accumulate, Iris expressed her opinion that there was little hope of getting the book published. With more than twenty years of effort and faith in the project, I refused to be dissuaded, and Iris agreed to sell the manuscript to me.

My faith in this historic document didn't waver and I kept at it. In 1977 I was encouraged by a Hollywood script writer who had some success with TV productions and claimed he could find a publisher for the manuscript. I agreed to let him try. To my chagrin he added some fiction, which discredited the manuscript. My hopes were dashed over the next ten years when he failed to interest a publisher. His efforts resulted only in more rejection slips. I discontinued our unproductive relationship.

After several more years, I enlisted the aid of my friend Phillip Wagner in Springfield, Illinois, to help me find the right person to produce a more accurate manuscript by going back to the original handwritten document. The new version—the one in this book—is the work of Walter Oleksy, an established author and a former feature writer with the *Chicago Tribune*. Oleksy, with great scholarship, studiously maintained the integrity of Adah Sutton's original manuscript and added editorial notes to clarify the Negro dialect in which Mariah Vance told her stories to Miss Sutton. He also added factual background information on people, places, and events before each chapter. This enables readers to have a better understanding of the Lincolns and their times.

Walter Oleksy's Afterword also helps clarify the reminiscences of Mariah Vance, putting into proper historical context the personal lives of the Lincolns and events that occurred during Lincoln's bachelor years in New Salem and married years in Springfield.

While these reminiscences may not be called "The Gospel of the Lincolns according to Mariah Vance," we feel they qualify as personal testimonials worthy of unbiased consideration. They deserve the same open-minded acceptance as other firsthand accounts of Lincoln that were written by his associates.

After decades of determination, Mariah Vance's stories of the Lincolns are at long last being published. Our thanks go to Hy Steirman, publisher of Hastings House, who not only read and accepted the manuscript as authentic, but made the decision that eluded all the other publishers: to publish the two volumes under one cover; the transliterated book for easier reading and the reproduction of Adah Sutton's original manuscript in her own handwriting to verify authenticity.

We enthusiastically present Mariah Vance's reminiscences for your historical consideration and enjoyment. We have attempted to report all that we have found and believe in, and ask you, the reader, to do as we have done—draw your own conclusions.

LLOYD OSTENDORF
Dayton, Ohio
March 18, 1995

PREFACE

by Adah Lilas Sutton,
Recorder of the Mariah Vance Reminiscences,
from 1900 to 1904

NO DOUBT THE READERS OF THIS BOOK WILL WONDER, WITHOUT THIS explanation, how I came into possession of these facts. Why they were never retold in a period of over fifty years. Especially since some of them are quite revealing and enlightening. I am making every effort to conscientiously repeat word-for-word the stories as told to me by [*Mariah Vance*] this highly respected and greatly loved colored servant of the Lincolns.

She served in their home at intervals from 1850 until 1858 and continuously from then until after Abraham Lincoln was elected the sixteenth president of the United States.

The greatest task in the retelling of these facts has been to change Mrs. Vance's Negro dialect into Mr. Lincoln's own words, where and when he converses. A. Lincoln's character of words is not easy to come by. He was truly an individual. His words were expressions of beauty and symmetry. They flowed freely from a truthful, pure heart and mind. I feel sure I've caught and expressed his exact meaning from her strange wording, though it has been a staggering task. To leave all these accounts in her [*Negro*] dialect would have become monotonous to the reader. I can only trust that the reader will enjoy and appreciate her stories as I did. Outside of the joy I witnessed, it gave this lovely Christian colored woman, as she again lived and cherished the life as a servant in the Lincoln home, I laughed with her and sometimes cried, I'm not ashamed to admit.

I feel duty-bound to go back to the turn of this century and will relate each step from there, so you will not fail to understand the whys and where-fores, the final garlanding and ultimate compiling of these stories in manu-script form.

I was just out of the Attica, Indiana, high school, a period in each young life, if not carefully planned beforehand, in which teenagers are at sea as to how to employ their time. In July of that year [*1899*] my brother-in-law turned over his interests in the LeClaire Brick and Tile Plant to his father and brothers. He wanted to embark in a new venture, the manufacture of concrete blocks.

As Danville, Illinois, a highly industrial city, seemed to him the right location in which to start, he moved his family (my sister and their baby daughter) there. At the last minute, I was asked to go with them, to stay until my sister became adjusted to her new home and surroundings. I was quite happy over their decision to include me.

Through church and social contacts, it wasn't difficult to meet and become acquainted. Nor in this city was it difficult to find employment. I sought and found employment as a bookkeeper and cashier in a shoe store.

As fall days shortened and it became quite dark at closing time, we realized it wasn't too safe to walk unescorted from the car line stop to their suburban home. My sister thought I should give up my work. I was reluctant to do so, as earning a salary was a new and entirely welcome experience. So the only sensible thing to do was to get a room close to my work.

About that time, the daughter of the apartment owner, where we were living, married. She offered me a room in her new home on the North Vermillion car line. This was not far from the business district. I was happy to accept. It meant not only being with someone I knew, but very pleasantly located. This, too, with being offered a much better position, opened a new era of life for me.

I liked this complete change as my new responsibilities made me feel quite grown up and no longer dependent on others. I could now return to Attica on weekends (via Wabash Railroad), visit with home folks, then return to Danville for Sunday church assignments.

However, the advent of winter weather finally made the trip home dif-ficult and sometimes a real hardship. Curtailing these visits home not only meant I would have to control my homesickness, but finding someone to do my laundry, for with only one sleeping room, such work as I did for myself when at home would be prohibitive.

I shopped around from one unsatisfactory wash woman to another. As spring came, I was told of a little colored woman (Mariah Vance) and her daughter Julia who did such very nice laundry. Finding the address of these two was such a short walking distance from my address, I hastened over to interview them.

On entering their home, the view of the interior was so neat and clean, one could only conclude their work would be satisfactory. The elderly lady who admitted me very graciously apologized for having to make me wait, as she had to finish waiting on her daughter who was, as she said, "ah littah undah dah weathah."

When she returned to the room, I told her of my experiences trying to find a good laundress. I can see her yet, standing there looking straight at me, with hands on waist, crossed in front, saying, "Well, honey chile, ef ah wah good 'nough fah dah Missy Lincolumn, ah shuh and be good 'nough fah mose anysone. Dat woman wah shuh ticklah [*particular*]."

I'll admit this "Missy Lincolumn" didn't register with me. However, as their work had been highly praised, I left my bundle wash, as it was called, with her. I returned every two weeks thereafter and never failed to compliment her on her splendid work. Often she repeated, "Ah wah mose good 'nough fah anyone, if good 'nough for Missy Lincolumn."

The first time I saw Julia [*then about fifty years old*], she came out in the yard where "Aunt Mariah" (as she chose to be called) and I stood talking. Julia looked very frail and ill. However, there was something in her bearing that emphasized her good breeding.

With a gentle, kind voice, she called a very beautiful, light colored young lady who was skipping rope on the sidewalk. This child was Julia's granddaughter, visiting from Crawfordsville, Indiana. She promptly came running and singing with a clear, rich quality, unusual today even in highly trained voices.

Her name was Eva Johnson (who later married Gene Jackson), an accomplished harpist on the Lyceum Circuit. This fact was verified by programs still in existence and by the Poston and Barnhill families from Crawfordsville, now living here. They stated that Gene Jackson also was a musician [*he played the cornet and violin*]. Eva and Gene (after moving to Danville) entertained for weddings, receptions, etc. [*In 1924, Eva Jackson accompanied Marian Anderson on the harp when the famous singer toured in concerts.*]

Aunt Mariah continued to talk about the Lincolumns. I lent, at first, almost a deaf ear, for it gave her great pleasure, I could see, to relate incidents in her early experiences. Finally I questioned her about these Lincolumns.

She seemed greatly surprised to learn that I didn't know anything about these Lincolumns, saying, "Ah's bewilderah'd ovah yoah all's nevah befoah heah howdly ah soul what wonduhs 'bout Abe Lincolumn or dah Missy. Dahlin', did'n yoah all evah know'd Mistah Abe wah da sixteenth president ob dah United States? But ah's oldah dan yoah all, an ah's don' speak good white folks' talk. 'Spose yoah did'n undastan. Ah loves ta tell ob mah life wid dah gran good folks ah work fah, when ah wah young, mah kinfolks wah sick an tied ob dees Lincolumns' hapnins."

From [*then*] on, I lent a listening ear. Even looked forward to her stories. Particularly the amusing ones. Then became quite interested in events historical, tying them with incidents my father had related. He met Abraham Lincoln at one time during his service in the Civil War.

My mother also told of riding in a spring wagon from Oxford, Indiana, to Lafayette, with a crowd who stood along the railroad track waiting for hours for the arrival of the Lincoln funeral train. She remembered every detail so vividly, for she was then only fifteen years old.

Finally becoming so deeply interested in Mrs. Vance's stories, I thought it would be nice to take these stories and incidents down, to tell them to my parents. She willingly repeated the ones she had already told, which I jotted down on any bit of paper available.

She was very happy to find someone to listen. She put new life and meaning in the telling, vividly portraying with picturesque zest, gestures, and Negro dialect these reminiscences. Laughing, joyously, giving expression by a shudder as she called forth some dangerous or revolting incident, or great tears would flow from her soulful eyes at some sad memory. She was never without a pipe, sometimes a corncob pipe. Often, a clay pipe with a little knob under the bowl [*by*] which she always held the pipe in place, shifting or removing it as she talked. When the weather was clement, we would sit together on her front step. When stormy or chilly, by her fire in the front room or spotlessly clean kitchen, where I was served corn pone, when convenient for her. The same kind of corn pone she made for the Lincolns, I'm so proud to relate.

Then, too, she had served the same fare to "Mastah Robert" (as she still called him) on his many visits. I sat at the same table and ate from the same plate used by Robert Lincoln, so this lovely colored woman told me.

I had tried to especially glean from her picturesque speech bits of her true meaning regardless of expressions or looks or actions, but back of it all shone forth the great love she bore for the entire family. Never antagonism or effort to smear their reputation. Just plain truth. Simply told, if sometimes in plainer English than I would have used.

These scraps of various shapes, kinds, and sizes of paper which notes of her reminiscences were jotted down on, grew into a sizeable pasteboard boxful over a period of four years. Never were her stories ever told in sequence, [*but*] just as they came to her mind. Being young, the thought never once occurred to me to put them in book form.

Often we were not able to talk for more than a few minutes, for Julia's illness became serious. Aunt Mariah had to take care of her, do all the washing alone, and have the Baptist Fellowship once every week. In her home, the Baptist church was born [*in Danville*].

After her death, this meeting was continued in her son Cornelius Vance's home, where the plans for the church were made and financed. No one but Aunt Mariah with such fine feelings and perceptions of righteousness could have carried on.

When Julia died that year in [*December*] 1900, she said to me, "Julia, mah beloved baby, when ah's wen' ta work fah dah Lincolums, es now en Heaben wid all does Lincolums 'cept my Robert."

No tears, just that supreme confidence and gladness that Julia was free from earthly cares and physical suffering. She said, "No mattah what befall me, Jesus doeth all things well." Until her own passing, she carried on nearly to the last with that same stoicism.

In January of 1904, her first-born, her dearly beloved Billie, died at 62. [*Mariah's son, William, who as a boy became good friends with Robert Lincoln.*] During his last illness, although she was past eighty years old and growing quite feeble, she cared for him and called it, "Putting mah shoulda to dah wheel."

Not until after he was gone did she seem to lag. I could see at each visit she was failing, though she didn't complain. She continued to tell of the Lincolns until on December 23, 1904, she passed on as peacefully as she had lived.

She left a heritage greater than money. Her stories were put away but prized as a treasure given to me by this wonderful little woman.

I took various office positions. In 1912 my dear father passed on suddenly. Mother would then be alone, for her other children were married. I felt it my duty to stay at home with her. To continue with office work and keep house as well meant neglecting one or the other.

It was necessary to do something that would add to our income, but nothing I tried seemed too profitable. It was suggested I buy and sell antiques. I started with a small investment. As I sold, I re-invested. I found it a dignified, interesting occupation. My mother loved it, for it brought into our home cultural, refined, and educated people.

The work also was fascinating. Always learning of makers of furniture, glass, china, and art. From literature I learned of rare books and the histories of them and great painters of fine art. Exact knowledge of types and patterns of primitives. Especially enjoying biographies of statesmen, something I never enjoyed in school.

Occasionally I sold bits of glass, china, furniture, or jewelry which I had purchased from Aunt Mariah after Billie's death, from what she called "plunda" from the Lincoln home. Both thrown away by them during her years there and when they rid out all excess when preparing to go to Washington in 1860.

But I always held on to the photographs of Lincoln's family, friends, and relatives. They seemed to belong to the stories she told. Quite often I showed them to clientele interested in historical items.

One professor [*Lloyd Ostendorf says it was probably Prof. J. G. Randall, a Lincoln scholar at the University of Illinois*] suggested I get in touch with Louis A. Warren, director of the Lincoln Life Association of Fort Wayne, Indiana. He said he might be able to help me put the stories (I told him of) in book form. That was either in 1937 or 1938.

Dr. Warren was very encouraging. We exchanged a few letters. In one, he expressed sincere conviction they should be put in book form for posterity and was willing to collaborate with me.

About that time, my mother became very ill. She needed constant care from the fall of that year until late spring the following year. I put the idea of writing completely out of my mind. Word travels fast, and I must here state that there were a number of people who offered help with such a book. About that same time, Mrs. Dr. Horner of Washington, D.C., president of the American Pen Women and a sponsor of [*restoration work in*] New Salem. Her aunt resided in New Salem at the time of the Ann Rutledge–A. Lincoln association. Also Dr. John Wesley Hill of Washington, D.C., who was chancellor of Lincoln Memorial University. But the undertaking, so foreign to my ability, was too great to even think of with my responsibilities.

My mother passed on in 1947. By then, the having of these notes had completely faded from my mind. Then in 1954 or 1955, I was scanning through and checking advertisements in *Hobbies* magazine when my attention seemed to center on an insertion by Lloyd Ostendorf of Dayton, Ohio, calling for Lincoln original photographs. After some correspondence, I sent the entire collection I had to him. He took them to various cities where there were large collections of Lincoln pictures: Springfield, Illinois; New York City; Detroit; Fort Wayne, Indiana; Cumberland Gap University (Lincoln Memorial University); as well as trying to identify as many as possible for me from his own fine collection.

Those he didn't purchase [*even*] at a very, very fair price after identification, he returned [*the photos*] with notes attached to each with suggestions. In nothing was he any way but trustworthy.

He later stopped over here when returning from a trip to Chicago where he attended the dedication of a Lincoln statue in the new Lincoln Square, which his illustration had been awarded the honor of being used as a design for same.

We talked on that short visit of his about the possibilities of a book from the notes I had taken. About the same time, Joseph Barnhart of Danville, a Lincoln historian and writer, urged me to write the book. He lived in a house once owned by William Fithian, from whose south portico Abraham Lincoln had addressed a political gathering.

Others who tentatively built up my courage were Mrs. Ramme of Terre Haute, Indiana, another Lincoln scholar; Herbert Wells Fay, custodian of the Lincoln Tomb in Springfield; his son Earl, an artist; and many others.

But Mr. Ostendorf gave concrete evidence of his willingness to see the book a reality. He said he would correct and edit it for me. I was, in a way, convinced I might be able to reassemble my notes. Having done systematic office work, I was schooled to go about it in an orderly way. However, it was a stupendous task to commence and expect to carry through.

I went over every note carefully. Many were badly worn, brittle, and writing so erased that they were not legible. First I pasted [*the legible notes*] on large sheets of paper. Rearranging as best I could in sequence and according to dates of historical facts which she [*Mariah Vance*] often mentioned. When at last I started to write, I had to look over the entire number of sheets of paper, to make sure I hadn't left out at the proper place any note that should be used. At each time I used a note, I underlined it with red pencil.

I had no literary ability and was conscious I could never add, as I went along, my own deductions. Nor did I mention at any times my opinions of traditional stories, even though some of her stories verified facts about [*the*] traditional. This took conscientious, exacting, confining labor. Nerve-wracking in the extreme sometimes. But rewarding for an accomplishment which Mariah Vance and the Lincolns would, if they could see and know that it was a labor of love, would thank me, and those who so graciously helped me.

Aunt Mariah could not say "Abraham" or "Lincoln" correctly. Although Mr. Lincoln never wished to be called "Abraham," and I sense the name "Abe" was too familiar, it was decided by Mrs. Lincoln that since Mrs. Vance always had called him "Mistah Abe," she could continue so doing, as well as continue to call her "Missy." However, she said it was a compliment from Mr. Lincoln, if he permitted her to do so.

Thus it was in her telling that she used these terms. Making her stories come to life after a period of forty years, by using "Mistah Abe," "Dah Missy," "Mastah Bobbie" or "Robert," "Willie," "Taddie," and their term for her, "Aunt Mariah." All of which adds up to the love and esteem the Lincolns held this beloved servant.

Even until her last days, Robert Lincoln visited her. In 1893, after returning from England [*ending his service as U.S. minister*], he stopped over in Danville on his way from Chicago to Springfield to visit with her. Perhaps he, too, longed to recapture some of his early home life and incidentally eat some of his early home cooking.

I feel sure Robert Lincoln appreciated Aunt Mariah's sterling qualities and trustworthiness far more than anyone else did. And there is no doubt from all I have read by various authors concerning him that Mrs. Vance was aware of Robert Lincoln's genuine fine character from childhood more than anyone. Understanding what others, even his father and mother, thought of seemingly, as a complex life. At least they never fathomed [*Robert's true character*], as Mariah did.

She once said, "He'n wah so quiet and serious. Nevah intah feahin' wid anyone's life. He'n wah so kind an hepful to mah chillun and precitate [*appreciate*] evah kindness what wah given. He'n wah bakard [*He was no braggart*]. Didn' wan no uns ta glorify him cause ob his pa. Dat man love mah Billie mose as a brothah. Nevah, nevah did he'n forget Aunt Mariah thro' her worstest times. He'n wah ah very true Christian foh he'n nevah let his left hand know what his right hand doeth."

No one knew from him that on his visits to her, he provided some for her future. That he paid Julia's and Billie's doctor bills and funeral expenses and, finally, Mariah's.

It must be recognized by all my readers, as I come to recognize, that he never would have given her more than a passing thought had he not admired and respected her very highly for her fine worth. She not only "put her shoulder to the wheel" as she said, by which she helped herself and hers, but neighbors testify of her charity, giving of her feeble strength to help.

By far one of the most, if not the most, rewarding outcomes by the release of these articles has been the genuine interest shown in the progress of this book. Not only Lincoln students and scholars have encouraged and offered willingly to help, but friends in general. I have also made new friends, sincerely interested in what I have endeavored to do.

Besides those already mentioned, I extend my sincere thanks to the personnel of the Springfield Library where I did research; the microfilm operator at the Federal Building at Danville (for copies of the *Commercial-News*); Benjamin Thomas, lecturer and author of Lincoln articles and books; Fanny Earnest of Champaign, Illinois, a colored lady who at one time lived in the Vance home; Mr. and Mrs. Gene Jackson and Mrs. Jackson's father, who furnished programs and photos; the recorder at the Court House in Danville for the Vance records; the caretaker of records at Crown Hill Cemetery; Dr. Maris of Attica, who explained the effects of the drug paregoric; and my niece, Mrs. John Weaver Frey, of Washington, D.C., who spent hours at the National Archives scanning microfilm, verifying records already in my possession.

Also the following Attica folks who furnished transportation so I could do research: Mr. and Mrs. Chester Cooper, Mrs. Laura Cook, and Mrs. Ava Stanfield. Not forgetting the well-wishers to whom I extend thanks.

Without the help of Mr. Ostendorf, I must repeat here that I might never have found a way to give this book to the public. It was his confidence and ability, his patience (for no doubt I have been very trying) that made me feel I would ultimately finish.

In ending, I have confidence that many scholars will conclude by comparison that this book has verified some traditions as facts, stated new facts, and separated legend from facts.

Sincerely thanking all for reading,

I am Humbly and Gratefully Yours,

ADAH LILAS SUTTON
Attica, Indiana
April 12, 1960

INTRODUCTION

Mariah Vance and the Lincolns
of Springfield

BY WALTER OLEKSY

*T*HE READER MAY WELL ASK, WHAT PROOF IS THERE THAT MARIAH VANCE WORKED for the Lincolns in Springfield and that she knew their personal lives? Besides census reports placing her in Springfield in 1850 and 1860 and her tombstone in Danville (which has an inscription that reads "Maid in Abraham Lincoln's Home 1850–1860"), the strongest evidence is two accounts—a document describing Robert Lincoln's visit to the Vance home and Mariah's obituary.

After the death of Robert Todd Lincoln in 1926, a eulogy appeared in the *Literary Digest* for August 14. Based upon articles in both the *Danville Commercial-News* and the *New York Herald Tribune* of July 27, it included a report told by Joseph "Uncle Joe" Cannon, former speaker of the U.S. House of Representatives, a close friend of Robert Lincoln's for a number of years. After telling highlights in Robert Lincoln's life and career, Cannon told this recollection:

> Mr. Lincoln, shortly after his election to the head of the Pullman Palace Car Company, after the death of its founder in 1897, was prevailed upon to make political speeches in the campaign of 1900, the year [*President William*] McKinley and [*Theodore*] Roosevelt were candidates. It required a lot of per-

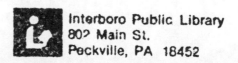

suasion to get him to come out in public and only when it was shown that the success of the Republican Party was not assured did he consent.

One of the few speeches that he made was in my home town [*Danville, Illinois, a small industrial city in east central Illinois*]. An incident that illustrates the private side of the man came up there.

It was the last and biggest rally of the year, the climax of the campaign. Mr. Lincoln arrived as quietly and unostentatiously as he could during the morning hours and registered at one of the leading hotels. A reception was started and then, because of complaining of being fatigued, Mr. Lincoln was excused. Several hours afterward when we thought he had rested long enough we sent the bellboy to his room. The door was locked. No one responded to repeated knocks of the bellboy. Half-frightened, we went to the room fearing that something had befallen him. A chambermaid soon opened the door, but the room was empty. Lincoln's baggage was there, however, and we started to hunt for him but without avail.

Then we did what few Republicans are supposed to do— we consulted a Democratic editor who was born in Springfield and was quite a bit of a boy before the Lincolns left there for Washington [*in 1861*]. He [*the editor*] had not seen him but he put us wise, and we soon found him. Lincoln, the orator of the day, was found in the north part of the city at the home of an aged Negress, Mrs. Maria[*h*] Vance, enjoying one of the finest meals of corn pone and bacon you ever tasted.

Mrs. Vance had been cook before the war in the Lincoln household at Springfield and nurse part of the time for young Robert Todd. Lincoln had heard that the woman was still living there and hunted her up. They had spent several hours together.

We hustled him away and to the park, where a great and impatient crowd awaited him. No sooner was his task over than Lincoln returned to the Vance home, humble as it was, and enjoyed more hours of talk with the aged woman, until it was near time for his train. From that day until her death [*1904*], "Mammy" Vance received a substantial check each month from Chicago.

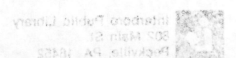

From this account by Cannon we know that Mariah Vance did, in fact, work for Abraham and Mary Todd Lincoln in Springfield. Over a period of ten years that she was employed there, she doubtlessly overheard many of their conversations.

Some critics have doubted this provenance that Mariah Vance in fact worked in the Lincoln home and that Robert Lincoln visited her, because archives did not confirm he was in Danville in the summer of 1900. Lloyd Ostendorf later found a copy of the *Danville Daily News* of October 30, 1896, with front-page headlines announcing a political rally at the Fair Grounds that Friday. A subhead read, "Welcome, The Immortal Lincoln's Worthy Son, Robert Todd Lincoln," who was to be a guest speaker at the rally. Joe Cannon forgot the exact date of the meeting that had taken place in 1896, not 1900.

Mariah Vance's obituary on the front page of the *Danville Commercial-News* of December 24, 1904, is headlined "Death Claims Mariah Vance," and subhead reads, "Aged Colored Woman Yields to Paralysis After a Week's Suffering, Lived in Lincoln Family."

The obituary said, in part: "Mariah Vance, the aged colored woman so well known to many in the city and who was the oldest colored woman in the county and perhaps in the state, is dead at the home of her son, Cornelius Vance." Then it said, "For years [*she*] was in the family of Abraham Lincoln."

The obituary concludes with: "No colored woman in Danville was so widely known as the deceased and not one held in higher regard. She was a good woman and faithful member of the colored Baptist Church. Mrs. Vance will be missed by many in this city."

It is unfortunate that the obituary did not go into detail about Mrs. Vance's years of domestic service to the Lincolns, but it is testimony to her high character that she received a front-page obituary, very rare for African Americans at the time.

The following is a chronology of her life, assembled from 1850-1860 U.S. Census reports and Springfield, Sangamon County, and Danville, Illinois, documents:

1819   Born Mariah Bartlett in Illinois
1838   Living in Springfield as of April 1838;
      Founder, Zion Baptist Church

January 20, 1842	Married Henry Vance in Springfield (Henry Vance born in Ohio, 1817)
1842–1862	Mother of twelve children (one stillborn)
April 1850–November 1860	Worked as laundress, domestic for Abraham and Mary Todd Lincoln in Springfield
November 1860	Moved with husband and children to Danville, Illinois
December 23, 1904	Died in Danville at age eighty-five

THE VANCE CHILDREN

William "Billie" A. Vance (1842–January 16, 1904)

Ellen Vance (1844–December 24, 1871)

Katherine Vance (1845–?)

Phebe Vance (1846–1854)

Julia Vance Patterson (1847–December 1900)

Mariah Vance (stillborn, 1850)

Lydia Narcissa Vance (1853–1924)

Rosa Vance Johnson (1855–?)

John Cornelius "Neal" Vance (1856–1923)

John Calvin Vance (1857–?)

Frederick Walter Vance (1860–1923)

Henry Vance Jr. (after 1862–1865)

Mariah Vance was born in Illinois in 1819 when James Monroe was president and Abraham Lincoln was ten years old and living in rural Indiana.

In 1850 Mariah was thirty-one years old and, according to the U.S. Census taken October 25 in Springfield, Sangamon County, Illinois, she was then the wife of Henry Vance, age thirty-three. He was an African American laborer, born in Ohio, who declared his worth to be real estate valued at $75. The couple had five children: William, eight; Ellen, seven; Katherine, six; Phebe, four; and Julia, three. The Vances lived in what Mariah called a shack. It was near the gas works, about six or eight blocks north and east of the Lincoln house.

Ten years later, in the census taken in Springfield on June 31, 1860, the Vances' assets had improved somewhat, since Henry declared he had $800 in real estate and $50 in personal property. There were five newcomers to the family: Narcissa, eight; Rosa, five; John, four; Cornelius, three; and newborn Walter.

Regarding Mariah's children, Adah Sutton has written: "Mariah Vance, despite her obligations to a large family that finally numbered 12, raised them to become highly respected for their honesty and talent. Each of those who lived to maturity had a good common school education. And as they learned, she learned. She got her start in spelling and writing when [*the boy*] Robert Lincoln, with her children in her home, taught them to read and write."

Mariah Vance was buried in Spring Hill Cemetery in a plot purchased for her and her family by Robert Todd Lincoln. Her grave remained unmarked until 1964 when, largely due to the efforts of Adah Sutton, a small stone marker in her memory was placed at the gravesite in a brief public ceremony. It was erected by the Ward Hill Lamon Civil War Roundtable.

A few words were spoken at the dedication by the Reverend Tobias Hutchins, retired Dean of Danville Clergy. Mariah Vance had been active in the organization of a Baptist congregation in that city years before.

Adah Sutton came from her home in Attica, Indiana, to attend the graveside ceremony. She reported how she came to know Mariah Vance and listened to and recorded her reminiscences: "Had I not taken notes during the period from 1900 to 1904, I could not now recapture completely the many wonderful experiences she related to me of her joys and sorrows while she was a servant in the Abraham Lincoln home in Springfield."

Before beginning Mariah Vance's reminiscences, some background on the lives of Abraham and Mary Todd Lincoln is appropriate.

Abraham Lincoln's father earned his living as a carpenter in rural Kentucky and supplemented his income by farming. He married Nancy Hanks and they had three children. Abraham's sister, Sarah, was born in 1807; Abraham, born on February 12, 1809, in a one-room log cabin near Hodgenville in Hardin County (now called Larue County); and brother Thomas, born in 1811 and died in infancy.

When Abraham was almost two years old, the family moved to a new homestead about ten miles away, a thirty-acre farm on Knob Creek. His father needed him to work on the farm, so Abraham went to school only for short periods during the winters when he was six and seven years old.

In December 1816, when Abraham was seven, the family moved to similar wilderness country in southwestern Indiana (now Spencer County). His mother died in the summer of 1818 during an epidemic of "milk sickness." Years later it was discovered that cows, foraging on the poisonous herb snakeroot, passed on the poison to those drinking their milk.

About a year later, Thomas Lincoln married Sarah "Sally" Bush Johnston, a widow with a son and two daughters. Lincoln was not close to his father, but he did grow to love his stepmother. During his eleventh year, Abraham had spells of abstraction and suffered periods of melancholy. The cause may have been frustration over his lack of education. He was mostly self-taught, reading books wherever he could find them, sometimes walking miles to borrow them. He fought his blues by reading and seeking out people to talk to and learn from.

Each Sunday, the family attended Pigeon Creek Baptist Church where the preacher's sermons were frequently against slavery. By the time he was seventeen, Lincoln stood six feet four inches tall and was strongly built. He left the farm for a time to work on flatboats plying the Ohio River.

Two years later, while back on the family farm in 1828, his married sister Sarah, whom he had loved dearly, died in childbirth. It was another great loss to him. At nineteen, after working on the Mississippi, Abraham joined his parents when they moved to central Illinois in 1830 to start a new farm along the Sangamon River west of Decatur. The following spring he piloted another flatboat down to New Orleans, then took a job as clerk in a general store in New Salem, Illinois.

In 1832 Lincoln was twenty-three and popular for his strength, displayed in splitting logs and wrestling matches, and for his flair in storytelling. That March, Lincoln entered politics for the first time when he became a candidate for the Illinois Legislature. He ran on a platform favoring universal education, improvement of navigation on the Sangamon River, and reforms in lending laws. He served in the brief Black Hawk War and upon his return to New Salem was defeated in the election.

The following January, Lincoln became co-owner of a grocery store in New Salem. When it failed, he was left $1,100 in debt, which took him years to pay. He became a surveyor, was village postmaster, and worked odd jobs, such as splitting rails for fences. He continued his self-education during this period.

Lincoln historians are divided on a controversial event in Lincoln's life: While studying to become a lawyer, Lincoln had reportedly fallen in love with Ann Rutledge, the daughter of a New Salem innkeeper. They supposedly were engaged; however, Ann died of typhoid fever on August 25, 1835, before they could marry and Lincoln went into a deep depression.

In 1834 Lincoln made a second try for public office and was elected to the Illinois House of Representatives. He served four successive terms (until 1841) and rose to prominence as a member of the Whig political party, which he later left to help form the Republican Party.

After obtaining a license to practice law in 1836, Lincoln moved to Springfield, the state's new capital. He arrived with only eleven dollars in his pockets and became the law partner of John T. Stuart. He quickly earned a reputation as an able lawyer with a good grasp of debate and the sincerity, color, and clarity of his speech.

While serving in the Illinois legislature, Lincoln practiced law on the newly organized Eighth Judicial Circuit. In 1840 he was reelected to the legislature for a fourth term. During the winter of 1839–1840 he met Mary Ann Todd, a society lady who would become his wife. She was born on December 13, 1818, in Lexington, Kentucky, ten days after Illinois became the twenty-first state of the Union.

Her father, Robert S. Todd, was president of the Bank of Kentucky in Lexington and served in both houses of the state legislature. He came from a family that had been among the founders of the city, a pride of the South. Her mother, Eliza Parker, came from another prominent Kentucky family.

The Todds were among the leading families of Kentucky. Mary's great-grandfather had been a Revolutionary War general and a great-uncle served as an officer under explorer George Rogers Clark. Her grandfather Levi Todd had been a major general in the militia in Indian battles. He lived in a mansion near the home of Henry Clay, a U.S. senator and leader of the Whig Party. Mary relished political talk at home and association with the important men of politics, even imagining herself one day being the wife of the President and living in the White House.

Her mother died when Mary was six. Her father soon remarried, and according to historians, she and her stepmother did not get along. A spiteful Mary once put salt in the woman's coffee and her stepmother called her "a limb of Satan."

A feuding relationship reportedly continued all during Mary's years at a private girls' academy and then four years at an exclusive private boarding school in Lexington, where she learned French, music, drama, dance, and other social graces of young ladies of good breeding.

Having been influenced by the politicians and political talk that were part of her father's world, Mary developed a strong interest in politics. When

Whig leader and family friend Henry Clay ran for President, sixteen-year-old Mary told him at a dinner that he had her support. She also commented that someday she, too, would live in Washington. Her ambition to become First Lady and live in the White House grew into an obsession.

When she was seventeen, Mary went to Springfield, Illinois, to visit her older sister Elizabeth who had married handsome, young Ninian W. Edwards, son of the governor. Two years later, in 1837, Mary went to live with them, reportedly to escape her stepmother. That same year her younger sister Frances married Dr. William Wallace, a Springfield doctor and pharmacist.

Mary was rather short, on the plump side, with a pretty face. Aided by a tight corset, she managed a fashionably small waistline so as to look slimmer in fancy gowns. Like other young belles of the South, she had a strong interest in fashion. She was reported to be high-strung and impulsive, a "creature of excitement," but also witty, warmhearted, and, at times, charming. She was also willful, demanding, and possessed of a hair-trigger temper.

Mary entered the high society of Springfield and danced with the most eligible bachelors whom she soon regarded as being "hypocritical, frivolous in their affection, or uninteresting." All suitors, she complained, were "hard bargains."

One who pursued her was Edwin Webb, a lawyer and state legislator who was fifteen years her senior. He was a widower with children whom Mary considered "two sweet little objections."

Among the eligible bachelors she did consider was Stephen A. Douglas, who was expected to go far in politics. He was a transplant from New England and had a slight figure (five feet, four inches tall and ninety pounds) and a reputation for being a ladies' man. Mary was impressed by Douglas and his political potential, but he had one drawback—he was a Democrat and she was a Whig. Despite this, friends considered them to be a "special pair." Douglas nearly proposed marriage to her (according to Jean H. Baker in her biography *Mary Todd Lincoln*).

Years later, Mary confided to a friend that Douglas had indeed proposed to her, but she turned him down, saying, "I cannot consent to be your wife. I shall become Mrs. President, or I am the victim of false prophets, but it will not be as Mrs. Douglas."

During her busy year in Springfield, at a dance in December 1839, twenty-year-old Mary became interested in a solemn-looking young lawyer and state legislator. He had a gift for oratory and it was said he might go far in politics. Abraham Lincoln was thirty and "very tall, awkward, homely, and badly dressed" (says Benjamin Thomas in his biography *Lincoln*). "His features were rugged and by nature and habit, he was a man of sad countenance."

Mary's sister Frances considered Lincoln "the plainest man" in Springfield—his coats were too short; his trousers shabby, patched, and short; and his socks rarely matched. Mary's other sister, Elizabeth, strongly rejected Lincoln as a suitor for her, calling him "rustic and socially primitive." It became painfully clear to Lincoln that the entire Todd clan, except Mary, opposed him for his appearance and considered him to be inferior to her and them.

By the standards of that time, Lincoln was old to be without a wife, especially for a man with high political ambitions. He was not wealthy but earned enough to support a wife, making between $1,200 and $ 1,500 from his law practice and an additional $100 to $300 as a legislator ($1,500 in 1842 is equivalent to $22,200 today).

Lincoln was nervous. Could he support a wife and family? Did he really love Mary Todd? He was aware that a pledge of marriage was then a legally binding contract. If he changed his mind, he could be sued for breach of promise. Marriage was for life in those days, especially for a politician. Divorce could ruin a career.

Mary Todd wrestled with her own doubts. Could Lincoln support her in the manner she was accustomed to? Could he rise politically to fulfill her ambition of becoming first lady? Did she love him? He was not physically attractive; should she settle for Stephen Douglas or another? Mary must have pondered these questions during their courtship.

To the surprise of friends and family, Mary Todd and Abraham Lincoln announced their engagement in 1840 and planned to be married the following January. But on January 1, 1841, the couple argued and parted. Although no one can verify what happened, one version is that Lincoln got cold feet and asked Mary to break off their engagement and marriage plans, and she consented.

Another version is that Mary was miffed when Lincoln arrived late to escort her to a New Year's Eve party. When finally he took her there, she showed how little she cared by flirting with Edwin Webb. Lincoln may have been jealous, which brought on the quarrel.

Mary's friends believed she had called off the marriage. The Todd family reported later that Mary stomped her foot during the argument and told Lincoln, "Go and never, never come back!"

Lincoln had a moody temperament and at times his melancholy (according to Benjamin Thomas) "became so acute as to be an actual mental ailment known as hypochondria, a lowness of spirits or a desponding habit of mind brought on by overwork, anxieties, or disappointments." This doubtlessly was aggravated by the uncertainty of his feelings about marrying Mary Todd. Thomas suggests that Lincoln confided this to Mary and she released him from his pledge, hoping that when he felt better, he would renew the courtship.

Lincoln did feel guilty about his failure to go through with the marriage. He sank into another deep melancholy, writing a friend that "I am now the most miserable man living. I must die or be better, it appears to me."

After a year and a half separation, a mutual friend, Mrs. Simeon Francis, wife of the editor of the *Sangamo Journal*, brought the couple together. The Francises thought Lincoln had a very promising career and that the couple made a good match.

Lincoln convinced himself that he now felt positive about marrying Mary. The courtship resumed and on November 4, 1842, the couple was married by the Rev. Charles Dresser, an Episcopal minister, in the Ninian Edwardses' parlor with only a few relatives and friends present. Lincoln slipped a plain gold ring on Mary's finger. Engraved on the ring were the words "Love is eternal."

Five days later, Lincoln wrote to a lawyer-acquaintance: "Nothing new here, except my marrying, which to me, is a matter of profound wonder."

Others wondered, too, because Lincoln and his bride were such opposites. Says Thomas: "She was short and inclined to corpulence, he was tall and lean. He was slow-moving, easygoing, she precipitate and volatile. He was a man of simple tastes, she liked fine clothes and jewelry. His personality and mind were the sort that grow continuously, hers remained essentially in a set mold. Both had ambitions, but her determination was so much more intense than his that it would be like a relentless prod, impelling him onward whenever he might be disposed to lag."

Lincoln was silent and moody. He dressed like a backwoodsman and often appeared to be dejected, preferring quiet evenings at home, reading. Mary was vivacious, liked fancy dresses, craved company, and loved giving and going to parties.

After their marriage, the Lincolns boarded at the Globe Tavern, a two-story wooden inn, for four dollars a week. This was difficult for Mary, who had grown up in luxury and lived in a beautiful home with servants. On August 1, 1843, their first child, Robert, was born.

The following January, Lincoln bought a house and lot for $1,500 in a nice residential part of Springfield at the northeast corner of Eighth and Jackson Streets. It remained the Lincolns' home until he was elected President.

The house had been built in 1839 by the minister who had married them. It was a story and a half in height and well built, with oak floors, laths of hickory, and doors, frames, and weather boarding of black walnut. A brick foundation for a fence was added in 1850. In the weedy backyard was an outhouse, a shed, and a small barn with horse and buggy.

Lincoln cut wood for the stove and fireplace, milked the family cow that stood outside tethered to a tree, and took care of his horse, Buck.

In 1841 Lincoln and John Stuart dissolved their law partnership and Lincoln went into partnership with Stephen Logan. The following year, Lincoln did not run for reelection to the legislature and devoted full time to his law practice. His association with Logan was dissolved after three years; he then went into partnership with William Herndon, one of a small group of men, including Stephen A. Douglas, whose company he enjoyed, sitting around the potbelly stove at Corneau and Diller's drug store, swapping stories and opinions.

Mary disapproved of Lincoln's choice of law partner because she considered Herndon, nine years younger than her husband, to be a drunkard, a "dandy," and a ladies' man. (Lincoln did not drink alcohol, but Mary sometimes served wine to guests. The Lincolns usually drank coffee, tea, unfermented grape juice, or water.)

Lincoln and Herndon's law office was a single, crowded, and cluttered room in downtown Springfield. Mary considered the office to be an untidy mess. Since her husband was often on the circuit and Herndon alone used the office, she blamed Herndon for its unsightly condition, complaining that during her surprise visits she smelled liquor on his breath.

Twice a year for periods of three months (March to May and September to November), lawyers traveled to villages and towns throughout the fourteen counties of the Eighth Judicial Circuit. They would stop at county seats for court terms of two days to a week as judges held court in makeshift courtrooms in general stores or saloons.

In his first years as a lawyer, Lincoln rode the circuit on a horse, then later, as roads came into being, he traveled by horse and buggy. When railroad lines were built in Illinois in the 1850s, he traveled by train but still had to rent a horse and buggy to get to the smaller towns. Not until 1857 was he able to reach every circuit town by train.

Lincoln defended all types of clients, from those accused of public intoxication to large corporations involved in complex business litigation. His popularity as a circuit lawyer and storyteller would later help him attract large crowds to hear him debate Stephen Douglas during the U.S. Senate race in 1858.

Mary Lincoln hated his traveling because it kept him away so much. Once she told a friend that "if [*her husband*] had stayed at home as he ought to, I could love him better." Some believe it implied that she wanted to be more sexually active. They slept in separate bedrooms with a connecting door. In those days it was considered "high class" to afford separate bedrooms for husband and wife. The arrangement suited Mary, who liked to read books (mostly romances) in bed into the wee hours of the morning. When he retired for the night, Abraham preferred to sleep.

While he was on the circuit, Mary hired cleaning women and other domestic help, both white and African American. She was a difficult and demanding employer, so they seldom stayed very long, complaining of her "fits of temper." Mary fired one woman because her potatoes were undercooked and the gravy was watery. Sometimes Mary was so loud and angry when firing help, her voice carried into the neighborhood.

Much of the time Mary did her own cooking in the kitchen fireplace, until Lincoln bought her an iron stove in 1849. According to records at the local general store, Mary bought large quantities of sugar (eleven or twelve pounds every two weeks) to bake cakes (she was known for her white cake), cookies, pies, and candy. She was frugal (some said a "pinch-penny") with food money and often made one meal last into leftovers for several days, yet indulged herself and the boys with desserts.

The Lincoln boys grew up being, what Herndon called, wild "brats," and Lincoln admitted that neither he nor Mary "controlled our children much." Herndon said that when the Lincoln boys came to the law office, they made it a playground. Perhaps the boys were on "sugar highs," a symptom unknown in the 1850s, from the sweets they consumed.

Mary was an excellent seamstress and spent a large part of her time sewing. She also knit well, making the family's socks, gloves, and scarfs. She bought large quantities of cotton goods to sew pillow cases, sheets, and curtains, but her joy was in buying silk and other fine materials, like ribbons and lace to sew onto dresses for herself.

As Lincoln grew more prosperous, Mary's dresses were made by skilled seamstresses, but she would add frills herself. She usually bought Lincoln's and the boys' clothes ready-made at the general store in town.

It was her habit, when Lincoln was away, to ask lady friends to visit. At times she had to plead with some of them to come, because her company was not that desired. Sometimes she would invite a male guest to the house, and on one occasion entertained one of Springfield's most eligible bachelors, Ozias Hatch, who later became Illinois secretary of state.

While Lincoln traveled, Mary was alone with the boys and spent many fearful evenings. She feared robbers, thunderstorms, and men who paid nightly visits to her hired domestic help (according to Baker's biography). She criticized her husband for not being important enough to make a good living practicing law in Springfield. His travels gave him the opportunity to establish his legal reputation for skill and honesty.

Lincoln worked hard. His fees ranged from $2.50 to $50, and averaged about $5 a case. Often he was paid in chickens or coal—anything but cash. The family had to live frugally on his income. The largest fee he ever received as a lawyer was $5,000 for a case he won for the Illinois Central Railroad.

Mary complained that when he was on the circuit he seldom wrote her. When he did write, he addressed his letters to her as "Dear wife" or "Dearest Mary" and signed them "affectionately."

Contemporaries said he was a henpecked husband and his wife's frequent tantrums caused him to stay on the circuit longer than his cases required. While other lawyers returned to their wives on weekends, Lincoln often didn't go home. When back in Springfield, he sometimes lingered in his law office with Herndon and other friends, swapping stories until the early hours of the morning rather than go home to face his wife's temper.

Mary would berate her husband in public, saying "He is of no account when at home. He is the most useless, good-for-nothing man on earth." Yet if someone criticized him, she came to his defense, saying she was proud of him and that he would go further than any man in the state.

In the autumn of 1844, Lincoln campaigned for Henry Clay in his Whig

Party's bid for the presidency. Mary Lincoln was very pleased with her husband's efforts on behalf of her old family friend, hoping Lincoln's stock would rise higher in the Whig Party. It would make up, in part, for her humble life with him thus far.

Edward Baker, their second son, was born on March 10, 1846. August of the same year Lincoln was elected to Congress. Mary's dream of living in Washington finally came true when the family moved there in November. But life in Washington failed to live up to her expectations. As one of many members of the House of Representatives, Lincoln did not achieve the prestige Mary had hoped for. He was a small fish in a big pond, and she was virtually ignored by Washington society. She was determined to set her sights higher.

Lincoln's most notable accomplishment in the House was to promote a bill in 1849 to abolish slavery in the District of Columbia. However, when the bill was abandoned by his backers, he never formally introduced it.

Lincoln sought the job of commissioner of the General Land Office. When he didn't get it, he decided to retire from politics. The family returned to Springfield, where he resumed his law practice with William Herndon.

Little Eddie Lincoln took ill in December 1849. While his parents worried over his health, Mary's grandmother, Mrs. Robert Parker, died in January 1850. Eddie, not quite four, after an illness lasting fifty-two days, died of diphtheria on February 1, 1850. Both parents grieved deeply over the loss of their son. It was more difficult for Mary, as she was often home alone with Robert, who was then seven. Years later Robert said that his mother's grief was so immense she wept constantly for weeks.

Lincoln realized that his wife was not well enough to manage Robert and the house, and needed help while he was away. In April, he personally hired Mariah Vance to do the family laundry and help Mary with other chores.

Mariah's help was some comfort to Mary. That July, when Lincoln was chosen to deliver the eulogy for President Zachary Taylor, she cheered up. She was hoping he would return to politics and was heartened by the honor bestowed on him.

When Mariah Vance first mentions working at the Lincolns' home in 1850, she speaks affectionately of Robert. He was a quiet, lonely boy who spent most of his time in his room, reading and daydreaming. Instructed by his father to be the "man of the house" when Lincoln was away, Robert grew up before his time.

Robert was the only Lincoln son who survived into manhood. The third Lincoln son, William Wallace, born December 21, 1850, died of "bilious fever" at the age of twelve in 1862, after Lincoln's first year as President. The fourth Lincoln son, Thomas "Tad," spoke with a lisp, having been born with a cleft palate on April 4, 1853. He died of tuberculosis in 1871 at the age of eighteen.

Mary Lincoln was troubled most of her adult life with emotional or psychological problems. In Springfield, to calm her nerves, Mariah Vance says Mary took paregoric, a popular drug sold in pharmacies in the nineteenth century. It was used for many ailments, including common aches and pains.

Paregoric is made of opium suspended in a solution of camphor and alcohol. It was first prepared in the eighteenth century. Because of the constipating effect of opium, paregoric was used to control diarrhea. It also was an ingredient in many patent medicines.

Little was then known about the drug's side effects. For Mary the side effects were depression, mood swings, and hallucinations. She believed she could communicate with her dead sons.

In the 1850s people were advised to take paregoric in small doses. Those taking the drug more regularly unknowingly became addicted. Nor were they aware of the effects of drug withdrawal when they tried to stop. Mary Lincoln and other heavy users of paregoric thought they were ill and that the medication would cure them. Despite the bad taste, they kept taking it. Actually, they got high on the drug, followed by depression. Without doubt, paregoric contributed to Mary's frequent mood swings, from her temper tantrums to what Lincoln called a "stupor."

Deaths in the family, drug addiction, and Mary's mental and emotional instability convinced Mariah Vance that the Lincolns had a very troubled and tragic family life. A deeply religious woman, Mariah believed it was her Christian duty to be helpful to the Lincoln family.

Mariah sympathized with Abraham Lincoln and greatly admired him for the all-suffering way he dealt with his personal problems. Her stories reveal the depth of sadness in the personal life of Abraham Lincoln and his courage in dealing with it.

Conflicting opinions persist about the personal lives of Abraham and Mary Todd Lincoln, individually and as a couple. Herndon's biography of Lincoln was criticized by some historians for revealing Lincoln as more human than heroic. Others allege it contained distortions and inaccuracies.

Herndon's negative portrayal of Mary Lincoln was said to be "exaggerated," and thus his book was largely discredited.

Actually, Herndon did not write the Lincoln biography. According to Dr. Wayne C. Temple, chief deputy director of the Illinois State Archives, "Although Herndon has his name on the three volumes, it was written by Jesse W. Weik in Indiana. Herndon collected the material and wrote Weik long letters, but did not write the book. Previously, Herndon had sold his material to Ward Hill Lamon, who himself hired a ghostwriter to do the book which in the end turned out to be very anti-Lincoln. It was Chauncey Black, a noted Democrat, who wrote it."

Mary's dislike of Herndon stemmed from their first meeting at a ball in which he commented on her dancing. He said she was the most smooth and easy waltzer he'd ever danced with, and that she glided like a serpent. He apparently intended the remark as flattery, but she took it as an insult and never forgave him or allowed him in her house.

After his book was published, Herndon lectured saying Lincoln had been in love with Ann Rutledge, but defenders of Mary Lincoln at the time said it was untrue. They accused Herndon of trying to get back at Mary by making her jealous.

For years, Carl Sandburg was one of the few historians who believed Lincoln and Ann Rutledge had been in love with each other. He writes in volume one of *The Prairie Years*: "She [*Ann*] had written McNamar that she expected release from her pledge to him. And no answer had come; letters had stopped coming. Her way was clear. In the fall [*of 1835*] she was to go to a young ladies' academy in Jacksonville; and Abraham Lincoln, poor in goods and deep in debts, was to get from under his poverty; and they were to marry. They would believe in the days to come; for the present time they had understanding and security."

That August, typhoid fever swept the plains and many of Lincoln's friends died. Though ill himself, Lincoln helped nail together the coffins for some of them. Then Ann took ill and lay fever-burned. Lincoln rode out from New Salem to the Rutledge farm at Sand Ridge to visit her. Two days later, at age twenty-two, she died of the fever. Dazed with grief, Lincoln could be found wandering in the woods along the Sangamon River.

My role in preparing the interpreted version of Mariah Vance's oral history for publication has been strictly as a journalist. I did not add anything to the original manuscript, but merely modified the heavy dialect for easier reading and wrote introductory and background material for those readers not familiar with Lincoln or the decade 1850–1860. Adah Sutton's explanations/comments are in parenthesis in the oral history; the editors' are in brackets. Copies of the provenance documents and photos described in this introduction are to be found in the photograph section at the end of Volume One.

The copy of the original handwritten manuscript reproduced in this book is exactly as Adah Sutton transcribed it from her shorthand notes.

WALTER OLEKSY
Evanston, Illinois
April 8, 1995

CRITICS AND
THEIR COMMENTS

SOME HISTORIANS, WHILE NOT QUESTIONING THE AUTHENTICITY OF this manuscript, have doubted the credibility of some of its stories. That is to be expected because they have lectured, taught, and written papers that varied from what Mariah Vance observed in the Lincoln home.

Mariah Vance may have had some memory lapses in dates or in the sequences of events. This is to be expected considering the time gap from the actual events to their recording. This oral history is presented as faithfully as possible—the human aspect, that of forgetfulness or omissions, comes with the territory. However, nothing was deliberately changed or distorted.

The following Lincoln experts have praised and endorsed the manuscript. Here are their acknowledgments:

Francis O. Krupka, historical architect of the Lincoln Home in Springfield, wrote the following letter of endorsement to Lloyd Ostendorf on December 29, 1992, regarding the Mariah Vance reminiscences.

As the historical architect of Lincoln Home National Historic Site, and the author of the *Lincoln Home Historic Structure Report*, I've found *Mistah Abe* [Adah Sutton's original book title was *Mistah Abe and De Missy*] to be an unusual source of information that is otherwise unavailable from the more conventional historic record of Lincolniana. With your permission, I have been using *Mistah Abe* as a reference since I first encountered a draft copy here in the park.

The Vance recollections include discussions of aspects of private family life not found in other histories and biographies.

For example, her repeated mention of the backyard laundry shed is entirely unique to her reminiscences. No one else has previously acknowledged the shed's existence, yet it is clearly present in both M. MacManus' 1851 and William Sides' 1858 land use maps of Springfield.

Vance also mentions her irritation that Mary Lincoln carved the home's large, original kitchen (that occupied the entire first floor of the east wing) into "cubbyholes" —the present kitchen and dining room. This too is a fact unmentioned elsewhere in the historic record, yet it's demonstrably true. Our physical (1984–88) investigations of the building clearly revealed that the wall separating the small, existing kitchen from the dining room was not part of the original Dresser cottage. The use of pine wall studs and machine sawn lath (rather than oak studs and hand split hickory lath) clearly dates this wall to the 1855–56 remodelling, an event that occurred during Vance's self-professed (April 1850 to November 1860) employment by the Lincoln family.

Others of her references such as those regarding other servants, the barn, the pre-wood shed (i.e., pre–1859–60) woodpile, the vegetable garden, the family livestock and pets, etc., also provide glimpses of domestic routines not found in other sources. Still others discuss events known to have happened— such as Mary wet-nursing the infant of a sick neighbor, Robert's eye operation, Mary's fear of lightning and storms, her headaches, etc.—from a different point of view that adds depth to the history of these events.

That Mariah Vance and her family actually lived in Springfield from approximately 1837 through 1860 can be documented from the historic record. That she worked in the Lincoln family's home as a domestic servant is known only from her reminiscences. Details of Lincoln family home life also have been preserved and interpreted from the unique perspective of the family servant.

There will, of course, be those who doubt the authenticity of these stories, but the discussions in them of architectural details of the home unknown prior to our pre-restoration investigations certainly suggest to me that these recollections are real and well worth publishing.

John T. Trutter, a director of the Abraham Lincoln Association in Springfield and Lincoln scholar from Evanston, Illinois, wrote Walter Oleksy on April 5, 1993:

> I have been much impressed with your manuscript about Mariah Vance and her remarkable memories about her services in the Abraham Lincoln household in Springfield.
>
> My maternal ancestors were close neighbors of the Lincolns (in Springfield) and my grandfather, Philip Mischler, was a playmate of young Tad Lincoln. My great-grandmother would be asked by Mary Todd Lincoln to help her braid her hair for some of her social events.
>
> The antics of the children and the Lincoln marital conflicts have always been a part of our family's oral history. But Mariah Vance has added a domestic's intimacy that is rich in description and, I believe, credible.
>
> As the first president of the Sangamon County Historical Society, a past president of the Illinois State Historical Society and, currently, the chairman of the Council for Illinois History, I feel that you and Lloyd Ostendorf are to be commended for a challenging job of editing an unique historic contribution.

In another letter, Trutter tells this amusing story about his maternal grandfather, Philip Mischler, and Tad Lincoln:

"The boys had been intently playing a game of marbles on a rear porch [*of the Lincoln home*], when Mary Lincoln summoned Tad for dinner. When there was no immediate response, she rushed through the door, broom in hand, and swept the marbles flying into the air. We assume that grandfather Phil took off for the safety of his own home with equal dispatch."

Another Trutter relative, Catherine Ramstetter, sometimes walked with Abraham Lincoln on her way to grade school. He was said to give her an apple as a treat, since he carried apples to counter problems of indigestion.

"My grandfather years later was in the dry goods business during the early days of the John Bressmer Company," Trutter writes. "After the

President's death and during the periods Mary Todd Lincoln would return to Springfield, she was one of his customers. He would report of her extravagance, how she would buy an entire bolt of yard goods from him so that no other woman would have a matching garment."

Dr. Wayne C. Temple, historian, former editor in chief of the *Lincoln Herald* for Lincoln Memorial University, author of a number of books on Abraham Lincoln, and currently chief deputy director of the Illinois State Archives, Springfield, wrote on December 21, 1992:

> It is my considered opinion that Mariah Vance's story as told to Adah Sutton is a valued piece of Lincolniana. Of course, this is not to say that Mariah might not have misunderstood some of Abraham Lincoln's remarks which may have been related to her as subtle humor and which she took for "gospel."
>
> But in the main, Mrs. Vance relates information about the Lincoln home which she could not have read in biographies, etc. For instance, she knew about the remodeling which cut up the huge kitchen in order to fashion a dining room, etc. Only recently did this fact come to light when the home was partially dismantled to study it and restore it.
>
> Mariah thoroughly understood Mrs. A. Lincoln's flights of anger and described them as she experienced them. Few servants ever worked for Mrs. Lincoln very long, but Mariah was not a live-in maid and could come and go as she pleased. Thus, she worked for Mrs. Lincoln during a period of years and not months.
>
> Some people have doubted that Mariah Vance existed at all, but I have traced her life in the United States Census, the Springfield City Directories, and other local sources and can vouch that she did exist and did live in Springfield, Illinois.
>
> Another scholar [*Francis Krupka*] has recently uncovered her church membership and also her marriage license to Henry Vance. She was a Baptist and a practicing Christian.
>
> Her oral history sheds new light upon the Lincoln story. Robert Lincoln himself visited Mariah Vance in later years at Danville and acknowledged that she had been a worker in the Lincoln home, even cooking for his family. So there is no doubt that she did labor in the Lincoln household.

If Mariah exaggerated some incidents, reconstructed long bits of conversations word for word years after the events and perhaps misunderstood some happenings, so have other sources of Lincolniana. Readers will have to judge for themselves the same as they do when reading Billy Herndon and others. Mariah's story deserves to be preserved in print so that it may be utilized by all in the future.

Mariah appears to have told her story as she saw and understood it. What more can one ask?

Dr. Wallace H. Best, founding director, chairman of the board, and editor in chief of the International Lincoln Association, Idyllwild, California, wrote on January 26, 1993:

> *Mistah Abe and De Missy* is as much a keystone to cap the arch of much better understanding about the personal lives of the Lincoln family in Springfield as the output of The Lincoln Legals Project has become to far more sophisticated knowledge about and understanding of Lincoln the Lawyer.
>
> Mariah Vance is truly "the other witness" who has been so sorely needed to counter the animosity toward Mary Todd Lincoln and all of Lincoln's children which pervaded William Herndon's *Lincoln* and thereby distorted the perspective of Carl Sandburg's *Prairie Years*.
>
> Vance adds much to our knowledge about the lifestyle of the Lincolns from day to day and year by year in Springfield from the beginnings of her service [*in 1850*] until their departure [*in 1861*].
>
> For myself, as a Lincoln psychobiographer, she is immensely important as a new primary source applicable to the highly complex purpose of arriving at reasonably balanced conclusions as to how the characters and personalities of the Lincolns—father, mother, and sons—transacted with each other during the Springfield years. In the case of the often maligned Robert Todd Lincoln, she also brings to life a large new reservoir of positive information.
>
> Indeed, Vance is to the domestic life of the Lincolns in

Springfield what Elizabeth Keckley (Mary's Black seamstress in Washington) and Frank Carpenter have been in regard to the White House years. Moreover, like Keckley, Vance provides much insight into the relationship problems of Mary Todd and Robert Lincoln in the dreadful years which followed the assassination of "Father Abraham." Because Vance lived until 1904, and because Robert Lincoln remained so lovingly bonded to her until her death, her testimony deserves thereby even greater credence than it might otherwise receive.

Of course, the stories of Vance come to us mainly through initial note taking and later writings of Adah Lilas Sutton as typed by Iris Sutton. Moreover, to the latter's manuscript, you [*Lloyd Ostendorf*] have edited admirably with Walter Oleksy to achieve outstanding readability.

It seems to me, especially given the evidence from Temple and Krupka, that the provenance of Vance cannot be challenged. But there is always the *Pale Fire* type of scholarship which will endeavor to put down Vance as "just another unreliable oral history." The Preface by Adah Sutton also conveys verisimilitude to me.

Moreover, Herndon's *Lincoln*, apart from his personal observations mostly in the Springfield law office and never in the Lincoln home, was based mainly on collection and editing of oral histories after the assassination. Many of those he [*Herndon*] interviewed though often descended from previous generations of fine oral historians among the English, Irish, and Scottish folks in Virginia, Kentucky, and Indiana *may* have lost some degree of traditional precision by the time they got to Illinois or became "more civilized" according to the customs of their own generation in the other states where Herndon so avidly pursued their memories and legends about Lincoln.

Dr. James C. Davies, retired professor of political science at the University of Oregon, wrote on June 6, 1993:

> The Mariah Vance manuscript is altogether absorbing; it took me back to the Lincolns in Springfield more vividly than I would have thought possible.

Benjamin P. Thomas, one of the most respected and authoritative scholars before his death, said that Herndon is the primary source of knowledge of Lincoln's private life. Now there are two. Mariah Vance's authoritative recollections give life to the family circumstances in Springfield, where Lincoln became more completely molded for his presidency. Only partly because Mary Lincoln kept Herndon away from the house, Mariah Vance's observations become the major primary source.

The reminiscences have a frank and innocent palpability that lends them credibility. Related orally to Adah Sutton several decades after Mariah Vance did housework for the Lincolns, they strike me as being as believable as the Four Gospels are about the life and teachings of Jesus, written similarly post mortem.

Extraordinarily sensitive and insightful to the interplay between Lincoln, his wife, children, the Vance family, and townspeople, the reminiscences are a precious, invaluable source of understanding of the psyches of Lincoln and his family.

The major contributions are to understanding two matters of great contention among Lincoln scholars and buffs: the romance between Lincoln and Ann Rutledge and the marriage of Lincoln and Mary Todd. B. P. Thomas tended to depreciate the romance, saying there was much fable but "nothing in Lincoln's writings to support" its existence. Mariah Vance's recollections confirm the deep effect Ann Rutledge had on Lincoln and his occasional, sometimes brutal use of her in his chronic conflicts with Mary Lincoln. Historians can no longer regard his love for Ann Rutledge as romantic creations of Herndon and Sandburg. The love, as Abraham Lincoln described it in these recollections, was of enormous importance in his life. And the reminiscences help explain why the marriage endured.

Miss Sutton's Preface is a fine piece of writing, and it lends credibility to her notes and to the reminiscences.

But the main sources of credibility are the reminiscences themselves. They present such meticulous detail and such insightful discussion of Mariah Vance's relationships to the

Lincolns and to her own family that it is hard not to accept her account.

Her "objectivity," if that is the right word for her deep and compassionate understanding, is repeatedly evident. She tells how Lincoln teased and sometimes tormented Mary and she him; how her addiction to paregoric intensified the effects of a probably inherited mental fragility, to make Mary a person "impossible to live with."

And she clears up a puzzle in my mind: why the youngest child, Tad, was named after his paternal grandfather, Thomas Lincoln: because Mary so decided. There was so much pre- and post-mortem hostility between Lincoln and his father, that I couldn't believe Abraham Lincoln had chosen the name.

She tells in detail about Mary's frequent rages, including a time she threw a stick at Abe. Mariah Vance reports conversations with Lincoln in which he asks her if baptism will help, and we get evidence that Lincoln was baptized in the Sangamon River before becoming President, secretly, so Mary would not find out. And Mariah Vance at one point observes that "Maybe Gawd got those two strange folks together to make both of them stronger." These two quotes lend strong confidence in her judgments.

The conversation between Abraham and Mary Lincoln on religion gives insight into the structure of his beliefs that is better than anything I've seen. Its straightforward presentation, by Mariah Vance as filtered through Adah Sutton, is so clear that only a theologian or a philosopher could misunderstand it. Lincoln had the enormous strength to maintain an open mind about matters that can be no truer than faith.

Overall, I'm awestruck by this manuscript and whatever further I could do to move it toward publication, I'd be happy to do.

In an effort to substantiate the honesty of her aunt's handwritten telling of Mariah Vance's reminiscences of the Lincolns, Iris Sutton wrote this letter to Lloyd Ostendorf in 1992:

> Enclosed are facts concerning my association with my Aunt Adah Sutton.

Shortly before my marriage [*at age 18*] in August 1941 to her nephew, James R. Sutton, I met Aunt Adah Sutton [*then 58*]. Aunt Adah was a prim little lady who still lived in the family home where she was born [*in Attica, Indiana*].

In spite of the 40 years difference in our ages, we shared a lively interest in antiques, history, and Abraham Lincoln. We spent many pleasant afternoons looking at her memorabilia; she was an avid "note maker" and kept notes, often dated, of family events for a family history she was making.

She had an excellent memory and would tell me the history of her antiques, where and when they were acquired, as well as discuss identifying features of periods and style. Among her many objects were several Lincoln family pictures of which she was especially proud because they had come from the Lincoln home in Springfield.

As I looked at them she told me about her conversations with Mariah Vance and her daughter (*Julia*). When she realized that Mariah was speaking of *The Mr. Lincoln*, she began to jot some of these stories down because she thought they would interest her father who was a Civil War veteran.

Many years later, she assembled her notes and wrote the stories in manuscript form in longhand, and it naturally followed that I would type it for her. It was our hope that these charming little stories would be brought to the public.

Unfortunately, this did not happen in her lifetime. She gave the manuscript to me, hoping these stories might be told, or at least, kept in the family.

After some time had passed, it was arranged for Mr. Lloyd Ostendorf to edit and illustrate the original manuscript and find a publisher.

All of my conversations with Aunt Adah were in a relaxed, family atmosphere, and there was never any reason to doubt her sincerity or veracity.

I am pleased to have this opportunity to express my belief in the authenticity of these memories.

(Signed) Iris Sutton, Attica, Indiana, November 28, 1992.

Lloyd Ostendorf says that the fact that Mariah Vance was virtually unknown to most Lincoln scholars and writers fostered doubt as to her very existence:

> Dr. Wayne Temple, eminent Lincoln scholar, found the 1850 and 1860 Census records proving she and her husband lived in Springfield. Francis Krupka found their marriage license and a document revealing Mariah helped found the black Baptist church there. The article in the *Literary Digest* of 1926 revealed and confirmed Mariah Vance's connection with the Lincoln family and especially the friendship between her and Robert Lincoln, who put her on a pension for her loyalty and services to the family.
>
> It is most interesting that Mariah Vance's tombstone, erected by local Civil War buffs in Danville, bears the inscription that she was "Maid in Abraham Lincoln's Home 1850 to 1860," and her obituary, December 24, 1904, made the top front page of the *Danville Commercial-News* and proudly told of her connection to the Lincoln family.
>
> After conceding from this proof that Mariah Vance existed and worked for the Lincolns, some Lincoln historians were still skeptical about Mariah's stories regarding Lincoln's love for Ann Rutledge and that he had himself baptized before leaving Springfield. We have published here the writings of others attesting that he loved Miss Rutledge.

Before closing, we turn to a brief analysis of Mariah Vance's influence on the Lincolns. She was a devoted servant and friend to both Abraham and Mary Lincoln and cared for their sons, particularly Robert, for whom she had a special fondness. As a boy, Robert would not run to his Aunt Liz when his mother needed help, he ran to Mariah.

Mary Lincoln placed a lot of trust in Mariah and both she and Abraham Lincoln repeatedly thanked her for her help to the family which often went far beyond a servant's care. Mariah became like a "grandmother" to the boys while being a trusted servant to the Lincolns. We may wonder how Mary could have gotten along without her, especially during the months Lincoln was away. By asking Mariah to "Stay with her, Mariah, stay with her" and paying her extra, Lincoln virtually left his wife, sons, and home in her care.

Mr. and Mrs. Lincoln separately confided in Mariah Vance, particularly Mary, who found it a comfort to share her thoughts and feelings with someone who reminded her of her Mammy Sally when she was growing up in Lexington. Mariah Vance's oral history reveals, for the first time, *both* sides of Mary Lincoln's complex personality—the good as well as the bad. While describing Mrs. Lincoln's tantrums in vivid detail, Mariah also reveals the woman's kind and generous nature that surfaced after she had upset someone with her temper.

Lincoln, who respected Mariah for being a good, hardworking Christian woman with a generous, caring heart, also developed some of his concern for and sensitivity to the hardships of Blacks from his knowledge of the hard lives of Mariah and Henry Vance. By Mariah's presence in his home and by visits to her home, Lincoln got a firsthand look into the lives of a typically poor, hardworking Black family living in a free state.

One of the most significant aspects of Mariah Vance's reminiscences is the affection between her and Robert Lincoln, which lasted until her death. Contrary to what some historians write, Mariah tells us that Robert was a kind and loving son to his parents and a wonderful man in adulthood.

Robert Lincoln taught Mariah's son Billie to read and write and, being present, she learned some reading and writing. But like most other uneducated Blacks of her time, she relied on the spoken word to communicate with others.

Storytelling apparently came easy and was natural to Mariah. Less literate people often tend to have good memories and a knack for repeating experiences to others. Mariah told her stories of the Lincolns over and over again for the next forty-four years. Indelible in her memory, she apparently could repeat them by rote.

Studs Terkel suggests in his book *Hard Times*, a collection of oral histories taken from those who remembered America's Great Depression: "This is a memory book, rather than one of hard fact and precise statistic." While Mariah Vance may err on some facts, which is seldom, she is true to her memory of events and conversations.

Mary Lincoln was used to living with housekeepers like Mariah, having been practically reared by Mammy Sally in Lexington. She was comfortable confiding in Mariah, as she did later with Elizabeth Keckley, her Black seamstress in Washington. It is interesting to note that Elizabeth Keckley's knowledge of the Lincolns, before being verified, was doubted for years.

Mary Lincoln had called Mrs. Keckley her "best living friend," and became especially dependent on her after the president's assassination.

Mrs. Keckley dictated her memoirs to a ghostwriter, about her life and years working for the Lincolns, and in 1868 they were published as *Behind the Scenes. Or, Thirty Years a Slave, and Four Years in the White House*. Mary objected to the book and it ended her friendship with Mrs. Keckley who later fell on hard times and died in the Home for Destitute Colored Women and Children in Washington in 1907.

According to historian Mark E. Neely Jr., an Associated Press article in 1935 claimed Elizabeth Keckley never existed and that her book about the Lincolns had actually been written by a White woman journalist. This attempt to discredit Mrs. Keckley and her knowledge of the Lincolns was later corrected by John E. Washington in his book about Negroes who had known Lincoln.

It seems appropriate here to include a short essay written by Adah Sutton in 1956 and given to Lloyd Ostendorf together with a tintype of Jack Lincoln, Robert's son, that she sold to Ostendorf that year. It was titled, "Story of Jack Lincoln's Tintype."

> On one of Robert Lincoln's visits to Danville, Illinois he called on a colored woman named Mariah Vance who had once served the Lincolns in their home in Springfield, Illinois.
>
> On a previous visit he had taken with him his little daughter Mary. They were on their way to Springfield to visit his mother who was indisposed at the home of his Aunt Elizabeth Edwards. Robert Lincoln changed trains at Danville, and while there took the opportunity to visit with "Aunt Mariah," as the Lincoln family called her. He wanted Mary, his daughter, to know this lovely old colored woman whom the Lincolns loved very much.
>
> On this particular visit in 1877, he wanted Aunt Mariah to see what his son looked like, so he brought with him a photograph (tintype) of little Abraham Lincoln, namesake of his famous grandfather Abraham Lincoln, President of the United States, 1861–1865. Robert Lincoln's son was nicknamed "Jack." He placed the picture in the album which he had borrowed and was now returning. This album was an old one that the Lincolns

had discarded when they left Springfield in 1861, and it contained many family pictures and [*those of*] other friends.

In reminiscing as he thumbed through the pages, Robert laughed about bygone happenings of his early life. After telling of incidents concerning various persons pictured, he asked Mariah if she remembered. But with his many laughs came tears from thoughts of his mother and of his martyred father, as well as other relatives remembered.

At one point when he spoke of his mother, Robert Lincoln dropped his head on the table and wept. Mariah put her arm about his shoulders just as she so often had done when he was a small child and shadows fell. To her, he was still a child and would always seem like one. . . her "Mastah Robert."

At length, he said to Aunt Mariah, "You know so much, that if divulged to the world, that would cast a gloom over my children. Would you just tell of the love and happiness that was in our home, for their sakes?"

Though Mariah Vance told this writer many, many incidents that occurred while she was working for the Lincoln family, I believe she never betrayed the trust Robert Lincoln placed in her. (Signed) Adah Sutton.

The tintype of Jack Lincoln appears in the photograph section.

Adah Sutton took no literary liberties with her notes. She respected the historical importance of her material.

If not for Miss Sutton's and Lloyd Ostendorf's efforts over decades, we wouldn't know this important African-American woman ever existed.

While Mariah Vance gives insight into the personal lives of the Lincolns, she also describes her own family and its struggles during the years 1850 to 1860. This reveals the parallel stories of two families, one poor and Black and unknown to historians, and the other, that of the future President of the United States. They lived their lives in tandem while slavery still existed and, as Lincoln said, "America lived half slave and half free."

Historians and biographers of the Lincolns have long wondered about their private lives in Springfield and wished there had been another outside witness in their home to reveal what their personal life was really like. Their housekeeper was that other witness. Here, now, are Mariah Vance's eyewitness accounts of her ten years with Abraham and Mary Todd Lincoln, shedding new, controversial light on America's most beloved but least understood President and his enigmatic First Lady.

VOLUME ONE

ADAH SUTTON'S MANUSCRIPT
OF THE WORDS OF MARIAH VANCE,
PREPARED WITH
EDITORIAL COMMENTS
BY WALTER OLEKSY

CHAPTER ONE

Mariah Meets the Lincolns

April 1850

After a bad storm in April of 1850, about four o'clock in the afternoon, Henry (that's my man), the kids and I was setting out front where we lived [*it was a rented shack on Washington Street in Springfield, Illinois*]. We was watching the coming and going of a rainbow what showed up after the storm in the east sky.

Henry fussed 'cause he thought it foolish-like, for me to tell the youn-guns 'bout Noah and the flood. It did done be a long drawn-out tale. I was 'bout winding it up, telling as how the rainbow was to remind us of Gawd's covenant that never again, no siree, there would never be another flood. I was trying to learn them that the flood had to come. It or something else had to come, 'cause folks was so wicked.

My Henry told me to keep my trap shut, we was going to have company. Henry had watched a tall man headed our way, coming up Washington. I never set eyes on him until up he stepped and turned the square into our front yard.

It was Mistah Abe Lincolumn. We all knowed him. We all knowed he was a good man. We'd heard tell stories 'bout him, that he was a friend of colored folks, just as how he was a friend of white folks.

My Henry spoke to him right friendly. He liked Mistah Lincolumn, but not most white folks.

Henry and his folks had been slaves. He never knew his real Pappy. He done got the name of Vance from a slaveholder who owned his Mammy when he was born. His Pappy had been sold off to another slaveholder. But my man and his Mammy got up North through the unnerground [*Underground Railroad*].

Now, me, I was never a slave. My kinfolks lived just across the Ohio [*River*] from Kaintucky. We often wandered down to the banks of the ribber to play. Well now I just don't remember rightly how many of us [*children*] there was. Only know that while we played, a big boat sailed up to the bank. Some mean white men got out of that boat and drove the older ones of us away. I was so young, I don't zackly remember, so as how I cain't tell it all. I heard tell I and a brother ran and hid. It was an older brother Neal what came up in time to save me.

Neal was not so big, 'cause as he done run with me, he let me fall on a stump. I was too heavy for him. See that white scar on my shin? Must have struck my shinbone a powerful lick. Yes siree! I'll carry that mark to my burying. It are the only white [*thing*] 'bout me. I's just plain black coon.

[*Adah Sutton says, "Mariah laughed then, showing a pink tongue in her toothless mouth. She was in her 80's."*]

But I's right proud I's real black. Had a black Pappy and black Mammy. African black, with good red blood and white hearts. Mammy grieved a heap over losing her chillun. Lawd goodness, it was no use trying to spunk her up. Poor Pappy, he'd go puttering 'round, out of her way. He paid no mind to anything in that Gawd-forsaken wilderness, but trying to do what was needful for Mammy. He'd fix a potful of possum. But the possum was tasteless to Mammy. Pappy would say, "Et hain't rightful dat you younguns should starve." So we et a gorge of possum.

A traveling parson done come along and set up a camp in that wilderness. Mammy and Pappy goes to the camp meeting. They done got the love of Gawd in their hearts. I's sure Pappy would have bust clean out of that meeting, but he see as how Mammy was getting happy, so he got up grit and stayed. He didn't dast go. He'd been a plumb fool not to see the home was going to be right as not again. You's can see I was raised a Christian woman.

After the meeting, we done went farther north and west. Wound up in Illinois, somewhere close to Springfield. That's where I met my Henry. I was just a skit of a gal when we got hitched. Five younguns in eight years was born to us by the time we set foot in Springfield in 1850. [*Mariah was sometimes vague about dates. Town records show she was living in Springfield in 1838 where she was a founder of the Zion Baptist Church; she married Henry Vance in Springfield in 1842.*] We didn't have much but younguns, an old mule, an old wagon, a cart and a wee bit of plunda.

We hardly got settled in our hut, 'til folks, good folks they be, wanted my man to haul wood and do chores. It was so cold in our hut, it froze to ice in our water bucket and outside in our cistern.

My man said we picked the Gawd awfulest time to move. We just had to go where we could find work, cold or no cold, or plumb starve. I got scrubbin's and washn's from folks. We got ourselves kitched up on food stuff and warmer togs. The lap youngun's stayed in, so didn't need shoes. Rent was only 75 cents a week.

That spring it rained a deal, especially April. I wasn't asked to work a heap. The mud in streets was black and sticky, and worse than black where cows roamed and pigs wallered. Guess folks figured, better leave well 'nough alone, while rain kept up, rather than have the muck in their homes.

I was spec'lating on getting most something to do, after the rainbow promised no more floods, and was about to tell my Henry, when I hear Mistah Abe say after greetings, "I'll come right to the point, Mrs. Vance. I believe you are the lady who did cleaning in my law office a while back. Anyone who could clean those windows so you could see through, really clean scrub that floor, and straighten up and make that office smell fresh, is the kind of woman we would like to do our washing and other household chores.

"I'd like most for you to come in the morning. I'm going out of town on the circuit for a spell. Mrs. Lincoln will be alone with our son, Robert.

"Now, to make a long story short, my wife is not well. We just lost our little boy, our precious Eddie. Then too, Mrs. Lincoln has lost other relatives she loved, and her heart is grieved. Besides, we think she is with child. She

69

has morning sickness, besides bad pains in her head. If you'll say you'll come, I'd be powerful much obliged."

But my man right pertnent spoke up. "Mistah Lincoln," Henry say, "Ah cain't no how find fault wid any you'ns doin or how you done treat folks. But ah don't want mah woman screamed at an chasted off'n the place, like you'se woman hab done did other workin' women folks, so ah's hear dem tell. Now my Mariah is a mild woman an ah's got a shield her an take her part. She might talk back a bit, but ah's feared she'd nevva fight a she-cat. Ah's not wantin' to hurt you'ns feelins, Mistah Lincoln, but I cain't 'bide by sich like, as dey say 'bout that woman of you'ns."

Mistah Abe stood right still, right there, as if rooted to that there ground. You could just see as how that man had a world of trouble. After a spell, he say, "Perhaps what you have heard is partly true. But you know when a ball starts rollin in the mud, it gathers more mud."

Then he look at me. "Now tell me, Mrs. Vance, what do you earn? When you wash, do you work by the piece, by the day, the hour, or by the week? I know with a very sick woman to work for, it's going to be a trial. But if you'll try to understand my missus, I think you'll learn to like her. And I think she'll like you. Sometimes it's all in getting acquainted. I'm not a saint. I know I have ways which sometimes jar on Mrs. Lincoln.

"Whatever you've been earning, I'll be glad to pay you more, because you'll have more trials than at most places."

Well, I says to Mistah Abe, "Since my Henry is not working now and won't need the mule and cart, he can stay with the older chilluns. If he says so, I can take the two wee ones. If you have a place to tuck 'em in, while I works."

Well, say Mistah Abe, "I'll be much obliged, and I'll find a place for the children."

My youngest, Julia, was still nursing, and I had to take her. I could put her to nap, but when she done woke up, if she had no company, her would cry. That's 'bout the orneriest thing for me to put up with when working. . . a crying youngun. So I took Phebe, too. [*Mariah's daughter Phebe was about four years old.*]

My Henry say, "Just this onst, Mr. Lincoln, an no more, if'n your woman 'buse'es my Mariah."

Mistah Abe says, "Now Henry, and Mrs. Vance, I'm ever so grateful to you. I feel relieved to leave my family and home in a good woman's hands."

He gave the chillun some stick candy. Told my man he'd get him all the work he could. Said, "I'll have the water pumped and the boiler on early tomorrow. You won't have to rush too much. Not so much you'll have to neglect your own family."

At that, he sauntered 'round the corner.

Well, I got to Mistah Abe's about seven o'clock the next morning. Sure 'nough, there was Mistah Abe poking wood—from a stack he had cut, piled in the yard—under the boiler on a brick contraption in the back yard. The lid of that old battered boiler was bouncing up and down like it had a hot-foot. The wood wash tub with a new-fangled washboard in it was on a stool, and plenty of lye soap. The wash was all in a pile on the floor of a shed.

I tucked my sleeping younguns in the corner of that shed and asked Mistah Abe if he done had his breakfast. He say, "All I care for. But there's a mess in the kitchen I fear I can't tackle."

I went in that nice large kitchen. In that kitchen was a big fireplace, a large table, a small work table, and a corner cupboard. The dishes, pans, and scraps of food was everywhere stacked. I figured while there was plenty of hot water, I'd be mighty smart to clean up the soil 'round about, before starting the wash.

I hardly started stacking dishes and brushing up 'fore I hear somebody coming down the stairs. It was a boy 'bout seven years old. For the life of me, I never set eyes on such a sober-looking boy. Proud-looking, he was, too. I felt a little queer 'round such a boy, so different from Mistah Abe's sad, deep-set, patient eyes. His eyes was so sunken.

Mastah Robert, I discovered later, had one crossed eye. But I loved that little man Robert right off. He then done smiled such a friendly smile that sure as you and I are sitting here on this doorstep, he washed off that sober-proud look right away.

He say, "Aren't I deserving of any breakfast?"

I say, "Land a goodness, Honey Chile, you is 'serving of all the breakfast you little fat belly can hold. I'd cook all day and all night to feed sich a dear, sweet little boy man what he likes best. But don't rub that smile off. That's worth heaps of shining gold."

Mastah Robert laugh. Really laugh out loud. He was a very, very still boy and most awful serious most all the time.

Mistah Abe say, "Robert, this is our new help, Mrs. Vance. I'm about to leave, son, and I'm going to put you in charge. I want you to help her as much as you can, for your mother is not well, you know. So be helpful and comforting. When I'm gone, you are all she will have."

I finished with Mastah Robert's breakfast and do the kitchen, then go out to the wash. I was sorting the clothes in the shed, when what should step right up to that door but the most prettiest woman I's ever laid eyes on. I say, "Howdie, Missy."

She pay no heed to my Howdie. She just walk over to the corner where my younguns was tucked in, and say, "What's this?", and give a terrible jerk on Julia's foot. Julia woke up with a Gawd-splitting ear yelp. De Missy scream at me, "Get those dirty yelling nigger brats out of here! Get them out of here, I say, right away!"

I was about to oblige her, when Mistah Abe come in. Quiet like, he say, "Mother, this is Mrs. Vance, the lady who is going to do the washing and help while I am away."

Say de Missy, "Well, what can she do with them whelps screaming? My head, oh my head!"

"Mother," say Mistah Abe, "you know full well what you'd do if a cyclone came up, sudden like, and jerked you out of bed. You'd do more than yelp. You'd raise the neighborhood, and after you got them raised, you'd swear that cyclone was possessed of a demon and raised them."

Mistah Abe had a powerful bad time with her. He turn to me and say, quiet, "Mrs. Vance, please pay no attention to what Mrs. Lincoln just said. She is such a sick woman. Go on with your work and I'll make Mother comfortable. She's a good woman, but so sick and troubled."

I just thought right there and then, I don't see no good only pretty to look at. She's a she-debil and ought to have them troubles, for how she troubles Mistah Abe. Even poor dear Mastah Robert ran to the barn like he was shot from a flipjack.

I settled Julia with my suckin and gave Phebe, the other youngin, a cracklin' I swept from the table. The washing was big and hard. I sure knowed it wasn't just a week's wash.

Mastah Robert, kind of timid like, come back to the shed bringing a kitten and a ball. He played in that shed with my two uns the rest of that blessed morning. He was being helpful, like as his Pappy told him to be. I just figgered he missed his little brother who had just died. He told my chilluns it was Eddie's kitten and ball.

When Mistah Abe lead de Missy away, I hear him say, "Can't I just for once leave here with a happy thought of you? Why, oh why do you always send me away to worry?" Most, he seemed to say it to himself.

But she spoke up. "If you were half as smart as I once thought you were, you wouldn't have to go wandering over the county, leaving us to get along the best we can with low life help. You'd stay at home like my people do and make a decent living."

Then he say, "Well, Mary, maybe we both made a mistake. And I declare I don't know which one of us made the worst mistake. But I'll do the best as I see it. I'll get you something to quiet you and then must be on my way. I don't want to keep the others waiting."

He pour something out of a glass jug and hand it to de Missy. Since then, I learn it be paregoric [*a mixture of opium and alcohol*]. He took her upstairs and put her to bed.

I finished hanging the wash. Some was dry and I was folding it. Mistah Abe come downstairs and say, "Mrs. Vance, your work is done right fine. The clothes are so clean, Mrs. Lincoln is going to be happy with them. I am glad you stayed. You must have an understanding head and heart. Mrs. Lincoln is always ashamed after she has one of these spells. I want you to come once a week, if you can. I don't think Henry will object when you explain to him."

I knowed my Henry a heap more than Mistah Abe knowed him. We'uns needed that money. Mistah Abe pay me 50 cents extra.

He pack the rest of his belongings in a bag. He come out to the clothes basket and searched out some clean bandannas and socks. He carry in the basket filled and packed down hard with clean clothes I taken down from the line. He put some papers in his tall hat. Took Mistah Robert on his knees, kissed and held him close.

I declare I remember as if twas yesterday, the big tears that rolled down and splashed. That man was a man of Gawd and he was crucified every day of his life.

He say, "Goodbye," and again say, "Thank God for your help."

Then he slumped away to the barn to hitch Buck [*his horse*] to the buggy.

I pitched in and finished straightening the house. Set Mastah Robert's dinner on the kitchen table, and sent food up to de Missy, then went to the barn. When I come back with my mule hitched to the cart, out come Mastah Robert carrying Julia and leading Phebe. Sad-like, he say "goodbye" and trotted back to the barn carrying the kitten. Such a lonesome little tyke.

I knowed right there and then that Mastah Robert was born to trouble, having such an ailing mother. If he didn' die from it, some day he would be a great good man, like his father, and good as to looks, like his mother.

How my heart plumb melted for that poor little lonesome like boy. He was so good and kind. I told my Gawd right there and then, I'd have to go back to that bedeviled house for that poor little boy's sake.

Getting Acquainted with de Missy

April 1850

One day while his father is away on the circuit, Robert runs anx-iously to Mariah's house and pleads with her to come quickly—his mother needs help. At the time, Mary Lincoln is with child.

THE WEEK OF MY FIRST WASH DAY AT MISTAH ABE'S HADN'T PASSED WHEN ONE afternoon about four I sees a small boy chasing all out of wind, right in on our front yard. Flashes of lightning and weak thunder was coming down out of the sky.

It was that poor, spunky Mastah Robert calling out, "Mrs. Vance! Mrs. Vance come quick! My Ma is in torment!"

I got him quiet in a spell. "What you mean, your Ma is in torment?"

(Though I just wants to say, "She's getting her just dues from Amighty Gawd.")

But sure as there is that Gawd in Heaben, when I looked at that poor scared baby boy, I say to myself, "Quit your infernal evil, debil thinking, and gentle-down." Then I say, "What's ailing your Ma?"

"Oh, Mrs. Vance, do come!" Mastah Robert say. "I've asked everyone I know and it's no good. No one wants to help her. One woman says to me, 'Let her die and go to hell!' They hate her! They hate her and they hate me! She's afraid of this thunder and lightning. She's got her head covered and screaming for help. Pa's gone and I'm all Ma has. You heard Pa say so."

My Henry sitting there says, "Mariah, think as how you better go? Ah'll mind de brats a spell."

Mastah Robert's eyes done lit up like one of those new-fangle oil lamps. Then he spied our Billie [*Mariah's son William, who was about eight years old then, a year older than Robert Lincoln*]. Billie was about the size of Mastah Robert. They took to each other about as how two monkeys in a coconut tree.

Mastah Robert forgot he was in a shake to help his Ma. But I did no fiddling. I wants to get going and get back before the storm broke.

Not a thing would gentle those boys down, so I say, "Mastah Robert, should I take Billie along in the cart with us?" He was so pleasured, he had an attack of chuckles right off. Right there and then I knows my black Billie and that blessed little white Mastah Robert was going to be everlasting, fast friends.

We loaded ourselves in the cart and you should have saw how away that mule, Maud, shoved along with each clap of thunder. The boys yelled and laughed with heaps of spirit. The thunder got louder and the mule got faster. I sure believe Mastah Robert was more joyful than he'd ever been before in his unhappy little lonesome like life.

About half way there, we'd gone about three or four blocks, out jumps a pack of rascals to try to stop that mule. You'd never know what that darn fool mule were about to do, until she done it. She pushed right smack through that mob, and did they scamper a spell! Then they got their heads together and give chase with mud balls and screaming at poor little abused Mastah Robert, "Ole rail-splittin' Abe's Bobby's a nigger lover!"

[*Mariah says the local boys called Lincoln a railsplitter in 1850, though the name was generally not applied to him until his campaign for President in 1860.*]

Then they catched up with us and grabbed that cart in the rear and pulled back hard. I pulled as hard on the straps and that mule seem to have horse sense for once. She slow down. I knowed my Billie and Mastah Robert weren't no match for that mess of heathens. They was the debil's own. My Billie would have gotten out of that cart quicker than a cat could catch a rat, but I grabs him by the seat of his pants while he was going over the end, and hauled him back.

Billie calls them white trash, a Gawd-condemned awful name.

Quick as a flash, I gives him a lick over his defiled, blaspheming mouth and knowed he'd been mixing around with them white trash on Jackson Street.

I gives him another lick for good measure, and warn him if I ever catches him with any of them lowdown white trash on Jackson Street I'll give him worse blisters than Shadrack, Meshack, and Obednego would of got iffin Gawd hadn't rescue them from the fiery furnace.

But all that talk of mine to them young'uns went plumb through both their ears. I swear I hardly got my speech out of my mouth than Billie howled, "Mammy, Mammy, here's Pappy's black snake [*black whip*]! Give it to 'em!"

Them blasted white trash was crawling in the back end of my cart. Just as I grab that Gawd-blessed black snake whip and crack it at them, Gawd sent a terrible streak of lightning and a clap of thunder that most upset us, and the mule give another lunge. We all screamed and that mess of rascals done must have thought they was struck by that lightning. I swear a war horse couldn't have catched them. They sure didn't molest us no more.

But oh, my Gawd in Heaben, when we done got to de Missy, it was worse than all the messes I was ever in, in my whole born days. There was de Missy laid up on the old black sofa, her feet twitching and kicking. Her head covered with a quilt and spew all over the floor.

I say to Mastah Robert, "Run for the doctor! Run, run, you scamps, run!"

But then my Billie, always snooping around, say, "Mammy, Mammy, look at her! There ain't no need for the doctor. She's peepin'! Her's playin' possum, like Grandpappy's pet possum. Just get that black snake and give her a good wallop and she'll forget it that it's blowin' outside or that it's goin' to blow this awful hell hole up!"

As quick as that lightning, those boys run out. I couldn't catch them, no siree. Before I uncovered her head or hold her feet from their jerking and twitching, back they come with that blacksnake whip.

Billie come busting in the door screeching, "Wallop that she-debil good, Mammy, and her'll stop scarin' folks out of their wits!"

Mastah Robert looked scared. Poor dear sweet little Mastah Robert. That angel chile had never been around any such as my Billie. Maybe I ought not to have done it, but I right there and then give Billie a cut with that black snake. He give out a howl worse than that thunder.

Up jump de Missy! Hair down and all tangle up, face covered with spew. There was no angel-pretty about her now.

I say, "Please, Missy, don't upset youself. I've come to protect you. This storm is bound to be over soon. My Henry always say, 'The harder the storm, the quicker it's over.'"

But Lawd God, her wasn't jumping about the storm. She was hair pulling-mad because I wallops my Billie.

She say to me, "Haven't you even got nigger sense? Billie only told the truth. This is a hell hole, and I've made it so! If anyone needs to be beaten, I need it. But no one needs cruelty and I won't lie still, no matter how I feel, and see it practiced in my house."

Mastah Robert done run to his Ma and cried, "Oh, Ma! Don't scold Mrs. Vance. She is a good, understanding woman in her heart and head. I heard Pa tell her so."

"Yes, oh, yes," say de Missy. "It was good of her to come over here in this storm, to be here to protect me. Leave her home and family. I shouldn't have had you go for her. But I was so sick and afraid."

Well, I just tell her, she'd have to get more love in her heart, for my Good Book says, "Love casts out fear."

She say, "If love have cast out fear, Mariah, love will cast out whip-pings, too."

I didn't want to argue with her, but my teaching never say anything about whippings.

The storm did just as my Henry say. It didn't last long. I got a basin of water for de Missy to wash her face. I ask if she would want as how I should clean out a clutter of parcels all around on the floor. [*Clothes and Mrs. Lincoln's yard goods, ribbons, etc., for sewing.*]

Do you know what she up and say? "Why, Mariah, those are little dresses I've made for your baby Julia from our darling little Eddie's clothes. I was so very sorry I disturbed baby Julia's sleep. I do so many wrong things when I have these headaches."

"Well, yes," I say to her. "You are a very sick woman. But you shouldn't carry on so with that baby you've got to have born. And bless your pretty heart, you didn't owe my black younguns any dresses."

We didn't see a strange woman soon enough, but there she stood right smack in the door. De Missy speak right up to her: "Nice time for you to be coming, Liz." [*Elizabeth Edwards, Mary's sister who lived about six blocks away at Second and Jackson Streets.*]

Then this Liz spied the spew on the carpet and her acted all upset. She went over to de Missy and say, "Mary, baby, why didn't Bobby tell me? Even though I've been swamped with work and must give a party, I would have dropped everything and come right over."

De Missy say, "Well you know how afraid I am when it storms and Mister Lincoln is away. All you think about is clean, clean, clean that big house and cook, cook, cook for parties."

"Well, Mary," Liz say, "if you'd think less of sewing up all the goods in the county to outshine everyone else in dress"—(looking at the material strewn around)—"and learn more about cooking and providing the right nourishing food for your family, you would have a happier and healthier family and home."

De Missy huffed up right smart about that. "Now, Lib (when she was mad, Mary called Liz, 'Lib'), if it's any of your nosey business, I'm just making a few little dresses for this fine colored woman's child."

Lib right smart up and say, "Since when have you become so patronizing to colored folks? It's time you're thinking of someone besides yourself."

"Well," say de Missy with her hands on her hips and those pretty eyes turned into a cyclone, but still looking straight at this Lib like her ruled the earth, "Mariah came to me when you wouldn't, and you know, Lib, I wouldn't send for you or anyone else unless I needed them."

This Missy sure have a world of spunk. Then her say in the sweetest voice Gawd Amighty ever put in a human being, "This is my sister Elizabeth, Mariah. Mrs. Edwards, this is Mrs. Henry Vance. She came to help us out last Monday, Lib. She is a good, clean, honest woman."

Right quick like, Elizabeth spoke out, "Mary, you need someone, and I hope you don't take any tantrums with this Mariah, and run her off."

I couldn't bear to hear that sick woman talked to any more like that, so

I say, "With her fixed up like her is, her's a mighty sick woman, with all her other complaints."

"I know, I know," say Miz Edwards. "But there isn't anything wrong with her that good common sense won't help some. Mother, Father, and I have humored and spoiled her, because she demanded it. And now her servants, Bobby, and Mister Lincoln especially have to take the brunt of all our foolishness. Abraham takes it or gets out. Many times, he gets out so Mary can have her way. I hope once in her life she has common sense enough to keep a good servant. All her other servants just couldn't take it, so they got out and stayed out."

That was all the sweet talk about me, but poor Missy, her spilled over a bucket of tears, crying her poor, poor sick heart out. Lib softened like Pappy's cotton balls, and as sure as Gawd made little apples, her went over to de Missy, kissed her, wiped up her tears with her silk handkerchief, and cried a little herself.

Lawd-a-goodness, I never once set eyes on such carrying on. Blazing mad at one another one minute, and the next minute loving and kissing like turtle doves. Maybe that's good raising. For I and my Henry, a little bit of fight, to get to make up, seem powerful good. But two kin, I just can't see. Who ever thought that was even good sense?

My Pappy would have given us a learning we'd remember, with his harness strop. There'd be no need for kissing and making up. We dasn't never fuss and fume in our home. I suspect they'd better kiss and smooch first, then there would be no fuming and fighting like wildcats.

But for ten years, I saw such doings, but they always parted friends and happy like.

Not with Mistah Abe. About the time he'd get his tank full of such foolishness, he'd just up and walk off, and wait until the fire cool off. Not that I could always abide by that. But that man were a man of Gawd. He just didn't like fuming around enough to take his own part. So there were no need to kiss and make up.

I hardly could help howling myself, but it was soon over and Miz Edwards went home. She say she'd come every day or send her husband to find out if de Missy need anything that they could bring or do.

When that Elizabeth left, de Missy say, "Elizabeth is very dear to me and I love her very much, but she has always tried to direct my life as she wants it. She would resent it if I meddled in her affairs. Elizabeth has been so kind through the years that perhaps I should look over her few faults. But I have both the Todd and Parker Southern temper [*Mary's mother's maiden name was Parker*], which I was never persuaded to try to control. Oh, I've so many evil ways."

Again she start to cry. I say to her, "You're not evil, you're just such a sick woman in your head. And you shouldn't be about tiring yourself, making these dresses for my Julia."

I was weaning Julia. I should have stopped a spell back, but she was so puny and the other chillun needed all the vittles we could get our hands on. We was so hard up. Milk sickness was going around, cholera, and I was feared.

"These dresses are most too flub-dub for poor colored folks," I tell de Missy. "Maybe you could let some of your rich folks have them."

Right then and there, I made a horrible mistake. I can't see why as how I can't leave well enough alone and keep my big mouth clamped, as my man say I should. For de Missy really wants to make up with us, because her pull Julia's leg and made her howl.

She say, "Oh, Mariah, won't you use them? Maybe I can change them some and they would be more like play dresses. They are made of good, strong material and colors that won't show soil easily. I have so many more. But if you feel you don't want Julia to wear little angel Eddie's clothes, I'll put them back in the chest."

There were a lot of love stitches in them clothes. Her had put a lot more in, to make up to Julia. So I say, "Why, bless you good Christian heart, Missy. I sees you have powerful lot of ideas about dressing little girls that are right good, even if you never have any of your own. I's just a plain black niggah and haven't got a heap of sense about clothes. My Henry's going have to change his mind about you." I clamp my hand over my mouth faster than that lightning, for sure enough, I let the cat out of the bag!

But just then, in bounced Billie and Mastah Robert with two stray kittens. Right then I see, if I never done did another thing, I had to get that Billie of mine out of that clean house of de Missy before all holla break loose. That house was so clean, it glisten-like. Only a wee litter around where de Missy been stitchin, and the wet spot where Miz Edwards have clean up the floor.

Mastah Robert say, "Billie, you can have the kittens, or you can give them to Phebe and Julia." Looking at his mother's frown, he say, "Ma don't like cats. Pa, he'd bring all the cats and dogs and other animals he found on the circuit.

"One time he brought us a white rat. It was in one pocket and a turtle in the other. He had put candy in each pocket for them. But the rat ate a hole in his pocket and was about out when he got home, and the turtle snapped his finger as he took it out of his pocket. It's the only time I ever heard Pa howl. Afterwards, he laughed about as loud as he howled."

This put de Missy at the same time in mind of a story Mistah Abe told: A parson was giving a toast to the really good things in life. He said, "Parsons are preaching for them, lawyers are pleading for them, doctors are prescribing for them, authors are writing for them, soldiers are fighting for them, but only a few are enjoying them! May we never forget that 'vice stings us, even in our pleasure, but virtue consoles us even in our pain.' At which one of the congregation replied, 'He makes no friends who never made a foe.'"

So Mister Lincoln said, "Let them bite and snap. Mother can have a pair of white ear muffs, and I'll have my turtle soup."

"You see," say de Missy to Mastah Robert, "Your Pa befriended a rat who chewed up his coat and a turtle that bit him after he gave him candy, but he still felt well paid."

Mastah Robert sure enough like the story, but my wild Billie say, "The dirty bums! I'd cram that candy down their dirty necks, and grab 'em by the tails and beat their brains out for not swallowing it!"

That speech didn't please de Missy too much like, but Bobby jump up and down and laugh and throw his hat in the air.

I know de Missy was going to quiet him down. But first she say, "Take them cats out and come right back in. I'm going to need you, Bobby."

When they come in, she was sweet as an angel. That woman have once again turn back to de prettiest woman I most ever seed. I don't know as how she done it so quick. But she took the boys careful like by the arms and told them to sit there and if they be quiet, they could have some cakes with raisins.

Billie hardly got sat 'til he screamed for cookies, but Mastah Robert was a little gentleman. Missy brought the cookies from the cookie jar and when they was et up, her brushed up the crumbs right quick.

Then she say, "Boys, stand up." Billie was a wee bit higher than Mastah Robert, who was heaps fatter. "Bobby, go up to your room and bring me your waists [*shirts*] and pantaloons and waistcoats."

Billie started to follow, but she grabbed him by the sleeve, what was so dirty I was ashamed. Now de Missy say, "You sit right there and be quiet, if you can for a little while."

For all that, I say, "I'll strap you, if you don't." I hadn't yet learned the lesson de Missy wouldn't abide by cruelty.

"Oh no you won't!" she says. "I run this house and you're going to do as I say. Do you understand that, Mariah?"

Billie yelled loud as thunder, "Give it to her, Missy, with both barrels!"

That pleasured de Missy and as black and dirty as he was, I thought sure she was going to kiss him. From that very Gawd-blessed day on, her love my Billie boy. And he was tooth and toenail for her. I still thought I'd strap him, when I got home.

I just can't figure out how that woman, as sick as her was when I left her on wash day, and as sick as her was the lightning day, could in betwixed done such loads of work. On wash day, I'd always wash and straighten up a speck, but there was nary a speck of soil on anything as big as a fly speck.

She was a fine housekeeper. Besides the house clean as the driven snow, she had planted flowers, onions, lettuce, peas, and Lawd, I don't know as how what all in that ground Mistah Abe have dug up. Her pretty, dimple hands was all scarred and that dirt grown in where that lye soap have made cracks. I told de Missy her shouldn't bend over, in her condition.

She say, "I would like to know who else would. Mister Lincoln is too tall to bend. He's bent so much already, carrying the boys straddled around his neck, bless them, playing piggyback. Then he carries the world on his shoulders."

Well, her tell Billie to put on some of Mastah Robert's clothes. Billie grabbed the bunch and went racing to the shed. I got there with a towel Missy hand me, and brush him up a bit. I swear, when you can see dirt on a black niggah, they's dirty. I got only the worse off of him.

I have a fight with him to keep a ruffled bedubbed waist on, and pantaloons buttoned at the knees. But I led him into de Missy by the ear, him screaming bloody murder.

I make him march right in to de Missy, screaming, "I don't want these sissy ruffly duds!"

At which Mastah Robert spoke up and say, "You see, Ma? That's why they make fun of me and call me sissy!"

So she say, "We'll see about some of the rest." She picked up the plainer, stout ones, and put them in a stack on a chair where the clothes for Julia were laying. She thanked me for coming, and say Mistah Lincolumn would pay me when I come to wash again.

I say, "Lawdy, Missy, I couldn't take no pay, after you give us all these duds. Bless you, bless you so much."

She say, "You're very welcome, Mariah, and bring Billie again. Bobby and I would love to have him. Now, Mariah, I believe you need come only every two weeks, since Mister Lincoln is not at home. I will wash out the few things we really need.

"I'm trying to get someone to stay at night. It's so lonely. Maybe one of Bobby's friends or perhaps an Irish girl I've heard of. She can get breakfast, then clear the dishes before she leaves in the morning. That would give me a chance to catch up on my sewing.

"Since Grandmother Parker died in January and my father in July, we've been in Lexington looking after affairs, or here caring for our dear little Eddie during his sickness and death. We've grieved so. I've neglected so much, too.

"Mariah, you and Billie have been who I needed all along. I feel I'm back home once again with Mammy Sally and all the pickaninnies." [*This term for black children would today be considered offensive.*]

At that, Mastah Robert spoke up. "Oh, Ma, can we call Mrs. Vance 'Mammy Mariah'?"

I don't know why, but that just didn't seem right. I say, "I's Mammy to my younguns, but I was never Mammy to no whites."

I ask, kind of scared, "How old be you, Missy Lincolumn?"

She say, "I'm thirty-two, Mariah. How old are you?"

"Well, I be twenty-eight in July," I say. "I's no ways old enough for you to call 'Mammy.'" [*Mariah was really thirty-one, a year younger than Mary.*]

"All right, Mariah," she say. "Maybe you wouldn't object if Bobby calls you 'Aunt Mariah.' Would you like that?" That was so blessed, being called "Aunt" to a little white boy like Mastah Robert. I say, "You's a powerful good woman, Missy Lincolumn."

She say, "Thank you, Mariah. If it's hard for you to say 'Mister Lincoln. . . .'" [*Adah Sutton did not complete this sentence. It was decided that Mariah call her employer "Mistah Abe," as she had trouble pronouncing "Lincoln." Lincoln disliked being called "Abe," but made an exception in Mariah's case.*]

". . . You can continue to call me 'Missy,' as I heard you call me to Billie. Billie, you can call me 'Missy,' too. It'll sound so sweet."

I told her I'd pay her in works, for the younguns' duds her give me. De Missy shooed me off.

I told Billie to get in the bottom of the cart, and spread all the clothes over him, so the white trash couldn't see him on the way home.

My Henry started to raise the very debil, when I was unhitching that mule, Maud. I went in. He was worn out with those four I left with him. Then he spied that stack of finery. He dug in that stack for some shirts for himself that Mistah Abe was tired of.

I say, "I guess Mistah Abe wears the tails off his own shirts."

Mad like, Henry say, "Didn' you bring any grub? We's starved."

Lawd, that Henry was de grubbingest man alive, and I told him to shut his foolish hoggishness. I'd fix him some flapjacks. He loved flapjacks. I told him all about our troubles with the white trash rascals. I knowed that big mouth Billie would spill the beans, if I didn't tell.

Henry say, "Lawd have mercy on our'n souls. Doze white debils ain't worth hog tyin' and killin', but that's what they'll do to us, every last black crow of us, if dey catch us. Dey done a heap more for less. Jes for walk'n on de street. When dey get a mean streak, dey string de black man up an laugh wid his dy'n jerk. We'ns just hab to stay unda cover."

I just told my Henry to simmer down. I wasn't going back to Mistah Abe's for two weeks, and the stink would all be blown away by then. Maybe Mistah Abe would be home by then, and if anyone could fix these things, that Mistah Abe could. He was a smart man. So my man quiet down a spell.

But you know, I's telling the truth. Henry was scared a spell, for a plumb week. But I did all the praying I could think of. I promised Gawd Amighty everything.

CHAPTER THREE

Mistah Abe "Cures" Billie's Lice

May–June 1850

Mariah returns to work for Mary while Mr. Lincoln is still away on the circuit. Mariah, too, is now with child.

On another visit, Lincoln returns home and helps Mariah and Billie through a "hair-raising" happening.

*I*GOT OVER TO DE MISSY AROUND SIX TO DO A TWO-WEEKS' WASH. THERE WAS A FIRE ready to light under the boiler and the boiler filled with water. I went in the shed and the clothes was sorted. The tubs were on the bench, the lye soap and board [*washboard*.], too. All I had to do was rinse the clothes in cold, clear water.

While the boiler done got hot, for hot suds to wash with, I had walked over to the yard, the spring weather was so beautiful. The flowers were up and still some blooming. I found I was coutched [*Mariah's word for pregnant*] as well as de Missy; I done weaned Julia in the nick of time. Just knowed I better walk and keep moving, to keep well for the next kid.

[*Mariah may have drawn upon the French noun,* couche, *for "coutched." Couche in French means marriage bed, child bed, delivery, birth. She may have heard the word while working for women who had learned French in finishing school and used couche when referring to their own pregnancies.*]

About seven, as I was hanging up the white clothes, Mastah Robert rushed out of the house and done took for a neighbor's where a boyfriend lived. Like the little gentleman he was, he called, "Howdy-do, Aunt Mariah!"

That "Aunt Mariah" made me right smart happy.

I finished the colored ones, emptied up around, and taken down the first ones dried, when I seed a redhead gal leave. She was young, maybe going to school. Her name was Lauri. [*Mary's helpers never stayed long on the job.*]

De Missy had done told me Mastah Robert's eyes was still weak and a little uncertain yet, after an operation on his eye by a German doctor and Doctor Wallace [*Mrs. Lincoln's sister Frances's husband, Dr. William Wallace*], that she wasn't sending him to school until fall. He was old enough and smart enough. She had taught him to read and write and some numbers. Oh yes, and a little French. He didn't like French, but just guess her crammed it down him.

The children at school had tormented him about his eyes [*they had been slightly crossed*], so she was still undecided whether to start him in school in the fall.

When I carried in the folded clothes, I saw that Lauri had straightened up a bit. De Missy heard me and called, "Is that you, Mariah?"

I asked her how was she, and she says, "I've been too busy, Mariah, to think of myself. I've made curtains for the entire house, made clothes for Bobby, if he goes to school this fall, and clothes for the new baby that is coming. I hope it is a girl. Mister Lincoln and I would both love to have a girl."

Well, I ups and say "I's wanting mine to be a boy."

At that, de Missy say, "Why, Mariah, why didn't you tell me you were expecting a child, too?"

"Well," I say, "'cause I didn't know I was coutched. Couldn't tell as how, as long as Julia was nursing. But since her are weaned, it showed up. I do hope it's a boy. Billie'll raise the roof if another gal shows up. Ellen, the oldest, he bats around. Guess it's just his way of saying he wish she was a boy."

De Missy say, "That makes me think, Mariah, why didn't you bring Billie? I've fixed over the clothes he called sissy. You must bring him the next time. Maybe Bobby will stay home a while, if Billie is here to play with. I never know where he is, or what he's doing when his father is away, and that's most of the time.

"I haven't heard a word from Mister Lincoln. I wouldn't blame him if he never wrote, or even if he never came home, the way I cut up."

"Well, now," I say. "Missy, you just don't know as how he's kind of ought to be 'nuvered [*maneuvered*]."

Her say, "Does anyone? I've tried every trick. If at the end of each trick it just doesn't work, I get discouraged and blow up. He just doesn't love me, and there is no other way to reach him."

"Oh, now," I say. "Back up, Missy. That man just love the whole world."

At that her say, and her have me stumped, "I don't want him to love me like he loves the whole world. I want him to love just me, as any man should love his wife."

I sure could think of only one thing to say after I pondered and considered. "Well, that man, that Mistah Abe, am a man of Gawd and my good preacher say, 'God is Love.'"

Her sent me home, saying, "Take care of yourself, Mariah. You're the only one I have to depend upon. Come in two weeks and bring Billie."

I went home with a downcast spirit. Everyone thought she was a bad, bad woman. She was only a badly mixed-up woman. A woman who didn't unnerstand her man, or her man unnerstand her.

I went back in two weeks. It was now June. I took my Billie with me. Mistah Abe was there this time. He was so poor and hollow-eyed. Look as how he have nary a thing to eat all month.

He had all the wash ready, and a heap of wood cut. I swear, I knowed he never seen me. I call out, "Mornin', Mistah Abe!"

He spied my Billie. I do believe he think it was my Billie saying, "Mornin', Mistah Abe!" He perked up by littles.

Billie, like his Mammy, never could keep his flytrap shut. Calls, "Hey, there! Are you'n deaf? Where's Bobby?"

Mistah Abe say nary a word, just pointed upstairs. Billie knowed none of this here sign talk. He took an old sock ball out of his pocket and socked it up on the house where Mistah Abe had pointed. That sure woke him up some. When it bounced off the house, he [*Lincoln*] caught the ball and throws it back to Billie. Billie slammed it back, and that got their acquaintance started.

They kept moving by littles down closer to the barn. I figured Mistah Abe wanted to get out of my way, and far enough away so that ball wouldn't strike the house again. They keep up that play 'til I was near done with my wash, and it was a hard one. Mistah Abe have brought home a heap of dirty clothes. Smelled bad, like he have a fever and forgot to take them off when he went abed.

Finally, they got tuckered out throwing and catching. Mistah Abe and Billie sat down on the wood pile. Billie squirmed around and finally went after the lice he'd catched in that black wool [*hair*] of his. Guess he done got them stirred up, playing what Mistah Abe calls a fast game of hand ball. That man sure loved to play that hand ball.

Mistah Abe noticed Billie scratching and say, "Mariah, what's Bill digging up there after?" [*Lincoln always called him "Bill."*]

"Mistah Abe, I swear if he catched them again, playing with that bad set next to us. [*Some white boys Billie played with in their neighborhood.*] I never know what to do with him. I always tell my younguns to stay away from them white trash."

Mistah Abe caught Billie and cracked a big louse with his fingers. He say, "Mariah, I know the very fellow who can get rid of these lice in a hurry, if you'll let me take Bill to him."

I say yes, so Mistah Abe take Billie to his barber. He bring back a shaved-headed, bald boy.

At first I didn't know my own son. Say, "Who that ape?"

When I recognize him, I got so all fired mad, I nearly left the Lincolumns then and there forever. I had no idea Mistah Abe would done get Billie's head shaved. It took a plumb year growing his wool back. The colored folks in those days was proud of their wool. I was worried until it began to grow back. Straighter, but still wool.

"Well, Mariah," say Mistah Abe, "I can't say I'm surprised that you love those kinks, after seeing my unruly black wig. At least kinks stay where you put them."

I raved again. "I's most about to give my Billie another punishment. A little peach oil, as you say, Mistah Abe. [*Peach seeds were made into a bitter oil. Some parents gave their children a mouthful of peach oil as a mild form of punishment.*] But I suspect he's had most enough. . . . lousy and a bald pate, for getting too thick with them white trash."

"Well," say Mistah Abe, "I'm white trash."

"Now look here," I say, "Mistah Abe, you done about enough already, without telling me I's working for white trash."

Mistah Abe laughed and laughed. I was about to pick up my youngun and leave, but he stopped laughing and say, "Well, Mariah, if Mother can stand me, you should be able to. And if my boy gets lice, I'll have his head shaved. But as for white trash, I was called white trash, my people were scoffed at and called white trash, and I must admit some of them were a little trashy. But if they'd all met a Mary Todd to put up with them and love them, maybe they'd tried to match her trying, as I did.

"Mariah, when you go home, give those 'white trash' neighbors a little kindness, if you can't love them. With your big, kind heart, I believe you can help to make them over to be as fine as your own family are. Remember there is only one power, Love. For God is Love."

At that, he took from his long coat pocket a sack of licorice sticks and passed them around.

I say, "I'll stay, and sure am shamed I cut up so."

I heard steps in time to push Billie's sock cap down tight over his bald head. Mistah Abe, Billie, and I all laughed.

[*Mary came out of the house, then.*] De Missy get suspicious and say, "So you can find pleasure with someone or something outside your family."

Well, that talk took us all by surprise. I sobered up.

Mastah Robert come up, grab Billie, and rushed for the barn, and Mistah Abe looked black. I never see such a downcast, black look.

[*Because his eyes were closed, Billie apparently stumbled and nearly fell when Robert grabbed him, and the boys must have made some noise that disturbed Mary Lincoln because she seemed upset.*]

As Mistah Abe leave with de Missy, I hear him say, "Now Mother, don't get upset again. I had to take Bill to the barber, to get his wool cut, for it was full of lice. Guess Aunt Mariah was ashamed of Bill's bald pate and pushed his cap down so tight it covered his eyes. That's why Bill stumbled and almost fell when Robert grabbed him and rushed away. Is there any harm in laughing at that?"

De Missy raised the paregoric bottle and drank from it. I knowed that bottle was a plumb gallon.

Mistah Abe say, "Mother, Mother, I wish you wouldn't. I suppose this means another day of stupor. If you'd only try to control yourself, for the child coming, if for no other reason."

De Missy say, "Little you care about me or the one we have, leaving us a month at a time without a word. When you do come home, with your hideous appearance and filthy clothes, how could you expect me to appreciate your return and fawn over you? Even the sight of you is repulsive. So get out! Get out, I say!"

He got out and drug his feet to the barn where the boys were. I hear Mastah Robert say, "Pa, I want my head shaved, like Billy's."

"Now, now," say Mistah Abe. "Not now. But if you get lice, off that beautiful hair comes."

"I'm going to get lice then!" screamed Mastah Robert.

"Well, Robert," say his Pa, "if you do, I might give you a little peach oil before the shave."

"Aw, gee, Pa," say Mastah Robert. "You never do what I want. You said you would take me to the woods sometime, but you never have done it. And I don't think you ever intended to. I want to see the flowers and the giant trees like you said you had split. I want to climb one of those giant trees and do what you used to do when a boy. I know for sure that's what made you so big and strong and good. I don't like to hear people say mean things about your rail-splitting as if it were a disgrace. Pa, can't we go? Can't we?"

I guess that was too much for Mistah Abe. He took Mastah Robert by the hand, picked up the ax, and they started off. Billie tormented me to go along with them. I have to box him, to get him to shut up.

I finished carrying in the wash, straighten up a little around, fixed some grub on the table, and went back home with Billie. All the way back, I was pondering what I would say when my Henry saw Billie's shaved head. I told Billie he sure must keep his cap on in the house when we got home. But the first thing he done did was to sling that cap across the room.

It was no time until Henry calls, "Come here, Billie!"

When Billie come there, my Henry grabbed him and before I could even think, had that boy 'cross his knees. Henry was short from his belly to his knees, so all I could do was to grab him by the feet and yank. Down slid Billie to the floor, and then made a dash for the door.

I grabbed Billie by the collar. I heard the buttons snap off and Billie was out that door like greased lightning, with me holding his coat that bust off of him.

That niggah man of mine was so mad, his eyes pop out of his mug and scowl up as big as a new red moon. He was that mad, a swearing something Gawd-awful. He would have bust out that door and after Billie, but I stood with my back against that shack door, and he knowed I'd taken my stand.

I say, "Now you big, black ignoran' coon, you go right back to that chair or I'll dent your old dumb head with this poker!

"Now you listen to me! Our Billie catched lice from those poor white trash he's been playing around with. Mistah Abe took him up to his barber and had his head shaved. I was mad too, when I saw that fine crop of wool gone. But it are gone, so are the lice. And I say, how you going to put them back? Not by scorching that poor boy's bottom!"

All my man could say was, "That long leg jackass scarecrow! That ugly lantern-jawed jackass!"

I waited until he run down abusing Mistah Abe, then I made it clear Billie had his punishment enough now. I let on it was settled and went about getting the vittles on the stove.

I made Billie wash the dung off his hands he got in Mistah Abe's barn. Made him sew the buttons on that popped off, before I give him any sow belly and beans and corn pone.

That seem to please my Henry. He still growled 'round once, now and then, but done tapered off as Billie's hair growed out.

Billie learned a heap, before that wool growed. The lice never hung 'round him any more 'cause he quit hanging around where he could catch 'em.

CHAPTER FOUR

De Missy Gets
Confidential with Mariah

June 1850

Adah Sutton wrote in her Preface that she thought it would be disre-spectful to have the Lincolns speak in the Black English speech Mariah Vance used. She transliterated certain words and grammar into the manuscript.

Henry Clay and Cassius Marcellus Clay are mentioned in this chapter. Henry Clay (1777–1852), a leader of the Whig Party, was a Kentucky senator with presidential aspirations and a Todd family friend in Lexington. Mary Todd admired him.

Cassius Marcellus Clay (1810–1903), Henry Clay's cousin, ran unsuccessfully for governor of Kentucky in 1851 on an anti-slavery ticket. He was a founder of the Republican Party in 1854.

95

I CAIN'T ZACKLY RECOMEMBA IF IT WAS THE NEXT TWO WEEKS AFTER MISTAH ABE HAD my Billie's hair cut off from lice or not, but somewheres near that time.

When I went to do the wash, the door was locked. There was no wash out and no clothes in the shed. I was plumb scared. I thought de Missy might have took too much paregoric and done laid up there daid.

I was pounding on the door and wringing my hands, and praying Gawd to have mercy on that poor critter Missy's soul, when Mastah Robert open up that very same door I was pounding on and say, "Boo, Aunt Mariah!"

I jumped as high as that doorknob. I almost fell in that door. I shouted, "Glory Hal-lulah! Glory Hal-lulah!"

That Mastah Robert near split his fat little sides laughing. I give that young tease a spank on his rump and say, "Where's de Missy? What's the fault with her now?"

"Nothing's wrong with her, Aunt Mariah," he say. "She had folks in after church yesterday. The preacher, his wife, Aunt Lizabeth and Uncle Ninnie [*Ninian Edwards*], Uncle Wallace and Aunt Francie, and some of the children. They ate dinner with us and stayed for supper. The preacher and his wife went home, but our folks stayed. They played chess and some other games until late. She's sleeping this morning, to make up for sleep she lost last night.

"Ma said, 'Go let Aunt Mariah in before she breaks the door down. The neighbors will tell I've been beating you and your father to death. Hurry, Robert, before I have another spell!'

"She tries to scare me, but I'm used to Ma's spells. Aunt Mariah, you'll get used to them too. Pa says, 'She's still just a little girl who has never grown up.' But I wish she'd grow up, or I would. I expect if I was grown up, I'd put her across my knees as your Henry does Billie. I suspect Pa feels like it sometimes."

"Now, now," I says to that. "Your Mammy are a powerful sick woman, and your Pa knows it. He wouldn't think of molessing your Ma. Her needs love and care the worstest way. Don't you never, never say unkind things about her, or to her."

"Aunt Mariah," Mastah Robert say, "I don't dare say them to her."

Then he stopped right there and then, because I pointed my finger at him and say, "Shew!" He skipped out that door, then come back and say, "I almost forgot, Aunt Mariah. . . . Ma said there would be no washing. She did

DE MISSY
GETS
CONFIDEN-
TIAL
WITH
MARIAH

it Friday and ironed Saturday. But she wants you to clean the kitchen and get dinner. Said use up what you can of the leftovers."

I swear, that woman was the mostest saving on vittles I ever see. Only [*except*] when her have company. I had the kitchen floor scrubbed until it was white as sand. I has to have a hot fire to heat water to wash the dishes. There was stacks of them dishes. I stood on some old hemp sacks in one corner of the kitchen while I washed the dishes. The floor was dried and I made the dinner of corn dodgers, chicken cut up in little bitsy pieces, and heat with the leftover sop. They call that some big name now, like frigasee [*fricassee, meat or chicken cut into pieces and stewed in gravy*].

It was just warmed over chicken, but de Missy when she smelled it and come down to eat, said, "Why, Aunt Mariah, with the leftover vittles, dessert, and that fine-smelling chicken gravy over corn dodgers, it really tastes better to me than our Sunday dinner. And this drink, Aunt Mariah, what can it be? It's delicious!"

Well, I just told de Missy, "I couldn't find any wine about for you. The bottles laying around was plumb empty, so I just parched some corn, rolled it down fine with the rolling pin, and then boiled it in water. I and my man and chillun like it."

Mastah Robert drank two cups of it. He said, "Ma, can't we drink this every day? Maybe I'll get stout, like Billie."

De Missy done didn't answer. I see, even if her did like it, to her it was black folks' or poor white trash food.

I had put a tin cup full of wilted wildflowers in the center of the table. De Missy spied them and said, "I'm glad you didn't throw these flowers away, Aunt Mariah. Robert brought them home from the woods last Monday where his father took him, as he had so often promised to do sometime. Robert and Mister Lincoln must have had a grand trip. Neither one could stop talking about it. It brought back so many memories to Mister Lincoln of his early life which he always seemed so reluctant to talk to me about, though he reviewed them in detail to Robert.

"I'm sure Robert's new impressions of his father as a woodchopper or rail-splitter will never again give him shame. He has been taunted by that in school, what little he attended last year. Now he has two battles fought. His eyes and his father's menial beginning. Now he looks at his father as a mighty oak, a man who has grown unsuppressed by the all-protecting hand of almighty God.

"I heard Mister Lincoln say to him, 'Son, I did split rails, but no railing about it is ever going to stop me, and don't let it ever stop you. Whether splitting rails or doing any other honest labor has its purpose in God's plan. To spur you on by first providing growth of body and sinewy muscles. As the body builds, the mind will build honest thoughts, deeds, and finally achievements. Honest labor goes into making honest men. Always remember that, Bob, and you'll never be hurt.'

"Robert on his own initiative gathered these flowers for me. That is one way Robert is like me. He loves every little, tiny blossom. Even weed flowers are beautiful and precious to him. So I'm making these flowers, this bunch of love, last as long as I can. It's his first full bouquet to me. I'm glad he's like what is best in me, if only a little. He is so like the Todds in body, but what pleases me most is he is so like his father, sensible and honest.

"Mister Lincoln brings me to task so often about the little fibs I tell. He calls them fibs, but sometimes they have gained the proportion of a black lie. It seems it has grown on me since childhood. My dear, dear father called them fairy tales and laughed at them.

"Mister Lincoln once said, 'Mary dear, I want you and my family to have all the good things I can provide. Don't think you have to fib to me. I'm so often embarrassed by bills poked at me, which you claim you have not run or have paid.'

"He patted me once and said, 'Mary if you have to fib, do make it such a whopper I can't catch you in it.'

"He's never been unkind to me. Since little Eddie went away he's gone out of his way to try to please me. But I know as God knows, it isn't because he loves me."

I was afraid to let her get too deep in that subject, so I says, "What was you going to tell me about their trip to the woods?"

De Missy say, "Oh, yes. They brought back slippery elm, bee bread [*honeycomb?*], and robbed a tree of honey. Mister Lincoln smoked them out by burning both of his socks on a long pole. That was a good excuse for getting rid of his socks. He just doesn't like to wear them, even in winter.

"You should have seen Robert when he and his father came home. He was honey from his chin down. It was a picture I shall never forget. He was so smeared and bedrabbled, but so happy.

"I believe his father was the happiest I have ever seen him. That trip will bind them closely. Closer than anything else. They've found a common

bond that will last. I pray God that Mister Lincoln and I could find a mutual tie.
I think we have both tried, but our foundations to begin with were so warped
and insecure, and our perspectives have grown farther and farther apart.

"I've even been afraid since Eddie went away that Robert will be taken
as a punishment for my gross sins. I even thought I should take my life so I
would not bring another one in the world to suffer for my sins."

"Now, now," I says, "look right here, Missy. You stop that rotten kind of
talk. You was brought here to replenish the earth. How as I know or anyone
know how as their chillun will do or hab a suffer? You suffer for your own
wrong. So as if you knows you so wrong. It's time to get right with God. Stop
that stubbornness and pride and if you can't kneel, bow to the Amighty
Gawd."

De Missy say, "But Mariah, if I should live to be a thousand years old, I
can never repay Mister Lincoln. He has been the kindest father and husband
in the world, and I'm the meanest, most exacting and demanding [*wife*],
even when I know I should keep still and keep my hand off, not ever try to
make him over. He's so perfect in his way, which is right."

I didn't want to say too much, because I sees her wanted to talk somethings out. I just had to tell her, though, what my Pappy used to say.

He was ignorant, but he'd ask us, "Cain't you brats see you're ornery?"
When we say yes, he say, "Well, no one ever quit their orneriness until they
can see it."

"I've tried so hard," de Missy say.

I say, "I believe if you'd humble yourself before the Lawd, he'd help you
out of this hell you're in. Now, I don't think you're bad, only to youself. Just
humble youself unto the Lawd."

"No, Mariah," she say, "I can't humble myself."

"I just don't see," I says, "what makes folks so gish dern proud. We's all
flesh, bone, and blood, and all born without sense, and all will die and then
[*it makes*] no sense.

"If you's proud of your Pappy's money, where is it now? If you's proud
of you looks, you only looks pretty when you's good now. Looks fade like
Mastah Robert's flowers. If you's proud of your French, who in this neck of
the woods understands a dern word of it? If you think you's going to get to
the White House, who'd want you there the way you perform?

"You'd better, I expects, just settle down to Mistah Abe's ways. If the
Lawd wants and needs Mistah Abe in the White House, you can bet your

DE MISSY
GETS
CONFIDEN-
TIAL
WITH
MARIAH

shimmy he'll get there. You just better depend on Gawd and quit you nagging. You just better try or you'll wind up always drinking that pisen, paregoric."

"Well, Mariah," say de Missy, "I believe you are serious and honest, but if paregoric were poison, the Todd family would have been dead years ago. Some never born. We were raised on it."

"Well," I says, "it's like the debil. It does its work slow and sneaking. Just you listen to Mistah Abe and stop that. It are worrying him most awful. Mistah Abe are afraid while he are gone, you'll kill youself or set youself crazy. Or maybe give some to Mastah Robert. You just better quit 'pending on that such like and 'pend on Gawd. That ole paregoric is the debil, and he's sure got you hooked."

She say, "First, Mariah, tell me. Has Mister Lincoln expressed his concern to you?"

"No," I says. "I heard him complaining about it to you. I wasn't listening, I just couldn't help hearing. Right then I knew as how he come home so little, for fear of upsetting you when he did come, or what might happen to you while he was away. That just why he come home all bedrabbled and looking starved and nigh out of his head. Cain't you use some common sense, as Missy Edwards say, and see it?"

"Well, Mariah," she say, "all you say may be true, but he hates me. I can see it in the sly looks he gives me, if he ever takes time to look at all. I don't think he ever did love me. He loved some common girl back in New Salem, and he loves that common cheap drunk Herndon he has in his office."

I don't know as how about that girl, right then and there. But I just up and says, "Well, Missy, I's feared you'll get hot if I says what I think about that cheap drunk Herndon. [*Mariah's knowledge of Herndon came from cleaning the law office.*] But I's just got this in my haid, and I's got to say it for your own good.

"He [*Herndon*] goes out and gets good and drunk on cheap rot gut. Then it's over with. You snow yourself under with fine wine and paregoric way too often for your own good and the good of your folks. Now you got a bad habit. A real bad habit for a good woman like you is. You better get down on your knees and pray for the good Gawd to root out that ole debil, before that debil pull you clean down to hell, and even take Mastah Robert with you."

De Missy say, "Mariah, I should be terribly vexed by that speech, if I thought you knew what you are talking about. I know I asked your help, and you've done the best you can. As for giving Robert either wine or paregoric, he'd scream his head off if I attempted it. When his eye hurt so badly, and I tried to ease the pain the only way I knew, the smell of it sickened him. He is his father's true son."

[*Adah Sutton inserted the following:*

Dr. Maris of Attica, Indiana, when called, gave me this information about paregoric: "Paregoric. Camphorate. Tincture of opium flavored by aromatic. Its various substances held in solution by 10 percent alcohol. It's a narcotic. Once used to console, soothe, or mitigate assuring pain or distress. If used in large doses or frequently, causes addiction, an intemperate habit. Once this habit is formed, it is no longer merciful. Can cause insanity or even death."

He went on to say that had the Todds and even other cultural families in those early days known the effect of promiscuous use of paregoric, they would have held their hands in holy horror.]

De Missy say, "But Mariah, my trouble dates back to my school days. You can't know of the thoughts that were instilled in my mind then, quite innocently by wonderful friends. Or the battles I have had trying to attain my ideals or ambitions. No doubt now obsessions.

"My early loves were ideals. My father, an ambitious and proud politician; Henry Clay, a learned politician who had accomplished at least a part of his ambitions; and Cassius Clay, a pure political reformer who would fight unto death for his ideals.

"Political views and dreams of the White House were instilled in my mind by these men whom I esteemed as perfect ideals to listen to. My studies were secretly for the ultimate purpose of someday perfecting me to become the First Lady of America. Not alone for the social distinction. At heart I had become a politician. I thought that someday I might be an indirect means of accomplishing my father's, Mister Clay's, and Cassius's political hopes that I continuously listened to.

"I would have even then married tottery old Henry Clay, because he seemed a potential candidate for president of the United States. My love for Henry Clay was as a child for a parent. [*Henry Clay was forty-one when Mary Todd Lincoln was born.*] At that early age, I did not distinguish the difference one felt for a parent and a husband.

"I believe my obsession to someday be the mistress of the White

DE MISSY
GETS
CONFIDEN-
TIAL
WITH
MARIAH

House was fostered right then, at that childlike period in my life. I had lovers [*in the nineteenth century, the word meant sweethearts*] in Lexington whom I could have married, but in the final analysis they did not fit in with my plans.

"Years later, after coming away from Lexington, I met a man who in every way met my needs. Even fell in love with him. When I felt sure he loved me, I was overjoyed, for he was young, immaculately attired at all times, was my social equal, polished, cultural, and educated. He had gained a political summit—a step only to becoming President. [*Adah Sutton adds in parenthesis here: Stephen Arnold Douglas.*]

"But his political views were opposite from mine. [*Douglas (1813-1861) was a Democrat, a senator from Illinois whose pro-slavery views conflicted strongly with both Mary Todd's and Abraham Lincoln's.*] After I thought he loved me, I tried to sway him to my way of thinking. Even became quite nasty with him at times, because I felt he was not as keen as I thought he was, since he could not be swayed from some of his brutal, unscrupulous tactics. But still I loved him.

"He became tired and disgusted with my nagging and bickering and turned me down. Not abruptly, that would have been kind. He was not kind.

"I was deeply hurt, but knew even crawling to him would never make him reconsider me. It would only enhance his conceit.

"I was young and proud and held my head high in the face of his apparent contempt. I would let no one know we were just more than good friends. I decided to show him I could find a lover who would be his political equal and could see from my point of view, even the road to the White House.

"Fate, or whatever one might call it, played in my hands. On my first trip to Springfield [*1837*], I had seen a Mister Lincoln whom a cousin of mine had said was very bright and would go far in the legal profession. On my second trip to Springfield [*1839*], one night while attending a highly social dance, I was introduced to this Mister Lincoln by my cousin who had brought him. We danced. At that time to my music. Now, to his.

"For years I held my love for Mister Douglas in my mind. But to thwart him, and outmaneuver him was always my way of showing him he was completely out of my life. So I went about using Mister Lincoln to this end.

"He was so gentle and pliable. Spineless, I called it. I actually thought he was in love with me, until one time I received an anonymous letter telling me that Mister Lincoln was and would always be in love with a girl in New Salem [*Adah Sutton inserts here: Ann Rutledge*]. She had started him on his legal and political career. I think she was just a common house servant.

"I didn't pay too much attention to the letter then, although now I know I had a twinge of jealousy. I planned how I would win his love, no matter who was hurt by it. No one will ever know how unfair I was to Mister Lincoln but myself.

"The unfairness of it was, I was still in love with Mister Douglas, but always comparing his suaveness with Mister Lincoln's awkward, ungainly ways and mannerisms. At times I had such a repulsion for him, it was hard for me to carry on my deception. But I had a method in my madness and I used every art given me, even to caressing him.

"At last, I succeeded in getting a marriage proposal from him. I felt sure now, he was clay in my hands. I accepted and we were engaged and the date set for the marriage. By careful tactics, I could still avenge Mister Douglas. Possibly, reach the White House before he could, for I had learned Mister Lincoln was a skillful and honest lawyer with ambition, also political views much like mine. When I approached him about his love for this girl [*Ann Rutledge*], he didn't deny it. He only asked that we would not dwell on it. That, with other things, I was continually trying to change him, subtly, but I believe he sensed it and perhaps resented it. I will always believe that my continual probing resulted in Mister Lincoln breaking our engagement.

"Down deep, Springfield people knew, even though Mister Lincoln tried to leave the impression that he was the one turned down. Later it was proven to me his only regret was for hurting me.

"Yes, I was hurt, but only my pride, for two men had not wanted me. I turned that over and over in my mind. Just think, now not wanted by this uncouth, ill-bred creature. I made a vow he would yet crawl to me.

"Oh, I know, Mariah, you will never again think of me as a good woman, just a scheming, wicked woman.

"I tried every approach, using all my friends. At last I cornered him where he had to reconsider me, if he was at all honorable. I cried not from shame or remorse but because men can't stand tears. Only his great good heart responded in sympathy. He begged to be forgiven for the wrong he felt he had done.

"After our marriage, often I would feel I couldn't bear him another minute in my sight. I'll not repeat all the cruel things I said and did. When

DE MISSY
GETS
CONFIDEN-
TIAL
WITH
MARIAH

Robert came, my father came to our apartment in that terrible rooming house. I was ashamed for my father, the epithet in my heart of all good, to see me living in such a place with such a man.

"But the minute my father saw and talked to Mister Lincoln, I knew, had he not told me later, that he was deeply impressed by his wit, intelligence, goodness, and honesty. As I loved my father so dearly and never thought of him as anything but right, I began to turn his viewpoints over in my mind and accept them. At least I now saw that by scheming and even driving the man, I might one day succeed after all in reaching Washington.

"We did go to Washington, after little Eddie was born. Mister Lincoln was elected to Congress. [*Lincoln became a U.S. representative from Illinois in 1847.*] I bought and sewed clothes for myself and the two boys for weeks. I was going to be a social leader in Washington, a grand success.

"You'll never know how disillusioned I was, to learn that a Congressman, simply because he had reached the U.S. capital city, was not always accepted in exclusive circles. We couldn't even live in a home by ourselves, but again had only quarters in a cheap rooming house.

"I didn't stay in Washington too long. I was as glad to leave as I was to go there. The children and I returned to my father's home in Lexington."

[*Mary and the boys, Robert and Edward, lived in Lexington during most of Lincoln's two years in Congress in Washington.*]

"Oh yes, I again heaped abuse on Mister Lincoln. And I believe it was right at that time that he saw me in my true light. A shrew!

"When Mister Lincoln finally came to Lexington, it was plain to see what good clothes, quiet, and a highly intellectual environment could do for him if it were his continual lot. My father even noticed the change and remarked about the difference Washington had made in him. It was then I took new hope, that after all, I might someday yet become the mistress of the White House.

"I was doomed for another disillusionment, for Mister Lincoln after several reverses politically, decided that he was positively getting out of politics. He went back riding the circuit. What little time he was home, I treated him in an exacting, unbearable way."

[*Lincoln had been disappointed in June 1849, at not being named Commissioner of the General Land Office. Two months later when offered the position of Governor of Oregon Territory, he said, "I cannot consent to accept." He had decided to give up politics and return to his law practice in Springfield.*]

Right there and then, that woman broke down and cried. That poor little soulsick woman. I say, "Now, now. Don't you cry you blessed little heart out. Mistah Abe never in this born world would have put that 'Love am forever' [*"Love is eternal"*] in that ring on you hand, if he hadn't loved you."

De Missy say, "Oh, Mariah, that's just it. He loved me for what I had tricked him into believing I was. I never loved him then, but I know I do now. With all my heart. But he hates me. He hates me. He hates me."

"You'se wrong, Missy," I say. "He don't hate. He's plumb scared of you. I can think of only one thing. You can start right now making youself back into the kind of person that he was getting hitched to. Just quit that paregoric so you get some sense in you head to think."

"But Mariah, these headaches," she say.

"Well, Missy," I say, "get happy and you won't have headaches."

Just then Mastah Robert dashed in for more corn coffee. The pot were dry. Only the grounds were in the pot. He scraped them out, put a load of sugar on, and et every last bit of them.

I listened quite a spell to de Missy. As my Henry and younguns was waiting for their grub at home, I pulled myself away.

Her said, "Well, Mister Lincoln will be home in July awhile before going to Chicago on some railroad business. I expect he'll bring home quite a few badly soiled clothes, as usual, so if you wish, you might bring Billie to keep Robert company."

At that, Mastah Robert throw his hat in the air and yelped out loud enough to split your ears, "Hurrah for the Fourth of July, Christopher Nye, and George Washington's cherry pie! Oh, I forgot. Washington can't have no cherry pie. He cut the cherry tree down with his little hatchet!"

De Missy say, "You see what I mean, Aunt Mariah? I'll ship those two boys out to the barn, out of our way. They play so nice together. Maybe I can take some of your advice, Mariah. I feel better since talking my thoughts out with you. Just as if I was back home with Mammy Sally. Take care of yourself, for the Lincolns need you, Aunt Mariah."

I stopped to get some grub and sure enough made tracks for home.

DE MISSY
GETS
CONFIDEN-
TIAL
WITH
MARIAH

CHAPTER FIVE

Robert and Billie Go Fishing

July 1850

Part of Lincoln's law practice in Springfield in the 1850s was handling cases for railroad companies, helping them obtain legal charters and defending them against increased taxation. The railroads doubtless paid Lincoln for both legal and political services.

As a lawyer specializing in railroad cases, Lincoln won a critical suit in which a canal company was trying to recover damages to a barge that had run into a railroad bridge pier across the Mississippi. He thereby helped establish the primacy of a new mode of transportation.

Lincoln also became active in patent law, after having an invention of his own patented in 1849. The idea came from seeing the steamship Canada *aground in the Detroit River. Although his invention of pumped-up air chambers to lift vessels off sandbars is used (in principle) in today's submarines, he never profited from it.*

Mariah tells the stories in this chapter to Adah Sutton while

107

they sit on Mariah's front porch in 1900. She starts by saying she came to the Lincoln house on July 1, a Monday wash day.

I REACHED THE LINCOLUMNS ABOUT THE SAME TIME AS BEFORE, BETWIXT SIX AND seven, on time to start the wash. I unhitched Maud and started to the shed, but turned around in the nick of time to catch Billie spitting out a cood of 'bacco. I boxed his mouth good and hard. He yelped and it brought Mistah Abe on the run. Mistah Abe say to Billie, "What's got you this time, a horse fly?"

I speaks right up. "No, Mistah Abe, I boxed Billie for chewin' 'bacco."

"Now, now, Aunt Mariah," he say. "Bill surely had his mouth too full of licorice candy, so he spit part of it out."

"No, Mistah Abe," I say and points to the ground. "See the cood at you big toe?" I hadn't notice he was barefoot, until then. That man have the most awful feet I ever see. Besides being two times as big as they oughta be, they have bumps all over.

He saw me looking and say, "When barefooted, I feel more at home, Aunt Mariah. But what are we going to do about Bill chewin' tobacco? That would be bad, if he taught Robert that. You know Robert thinks the sun wouldn't rise if Bill weren't on earth."

Just then Billie heaved up. It was his first chew of 'bacco.

Mistah Abe laughed and laughed. "Guess that ends it," he say. "Aunt Mariah, we won't ever need to be afraid he'll teach Robert that bad habit."

De Missy hear the noises and done come a tearing. What a sight that poor Missy was. Her have been doing the wash, and Mistah Abe was hanging out the clothes.

"Well, I swear!" I say. "Here I comes over with Billie, as you said, and now you don't need us."

De Missy say, "I declare, Mariah, when I told you to come on the Fourth of July, I thought today was the Fourth. I found out yesterday that today is only July the First. The preacher had mentioned in his sermon about celebrating Independence Day coming this Thursday. So I felt sure you wouldn't come until Thursday."

"However, the washing is only started, as you can see. Mister Lincoln has hung them on the line to dry as best he could."

You shoulda saw those clothes. It was the mostest mixed-up mess you ever seed. De Missy winked at me and shooked her head just in time, so as I kept my big mouth shut.

Mistah Abe wasn't fooled. He wented away grinning.

I took off my slat bonnet, rolled back my sleeves, and have the white ones on the line in short order. I straighten out those on the line, what Mistah Abe had hung. They wouldn't have dried in a week.

De Missy say, "I'll go in now and clean the house, then clean myself as Elizabeth is coming, to go with me to German's Gallery [*a photography studio in Springfield owned by Christopher Smith German*]. Elizabeth insists that I should have my photograph taken, before I get any larger.

"Dear, good Elizabeth. I know that she thinks I may die [*in childbirth*]. I was torn when our dear Eddie was born, and haven't been exactly in good physical condition since, carrying this child.

"Mariah, will you find Robert? He's going to go with us to the gallery. And when you finish with the laundry, will you straighten the kitchen and fix our dinners? We have leftovers again. And do make corn coffee. Robert has never quit talking about it and begging me to learn how to make it. He has his father in the notion for some corn coffee too. Mister Lincoln said he never had any other drink but it and water when he lived in his father's home. I'd burn the corn, if I tried to parch it.

"Reverend Smith and his wife came home with us after the service yesterday. Lauri wanted today off, so she helped prepare dinner and helped serve. But after dinner, she refused to wash the dinner dishes and cooking utensils, since she had an afternoon engagement with a gentleman friend to go for a buggy ride.

"I swear, if it wasn't for being alone at nights, I'd dismiss her. Unless I watch everything she does, I have it to do over.

"I could get Howard Powell, Robert's friend. If we needed help in the night, he could go with Robert to get whatever we might need. You couldn't awaken Lauri if a cyclone struck. Still, she's always here, at least during part of the night, while Howard can't always come. His folks are talking now of moving."

Mistah Abe then say, "Well, Molly, you think of everything." [*Lincoln's pet name for Mary was "Molly." Most of the time he called her "Mother."*]

De Missy answered him right sharp. "Yes, and I'm still wondering what made Billie sick and yelling, out at the barn."

I oughta have my big mouth smashed, like I smashed Billie's. I told de Missy about Billie chewin' 'bacco, and that like the whale that swallowed Jonah, Billie heaved up worse than when the whale take the notion to get rid of Jonah.

De Missy and Mistah Abe cut loose the most awful laughs I ever heard about that house. She choked on that laugh so hard, Mistah Abe, sure as I's sitting here on this doorstep with you, beat her on the back to make her stop choking so hard. I thought sure he would break her back off before she stop choking. I thought they was both going plumb daff, because I couldn't see a thing to laugh about. I's just telling the plain gospel truth about Jonah and the whale.

When they stop laughing and screaming, I say, "Glory Hal-lula, praise Gawd, you ain't daid!" That start them up again. They must have had something to make them powerful happy before I come. Maybe she just decided to get happy, as I told her to, and that would drive the headaches away.

Mistah Abe picks hisself up and moseys to the front hall, props hisself against a chair back with a pillow, pulls up his knees, and settles down to read. It must have been another Artemus [*Charles Farrar Browne used the pseudonym Artemus Ward to write humorous/folksy letters on current events to newspapers*] he was reading because he keep the house noisy with his loud laughs.

De Missy got herself dressed and sat down with her sewing and waited for Elizabeth.

I went to the barn for to hitch Maud and there were that blessed Mastah Robert, teaching my Billie schooling.

Before we left, Mistah Abe come out and say, "Mariah, has Mrs. Lincoln paid you for these weeks you've worked?"

I say, "Yes, suh, Mistah Abe. De Missy have more than paid me. You can see for youself—Billie's nice pantaloons and shirts, and she dress my Julia like her belong to Pharaoh the King."

"Mariah that isn't pay," he say. "That's a gift."

And do you know what Mistah Abe do? He take a big ten dollar out of his pants pocket and give it to me. My eyes watered and spilled over. I was that both sad and happy. I never have that much dough all at once in my whole life. If he have let me, I'd get down on my knees and washed those dirty feet of his with my wool. Like the woman Mara Magdalen wash Jesus' feet.

Mistah Abe say, "I'm leaving for Chicago on the Fourth, Mariah. I have business there and attend the United States District Court meeting. I believe Mrs. Lincoln will be looking for you and Bill then."

When we reached home, Billie was as proud as a struttin' cock. He knowed letters and numbers. How Mastah Robert ever got him to sat down long enough, I'll be blessed if I ever knowed.

My Henry was as proud of Billie's learning as Lucifer, as the Good Book say.

I put our grub on the table and we hardly got started eating when Billie began to beg his Pappy to go fishing. Henry was kinda tuckered out from tending the younguns while Billie and I was gone.

Right sharp, my man say "No!" "No" meant "No!" when Henry say it. But he was so all fired proud of Billie learning letters and numbers, he say, "Maybe tomorrow."

Well, Billie say, "Dat's zackly wen ah waned to go. To-morrow to da ribba."

Then Henry say, "If you'n tink I's 'bout to walk six mile to hold a string in da watah, you's plain dumb."

I spoke up and say, "Well, if you don't, you're plumb lazy! You sure can do that much for your boy what wants to be educated." [*Henry agrees to take Billie fishing the next morning.*]

Billie throwed his sock cap like always. Then sat down and made all the letters and numbers Mastah Robert have telling him how. He keep singing over and over about 'morrow at eight.

I fixed them a packet of corn bread and sow meat. My Henry made fish poles and pin hooks for our Billie. Then they dug up some squirming worms.

I was glad when they was gone. Henry was always in my way when I was working at home. He could be a most aggravating man when I wants to clean. And Billie was always fighting with the girls, or I was feared where he was, if out of my sight.

They come home as the sun were about to go down, and don't you know, they have a string of fish. About eight or ten nice fat fish. They was both tired out, but sat right down and cleaned them fish like the store fish. Not a gut left in any of them.

I made a pile of griddle cakes and fried some of them fish right off. They was so hungry, and the fish was so good, we liked to bust, eating them.

Then Billie up and say, "I bet Mister Abe and his Bobby wish they had some of the fish they give to us."

My Henry look down that flat nose of his.

I say, "Now Billie, what you been up to? How come Mistah Abe and Mastah Robert was fishing there with you? No wonder you knowed just when to start this morning!"

I say to Henry, "Ole man, is you going to sit there like a bump on a 'notty log and let him lead us and the Lincolumns 'round by the nose? I bet my best shimmy, Mistah Abe saw through Billie's schemen, if a knothead like you couldn't. Seems you and that 'scarecrow,' as you calls Mistah Abe, must have made up. Well, the Good Book say, 'A little chile shall lead them.'"

My Henry say, "If you'sn' stop dat damn preachin', dat ah get so 'fernal tired of hear'n, ah'll let you know—a blind man coulda seen what dose two scamps done did, an how dey put da hooks in us'n', 'fore we'n put da hooks in da fish.

"First, when we gets to da ribber, Billie wants to climb a tree. I say, 'Go 'head.' He climb clean to da top an look 'round and 'round. Den come down slow, all tuckered. He'sn got his'n wind 'bout five or ten minutes aftah that. Den put both two fingers in his mouth an whistle sich a Gawd awful loud blow, 'bout scared me stiff.

"I say, 'Billie, if yous'ns dare do dat again, ah'll break dose fingers plumb off, so youse cain't scare hell out of me again!'

"But just then, not so far off was a whistle, not so loud as Billie's blast. At dat, ah knew if it warn't a bird answerin', sometin' war up. I say, 'Billie, you blow again.' Billie right away blow. 'Fore that blow got two feet away, you nevah hear such a ear-splittin' noise in you'se'n born day. Dat Mistah Abe know as well as ah what was up, and he done have answer.

"When we met, Mistah Abe put out his'n big hand to shake hands and laughed, but say nary a word. Ah thought, if Mistah Abe can keep his'n fly-trap shut, so can ah.

"Wes'n went right down to da Sangamon and start fishin'. Dar warn't any talk.

"Mistah Abe and his'n Bobbie got da first fish and kep gettin' more. But they sure have a good long fish pole, and cooked bait with meat, cotton, corn meal, and sweet oil. Mistah Abe say he hab some 'portant work and muss go. He took Bobbie by da hand. Bobbie want to stay, but Mistah Abe say, 'Let's give Mister Vance—(juss like I war a gentleman)—and Bill our fish.' Den he wish us'n 'Good luck.'

"That Mistah Abe sure taught me a lesson. He'n didn't fuss at Bobbie or whip 'im. He'n hab sense 'nough not to spoil da day for us, or scare da fish by rantin' and ravin'. Ah took a nap, 'fore we come 'way."

Then my Henry say, "Well, ole woman, what you'ns goin' ta do 'bout it? Is you'ns ole man got brains or hain't he?"

I say, "The best thing Mistah Abe taught you, as he say, 'A still tongue make a wise head.'"

My Henry's like an old woman. Have to have the last word. He say, "'Spose you take some dat larn'n, too!"

CHAPTER SIX

A New Tantrum

July 1850

Lincoln intends taking the family to the fairgrounds for the Independence Day celebration, then go to Chicago on business.

While in Chicago for the U.S. District Court session, Lincoln delivers a eulogy for President Zachary Taylor at City Hall on July 25. Taylor had died of cholera on July 9.

During his term in Congress (1847–49), Lincoln had supported Taylor's bid for the presidency and his position against expansion of slavery. Lincoln hated the sight of slaves in Washington and wanted the government to pay owners who released their slaves voluntarily. The plan was not accepted.

Lincoln also sided with Taylor in opposing the Mexican American War, considering it to be a Democratic Party excuse for a landgrab. (After defeating Mexico, the United States acquired the Southwest territories, including California.)

*I*DRESSED MYSELF IN MY BEST DUDS AND DRESSED BILLIE IN HIS BEST. PINNED A WEE flag on his sock cap, and walked over to Mistah Abe's on the Fourth of July, 1850.

When we got there, I found Mistah Abe have hitched Buck to a new buggy. De Missy was dress up pretty and was dressing Mastah Robert in a "Little Lord Fauntleroy." Her call it that.

[*This is an anachronism.* Little Lord Fauntleroy, *a novel by Frances Hodgson Burnett, was published in 1886, and tells of a rich boy dressed in a dark suit, short pants, a high white collar and dark tie. The style for boys became all the rage.*

It was a memory mistake on Mariah's part; as a laundress she washed many such outfits (Robert termed then sissy suits,), which subsequently were called "Little Lord Fauntleroys." Or perhaps she remembered reminiscing with Robert on one of visits with her when he may have referred to his sissy suits as Little Lord Fauntleroys.]

Mastah Robert twist and squirm this way and that. He wanted no such clothes. De Missy held him tight as bee's wax, and got him rigged up for that celebration.

I felt plumb silly when her say, "Why, Mariah, what did you and Billie come over today for? There is no work to do today. You know you only come on Mondays every two weeks."

I backed away. Her looked cross as old satan. I done thought maybe her are crazy, as some folks say. But I pondered and considered in my heart, maybe it are the weather. Maybe Mastah Robert twisting and squirming, or her carrying a kid in her. Maybe something again about Mistah Abe.

I say to de Missy, "Ain't this the Fourth of July or ain't it? You done said come the Fourth of July and here I are."

"Mariah, listen to me," say de Missy. "Haven't you got a lick of brains in that black skull of yours? You're so all fired dumb. A two-year-old would know better. I told you Monday that I thought Monday was the Fourth of July, until the minister reminded me of my mistake.

"Surely any servant, especially a black one, would have sense enough to know we don't include them at any time or place in our social life. Yet, you come over here dressed, thinking we would think you our equal."

Just then Mistah Abe come down the stairs with his valise. Mastah

Robert grabbed Billie's hand and started to run to the barn, but Mistah Abe call to them.

"Just hold your horses right there, boys, and not so fast about getting away," he say. "Just trot right back here." He pointed to a spot where he wanted them to halt. "I've a crow to pick with you two boys, and I want to pick it before your two mothers.

"When you two little rascals put for the barn, it isn't all for reading, writing, and arithmetic. Understand this first: I want you two to be good friends. I'm more than glad you want to learn, Bill—and Robert, you're willing to teach him what you've already learned and it's fresh in your mind.

"I want you two to have all the fun life holds for you, unless that includes trickery and scheming, as you two pulled over on Mister Vance and me about a fishing party for four."

Mastah Robert speaked right up, like a little gentleman, and say, "Pa, Billie didn't trick or scheme. He wanted so very much to go with us to the woods the other day, but you didn't insist and Aunt Mariah wouldn't let him. She told him he should know his place with white folks. Pa, why if one is white and the other darker, what makes the difference?"

Then de Missy was going to put in, but Mistah Abe hold up his hand to make her keep her mouth shut.

"Well, son," say Mistah Abe, "let's forget the white and black right now and continue with your explanation concerning our fishing episode."

Mastah Robert went on then. "I told Billie I was going to try to get you to take me fishing. That was while I was teaching him numbers and letters. He was writing them down and I was waiting until he got through copying the twenty-six letters and ten figures which I had set down for him to learn from.

"Well, Billie jumped up and he almost cried, that he wanted his Pappy to take him fishing also. I told him if his Pappy knew how hard he was trying to learn, maybe he would take him. Well, he said, 'If I can get him to go, maybe we can meet you and your pa at the river.'

"So I said, 'If we could both start about the same time, maybe eight o'clock tomorrow, we might get there at the same time.' But I knew, Pa, your legs were longer than Mister Vance's legs, even if you do walk dragging them, and I knew Billie's Pappy was mad at you for having Billie's hair cut.

"So those were two problems which presented problems. I don't know what Billie did or said when he reached home, but the last problem must have been worked out satisfactorily, for when we met at the river, Mister Vance seemed to like you, Pa.

"Billie said to me, 'Maybe we would reach the river at different places.' I said he could whistle, if he didn't see me, and I would answer his whistle. That was all there was to it. Now where do you find a scheme or a trick?"

"Well," say Mistah Abe, "I want you two boys to be good friends always, but I was beginning to think you were bad for each other. I see now how wrong I was and apologize."

"What's 'apologize'?" Billie put in.

"That's one way of saying I'm sorry," say Mistah Abe. "But it wouldn't have been too hard for Robert and you, Bill, to have put confidence in your Pappy and me."

"What's 'confidence'?" say Billie. That Billie of mine want to know everything.

Mistah Abe say, "That word was a little too big a jaw breaker, but it means both you and Robert could have told your Pappy and me your plans to meet."

Well, sir, that Billie of mine speak right smack up. "Dat weren't Bobbie's fault. I knew my Pappy war mad at you, on 'count of my hair, for he called you a scarecrow."

Mistah Abe let loose a big laugh. "That's what I am, Bill. But you did scheme a little, didn't you?"

Billie say, "I thought of course my Pappy wouldn't go, or if he did go, he'd sock hell out of you."

Mistah Abe look to bust his very sides laughing, but wound up saying, "Thanks, Bill. You're a real protector. But always remember to try kindness before you try your fists."

De Missy couldn't hold in any longer. She was so mad, her fairly shook, but sent the two boys to the barn, as those two Lincolumns don't quarrel before Mastah Robert. Then she let loose.

Looking right at me, she say, "I don't want Robert to associate with the likes of Billie, that scheming little trickster. The barn's the place for them, where no one can see them together.

"Now, Mister Lincoln, you big baboon. I'm ashamed I'm your wife, or who do you think I am that you can't confide in me your doubt and fears concerning Robert's welfare? Or am I nothing to you or Robert, in your point of view? Whose opinions and mother love don't count?"

Mistah Abe looked black and his bad eye shot up to the left half corner.

"Mary, Mary," say Mistah Abe, "can't you see I tried to shield you? I didn't want to worry you. The time to judge is after all parties meet, discuss, and defend, as in a court.

"I heard what you said to Mariah, Mary. I told her to come. I wanted to discuss other angles of her employment with both of you, but this fishing episode came up and I felt that should be cleared away first.

"Mariah, I am sure you can find it in your good Christian heart to forgive. Mrs. Lincoln is just not herself these days."

Then De Missy blurts out, "Who could be themselves around a glum monstrosity? I wish I were dead! I wish I had died with little Eddie. I wish I could die with this one I'm carrying!"

Mistah Abe say, "Now, now, Mother, quiet yourself. I'm going to Chicago in a little while. I'll take you and Robert with your picnic lunch to the fairgrounds."

De Missy say, "You can relieve your mind right now, my Lord and Master, of your responsibility to a wife and your child. I'd see you in Glory before I'd go one step with you. Now get out! Go to Chicago. I'm not in the right shape to go with you. Billie's Pappy is right, you long-legged awkward scarecrow. If Robert and I go, we can walk."

I wanted to run. I wanted to grab Billie and never go back to that hell hole. I wanted to pray for the both of them. Her was sick in both soul and body. Mistah Abe was about at the end of the rope with de Missy. I swear I'd rather live in the hovel with my man I had, than in that fine home on Eighth.

Mistah Abe unhitched Buck. He took de Missy at her word. He took Mastah Robert by the hand and started for the front and his valise.

I decided to go the front way home, because I was with my best clothes on. So I took Billie by the hand. We got to the corner in time to see Mistah Abe kiss Mastah Robert goodbye.

De Missy say nary a word. Her eyes was red as her stood on the front. Mistah Abe nary even wave. I thought, what are going to become of that blessed Mastah Robert? He say, "Goodbye, Aunt Mariah. Goodbye, Billie."

I went home and told the whole story, except what de Missy say to me. Henry say, "Dar's nothin' wrong wid dat woman 'ceptin what a darn good beatin' would settle. Kid or no kid in her'n, I'd cook her goose so damn brown, a hawk wouldn' touch it. Den I'd make her eat it, carron' [*carrion*] an' all."

I didn't want to say too much. I was all upset and felt a bit squirmish in my stomach. Walking over and back from Mistah Abe's without setting a bit had got away with me.

That night, I thought I'd die, I was that pained. I lost my child I had in me.

Henry was scared. He ran for the colored preacher's wife and her took good care of me. But I didn't mend as quick as when I had my younguns. So I was still in bed when Mastah Robert come tearing in, about three days later.

He says his Ma was sick and would I come? Poor Mastah Robert looked scared and hurt when he see me. Guess I was a coon three shades lighter than when he see me last. I sended Ellen, not yet seven. But I really needed her. Her didn't stay long. De Missy send her back with a kettle of soup, beef soup, noodles, and lots of good vegetables, a sack of meal, and a whole dollar. That poor Missy have robbed themselfs of their dinner for us, as sick as her were.

That done put the screws in my man. He say, "Maybe dat poor ting needed lovin', stead of beatin,' an ole Abe hab forgot, if he'n evah knew how to love. But he's right, dare say. Ets bess to keep usn's noses out ob dare 'fairs. We'ns hab enuff ta sweep our own backyard."

De Missy send over every day something. Fruit, mostly. Onct, three or four kinds of vittles, and fancy stuff. Her had a party. A lot of folks been there, and brought in stuff, Mastah Robert say, that wasn't touched, and send another dollar.

Ellen have told her I'd lost my chile. As soon as I was able, I hitched Maud and go over. Mostly, to take her pans and dishes back. I was surprised when I got there to find her up and in such good spirits. Someone had took her a message that Mistah Abe had been selected to speak the services in Chicago for Henry Clay who had died about then.

Her went clean overboard about what an honor that was. She say Henry Clay was first after her father, next to Gawd. Now [*her husband was*] no more a baboon or monstrosity, but a fine high-minded man. But I always knew Mistah Abe was a man of Gawd.

[*Adah Sutton got the eulogies out of sequence. Mariah spoke of Lincoln's going to Chicago in July 1850 to deliver a eulogy for President Zachary Taylor. Clay died in 1852 and Lincoln delivered his eulogy in Springfield.*]

I was to return, if I felt able, on regular wash day. There would only be a small wash, because Mistah Abe would not be home yet, and her washed out the party things.

[*Mariah, still upset with Mrs. Lincoln, did not return for the rest of that year. Mary hired a live-in maid named Catherine Gordon, who was listed in the U.S. Census of 1850 as residing in the Lincoln home.*

On the subject of Abraham Lincoln's position on and attitude toward slavery, which came up for the first time in Mariah Vance's reminiscences, Lloyd Ostendorf brings to our attention the references to Abe's encounters with slaves and slavery in his youth, as described by Francis Marion Van Natter in Lincoln's Boyhood: A Chronicle of His Indiana Years, *published in 1963 by Public Affairs Press, Washington, D.C.*

"Van Natter helps reveal Abe Lincoln's early concerns for the unjust conditions suffered by Black people, which was very early rooted in his character," says Ostendorf. "Lincoln's interest in and concern for slaves in bondage and for the welfare of African Americans in general was developed largely in his formative years in Indiana."

Van Natter tells how Abe associated with Blacks, worked with them, and they in turn responded to his interest in their plight at a much younger age than previously believed by many Lincoln historians.

Van Natter tells us that in 1826, when Abe was seventeen and ferried a boat on the Ohio River, he saw slaves working on the plantations in Kentucky and heard their mournful songs as they chopped cotton or stemmed tobacco. Sometimes Abe sauntered up to Troy, Indiana, where the log-house-lined streets were crowded with boatmen, river pirates, Negro slaves, prostitutes, gamblers, and planters.

Negro clog dancers fascinated Abe. He had seen them oar their masters across from Kentucky to trade in Troy and watched slaves dance in the streets while their owners traded. He tried to learn some of the steps, which attracted passersby who laughed, waved whiskey bottles, and urged Lincoln on. Black slaves grinned and hoed it down. Abe's long legs swung and missed the rhythm, but he kept trying. The slaves took an interest in him, showed him the steps in slow motion. While the crowd shouted and emptied their bottles, Abe concentrated on clog dancing. He caught on. According to Moss Emacoal, a neighbor of the Lincolns, Abe got to be one of the best clog dancers in southern Indiana.

Back home, Abe eagerly read the Western Sun *newspaper in Gentry's store in Spencer County, near his home, and formed his admiration for the Kentuckian Henry Clay, who was then President John Quincy Adams's Secretary of State. Clay believed in the gradual empancipation of slavery, and in compensation for slave owners, should slavery be abolished and result in financial loss. Even in his youth, Abe was quick to comprehend both sides of the slavery issue, long before the Civil War resolved the national dilemma.*

In the fall of 1826, while he and his friend Jefferson Ray were taking a flatboat down the Ohio and Mississippi Rivers peddling their cargoes to planters along the Arkansas shores, Mexico suddenly freed all slaves in Texas.

"Standing on the north bank of the Ohio River, Abe Lincoln often watched boats going downstream loaded with Negro field hands, house servants and worn-out breeders," says Van Natter.

"He saw them sitting chained together, saw them rocking back and forth in misery; heard them singing, praying, weeping. Such scenes must have disturbed him deeply. In his ears dinned the propaganda for and against the slavery system."

After his river work, Abe worked alongside slaves at the William D. Ferguson plantation in Arkansas, cutting tupelo gum trees for firewood, which he soon learned was a much harder job than chopping Indiana trees for rails. He learned that a slaveholder in the area, Miss Frances Wright, was conducting a self-emancipation experiment at her plantation at Nashoba.

"It can only be surmised that the Ferguson slaves told Lincoln what they knew about the experiment," says Van Natter, "and Lincoln told them what he had heard elsewhere in Indiana. Surely here Lincoln was seeing a different side of the slavery issue. This must have brought more forcefully to his attention the idea that slaves were property; that freeing them without compensation to their owners was not consistent with justice or property rights under the Constitution."

By March 1829 Lincoln was home again and showed a big scar over his right eye, made by the club of a Negro bandit. Soon after he went to Louisville, Kentucky, where he got a job in a tobacco warehouse working alongside Negro slaves handling heavy casks of tobacco. One day, Abe saw a white boy accidentally knock a pitcher of drinking water off a shelf. The warehouse owner's son mistook a slave for the culprit and began flogging him with a blacksnake whip. Aware of the injustice, Abe said sharply, "Don't do that! A boy came in here and broke your pitcher."

The owner's son then twice lashed Abe with the whip for interfering. "The sting of that whip detonated in Lincoln's mind an accumulation of explosive resentments against slavery," says Van Natter. "He knocked the man to the ground and smashed hard fists into his bleeding face. Some white Kentuckians who also hated slavery advised Lincoln to run to the ferry and escape across the Ohio to Indiana." Abe managed to escape a mob that came after him, rowing a skiff across the Ohio River to the Indiana side.

"Lincoln darted into the thick woods, heading northwestward," says Van Natter. "As he pushed his way through briars and tangled grapevines, he began to realize the enormity of his act. He had defended a Negro slave. He had struck a Kentucky slave owner's son. Slavery sympathizers. . . . would surely cross the river and try to catch him. To throw pursuers off his trail, he avoided well-traveled paths and highways. Abe Lincoln skulked through the Indiana wilderness, living on roots, dry berries, acorns, beech-nuts, wild honey—anything he could find that was edible. Finally, he reached Terre Haute on the Wabash. Fox-like, he circled back, throwing real and imagined pursuers off his trail, and arrived home."

The episode was probably one of Lincoln's last contacts with slavery during his formative years in the Indiana border country.

"It helped him shape his total impressions of this controversial institution," says Van Natter. "He had seen slavery and had taken part in discussions concerning it. But like the nation itself, he was no doubt still confused over the problems—and their solutions—relating to man's ownership of man. He had grown to hate slavery; he had promised himself that if he ever got a lick at the evil, he would hit it hard. Yet he realized that there was a wide, deep gulf separating the viewpoints of pro-slavery and anti-slavery people."]

CHAPTER SEVEN

"De Missy Pile Up the Hurts"

August–December 1850

The Lincolns' third son, William Wallace, is born on December 21, 1850. Lincoln continued to divide his time between practicing law with William Herndon in Springfield and going out on the circuit to represent the railroads and individual clients.

WHEN MISTAH ABE COME HOME FROM CHICAGO [*JULY 1850*], HE MUST have goes right out on the circuit. De Missy send Mastah Robert over for me to come quick. I just couldn't go. My Henry were out with the mule and Billie was with him. I was done head over heels then at home.

I hated it [*refusing*] the worst way, on account of Mastah Robert. I swear that boy look about as glum as his pa done did about most of the time.

We needed the work the worst kind. Times was bad and winter was coming on to prepare for. The fruit we have was mostly wild fruit.

My man had clean out some attics and lightning caves. He brought home a heap of plunda. Among it was a pile of lightning jars [*"white lightning" or moonshine*]. They was top-heavy with big globs of glass on the top, but I cleaned them up. Most of them held plumb a half gallon.

I canned fruit and some vegetables out of our garden. Tied the tops shut with pieces of muslim I'd wash. Then cover over with wax to seal all of the air out. Then I fill the crocks Henry got with the plunda, with cabbage kraut, and made some cider vinegar and cider. I figured with the fish my man and Billie would catch live, and the possum, coons, wild turkey, and wild hog, we could live. All we need buy was [*corn*] meal, a few duds, and pay the rent on the shack.

We didn't need much duds, because de Missy give us stacks of clothes. Besides clothes Henry brought home from attics. Mistah Abe have help Henry by giving him a good name to anyone that need work done. Those were sure hard times. There was a few I work for, before I went to the Lincolumns. I couldn't put the Lincolumns first.

I still didn't like the slack de Missy gave me on the Fourth of July. I like to forgive even to seven times seventy, but de Missy would pile up the hurts to seventy times seventy.

About two o'clock that same afternoon, poor little Mastah Robert comes back. "Oh, Aunt Mariah!" he say. "Won't you come? Ma needs you so much. She is giving a party. Lauri got out of patience and left. Aunt Lizabeth can't come until time for the party. She has her hands full in her own home. Ma has sent for almost a dozen [*women*]. They say, 'I wouldn't work for her if she gave me a million! She's too mean or bossy. Let her go down to Kentucky and get her a nigger she can flog.' Won't you come, Aunt Mariah?"

My heart was plumb broke for that little tyke, but I just couldn't go. After hard thought, I sent my oldest gal, Ellen, though I needed her to run errands and tend Julia. Ellen put up a howl, her sure didn't want to go.

Ellen was a pretty, light-colored gal, and when slick up, was fit to be a queen's maid. Her have spunk and pride. I tried to teach my chilluns it was a black sin to be proud. I sometimes wonder if some white master's blood didn't run in my chillun. It must have been on my side, because Henry was black as night with a flat spread nose. His mouth turned wrong side out, and his wool was so matted, I couldn't comb it out with Mistah Abe's comb he use on Buck's tail and mane.

Ellen didn't come back until it was getting dark. Her still nary like de Missy. Say de Missy sure was a slave driver. But right there I told her, I expected that before her died, she'd have to do a lot of hard work. Trouble was, I never put much on my chilluns' shoulders to carry.

I never been a slave, and my Pappy and Mammy let us putter and play. We were puttering and playing on the Ohio [*River*] when those white men drag Mammy's and Pappy's chillun off in their boat. I have an easy chile life.

When I told Mistah Abe, he say, "Mariah, you had an easier, more care-free life than I. Perhaps you were far better cared for than I. Even today there are many more colored folks than white people, even of the slaveholders, who have a happier life. They do not strive for things as white people do. I believe their spiritual values are higher. They only strive and want, above all else, happiness. True happiness comes from only one thing, a clean mind. A mind lacking jealousy, greed, and hate. A heart of love.

"You have much to be thankful for, to God. You weren't a slave. You had fine Christian parents who taught you their Christian way and wanted above all else to make you happy. I shall endeavor to give my children all I can, both of this world's goods and happiness. Then in later life, with a foundation of love, they can more easily judge their fellow man and cope with the vicicatude [*vicissitudes*] of life."

Ellen say when her first went to work for de Missy, she put her to wiping dishes. The first thing her did was to drop a sassa of fine china what de Missy never use for common [*everyday use*].

Ellen grab her bonnet and was about to run home. De Missy say, "Why Ellen, that was only an accident. You are just nervous. You didn't do it on purpose. So come right back and finish these dishes."

Ellen stayed scared stiff all the time, for fear she would drop and break more of those thin, posied dishes trimmed in gold. De Missy have some heavy ones with blue pictures on that her give to me later.

Ellen then have to polish silver. Some was heavy. Too heavy for Ellen to lift. Her was not seven then. Her help lay the table, did dusting upstairs and down. Her come home lugging a big basket with something of all the fine vittles, the fine salads, jelly cakes, fruits, and a big ham bone for me to cook. Lots of good meat on it yet.

I knows my Ellen was tireder than her ever been in her life. The only way she was happy was because her have the first dollar in her life. But I say right there and then, I'd never send her again. I go first, if it kill me.

Several girls work for de Missy before little Willie was born. I declare if I have to depend on someone to do my work, I wouldn't be so fin-a-ky. I couldn't get my Ellen to go back even if I wanted her to. Her was plumb scared of de Missy.

It was only a week or so until Willie was born, the first part of December [*December 21*], and de Missy wasn't so well for nigh a month. Doctor Wallace that was her brother-in-law, wanted her to be quiet. Her wanted to get out and go to the parties going on [*holiday festivities*], but he put his foot down. I don't know of anyone that could make her behave, but Doctor Wallace. She even named the baby William Wallace for him.

My Billie thought that the William was for him. I told him to come off the high horse, that he was just getting too big for his breeches. De Missy wouldn't name one of her precious little boys after a black coon. No siree. Even if they done did like him a heap.

At Christmas, here come that blessed Mastah Robert with presents for all of us. A lot of clothes. The dresses for me was too high-falutin'. Some of her's after de Missy dropped that precious baby Willie out of her. The dresses was too out of shape and too big.

Henry got shirts and bandannas, our Ellen a right pretty hood. Then toys for the rest of the kids, and candy. Store candy. Her [*Mary*] wasn't up until New Year's or later. I forget, her send two silver dollars.

Mastah Robert stay a long time. He was sure learning at school. I don't remember if it was Mister Estabook's school yet or not. [*The school run by Abel W. Estabrook.*] He sat right down at our kitchen table and learned Billie and Ellen what he have learned. My Ellen learned faster than my Billie. But Billie did done put letters together and made words. Mastah Robert come back after that every few days. My younguns learned to read and count. My Henry never catched on, but there and then I went and got my learning.

Every time Mastah Robert came, he bring vittles, chestnuts, and taffy. I took the dishes and pans back after Christmas. I wanted to see that blessed little new baby, William Wallace.

They always call him "Willie." It was never "William," "Billie," or "Bill." Mistah Abe called my Billie "Bill." No one else ever did call him that until the day he died.

I never knew the little angel, Eddie. But they say that Willie was the spitting image of Eddie.

I learned why they send Mastah Robert over so often. They wanted to get him out of the house so he wouldn't disturb the baby or de Missy. I wanted to tell them they was making a mistake, but her wasn't fit to talk to, because her mind was set. She run that poor little Mastah Robert out everytime he comes near. He tip-toe around like a little mouse.

De Missy told me her got coutched [*with William*] while visiting in Kaintucky. Her had come home after Mistah Abe had about a month before.

Doctor Wallace said, "Mary you are so nervous, the trip has been difficult for you. Unless you relax completely, you may experience nausea and may even lose your child. I want you to go to bed and rest completely."

I think that was about the time I first went to the Lincolums to work. I never saw another perform as her did, when her carried Willie. If old woman's stories was the truth, that baby Willie would have been a screamin' little debil. He did done hold his breath.

Mistah Abe say, "We'll have to help him over that someway, for with him holding his breath, like I have to hold my tongue and Robert have to tip-toe, the neighbors will think the Lincolns have moved out."

I put the pan and other things Mastah Robert have brought our presents in, where they belonged. I wash the baby Willie for de Missy, straighten around some, too. That gal they now have was not so bad, but have her hands full trying to please de Missy. I didn't stay only a speck there. Her told me if I felt able, I could come on regular wash day, for there was a little wash her could not trust to the maid.

I never took Billie next time, and I didn't see de Missy or Mastah Robert about. The fire and all was ready. If it hadn't been all made up, I would have gone home, but I was glad afterwards I stayed. Her was a sick woman in bed by the doctor's orders. When I went in, after the clothes was dry and folded, there was no dishes or kitchen to clean. Mastah Robert catched up with me before I reached the barn, and say, "Ma wants you, Aunt Mariah. She says she owes you an apology."

I didn't much want to see her again, and I wanted to get home. There was so much work at home to do those winter days. I was afraid us might have words yet. Then that would finish us for good. It would be an awful thing if I rebuke a sick woman. Some way, I didn't feel so good towards that woman. I prayed the Good Lord to take that awful sin of hate out of my heart, but he no have done cleaned my heart yet, even with all the Christmas Mastah Robert brought.

I went upstairs to where her was. Her started right in. That poor thing was more strick with her misdeeds to me than I ever thought that proud woman could be.

De Missy say, "Mariah, I owe you an apology. I know I have hurt you deeply and so injustly. I am sorry for what I said to you on the Fourth of July, and I sense you haven't gotten over it. Can't you find it in your heart to forgive me? I just couldn't think of starting a new year without making an effort to get your good thoughts toward me again."

I declare I wilted plumb down like the little snow man Mastah Robert have made. I almost thought I was the sinna 'stead of de Missy, for the sin of hate in my heart. Maybe it was not hate, maybe I was just proud. I don't know what of the two are the worse. I was pracsin what I preached and told my youngun the worse sins was to be proud and to hate, and I done did both of them. I told de Missy I would forgive her so I too could start the new years right.

De Missy go on, "If I was the cause, even indirectly, of your losing your child, I know God will punish me. I just can't seem to learn in time that I'll be punished. And I have been, for the guilty conscience that has been mine since I was so rude to you and Billie.

"I was terribly upset that day. I had planned and had wanted so very much to go to Chicago with Mister Lincoln. At the last minute, I had a little upset physical condition. Mister Lincoln decided the trip would not be too good for me.

"But that wasn't all. I never receive the least attention from him, unless I approach him first. You saw how when he left, he kissed Robert over and over, but he didn't even wave goodbye to me."

I laughed and said, "Maybe he thought you think it was a baboon waving at you." She really smile a wee bit. "I try to tell you, honey catch more flies than vinegar."

De Missy say, "God only knows how this will end. All he thinks of is the circuit, or some other trip. Anything, it seems, to get away from me. I believe if he felt justified, he'd take Robert and leave for good. Now that Willie has replaced Eddie, or at least has softened the blow of dear little Eddie's going, he may come home more often and find more happiness here.

My only hope, so far as I'm concerned, is that my deep love for him will find a way to save our marriage."

I just wasn't able to go back again until almost spring.

I don't know how her and Mistah Abe made out. Her told my Ellen before I made this last trip, that I have spoiled her so with my fine wash, her would do it before [*hiring*] just anyone else.

Mastah Robert come over often. Every time my chillun learned something from him. Sometime he brung a few duds for to wash by hand.

Folks say that Mastah Robert was mean to Eddie and now was mean to Willie. I know that was not so. If anything, Mastah Robert was shoved off and out, so as he wouldn't disturb. I know Mistah Abe seed it that there way too. It was a terrible mistake. Not intention at all.

I do know Mastah Robert wanted to hold Willie and they said he didn't know how. That wasn't no excuse. They should have teach him how. Other chillun could come in and play around Willie, but not Mastah Robert. I's not zadgeratin.

That Mastah Robert was a little lonesome boy when at home, unless Mistah Abe was there. I think Mistah Abe should have come oftener on Mastah Robert's account. Mistah Abe was a terrible busy man and folks say he was making heaps of money now. I knows they sent us money all that winter.

CHAPTER EIGHT

All's Well That Ends Well

Spring, 1851

*If the Lincolns' speech seems formal, the editors wish to remind read-
ers that Adah Sutton explained in her Preface that Mariah Vance
spoke in dialect (today called Black English by African-American
scholars), repeating what the Lincolns said. Out of respect to them,
Sutton says, she interpreted Mariah's words into euphemisms of correct English.*

THAT WINTER WAS LONG, BUT PASS QUICK LIKE, IT SEEM. HENRY HAVE LOT OF
hauling for stove wood. He haul the Lincolums about eight or ten
cords. The poles, Mistah Abe chopped himself. People never forgot Mistah
Abe was a woodchoppa. I always wonder what was so strange like about
that?

133

But Mastah Robert come home one day in the spring, complaining that the boys was now making fun of his pa because he was a woodchoppa. It used to be Mastah Robert's eyes they made fun of. Now it was his pa woodchoppin.

De Missy say that Estabook school should have better control over their pupils. She told Mastah Robert to tell them his father had eight years in the State Legislature, was in Congress of the United States at Washington for one term, is a successful lawyer, and someday would be President of the United States, so if woodchoppin started all that, maybe some of their fathers should go to the woods to see if it would make something of them.

I tells you, her was mad. But that didn't stop Mastah Robert's hurt feelings a bit. He just never got over folks throwing up things about his pa and ma to him. He have such a tender heart, and would never say things tit for tat to them who tormented him.

Never the world over could you find a finna man than Mastah Robert turn out to be. He wasn't stuck up. He come to my house whenever in Danville and he ate corn pone at my table [*years later, as an adult*].

After they tease Mastah Robert about his pa being a woodchoppa that day, his pa came home and took the poor little hurt boy by the hand and say, "Son, I'm not ashamed of any honest labor I ever did, or am I ashamed I am a son of a common, illiterate, laboring father. They have all been stepping-stones to the better life I now enjoy, so far as education and material gain is concerned.

"Yes, son, I split rails, though no rail is ever going to stop me. So let us let them rail on. Their railing only spurs me on, as most all pioneers have been spurred on and have achieved. Some have accomplished great things, others just have become honest men, men with honest thoughts and deeds that is producing a progressive America.

"So son, just push all that teasing that those youngsters are up to, in the back of your mind. Just feel sorry for them, that they use this precious time and their God-given power, to think so foolishly. They are the losers, not you.

"Robert, I can't wish harm for them, so don't you. The Bible says, son, 'The bread that is cast on the waters comes back.' They may reap someday the humiliation they are trying now to afflict you with. They may then think.

"Never let anyone show you they are master over you. If they start you to worrying, they are masters in a wrong way. They are really below you, for they are not good to listen to.

"I want your childhood and in fact your entire life to be happy, above all else. But without the foundation of a happy childhood, you have a poor chance for a happy outlook in later life.

"I want to tell you about the engineer on the train I last rode to Chicago. A big hog and a litter of pigs were on the track. He stopped the train, dismounted, and by throwing some food from his lunch pail far off the track, succeeded then in driving the mother hog to the food. Most of the litter followed. The little stragglers, we helped him pick up and also remove from the track. He quickly hollered, 'All aboard!' The bell rang, the whistle blew. We scrambled back in and were on our way again. Not one of those swine could think of us as anything but friends.

"It might be a good idea to shame them [*Robert's tormentors*] or perhaps make friends of them, by doing each one a kindness. Never say rude things to them and put yourself on their lower level. It'll pay off, son. You try it."

Mastah Robert say, "Pa, I just can't see where the engineer getting the hog and pigs off the track applies to what the boys say to me about you and ma. If I'd call them hogs and pigs, that would be rude, wouldn't it?"

Mistah Abe laugh. "Son, I meant to emphasize the fact that the engineer didn't rudely plow those swine off the track with the engine cow-catcher. If he had plowed into them, he may have derailed the train, perhaps thus injuring the passengers on board, or otherwise costing a large amount to have the train or tracks repaired. He no doubt would have killed most of the swine. This would mean a loss to the farmer who owned them and could ill afford to lose them.

"You see, son, though it delayed our trip a little, that engineer's gentle thought, level head, and kindness paid off. So will it pay you, Robert, to deal with these boys and all difficulties with careful thought and kindness. If it can't be done that way, then they are not worth an effort, so then steer clear of them as much as you can. If they see it isn't bothering you, they may cease. That has been my experience, so often. In other words, if you can't cure, learn to endure."

You knows what? I believe what Mistah Abe preached to Mastah Robert's head help a heap, because right away, he have some boy friends he never have before. He was more cheerful like and happy for a spell. But I did done wonder after all, which advice he done took. That of his pa or his ma? I always thought that it was good that they didn't give their advice before each other. They was both of them so different. Could have end in a rumpus 'tween them.

It was I think, I may be mistaken about the time, Easter vacation for Mastah Robert, and Mistah Abe was going out on the circuit. Mistah Abe went in, pick little Willie out of his crib, in the room off the parlor. De Missy have made a nursery there. They have an old-fashioned crib that looked like a hollow-out log. It was cut with a hood at the head and a set of rockers on the bottom. De Missy have it all flub-dub up.

That Willie was just like a picture. He was dress like I dress my girl babies. Maybe de Missy want a girl so bad, was why her dress it that way. Her dress Mastah Robert with flub-dub and ruffles 'til he for once got his dander up.

Mistah Abe walk 'round about the house carrying Willie on his shoulders, as young as he was. He kiss Willie and for the first time since I know them, kiss de Missy.

Mastah Robert walk to the barn with his pa until he hitch Buck, then come running back for his pa's stovepipe hat. He carry it to his pa with the top down, so not to spill out Mistah Abe's papers. That's the only time I ever did know of him leaving his hat. Must have had a heap of something on his mind, to forget that hat.

De Missy was so happy that morning, her didn't act natural. I think that blessed Willie was a blessing.

I went every two weeks and there was nothing new. I didn't help at parties, cause her have an Irish maid again. And her have parties all the time. It should have been hard for her. That Missy have such a time. Have to be in bed after that blessed Willie Wallace born. But her just have parties on the brain. And I knew it would be of no account to tell her it was not so good for her.

Once de Missy say, "At least my guests won't have to wade through cow and hog tracks to get to my parties, thus ruining my carpets. The law has taken a hand and made those folks who have hogs and cows keep them home."

[*In the early 1800s, Springfield's unpaved streets allowed livestock to roam freely. An 1851 ordinance forced livestock to be penned.*]

I thought she should go slow, about using so much money to have parties. I heard Mistah Abe say to de Missy, "Outside of being retained by the Alton and Sangamon Railroad, my business is slow. We now have this little account in Jake Bunn's new bank. I can't permit any large withdrawals. With a new baby and all expenses related to his birth, a sizable hole has been made in our checking account.

"Please, Mary, don't dissipate our deposits drawing interest. If you run out, Billy [*Herndon*] will supply you with my share of our receipts here." [*Lincoln and his law partner split fees evenly.*]

The very name of Herndon made her blow up. "If you'd use any judgment, you'd send that lazy Herndon out on the circuit, at least half the time. You're so determined to share half with him. Then spend more time in your office, as all big lawyers do. And incidentally, more time with your family. We miss you so. Then too, you have two sons again to guide. At least share part of the responsibility with me."

He say, "Well, Mother, I know I have an equal responsibility with you. And I'm trying my best to assume it. We have, I hope, a long life ahead of us, and we must both be more patient."

After that, things began to cool down for a spell. When Mistah Abe left then to go on the circuit, I thought everything was right between them. He hardly got away with Buck until her begin planning for parties.

Her say to me, "Mariah, I just must get out some from now on. I must return to my place in society. I've isolated myself and have withdrawn myself too long already. People will forget there is a Lincoln family in Springfield. Since the slave question has been quieted down, Mister Lincoln wants no part in politics.

"I'm sorry for that, because it gave him prestige. The Todds have always enjoyed social distinction. I'm determined the Lincoln family will not lag behind."

That Missy have one party after another. Her even took a party to the show, and then brought them home and feed them. Mistah Abe didn't come home for eight or nine weeks, without a word from him. Her have use up that check account. Have run bills at the grocery, the dry good store, and even say her would have to let my pay go until Mistah Abe come back.

At last her have to go to Mistah Abe's office to get his share of what Mistah Herndon—that man what she hate—have save for Mistah Abe. Her would have use all that, but Mistah Abe come back the very next day.

Just think, use all that money on parties for folks what say all sorts of mean things about her. Such as one her always include in her society told me, "Mrs. Lincoln entertains more fine than any of us who could far better afford such. And we don't give a fiddler's damn for her."

When Mistah Abe come home, her was delighted with the two hundred dollars he put in her lap, but not with him. De Missy wouldn't let him kiss her foot then, even if he want to. Her was mad because he stay away so long. Her was smarting because her have to go to that Billy for more money. That filthy man and that filthy office.

I hear her say, "What kind of clients would go to such a filthy office and be interviewed by that filthy character? Yet you would have your wife be humiliated, before you would get a partner who is gracious, at least. Who would see to it that his office was not offensive. But you deliberately make it necessary, by staying away almost two and a half months. Other lawyers on the circuit appreciate their family. If and when it isn't possible to come home, they write, showing their love and concern. Robert wonders why you stay away, and people are gossiping because other lawyers on the circuit come home, yet you stay away after all I've endured this last year by grief and sickness. Or hasn't it concerned you in the least?"

Mistah Abe say, "Well, Molly, I'm sorry if you ran short of money. I thought our checking account was sufficient. I'm truly sorry you had to bother Billy Herndon."

At that, she fairly tore the roof off. She ran at him with a butcher knife. I got out of the house quick. Her scream worse than a panther. Mistah Abe grab her hand and took the knife away. That was the worse wildcat spell I ever saw.

He sat her down and I declare, he say, "Molly, did you run any bills?"

Her lie and say, "No."

Well, he say, "Maybe the money did run short. I don't feel too surprised now. I want you and the boys to have all the comforts of life. Since your indisposition for a year, besides your change of figure, you did need clothes."

That man give her every chance to tell him, how her have spent so much money. Her only look blacker and blacker and held on to that money, that two hundred dollars from Mistah Abe's share at the office.

Finally, he leave the house. But he wasn't gone long. I could tell he was dreadful disturbed. He went right in the back room of the parlor where de

Missy was. When he get wrought up, he talk squeak like and like he was choked.

I couldn't help but hear him say, "Mary, little did I think that my wife is both a liar and a cheat. I've tried to tell you that I can't tolerate a habitual liar. I'm afraid I'll have to call you that.

"I've overlooked occasional fibs and I've put up with your senseless tantrums, your incessant false front. But with that I've found out you are a cheap little cheat!"

I tells you, he must have had all that stored up for a long time, 'cause he laid it on like he was exploding.

"You've charged bills every place you can. When I found you owed so much at the grocery, I thought I should go the rounds of the stores. You must have fed half of Springfield on fine foods. But we've always sat down to the plainest of fare, since you said you wanted to economize. For what? To feed, or rather splurge, on what you've robbed your family of?

"I can't object to dry goods, but why rolls and rolls? What do you do with it? Don't answer me. I can expect another lie.

"But the worst is so little, I'm ashamed almost to face the good people of Springfield. At the drug store, you took out bottles of perfume, broke the seal, used what you wanted, then took the bottles back saying they were poor quality. It's common talk, among the hundreds you entertained while I was gone, about this one act, besides your extravagance.

"Now Molly, hand me that money so I can go downtown and try to settle up. It may not be enough, but I'll try to make it stretch as far a I can."

She threw that money at him and say, "Take your pinch-pennies and get out! I wish I had never laid eyes on you, you homely, uncouth brute! I wish I had married in my circle. Elizabeth warned me. I wish I had married Stephen Douglas!"

Mistah Abe say, "I wish you had, too. But I said, 'Until death do we part.' Maybe this is death. It's worse!

"I must say this, since you brought up the subject of Stephen Douglas. There's one reason you didn't marry him. He was smart enough to learn soon enough what it has taken me nearly ten years of sad experience to learn. You are a spitfire, a cheat, and a liar!"

I didn't approve of all he said. I really felt sorry for de Missy, for once. I still believe her love him. It was only a mad cat-fit, another tantrum, when her call him names.

Mistah Abe was in earnest and her knew it. But her wound up with the last word: "I'll have Grandmother Parker's and my father's estate. And when they are settled, I'll penny-pinch with you no more. I'll take my sons and get out."

[*Mary's father and grandmother both died in 1849. Their estates apparently had not been settled by 1851.*]

I really don't think he heard. And I done think he wouldn't care, only for Mastah Robert and Willie.

He left the house and went to the barn. There, Mastah Robert was playing with a bunch of his new friends. They have a theater with boxes for seats and covers from the house for a stage curtain.

Mastah Robert jump up and down when he see his pa. "Oh, Pa, I told the boys you would take us to the woods and show us how to chop trees down, like you did in Indiana."

Them boys all gather around and say, "Will you, Mister Lincoln? Bob said you took him once and he climbed trees. Then he told us about your fishing trip to the river."

I wondered if he told them about my Billie and my Henry going fishing, too. I expect he did.

Mastah Robert was not proud. He never mistreat Billie because they call him and his pa nigger lovers.

Mistah Abe say, "Now's as good a time as any, to take you boys to the woods. You boys run home and tell your mothers where I'm taking you, if they have no objections. Robert, you go in and tell your mother."

But Gawd Amighty, they never went to the woods. Mastah Robert come a running to me and say, "Ma's laying on the bed with her head hanging over the floor, and baby Willie just look awful!"

I push him and say, "Get your Pa, quick!"

Mistah Abe must of take only two steps to the house, and tore his shirt to get in to where de Missy was. Her have taken a big swig of paregoric and then let Willie nurse.

Mistah Abe shook her and shook her, but she didn't budge. Then he pick up baby Willie who might have just a natural sleep, but Mistah Abe thought maybe her have give him some paregoric, too. He rush Mastah Robert off to get Aunt 'Lizabeth and Doctor Wallace. Told Mastah Robert not to tell anyone, but those two.

Doctor Wallace come in three shakes, as did Aunt 'Lizabeth. Doctor Wallace knowed at once what I do. He have had some of that same in his own home. [*Apparently Mariah meant that Elizabeth also took paregoric, as Mary had admitted that most of the Todd family had.*]

He told 'Lizabeth to make some black coffee, but there wasn't any in that house. The coffee and everything have been gobbled up by her parties.

Mistah Abe hurry to the peoples who wrote the paper there, a Missy Francis. [*Among the Lincolns' neighbors were Mr. and Mrs. Simeon Francis who lived on Jefferson Street at the corner of Sixth Street, about six blocks from the Lincoln home at Eighth and Jackson streets. Francis was publisher of the* Sangamon Journal *newspaper.*]

Her gave Mistah Abe a pot of cold coffee what we put on the stove and get it hot. Doctor Wallace taste it, made it weak like, and gave a little at a time, with a spoon, to Willie. He say, "I hate to give this awful stuff to a baby so young, but it's about all I can do until he awakens. Then I can see if he's had any paregoric given to him."

Mistah Abe have shoo Mastah Robert out before Doctor Wallace come, so he wouldn't hear what was said, so he [*Robert*] could tell the boys. But he [*Lincoln*] told him to tell the boys his ma was sick and they would go to the woods another time.

Doctor Wallace say, "The child could not have nursed that from Mary. It has been too short a time for it to take effect. She has given him a little [*paregoric*], perhaps. But I wish she wouldn't. He has been such a fine, healthy baby. But Mary has been under a heavy mental strain to have done this."

He give her some black, thick-looking medicine, then had Mistah Lincolumn to take one arm and he took the other and walked her.

Her head lolled from one side to the other. Her was a plumb awful sight. Doctor Wallace say, "She'll become sick and both the medicine and the paregoric will come up."

It sure did. 'Lizabeth clean everything up and say [*to Mary*], "Poor baby, poor baby, you were awful sick. Now you'll be all right."

But she wasn't, nor Willie, for a number of days. Doctor Wallace watched them both carefully.

All this cause Mistah Abe catched her in a lie and cheating. I never did see such a fernal mess as those Lincolumns could get themself in. I was getting out of that house as fast as I can. Mistah Abe grab the paregoric, bust the bottle with the ax, and bury it in a hole he dug. I made up my mind I never complain about my folks again.

I straighten up the kitchen and was on my way to hitch Maud and get for home, when that blessed Mastah Robert come tearing up from the barn and say, "Aunt Mariah, bring the meat cleaver and come to the barn quick! Pa got caught in the trapeze he hung for us when he was trying to show us how to skin the cat!" [*Lincoln had gone to the barn to get his mind off his family troubles and entertain Robert's friends. He had rigged up a rope trapeze at the top of the barn and was showing how to "skin the cat," an acrobatic somersault.*]

"Aunt Mariah, hurry, hurry!" say Mastah Robert. "He is all tangled up in a knot!"

I couldn't move, I just have to stand there still and hold my sides. I about to bust, laughing.

Mastah Robert rush in, get the meat cleaver, and bust out again. He grab my hand and say, "Run, Aunt Mariah! Run quick!"

When I git out there, there was Mistah Abe hanging by the feet and haid, all tangled up in that 'trapshun he fix for the boys. They have come back to go to the woods.

Mistah Abe was getting them settled about not going to the woods and he was wanting them to stay out of the house and not run into that mess.

He was laughing at the top of his voice. I was splitting my sides, and the boys, all but poor Mastah Robert—(he had the daylights scared out of him two times that day)—was yelling and jumping around like wild Injuns.

Mistah Abe got a little settled and say, "I just can't hold on much longer. I'm mighty uncomfortable." He was high up. He say, "Aunt Mariah, just chop that rope up close to the plank it is tied to, and let me drop."

I swear I was so weak for laughing, I could hardly raise that meat cleaver to chop. But when I give it a sound whack, down Mistah Abe fell. I's scared he would break his back or neck. But you know what? He lands right smack on his feet, like the cats he love.

I put for home and Mistah Abe put for the office. He told the boys, "Boys, don't go to the house. Be good boys and I'll take you to the woods the next time I come home from the circuit."

When I reach home, I never told my man about that fracus at the Lincolumns. I told him about Mistah Abe's 'trapshun and I thought that fat belly of his [*Henry's*] would wiggle plumb off him, he laugh so hard.

I was glad I didn't take Billie. He would have spilled the beans if he heard the fracus of de Missy and Mistah Abe. But he was mad he wasn't there to see Mistah Abe's 'formance.

[*John Thomas Trutter, a Lincoln scholar from Evanston, Illinois, whose great-grandparents lived a few doors away from the Lincolns in Springfield, says his family's oral history explains that Mary Lincoln bought entire bolts of a particular fabric in order to prevent any other lady in town from wearing a dress of the same pattern or color as hers.*]

CHAPTER NINE

The Talk of the Town

Summer–Fall, 1851

Lincoln gives his son Robert and Mariah's son Billie some words of wisdom about the business of being a lawyer and the importance of friendship. Again, Lincoln's words are as Adah Sutton interpreted them into correct English from Mariah Vance's dialect. Also, when talking with those less educated, Lincoln put them at ease by speaking less correctly or in their dialect.

When Lincoln learned that his father was gravely ill, he was unable to visit him because of sickness in his own family. Willie had been born the previous December and may have been ill at the same time that Lincoln's father was dying. Thomas Lincoln died on January 17, 1851, and Lincoln did not attend the funeral.

Lincoln wrote his stepbrother John Johnston that he hoped his father would recover, then added: "Say to him that if we could meet now it is doubtful whether it would be more painful than pleasant."

In this chapter, Mariah says Lincoln explains why he and his father were not close.

Thomas Lincoln resented the time his son spent at school or reading books when on the farm. Young Abraham had an overpowering desire to learn, and besides reading books, asked questions of those he thought he could learn from. He never forgot what happened one day. . . . As a boy, he was sitting on a fence when he asked a passing neighbor a question, and his father knocked him off the rail.

Abraham was of the opinion that his father hated books. More than once he heard him say it would be bad if someone got "too much eddication."

Like typical farming fathers of the 1800s, Thomas Lincoln found the days and seasons were short, if all the work on a homestead was to get done. For this reason, he placed more value on work than on getting an education. But Abraham craved knowledge. He was determined to be different from his father. Their conflicting interests and priorities doubtlessly distanced father and son. Yet Lincoln worked hard for his father until he was twenty-two, a few months longer than most young men of that time worked for their fathers, before going off on his own.

Lincoln may also have preferred not to visit his dying father or attend his funeral in order to avoid seeing his stepbrother, whom he considered lazy and shiftless.

Also in this chapter, Mariah Vance tells Adah Sutton a very touching story about Mary Lincoln and the care and tenderness she showed to a neighbor and her baby. It demonstrated how good a person Mary could be, when not beset by her own personal problems and obsessions.

Lloyd Ostendorf refers to this as "the river of milk" episode. "It was one of the best stories in the manuscript," says Ostendorf. "I remember typing it from Adah's handwritten work. I also found it verified in an old Springfield newspaper account."

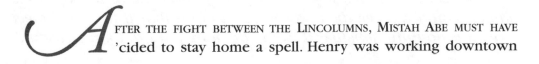

AFTER THE FIGHT BETWEEN THE LINCOLUMNS, MISTAH ABE MUST HAVE 'cided to stay home a spell. Henry was working downtown where they was tearing down old ramshacks and building new brick build-ings, some three stories high, or nigh about.

Henry saw Mistah Abe about every day. One morning Mistah Abe come out of his office as Henry was starting in to work.

My Henry say [*to Mariah at home later*], "It's the talk he [*Lincoln*] do most anything to get away from de Missy."

Now I say, "Mistah Abe have a heap on his mind. He makes his living with his mind, and he have to be where he can think everything out."

My Henry say, "You dumb as a ox, Mariah. Why, that man air on da street most of his time when here, crackin' stories. An ah bet he'n hab a bunch in his office 'til two or three in da mornin', jus raisin' hell and laughin 'til it war too late to go home. Dat would be tough after so much fun. After such a damn good time, to go home to dat hell piece he'n got for a wife."

I couldn't get it out of my head what Henry say about Mistah Abe and the talk of the town. Well, I know people talk. I know they talk to me about de Missy, but I was surprised they talk about Mistah Abe.

I felt like I should go his office and tell him. I might have, only Henry told me so often to keep my nose out of their business.

I knew there was some truth in Mistah Abe having hell at home, and maybe no human can hold their tongue forever. But I swear, Mistah Abe did raise some hell. He told her [*Mary*] all he have stored up in his head about her. And he didn't choke on lies, 'cause there was no lies.

Still, I thinks de Missy 'serves to be forgive, for her was so mixed up. And I believe her love the man and was near dying because her thinks he don't care for her. But he say, "'Til death do we part." So I thinks he'll stay with her until death, and maybe they'll patch it up.

I told my man to keep his lip button about both of them, 'cause they both are our friends and help us. And Mastah Robert right then was giving his education to us.

Mastah Robert come over and say, "Ma has been sick again with headaches. She doesn't want my friends and me around making noise. She sent me over to play with Billie."

That please a whole bunch of my younguns. I couldn't hardly help from going right down to Mistah Abe's office and tell him he should be at home with that poor woman and that blessed Willie Wallace. I ask Mastah Robert how was baby Willie.

He say, "Oh Willie, he's fine. Only once he had colic, and he holds his breath until he's blue in the face. That scares Ma. I wanted to hold him, but they are afraid I would let him drop. I'm almost ten and Ma still thinks of me as a baby."

I say, "Hold your horses, Mastah Robert. You was born in 1843 and this is only 1851." [*Reminding him he is eight.*]

"Well, anyway," he say, "I'm taking Latin and Pa's studying with me."

He ask Billie if he would like to study some Latin.

"No," say Billie. "I'd rather learn how to spell and read."

My kids all join in and say they all want to learn how to count and put letters together, so they could read. Whenever Mastah Robert come to our place, it please the whole bunch so.

Then, Gawd bless their little hearts, they all set on the floor and have school. I was learning too, to read and count.

I send my Billie up to the town to tell his pappy to bring home some corn for hominy, and to make parch corn. I couldn't go 'cause my man have Maud and the cart. Mastah Robert went along. They didn't stop with Henry long. They went on to town and ran into Mistah Abe. They coax him to take them fishing.

It was a nice day, but he say, "I have some important work to do. Not today. Maybe tomorrow."

But right away he want to know why Bobbie was downtown with Billie. Mastah Robert say, "Ma sent me over to play with Billie because she wants the house quiet. She didn't want it overrun with boys all day. She wanted Willie to sleep because he didn't rest last night. Then when I was playing with Billie, Aunt Mariah wanted Billie to come here to see his pappy and tell him to bring home some corn for hominy and parched corn."

"That all sounds first-rate," say Mistah Abe. "Now here is a nickel apiece. Go get some candy. And get off the street because it is so torn up from the building going on."

Say Mastah Robert, "How come you are on the street instead of in your office?"

Mistah Abe was always willing to explain things, but my Henry would say, "Shut you'n imp'dence [*impudence*] 'fore ah knock you'n teeth down you'n throat!"

Mistah Abe say, "You must learn, Robert, that men can do a great many things little boys can't. But to get to the point, son, I have business on the street."

Billie say with his big mouth, "Stan'in' 'roun crackin' jokes wid da bums?"

"Listen, Bill," Mistah Abe say. "I don't know where you get such notions, but that 'crackin' jokes' as you call it, or telling stories as the truth of the matter is, I must be friendly with all people. That's my way of being friendly, and if I make friends, I may get their business. If they like me they will come to me. There're too many lawyers around these parts to neglect all you can do to get a share of the law business.

"Some of these folks you call 'bums' are mostly poor folks. Their business, to be sure, cannot be very profitable. But it gives me experience and sometimes helps these poor souls. I do the same thing on the circuit and in court. I make friends and I like friends.

"Always remember, boys, you can't buy friends. You have to merit them. People will be more apt to be your friend if you make them happy than if you made them angry. But as I said, I like friends.

"Until I came to Illinois, I was never in a position to make many friends. The country where our family lived was sparsely inhabited. It was a wooded and desolate country. I often longed for companionship that I could talk with and learn from. Especially discuss the learning one gets from books.

"Don't misjudge this last statement, boys. Always remember you can learn from everyone, even the lowliest. If not anything else, often good common sense.

"My father and mother had no book learning, but each in their way had good common sense. Did the best their meager education permitted, and above all, were happy."

Mastah Robert spoke up and say, "Pa, then why don't you act happy at home?"

"Well, son," say Mistah Abe, "maybe I don't act all I feel. Often I must think out how to plead a case, or meet obligations. At home, when away from the hubbub of the public, I can concentrate and plan. I guess I must have formed this habit early, of thinking things out, trying first to be right before going ahead. You see, the habits you form when young are almost impossible to break.

"Maybe I haven't spent enough time with you, Robert. We'll go fishing tomorrow. Bill, ask your pappy to go fishing with us,"

Mastah Robert, he stayed for dinner, then put off for home. When my man come for his dinner, Billie like always popped off about everything.

Henry say, "Well, ole Abe Lincolumn can go fishin' wid you'ns, but how da hell do he"n think ah can go fish an work at da same time? Jus 'cause he'n know ah cain't go. Cotch a white lawyer goin' anywhar wid a niggah. 'Specially one what got hitched to a white-high flutin' 'ciety woman like Mrs. Lincolumn."

Billie say, "Dat ole woman didn't want Mammy and me to go with her on the Fourth of July."

I hush him up by saying, "Well, we didn't want to go, so we's even."

But Billie stuck up for Mistah Abe by saying, "Wan we'ns war fishin' t'gether, he'n walked plumb home wid us'n."

My Henry have hardly got away when that blessed Mastah Robert come tearing back and holler, "Billie, oh Billie! What do you think? The whole gang is going fishing with us!"

Billie look down his nose. "Whose the gang?"

Mastah Robert up and say, "The bunch of boys I play with now. I told them you could whistle like all the birds. You could get the little wild animals to come to you, then we could catch them. And that you are a peck of fun. They all want you. You come over in the morning, early. We'll fix a picnic lunch for you, too, so don't stop for that. He can go, can't he, Aunt Mariah?"

When the gang all got to the Lincolumns, de Missy say, "That Bobby of mine will be a diplomat someday, or an ambassador." And sure enough, what de Missy say come true.

They all went to the woods, and Billie done made all them boys his friends. Some of those boys was the ones that I had to cut with the black snake, to get them to leave us alone that time in the cart. Mastah Robert made friends with them. Then he fix it so they was Billie's friends.

Mistah Abe brought my Billie home first. Billie had caught a 'possum. Mastah Robert have a crow. Billie climbed a tree and coax it to him. Mistah Abe left a long string of nice fish.

Billie say, "If'n you cut da crow's tongue, it'll talk. If you leave it here, Pappy will do dat."

Mistah Abe thought that a little cruel. But Billie tell him, "Pappy know how, so it won't hurt a bit." So Mastah Robert kissed the crow and gave it to Billie. All the boys wanted to go back the next day and get a crow for each of them.

Mastah Robert, like a little gentleman, introduced each friend to me before they go home. Just like I was the grandest lady in the land.

Oh yes, he tole me his ma wouldn't want me for a while. I didn't go back until in November.

De Missy done did the wash and house and all her serving, besides taking the best care of Willie 'twixt the time I worked for them last and the time I went back when Mistah Abe come home from the circuit for the winter. Her was making up for the parties her spend so much money on. And her sure enough look like a work woman.

I worked for other folks. Land, some of those folks gave the Lincolumns fits. They say when Mistah Abe's pa died, de Missy want Mistah Abe to wear a band of crepe around his hat. She say he was showing no grief and no respect for his pa.

He say, "Pa was never in Springfield, and they'd think I was mourning for one of my cats. I did all I could for him when he was with us. I left money with Ma, when I was there last, for just whatever might happen to either of them. Ma promised to keep it for that purpose. I know she didn't spend a penny of it for anything else. She is so honest.

"If I had gone back when Pa was still alive, brother John [*Lincoln's stepbrother, John Johnston*] and I would have had to fight it out. That would have hurt Pa more than what pleasure my visit would have been to him, so I stayed away. John is a shiftless spendthrift."

De Missy say to Mistah Abe, "Hadn't you better write to John now and relieve your mind of all your pent-up feelings? Maybe then you can take care of business pending."

"Perhaps I should, Mother," he say. "If I don't, he'll skin Mother out of her home, and then write me for a Christmas present of a few hundred dollars for relieving her."

Mistah Abe was walking the floor when I got back there in November. He was talking to himself or perhaps to little Willie.

He have Willie in his arms. He paid no attention when I say, "Good morning, Mistah Abe."

Directly, de Missy come and took little Willie from him. Mistah Abe wake up a speck and say, "Do you know, Mother, I can remember my little brother somewhat. [*Lincoln was a boy when his younger brother, Thomas Jr., was born on Knob Creek farm in Kentucky. He died of milk sickness in infancy.*]

"My father called him 'Tim Tom Tinker.' I believe I've figured out who our baby looks like, besides little Eddie. It is my darling little brother buried back near our last home in Kentucky."

De Missy say, "That may be, for Willie does favor you."

Then, as in a dream, he was looking far off and say, "Mother took sister Sarah and me to his [*Tom Jr.'s*] grave, before we moved to Indiana. Pa left us in Kentucky while he went to find a place for a home in Indiana.

"Mother knelt down at his grave. She had Sister and me kneel, too. She told us to bow our heads as she prayed. She asked God to stay near him, so he wouldn't be lonely after we were gone. Pa was religious too, but not the kneeling kind."

De Missy say nothing, but walk away with Willie crying for his titty.

That woman was so full of milk, it run from her all the time. Mistah Abe once brought a poor little starved neighbor's baby to her to feed, to wet nurse, so it could live. It was a help to her too, to get rid of that rivva of milk. And that poor baby get well and fat.

It was getting about the last of November and Willie's birthday was soon in December. He would be one year old and de Missy was planning a party for him.

After my wash was done for de Missy, she ask me to go upstairs and straighten. When I got up, there was Mistah Abe sitting right on the floor, his knees up almost to his chin, a reading. Maybe Shackspa, for he was motioning like a actor in a show. [*Lincoln loved to read and reread Shakespeare's plays.*] He always read out loud. Once he say he learned that in the "blab school." The kids all blab at once [*reading their lessons aloud*] so the teacher knowed they's not fudgin'.

Well, I took the broom and say, "Mistah Abe, I has to sweep you out."

He sat for a spell, until I nudge him with the broom. Then he moseyed out to the stairs and sprawled on the three top steps.

In a little while, I heard de Missy scream, "Can't you move? I'll give you until I count three. Then if you aren't up and going downstairs, I'll grab a bunch of that black hair and pull you down the steps!" Her started her count. "One, two. . . ."

Mistah Abe look up and say, "That puts me in mind of an experience I had in Indiana. I was on my way to the home of a man who had lent me a book to read. I was busily reading some lines I wanted to be sure I had committed to memory correctly. As I walked, I paid little attention to where. I was reminded where by falling head-first over a billy goat eating the long grass in the road. I landed in a mud hole.

"I was leaning over to retrieve the book that went in the mud with me, when Mister Billy goat, having a vindictive disposition, decided that my posterior was just in the right position to retaliate for the way I had disturbed him.

"My second header seemed to strike him as a game he liked. After a few 'baa baas,' he put his head down and made another lunge. This time I was ready for Mister Goat. I stepped to one side and grabbed his whiskers. After tussling for a while, swung him over my shoulder and he landed head-first in the mud hole. He picked himself up and shook his head, as if to say, 'I've decided this game of leapfrog is not for me.'"

De Missy say, "You wouldn't dare!"

He say, "Anyone who takes a dare, kills a horse and eats its hair."

At that, he got up and turn 'round. He put one of his big feet on the top step, lay de Missy over his knee, and spank her bottom!

Her come into where I was working as pleased as a grinning kitten. I swear, you never could decide how those folks would wind up in their argufying. Mistah Abe went down the stairs laughing fit to kill. And her smiling and singing at her work.

I guess they patch it up, about the cheating and lying business. Although de Missy told me later that Mistah Lincolumn would never temporize with evil, least of all the lesser evil morals that lead to crime.

When my work was done, I went home with a load of food, clothes, big pay of two dollars for the wash and cleaning, and my back pay that we sure could make use of. And an invite to bring Billie the next time.

[*The infant Mary Lincoln wet-nursed was Charles Dallman Jr., son of Charles and Harriet Dallman, who lived nearby. Dallman, a carpenter, became known as a pioneer builder in Springfield, and was later an alderman from 1864 to 1866.*

The following item appeared in the Springfield, Illinois, State Register *newspaper on Sunday, February 27, 1938:*

> The Dallmans made their first home in a red brick bungalow that stood on the north side of Jackson street, a few doors west of Eighth street and only a stone's throw from the Lincoln home.

On April 4, 1853, Tad Lincoln was born. About this date came the second child, Charles, to the Dallman family. Mrs. Dallman was at that time unable to nurse her baby. When Mrs. Lincoln heard of that fact, she sent her husband over to the Dallman home and had him bring the infant to her for nursing. . . for the necessary time. She also said Mr. Lincoln rocked the cradle until the child was happily asleep.

Mariah Vance told Adah Sutton the "river of milk" episode happened in 1851, but according to the newspaper account it occurred two years later. For the purpose of following both Mariah's and Adah's chronology as closely as possible, the episode has been left in the year Mariah remembered it.]

CHAPTER TEN

Of God and Fortune-Tellers

1851

Abraham Lincoln's parents were members of the Little Mount Baptist Church in Kentucky. His older sister, Sarah, joined the Pigeon Creek Baptist Church when the family moved to Indiana. Biographers say Abe never joined any organized religion.

An Episcopal clergyman married Abraham Lincoln and Mary Todd. Mary was a member of the Presbyterian church and Abe often attended Sunday services with her and their sons when he was in Springfield. He had grown up reading the Bible. He knew "the Good Book" so well, he could quote it and often did in his talks to juries, in political campaigns, and in his speeches and letters.

Lincoln's independent views on religion did not help his political career. His political enemies called him a deist, one who advocates natural religion based on human reason rather than revela-

155

tion. Speaking to a young men's group in Springfield in 1838, he praised "Reason; cold, calculating, unimpassioned reason."

Lincoln also was called an infidel, one who is not a Christian or opposes Christianity. Even his friend and law partner, William Herndon, considered him to be "a sort of infidel, a theist, a fatalist." Lincoln was accused of infidelism during his campaign for Congress in 1846. In his defense, he released a handbill to the press that explained his religious views. He said, in part:

> *I am not a member of any Christian church, it is true; but I have never denied the truth of the Scriptures; and I have never spoken with intentional disrespect of religion in general, or of any denomination of Christians in particular.*
>
> *It is true that in early life I was inclined to believe in what I understand is called the "Doctrine of Necessity"—that is, that the human mind is impelled to action, or held in rest by some power, over which the mind itself has no control; and I have sometimes tried to maintain this opinion in argument.*

He said he could not support a man for office whom he knew to be an open enemy of or scoffer at religion, but no one should make such a false charge against him. He also said he had given up arguing for fatalism more than five years before.

Newspapers did not print his religious defense until after he had won the election.

Neither his wife nor his closest friends could say they knew Lincoln's true feelings regarding religion. David Davis, his campaign manager and long-time friend, said, "I don't know anything about Lincoln's religion, nor do I think anybody else knows anything about it."

Many evangelical Christians considered Lincoln to be a solemn, earnest, religious man. Regarding this, Mary said, "He never joined a church, but still he was a religious man. But it was a kind of poetry in his nature, and he never was a technical Christian."

Lincoln once made a correction in a book of sermons that said, "Ye have loved me, and have believed that I came forth from God." Lincoln crossed out the words "from God" and replaced them with "from nature."

Lincoln sometimes joined Mary in attending revival meetings held by the Presbyterian church, but when asked to join the church, said he "couldn't quite see it."

Ruth Painter Randall says in her biography of Mary that Lincoln wrote a friend in 1837 that he was lonely in Springfield. "I've never been to church yet, nor probably shall not be soon," he wrote. "I stay away because I am conscious I should not know how to behave myself."

Typical of many other Christians and churchgoers in the 1800s, the Lincolns also were drawn to other spiritual influences. Like his father, Abe believed in dreams that foretold events to come. He often tried to understand what influence his dreams might have on his future. Mary believed in signs and told him about their portents of coming events in their lives.

Mary Edwards Brown, granddaughter of Mary Lincoln's sister Elizabeth (Mrs. Ninian) Edwards, said in an interview in 1959, "The night before their boy Eddie died, Lincoln had the same dream he always had when something unusual was going to happen—you know, about a ship sailing along fast, that he had the night before he was assassinated."

Both Lincolns were superstitious. Lincoln once wrote to his friend Joshua Speed, after learning of Speed's marriage to Fanny Henning: "I was always superstitious; I believe God made me one of the instruments of bringing your Fanny and you together, which union I have no doubt he had foreordained. Whatever he designs he will do for me yet." (He was apparently referring to his possible marriage to Mary Todd.)

One day in 1851, Mariah Vance spoke with Lincoln about religion and spiritualism. His comments in this chapter need some explanation. As in previous chapters where Lincoln is quoted, Adah Sutton copied Mariah's Black dialect in remembering what Lincoln said to her, then transliterated it into her (Adah's) own narrative style. The gist of what Lincoln said remains as Mariah remembered it.

I ASKED MISTAH ABE IF HE BELIEVED IN RELIGION AND WHAT CHURCH HE WOULD JOIN. He say, "I remember going to a camp meeting in Kentucky. I was a little tyke. We drove several miles with folks who picked up my mother, sister Sarah, and myself. Then on down a few miles they took on some of our neighbors.

"Dennis [*his cousin, Dennis Hanks, who lived with the Thomas Lincoln family*] was bent on going, but he hadn't finished the work laid out for him. He was punished by having to stay home.

He licked through his work and hit the road, getting there about two hours after our load. And it was a load, for a cart not much bigger than yours, Mariah, and an old broken-down horse. Part of the way, we got out and walked to relieve that poor nag when the going got rough.

"There was baptizing. Immersion was novel in those parts, so much so that many from a distance were incited to come. There were houses of worship, but few parsons. The churches, such as they were, had 'gospel droners,' as those professing to be preachers were called.

"I remember I was more impressed by the dunking that Dutton Lane (I believe that was the Baptist preacher's name) gave those who repented after being enchanted by his exertions [*exhortations*]. They testified, after swooning, that they were delivered by a vision, a dream, an uncommon appearance of light. Some, by a spoken voice to them: 'Thy sins are forgiven thee,' and by seeing the Savior with their natural eyes. All of whom were received into full fellowship.

"Knowing no better way, I, as did my mother, considered this to be the work of God. I still believe a part of what those people testified to, because visions are not uncommon to me. Nor were they uncommon to that blessed mother of mine. Until her death, she was a devoted Christian.

"She often spoke of things that would happen even foretold her early death. Once I heard her tell my father, when she was in seemingly good health (that was in Indiana a number of years after the Baptist camp meeting in Kentucky), just when she would die, and asked him to marry some good Christian woman to care for him and their children.

"I believe that promise he made her was sincere. He could have married a short while after my mother was laid away on that knob [*a rise or hill, as in the Knob Hill country back in Kentucky*]. But he waited a respectable time and brought us to a good woman.

"No better woman ever lived than our [*step*] mother, Sarah. To her I owe a debt of gratitude that can never be paid in acts of appreciation, outside of help financially. I often worry because I can't give her more."

"Well," I say to Mistah Abe, "then you are a Baptist?"

He then say, "Mariah, I can't remember, and don't know too much about the doctrine of any church. I believe, though, since my dear mother and stepmother were both good women, and were Baptists, and taught me nothing but good, I'd join the Baptists, if any church.

"But I've ideas of my own. I pray God they are not false ideas. They have a way of directing me. And if I'm in doubt—Mrs. Lincoln and I both agree on this—since our dear Eddie's death, we go to three good women who are in touch with the spirit world, and can straighten us out. This, Mrs. Lincoln and I do find comfort in."

[*Mariah then told Adah, "And you knows, the picture of those three ole 'fortune-tellers,' I calls them, I still got."*]

I just couldn't think Mistah Abe and de Missy could go to these cheats. I say to him, "Do you pay 'em?"

He say, "Why, Aunt Mariah, of course we pay them."

I say, "I just can't believe you put them before a good parson."

"Mariah," he say, "I believe in God, as I know you do. I believe in Christmas, as I know you do. I believe God created all that was created. I believe he spoke the word and all was created good. I believe God is love, that universal love is all, since God is all in all. This because I believe thoroughly in the Bible.

"And that same Bible says God is spirit. So if all things are created in his image and likeness, as the Bible says, and I believe that also to be a main truth, then his Son was spirit. Then we are spirit. We could go on and on and say the birds of the air and fish of the sea were spirit, and so on.

"Christ was crucified, returned, and ascended into heaven. Christ said we could do even greater things than he did. If that is so, and I believe it is, for the world has only begun to touch the hem of his garment through faithful prayer, then why couldn't we, or our loved ones, return after the state called death?"

"Well," I say, "Mistah Abe, the blessed Christ didn't have to return because three old cheats call him back. So if the dead do come back, they can do the same as Christ, if they are like him, a spirit.

"I know you and de Missy need comfort. If you know little Eddie are in heaben, why would you want him to come back to this bad world? Don't you think that's selfish? Cain't you find comfort in knowing he's out of all this wicked world? Our Christ haven't come back since he went up to heaben. He was right here when he return from the tomb. He wanted to talk to his 'siples [*disciples*]. Cain't you find comfort in knowing Gawd does all things well? Christ says, 'These little ones, for of such is the kingdom of heaben.'"

[*Mariah was referring to Matt. 19: 13-14, King James version: Then were there brought unto him little children, that he should put his hands on them, and pray: and the disciples rebuked them. But Jesus said, "Suffer little children, and forbid them not, to come unto me: for of such is the kingdom of heaven."*]

I believe I do Mistah Abe good. He say, "I'll think, and think hard, about what you have said. I want to think right. Maybe I've missed an important point some place."

I say, "I just pray and I believe, and I know Gawd hears and will answer."

Da Mistah say, "Mariah, I'm ashamed to say your way of the Christ cross is so new to me. You are a good, devout, wise Christian. Maybe your coming into our home has been a wonderful blessing, besides the good work you have done for us. Sometimes I have believed little Eddie was taken to lead me to study, to see, and to be redeemed. For 'a little child shall lead them.' That could be, in death, the same as in life.

"The minister who preached little Eddie's funeral has helped to open my eyes. I now have a book this minister wrote, *The Christian Defense*, and I'm trying hard to believe it. [*The book of prayers and Christian guidance in daily life was written by the Rev. James Smith, pastor of the First Presbyterian Church in Springfield, the church Mary Lincoln attended.*]

"It seems so hard to believe we had to sacrifice a precious child in order to gain insight into the divine road of life and to life eternal. The way, so says the Bible, is straight and narrow. Maybe we are trying to take the easy way.

"But I'll assure you, Aunt Mariah, it would be a cross I couldn't forgive myself for, if I disturbed that angel baby, so that he could shoulder my cross. It would indeed be a dear price of conscience to pay for a momentary comfort."

I don't know if de Missy ever gave up the fortune-tellers, but I heard that Mistah Abe had a time with her after Willie died in the White House [*of pneumonia, on February 20, 1862*], for her have fortune-tellers there. Mistah Abe thought her was going crazy.

De Missy grieved over everything too much. She was a good woman, but powerful odd.

[*Lincoln apparently did place a great deal of importance on prayer, especially after becoming President. He is credited with having started (in 1861) the regular national observance of Thanksgiving on the last Thursday in November.*

The observance had been promoted by Sarah Josepha Hale, editor of a popular women's magazine, who had recommended that an annual day of national thanksgiving be established. Her letters to Lincoln on this cause prompted two of his nine proclamations of fasting, prayer, or thanksgiving.]

CHAPTER ELEVEN

Where There's a Will

Winter, 1851–Autumn, 1852

Lincoln loved animals and often brought home strays, among them a collection of cats and a crow. A diverse cast of characters enters this chapter. Henry Clay, Daniel Webster, Harriet Beecher Stowe, President Millard Fillmore, and Jenny Lind.

Henry Clay (1777–1852), a lawyer and orator, was a U.S. senator from Kentucky and later speaker of the U.S. House of Representatives. In 1820 he helped push through the House the Missouri Compromise, which prohibited the expansion of slavery into new territories.

Clay, a friend of the Todd family in Lexington, was an unsuccessful candidate for President in 1824. He returned to the Senate in 1831 and became leader of the Whig political party. He made several more unsuccessful attempts to become President again in the

1840s. For his efforts to hold the Union together he became known as "The Great Compromiser."

The Missouri Compromise was a series of laws enacted by Congress in 1820 and 1821 to maintain the balance between slave and non-slave states, a compromise measure between North and South admitting Missouri to the Union as a slave state in 1821. The North feared that admitting a slave state would mean a shift of balance in the U.S. Senate in favor of the South, since prior to Missouri, the Union's twenty-two states were equally divided between slave and free.

The situation was stalled until Maine petitioned for admission as a free state. Henry Clay led the forces that evolved the compromise, admitting Maine as a free state and allowing Missouri to frame a constitution with no restrictions on slavery.

The compromise banned slavery in the rest of the Louisiana Purchase territory north of Missouri's southern boundary. It was repealed by the Kansas-Nebraska Act in 1854 when the doctrine of "popular sovereignty" was introduced. Lincoln's opposition to the repeal revived his interest in politics.

The Kansas-Nebraska Act allowed those in the territories of Kansas and Nebraska, north of the Missouri Compromise line, to choose whether or not to allow slavery. Lincoln strongly opposed the concept of new states having a choice. "Bleeding Kansas" became a battleground between pro- and anti-slavery forces.

Millard Fillmore (1800–1874), a lawyer from New York, became a leader of the Whig Party in 1840. With Henry Clay's backing, he was nominated for Vice President on the Whig ticket with Zachary Taylor for President. They won the election of 1848. Taylor died of cholera two years later, and Fillmore succeeded him as President.

Fillmore signed the Missouri Compromise and took a middle ground on the issue of slavery, trying to keep extremists from gaining power. The Whig Party declined over the issue of slavery, and Fillmore's political career came to an end. He later opposed Lincoln's election as President.

Fillmore also was a supporter of the Fugitive Slave Act of 1850. It provided for the seizing, return, and sentencing of runaway slaves between states. Northern opponents created the Underground

Railroad helping runaway slaves reach safety in the North or Canada. They also enacted personal-liberty laws in the North that guaranteed jury trials to fugitive slaves. The law was nullified by several Northern states, and on December 20, 1860, South Carolina became the first state to secede from the Union. The law was repealed by Congress in 1864.

Harriet Beecher Stowe (1811–1896), the daughter of a Connecticut minister, strongly opposed slavery and aided at least one runaway slave. After the Fugitive Slave Act was passed, she wrote a novel about the injustices of slavery. Uncle Tom's Cabin *was serialized in an abolitionist newspaper in 1852, then was published as a book, which stirred the conscience of a nation, especially the North.*

Daniel Webster (1782–1852), lawyer and member of the House of Representatives from Boston, was one of the greatest orators of his time. He was also a leader of the Whig Party and a presidential hopeful. Some of his greatest speeches were in support of the Missouri Compromise.

Jenny Lind (1820–1887), "The Swedish Nightingale," was a soprano who toured the United States with great success between 1850 and 1852.

After telling how these men, women, and events touched the lives of the Lincolns, this chapter closes with Mary Lincoln confiding in Mariah about her lifelong ambition and her troubled marriage.

Mariah tells Mary she believes she knows the root of the problem "De Missy" has with "Mistah Abe."

T HE NEXT TIME I WAS BACK TO THE LINCOLUMNS, I HAVE TO TAKE BILLIE AND THE crow. That crow was under my feet and in most everything in our shack. We didn't dare let it loose. When Billie did take it out, he have to hold fast to it.

It caw-caw so, the white trash could put Billie in the jug or worse still, string him up. But I declare, those white trash have simmer down some, since they found out Billie now have high-falutin' white friends. And my Henry plumb simmer down after he see the respect the Lincolumns and their friends show Billie and his Mammy.

My man's boss on the building tearing-up was saying some mighty mean things about the Lincolumns one day. My man knew to keep his job, he'd have to keep his mouth shut and keep his fists to hisself. It was all he could do, but he come home madder than a poked hornet. I have the chance to tell him now. He knowed how he sound when he pop off 'bout something that he only suspect and have no sense in his blabbin' about.

That man of mine say when his younguns get education from Mastah Robert, they'll know how to help all the poor niggahs what's being lashed down and driven. He wish Mistah Abe would get back in politics and go to Washington. This time, maybe he could put some sense in them legtators' heads and they see, black and wool am no different than redheads and freckles. He say, "Igmowance am igmowance, and the worstest igmowance is to think God made a difference in our souls."

I was so happy to hear my Henry say Gawd, for he always say he didn't go in for that religious stuff very much.

It was a little late that morning 'twixt Willie's birthday and Christmas, when we got over to my wash. We have to walk to the Lincolumns because Pappy was hauling [*with the mule and cart*], and it was cold.

Everything was ready and I washed in the shed. Mistah Abe have made the water hot outdoors [*on the backyard boiler*], then carried it in. I have to boil the clothes outdoors.

When I got done, Mistah Abe build up more fire for the hog he was killing. He killed two chickens and picked them, after scalding. I dressed them, but didn't know those chickens was for me 'til we started home. They gave us lots of that hog, too.

Mastah Robert and my Billie stay in the shed, 'cause it was too cold in the barn. They manage to keep quiet until I went to the kitchen to clean that while the clothes dry. They froze dry.

De Missy have knitted a pair of mittens for each of my chillun and me, too. That took a lot of knittin'. And they bought a pair of those horsehide gloves lined with wool, for Henry. Those new wool yarn mittens sure keep my hands warm when I taking down the clothes.

Billie didn't get much learning from Mastah Robert. The crow got the learning. My Henry done did a good job of fixing that crow. Those boys say "Stop!" so often, that crow learn to say "Stop! Stop! Stop!"

Mastah Robert laugh 'til he cry. He beg his Ma to let him have the boys [*his other friends*] come to hear. But her say, "Another day."

I stirred up a batch of fresh cracklin' bread with fresh chops and gravy sop for their dinner. I want to put off for home, to get my Henry something hot, so they couldn't coax me to stay. Mastah Robert coax me to let Billie stay, but de Missy put her foot down.

Her say, "If Billie stays, the rest of the gang will get here some way, and this house will be overrun with boys. Wait until some warm day when you can all go to the barn. Anyway, Bobby, you have to practice your recitation which you are on the program to give Christmas Eve at church."

Mastah Robert say, "Oh, shoot, Ma!" But he got no further.

De Missy say, "Bobby, go upstairs!"

Mistah Abe say, "Well, Bill, since you can't keep the crow and it's about to become a bone of contention here, I've made a cage for it. Maybe when it learns this is its home, when it becomes more tame, it won't go far when let out. It will easily find its way back here to its friends and food.

"I've always loved a parrot. I saw a cockatoo at a circus. It could talk better than a parrot. But I like this crow. Maybe I can talk to it once in a while, instead of talking to myself. It just might be able to prompt me on some of my pleas I practice, when it learns to talk better." Then he laugh.

As he was about to go out that door, that Jim Crow right up and flew on his shoulder.

[*"Jim Crow" was a name given to laws enacted in the South in the 1880s that legalized segregation between Blacks and Whites. The term originated in the play* The Rifle, *in 1828.*]

Mistah Abe patted it and brush down its feathers as it caw-caw. Then Billie hold out his arm and the crow flew to him. Mastah Robert come back downstairs. He was a little scared when his turn come. That crow done act just like it was going to fly at his face. Instead, it lit on his head. Mastah Robert laugh so loud and long, this is no lie, that black crow laugh too!

Mistah Abe say, "I hate to cage that bird. But these six cats, especially the black tom, will have to be tamed a little more, as well as the crow. The crow may come up missing its wings and tail, and the tom may have his eyes pecked out. If anything should happen to the little kittens, I know Mister Crow would have to go back to the woods.

"Mrs. Lincoln doesn't care too much for the noise of the crow, as Willie, the precious little rascal, is here and mustn't be disturbed. Since a cat jumped into the crib with Willie, she keeps them out in the shed or barn. I suspect the shed is where Jim will have to go.

"Our little white rat that I brought home in my pocket at one time—remember it nibbled a hole in my pocket? It had to be caged. You know cats like rat meat and don't go slow on eating birds.

"Our turtle has hibernated somewhere, perhaps just for the winter. I had it tied in the barn and part of the rope is still there. Mister Turtle may be miles away to the South where the weather is warmer. Turtles know what they want and go after it, slow but sure.

"I'd love to know their minds. In fact, all living creatures' minds. Maybe they think better thoughts than we. Maybe someday, who knows, they will rule man instead of man ruling.

"Take that crow. It can talk our talk, so we can understand. Can we talk their language? No. They wouldn't recognize what we were trying to say. Nor would we know how to go about trying.

"Can any living thing but a bird fly? Some birds such as a duck can fly, and swim too. I've often wondered, when seeing birds fly, if man will ever attain their height? Maybe mechanically. A balloon is not the answer. Maybe breath control. The Bible says, 'The last shall be first and the first last.' Maybe we, as mighty as some really believe they are, are only the last.

"The nearest I ever knew anyone coming to understanding all creatures, especially birds, is Bill. Bill answers them and they answer him. Maybe I'm giving Bill too much credit for understanding. It's that God-given talent of the finer shadings of tone that he can execute, perhaps.

"Bill will be a fine man. God must love Bill greatly to have given him these greatest of talents, and Bill is using them. The Bible say, 'If you don't use your talents, they are taken away.'"

Mastah Robert spoke up and say, "What's my talents, Pa?"

Mistah Abe say, "Well, Robert, you are a very sincere, kind, lovable boy. You make friends who are worthwhile. You love friends and you keep them. Didn't your Ma say, 'Someday our Robert is going to be a statesman, an ambassador, or a diplomat?'

"Why? Because you smooth out the hurts that might develop into worse hurts among your friends, and with them. Now just to show you what I mean, you made friends with your friends and Bill."

Then my Billie, that awful blab gut, up and say, "Mah pappy war mad as heck tord Mistah Abe an you ma, 'til he'n found you'n warn't stuck up. He'n fight hell out of dat bums, he'n could, ef da got lippy 'bout you'ns. He'n mad at he'ns boss fa talkin' 'bout da Lincolumns. He'n war 'fraid to fight da boss, 'cause he'n loose his'n job. But ah bet someting awful will happen ta dat boss, fa sayin' lies 'bout you'ns."

I finally grab Billie by the arm and marched him home. I preached to him all the way, about being a tattle-tale.

We got home before Henry. The kids was all hungry. I made corn cakes and cooked those chickens. We have a meal as fine as anyone's Christmas dinner. That chicken with chicken sop and some flub-dub food from Willie's birthday party was licked up clean by we'ns seven.

It was in January 1852 before I went back to wash. The Lincolumns was in a funk 'bout Grandma Parker's estate. [*Mary's grandmother Elizabeth Porter Parker died that January and relatives contested her will.*] Something 'bout a law suit in connection with two colored people that have a high education and then was ship off to Africa. [*Though anti-slavery, the Parkers owned a few slaves.*]

The other was about de Missy's stepmother getting too much. Her stepsons, de Missy's brothers, was making trouble. Mistah Abe was in the middle of all this, since he was a lawyer for de Missy, Aunt 'Lizabeth, and Aunt Francie. It was all so mixed, I couldn't get much sense. But Mistah Abe was going to Lexington. He go on the circuit as usual that spring and would go to Lexington in the summer.

There wasn't too much excitement of any kind that I could tell. Only de Missy raving first about one, then another of her folks. Mistah Abe say, "It's no use crossing a stream before you get to it."

I hear de Missy say, "Well, if you could see beyond your nose, you would know we are in the middle of a big puddle now."

Her tried her best to keep Mistah Abe off the circuit. She said he'd make more all around by settling the estate. But he knowed there was too many to get that estate money, for anyone to get rich off it, 'cause her pa owed money that have to come out first. I didn't know much that went on that summer, as de Missy done did her own work and wash.

Her was all work up that fall. Such fussing over a little dab of money by her brothers and sisters.

They was all smart enough and could get out and make more than they got, in less time than it took to fuss about it.

I hear Mistah Abe say, "I wouldn't drag out all the family skeletons for people to snicker and gossip about, for all you will get collectively."

But he was the lawyer and have to do as she said. She say when the estate was settled, she would take her money and get out, and take the boys with her. Her said that, when her was mad. That woman would come slipping back, because that money wouldn't keep her in a shack for long.

Not long after Mistah Abe come back from the circuit that spring, their friend Henry Clay died [*on June 29, 1852*]. My, but de Missy was grieved.

Her tole of what a fine man he was, and about his cousin who was bitter against slavery.

Her say Mistah Lincolumn was chose to eul'gize Mistah Clay. It was in the State House or some other big building in Springfield. Her brag and brag about what a big honor that was.

[*Lincoln gave an impressive eulogy for Henry Clay in the Hall of Representatives at the State House on July 6, 1852.*]

Henry Clay was first, after her father, next to Gawd. Her say, "When young, I dreamed and planned to marry Henry Clay, because he would be President of the United States someday. Then I would be the First Lady of the land.

"I knew little then that love entered into marriage. My love, or rather the great respect I entertained for him, was as one would love a kind, good, and indulgent grandfather [*which Clay was old enough to be*]. He was in our home so much, always discussing politics and government, or we in his home. The Whigs have lost another fine and strong supporter, Daniel Webster." [*Webster died October 1852*].

Mistah Abe talked a lot about them.

He got hold of a new book, *Uncle Tom's Cabin*, that year. I wanted to stay and hear him read it plumb through. He read so loud, I could understand, but I have to get on home.

He was terrible worked up over that story and say, "Maybe someday I can take a crack at slavery. And when I do, I will make it count, if I can't bust it completely up."

He say, "I'm glad for the Underground Railroad. This system has been in operation for at least two years. It has stations at regular intervals. Already, many thousands have been brought North and are now living as free people. The main route is from Richmond to Philadelphia. They are even coming through in coffin boxes."

He said of [*Millard*] Fillmore, who was made President after [*Zachary*] Taylor's death, "I like Fillmore as a man, but he has lost prestige by signing the Fugitive Slave Law. The North doesn't want slave owners invading the North, seizing any colored person they said was theirs, then without process of law, draw them back South into servitude. Many free Negroes who were always free and had always lived in the North were virtually kidnapped."

I didn't tell Mistah Abe, but my Henry was sure scared stiff. Mistah and Missus Lincolumn talked of all the new things what have happen since I went to work for them in 1850.

I may not always get the date right now, since it is getting hard for me to remember them, but I do remember them talking a lot about a beautiful and fine singer from Sweden. Her name was Jenny. Her travel in a private railroad coach and visit the White House and the Fillmores.

There was yacht races. America won the prize from a bunch of English yachts. I bet that made them English mad as blazes.

Every time they would talk about boats or railroads, de Missy would plan to travel somewhere. When they talk about the trans-Atlantic steamer crossing the Atlantic in ten days, her was going to get ready for a trip to France.

I swear I never seen such a mixed-up woman. Instead, her got coutched again. It was sure going to be a girl this time, her say.

That fall, de Missy tole me that Mistah Abe have been sulking or something strange. He wouldn't talk to her or stay home after coming home from the circuit last of June 'til he caught her with morning sickness in August.

She said, "Then he was ashamed and has been more like himself. I tried everything I could think of to try to draw him out of this mood. I talked to him about this same book he is now reading, *Uncle Tom's Cabin*. But he acted always as if he didn't hear me.

"Mariah, we've had so many fights, I now sometimes doubt my sanity. I really threw a stick of wood at him and hit him."

I thought to myself, maybe Mistah Abe didn't really love that poor woman. But then how could he, the way her carried on? If he'd talk, he was wrong, and if he didn't talk, he was wrong.

Maybe what they say then was true. He have so much hell at home, he hated to go home.

But he told Mastah Robert he liked to be alone. Alone with his thoughts, to think things out.

I just often wonder, as smart a woman as de Missy was, and as hard as he worked to give her all her was raised to, why in the born world her didn't simmer down? Let her boss her housework and her 'ciety, and let Mistah Abe take care of his business.

But no. De Missy have to boss it all. Mistah Abe was his own boss too many years to be bossed by what they now call "petticoat government."

My man say when two head-strong bosses gets together, one from the North and the other from the South, it just have to be a fight to settle it.

CHAPTER TWELVE

Thunder at the Lincolns'

1852-1854

While Lincoln is away again on the circuit, Mary tells Mariah she is often afraid when home alone. Her fear may have been rooted in the influence of Mammy Sally, a slave in the Todd household who worked as cook and helped raise her. Mary and her sisters grew up hearing Mammy Sally tell tales of Indian battles on the frontier, which frightened the girls. Mary's fear of being alone may have gone back to the time when, according to Jean Baker's biography of her, Mary was a girl and some friendly Cherokees were said to be nearby. She was afraid they were going to scalp her. With no place to hide she just stood in a room of the house and cried in terror.

Mammy Sally also frightened Mary with tales of spirits, the devil, and a mythical West African jay bird. She also told Mary the dead can return to the living in friendly spiritual visitations. Mary apparently believed this and years later sought comfort in trying to

173

communicate spiritually with her young son Eddie and then Willie, who died in 1862 in the White House. Mary goes on to clear up a misconception historians have had about her feelings for her stepmother.

When Lincoln returns home, he has a very unorthodox way of handling one of Mary's tantrums. Thomas "Tad" Lincoln is born and Mariah is "coutched" again. In 1854, the Missouri Compromise is repealed and, for the first time, Mariah learns more of Lincoln's thoughts on slavery.

Abraham Lincoln had been born in a slave state, Kentucky, and his uncle and other family members had owned slaves, but his parents had left a church because of their opposition to slavery.

He claimed later that his father had moved to Indiana, a free state, "partly on account of slavery." Lincoln was not an abolitionist, but considered slavery an injustice and an evil, and was strongly opposed to its extension into the territories and new states to join the Union.

"I hate slavery," Lincoln said [not to Mariah] in 1854, "because of the monstrous injustice of slavery itself. I hate it because it deprives our republican example of its just influence in the world; enables the enemies of free institutions with plausibility to taunt us as hypocrites; causes the real friends of freedom to doubt our sincerity; and especially because it forces so many good men among ourselves into an open war with the very fundamental principles of civil liberty, criticizing the Declaration of Independence, and insisting that there is no right principle of action but self-interest."

In a speech in 1858 he attacked compromises over slavery in the territories, saying, "As I would not be a slave, so I would not be a master. This expresses my idea of democracy. Whatever differs from this, to the extent of the difference, is no democracy."

While running for the presidency in 1860, Lincoln told a friend, Newton Bateman, the State Superintendent of Public Instruction: "I know there is a God, and that He hates injustice and slavery. I see the storm coming, and I know that His hand is in it. If He has a place and work for me, I believe I am ready. I am nothing, but truth is everything."

He spoke on, then concluded: "I may not see the end; but it will come, and I shall be vindicated; and these men [pro-slavers] *will find they have not read their Bibles aright."*

MISTAH ABE WENT OUT ON THE CIRCUIT THAT FALL *[1852]* IN GOOD spirits and promised de Missy to come back soon as he could. But I swear, the circuit kept that man, as always, the full time.

De Missy was debilish mad, and hurt, too. She say, "Mister Lincoln knew my condition. How I suffered while carrying Willie; of the care of two instead of one, and doing my own work besides. I can't get a fulltime nurse or maid, or they are worse than if I did my own work.

"Thank God Robert is in school part of the time. He loves to play with Willie, especially now since Willie walks and talks some. Willie has learned faster than either Robert or precious Eddie. I believe he will be very bright.

"Robert is seven years older than baby Willie. I'm always afraid he will hurt the darling child, who took the place of our little Eddie so soon after he was taken. Robert doesn't mean to be rough. He has played with some very rough boys and has learned from them.

"Then, too, he tries to emulate his father, or perhaps surpass his father's stunts of entertaining children. I believe Mister Lincoln had so few play days with other children when he was a child, he is fulfilling that longing now. At times, he acts so like a child.

"Robert tries to imitate his father in games such as piggy-back. Then he jumps with Willie on his shoulders, something I've never seen Mister Lincoln do. He takes him by one hand and whirls him around in a circle. The last time, I caught him trying to teach Willie how to slide down the stairs banister.

"It's all in play, but I just had to reprimand Robert. I wanted him to understand the danger to baby Willie's life and limbs. Incidentally, also that he isn't as grown up as he thinks he is.

"Mister Lincoln says if I keep on picking at Robert, he'll eventually resent it keenly. Either by withdrawing from me, then seeking the company who may mislead him, or perhaps withdrawing into his shell, thereby becoming as a stranger. Maybe backward and unnecessarily quiet.

"He says that is Robert's way of self-expression, that he loves Willie, wants him to be a companion. He needs Willie and Willie needs him. Mister

175

Lincoln says, 'If you want Robert to stay young, playing with his baby brother is a good way. Not force French and subjects too old for him to grasp. You'll cause Willie to fear Robert by your constant raving. I don't want my sons to dislike or to fear each other. If Robert can't play with Willie, Willie will seem a pest and intrusion in his young life.' I told him if he was more capable than I of directing our children, perhaps he'd better quit the circuit and settle down like a husband and father should. Get rid of Billy Herndon. Clean up his office. Get respectable office furnishings and assert himself as he should, as a first-class, respectable lawyer.

"Mariah, you see how we conflict. He doesn't seem to realize my feelings, or how I am so continually embarrassed. The fear I so suffer, alone so much. He seems utterly without fear. I fear my shadow. I walk the house all night without someone to stay with the children and me. Every little noise is a torture.

"I have even feared my shadow. The shadow has made me really believe that a robber has broken in, to cut our throats, or worse, carry our babies away. I say babies because Eddie is still with me. I've even screamed out the window in the night, that we're being robbed. That a cutthroat is after us.

"Once, the constable came. He searched the house, but found no one. Another time, the sheriff, who lives only a stone's throw, came. He told me I had a nightmare, and that the neighbors were complaining about my continual disturbances in the night. I swore to him that the intruder ran out as he came in. He said, 'Poppycock.' See how I'm ridiculed?"

They say boys played jokes on her sometimes, 'cause they knowed her was afraid. I told her the Bible say fear are our worst enemy. Her told me about when her was a chile, that when her was crying because her was afraid to go upstairs in the dark, in their country home in Lexington, her stepmother say that was the debil in her.

She say, "My father took me in his arms and said, 'I'll go upstairs with you. You can see there is nothing to fear, my baby love.' He said I was so like my mother. She was always so afraid.

"Now don't misunderstand me, Mariah. My stepmother had much to contend with. Her stepchildren were a problem. If any little thing went wrong, we would run to our grandmother Parker, who resented her taking our own mother's place. She demeaned this good woman who was trying to do her best, by both her brood and my father's first children.

"After Grandmother's thorough lashing her to us, our childish complaints, often unjust, became problems unsolved.

"I believe that was one reason my father sent me to boarding school. Bless my gentle, kind father. He dearly loved my stepmother. She was a highly cultured, beautiful, attractive woman. Her children all show the good stock that was in them. Emilie, my choice, is a beauty [*Mary's stepsister Emilie Todd Helm*]. Maybe because she is so beautiful. I've always loved the beautiful. Sometime before long, I want this little sister to come visit us.

"My father so loved all his children. I know he humored me the most. Maybe because he and I had much in common. I clung to him so. Maybe because I was so like my mother. Maybe as Abram says, I was never picayunish with her. [*Abram was Mary's pet name for her husband. She also called him Abram when she was excited or feeling flippant.*]

"After my mother's death, Mammy Sally seemed closer. We had Aunt Ann with us. [*Her father's unmarried sister, Ann Maria Todd, was in charge of the house after her mother died.*] My father needed companionship and a wife, and I was glad he married a woman we could never be ashamed of."

But about fear, I remember once that before Mistah Abe went on the circuit, and de Missy was with Taddie in her, a big storm come up. I looks out the window and there was Mistah Abe tearing down the boardwalk towards home. He bust in the door like there was no door there.

De Missy have put down the windows where she was, and put down the rest, upstairs and down. She have lay down on the cot in the back parlor, all roll up in a knot with a cover over her haid. Mistah Abe thought her was home alone. He found her and begin to talk the roughest talk I ever did hear from him.

He ask, "Molly, don't you have anything else to do, with your head under the covers?"

Lord, how that woman got up like a whirlwind and screamed, "Abraham Lincoln, don't you ever speak to me again as if you were addressing a woman of the streets! Now get out and go back to that class of loose women you've been associating with."

He picked her up in his arms and held her so close her couldn't breathe or talk. As soon as he let go of her a little, that woman begin pounding that man. How he did laugh and laugh.

I wonder, was he gone out of his mind, too? Then he say, "Puss, dear, that's the way I'd rather see you, of the two evils." He kissed the back of her neck and then her face, and put off downtown.

Her was still mad, too mad to know it was lightning and thundering outdoors. As the storm quiet down, her quiet down. Her say, "Please, Mariah, don't ever tell anyone Mister Lincoln talked that way to me. He knows that I so dislike incorrect grammar from him, let alone disrespect. I wonder why he takes such an ill time to approach me that way. He knows it makes me furious."

I says, "Missy, that's easy to explain, or ain't you got the reason in you haid now to do that? He wants for to make you so mad you would forget the storm. You see he did it, too."

"Well, I'll think that over," she say, "and I promise I'll never let him curb me again in that way."

She went back to the back parlor, picked up Willie who was fussing, and took him out to see the beautiful rainbow coming up east of the Lincolns' in a clear sky. I says they is so much to be happy for. We should all think of as a why for rain. The air am so sweet and fresh. Everything is so wash clean, and that promise Gawd give us with the rainbow.

That spring, when Mistah Abe come home from the circuit, he was so glum he look like a storm cloud for sure. After a while, I caught on, it was about that Todd state [*estate*]. He say he'd spent more time and worry over that state than any case he have.

Now Mistah Abe got a letter saying he owed the state. He knew what was at the bottom of it. That was Levi, just for spite. [*Levi Todd was Mrs. Lincoln's older brother, born in 1817, a year before her. Her younger brother, George, was born in 1825.*]

De Missy say, "Did you answer the charge?"

He say, "That letter was forwarded to me from Danville [*apparently from a legal asscociate there*]. I answered it. As for collecting and keeping any money belonging to a firm your father was connected with, that is without question a cooked up lie. The only money I ever received from your father was fifty dollars in 1846. I did collect it, but as you well know, your father gave that to us. That was his own personal affair.

"I still say Levi and George have no self-respect or shame. I wish I could wash my hands of the whole thing. Ninian Edwards wouldn't have wasted his time with it. However, Ninian and I had to enter suit against Levi. This was the upshot of this attachment of seven hundred and fifty dollars against us. Now it's up to them to prove it and they will never find, by any man or firm, a claim against me."

That same spring, I think it was the first part of April, Mastah Robert rush in our shack and say, "Ma wants you, Aunt Mariah. She's awful sick. I have to hurry to catch Pa at the office, before he goes out on the circuit. Ma says to tell him to hurry, too."

By the time we got there, Dr. Wallace and Aunt 'Lizabeth was on hand. The little big-head baby didn't squall like my babies, when the doctor turned them up and spank their bottoms. Dr. Wallace turn-round to 'Lizabeth and shook his head. Mistah Abe went up to the bedroom. He see the baby have a large head. He joke and call him "Tadpole." De Missy get a little excited and say, "Oh my, oh my. Is my baby deformed?"

Dr. Wallace say, "He's a fine baby, a really beautiful child." And you know, Taddie, as they nicknamed him for Thomas, his real name, was always their best looking. De Missy say to Mistah Abe, "His name will be Thomas, for your father. He should be honored for giving to us such a fine husband and father as Abram." Mistah Abe say, "Oh, shucks, Mother. You wouldn't be soft soaping me?" He was a wee bit 'barrassed.

I helped out what I could. 'Lizabeth greased the baby and dressed it, and bossed me. I think of all the ladies I ever worked 'round, Aunt 'Lizabeth knew the most about managing and was the kindest. Her did everything in its time. Never wanted to do too many things all at once, as de Missy. She was never bossy, extravagant, and was a fine cook.

Mistah Abe sat in the kitchen when we was getting the meal. He seemed overjoyed with that new baby boy. 'Lizabeth have me make the corn bread with meat cracklin' in it. She bragged on my good baking and cooking. I took some things home to wash.

I was due to have my next baby, another girl, Narcissa. I didn't show. I was so thick at all times anyway, no one ever knowed, and I felt fine this time, so as how I didn't tell. Altogether, I have eleven and there was not as much fuss or doings over those eleven as over this one, Taddie.

When I went back the next time and told de Missy I had Narcissa, that woman about called me a liar. Her say, "Mariah, how on earth did you carry that child without me knowing? Of course you hadn't been here for some time, until Taddie was born. But I'm hardly up and around, while you are out working."

And I went on with my work, carrying my baby with me as I did all the rest. Sometimes I hated to leave my home, especially if any chillun was not well. Phebe was always my weak one, so tiny, and coughed a heap. The chillun was all good to her. I had good, happy chillun, so I wasn't afraid to leave them. It was only that they have a right to a mother all the time. But my Henry couldn't make enough to feed and keep that whole kitten possy.

Aunt 'Lizebeth told me that de Missy didn't know at first there was a fault with Taddie. [*Tad was born with a cleft palate, and lisped.*] She thought that the running of milk over her when Taddie sucked was because her was so full. When her found out that milk was coming in Taddie's mouth and running out his nose, 'Lizabeth say they thought Mary was going into another of her spells.

Dr. Wallace said for de Missy not to worry about that. Taddie was getting plenty of milk without what ran out. He expected there was thousands like that. He say "expect" for not sure. That ease de Missy a little. Her finally found a way to turn that baby so the milk stayed in him.

Mistah Abe say right away, "Dr. Wallace assured us that when Taddie is weaned, that condition will clear up."

But that was a long time, because de Missy put everything on her, bitters and lamp black, but if her sat somewhere where Taddie could pull himself up, he'd tug at her. That chile was so long walking and talking, everyone say he never would.

Mistah Abe say, "Mariah, I don't have to ask you not to discuss Taddie with anyone. It'll make it hard on Taddie in later life, and Mrs. Lincoln. She already is beginning to borrow trouble."

But that news leaked out just the same. I know this, the Lincolumns have a lot of neighbors, but only to speak to, when out somewhere. But de Missy say she didn't encourage neighbors to run in and out at their pleasure.

"I don't go into their homes unless asked," her say. "When I went to the Ward School in Lexington and later at Madame Mentelle's [*boarding school*], they were very strict about our social relations as well as our studies. Perhaps that is why I'm such a hard person to work for.

"Besides, I only have and only want callers when I invite them. There is gossip, more than enough in this town, without calling for more. Maybe the [*neighbors*] don't like me because I hold myself aloof. I want to be friends to people. I have a few very close friends. . . . Mrs. Francis. . . .[*Eliza Francis, one of the few women in Springfield who, like Mary, was interested in talking politics.*]

"No better friend could be found, even if she is a little nosey. If it hadn't been for that dear woman and her husband, I doubt if Mister Lincoln and I would now be man and wife. Then there is the Presbyterian minister's wife, Mary Black, who married a very true friend of Mister Lincoln's, Henry Remann. She is now a widow. Poor dear, I really should go to see her. She has had so heavy a load to carry. Shortly after her husband died, a baby boy was born. He wasn't a year old when I took him to a photo gallery and had a picture taken of him. Elizabeth had a picture taken of one of Mary's daughters at the same time.

"I dressed Henry. Mary named him for his father, and the little girl's name was Mary. She couldn't have been over three years old.

"I liked her, as did Elizabeth. But Mister Lincoln liked the older one, I guess because she wasn't so shy and he could be more at ease with her. Mary's picture was so natural, but poor little Henry looked more like a shadow than a picture. Parts were so blurred. Perhaps he may have moved, or was dressed too fairy-like to take good. Mary declared it was a sign he was now crossing into the spirit world, to be with his father.

"She had so much trouble and grief while carrying him. She really thought he would not live, or would not be right. He is now a fine, healthy, sturdy boy, though a little unruly. At his age, almost four now, one can expect a problem. I think Mary is about seven now. A very pretty girl.

"I have other good neighbors. If I let one come, the rest would be antagonistic if I didn't let them come also."

My Henry don't want the white or the colored in our parts to come in. He say we both work too hard to be molest by them.

About the time I was back there to work again was in 1854. I know that because there was quite a stir about that time. Henry come home one day all excited. He say, "Da Black Flag will be aftah us'n! Let's get our'n duds an tings, pack an get Noth! Day's goin' 'peal da Mizzur Comprize [*Missouri Compromise*] and dat's goin' ta let da Noth hab slaves. Maybe we'ns can get ta Canda. [*"The Black Flag" represented dealers in slavery and was a scourge that all Blacks dreaded. Henry Vance, a fugitive slave, had to be wary of such dealers who didn't care if a Negro was a fugitive or not. Black men and women who were captured by dealers were sold, even those who were free.*]

"Mariah, you'ns nevva been ah slave, naw usn's chilluns, but ah hab, and, ef da kotch me'ns, dale flog me'ns mos ta death, an maybe da rest of our'n folks."

I quiet Henry because Mistah Abe have come home in June, excited too. He say, "That dirty rat Douglas is stirring up a mess that's going to be hard to settle, and only for political favors. Outside of that, I can't understand why he would do such a thing."

Just then, de Missy come in and say, "Why, Abram, I never heard you call anyone a name before. I do believe you are jealous of Stephen."

Mistah Abe say, "You should know how I deplore slavery. He's using his position as senator to champion the Kansas-Nebraska bill in order to repeal the 1850 Missouri Compromise.

"These squatters' rights are just a prelude to moving slavery little by little farther into the North. He declares this is the way to settle the North-South controversy peacefully.

"He's only courting the Southern votes in order to be re-elected senator. Already there has been blood shed in Kansas between pro-slavery and anti-slavery factions. Mark what I say, Mary. I will kill that killer!"

After that bust out of him, Mistah Abe began to write notes and write notes that he almost fill that plug hat of his. One time when I was there, Mistah Abe and de Missy have those notes all spread out on the table in the big kitchen. Little Taddie was squalling his head off when I come in the room from out where I have been washing.

I told Mistah Abe, "Boss [*the Lincolns' cow*] is full and should be milked."

He didn't hear Taddie or me. Willie come romping through the house, grab Mistah Abe's coattail, and screamed for him to play with the two. It was a nice day and those kids need the outside. Mastah Robert wasn't there, but it wouldn't made a form of difference, because Taddie always bit Mastah Robert when he come near.

Once Taddie have a big welt on him and de Missy claim Mastah Robert have hit him or pinched him. I searched and found a great big bed bug in Taddie's crib. As clean as de Missy was, I declare I don't know where it come from. When her asked me, I hadn't been there for months. I was right smart mad and was going home and never come back.

Then she accuse Mistah Abe of bringing the bed bug from one of the "dirty taverns" he lodged in on the circuit.

Mistah Abe say, "Well, Mother, if little Taddie never gets anything worse than a bed bug bite, he'll come out in tip-top shape. I've had worse bites from vicious tongues."

Willie pulling and Taddie biting, Mistah Abe let loose, after de Missy scream for him to do something about quieting them. He put all the notes in his hat. Her wanted him to leave them on the table and let her arrange them. But he scooped them boys up, put a boy under each arm like they was sacks of meal, and went out with them.

De Missy say, "Well, Mariah, we'll need the table in a little while anyway, for dinner. I'll need you a little while longer today because I must clean the rubbish out of this house.

"I'll plan on a maid this summer. There's a colored girl, Eliza, I'm sure I can get. Frances found her. And I do need an all-time girl now. I wish I could have you all the time, but your family needs you, since Phebe is so ill, and the new baby, Narcissa, has added another one to your already heavy load."

We got through dinner early. Then her begin to pile things that have to go upstairs. Pick up what was strewn around by the boys and Mistah Abe. Sweep here and there into a cleaning pan. While I folded the clothes, wash the dishes, and straighten up the back part, inside and out.

When her come downstairs from fixing beds, she had emptied drawers of a lot of plunda. Dresses, shoes, bottles of all kinds, and some jewelry her have mended and it didn't suit her.

Her say, "Mariah, pick out anything you want and I'll have Mister Lincoln take the rest out and burn."

Just then, Mistah Abe come in. I was pulling down my sleeves. I'd rolled them up to keep them out of the wash. You might think that man didn't see things, the way he went around with his head down. But he spied the long slit in my sleeve. De Missy had handed me a pair of earrings with white heads on [*cameos*] and breast pin to match.

Mistah Abe say, "Mother, I expect Mariah could make better use of a new dress." She look up, as he put one of his long fingers in the slit of my sleeve and torn it clean down.

The next day or so, she send Mastah Robert over with two new-made calico dresses. [*Mary had sewn them herself for Mariah.*]

CHAPTER THIRTEEN

Lincoln's First Tiff
with Douglas

Summer–Autumn 1854

After devoting most of his time from 1849 to 1854 to his law practice, Lincoln's opposition to the Kansas-Nebraska Act and Stephen Douglas's "popular sovereignty" doctrine brought him back into politics in the summer of 1854. He campaigned for the Illinois legislature saying the doctrine was against the Founding Fathers' wish to limit the expansion of slavery in America. Campaigning took Lincoln away from home part of the summer and fall as he traveled the state speaking to crowds wherever he could gather them.

One of his greatest speeches against Stephen Douglas was given in Peoria on October 16, but according to Mariah Vance, she got the brunt of Lincoln's oratory a few days before that.

Lincoln was elected to the Illinois legislature on November 7 but resigned on November 27 to run for the U.S. Senate against Douglas.

Mariah's husband, Henry, fearful of being caught as a runaway slave, plans to move the family farther north. This prompts Mariah to speak with Lincoln about the equality of the races and he has his own advice for Henry. In the midst of Mariah's anxiety, another personal tragedy strikes her family.

*I*T SEEM I JUST COULDN'T GET AWAY FROM THOSE LINCOLUMNS, OR THE LINCOLUMNS get rid of me. That Eliza only stay two or three weeks, then de Missy send for Mariah.

Phebe was getting worst and worst. With Narcissa, I have two babies to carry to my work. I work for some doctor's family. One doctor say it are TB of the bowels. Phebe, the poor little chile, was passing blood and having hemrige too. So this Doctor Henry say he could do nothing but something to quiet her.

[*She must have meant another doctor, because Dr. Anson G. Henry had left Springfield two years before.*]

Another doctor, Elias Merryman, say it was the lungs altogether and it was catching. I quit that place, because I couldn't keep Phebe close enough to watch. They say to take her to the attic. So when Mistah Abe come for me, I went back.

De Missy was plumb flustered when I got there. Mistah Douglas have make a speech in the Hall of Repsentas. Mistah Abe was going to give his "killin' of de killah" speech that day. Her was near crying.

She say, "Mariah, I feel like kissing you. I can't imagine why Eliza left. I liked her so much. She was such a neat, nice little girl. Did just as I told her. I worked right along with her. I have so much to do. Mister Lincoln is back in politics. Thank God. He may stay at home more now, although he has done so well since Taddie came. Mister Lincoln was back in three weeks after April 4, when Taddie came. We have had several very companionable talks. I believe we understand each other now. We both love Taddie so much.

"I'm trying to prepare his clothes for him to wear today. He will give an address in the Hall of Representatives where Douglas spoke yesterday. It's an answer to Stephen Douglas on the Kansas-Nebraska bill and the Missouri Compromise which Douglas has backed.

"I want a driver for our new carriage, but Mister Lincoln insists he will drive it. Our estates are now settled and I can have some freedom now, spending money.

"I would love to have kept Eliza. She made no explanation why she was leaving. I tried not to work her too hard. I've been called a slave driver so often by the careless Irish whom I have to put up with. Eliza reminded me so very much of Mammy Sally's little girl, Judy."

I knowed nigh what Eliza left about. But my Henry had say, "Keep quiet, Mariah. We'ns all get'n tings en shape ta move wen da time es rite, so must keep et a secret. Day mus not fine out. Day wood move in on us'ns an drag us'ns all back South."

I suspect Eliza's folks was moving before any trouble begins. We colored, down by the African church where the colored folks live, have discussed it. They first plan to move to the unda-gron in Indiana. There was swamps there. It was close nigh an Injun mound. Some Shawnee Injuns what have marry some black would help us. My Henry thought that up North in Illinois where he could get work in the coal mines would be better for us with our big family.

I'd like to talk it over with Mistah Abe, but Henry say, "No. Jus as shur as God made litta green apples, ef it got 'roun, we'ns ware dead niggahs. We'ns hab all plan ta fight, even ef we'ns war kill."

We all would of liked to kill that Stephen Douglas, but our preacher say, "Don't start a row. If you do, our cause is lost. Let all the colored folks pray for protection, from the only protection, for God sees and will [*protect*] if we believe."

I tell you, I backslide a heap, but was still praying. I pray and pray for Phebe then, too. But I guess Gawd gives and Gawd take 'way. Gawd take most all my children now.

[*Mariah told Adah Sutton in 1902 that only four of her twelve children were still living. Billie died two years later in 1904 as did Mariah; Fred and Cornelius both died in 1923, and Lydia died in 1924.*]

I went to the kitchen. Mistah Abe was in the parlor with his papers out of his hat. De Missy take little Phebe in her arms and carry her upstairs. Her say, "Mariah, I'll take Phebe with me. You watch Narcissa." Those two babies was both asleep. "When you finish the kitchen, wash out the diapers that Taddie mussed. Then go into the back parlor and straighten and dust."

I was through in three shakes and run into the parlor just in time to get a hard punch in the eye from Mistah Abe's fist. He was standing before a long looking glass, practicing speechmaking. He was so earnest, making gestures, he didn't see me until I screamed. That scared him plumb out of his speech what he was just saying, "If a colored man is a man, then. . . "

And then's when he strike. De Missy come running. Narcissa begin squalling. I say, "You great big galoot! You put my eye 'most out!"

He still didn't understand. When he did, he laugh and laugh. He near bust both his suspenders laughing. That made de Missy mad as blazes. Her say, "Don't stand there like a laughing idiot! Do something for Mariah! Get Doctor Wallace!"

Her love that Doctor Wallace since he coaxed her not to have a midwife for Taddie to be born by, and get her Doctor Wollgemuth.

But Mistah Abe didn't stop laughing. He say, "I'd hate to think how I'd look if they hadn't turned up so much for hands and feet."

De Missy pick up Narcissa and walk the floor with her. Mistah Abe finally go to the shed and bring a piece of fat meat for me to tie on my eye. This nary please de Missy. Her say, "Get out and get Doctor Wallace!"

When the doctor come, he say, "Brother Abraham done the best anyone can do, Mariah. But who are you going to tell Henry you've been in a fight with?"

De Missy say, "Don't tease Mariah, William. She has this to add now to her already heavy burden. She has a very sick child upstairs. I want you to see her. Do what you think is best for the little one."

He went upstairs and come down with Phebe in his arms. He feel her pulse and push down on her fingernails, examine her nose, to see if it was pinched, and then say, "Mary, why on earth haven't you drawn my attention to this child before?"

Her say, "Well, Doctor William, this is the second time I have seen this child in almost four years. It was only a few weeks ago when I learned that the child was not well. Then all Mariah said was that Phebe has always been puny and coughed. Is it serious?"

Doctor Wallace first look at de Missy, then at me, and say, "Mariah, do you want to know the truth?"

I told him I already knowed the truth. My Phebe was going to heaben. He look straight at me and ask, "Have you had any medical care for her?"

I say, "Doctor Anson Henry told me to make some hore-hound tea."

"He gave you no medicine?" Doctor Wallace ask.

"No, he didn't want to bother with black folks," I say.

The doctor say, "What a shame, what a shame. Some of these doctors can't see. There is no difference between black or white. Just the color of pigment in the epidermis is different. In most cases now, that difference is slight."

I say, "Maybe that doctor didn't want to fool without getting a heap of money."

"By the gods!" he say. "Can it be any doctor can be that mercenary? A life is a life, whether it be saved by a veterinary or an M.D. That is our responsibility. A tithe to God, if one will think to put it that way. Mariah, does the child eat?"

I told Doctor Wallace, "A little. Such as we have."

He say, "I'll give you a little medicine. It may give her an appetite. Get a soup bone. After it is well cooked, skim off the grease. Take out the bone and cook some barley in the skimmed broth to a consistency of a gruel. Don't begin with too much water, but don't add more water after the meat starts to boil. Cold water, Mariah. Hot water will keep the strength of the meat from the soup. Just enough salt to keep it from tasting flat.

"I've had to teach Frances to cook. These Southern belles have good tasters, but are the world's worst cooks. Have you given the child plenty of milk?"

I told Doctor Wallace, "My Henry milk our cow until it went dry. Then that poor Bossy have got thinner and thinner and cough too, then done lay down and die. Since then we have skim milk from where I works. The young-guns of ours love skim milk, 'specially when it clabba [*clabbered; milk that becomes thick in souring*]. Then they eat it with a little sugar and break up corn bread in it."

"Well," say the doctor, "how are your other children? If they are like this new baby of yours, you have nothing to give you anxiety about them."

I spoke right up. "I do the best I can. I haven't much time for worry. Our preacher say we should weep at a birth and rejoice at a death. So if Gawd wants my little Phebe in his colored heaben, I'll just go on getting the rest of them in shape to be with her when Gawd calls them."

Up spoke that doctor. "Mariah, you are a brave, good, God-loving woman. Don't hesitate at any time you need me. Bring any or all of them to me. I have a country route to make every day. Unless a call comes from the country at night that is urgent, I'm at home or at my office."

I thank Doctor William. I could see de Missy was nervous.

"Mariah," her say, "now that the children are resting, let's get this house in order. I declare I send my children away for Liz to take care of, so they won't interfere with my work. I still have the meal to prepare for our party this evening. There's more commotion than my children would have caused."

"Well," say Doctor Wallace, "I want to know who called me here, and who sent for Mariah? You and Frances are the least respectful of anyone's feelings or wishes I ever encountered. Ninian Edwards has taught Elizabeth that all aristocrats didn't come from Lexington and that the most aristocratic are the most tolerant. I want to know, Mary, did you ever in your life consider anyone's wishes or feelings before your own?"

I speak right up for that poor Missy. "Doctor Wallace, you are awful kind, but no kinder than de Missy. This dress I have on, de Missy make out of new calico and give to me. She have give us so much fine food. My Henry say, "We'ns all done got a rich man's aptite on a poor man's pay.""

The doctor laugh and say, "Let me know about Phebe, will you, Mariah? And be sure the next time you catch Brother Abraham propped against the wall in one of his dense moods, sock him a good one in the eye! Abraham, make that answer to Douglas a scorcher!"

Mistah Abe laugh. "I wish I could. When Mariah screamed, it scared all the speech out of me."

"Just remember," say the doctor, "these poor colored folks need all the help you can give them. Try to meet, if not do, a better job than Cassius Clay did in July. [*Cassius Clay, publisher of an abolitionist newspaper in Lexington, was speaking strongly against slavery at this time.*] I'd suggest you scare them into thinking that the black man will prevail someday."

Like my Billie, I ask, "What is 'prevail'?"

"Well, Mariah," say the doctor, "the way I've used it, they, the colored, will rule over the white man."

I declare, that doctor didn't know, that's what got us in this mess in the first place. The preacher say, "King Pharaoh was a black man and he made slaves of the white. Turnabout's fair play. It's what we are, slaves."

Doctor up and say, "If the whites now think they are so much better, why don't they do different than they did back in the black man's rule? Why don't they start a new era? A new thought. As our Constitution says, 'All men are created equal' and are to be given equal right to life, love, and the pursuit of happiness."

[*Actually, the quote is from the Declaration of Independence and specifies liberty, not love. Mariah apparently got it wrong and Adah Sutton did not correct her in writing the reminiscences.*]

But Mistah Abe speak up. "That eternal cycle. . . . the earth is round and never ceases to go around. The moon and sun and, although no one knows, even the twinkling stars may be round. We know they travel, or are visible at different times in different places. Oh, that mastermind, how marvelous. We the little minds who can do likewise. At least we are here to continue the plan; to seed, bloom, and grow into mighty plants, animals, and men. To enjoy to the fullest, to have dominion over. Not to destroy this cycle. Yet the mighty are so wrong, stooping to such little views that lead to little deeds."

I say, "The preacher say that Christ went in among them black men and found a lot from them that he couldn't learn from the Jews, what was his own folks. They just think about money. They make the house of Gawd a den of thieves. But he upset their applecart. He threw the moneychangeas out of the temple. That why they didn't like him. They say all manner of evil about him. That why they nail him to the cross. They still think money the only power."

Mistah Abe have his say. "All Christ said made good sense. Even a child could understand. Yet he was crucified. I think we should all do as the Catholics do. Wear the cross, as an emblem of his suffering, to show us the right way. . . the easy way. . . to live. And have life without suffering, cheating, lying, or in any way abusing our fellow man, which would put our minds at peace. No strife, no fear. An all-encircling love, he taught. But about the Jews, there are many good, God-fearing Jews."

De Missy say, "I'll teach both of you men something, if you don't leave Mariah free to get her work done."

The doctor snap back, "Mariah is doing more work while listening than you are. But Brother Abraham, try to squelch that Little Giant. [*Stephen Douglas got the nickname "The Little Giant" because of his short, stocky figure.*]

"Do as good a job, if you can't do better, than Cassius, if he gets up to oppose you. He'll be there, all right. You reach out with one of your long arms and push him back in his seat. That's what Cassius would do, or maybe use his Bowie knife."

That make me think I was at the Lincolumns when that Cassy [*Cassius*] Clay, Henry Clay's cousin, spoke in the grove. They wouldn't let him speak in any public building because they say he was a radcal. Mistah Abe went to that grove and sat on the ground in the hot sun and listened to his speechmaking for two hours.

De Missy have sent for this Cassy to eat with a number of her friends that evening. Her want Mistah Abe to know Cassy. Her say she want them to get acquainted, so both would know just what the other stood for.

This Mistah Clay have notice Mistah Abe on the ground. He was glad he stay, to learn who he was, and just why his fine friend, de Missy, have selected him [*Lincoln*] of all her lovers. I declare, the way he look at de Missy, and her look at that man [*Cassius Clay*], you'd think they was lovers, if I didn't knowed her was so bad in love with Mistah Abe now. Even though that man was a Kaintuck, he hate slavery worse even than Mistah Abe. But that's what make me think Mistah Abe have a big job on his hands, to beat that Cassy's speech.

The Lincolumns took the carriage away in time to pick up a few friends. That Julia Jayne and her husband, and Lyman Trumbull, and another I forget.

[*Lyman Trumbull was Illinois Secretary of State in 1841, a justice of the Illinois Supreme Court in 1848, and was elected to the U.S. Congress as a Democrat in 1854 and elected to the Senate in 1855. In 1860, he joined the Republican Party on the anti-slavery principle and supported Lincoln's presidency.*]

Mistah Abe was all slick up. A nice white shirt de Missy have made, a stock [*high white collar*] that was straight when he left, boots shine, and clothes clean and press out smooth, and hair water down like it have been plasta to his haid.

Miss 'Lizbeth wasn't going to the speechmaking. Her come with the three 'bout time I have all my work done. Her say my bake chicken and sage dressing smell good enough to sample, but her didn't. Her younger boy, Charley, come along to play with Mastah Robert. Her put Willie Wallace and Taddie to bed upstairs and told them if they would take a good long nap, they could stay up for the party that evening.

Mastah Robert wanted to know where was Billie. I say, "Billie are now twelve years old. He keeps us in wood, 'cause Pappy am so busy hauling. Sometime, Billie even help Pappy."

"Aw, shoot," Mastah Robert say. "Charley and I can't have fun without Billie."

But they went out to the shed and the first thing I knowed, Jim Crow [*Lincoln's pet crow*] made them heaps of fun.

Miss 'Lizbeth never notice my eye. I took the meat off. I have to see what I was doing with both eyes. Her have such good manners, anyway. Her never stare you in the eye like you was lying, like some white folks do.

I help her around a spell, until first thing I knowed, all the Lincolumns and friends come in. Mr. Lincolumn was happy, talking and telling stories and joking with all their friends.

They was 'gradulating him on his wonderful speechmaking. It was grand, it was. The best in the world. He have Douglas over a limb. But Mistah Abe say, "Let's wait until this is all over. The Little Giant isn't going to let it stop at this. I'll admit, he had me sweating."

De Missy say, "Abram, I'm so humiliated and ashamed of you, I could cry myself sick. The work I went to, to make you appear genteel, and you got up there with no coat on. Your shirt sweated out. You raked your hands through your hair and even took your stock off, right on that platform. But it was crushed and under your ear anyway. And the mud on your boots. Looked as if you'd tromped through a hog pen!"

He say, "Well, Mother, I knew if I waited until after the meeting, it might be too late to round up some of the things I knew Mariah should have for Phebe. Here's part of it, Mariah."

He pulled out of his big pocket a sack of barley, and a big sack of candy for the chillun, a Jenny Lind doll for Phebe, a rattle for Narcissa, and a cut of bacon for my man. Then he say, "Robert, Charley, and I will take you home. We'll go past the butcher for your soup bone."

I wrap Narcissa and Phebe. I held Phebe and Mastah Robert slide in the back seat with Narcissa. Charley was about to get in the front with Mistah Abe when Doctor William say, "If you're taking Mariah home, I may as well go along and see if there is anything I can do for the rest of her children."

While Mistah Abe was after the soup bone, the doctor goes in the grocery and when he come out, he say, "Here, Mariah, is a sack of prunes for you."

There was about ten pound, and in a paper was six loaves of good yeast bread. They'd just been bake, still stuck together in squares and warm yet.

The doctor say, "When you're getting supper, cut a slice and put it in the oven to dry out for Phebe to eat with her milk."

Then he hand me a brand new tin bucket with two gallons of milk. I was so happy, I right there and then bawled. Mastah Robert notice that the doctor have another package and say, "What's that?"

Doctor Wallace grin and say, "That's mine."

"Well," Mastah Robert say, "what is it?"

"All right, little snoop," say the doctor. "That's crackers and a wedge of Swiss cheese."

"Well," Mastah Robert say, "aren't you coming to Mother's party?"

"Oh yes, you bet I am," he say. "That cooking your Aunt Elizabeth and Aunt Mariah did smelled too good for me to miss. I eat cheese and crackers where I have calls and have to miss my meals."

Before Mistah Abe and the doctor got away, my Henry come in. He have a big wooden box in his cart and brought four or five big hemp sacks around to the back of our shack.

The doctor explain about the chillun. Told Henry he have a fine family of healthy chillun. But Phebe would need close attention, and he would come back if called.

Mistah Abe had spied the sacks and box and ask my Henry if he was fixing to move. Henry look sheepish, but look cross to me.

Mistah Abe say, "Those sacks look like the ones we packed our plunder in, when we came to Illinois."

Henry call Mistah Abe to the back and done told him his plan. He sure that I spill the beans. When Mistah Abe come back to get in his buggy, he look worried. He say, I heard him, "Don't do that, Henry. It's a foolish move. Discourage the rest."

He pay me my wage and say, "Here, Mariah, you may need this." He give me another five dollars.

Then the doctor say, "Take this, too. It won't strap me, and you may need it soon."

I did need it. In a few days, my Phebe just went to sleep with Jenny Lind in her arms, a happy smile on her little peaked pale face, and wake up in heaben.

The only time de Missy ever was in my house was to bring the clothes Phebe was laid to rest in. Her cried when her saw my pale little Phebe, almost white, with that doll in her arms. The dress and fluffy little petticoats. The ribbon in her hair, and little moccasins de Missy done knit. Made my Phebe look like a little princess of fairyland.

Her was bury in the poor lots of the graveyard where Mistah Abe was first laying when they brought him back from Washington.

CHAPTER FOURTEEN

Old Times Are Not Forgotten

1854–1856

Most of this chapter takes place in 1854, but Mariah digresses at times a year or two ahead.

Lincoln tells Henry Vance what he hopes will happen to slavery in America, and his determination to end the institution. Mary has high hopes that her husband will win a seat in the state legislature and get a chance to become President.

A beggar comes to the Lincoln house and Abe and Mary disagree on how to welcome him. Lincoln tells Mariah about his youth and the years he spent in New Salem.

Lincoln had left his father's farm at the age of twenty-two and in July of 1831 started on his own by moving to New Salem, a village in farm country along the Sangamon River. Only about a dozen families lived there then, but their hopes were that New Salem would become a prosperous town.

Lincoln got a job as a store clerk and shared a loft and common bed with several other men above James Rutledge's tavern. Rutledge's daughter Ann was eighteen when Lincoln first saw her working in the tavern, helping her parents. She was a pretty girl with long auburn hair and blue eyes.

The Rutledge tavern was a social meeting place, and Lincoln enjoyed talking with townspeople and farmers he met there. The Rutledges enjoyed singing hymns during the evening and guests and lodgers, including Lincoln, frequently joined in. Doubtless, Lincoln looked up from his hymnal occasionally to admire the young woman.

Lincoln joined the New Salem debating society and ran for the Illinois legislature in March 1832. He became a captain in the New Salem volunteer militia in the Black Hawk War that spring and after the uprising was put down, returned to New Salem in July.

He lost the election but continued reading and studying, mostly on his own. Sometimes he asked questions and guidance of a local schoolteacher, Mentor Graham. One of the books Lincoln read at this time was Kirkham's Grammar, *which he shared with Ann Rutledge. Sometimes they would read and study together from the book. He later gave her the book with the inscription, "Ann Rutledge is now learning grammar."*

In January 1833 Lincoln became partner with William F. Berry in buying a general store, but Berry's drinking and mismanagement of the business caused it to fail. It took Lincoln years to pay back their debt, about $1,100, a considerable amount at that time.

In May 1833 Lincoln was appointed village postmaster and the following January also became deputy county surveyor. He studied law on his own by reading law books.

He ran for state legislator again in the spring of 1834 and in August was elected to the Illinois House of Representatives. That December, Lincoln began commuting to Vandalia, which was then the state capital and home of the General Assembly.

While a legislator, he met Stephen Douglas, a Democrat from Vermont, who was four years younger.

Ann Rutledge, meanwhile, had become engaged to a handsome Easterner, John McNamar, when she was twenty-one. McNamar had changed his name to McNeil when he moved West to seek his fortune, claiming he wanted to succeed on his own, without any influence from the family name. He prospered in New Salem, becoming a store-keeper and farmer.

Some time after his engagement to Ann, McNeil left to see his family in New York State. He wrote Ann several letters over a period of several months, then said his father had died and he was obliged to remain until his father's estate was settled. He never wrote Ann again.

During her fiancé's absence, Ann's father sold the tavern and bought a farm seven miles northwest of New Salem. Lincoln visited the Rutledge farm on some of his travels surveying the county. Ann contracted typhoid fever (then called "brain fever"), and she died on August 25, 1835, at the age of twenty-two.

Years later William Herndon interviewed people who had lived in New Salem at the time Lincoln resided there. He got conflicting reports on whether Lincoln and Ann Rutledge had been in love and had become engaged. He concluded that their love was mutual, and that Lincoln had loved Ann with "all his soul, mind, and strength." Herndon reached that conclusion from reports that Lincoln was very despondent after Ann's death. He became reclusive and melancholy and it was months before he pulled out of his despair, leaving New Salem and returning to the legislature in Vandalia.

Mariah tells of a day in autumn of 1854 when Lincoln recalls to Mary his youth in New Salem and his feelings for Ann Rutledge. Mary explodes at him for opening an old wound.

*M*Y HENRY COULDN'T GET OVER THE PICKLE HE THOUGHT HE HAVE GOT us in, by tattling to Mistah Abe all we blacks have planned. He say everybody was talking about how Mistah Abe have lambashed Stephen Douglas, and the help he was trying to give the black man.

The black man, most say, is best to get out. Mistah Abe say nary a word about us moving, because if he have dare to, there would have been talk, and Henry would have heard it.

Mistah Abe have told my Henry if there was any movement, he'd get it to Henry right away. He say, "Springfield is full of people who once lived in the South. Highly educated and good Christian people who hate slavery. Until Nebraska and Kansas are invaded by the slave trade, which will never happen, no one will start the slave traffic in Illinois.

"What I would like to see, and thoroughly believe will happen in time, is for the North and South to come to a reasonable agreement and gradually free all slaves. Perhaps for a price. But free them. And I'll continue to try to free the slaves, until the last breath is gone from my body."

I told all the folks about de Missy coming with the dress she make and laying my Phebe away with the little dollbaby Mistah Abe bought and she held in her arms when Gawd took her. Those folks I work for was sure stonish. But some of them say they knew she did [*come to the house when Phebe died*], because they watch her in her fine carriage and where she go to.

I told them all about what Mistah Abe and Doctor Wallace did. I think right there and then, they going to get ashamed, how they have talk about the Lincolumns. They all begin giving us good stuff instead of cast-off skim milk, and dog bones that we could eat. Fritz, our dog, got all of them bones. What he couldn't eat, he bury for a slim eating day.

There was a lot more speechmaking [*as Lincoln ran for the Illinois Legislature and spoke more against the Kansas-Nebraska bill*]. They say Mistah Abe worned [*wore down*] that Douglas so, he [*Douglas*] ran out of something to say. Douglas keep repeating what he have already spout off. Right there and then is when I think, and so did my Henry, Mistah Lincolumn started for the White House for Pres'dent.

De Missy was so full of joy, her nearly bust! Her ride 'round in that fine carriage with a driver. People was green 'cause they was so jealous. Her didn't bother about taking them.

Her was the same 'bout that as her was about folks popping in at any time at her home. When her want them, her ask them. And her ask them to parties. Parties, parties, parties. 'Specially after her little stepsister Emilie come to visit.

Mistah Abe went out on the circuit, but went to Chicago and other places, too. He now have a big job with the railroad, about righta ways. They give him a pile of money, about $200 or $300 before he even started to work for them.

[In the 1850s, much of Lincoln's law work involved cases related to rail traffic in Illinois. Most of his greatest successes as a lawyer came from representing the Illinois Central Railroad and other rail companies in the state.

He was on retainer for the Illinois Central from 1853 to 1860. As attorney on their behalf in the McLean County Tax Case (1854-1856), he estimated he saved the railroad a half million dollars, receiving his largest fee for winning the trial, $5,000. Mariah apparently was referring to an advance or bonus he received from the Illinois Central for agreeing to take on the case in 1854. Eventually he had to sue the railroad to get his fee.]

I do believe the Lord prosper those folks because they was on the colored folks' side.

Mistah Lincolumn say, "I've got to be comfortable or no speech comes. If I have a tight collar or tight boots, especially, that's all I can think about until I'm easy like."

He say wool socks make his feet burn and sweat. He never could get used to them. That makes me think about one time when de Missy was going to have a party. All the good things to eat was on the big table in that nice big kitchen her have before her ruin it by cutting it up into little cubbyholes.

Besides being called "Abe the woodchoppa," he was called "Sockless Abe." I know he never wore socks, only when made to by de Missy. Her make such nice knitting, and took special care making Mistah Abe's socks.

The day of this party, I was about to carry some of the fancy food in so as to be handy when the guests come, when Mistah Abe come 'round the house to the back door with the raggedest, most forlorn beggah I ever did see the likes of.

Mistah Abe say, "Mariah, you see that this traveler gets something good and hot to eat."

He sat down by this tramp and nibble as the tramp ate some of the good solid food I thought would be best for a poor starved man. Mistah Abe say to him, "Are you warm?" He look down at that tramp's feet and say, "Look's like your toes are out."

Then he begin to tell what his pa did to keep his feet warm. "We were very poor and had no money to buy wool to be woven into yarn. Therefore, no yarn to be knit into socks. My Pa discovered that paper could be wrapped around his feet. This paper he used instead of socks and was a greater protection from cold than wool. Wool made his feet sweat, and when the feet are damp, of course they will freeze much easier. Wait a minute. I think I can find you some socks I am not wearing."

Then he pulled his pants legs up high enough so the tramp could see his bare legs and a bit of paper that had slipped up to the top of his boot.

After Mistah Abe have started for to find those socks, that tramp push his chair back. He praise and praise that good man and thank me. I think I should say something, so I say, "Mistah Lincolumn is a very obliging and good man."

When I say "Mistah Lincolumn," that bum grab his hat and rush to the door, not waiting for Mistah Abe and his socks. He didn't get out though, before de Missy come in, all dress for the party. Her say, "Mariah, what was that culprit doing in my house?"

Her spied the dishes dirty on the table and was so mad, her like to bust her bustle off. "Don't you ever let such a character in our home again. The effrontery of you sitting such as he down at our table to dine!"

Well, I spoke up and say, "Just keep your petticoat on. Mistah Abe brought him here and sat down and eat with him."

Just then, Mistah Abe step in holding a pair of socks in each hand. De Missy put her hands on her hips and pierced him with those mad eyes of hers. "Abraham Lincoln!" she say. "Explain this new insult from you. Is this the class you associate with? But over my dead body it's the last of his kind you'll bring into my home! No wonder you have no refinement. Sprawling around on the floor, eating in your shirtsleeves, wiping your mouth on your sleeves, and raking food from the meat plate or food bowls onto your plate with your knife. No wonder all these social blunders humiliate me before my friends."

He let her spout off. Then she spied the socks he was holding. He didn't give her time to jump straddle him about that. He say, "Mariah, where is my 'culprit' friend?" He have heard de Missy call him a culprit.

I say, "He flew the coop when I just said, 'Mistah Lincolumn am obliging and a good man.' He went for that door like he was chase by the debil."

Mistah Abe laugh and laugh, split to kill. The more he laugh, the madder de Missy get. Her prance that kitchen like a wild woman.

Finally, Mistah Abe hold up the socks before her very eyes and say, "When you cool down, Molly, you can ask me about these socks."

Her threw back her haid and scream at him, "Take them back where they belong! I know about them. Little do you care how much I work so you can live less like a freak. I spend hours knitting so you'll have nice wool socks and live like a gentleman. But no, you wrap your feet in paper, and give decent clothing to your indecent friends!"

"Well, Mother," he say, "I'll admit that the case in question looks black against me. If you'll come down off your high-horse, maybe the case will prove less formidable. Really, Mary, you do look pretty, all strung around about with flowers. If you'd manage to smile, maybe I could manage to like you."

The more he tease, the worse her carry on. Finally, he say, "Mother, you've got yourself in a fine fix to receive your guests. You've pranced your hoops and bustle over to your left side and the posies are falling out of your hair. Now straighten yourself and listen to what I have to say, before you go any farther.

"I did know that man, and he is a bum and a culprit. Once when I made a speech in Vandalia, he was a successful lawyer. I went before my audience perhaps as disreputable looking to him as he is to you today. He looked at me as though I was an intruder in their midst.

"Through the years that have intervened, he has come down considerably from his lofty false airs. A social drink finally developed into the drunk and derelict he now is. His lovely home life, good practice, and respectable friends are no more.

"Yes, Mary, he is a culprit. A petty larcenist and a vagrant. I knew he didn't know me. But perhaps he has learned of me getting this lucrative railroad job. That is no doubt why he ran when Mariah mentioned my name. He couldn't face a man he had once shunned and sneered at.

"I'm sorry he didn't get the socks. His toes were out and he looked cold. I hope the little he ate did him some good. If it hadn't taken me so long to find these socks, I'd have made it back before Mariah gave me away. I guess I hid them so good, I couldn't find them. I'll try to do better next time."

De Missy snatched them socks and put them nice wool socks in the kitchen stove fire. Mistah Abe say, "Why, Mother, you're only making yourself more work. You'll knit more for me. Or will I have to continue wearing my 'everlasting socks.'"

That's what he call his bare legs when there was no paper around to wrap his feet in. He say, "That would be another relief to you and Mariah. Never a hole to darn, and best of all, Mariah will be relieved of washing them. That's a job, after I've worn them on my vile feet."

Missus Lincolumn was still mad and say, "I never want another tramp in this house."

But Mistah Abe spoke up pretty quick like. "If you would think of anything but your own wishes, and be a little more human, you might see that no one should be turned away hungry. Especially on a day like this. Here is plenty for half the town, yet you begrudge a small morsel to this poor unfortunate.

"Mrs. Lincoln, maybe as you have said many times, it is encouraging these beggars to raid us when coming to town, encouraging this easy way out of work and thrift, inviting others of these slothful, but my intentions are good and my conscience is clear.

"I pray God my boys will never be cold, hungry, or ill-clothed. We have tried to set an example of clean and decent living before them. We have given them loving care and protection. But who knows the course of human events? God grant they shall never have to ask for food or shelter, as I have had to do. But if that day should come, I don't want them to feel that 'the sins of the parents have been visited upon the children.'

"But begging is honorable, rather than stealing. When our family traveled from Indiana to Illinois, though we brought along some food, at various stops along the way those kind-hearted Hoosiers gave us food and shelter. Each time I live that trip over, I ask God to bless them and prosper them. Sure, we were not bums. But it never hurts anyone to lend a helping hand."

And you know, de Missy never, never turn away another beggah.

I ask Mistah Abe now that he was getting along fine and have a nice family, did he ever long for earlier days in Kaintucky and Indiana.

"Yes, Mariah," he say. "I hardly believe there is a person living who hasn't wanted to be a child again. Their childhood may have been devoid of luxuries, even very frugal. Luxuries weigh us down. Any material does. The more one has, the more cares.

"As for the three states, I find the people very much the same, although I was only seven years old when I left Kentucky. I got my sprouting start there. I learned to love everyone and everything under God's blue sky, and all above in God's blue sky.

"I got my first taste for learning, for work and play. More play than learning or work. My mother could read a little. When not busy, she read the Bible to sister and me. She could sew and made a quilt from patches she gleaned from her early dresses and her aunt's dresses. Her aunt raised her. She wove when she could find material necessary to make up the skeins.

"I could weave, and in later years helped my stepmother weave and wind. I was born under a quilt my Ma made.

"Oh yes, I was born under a buffalo rug covering. But to pretty it up, this quilt was thrown over it. Mother gave this quilt pattern to the neighbors who were so good to us during our home in Kentucky. Their names were Mister and Mrs. Abraham Enslow."

I say, "Then that's how that big name Abraham was hung on you."

"Yes, partly," say Mistah Abe. "And partly for Abraham Lincoln, my paternal grandfather. I've always been called 'Abe.' Outside of Abe being shorter, I can't see it's any improvement. Abe seems too familiar, and familiarity breeds contempt.

"My home in Kentucky will ever be dear to me, as will my home in Indiana. Under God's blue sky there never were kinder, more accommodating and generous folks than the Hoosiers.

"I've often wondered why Pa had to take it in his head to leave Indiana. But guess he was struck with wanderlust. Guess I took that attribute from Pa. I love to wander.

"I've enjoyed every minute of my circuit riding. And I've relived my Kentucky and Indiana life on my fishing trips with Robert, Bill, and the boys. I'm a boy again. Now I understand much better the why of creation. The never varying plan of the universe. A continuous cycle of rotation.

"Once I was led to believe by reading the wrong books, and not sticking to the most worthwhile book ever written, that science explained all. But Mariah, by your unshakeable faith and your Christlike mind, you have lifted me out of believing only in material values.

"Now I know that without the spiritual values behind them, the material or scientific things would not function. For thought or the spiritual, whichever you choose to call it, is the power that operates the universe.

"I'll never be sidetracked again. For I know the spirit is the ruling power and principle. No material can explain it, but the spiritual can explain the material. There is still a creative principle we should all strive for.

"Christ said, 'You can even do greater things.' He multiplied the loaves and the fishes. He made wine from water. He healed and lifted the dead. He did this by faith alone in the Father, the God creative principle. This he tried to teach, but was led to rebuke, 'Oh ye of little faith.'

"When I reached Illinois, I was [*just over*] twenty-one. Then labor of a different sort began, and what spiritual values I had gained were pushed to the background for material gains. Maybe it was a poor swap, and maybe it will prove to be just what an Almighty God knew was best for me.

"I've enjoyed my new life here. I've had material help I never had in Indiana, although the location in which we lived in Indiana gave us the best it had to give. At least I grew strong and was isolated from detrimental environments.

"I believe I can credit Indiana with giving me the basis for clean thinking, therefore clean living. The folks there were kind, clean, and honest, as were my father, mother, and stepmother.

"There those traits were instilled in my make-up, so much so that it amounts to almost a hate of the reverse. In court, I deal with cases so revolting sometimes. Cases that only the blood-thirsty for social, political, or material gains could perpetrate. I often wonder if I wasn't led to the courts to test my strength of character.

"I often review my life in New Salem. Especially my association with one person, a young girl some five years younger than me. We often talked about the new beginning, after coming to Illinois. About what was the best thing for me to start out in, as a trade or profession. I had made some bad business ventures.

"After I had made a political stump speech, which the New Salem people liked, she encouraged me to study law. Had I not had great respect for her, for her sincere interest in me, and her intelligent judgment, I would never be where I am today. When God saw fit to take her, for a while the bottom seemed to drop out of everything. Only knowing that I wanted to do what she wished and planned forged me ahead.

"I have had setbacks and discouragements, but I've never doubted that I was led by her [*Adah Sutton inserted the name "Ann Rutledge" here*] right advice and warm encouragement. She seemed more anxious for me than I was for myself.

"Even her memory brings forth my grateful thanks. By her help, I went to the Legislature in 1834. She died in 1835."

De Missy have listen, but guess her have all her wanted to hear. Her say, "Let that dead girl rest. You've got a wife and family. A wife who has sacrificed and still is sacrificing for you. But what thanks or appreciation do I get? Even the little things you could do to show me you value my efforts, you shrug off. Never even mention. But this common kitchen servant you flaunt in my face!"

He say not another word, but took his stovepipe hat and old gray shawl down from the hall tree and started for town.

That woman was so mad, her eyes flash fire. "Now you see, Mariah," she say. "Now you see. Is he still such a 'God-man' to you?"

I say, "If my Henry have said such as Mistah Abe say, I praise God he was on the right track. No different who or what put my man on that track. I don't want to hurt you, but that man is working and giving you all the good clothes and what else you want.

"I heard him say, 'You know what you want, so go and get it. I wouldn't know how to select thing-a-ma-jigs for you.' He don't drink or smoke or curse or blaspheme. He don't nag you. And he going to be a big blessing to you and your boys.

"I'd simmer if I was you. And if you can't stand what he say, why don't you just walk away until you cool off? That's what he did just now. He don't start fights, and he don't let you finish them. Now, my Henry wouldn't walk off. He'd finish that fight if I started one, or slap me down."

What I knowed and didn't say was, that her was jealous. Mean jealous of her man. I felt sorry for her. Her was a good woman in so many ways, but just couldn't get on the right track to be happy or make her folks happy.

That fall or winter [*1854*], Missy's little sister Emilie came. De Missy sew and sew for her and make pretty hats for her. That child-lady didn't have too many clothes when her come. Her make Emilie fine dresses and crochet nice gloves to go with each dress. Her would hire a driver for twenty-five cents to drive them through town to show this little sister off. Her was sure that this pretty sister would find a rich husband in Springfield. They went to parties and had parties. The whole kitten possy of them tried to get Emilie married.

Mistah Abe like Emilie and didn't stay away so long while her was there. Her say "Brother Lincolumn" was an ideal husband and father, but there was no more as good [*a man*] or as smart loose in Springfield, so in about four months or so, her went back to Lexington. When de Missy was building a bigger upstairs and a littler kitchen downstairs, while Mistah Abe was on the circuit in 1856, her heard from Emilie and she had married.

Mastah Robert was about thirteen now and was a nice quiet boy. But just as Mistah Abe say, Robert, Willie, and Taddie would grow apart. Willie was five and Taddie three and such mischievous little pests you never saw. De Missy say one reason she change the upstairs was so Robert could have his own room, away from those precious little torments.

She say, "Taddie never lets Robert alone when he is at home. Robert really is not a student and needs all the privacy he can get to study. I think a change of school will create new interests for him. He really is studious, if not a student."

When Mistah Abe come home and found the house so changed, he pretend it was someone else's home. But I could see he was happy of it.

[*A second story was added to the Lincoln house in 1856 at a cost of $1,300. Mariah jumps ahead a year in her history to tell about it, then returns to 1855. She also implies that the addition was more Mary's idea than her husband's.*]

Mistah Abe like his new bed. It was big and long. Long enough so his feet didn't hang over the footboard. [*The Lincolns continued to sleep in separate bedrooms.*]

De Missy spent her money and went in debt over $500 for decorations and furniture. Mistah Abe paid and said nary a word. Her didn't lie about her debts this time. So her didn't have to take another tantrum and paregoric for lying to him.

Mistah Abe was growing bigger and bigger in Springfield and all around the country where he made speeches. I hear them say Mistah Lincolumn is now in politics up to his neck.

De Missy still rode 'round in her carriage with a driver. Her sewed, sewed, sewed, and clean, clean, clean. Go to shows with the chillun, give parties, and go to parties, even after her little sister go, her keep that up.

Mistah Abe, 'twixt riding circuit and going to Chicago speechmaking, saw little of his home. When he got home, he had so much to think about away from home, he hardly knew he was there, except when those two, Willie and Taddie, stuck him with de Missy's hat pin or trip him, when he was walking. Or made mud balls and pasted him with them, or about a million other things. Then he would wake up, take them for a walk, play piggyback or somersault.

He would set at the table and not eat or talk to anyone. One day, de Missy fill a teaspoon of salt and say, "Here, Mister Lincoln, taste this. You may like it. You don't like anything else I prepare."

Like a child opening its mouth to grab titty, he open his mouth and she put the spoon of salt in. As always, he said nary a word. He went to the back door, spit it out, and started on more paperwriting.

Willie tormented him, asking why his Pa didn't eat.

"Why," say Mistah Abe, "didn't I eat?" Then he say, "Mariah, are we out of [*corn*] meal?"

I say I'll look and see. What was there was stale, so I say I'll go by the mill and get some in the morning. I was going back the next day to help clean.

I was returning from the mill close 'round Springfield. I have that meal in my cart. All to once, that mule of mine buck. I crack it with my black snake and do about everything to get it started. I even got out and tried to coax it.

Mistah Abe come along and say, "I thought maybe you would forget to bring the meal, so I was on my way to the mill. Back in Kentucky and Indiana that was one of my chores, either grinding the corn for meal or going to the mill for it."

Then all at once, he see I have the meal and that that ornery mule was bucking. "Well, so Mister Mule is hungry," say Mistah Abe. "We'll fix that."

He turned that cart around so Maud was facing the cart. I thought, has that man plumb lose his senses? He say, "She'll smell the corn meal and start reaching for it."

Sure enough, the dash her make with me in the cart like to upset that cart. I scream, let loose the line, and wave both hands in the air. I 'spect that sight would of made a dog laugh. 'Specially Mistah Abe dashing after that mule.

With his long legs, Mistah Abe catched up with the mule. He give Maud a little meal from his hand. That stop the chase. He turn that mule around like he sure should have left her in the first place.

He took a candy bag from his pocket, fill it with meal, tied it under that stubboren mule's nose, and her ran after that bag of meal right under her fool nose so fast, I could hardly guide her or stay in the cart.

Mistah Abe followed laughing every step and manage to reach home when Maud did. And what a Gawd for sure blessing. I was near tuckered, see-sawing on those lines.

CHAPTER FIFTEEN

The Circus Comes to Town

1855–1856

Lincoln ran for the U.S. Senate in February 1855 but was defeated by a vote of the Illinois legislature. Lincoln returned to his law practice; Mary, however, was disappointed because it would have returned them to Washington.

Mariah then digresses, recalling what Robert Todd Lincoln told her years later about the happiest time of his father's life. After that, Mariah tells of her "shock" at overhearing Doctor William Wallace reprimanding Mary for taking paregoric and giving the drug to her son Edward. Chronically ill most of his life, Eddie died of tuberculosis on February 1, 1850, one month before his fourth birthday.

211

Lincoln grieved deeply over the loss of his second son, and Mary fell into a long period of depression.

On a more cheerful note, Lincoln's and his sons' fondness for animals and the circus parade, which Mariah describes in this chapter, calls to mind other writings concerning Lincoln's interest in circuses.

Lincoln's friends in New Salem and Springfield wrote in 1898 about the excitement created when the circus came to Springfield in 1833. Harvey Ross, who ran the mail route for the government from Springfield to the Illinois River while Lincoln was postmaster in New Salem, wrote how Lincoln got dressed up for the circus. He described his coat and pants of brown linen, vest of white with dots and flowers on it, fringed black silk handkerchief for a necktie, and low shoes with double bow knots on the instep.

A Lincoln neighbor, Olivia Leidig (later Mrs. Olivia Whiteman), told of circus day in Springfield as she remembered it. She recalled in the Decatur Herald and Review *of February 10, 1929, of a day probably in the early 1850s:*

"Lincoln really became a king for the children of the neighborhood. It was his delight to seek out the boys and girls in reduced circumstances who were unable to purchase tickets, and with his own children would start out for the white tents. He would hold up the smaller children so they could get a good view of the animals and other attractions."

EARLY ONE MORNING WHEN I REACH THE LINCOLUMNS TO DO THEIR WASH AND SOME work, the table was cleared and papers from Mistah Abe's stovepipe hat was piled high on the center of the table. De Missy would take a paper and write down. Then he would do the same. Some was clips from papers all over the United States.

[Mary was helping Abe go through newspapers, researching for material in preparation for his speeches.]

Once, her cuss the newspaper 'cause he took so much time reading them. Now she'd read them all and cut, cut, cut from them. Then Mistah Abe would take the stack from her, and his writing, and read over them all.

He would say about this and that, "This cannot be this man's conviction. Or it's a political maneuver to get votes. I'll jot down only the nib of the points I wish to make. God will place on my lips the words to speak on each point. If I wrote out a hundred addresses, I'd never speak them as I wrote them, so that's no good.

"I heard all I wanted to hear of that when I was in Congress [*1847-1849*]; political scoundrels gained support of other scoundrels by twisting an issue. I'll tell you, Molly, there are more scoundrels in politics, especially on the slavery issue, than there are in the penitentiaries."

"Oh, Abram," she say, "you are a radical on that one subject."

He say, "Yes, Mother. I'm a radical in the same way Cassius Clay is. I'll dare to do right and be true to my convictions. Even in the face of ridicule and failure. Even death, if that must come."

Mistah Abe run for the Senate against Stephen Douglas, or so de Missy declared he would in 1855. In the primary, they call it. Mistah Lincolumn and Julia Jayne's husband, Lyman Trumbull, were both on that ballot. At that time, the Legislature select the ones to run for Senator.

Mistah Abe win, at first. Then on the rest of the ballot, he slip and slip, 'til he thinks it best to give his votes to Trumbull who was elected.

[*To prevent the election of Joel A. Matteson to the U.S. Senate by the Illinois General Assembly, Lincoln threw his votes to Lyman Trumbull, who was elected on the tenth ballot. Lincoln said he only "moderately" regretted his defeat, but his wife took it much harder.*]

De Missy, without any sense at all, hate that friend Julia Jayne from that on. [*Julia had been Mary's bridesmaid.*] And her so mad at Mistah Lincolumn, her rave and rant, get headaches, and take paregoric.

Those tantrums of hers got worse instead of better. Her act more out of her head, more like a crazy person. For days, her not clean up, not even comb her hair. All just 'cause her thought they sure was going to the White House again and finish Stephen Douglas forever.

Her wouldn't go to the door if anyone came, or wouldn't go out even in her carriage, and no parties. Her carry on this way more than a month. Her neglect the chilluns, until Willie and Taddie took sick. Taddie near die with lung fever. Doctor Wallace work night and day to save them.

Mistah Abe was in Chicago on business. Willie was left with weak lungs.

De Missy send word to him. When he come home, she blame him 'cause her have so much with the care of those boys alone. Her couldn't handle it all.

That's the first time I ever felt like chipping in right there and say what I knew was so. It was just 'cause that woman couldn't go to Washington again. And maybe Julia Jayne Trumbull would get to go.

I do believe that woman's jealous thoughts was the very debil in her. Her sister 'Lizabeth for once didn't pet her. Or 'Lizabeth wasn't even disturbed 'cause Mistah Abe wasn't chosen.

The Edwards have a big party ready for Mistah Lincolumn that night of the election. They that sure he was to be chosen. It didn't bother them at all, 'cause the party have to be call off. De Missy didn't give nary a party or go to parties for weeks. Her say she was too humiliate.

Mistah Abe went back to the circuit and to what other business he have. Then he say he work and pray, day and night, for the colored people. He would help free them or die in the attempt.

[*Mariah tells Adah Sutton then, in her own words*]:

He'n say right. Only he'n free dem an die, too. He knew someway, somehow, someday Gawd would liberate them.

I don't believe his heart was on law or politics after that. He say once that humans were held in bondage, abused and not permitted to rise above servitude, made him miserable. That man was so sad, he hardly have a smile even for his little boys.

One rainy day when her got over her huff about something, de Missy send out invitation a week before for a party for the boys. The mothers could come to sew for the church missionary. Her put all the boys' playthings in the shed. Her have the barn clean and fix with a stage and seats.

After the sewing, de Missy serve what have been agreed on by the business of the circle. Just two things. Cake and fruit, and of course coffee, or what they want to drink.

Her fix cakes and candy and lemonade in the shed for the boys. [*Willie, who was then about four and a half years old, and Taddie, who was then three, and their friends. Robert was twelve and apparently at school that day.*]

Emilie [*Mary's stepsister had come to visit*] hadn't gone home yet and her help serve. It sure was a nasty day [*apparently a rainy day in March or April 1855*], and de Missy say her expect most of them wouldn't come. Her put a piece of carpet out for them to wipe their shoes on. And as little sister

Emilie and de Missy receive them, they put their wet 'brellas and wraps on the new hall tree, what finally got there from her Pa's estate. They have ordered it about a year or so before it came. [*Besides some money, Mary inherited some furniture from the family home in Lexington.*]

The sewing was over, as well as the gossip about those who wasn't there. Then the serving begin. Then in march Willie and that whole kitten possy of boys. Each one have an animal. Willie first let down the white rat on the floor. The women begin to put up their feet and scream. Some even stood on their chair.

Then up step a boy with a turtle. Some kittens come next. A whole slew of chicks, one from each boy. A hop toad, a big bull frog croaking for to go back to the water. An old hen, and Jim Crow that repeat over and over, "Get out, ya bums!" The boys have taught him that.

At last some boys let down on the floor the big tom cat. The screaming scare that black debil and I never, never seen such racing 'round in a house in my born days. The womans put for the door, grab their 'brellas and coats as they departed and they scream at their kids to come or they would beat the daylights out of them.

Emilie laugh until she cried. I busted my sides, and de Missy was again humiliate. Her grab Willie and scream, "Why did you do such a thing to me?"—It was always "Me."

Little Taddie like it so much, he roll and roll on the floor and clap his little hands. I bet that was the best party those boys ever have.

De Missy kept repeating, "Why did you do it?"

Finally, Willie say, "The boys got tired of all but Jim Crow. So we decided to have a circus parade and let the animals act. We wanted the ladies and our Mas to see our show. I was to bring in the chariot driven by the white rat. Each animal was to have an act, but they acted better than we taught them.

"Jim Crow was the clown. He was to say, "Get out, you bums!" just as the circus clown said in the circus you took us to. You remember that, don't you, Ma?"

De Missy didn't answer, her was so mad.

Then Willie say, "Well, Pa will laugh. He don't like a gang of women here all the time anyway."

Her eyes spat fire and her yell, "William Wallace, did your father say that?"

Willie was smart. He grin and say, "No, Ma. But I can tell when Pa does-n't like a thing. He's sad and quiet. But I bet he'll like our circus."

Sure enough, when Mistah Abe come home and de Missy told him all 'bout the fracus the boys have raise, he in his high-pitch voice scream, "Good!"

Then all talk at once, telling about it. Emilie who had been double over laughing bust out and say, "Brother Abram, you missed the biggest show of your life. Why can't we have another party soon, when you are home, and have the boys put on their circus parade?"

They laugh so loud and long, de Missy really scream and pull her hair. Mistah Abe pay no attention to her ranting. He was sure happy again for a while.

He say, "Little sister, I do believe I like you better than ever. I'm in on that party, if I have to miss the circuit. I'll never again tell a story that tops that one."

De Missy rush upstairs. I don't think her was so sorry when Emilie went home.

For days after that, Mistah Abe would bust out laughing, if Willie or Taddie was near. They would almost always say, "Pa, when can we have the circus?"

He would pat and hug them. Then they would run for some of the animals. The chicks, white rat, and Jim Crow climb over that man with those two boys pestering, pestering even when he read. He would join in the fun with them once in a while.

When Mastah Robert come home from school, the boys tole him about the circus parade they have. Mastah Robert couldn't help but laugh, for he knew what torments those boys were. He couldn't call his life his own. If he complain, de Missy would scold him and say, "You had freedom, why are you always complaining about the fun these boys have?" But Mastah Robert never have such freedom.

Mastah Robert loved his mother. He was so kind and thoughtful and good, and so senstive, he felt sorry for his poor Ma. He always put his arm around his Ma and comfort her, if anyone took sides against her. He try to smooth over the hurt places.

I think all the boys like their Pa the most. They never stop to think, their Pa could preciate them more, 'cause he was not with them much. But their Ma sewed, cooked, sometime wash. Nursed them, kept a nice home for them, kept them clean. Took them to shows and church, waited on them when sick, and welcome their friends. Even if her wasn't much fun, her never abuse them and did the best in the world for them, as well as herself, as her see it.

I think Mastah Robert knowed more than he let on. I think he knowed his Ma was a sick woman in her mind.

Once when Mastah Robert [*then a grown man*] was on his way to see his Ma, who was then sick at Aunt 'Lizabeth's in Springfield, he stop in Danville to see me. I don't think he ever went through Danville without stopping at 812 Oak Street. That was our home close to the Big Four track as it is now [*in 1902*].

[*Mariah or Adah got the street and house numbers mixed up here. Mariah's daughter Julia Vance Patterson lived at 714 Oak Street in Danville. It was near 812 North Gilbert Street, where Mariah resided and where Miss Sutton visited her and heard her Lincoln stories.*]

He talk a heap about his Pa. Say, "I'll never believe that Pa was ever any happier than after he signed the Emancipation Proclamation."

[*The Emancipation Proclamation was an executive order issued by President Lincoln on January 1, 1863. It abolished slavery in the Confederate states and opened the U.S. army and navy to Negro volunteers.*]

He tell, "One time on a trip from school to see the folks at the White House, I happened in to Pa's room unexpectedly. Pa was kneeling, praying earnestly to be directed aright. The North was besieging him to free the slaves so they could fight. The officers, especially Stanton [*Edwin McMasters Stanton, Lincoln's Secretary of War*], said he was so slow, he was ruining the country.

"But Pa said, 'I trust a mightier guide than these mortal men. The emancipation will be signed. But when it is, God will direct my hand that holds the pen.'

"He suffered for the fallen soldiers of the South as much as for those who fell in the North who were injured or were killed. He excused the rash abuse that was heaped on him. Once he said, 'Father forgive them.'

"He died many deaths before [*John Wilkes*] Booth killed him. I firmly believe," Mastah Robert said, "if there is a heaven such as is written, that God would choose Pa to sit on His left as Christ is chosen to sit at His right.

"Ma's a good woman. She did much to smooth away Pa's primitive habits. But she or anyone could never for one second influence Pa if he didn't think they were right. He would often say God would act in His own good season. He never took credit for a thing. It was always God. He never intentionally hurt another's feelings. I wish I was like him."

Mastah Robert was always a good boy. So tender and easy hurt. He put a brave front on before men, but I saw him cry 'til would break your heart, about the passing to Gawd of his brothers, his son, his Pa, and the shape his Ma was in.

I don't think I ever hear Mastah Robert cry when I work in their home in Springfield. It was the years [*afterward*] that make him sad. He saw Garfield and McKinley both kill, and he cry for them both.

[*James A. Garfield (1831–1881), served as twentieth President of the United States from March 1881 until his death in September from an assassin's bullet in July. William McKinley (1843–1901) was the twenty-fifth President of the United States, from 1897 until his assassination by an anarchist in September 1901.*]

Maybe they brought back Mistah Abe to him. He was tenderheart to animals. When a little boy and even when he was sixteen or seventeen, when Willie and Taddie abuse the birds and animals all over their home, he would pet and even kiss those poor abuse creatures. Often when his Ma was upset, he would go up to her and put his arm around her, and pet her.

Mistah Abe never encourage de Missy in her tantrums. Those last two years I work right steady at their home [*1858–1860*], I hear Mistah Abe say, "Mother, you'll make yourself sick," or "Can't you be more considerate?"

He more often would leave, but sometimes kiss her goodbye. The minute he was out the house, that woman would settle down and be herself, less her took a notion to take paregoric and go to bed. All the talking Mistah Abe, Doctor Wallace, 'Lizabeth, and I give her didn't do no good. Her love that paregoric.

Once de Missy say [*to Lincoln*], "Your mouth is black all around with that licorice you're forever chewing. Your mouth is ugly enough without that."

That man have the prettiest teeth I ever saw. But they did get black when he chaw licorice. He say, "Well, Mother, I like licorice like you like paregoric. The difference is in the effects. Licorice, if it be a vice, will not injure me or anyone else. But someday, unless you stop, it [*paregoric*] will destroy you."

When Doctor Wallace was doctoring the boys, I hear him say to de Missy, "Now you listen to me, Mary. If you give another drop of that damn stuff to these children, I'm through. Do you want to kill these two also?"

I was plumb shocked.

He say on, "If I knew where you get it, I'd take the law if I had to, to stop it. Abraham has done the best he can. Gurgle it if you must, though I swear by the Eternal God, I'll not stand by and watch you ruining your own sons."

They didn't say paregoric, but I say to myself, what else are it?

Her was so good, when everything went her way. I mean, like when Mistah Abe get Stephen Douglas all tangle up in his speechmaking. But when Mistah Lincolumn made that first speech, and stand there beside that primp-up Douglas, all rumple hair, without coat or collar, and muddy boots, her was humiliate. Then when Mistah Abe give his votes to that Trumbull, her was furious and jealous.

When he say nice things of Ann, the New Salem girl, her was mad and jealous again. Her got so her didn't want Mistah Abe to praise anyone what her didn't like, and some of them she did like, like little Emilie.

After de Missy fix the house different and was busy getting it all prettied up [*after the second story was put on in 1856 and the house was redecorated*], I think that woman was happy some. I believe Mistah Abe really like his home better and was happy about it for a while. He never say a word about what was spent on it.

He still have his spells of deep thought. He was asked here and there and everywhere to speech-make. Sometime he take de Missy.

After he answer Stephen Douglas in Springfield, he speech-make in Peoria, Urbana, Quincy, Jacksonville, and even Chicago.

[*Mariah was referring to the more than fifty speeches Lincoln made during the spring and summer of 1856 when he was a presidential elector and helped organize the Republican Party. He received 110 votes for vice president in an informal ballot during the first Republican National Convention on June 19, 1856, held in Philadelphia. The party's unsuccessful choice for President was the explorer, soldier, and California senator John Charles Frémont.*]

Those speeches came from his heart, against extend of slavery. De Missy was glad he was back in politics.

But Mistah Abe say, "If it's a means to an end in right, I must go back. But I'll be on the side and with the issues I think are right.

"The end in question is the recognition of our Constitution. The main issue involved here is that all men are created equal. The extension of slavery is flaunting disloyalty in the faces of free-loving peoples. Slavery as it exists is so wrong and we in this republic are taunted as hypocrites who, for economic reasons alone of self-interest, would sacrifice human souls and bodies in dastardly, brutal acts. Acts against fundamental principles of civil liberty."

CHAPTER SIXTEEN

Pretty as a Picture

Autumn, 1857

While Lincoln is away on the circuit, Mary throws her most lavish party. Afterward, she wrote her sister in Lexington, "I may perhaps surprise you when I mention that I am recovering from a slight fatigue of a very large, and I really believe, a very handsome entertainment. . . . About five hundred were invited, yet owing to an unlucky rain three hundred only favored us by their presence."

T ADDIE MUST HAVE BEEN ALMOST FIVE AND WILLIE ALMOST SEVEN WHEN I COME TO wash that morning [*in autumn, 1857*]. It was cold. Mistah Abe was out speechmaking or on the circuit. I just don't rightly remember. But this time I have to build a fire to heat my water. That was sure a surprise, as the

221

water was always hot for me, the clothes sorted, and everything ready.

I didn't see a soul around. I counted my fingers to be sure it was the right week. I have left Narcissa and Rosa, my last girl, at home, and only brought my wee chile, John. He was such a little sleepy-head, I never had trouble with him.

Because I have to make the fire in the kitchen, I have to carry the water out to the shed, where I wash. While I was busy, I never stop until I'm done. This morning, I smell smoke. I look up and see the smoke coming from the kitchen door. I says, "Holy Gawd, the Lincolumns' house is burning down!"

I dash in the kitchen and there stand Taddie and Willie in their nightclothes, each with a soap bubble pipe in his mouth. But no soap bubbles. They have torn paper and dried corn silks in their pipes. They have start their pipes with my kitchen fire.

I scream at them that they would set the house on fire. But they paid no heed and each spit some black spit in the fire. That scared me, until I found it was licorice juice they was spitting out, pretending it was 'bacca juice.

I say, "Where's you Ma?"

Willie say, "Don't you dare wake Ma, Aunt Mariah. She was up late with guests and wishes to sleep this morning. We are the men of the house."

I say, "You'se not men, you'se two bums! Smoking and spitting and scaring the daylights out of me with your smoke and black spit. Your Pa is a man, and he don't smoke and chew 'bacca."

"Well," say Willie, "Ma's guests are the cream of Springfield and they smoke and chew, because we saw them last night."

I up and say, "Who do you think are the best man in the world?"

Both say, "Pa is!"

"Well," I ask, "who would you rather be, your Pa, or one of those 'bacca-chewing or smoking men?"

Taddie threw his pipe and wad of licorice from his mouth in the stove and scream, "Papa Da!"

Willie say, "Now get out and leave us alone."

De Missy come tearing in. Her have an idea I was the cause of the bedlam. But Taddie gave it away. He grab Willie's pipe, what Willie was holding behind of him, and say, "If you tell Ma, I'll hit you, Aunt Mariah, with Willie's pipe!"

Taddie didn't talk as plain as that, 'cause he couldn't [*because of his lisp*].

De Missy always seem to favor Willie. Her say, "Willie, precious, tell Mother what you and Taddie were doing?"

Willie was smart, and he say, meek like, "We was only playing."

But de Missy say, "How playing? Tell me about the pipe and this smoke. Give me the pipe, Taddie."

He held it back of him for a spell, then finally shove it at her. De Missy look at it, smell it, and say, "Come to Mother, boys."

Taddie step up bold like, but Willie hung his head and went slow like.

"Now, boys," her say, "I know you were playing, but this is an order from Mother. No more such playing."

"But Mother," Willie say, "those men at your party last night smoked and chewed and you didn't tell them to stop. Why should they have more privilege in our home than we have?"

Her say, "Men can choose or can limit themselves, when it comes to vices. But little boys must be guided or directed by parents who love them. Your father would not do what he would not have his boys do. You know he would not want you to pattern after men who are careless about their habits. Don't you want to please your dear father?"

They both of course say they do. No spanking, no scolding. That was the way Mistah Abe and de Missy manage those boys. I never did see the like, for those boys went back to their making soap bubbles without another word.

As always after parties, I have stacks of dishes and the house to keep clean. Now that de Missy was up, I knew I'd never get away until the last speck of dirt was out of that house.

I hurried with my wash, 'cause it was a big one. Her must have stripped the beds of coverlets and chairs of didies [*doilies*] and the windows of curtains and sash curtains. There was a lot of cleaning rags, besides the regular things.

Her tell the boys to play in the yard and not get in Aunt Mariah's way. But mercy alive, those boys went from one thing to another so fast, they kept me yelping at them to keep from tromping them down.

They always scared me when they climb the wood pile. It have poles at the ends but the stack was so high and they climb to the top. Willie always drug Taddie up. If those poles have busted and start the wood to roll, those boys could a been mashed plumb flat as spanked taters with that wood. Some of the chunks was big and heavy.

All my kids seems as how never got into so much debilment as those two. I never know why I worried so much about those little scamps. Their Ma and Pa didn't.

My work wasn't over until it was time for dinner, so I have to fix more leftovers, as always after parties. De Missy let me bring John in. Her say once that her didn't like smelly colored babies. Her have give me powder to put on after I didied John, it help him from gallin' [*his skin from chafing*]. But I knowed it make him smell good, too.

De Missy give me a bag of assafidity [*asafetida, a bitter resin thought to ward off diseases*] to hang on a string around his neck. Her boys always wore them, to keep away 'seasas. John was too little to eat, so I give him titty from me.

De Missy always say, "Aunt Mariah, don't say that vulgar word—titty. Say nurse." I do forget once in now and then, but before Gawd, I don't mean to be vulga.

We have hardly started eating when Mistah Abe come in, by surprise. I think by their talk, he have got a wire to come to Chicago on some business or other. Right away her plan to go along.

Mistah Abe was heap pleasurable about something. That change soon enough. They had fracuses before, but it wasn't a patch to this one before he was home long.

After he have eat a bite or two at the table, he say, "Mother, I have something here—(he reached in his pocket and drew out a picture)—that you've asked me about so often.

"Now, this is not a picture taken of the little girl I knew and who was very dear to me in New Salem. However, it couldn't look much more like her if taken of her. I picked it up in a picture gallery to bring home to show you."

De Missy take the picture and look at it and look at it. And the more her look, the blacka her look. I hope to die right here on this spot if that woman didn't push her chair back, stand up, and slap that picture down hard on the table and say, "You'll never make me believe, if you tried to convince me before a tribunal, that a girl who looked like that cared an iota about you! The way she is dressed shows she is not a common country girl."

"Well," say Mistah Abe, "It's the face. The face of a young innocent angel."

"Boo Boo!" say de Missy. "Innocent! When she would go with you, while engaged to marry another?"

Her look like thunder and he look like he was struck by lightning. Her grab the picture up and start for the stove.

He quick—quicker than I ever see him move afore—grab her and squeeze the picture out of her fingers.

That woman plumb act wild. Her scratch at his face. Pick up a fork and I believe her would a dug his eyes out with it. But Mistah Abe grab her hand and got the fork away.

Then he sat her in a chair. Drew another chair out from the table, and sat square in front of her and look her right smack in the eyes and say, "Woman, how long-suffering do you think I am? Had you destroyed that picture, you would have destroyed the symbols of some of the greatest happinesses I've had in my life. Not only because it is so like a little lady who tried and did help me start what I've now accomplished, but because it is also so like my angel mother.

"Had you destroyed it, you would have destroyed a part of me that can never be replaced. You would have destroyed something that would be encouragement to go on to better things—every time I looked at the picture, could help me live through trials. Could help me live over and over some of the greatest happinesses I've had in my life.

"I wouldn't lie to you, woman. If you continue these fits of insane contemptibleness, I'll promise you and myself before God, you'll just be a mother of my children and no more.

"If you try, you can stop this silly jealousy that has ruined what could have been a loving disposition. You've let yourself go unchecked until it has become an obsession. I thought I was marrying a woman who would be a helpmate instead of a hindrance. No man can go on and up shouldering such. You can make up your mind."

He started for the door. She screamed. Ran at him. Throwed her arms 'round his neck. Tried to drag his head down to kiss her, or her kiss him. But Mistah Abe stood like a statue. Before her let loose with both hands around his neck, her draw back one hand and slap that man a Gawd-awful slap in the face. Then her ran to the door, lock it, and told him if he left, her would kill herself.

Then we hear pounding at the door. Taddie was crying to come in. Mistah Abe say, "Give me that key or I'll have to take it from you."

She threw it on the floor at his feet, and when he stooped for it, she jumped on his back and pulled his hair and tried to choke him. He straightened up quick and her sat hard on the floor. He opened the door and in rushed the boys, who had been shuved out when the fracus begin.

Taddie have a big splinter in his foot. Willie have drug Taddie up on the wood pile again.

Mistah Abe pull out the splinter and wash the foot. Put on some turpentine, wrap a clean rag around. He kiss the boys and start them out again.

But again de Missy tries to lock him in. He pushed her to one side and goes out. Her goes out too. Grabs his coattail and hangs on.

Well, that woman sure have him, ' cause Mistah Lincolumn didn't want a public spectal. No one on the outside knew his trouble, 'cause he tole no one. Guess he was too 'shamed.

He come back in. Her try and try to talk to that man, but guess he said his say and meant every word of it. He sat with his chair lean back against the wall, with his head down and his arms wrap around his knees.

John was asleep all through that hullaballu. I have to pass Mistah Abe to go home. He say narry a word. Reach in his pocket, take out some money, and hand it to me.

I didn't know it was five dollars until I stop at the store and the store keepah hands me the change. Four dollars and a quarter. I was sure Mistah Abe didn't mean to give me more than two dollars, so I walks back to the Lincolumns.

Before I got there, I knew he or somebody else was coming, 'cause I sees a brush limb of a tree over the fence wigglin' and a long stick stuck through the bottom of the fence that struck the boardwalk. It was Mistah Abe coming with his head down.

That man never would a come out of that sad look if that brush limb hadn't knocked his hat off and a long stick got between his legs and stop him. Those little scamps [*Willie and Taddie*] laugh at the top of their dear little voices and Mistah Abe reach over the top of the fence, put one on one shoulder and one on the other, and that's the way they was when I met them at the corner of the street.

Mistah Abe say, without a smile, "I'm taking these two sacks of corn to the mill to have ground into meal."

Those two boys began to wiggle. Taddie say, "No meal, Papa Da!" They have teached their Taddie to say Papa. The others all say Pa and Ma.

Then Taddie begin to kick with both feet. Mistah Abe let them both down, kissed them, gave them each a love pat, and send them down back home. After he tole them to be good boys, and not forget to close the gate.

Never once did that man smile again after those boys run back. He say, "Aunt Mariah, did you forget something?"

"No," I say. "Mistah Abe, you make a heap big mistake. I stop at the store for some grub and they gave me these four dollars and a quarter back. Now I knowed you'd done made a mistake, 'cause the five dollars what you give me wasn't the two dollars I 'specks it was."

Well, Mistah Abe say, "You're a very honest woman, Aunt Mariah, but I made no mistake. I knew that five dollars was all I had in that pocket.

"When you first came to work for us, all you was supposed to do was wash. But you've been ready and willing to take time from your family to help with all the other work. Have you always been paid for this extra work you've done?"

I say, "Why, Mistah Abe, I'll never be able to pay you for all the extra you've given me. You and Doctor Wallace and de Missy."

"Gifts are gifts, Aunt Mariah," he say. "And work is work that is only compensated for by pay in dollars and cents. I would never forgive myself, or expect to gain, if I withheld from you out of what you rightfully earn."

No one will ever know just how really Gawd-like that man was.

I was sad for the next two weeks, about those Lincolumns. I couldn't do or say a thing to help them. But I guess something must a come up to partly straighten things out, as de Missy goes to Chicago with Mistah Abe. Her tell me about the wonderful time they have at the shows, and her buys dress goods and more curtain stuff.

CHAPTER SEVENTEEN

A House Divided

1858

Lincoln was opposed to Stephen Douglas's philosophy of "popular sovereignty" in the Kansas-Nebraska Act, which allowed territories to be admitted into the Union as new states with the choice of being free or slave. It prompted him to run for the Senate against Douglas in 1858.

Lincoln opposed slavery because he believed it violated the doctrine of equality in the Declaration of Independence. Still he was not an abolitionist. He supported the Republican policy of containment, allowing slavery to continue to exist in the Southern states on the belief that it would eventually die out there, while preventing its expansion into the North or new states.

Because the Whig Party did not share his support of containment, Lincoln became a Republican in order to unseat Democratic Senator Stephen Douglas of Illinois.

On June 16, the Illinois State Republican Convention, meeting in Springfield, unanimously chose Lincoln as their candidate to run

229

against Douglas. Lincoln accepted the nomination and that evening delivered a speech that caught the attention of the nation.

"A house divided against itself cannot stand," said Lincoln. "I believe this government cannot endure permanently half slave and half free.

"I do not expect the Union to be dissolved—I do not expect the house to fall—but I do expect it will cease to be divided. It will become all one thing, or all the other. Either the opponents of slavery will arrest the further spread of it, and place it where the public mind shall rest in the belief that it is in the course of ultimate extinction; or its advocates will push it forward till it shall become alike lawful in all the states, old as well as new, North as well as South."

The speech and the Lincoln-Douglas debates that followed that year brought Lincoln national recognition. Their speeches drew large crowds, even though at that time, senators were elected by state legislatures and not by direct vote of the people.

During the campaign, Lincoln is said to have remarked about Douglas, "You can fool all the people some of the time, and some of the people all of the time, but you cannot fool all the people all the time."

The debates became high excitement for entertainment-starved people of the prairie state. Crowds came by horse and buggy, oxcart, boat, special excursion trains, and on foot to hear "Tall Abe" and "The Little Giant" debate each other in carnival atmosphere with brass bands, bunting, balloons, and free refreshments to cool them in the hot summer sun. But many turned out in the rain too, and stood under their umbrellas to hear them debate.

Douglas, short and stocky, was the more sartorially polished politician, usually wearing a blue or white coat, frilled shirt, well-tailored trousers, and polished boots. Lincoln towered twelve inches above his opponent, wearing his old black coat with sleeves too short and exposing his long wrists, often a rumpled shirt and tie listing to one side of his collar, and often carrying an old gray shawl and an umbrella.

Some called Douglas a fox in his speechmaking and Lincoln a fox catcher. Their words were taken down by reporters and wired to newspapers across the nation.

After the debates, seven in all, Lincoln retired to a hotel room in whatever hamlet he spoke in and was alone with his thoughts. Writer David R. Locke talked to Lincoln one evening after one of the debates and said, "I never saw a more thoughtful face. I never saw a more dignified face. I never saw so sad a face."

Lincoln long had worried that slavery was pulling the nation apart. In 1854 he said, "Much as I hate slavery, I would consent to the extension of it rather than see the Union dissolved, just as I would consent to any great evil, to avoid a greater one."

Lincoln chose the phrase "a house divided" from the New Testament, Mark 3: 25: "And if a house be divided against itself, that house cannot stand."

In this chapter, Mariah Vance tells what was going on in the personal lives of the Lincolns that summer and fall. She began working at the Lincolns' on a daily basis in 1858.

Mariah recalls a day when Lincoln tells Mary that he would not defend a client if he thought the person was guilty as charged. However, Lincoln historian Dr. Wayne C. Temple, chief deputy director of the Illinois State Archives in Springfield, wrote the editors of this book in 1992: "It was a piece of folklore that Lincoln only took cases that he believed in, or that the client was not guilty. The truth is that Lincoln took whatever case came along. He once defended a slave owner. It was a case, and it paid a fee."

Mariah goes on to tell that Mary wants to give her input into Lincoln's speeches, but he says he will instead follow his own principles and only be guided by God. Mary becomes increasingly tired of his speeches at home, preparing for the debates with Douglas.

Lincoln refuses to be present at the home parties Mary holds for the "aristocrats" of Springfield. While his house is full, he instead takes long solitary walks. Lincoln frequently walked alone at night with his thoughts, when at home, while on the circuit, or away throughout the state while debating Douglas. He said he often reflected on his own life and experience in mentally preparing his speeches.

On one of those solitary strolls on the empty boardwalks of after-dark Springfield, while he sought inspiration for his nomination speech, had Lincoln thought of his own house, and how divided it was? As Mariah's history reveals of the Lincolns at home during the years she worked for them in Springfield, a civil war was fought there almost every day.

MISTAH ABE NEVER BRAG ABOUT NOTHING. HE WHIP STEPHEN DOUGLAS' pants clean off, just by telling the Gawd's truth in his speechmaking. He never, never took credit for being smart. He say while he was speechmaking, "All I want and all I have are the points I wish to speak on. I sift Stephen Douglas' argument down to the subjects he evades or handles recklessly. I jot down those points and store them in my hat. The good Lord God in some way of his carries me through from there."

Once de Missy ask if he wasn't afraid he would make a hobble if he didn't go over all the points with her. She say, "Maybe I can suggest something from a political angle, as that is my forte. I've been versed in politics since a child. Henry Clay was a mighty politician and he knew all the tricks of the trade. So does Stephen Douglas. You must hold in mind always that he is a powerful weapon for the slaveholders, and against any opponent who gets in his path. Abram, don't let him slay you."

Say Mistah Abe, "Well, Mother, I am well aware of the fact that you are a real little politician. And I understand perfectly your earnest and abiding faith in politics, and your ambitions that have never cooled off. However, I have faith, if I am true to my convictions no matter what side I am on politically, if I show the principles of the Republic, that is, the principles of the Party, I can depend upon God to put the right ideas in my mind and voice to speak. He always has, when I yield to him.

"A long time ago, I sensed if I chose God as my prompter, He would fill my mind with the right. Nor would He forsake me in any difficult undertaking. To me, it's not a question of who is mightier or righter, God or Stephen Douglas. Right is might.

"I know if at any time my frail mortal mind attempts to lust for might, if it is not right, God will either set me on the right track by some example, or I will fail by failing to recognize His loving care. The Bible says, 'to trust, not to meditate before what ye shall say, for I will give you a mouth to speak wisdom.'

"It's unexplainable to me, as so much has been, especially since my residence in Illinois. At that time, out of a clear sky came the thought, 'You are [*just over*] twenty-one. No longer should you depend on another's orders.'

"I had always felt that I was subject to my father's direction and care. I'll admit I had some fear of this new adventure, embarking alone in a new country. Immediately upon my decision to go it alone, I found new, helpful friends. Every step until now has been test and try, with many trials, I'll admit. But somehow I've learned there is a mighty power outside of the physical or mortal mind that directs us, if we'll put our trust in it.

"Some day I hope to gain Mariah's faith. The faith 'bigger than the mustard seed.' The faith that will remove the mountains of trouble for the colored people. Involuntary slavery is so wrong. If I can, through God's help, utter one word that will produce a chain of reactions which will eventually free the black man, I shall never cease to thank God for that one word. I know now God has put many words in my mouth.

"When I started to practice law, I promised God if I found anyone whom I was hired to defend were guilty, I would quit the case. Even in unexpected ways that promise which I have kept has paid off. Many times when it seemed I was about to fail, a true story of some happening in my early life would come to mind. I unhesitantly used them to illustrate a point, though it seemed not to come clear how that story really would fit in.

"Sometimes even the point I wished to make was not too clear. I'd seem to be treading on thin ice. But I never was let down. The finish of these stories seemed not of my own mind, or how they applied.

"The outcome of the story and points gained were so surprising. I often laughed more heartily than anyone else. By steadfastness in this promise to do right, as God shows me the right, or as I submit to His guidance, I know I cannot fail.

"Christ said, 'It is the Father in me,' and 'Not my will, but Thine be done.'

"Remember how Mariah gave up her little Phebe? How she accepted it and was comforted? Did we do, as she did, with Eddie, Mother?"

De Missy began to get powerful nervous and say, "Abram, let's not have anymore sermons from you. Once a week at church is enough, and the place for that. That's all I can digest. Let's get down to earth and be practical. Sometimes I think you talk like a crazy man."

233

You see, her wasn't a Gawd-woman, but Mistah Abe was a Gawd-man. He try to be patient with that woman, and say, "Mother, I've so often gone over your plans. You have helped me in many practical (as you say) ways. However, when it comes to our planning an address, it just doesn't work out. I've stood for hours, reciting what I thought I would say in defense of a client or a conviction of mine. Those words just didn't come out. New triumphant words came from my life. Often strange statements. But they never failed to be the right.

"You remember what was the outcome of one of my rehearsals? Mariah got a black eye!" He laugh and laugh.

De Missy say, "Now I know you are crazy."

I think it was just like Doctor Wallace say. That false 'ristocracy of her am "Big me" and "Little you." Even Gawd is the little one.

Mistah Abe have all the laugh taken out of him. That man, as always, look sad. He put on his hat and shawl and put off outdoors. It was no use. Everytime her open her mouth, that woman drove a wedge 'twixt them farther and farther.

Her talk and talk to me after Mistah Abe was gone. I couldn't say nary a word. I knowed they was as much different as day and night. And if I spouted off, I'd get my foot in it up to my neck.

Her say, "It's a wonder Mister Lincoln didn't mention that common Ann, from the backwoods where he came from. He's never directly told me he loved her, or that she loved him. He's mentioned her many times. He's even given her credit for his start in the practice of law.

"I've so often asked him what she looked like, though I suppose she was a straggly, ill cared-for farm girl. He's always said, 'She's too ethereal to describe.'"

Once I heard Mistah Abe tell de Missy, "She's the only one who ever reminded me of my mother, buried back there in Indiana. My mother, as I remember her, was a gentle Christian, as was Ann."

De Missy say, "Whenever he speaks of his mother or this Ann, he always becomes quiet and sad afterwards. He won't talk to anyone for a day or two, and wanders around as if in a daze. It leaves one wondering if it's his mother or this Ann who occupies his mind so completely."

Well, I thinks maybe I'd feel hurt too, as her does. But I'd sure try, if I love him, to change my ways. Be more like the ones he loved, for their gentle Christian ways, and try to understand my man more than her do.

It are so plain to see when he got on a subject he never, never got off that subject 'til he have thought it out. Her could help both herself and that man by stopping blabbing and scolding and those wild tantrums. Beat the world how he could seal that mind of his off against her outbursts. He didn't realize it was causing talk that maybe wasn't true. And causing her thoughts that was bad for her.

Maybe Gawd got those two strange folks together to make both of them stronger. But it was a tussle for her because her could never been happy with Mistah Abe doing something good, 'stead of always wanting him to do something big. A common circuit rider and common friends make her mad.

I'd wonder, if I hadn't knowed her like me, 'cause I remind her of Mammy Sally back in Lexington. How could her like me and be so good to me and my chillun. It may be Mammy Sally was a 'ristocrat coon, 'cause her belong to 'ristocrats. Mistah Abe belong to her, so he should be 'ristocrat. But none of his peoples. Her didn't want his people around, nor any of his friends 'cause they was common no 'count, her say.

When her have a party, her pick the cream of Springfield. Mistah Abe nary care, though. He wasn't there half the time anyhow. When he was, he act just as natural as if they wasn't there. He go to the table with no coat or collar. In his sock feet, if his feet hurt. Maybe even without socks. He slid bones from his plate on the table cloth. Drink juice left from the dessert out of the sauce dish. Scoot food stuff to his plate from the tureen or the meat platter. And worse of all, wipe his mouth on his shirt sleeve.

De Missy would act as if her didn't seen. She be sweet about it, 'til the guest leave, then her would raise 'ticklah hell. Even my Henry have better table manners. But Mistah Abe did just love to tease her. When her finally stop raving, that man stop doing. He just couldn't be driven. If her stop driving him for a while, that man would go higher and higher in law and big jobs.

Those Lincolumn boys must have taken their teasing from their Pa, 'cause they was the worst teases I ever saw. Once when de Missy have a big day-time party, some of the lady brought their brats along, as de Missy call them. Her say they put her boys up to mischief. But Willie and Taddie love mischief better than their toys. If those womans' boys could teach them two Lincolumns any new tricks, de Missy should have give them one of the party prizes.

Mistah Lincolumn have just told them about always tying his step-mother's apron strings to the slats in a ladderback chair everytime he could.

'Til her finally made him repair the damage cause by this trick to the strings and sometime the apron.

Then he told about holding a little barefoot boy upside down so's he could walk on his stepma's whitewash ceiling with his dirty feet. Course his stepma made him wash his feet, before he track in on her clean scrub floor.

He make a funnel from a leak in the log cabin roof to a wooden stove tub. There he caught water, good rain water, so he wouldn't have to go to the spring to carry the water. One day his Pa rave 'cause that spring water taste just like roof rain water.

He [*Lincoln's father*] went to the spring to try to discover the cause. When he come back, he climb to the loft of their cabin and found Mistah Abe's funnel. The funnel and the fun end right there, 'cause his Pa lam him good. His stepma took that boy's part, and laugh about the tracks on the ceiling and the funnel.

Mistah Abe was never like his Pa. Only he did like to wander from one place to another. He love to wander under the stars at night. Love the woods and the circuit. He make extra trip to Indiana to his poor Ma's grave. He go to see Dennis Hanks and his wife who was Mistah Abe's stepsister. Anywhere so he was on the go.

Mistah Abe once tell de Missy if her would make one circuit trip with him, her would enjoy the change of scenery. The various court proceedings and the fun they had. Or if she would take the boys fishing, she learn to love nature. The only nature her love was her flowers. Her say her got enough nature at their country home in Kaintucky. Her was always afraid out there, and say, "I can't see any sense in rambling around when there is so much in this big world to see. Like Niagara Falls, the Liberty Bell, all the culture of Boston, then London and Paris. For you," her say to Mistah Abe, "if you speak of a trip, it's going to the wild country like California or Oregon."

He say, "I want my boys to learn of the real wonders, those still in the primitive state as [*God*] created but never desecrated by man. Should man by his meddling change the course of the stars, sun, or moon, then the end is near. That, perhaps if ever, will be ages from now.

"The Bible says, 'There will be no seasons, no time, and the powers of the heavens will be shaken.' This couldn't be by a God who created them and called them good. It must be by meddling men. Men who are prone to heed the wrong instead of the right."

In spite of that man's good ways, he provoke that woman. If her could have been provoked as much by her boys, that home would have been worse than a hell, but her couldn't see a fault in her boys.

Those boys at the party, with those other boys there, tied all the ribbons and sashes those ladies have strung from their hats and dresses to the back of the chairs. They was like little mice at their jobs. They left the streamers loose, but tied the knots tight.

When the ladies moved or turned their head too far, off pop the hat to one side or the other. Sometime their bonnets fell to the floor. The streamers from their necks would choke them. Some of the sashes was pull clean off when they got up from their chairs.

That party end with those woman screaming at their kids. The kids whooping and laughing. Some of the woman blaming the other woman's brats.

Mistah Abe fairly roll off his chair laughing about it, when told. He hug those little rascals to him as if they was little angels, 'stead of little torments.

He say, "I couldn't reprimand them for doing what I so often have wanted to do, especially when in church. When women there fling themselves about, wiggling their gee-gaws, attracting attention to their finery."

De Missy say it wasn't her boys at the bottom of it. The older boys were to blame. "But I'm sorry it had to happen in my home. It broke up the party and was a reflection on my ability as a perfect hostess."

My goodness, but that house was sure pretty after de Missy have it made over. Her even have wallpaper from Paris. And the most new orments on the mantel, and what-nots. A new banjo clock. New carpets and curtains and drapery and tiebacks. A crystal light from the ceiling of the front parlor with lots of bangles of glass and candles. I think maybe a dozen candles. And candles on her mantel.

When her have a party and the table was all set with her fine china and crystal, with all the mounds of good eating, it was wonderful. But I never would a give up that good old big kitchen and that nice long table for all the rest of the house's fixings. When her have much company, they have to set the table in the setting room. The dining room her cut off from the big kitchen sure wasn't big enough.

Her give us the nice kitchen chairs. They was black painted with bright fruit and flowers on top the black. The old bed Mistah Abe say he outgrown, and a load of pretty little orments. Some blue china dishes and almost my cart full of pots, pans, old carpets and old clothes.

My Henry help me unload this plunda in the shed. He say someday maybe we could add another room to the shack, made of plank. But he never did.

Most of that plunda stay in the shed 'til we move to Danville [*late in 1860*]. My chilluns broke up most of those orments, playing with them. We wore the carpets, and clothes out. But the rest I have, and I'll sell for the money I need.

I'm old now and they are in the way to clean. Since Julia's dead, and my chillun don't care for them, or my stories 'bout them. They got tired years ago listening to the Lincolumn talk, I guess. I get what I can out of them [*what Lincoln gave her*].

[*Adah Sutton adds here: "I bought what she had left of ornaments, china, jewelry, books, furniture, and pictures."*

The Lincoln home in Springfield today contains a blanket chest given to it by Adah Sutton and believed to be one of the few authentic relics placed back in the house. Miss Sutton sold other itmes to various collectors and museums. Co-editor Lloyd Ostendorf purchased some of these from Miss Sutton, including photo albums, tintypes and photographs of the Lincoln family, a pair of Staffordshire vases from Lincoln's mantel, and Abraham Lincoln's old walnut spool bed, circa 1850, which Ostendorf gave to his daughter.]

CHAPTER EIGHTEEN

Right from Wrong

November 1858

Adah Sutton begins this chapter by saying she asked Mariah if she knew why Lincoln left the Whig Party.

WELL, I DID HEAR TELL, ONE TIME WHEN MISTAH ABE WAS TALKING POLITICS. This talking was with big folks. Some what come, what wants to get artcals to put in the paper. Others what wants jobs when he get to Washington as senator.

Mistah Abe say, "It might surprise you to hear that I was once an Andrew Jackson man. All the Lincolns were Democrats. My father, the Hanks [*Lincoln's mother's cousin Dennis Hanks and his family*], and Johnstons [*his stepmother and her parents*] were Democrats."

I did hear tell—let's see, I think it was Mistah Sam Graveses —his little boy was Willie's playmate after Eddie died and before Taddie came to town. He say not one of Mistah Lincolumn's no-count relatives voted for him. But every last one of them would be after that poor Mistah Abe for money if'n he got to the White House.

Every last one of the Lincolumns' neighbors voted for him, and they did again in 1860 for President, 'cause they all say so. There was the constable, Abner Watson; William Billington, the engineer who Mistah Abe sometime help fix things and like a heap. Then there was the county sheriff, Charles Arnold, what didn't like de Missy 'cause the screaming 'round. She disturb the neighbors who send for him in the night. Then Mistah Ben Moore, the surveyor. Mistah Abe help that man too, when he get in a pinch. Mistah Abe say, "Sometimes that Benjamin Moore in his surveying doesn't know where to start and then where to stop."

About all he knew how to do was drive a stake and drag the line straight, he say. But Mistah Abe love his neighbors and all the neighbors besides the Francises, the Trumbulls, and the Brownings, who was his friends. [*The O. H. Brownings lived in Quincy.*]

Some of the woman folks didn't like de Missy too much. But when the Lincolumns got in high politics and make lots of money from the railroad job, and de Missy have a fine carriage and went in big city high society, they all hover around to get an invite. [*The Illinois Central Railroad hired Lincoln as a lobbyist to help gain a charter from the state. He later became the railroad's regular attorney.*]

And that's just what de Missy did, for she could show them "hangers-on" as her called them, how 'ristocrats entertain right.

That blessed woman was forgiving. Her look over all the mean things they done to her. But her also have a heap of politics, and know how to get votes for Mistah Abe.

But Mistah Abe wasn't made senator. The "Little Giant," as Mistah Abe call Douglas, beat him to it.

Mistah Abe say that if Stephen Douglas fall smack dab in the Sangamon River, they would pull him out with his pockets full of fine fish.

He say, "One thing I don't like about Mister Douglas' defense, which should be clear and concise, from moral, Christian, or political angles, was sidetracked for nothing, more or less, than dirty attacks on his opponents. Always laden with nasty insinuations or quite often smears that were heavily laden with untruths."

[*Adah Sutton again asked Mariah to tell her why Lincoln left the Whig Party. Mariah told her the following*].

I gets so all fired excited when I think of how Mistah Abe was abuse by everyone of those newspapers by the Democrats, with all those horrid pictures. Those Democrats most everyone pig heads at that time, making fun of that smart man, smart enough to become President. I just get all rattle up. Now where was I?

Oh yes. Mistah Abe say, "At the time I turned Whig [*Lincoln was the Whig member of the Illinois State Legislature, which elected him four times, from 1834 to 1840*], the uncertainty of the currency was the deciding factor.

"My friends in New Salem at that time were William Jones and William Woods, who were strong [*Henry*] Clay men. They gave me Clay speeches which had been written up in newspapers published in Cincinnati. I became a fervent supporter of Clay's great principles. I read other papers from Louisville, one called the *Journal* and another given me by friends, called the *Telescope*. I learned what I read, word for word, so I could repeat correctly. They called me their walking newsboy. But the Whig Party finally petered out.

"From the Whig Party, this new Republican Party has been born, named for this our Republic. The Republican principles are not wholly unlike the Whigs'. It supports in every way the original Constitution of the United States.

"I feel quite certain this original principled Constitution, which was conscientiously thought out and prayed over, will keep us a United States as long as the world stands. Should all nations everywhere follow its precepts and leadings of this new party, all men everywhere can eventually become free. Those who oppose freedom will become extinct.

"Men, from the beginning, were given the free moral right to choose between right and wrong. Some may choose wrong because they have been deprived of their right to think. [*They*] have been misled. But with strength of character and the power of a good mind, one can seek and find the right road. We need not follow a wrong choice as mainly lack of mental development causes.

"Once my Pa said he'd know right from wrong if he was raised in a rat hole. My poor father was a good man, but without a developed mind, was often misled. Pa did right as he saw the right, but Pa never had even a good start.

241

"As for me, I had an angel mother and stepmother and wonderful good friends to guide me aright. Such help as I received from them helped to develop my mind and overbalanced those who opposed my desires to learn and rise.

"Pa opposed me, but he thought he was right. A great many people here in Springfield think Mrs. Lincoln and I are not bringing our children up right. The first step in blocking anyone's progress, through development of mind, is to not allow them freedom. One should set a good object lesson, for one thing, before their children. Then give the children freedom to learn from the object."

Mistah Lincolumn only have two Sundays to home during his debate with Stephen Douglas for the senate job. [*There were seven Lincoln-Douglas debates, but Lincoln gave a total of sixty-three speeches across the state between August 12 and October 30, 1858. His two weekends at home were September 25–28 and October 16–18.*]

But those Sundays [*weekends*] from Friday until Monday was so full with parties by de Missy and others, there wasn't a single moment of rest. There was a heap of peoples come to see Mistah Abe. They was all so sure he would be 'lected.

What time Mistah Lincolumn wasn't traveling from one speechmaking place to the other, during the debate, he have no time to take care of his poor feet. 'Sides corns and bunions, there was an old case of frozen feet [*frostbite*] that bother those big feet of his. I don't think that man would have come home those two Sundays, but it give him a chance to soak and doctor those poor feet.

When he was home, it was a "whirl," as de Missy say, of parties. 'Sides my work for them, they have Mary, the maid. I was call "the servant." But de Missy keep Mary so busy, her 'bout fall in her track.

Then one day when us was giving to fix for a big party 'cause Mistah Abe was home, this was a politics party, Mary got plumb play out and sick, so couldn't come. Mistah Abe go upstairs. I thought maybe he was up there resting his poor burning, aching feet. I hadn't seen him take the foot-tub of water up. I never seed a man wash his feet so much.

There was lots of work upstairs I have to do after my kitchen work. When I got upstairs, there was Mistah Abe and the two boys [*Willie, not yet eight, and Taddie, about five*] right there in my way. The boys tearing around as always. Mistah Abe with his two poor feet in the water.

Mistah Abe call to the boys. They went to their Pa on a gallop. He say, "Keep out of Aunt Mariah's way."

Just then, Taddie spy a picture he never saw before, on the tub. He and Willie both squat down to look at all those pictures on that tin foot-tub. Seems they never could get 'nough looking at those pictures [*on the tub manufacturer's label*].

Mistah Abe carry the water upstairs from the pump in the back yard. Summer or winter, that man wash his feet in cold water.

When I first work there in 1850, Mistah Abe use soft soap, but when he make lots of money with lawing and the railroad, they have castile or such-like soap.

On this day of the biggest party, when about the whole of Springfield would come in their carriages with their finery on, I was working so fast I was all out of breath upstairs and de Missy was working like a niggah, sure 'nough. In the midst of all this hub-bub, up come a bunch of men down in front.

De Missy was just then 'ranging the table after dusting and 'ranging the furniture and couldn't go to the door. I sure was a mess, from top of my wooly haid to my flat feet. So Mistah Abe pull his feet out of the tub. He give them a wipe, put on his carpet slippers, and as cool as you please, let that mob in.

He took their hats and hung them on the hall tree, then led them into the parlor that was only about half done clean. He say, "Be seated, gentlemen," and then they give to talk.

There was de Missy, caged for a full half-hour in the kitchen. Mistah Abe call her, then went to look for her to introduce to the gang of those men in the parlor. Not seeing her, he said, all joking, "I suppose Mrs. Lincoln is out mussing up something so she can find something to straighten up. That little woman is the busiest little body in the world." They all laugh hartly.

I was doing my best to keep those boys quiet upstairs. I say, do this and do that, to help. When I say, "Your Pa have left that tub right in my way," I sure start a hulla-ballu, but I still didn't stop gabbing to them boys. "Your Pa always throw the water out of the upstairs window. He can throw it far enough, it done didn't drip down the house."

I tole the boys I'd make them johnny-cakes with maple syrup—(they like johnny-cakes)—if they would be quiet and not scatter trash about faster than I could clean.

When they got too quiet, I have to see what was up. Sure 'nough, those two was working like little scamps that they was, pulling that foot tub. They say so it would be out of my way.

I say, "You is good boys, to help Aunt Mariah."

They was whispering. I thought it was 'cause I ask them to be quiet. Right there I say those two little angels is being good for johnny-cake.

In less than a shake, I heard that foot tub tumble down those stairs. I ran to see.

"Holly Gawd!" I say. Those boys bust out so loud laughing. With the noise of that tumblin' tub, Mistah Abe and de Missy come tearin'.

Mistah Abe take one look in that parlor. He excuse himself to the men and say, "I have a little job to take care of for a second." De Missy was wringing her hands. Mistah Abe tell her, "Mother, it's nothing much to worry about." But he put his hand over her mouth, for fear her would rant and scream.

Then he pick up that foot-tub, put Taddie in it. He stood up and hug his Pa around the neck. Mistah Abe lead de Missy with his arm around her. He know that was the way to quiet her, if he made a little love to her.

That other rowdy, Willie, follow with his Pa and Ma and Taddie, out to the shed where Mistah Abe lock the boys in with Jim Crow and the other pets and pests. He kiss de Missy and pat her. Her was fit to be tied, but then he come back laughing.

When he ask the boys why they do it, they say, "Well, Pa, besides helping Aunt Mariah by getting that tub out of her way, we remembered you told us about Niagara Falls and the cat-racks [*cataracts*]. [*Mr. and Mrs. Lincoln visited Niagara Falls in July 1857*]. That made us want to make the cat-racks. That tub was just the boat bouncing on the rocks going over the falls."

Mistah Abe say, "Well, boys, you got the right idea, but in the wrong place." And as always, he laugh split to kill.

But those stairs was sure a big mess to clean and dry, with all the pile of other work. All Mistah Abe say was, "Well, that's one way of cleaning the stairs and carpet in short order."

He never left his foot-tub of water standing again. De Missy say that was another example he'd have to set for his children to follow. The stairs get clean for the party, but Mistah Abe help.

I really don't think those men zackly knew what all that rumkus was about. Mistah Abe went back in the parlor as cool as a cucumba and talk a while.

He come out from the parlor to the hall, give them their hats from that hat-rack. They wish him luck for his 'lection to senate. Mistah Abe thank them, bid them good day, and then close the door after the full hour of 'citement.

Mistah Abe put out to the shed to let those little rascals out. No whipping, no scolding, no do this or do that. But there they was, perched on his shoulders, laughing like they was on one of those new-fangle merry-go round. Jim Crow was screaming to them, "Come back, come back!" That crow missed them when they out of its sight, like it was their lost brother.

Mistah Abe keep them out of the house until dinner, playing hand ball, aunty over, and Lawd know what all. 'Cause that man knew de Missy was fit to lay down and die, her was so worked up. It just wasn't possible to leave those boys out of sight for a blessed minute.

When Mistah Abe did leave to go to the office for a spell, those boys went into the barn and play with their little wooden wagon.

The whole Lincolumn family love cats. They have cats of all colors and kinds. Little kitty baby ones nursing their Mammy cats, and big toms. De Missy wouldn't have them in the house, so they have to stay in the shed or the barn.

This day, only a speck after Mistah Abe left, the boys decide to take the Mammy cat and some suckin' baby kitty for a trip to see their brother, Robert, who they thought was in school there. They say those cats need educatin', too.

They hitch two toms to the tongue of the wagon. Willie hold them so they couldn't start off 'til Taddie put the mother cat and babies in. Then Willie start to lead those two tom cats. 'Bout that time, Taddie 'cided they have better go faster or they won't get to school that day. So he give that wagon a push from the hind side by running and shoving the wagon.

The wagon twist and turn one of the toms 'round. I guess those toms thought that the other one have 'cided to fight. They give the Gawd-awfullest rumkus you ever did hear.

Taddie runned up to hold the black tom, while Willie hold the stripe tigah tom cat. Those was big cats, and hard to hold, 'specially when they have fight in them.

In the tussle to keep them cats from scratching each other's eyes out of their haids, them boys got scratch on their face and arms. Those cats hiss and hiss at each other and screech and scratch, but those boys hold on.

Finally Taddie say, "Willie, let's make them up. That's what Pa and Ma make us do."

So they hold thos toms' snoots right up to each other's snoots, to kiss. But do they kiss? No, it's more scratch, screech, and claw.

This was just too much. So here thos boys come screaming for Aunt Mariah for help. I throw up my hands in plumb horrah, at the sight of those boys. Blood all over their faces and arms, and their clothes torn.

They screaming, "Aunt Mariah, make those blasted toms make up!"

I took both those torments by the hands and took for the barn. Those cats have broke loose the strings from the wagon and was in a real cat fight. Hissin', spittin', clawin', cryin'.

The tigah got the best of that fight. The old black tom come up with a clawed eye. I have to get a buggy whip to sep'rate them.

Those boys cried 'cause I whip those toms. All through that hulla-ballu, that Mammy cat and her little kitten lay in that wagon bed as content as if there have been no cyclone. But cats are the laziest critters on Gawd's green earth, and the dumbest. All they know is to lay 'round in folks' way, to stumble over.

I got those boys back in the house, wash their dear little dirty, bloody faces and arms. All de Missy ever saw was the torn clothes and scratches. And that was nothing new for those two boys.

I swear have she seen them before I clean them, we would have to send for the undataka. Her was ready to drop with that Niagah Falls and the hard work on the party for that afternoon and night. Why that woman could-n't see what it was doing to her is plumb a mystry. All her think 'bout was how they was going to manuva to get to the White House.

CHAPTER NINETEEN

The Road to the Presidency

1858–1860

After the last Lincoln-Douglas debate, on October 15, 1858 in Alton, Illinois, Lincoln tells Mariah that Stephen Douglas may win the Senate race, but can't become President.

Lincoln loses to Douglas by a vote of 54 to 46. Douglas won because of gerrymandered southern Illinois districts, so the Democrats had more senators and representatives and they decided the winner. Mariah later overhears Lincoln tell Mary why he wants to be President. Lincoln returns to his law practice and temporarily drops politics in 1859.

The nation is stirred that year by the crusade of John Brown, a Northern abolitionist who leads a raid on a federal weapons storehouse in Harpers Ferry, Virginia. His plan is to set up an independent nation for runaway slaves.

Southerners accuse Northerners of encouraging a slave revolt and begin to talk openly of seceding from the Union. Jefferson

247

Davis, a senator from Mississippi, says the raid could lead to "civil war." Lincoln's anti-slavery Cooper Union speech in New York City in February, 1860 strongly attacks Stephen Douglas's pro-slavery views. The speech is enthusiastically received by many in the Eastern states and by leaders of the Republican Party. Lincoln follows it with a speaking tour of New England and stops at Exeter, New Hampshire, to visit Robert, who was attending Phillips Exeter Academy.

The Illinois Republican Convention meets in Decatur May 9–10, 1860, and a movement begins for the nomination of Lincoln for President. Lincoln admits that "The taste is in my mouth a little." At the convention, he receives his nickname, "Rail-Splitter." At the Republican National Convention in Chicago on May 18, Lincoln, on the third ballot, is nominated the party's candidate for President.

Mariah digresses to tell about a visit from Robert Lincoln some years later when she lived in Danville and he speaks about his mother's emotional condition and her later confinement in a mental institution.

After Lincoln's assassination, Mary increasingly was unable to cope with some of the problems in her tragedy-plagued life. On one occasion in Chicago, she attempted to leave her hotel room without her clothes. When Robert tried to restrain her, she screamed, "You are going to murder me!" Her old eccentricities, such as buying more clothing and yard goods than she could ever use, developed into a mania.

Mary had unfounded apprehensions that she was being followed and feared for her life or that Robert was dying when he was in fact in perfect health. She carried large sums of money around, but feared she was poverty-stricken. Robert, in an attempt to restrain his mother from possible self-injury and get her medical treatment, finally made the agonizing decision to have her committed to an institution.

Mrs. Lincoln became embittered toward Robert, but he was only doing what he thought best for her. In 1875 doctors and court hearings certified to her emotional instability. She was adjudged insane and Robert became conservator of her estate. A year later, agreeing not to trouble him any longer, she petitioned for a new hearing, was found to be sane, and was released.

She traveled abroad and returned to live out her last years under the care of her older sister, Elizabeth (Mrs. Ninian W. Edwards), in her Springfield home, the house where Abraham and Mary were married.

Mariah describes the excitement in the Lincoln house and in Springfield when Abraham Lincoln is elected President of the United States in 1860.

On October 19, Lincoln receives a letter from eleven-year-old Grace Bedell of Westfield, New York, suggesting he grow a beard. He does.

Mariah skips ahead some years in this chapter to give her evaluation of William Herndon's biography of Lincoln after the President's assassination and her opinion of Herndon himself.

Herndon conducted an intensive research campaign after Lincoln's death to lecture and write a biography of the martyred President. In his most controversial speech, on November 16, 1866, he painted a very different picture of Lincoln.

He said Lincoln was not warm or a man of heart but was dominated by reason and was very ambitious, even possessing a "greed for office." In that speech, Herndon was the first to contend that Lincoln had been in love with Ann Rutledge, based upon information he obtained from some residents of New Salem.

Herndon said the death of Miss Rutledge made Lincoln a melancholy man who led a tragic life. Robert Lincoln objected to the negative characterization of his father. Mary Lincoln was mortified at Herndon's contention that her husband had been in love with anyone before marrying her.

The controversial lectures backfired on Herndon and his fortunes fell. He turned to farming in 1867 and neglected his law practice. Pressed for money, he sold his research notes on Lincoln. He took to drinking heavily.

In 1881 Herndon stopped drinking and began writing his biography of Lincoln. Herndon's Lincoln: The True Story of a Great Life, *published in 1889, did not bring him the wealth he had hoped for and some historians contend it was full of inaccuracies. They dismissed the Ann Rutledge romance as being untrue, believing that Herndon had made it up in order to get back at Mary*

Lincoln. Mary died seven years before Herndon's biography was published.

Despite some inaccuracies, Herndon's biography has been one of the major sources of information regarding Lincoln's years in New Salem and Springfield. The Lincoln-Rutledge romance grew into the stuff of legend. Now in the reminiscences of Mariah Vance, we learn that the romance was real and had a profound impact on Lincoln and his marriage.

MISTAH ABE AND DE MISSY HAVE JUST COME BACK TO SPRINGFIELD FROM the last debate at Alton, Illinois. De Missy was argufyin' about some mistakes Mistah Lincolumn have made, that gave Mistah Douglas the best of him.

Well, he say, "Mother, you'll see some day I've tricked him into really asserting himself for what he really is. He may become the senator, for with his beautiful and gracious wife and the idol he has made of himself for so long, he can win. But when the South wakes up, he's a dead pigeon on a presidential ballot. The South is bound to see, he is really at heart no slavery man.

"Even though the North and South differ on this subject, I don't condemn them as blind and ignorant, for I wouldn't honestly know what to do if I was placed in the South to decide.

"There are a great many good and kind slaveholders. Better than some whites in the North are to the whites. And I'm convinced that their conviction is as sincere as ours, and they are not going to like a hypocrite. They will see he has been maneuvering for votes from both political parties. That Little Giant is a wonderful politician, but I believe I've tripped him up this time.

"Another thing, Molly—I'll be better known throughout the country on account of the publicity given me. You see, this association—my name in debate with a name like Stephen Douglas, with one already nationally and internationally known as a power—cannot help but give me some prestige.

"The question is bound to arise: Who is this man, Lincoln? As a Douglas opponent, they will reason. Douglas is too smart a man to consent to debate with anyone easy to defeat."

Sure enough. Even before Mistah Abe was nominate for President, he was ask to speech make clean through to the Atlantic Ocean. I just cain't recomemba where all or when. But one was Coops Institute [*Cooper Union in New York City*]. And at the school where Robert was going in the East [*Phillips Exeter Academy in New Hampshire*].

I guess that school didn't think they was going to get much of a speech when they first saw Mastah Robert's father. But after he spoke, that blessed Robert was awful proud of his Pa. They want Mistah Abe to speech-make more and more.

De Missy got a letter after that from Mastah Robert, telling all about his Pa's visit and how proud he was of him and what a difference it made with his classmates' opin' of him.

Most of the time when Mistah Lincolumn have to go away, de Missy go along. Her went to Ohio. I think, Columbus, Dayton, and Cincinnati. They left the boys to home. [*Actually, they sometimes took Tad with them, as they did on their Ohio trip.*]

I think that time [*the Lincolns were away*] Aunt 'Lizabeth come each day. Mary, the maid, and her [*younger*] brother Georgie stay at night. I go home at night to fix for my man Henry and my chillun for next day. I went back 'most every day.

Willie and Taddie [*if Tad wasn't traveling with his parents*] wore us 'most all out, clean thread bare worn out, but we dassn't punish them.

Georgie went to day school and so did Willie, when he want to. When he didn't want to, he didn't. Georgie didn't go in Willie's class, so was not pestered by Willie during school. But those two Lincolumn boys made up for it at night. I knowed that Georgie was the gladdest boy alive, when Mistah Abe come home. It was in the fall of the year.

Before they go, they give some orders: Aunt Mariah, do this and that. If they have a cold, give them vinegar tea, made with sugar, red pepper, ginger, and hot water. No screaming or scolding the boys. They say to Mary [*the maid*], do the same. But Aunt 'Lizabeth make Taddie keep clean and spruce up while her was there. And when he got too frisky, her sent that scamp to bed or made him sit on the kitchen chair. Her would always use the kitchen chairs 'cause Taddie kick and squirm so much, he have all the stuffing pull out of the better ones.

De Missy come back bragging 'bout how 'ciety invited them to their manshuns in all those Ohio places. General this and Doctor so and so, and the mayor of all the cities.

Her kind of got over the tantrums about Mistah Lincolumn not getting 'lected to the Senate. That woman never get enough 'ciety.

Mistah Abe once say, "Mother, you want to go to Washington for no other reason than to be in the highest spotlight in society in America, Mrs. President, while I have only one desire, to go to Washington this time as President to save the nation. If to save the Union means saving the colored people and lowly whites from bondage, indeed, we shall be twice blessed."

Those two folks was as far apart in all they thought and strive for as the North and South. And the sad and sorful part was, they never, never was any differment!

Mistah Abe ask de Missy after that trip if her thought her could settle down for a while, 'til he made some more money. That debate business with Stephen Douglas have about strapped him.

That was a hard job. Her did try to save by staying home sewing together all the lace and material her got while away.

Mistah Lincolumn have lots of work. Lots of big men in poltics from all over the country come to see him.

I know that man never want to be President. He told one man that he really wasn't fit for the job. His stepmother didn't want him to be, either, he done tell de Missy.

But de Missy say, "She may be a good woman, but she doesn't know enough to use good judgment."

[*Lincoln's stepmother, Sarah Bush Johnston Lincoln, was born December 13, 1788, and died December 10, 1869, surviving by four years the assassination of her stepson in 1865.*]

But de Missy egg him on and on. The only rest that man got was when he clam up and wouldn't talk or when the boys demand a romp. Of course, that was every time he step in the house.

Mistah Abe get too busy to talk, too. He still chop wood, milk the cow, feed and tend to the horses, go on the circuit, joke with the men downtown, and walk the street late at night, both before and after he was nominate for President. He done did all this, most to be alone and not be pestered. He still have his trip to Chicago and speechmaking.

The speeching would come out in the paper. When I go home, my Henry have me or one of the younguns read these papers he pick out of trash he haul. [*Mariah had picked up some reading ability by watching*

Robert Lincoln teach her son Willie to read and write.] My Henry near had a hemrig 'bout the slams and awful pictures of Mistah Abe.

It was a shame, my man say. Those fellows that make up such blasphem pictures should be strung up like they do niggahs. If niggahs write such stuff and draw such hellish pictures 'bout whites, they would be burn and cut up inch by inch.

Mistah Abe would only laugh. But de Missy have headaches from raving, then take paregoric. Not so much as once, but too much. And Mastah Robert would write. His poor baby heart was broke.

But Mastah Robert come home after his Pa was nominate. But the poor boy got no peace from those two little imps. He try to play with them, to keep them home and content.

When he was played out, he went to his room. They follow, crawl all over him like they do their Pa. Write with pencil over everything, then scream and fight like little demons. If that blessed Robert held their hands, de Missy say he was 'busin' them.

Finally that poor boy have to lock hisself in his room, to get any rest. Then those scamps would pound on his door.

Mastah Robert want to study up to go to 'nother school that fall. He want to go to Harvard. He try to get in once, but wasn't good 'nough. Now with some instruction they gave him at Exeter, with study in the summer at home, he might succeed, and he did. But with all the torment that boy went through, I just can't figure how he done did it. That poor boy rarely went anywhere. His old friends he play with, when a little tyke, say he have the swell head. But wasn't so. He couldn't step out, that some one of those Demcrats kids wouldn't make fun of his Pa and Ma.

They tell him how Douglas have wallup his lyin' Pa, and that Douglas would wallup him again for President. They say even his Pa couldn't speak good English. That Missus Lincolumn and his Pa talk niggah talk.

Robert knew he didn't say words just like his Pa and Ma say them. He spoke correct. He spent a lot of time trying to get them to say words so they would sound different, but it was no good. Both Mistah Abe and de Missy did talk like Kaintucky folks, what they was.

Mastah Robert spent lots of his time with my Billie when Billie was not at work and to home that summer. His Ma and Pa was gone most of the summer, here and there. They would sometime take the boys, sometime just Taddie.

253

Uncle Ninian couldn't abide those boys [*Willie and Tad*]. He say they was ruffians and 'ruptin his house, and was a bad influence for his boys and grandchildren. It was impossible to keep them from debilment. When their Ma and Pa take Taddie or both with them, that's 'bout the only time anyones have any peace.

To entertain them have to be some debilment, like making tick-tack on the window or punching up through the bottom of chairs with darning needles, so when you pull the string, the darning needle would pop up through the seat and stick anyone what sat down on that seat. If you pull three times, the needle punch, punch, punch up through that seat three times, and then those who got that good hard sticking, howl three times.

I do believe Mastah Robert enjoy some of that, once when de Missy have a party for those who come to 'glatulate Mistah Abe after he was nominate, since he couldn't abide the airs of some folks that come calling.

One party was at night, and Mary, the maid, have put the boys to bed. She read to them 'til her thought they was asleep, but they was playing 'possum. When the party got going, down they slip in their red flannel nightclothes what de Missy make to keep them from catching cold.

Outdoors they go with the tick-tack on the window. Some of the ladies thought it was spooks from the other world and say it was a sure sign of bad luck. Maybe someone there was goin' die. Maybe Mistah Lincolumn wouldn't be 'lected. Maybe he would get 'sassinate. [*Mary was entertaining friends who, like her, were interested in spiritualism, which was popular at the time.*]

Mistah Abe went out, carry those two rascals in, and say, "Here are our spooks."

The ladies all pull away from them scamps. But as soon as one big, fat gal sat down on the chair with the darning needle, pull, pull, pull went that string. Her jump up and scream worse than a Injun. Her say debils and hornets was in that house.

Mistah Abe and Robert knew, but look 'stonish and say nothing. I could see they was shaking their hides off, mostly 'cause they want to laugh so bad with those boys, what laugh and laugh and roll over.

Mistah Abe march out, get a flat, round board we used on the clabba crocks, put it on that chair and sat right down on that board. The boys didn't know, so pull the string. No punch, no sticking from the darning needle. They thought the fun was over, so put to bed looking sour, but as meek as little lambs.

I think Mistah Abe and de Missy was most awful proud of Mastah Robert. He was quiet, and such a gentleman always. Then he pass the 'zamnation and they let him in Harvard. I think Robert was proud of his Pa and Ma, but never, never proud or show-off kind.

He told me once, when he pass through Danville and stop to visit a little with us, that he have want to go in the regular army as a private [*during the Civil War*]. He never wanted to take advantage of his Pa being President, then or never in after life.

His Pa want for his Ma's sake that he should stay out of the war or take something easy like an officer under [*Ulysses S.*] Grant. He was under Grant, but took dangerous missions.

Mastah Robert say, "I knew my Pa would be criticized, but Ma was Pa's problem."

Her was for a long time bad in her mind, and should Robert be killed, her would have to be put 'way, as Robert [*years later*] have to put her 'way, when her perform so in Chicago.

Robert left his home to stay with her [*Mary*]. When he went back home to his beautiful wife, de Missy ran 'round naked in the hotel. Would have gone out that way to the street, if not stopped.

Her spent money so foolish that poor little Taddie would have been without money for an education. Mastah Robert cried and cried 'cause the 'thorities say he must put her 'way. His heart was broken. Then his Ma blame him. Say he want to rob her. What was he to do? He couldn't be with his Ma and he couldn't be away from her.

'Lizabeth even was mad for a while, until de Missy stay with her. 'Lizabeth have to put up with so much of that poor mindless woman. Her dark room, with a candle or lamp burning that might be [*cause a*] fire. Heaps and heaps of trunks full of dresses and stuff to make dresses. That woman then accuse 'Lizabeth of stealing her money. Aunt 'Lizabeth then have at last to ask Robert to forgive her.

When Mistah Lincolumn was 'lected President, there was another change in that parade what have start to come to their home [*in Springfield*]. Mistah Abe have to see so many politic men and those that want him to get them jobs in Washington, he have to move to the State House.

De Missy couldn't have them tramping in at all hours and his office wasn't big enough. The South was 'ceding and Buchanan sat there stiff as a poker and did nothing.

[*James Buchanan (1791–1868), fifteenth President of the United States (1857–1861), was glad to leave his presidential responsibilities. During his administration, while states were preparing to secede from the Union, he did not make any decisions that might create trouble.*]

Mistah Abe needed most awful to be alone, to think and write. But no, it have to be a hulla-ballu he have to face. Then too, that Herndon, who turn out to be a no-'count lying scalawag, just as de Missy always say he was, tried every way to run Mistah Abe's business. But for the good Mistah Abe always saw in him, he stay friends. Mistah Abe say, "Billy Herndon is a bad enough friend at times. I can't afford to make an enemy of him. What Billy wants is to be my man Friday." And he laugh.

He always smooth things over for that man. I think he always knew how he would end, if contraried. So Mistah Abe say when he left their office for the last time, "Leave the sign 'Lincoln and Herndon.' I'll be back and we'll continue together." But that never stop Herndon. Even after Mistah Abe was 'sassinate, he wrote mean lies about de Missy and then some about Mistah Abe.

Mastah Robert say he try to have Herndon take back what he told in a speech and wrote in a book. But it have gone too far. Too many want to believe bad instead of good. 'Specially about de Missy.

Mastah Robert was plumb crush. That dirt they blame on Mistah Abe at their office was not Mistah Abe's fault. Truth is, the Lincolumns sent me to the office to clean many times. I would go, but could I get in? No. 'Cause that Herndon was lock in there stone drunk. You could even smell him in the hall.

Once I went just as he was coming out. He say, "You can't go in. I'm locking up to leave."

So you see who was the cause of that dirt he done blame on Mistah Abe. When the truth are, as sure as Gawd is, was all Herndon dirt.

De Missy plead and plead to get rid of that man, that dirty bum, to get a nice boy like one who have come to their home to eat sometimes.

Mistah Abe say Herndon was smart and could help him. Mistah Abe done all he could to lift that man out of the gutter. Then you see how he pay back. He tell just 'nough truth to make it all sound like truth, Mastah Robert say.

That ornry man pay for it. He died in rags. We got the book he wrote. We read the lies and lies, and got so all-fire mad, we burn it up.

There was a bunch come to notify Mistah Lincolumn that he was 'lected President. The boys [*Willie and Taddie*] was all dress up for the 'casion. They shook hands as those gentlemen come through the gate. Mistah Abe met them and introduce them, as they enter the parlor, to de Missy, all dress up waiting there.

Her plan a little party for those who stay that night. Her told the boys if they stay clean, what her would get them as pay. They go upstairs to their room and was as still as little mice. I say, They can be good little angels if they get what they want for being good. Well, they have chicken and some fancy fixings. Mary the maid wait on the table.

I always keep things going in the kitchen. On parties, I could hardly turn around in it, de Missy have it cut up so. That nice big kitchen have to go for bathroom and dining room. When the boys come in at last to be seated at the table, there they was with ravel out sock yarn pasted and tied all over their faces, for whiskers. Their Ma have call them little men so often, they 'cided to look like their Pa and have whiskers what he have growed.

Mistah Abe growed them 'cause a little girl done wrote him he would look better if he would done grow them whiskers. And maybe that would help him to get 'lected President.

Mistah Abe was always proud when his boys want to look like him, and it please him powerful, those whiskered sons. De Missy was shock, but wouldn't scold them before company. So there they sat eating chicken and soup with them black sock yarn whiskers full of dripping soup.

Mary [*the maid*] come in the kitchen choking with laughing.

I thought when I saw them, Gawd in heaben, what those little imps of the debil going to do next to 'barrass de Missy? But Mistah Abe laugh and laugh about it and say, "They held the stage and attention of the audience and saved the day for me. I got out of committing myself to those men, thanks to Willie and Taddie."

De Missy say [*to the boys*] as she cut off those whiskers, "You don't deserve all I was going to do for you. And until you learn to behave, you will have to be left out of parties given for your father."

But I notice Mistah Abe edge them in, everyplace he could when there was a party.

257

CHAPTER TWENTY

Mistah Abe Comes
to Billie's Defense

1860

Mariah did not say when the following incident happened, but it was probably in 1860, just before Lincoln was elected President and before Mariah and her family moved from Springfield to Danville in November.

M ISTAH ABE LOVED MY BILLIE'S SINGING. I NEVER DID KNOW OF another kid who could sing a tune clean through like grown-ups, and never miss one single sound like my Billie could when he was only two years old. He could whistle like all the birds, and even get them to fly to him when he was five.

De Missy say, "God was good to our Billie." She have a little spinet. Her would play, but my boy say she couldn't play a horse fiddle. But Gawd bless de Missy, her tried, and I told that boy of ours if he ever hurt that poor woman's feelings, when her was a trying so hard to help, and trying so to show as how her like his singing, I'd plumb wring his black haid clean off his shollers.

My Henry loved to sing, and I could sing what suited me. My chillun all them could sing, but Billie the best. Mistah Abe wanted sad songs or the church. 'Specially the colored folks' religion songs. He often laugh, when Billie would sing 'em, though. 'Cause Billie clap his hand, roll over on the ground, and act sometime like he was flying to heaben.

Mistah Abe ask him once, "Where did you learn such monkey-shines, Bill?"

Billie ups and say, "Day hain't monkey-shines, dat's da way dey 'spose to be sung. Dat's da way dey all do in church."

After that, Mistah Abe would sometimes join in with clapping and flying jestas. Mistah Abe couldn't sing no more than de Missy could play the spinet. But de Missy say, "I always know when Mister Lincoln isn't worrying, if there ever is a time when he isn't, for he goes about singing or whistling." Sometimes he play the mouf organ. He could do that better than sing.

You never could get my Billie to sing low [*softly*]. He always sing loud and clear. He even wake up in the night and let out such a blast, all the younguns would get stirred up. At last, my Henry lammed him a good one and told him if he must cut loose, to get outdoors.

Well, Billie have one hitch at that, singing out at night when he was eighteen. The white trash-round there went hog-wild. They have Billie 'rested and he have to go up before Mayor Sutton. [*Goyn Sutton was mayor of Springfield in 1860.*]

I just 'bout went crazy, 'til Mistah Abe say he see what he could do. My Henry say even if Mistah Abe get him off, them damn white trash would grab Billie and string him up.

Well, Mistah Abe was right there that day to stand by Billie. The white trash was there, too. They done have him down for disturb the peace. They say he go out at night and screamed, after they'd gone to bed and sleep. Brayed like a jackass and hooted like a owl.

Billy was mad as blazes, saying such about his singing. He spoke up and scream, "They's damn liars! I war sing'n!"

"Order in the court!" say Mayor Sutton.

Billie say, "Ah'll show you'ns ah can sing, if you'ns let me."

Well, Mistah Abe say, "Bill can sing, your honor. Maybe you will favor me by giving Bill a try. I believe you will be a fine judge of his voice, as you have a marvelous voice and are versed in music. That may be a good way to prove right now, whether he sang or hooted."

Mistah Mayor Sutton say, "Request granted."

Billie broke loose with all his heart and soul and with all his acting up. Mayor Sutton and Mistah Abe laugh almost as loud as Billie sang. The white trash done got out of there faster than lightning, and between Mayor Sutton and Mistah Abe, they say, "Case dismissed!"

Billie started to run too, but that Mayor Sutton call him back and say, "Not so fast, Billie. You and I need to talk this happening out, as man to man."

That please Billie a heap, to call him a man.

Later, Billie says to his Pa and other men, "Dad Mayor Sutton air mose da best man 'sides Mistah Abe. He'ns got a good word fa eber one. He'ns say dar air no white trash, just unfortune, and we'ns no worser or no betta dan dey."

The mayor say, "Billie, you have a fine voice. God has been good to you. You should use it for the glory of God. From now on, don't waste it on anyone who doesn't appreciate it. You really did disturb the peace, but as this is your first offense, I'll let you go if you promise me, you'll not get out at night and wake your neighbors up.

"Billie, you have a wonderful voice, though from now on when you want to sing, come and sing for me, or go to the Lincolns, who love your singing and want only the best for you. You may go now."

Billie rush out singing at the top of his voice, "Glory, glory, halla-lula, ah's on my road to glory now!" He throwed his hat in the air and dance and clap every step until he was gone.

[*Adah Sutton adds here: "Mariah told me, as did a number of members of the white churches in Danville, that from the time the Vances moved to Danville in 1860 until his death in January 1904, Billie, because of his beautiful voice, was much in demand in churches, including those attended by white people."*]

CHAPTER TWENTY-ONE

Mistah Abe's Secret Baptism at Night

1860

The most controversial passage in Mariah Vance's reminiscences is her revelation of Lincoln's "secret" baptism.

After becoming President-elect, Lincoln told Mariah that before he left Springfield, he wanted to do all he could to have God's help in the work ahead of him. This led to a discussion of whether he should become baptized.

For those who question Abraham Lincoln's baptism, we quote from Adah Sutton's letter to Lloyd Ostendorf on March 25, 1957:

> *The thought of this baptism as a proposed article for the* Lincoln Herald *by Dr. Taylor seems to prove lst, the story is not questioned by Dr. Taylor* [curator of the Lincoln collection at Lincoln Memorial University, Harrogate, Tenn.];

263

*2nd, in face of the fact (tradition has it) Lincoln was in
no way affiliated with any church, he could have been
baptized.*

*So many false stories have been told, which are
now considered true, and so many true stories are said
to be traditional. This alone has and still is confusing me.
Makes me hesitate to be set up and shot at even on any
one point. Especially since in my heart and mind I know,
every story that Mariah Vance told was as true as there is
a God in Heaven.*

DE MISSY WAS PRESTAREH *[PRESBYTERIAN]*. WELL, THAT WOMAN EVEN SAYS SHE
was nigh up in heaben when she sets in that pew on the Sabbath.

Once when she was carrying on so [*at home*], Mistah Abe say, say he,
"Mother, can't we find a place here, somewhere, for that pew, so you can sit
in it every day?"

De Missy would beg him to join them [*in becoming a member of the
Presbyterian church*]. She sure say it would help him up in the world.

Mistah Abe then and there says, "Mother, I don't want to be helped up
in the world, the way you see it. I want to live so as I can help up. If I can't
sit on a storebox in front of Hoffman's Row and with only one of my unpolished common stories help one of them boys, one of the 'common herd' as
you calls them, a story that would lead a boy to Christ as I know Him, I'd
give all my chances to be President, as you hanker for so much."

[*Hoffman's Row was a string of brick stores and office buildings on the
public square in downtown Springfield. The Sangamon County Courthouse
was there, as well as the building in which Lincoln and Herndon had their
law office. Lincoln frequently joined his fellow lawyers and others who gathered on the street or in Corneau & Diller's drug store or sat on the "liar's
bench" out front and talked about news of the day or swapped stories.*]

Yes, Mistah Abe would sometimes go to (church) meetings with her. I
don't think he done liked their high-falluting airs in that there church.

He once say, "It sure wouldn't be any harder for them to go down on
their knees than to do all that bowing and scraping."

Another time he say, "I sometimes wonder if it is a church or a circus. They're all decked out in so much trappings and perform so."

He sure knowed of their unpaid bills, for he say, "Mother, how can those folks go out and make such a show in unpaid finery? And others there are robbing their homefolks of bread, meat, and milk, just to make a show."

He always want to be babsized. He done promise his mother, when a little tyke 'way back there in Indiani when he was old enough to know the meanings, he would be babsize. And them Prestarehs don't go by being dunked down under water.

De Missy say, "That is 'backwoods' now." Besides, Mistah Abe has shamed her and the boys enough with his old-fangled ways.

Once he say to me, "Mariah, do you think it has helped save your soul to be baptized?"

"Yes, Mistah Abe," I say. "It sure always make me knowed I done one thing Christ done did. He let John babsize him in the Ribber Jordan. He sure must thought that it was good, so I's that good."

"Yes," Mistah Abe say. "It shows you are in earnest about your soul. You want your sins washed and clean as water can make your body."

A few days after that, he say, "Mariah, I'm going to be baptized. Do you think it would be sinful if I was baptized and not let on to Missy Lincoln?

"Now, I am not ashamed, but she'll raise Ned [*hell*] and it would be a worry on my mind. I don't think that would be a good way to go to my baptism. Besides, like as not, it would start another misery up in her head. I've got too big a load now to tackle getting over that and still try to have the mind that also was in Christ Jesus when I go to my baptism.

"Another thing that bothers me a heap, Mariah, gossips and sightseers would most likely come in mobs. Not to reverence but to mock and beguile my intensions. I don't like show of any kind, when it can be helped. I'd like to know just how to help it.

"Mariah, you've a good head for planning. Just how can I be baptized so Mother won't be upset? Somewhat of a crowd is bound to congregate."

I say, "Mistah Abe, you can think and think, but there's only just one way. You got to go at night."

He just stood there and stared at me. I just knowed I'd given him a ter-bul shock. He was the saddest looking critter I most ever set eyes on in my life. I thought he was going to bust out crying. He just walked off muttering, "God help us!"

I say, "Hal-lulah, Mistah Abe!"

In a little while, he comes to the kitchen and, more cheery like, say, "Mariah you saved the day for me. I'm not going to Washington without doing all I can to keep this one of Christ's commandments. I couldn't expect God to help me lead the nation so full of woes, if I failed Him.

"I'll write to Parson Elkins and have him come, if he will. Let's pray he will."

[*Adah Sutton inserts here: "I've always thought, especially since I read somewhere that Elkins was the name of the minister who presided at (Lincoln's) mother's grave, that Mariah got the names mixed. Perhaps he, if still living after forty years, was around seventy years old. He could have been a very young minister when he came to preach the sermon at Lincoln's mother's grave. In that case, it might possibly have been the same minister who came to Springfield to baptize him. He must have had in mind a very large minister, because he said"*]:

"Any one of these parsons around here could let me down in the river, but none I'd be certain could heist me up.

"Now, Mariah, it's just got to be a little secret betwixt us and our God."

I just say right there and then to Mistah Abe, "Yes, suh," I say. "I swan, Mistah Abe, you never need be jumpy. I won't ever even tell my Henry."

He [*Henry*] would look at me and scowl onery like and say, "Bettah mind youse own 'nitten und stop mouthen' other folks' complaints."

And to this very live-long day, I never once told a soul but you.

[*Adah Sutton wrote here: "Meaning me, and I believed her. I've learned since that the minister did tell of the baptism years later, after Lincoln's death. Possibly after Mrs. Lincoln's death.*

"*Later I will give an account of the baptism, as told by the Reverend Ankrum, and will write a copy of the letter written to me by Anna Deal in which she relates the story of the baptism as told to her by her father, David E. Wagner."*]

We never talked it over no more until early one cold morning. I always went early, the days was getting so short. I was toting my last youngun with me that morning. [*Frederick Walter Vance, born in 1860 and died in 1923.*] Mistah Abe was never a one to get up early, but I swan there he was along the plank 'way out front, with his haid down, pondering and considering. I went into the shed and tucked my youngun in. I was straighten up the kitchen first. It was such a teeny cubbyhole, after de Missy changed the whole house 'round. Things just got in a fierce pile with the leftover dishes to do.

I was on my way out to the shed to get some soft soap when Mistah Abe come up. He kinda sad-like say, "Mother has the misery again. I gave her some paregoric. She's quiet now."

Well, I knowed good and well she was in a tantrum. Poor Missy, she was such a sick, sick woman in her haid. Well, there was nothing in this living world to stop that streak in her 'cept paregoric. No siree.

I cleared away all the soil and done fixed Mistah Abe some breakfast. I fried some mush cakes. He sure liked mush cakes and sorgam [*sorghum, a sweet syrup*]. He just didn't want more. He ate a bit and shoved his chair back on the two back legs.

He say, "Mariah, I've been baptized."

He didn't say more for some bit.

I say, "Mistah Abe, you want to tell me how it all comes off?"

"Well," he say, "the Reverend Elkins came in the night time and baptized me and went back in the night time. We didn't go the regular cow path, just waded through persimmon scrub, hazel brush, and wild grapevine. I knew if that parson felt as I did, he was as glad to get in that river [*the Sangamon*] as I.

"Now, Mariah, I don't mean I wasn't pondering and considering, but I swear the needles were thicker on us than dog fleas on Rover.

"The parson and I had a mighty sacred charge to keep, and deep inside of me I was praying. Now I really praise my Lord and my God I took the right step. You know, Mariah, many weeds have to be trampled to reach the right path."

I say to Mistah Abe, "Glory to Gawd Hal-lulah!"

Then he say, "My mother was a Baptist. I had a Baptist parson say the words over her body back there in Indiana and I'm sure she would like it if she knew I had a Baptist parson baptize me.

"You know what, Mariah? I feel free now. I know God will watch over me and do all for the best.

"Mrs. Lincoln thought I was with Billy Herndon. That's all I regret. I can't tell her where I was."

After I cleaned and prepared dinner, I went to the barn for the mule and cart, and there was Mistah Abe's wet shoes, shirt, long underwear, and pants hanging up drying.

The next time I returned to do the washing, the clothes was down from the nails where they hung in the barn, and there were two shirts and two suits of long underwear in the wash to do.

The ones that hung in the barn. I know they was the same he gets bab-size in.

[*Adah Sutton adds: According to Anna Deal's account of the baptism, told to her by her father, which follows, Mr. Lincoln did supply the minister with clothing for the baptism.*

From the Maryland and Pennsylvania Historical Sketches *by Reverend Freeman Ankrum, A.B., Masontown, Pennsylvania, 1947, page 121, chapter 3, I quote:*

> *Elder D. P. Sayler was a great admirer of President Abraham Lincoln, and a frequent visitor at the White House. He spent many an hour with Lincoln who was always glad to see him and called him "Bishop Sayler." The President told him that he considered him capable of filling any office to which he might be called. Then, addressing him earnestly, he said, "But Brother Sayler, I ordain you a Dunkard preacher forever."*

And on page 237, chapter 7:

> *When Abraham Lincoln viewed the desolation around the Dunkard church (Antietam, Maryland), he had more than a passing interest.*
>
> *Before taking office as President, and while still in Springfield, Illinois, Lincoln sent for a minister of the German Baptist church, commonly called 'Dunkards'* (because people were immersed during baptism), *and was baptized by him in the river.*
>
> *He promised that after his term of office expired, he would conform to the church.*

Adah Sutton then adds: From a letter to me by Mrs. Anna Deal of June 30, 1956, I copy the following account:

> *My father, David E. Wagner, past 76 years of age at this date, February 12, 1935, relates a circumstance told him by*

Elder Isaac Billheimer, at one time a resident of Tennessee and later a resident of Heath, Indiana.

An Elder of the Fairview Church, Isaac Billheimer told father he was acquainted with the minister who baptized Lincoln. (Father doesn't remember the name.)

The minister who baptized Lincoln was a member of the German Baptist Church (nicknamed Dunkard). *Lincoln sent this minister word to come to Springfield on a certain train which arrived there after night.* (Lincoln had sent him twice as much money as he needed.)

Lincoln met him and they went to the river where Lincoln was baptized, yet that night. Lincoln had brought extra clothes needed for both, and having changed clothes they went and waited for the train to arrive, and the minister left after midnight. Lincoln promised that after his term of office expired he would conform to the Church.

Adah Sutton adds: This is a copy of the original account written by Anna Etta Wagner Deal, dictated by her father on Feb. 12, 1935, Lincoln's birthday.

Editor's note: This description of Lincoln's baptism also is described in a book, Sidelights on Brethren History, *by Freeman Ankrum, published 1962 by The Brethren Press, Elgin, Illinois. Ankrum also says in his book:*

> *We are concerned here largely with his (Lincoln's) relationship to the Brethren (the German Baptist Church). Concerning Lincoln's being a Christian, there remains no doubt. But the churches with which he was most familiar did not appeal to him because he felt that they minimized the Lord Jesus Christ and put manmade ordinances ahead of Him. Although little has been published about it, there is strong reason to believe that Lincoln espoused the Brethren faith.*

> *D. W. Cripe, of Peoria, Illinois, a number of years ago said, "I am personally acquainted with David and Anna Wagner (sic), to whom the elder told the incident of Abraham Lincoln's baptism at Springfield, Illinois, just before he went to Washington to take the Presidential chair. I can recommend Brother and Sister Wagner as honest, truthful Christians who*

can be depended upon. I am also acquainted with, and personally know, a man by the name of Theodore Swanson, an honest, truthful man who has read in a number of historical books about Lincoln. He told me that he read of the incidents of his baptism in one of the histories."

It has been pointed out to the writer that when Lincoln decided to wear a beard, he wore the type popular with the Brethren of the day.

It is a well-known fact that Elder D. P. Sayler, of Carroll and Frederick counties, Maryland, was a frequent visitor of the President in the White House. He and Lincoln were rather intimately acquainted. Lincoln would call him "Bishop Sayler" and once told him that he considered him capable of filling any office to which he might be called.

Mariah may have been mistaken in the name of the minister who performed Lincoln's secret baptism, saying it was Parson Elkins. It was Parson David Elkins who presided and spoke at the grave of Lincoln's mother in the fall of 1818. Nancy Hanks Lincoln was buried in Indiana, and Reverend Elkins, pastor of the Little Mound Church in Kentucky, came at young Lincoln's request to preach her funeral sermon. If this was the same Parson Elkins, after some forty years, it would be noteworthy because of his age in 1860. But at any rate, that was the name remembered by Mariah Vance.

Adah Sutton's research led her to learn that the minister who performed Lincoln's secret baptism was another man, a parson of the German Baptist Church whose identity she could not discover.

These two accounts of the baptism, from widely different sources, agree in every detail with Mariah's story that Abraham Lincoln was baptized Christian, even though he was not a formal member of any church, as has been so often stated. That he attended church services in Springfield and Washington quite regularly has been verified many times.

Lincoln was thirteen when he witnessed his beloved stepmother's baptism as an adult. It seems appropriate here to include the description of her baptism, quoted from Lincoln's Boyhood: a Chronicle of His Indiana Years, *by Francis Marion Van Natter, published 1963 by Public Affairs Press, Washington, D.C.:*

Next day (June 7, 1823) *being the second Sunday in June and baptizing day, Abraham stood on the cool, wooded banks of Buck Horn Creek, a branch of Pigeon Creek, and heard the* (Pigeon Creek Baptist) *church members singing hymns. He knew that Article 8 of their Articles of Faith declared: "We believe that baptism and the Lord's supper are ordinances of Jesus Christ and that true believers are the only proper subjects and the only proper mode of baptism is immersion." Abraham watched his stepmother calmly walk into the pool of living water and, as the singing stopped, saw the preacher "bury her with Jesus in baptism;" then saw her go "straightaway out of the water" as the Saviour had done from the river Jordan.*

(Van Natter says Lincoln's baptism took place on June 7, but the 1823 calendar shows the second sunday in June was the 8th.)

Lincoln's father, Thomas, had been a member of the Freewill Baptists and had been baptized in Kentucky by the Reverend William Downs in Knob Creek. He was "boss carpenter" in building the Pigeon Creek Regular Primitive Baptist Church.

When Abe was sixteen, he was given a job as sexton at the Pigeon Creek meetinghouse, responsible for taking care of the church property.

One Sunday morning, while Abe sat on a sinner's seat and listened to the sermon, the preacher announced, "I am the Christ whom I shall represent." Almost immediately, the preacher began fidgeting, then dropped his pants. The congregation was astounded, then saw him continue squirming and then pull off his tow linen shirt. Everyone sat dazed as, standing in the pulpit, their pastor was naked as Adam on the day of his creation. Finally, in the back of the church, an old lady stood up and looked sternly at the preacher. "If you represent Christ, then I am done with the Bible!" she shouted.

Only Abe knew why the preacher had been so discomforted as to disrobe. As the preacher had begun his sermon, Abe had seen a little blue lizard climb up the minister's pants leg.

This light story aside, regarding Abe's churchgoing as a youth, it seems possible that having witnessed his stepmother's baptism as an adult, including her total immersion in Pigeon Creek, may have been a strong contributing factor to his decision to also be baptized as an adult, and to have it done by a Baptist minister immersing him in the Sangamon River.

To those who may feel that it was out of character for Lincoln to be baptized, Lloyd Ostendorf responds, "It was not unusual in Lincoln's time, nor is it today, for adults to feel the need to become baptized Christians in certain thresholds of their lives. We know that Confederate Generals John Bell Hood and Joseph E. Johnston both asked for and received baptism during the heat of battle in the Civil War.

"In November of 1860, Lincoln had already been elected President and was soon to leave for Washington to embark upon the monumental task of trying to hold the nation together over the issue of slavery. The possibility of civil war was great. It is understandable that he felt the need for the Lord's support and, if that meant getting baptized, that's what he would do. But he would want it done in secret because religiously he was a very private man and wouldn't want it to get around.

"It is not hard to believe that Lincoln desired to be on God's side when he assumed the awesome job of the Presidency."

On August 8, 1994, Ostendorf sent me the following letter, after having conducted additional research into the subject of Lincoln's "secret baptism" and having recently interviewed the Rev. Calvin Bright, pastor of the East Dayton Church of the Brethren in Ohio:

> *He (Rev. Bright) told me he had made a lifelong study of the facts and oral history given to him by various members of the Dunkard Brethren about the secret baptism of Abraham Lincoln, mostly to Brethren Societies in Illinois; places like Cerro Gordo, Illinois, east of Springfield.*
>
> *Reverend Bright visited Albert Harshbarger (an elder of the Church of the Brethren) in his later years and was told by him that when he was a boy, the account of Lincoln's baptism was a matter of local knowledge with the membership of the local meetinghouse. Harshbarger died in January 1994.*
>
> *Harshbarger claimed that it was Bishop Daniel P. Sayler (of Carroll and Frederick counties, Maryland) who actually performed the baptism, and though it was supposed to be kept*

secret, he could not keep it secret among his brethren and told certain ones at Cerro Gordo, where he changed trains on the Wabash railway to Indianapolis, Indiana, enroute back and bound for the Fairview Brethren Church in Indiana.

Reverend Bright claimed that no written record was made of the baptism, not only because it was to be secret, but because if the baptized person was not to become a member of a local meetinghouse congregation, his name would not have been recorded in their records. Thus, it remained an oral tradition and even to the present day in old Brethren communities, various versions quite similar in contents found their way into writings by Brethren historians in the historical collections of Church of the Brethren General Board writings in the church Archives in Elgin, Illinois.

Brethren Historian Freeman Ankrum said that Brother Sayler was known to have been against slavery, and in 1858 followed Lincoln from town to town during the Lincoln-Douglas debates. He also claimed Reverend Sayler spent time in the Lincoln home in Springfield, and that the friendship established in Illinois carried over into later visits to the Executive Mansion in Washington.

The Brethren Family Almanac of 1908 tells how President Lincoln was always glad to see Bishop Sayler at the White House. He called him "Brother Sayler" or addressed him as "Bishop Sayler," and earnestly said, "Brother Sayler, I ordain you a Dunkard preacher forever."

What could be more normal than for Lincoln to have engaged Brother Sayler to baptize him, as his friend and confidant?

Some historians who have trouble believing Lincoln had himself baptized say they doubt it because they wonder why he would have kept it a secret, especially from his wife. But that may have been because Mary was not one to be able to keep a secret, especially one of that magnitude. She also would have wanted his baptism to be a public ceremony, and since Lincoln was a very private person and kept his religious feelings to himself, he would not want the event to be a spectacle. Then, too, Mary was a Presbyterian, and Mariah says Lincoln chose to be baptized by a Baptist minister, as his stepmother had been. If Mary had learned Abe was baptized by anyone but a Presbyterian, it would likely have caused major arguments and perhaps even a religious war between them, which, on top of everything else, he did not need.]

CHAPTER TWENTY-TWO

The Ann Rutledge Likeness

November 1860

Soon after Lincoln is elected President, while Mariah is working in the Lincoln home, he and Mary are going through their personal belongings in preparation to pack for their move to Washington. A photograph falls out of Lincoln's family album and Mary asks him about it. It opens up an old wound inside her, but this time Lincoln has a solution for how to heal it.

    As has been pointed out earlier, out of respect to the President, when Mr. Lincoln or Mary is speaking, Adah Sutton translates the Black English into American English. This particular chapter is being told by Adah Sutton, though closely based on her shorthand notes of Mariah's reminiscences.

*O*NE AFTERNOON, NOT LONG AFTER MR. LINCOLN WAS ELECTED PRESIDENT OF THE United States, Mr. and Mrs. Lincoln had for several days been gathering together articles precious to them, which they wanted to either store or take with them to their new home. From a long list Mrs. Lincoln had made of the necessary and desirable, she said, "Perhaps we should look through the pictures while we are in here [*in the parlor*]."

They had finished disposing of a few ornaments that had been cracked or broken. Some of which she gave to Mariah, saying, "You can throw these away." But Mariah treasured them as little keepsakes of her association with the beloved Lincolns.

She said, "I think it best not to clear the house of all decorations now. We'll just remove these things that are damaged or the ones we will not care to keep. You know we'll have to live here and do some entertaining almost until the last day before we leave."

At that, she had Mariah remove several pictures from the wall and take them to the shed. A few family pictures were grouped together on the wall. Among them were two photos of Mr. and Mrs. Lincoln which had always been hung together. They had been in the same place on the wall ever since Mariah had worked there.

When Mrs. Lincoln took them down, she brushed them carefully and caressingly held them to her, saying, "These are my two most precious pictures, taken when we were young and so desperately in love. They will grace the walls of the White House. They belong there to the last."

Mr. Abe laughed and said, "I trust that that grace never slips a peg and becomes disgrace."

They came to the photograph albums which had always held a place on an attractive marble-top table in the parlor. One of these albums belonged to him and one to her.

Her album was larger than his [*made*] of fancy brown leather with two clasps. It contained her family [*the Todds*] pictures. Others were friends —some Lexington belles.

The album was pulled apart and badly worn. From it, she removed many pictures, and after remarking about some, discarded them. Others she put to one side, saying, "Those I wish to keep, I'll buy another album to put them in. And no doubt we'll have new ones in Washington. This album is quite badly worn."

She sorted from a stack of photos in cases a number she wished to keep. She then handed the remaining ones to Mr. Lincoln who also kept a few and discarded others. Always he laughed and reminisced. Each one called forth a funny or strange incident. A few of which I have retold in precious chapters of this book.

After they had finished with the ones in cases, picking up his [*Lincoln's*] own album, which was a much abused small brown one with white porcelain buttons, he said. "We'll now take a peep in the rogues' gallery."

Most of the pictures in his album were small tintypes or of cardboard. Many of the slats for pictures held name cards, old-time campaign badges, cartoons, and a few programs. The sides bulged with little keepsakes he had placed between the pages.

He said, "By the looks of these, I think the boys have decorated them with sticky fingers. Look here, Mother, the precious little rascals have given this one a black eye with licorice candy." They both had a hearty laugh.

When he came to his father's picture, he remembered the story of how and why it had been taken, as if it had been quite a while before.

He said, "I remember distinctly riding off the circuit to reach Pa and Ma's place in Coles County. That road would have mired a horse to its belly in rainy weather. It wasn't too good at that time, but the boys [*his sons*] had so often asked me about my family, I decided if I could get them to consent, I'd take them [*his parents*] somewhere and have their pictures taken.

"It took some pleading. Ma said she didn't want to break the camera. I told her she just wanted me to tell her how pretty she was. Ma was good, and in her face she looked it. I'd have called her a pretty woman even then.

"Pa said he didn't have clothes to have a picture taken in. I said, 'That's right, Pa, but I'll fix that.' So I took him [*into town*] to get him a new suit. I expect he was buried in it, if John [*Lincoln's stepbrother John Johnston*] didn't wear it out.

"I hitched up my horse to an old wagon Pa had, and while I was doing so, Pa bathed. I don't remember Pa ever having shaved, but I never knew a cleaner man."

[*Lincoln's father was always clean-shaven. Lincoln could have meant that his father had a stubble of hair on his chin and face that he didn't shave off.*]

"Why, back in Kentucky, he'd even take soft soap and sheep's wool (perhaps before being carded) to the creek, cut the ice, and bathe.

"Ma usually cut his hair, when it was cut. His hair was black but not stiff and stubborn like mine, and she did a pretty good job.

"He came out to the wagon with a new wool plaid shirt on that Ma had made for him, and a white stock [*collar*] and tie. I can still see that look of pride and happiness. Pa hadn't been away from that farm for ages.

"He said, 'I wish Sally [*his wife*] would go too, but I couldn't coax her to.'

"I got him a suit and, by the time the picture was taken, it was about three o'clock in the afternoon. I had promised the boys to meet them on the circuit, so we couldn't loiter. I'd have liked to have seen and talked with Ma more, seeing her expression when she saw Pa in his new suit. I always knew he was a good-looking man, but clothes made me pretty proud of him, and glad for him."

At that, Mary Lincoln took the picture and looked at it long. "Yes," she said. "He looks like an aristocrat. If he were just as cultured as he looks." [*Adah Sutton added here:* "*She* (Mary) *never wanted Lincoln's people around.*"] "That suit is nicer than any you ever purchased for yourself, and fits him better."

Lincoln laughed and said, "Pa was a better clothes-horse than I."

Another one he discarded was a group, supposedly Mr. and Mrs. Lincoln and Robert when young. At that time, I was not familiar enough with these pictures to judge the authenticity since Mariah evidently failed to put them in a container I purchased. I've searched for this family group of three among the grandchildren and friends, but never unearthed them. I feel sure if not in some Lincoln collection, the rest must be lost.

As for the Lincoln group of the three, Mariah related, "Mistah Lincolumn said, 'That photographer sure mixed us up. Gave us this picture of a giraffe, a bear, and a baboon instead of us.'" It was of the three standing [*the Lincolns and Robert*].

The last picture he opened the album to was a tintype a little larger than the others (measured by my eyes about 2 1/2 inches by 4 inches or maybe a little over). It was a three-quarter figure of a very young, beautiful girl with a lovable, innocent face, a childlike face.

He looked at it long and intently, but made no remarks while studying the picture, which Mariah said he had found in a gallery some five years before and brought home.

At that time he showed it to Mrs. Lincoln, she asked who it was. He said, "Well, Mary, you have always wanted to know just how Ann looked to me. This is not her picture, but one so much like her, especially at the time I first met her, it could be her. To me it is her."

Mariah said, during the intervening years she had come across him looking at the picture. It must have always reminded him of their love and proved his appreciation for her help and happy association.

In placing the picture back, which was partly secured in a slot, the album accidentally slipped from his knees and fell to the floor, scattering contents but staying open to where he had fastened Ann's likeness. He picked it up and replaced it on his lap.

Mrs. Lincoln got up from her chair, stood behind him, and looked down at the picture. She, too, did not speak. But they both looked during the silence as if each sensed a benediction, as if to speak would make the silence less hallowed or consecrated. There had been so many hard words from her before that, called forth by her jealousy. Perhaps more to be assured of his love (now perhaps she knew her life's ambition had been attained, a new life was before them that needed all their attention).

But she asked softly, a question which so often before this time had resulted in bitterness on her part, "Mister Lincoln, have you never put her out of your life?"

As if dazed by his reflections, he hesitated quite a while to answer her. She began to twist her hands and show signs of becoming hysterical.

Sensing what might happen if he didn't speak, he looked her squarely in the face, put his arm around her waist, and drew her to him, a demonstration rarely indulged in before any of his household.

Then he said, "Mary, perhaps Almighty God reopened this chapter in my life, so we could renew and review it and then close it forever. No, I have not put her out of my life. She was put out years ago. Since the Higher Power seen fit, we cannot question the ways of such Divine Intelligence."

Mrs. Lincoln [*a Presbyterian who believed in predestination*] then said, "Then you do believe our ways are planned?"

He answered, "No, not in the sense you have in mind as you are questioning me. Sometimes I think God should have always been spelled 'Good.' God as an individual mind seems narrowing, and hampers the power we should feel is omnipotent.

"Good is all inclusive. All things, if good, are relative, hinge, help each other, and work together for good for those who love good. Thus to love good is to work out our own destiny with the help of all good. Regardless of our own plans and often highest desires, our destiny is gauged by our own thoughts and actions often come to pass far better than we ever hoped for. Love—Good—leads the way, if we cooperate.

"When I was experiencing hardship in my youth, I never dared hope for the blessings I now enjoy, or such privileges and blessings as my family may now have. My blessed mother and conscientious, hardworking, honest father started me in a way I never forgot. May God help me to always stay in that way.

"Above all, it has ever brought me in contact with the elements and people that have made it possible to climb to the highest place in this good Nation. Mary, among those who helped me climb, who instilled ambition in me, was Ann. She had her part; not because it was planned at my birth, but because I tried to be good, and she was good. Like begets like. I attracted her, and she attracted me. At that time we needed each other in our lives. Assuredly at that time she was most dear to me, and her memory has been so since—a lingering part of my existence.

"But tonight she seems strangely far away and going out farther and farther. Our associations, as I tried to review them a while ago when looking at this likeness, are blurred. In some cases so blotted they were as, perhaps, a partly forgotten, beautiful dream which I could only vaguely recapture. Only disconnected parts would return to my memory.

"To you, Mother, I now owe my love and devotion. You too have helped me climb, and are still helping me. Ann is a memory. You are a living reality, not to be put aside an instant for anything or anyone whomsoever.

"Let us live the Good-Life not alone for ourselves but for our precious children we have brought into the world, so that only good will come of them. Let's improve our remaining life with good, unwarped thoughts and deeds. Let's let the past remain the past, and thank God—Good—it was so. The past has played its part, and played it well, to make today for you and me."

He waited a moment, then said, dropping the album to the floor, "Mariah, you can take this heap out and burn it."

Mariah told me, "I done didn't burn it, for here it is!"

[*Mariah Vance kept Lincoln's family album until she sold it to Adah Sutton between 1900 and 1904.*

Lloyd Ostendorf later bought the album from Miss Sutton and some of the photos in it are reproduced in this book, including the original tintype of the Ann Rutledge likeness.]

CHAPTER TWENTY-THREE

The Last Time Aunt Mariah
Saw Mistah Abe

December 1860

Because of his fears of hostility against Blacks, Henry Vance moves his family to Danville, Illinois, near the Indiana border, soon after Lincoln is elected President on November 6, 1860. Henry has prospects of getting steady work there in the coal mines. The Union is suddenly "dissolved" on December 20 with the secession of South Carolina. The Lincolns are not scheduled to move to Washington until the President-elect's inauguration in March.

With this chapter, Adah Sutton concludes Mariah's oral history. She begins with some commentary of her own: "I asked Mrs. Vance if she ever saw Mister Lincoln or his family after the Vance family moved to Danville. The reason for this question was that a number of people told me that Mr. Lincoln had called for her, to see if [she was] *in the crowd that met the Presidential train when it stopped at Danville en route to Washington.*

"Others said that after the war, Mrs. Vance made a trip to Washington to have her husband released from the army but that Mrs. Lincoln refused to see her.

"These were Mariah Vance's answers to these reports, which I am convinced she answered truthfully."

O H, YES, I SAW MISTAH ABE ONCE. YOU SEE, WE LEFT SPRINGFIELD SHORTLY AFTER Mistah Abe was 'lected President in November in 1860. My Henry have got work in the mine outside Danville. He and my Billie have gone on [*ahead of the rest of the family*] with a load of plunda. Then Billie come back for us [*Mariah and the children*] and the rest of our stuff.

You see, the whole country was in a mess. President Buchanan, 'cause he was going out of office. And of course, lots in Washington under him was for slavery. He just sat there and nary tried to stop that war what was brewing. So the colored folks was near skeered out of their hide and most moved farther north, as we planned before.

No, Mistah Abe never call for me or any of my family that I know of, or hear tell of, when the President train stop at Danville.

Mistah Abe and Mastah Robert have come to Danville 'bout Christmas time in 1860. They stop at the Etna House, if I rightly recomemba, for some meeting with some big men in politics and some of their friends. One was Dr. Fithian, I recomemba.

'Bout noon on that day, a messenga boy bring a note to our house. I tell you I was sure my Henry have been kill or hurt in the mine. But the telgram was from Mistah Abe.

It say on a slip of hotel paper he have send by this messenga: "Am at this hotel for a short time today. Robert is with me. I would like for you and Bill to come here between the hours of 3 o'clock and 4 o'clock. We will be very, very disappointed if you don't come. Give messenger your answer. With esteem, A. Lincoln and Robert."

Well, Billie have come in for dinner. He was doing some work for the

Hegler. That is a nice rich family who have made money in the smelta [*smelting*] works. They was German folk. All those German folks was good to us. Seems as how, since I recomemba again, that was for the Hegler work. Maybe it was some street work my Billie was doing.

Work or starve, nothing not a soul thing on this earth, could have kept my Billie away from going to see Mastah Robert. When we move here, Mastah Robert was in some school in the East. Maybe Phillips' 'Cademy at Exeter, New Hampshire, or Harvard. So Billie have to come away without a sight of the blessed Mastah Robert.

[*Robert Lincoln graduated from Phillips Exeter Academy September 15, 1859. His first year at Harvard was 1860–1861, the class of 1864. He was with his father during Christmas vacation.*]

We dress in our best clothes. I comb the braids out of my head and made my hair neat, as if it have beeswax on it. Billie slick up, too.

Right at 3 o'clock sharp we reach the steps up to the door of that hotel. Mistah Abe and Mastah Robert almost run down the steps to meet us. I thought Mastah Robert and Billie was goin' to kiss.

Those two Lincolumns was sure pleasured to see us again. Just smiling and laughing and shaking hands. Like no one was on this earth but the Vances. Just like no white folks was around gapin', like they have never saw the like before.

Right there and then I know, President or no President, nothing would ever change Mistah Abe and Mastah Robert. They would never on this earth ever get the swell head. If being President wouldn't cause it, nothing would.

Well, Mastah Robert put his dear arm 'round Billie's shoulda and say, "We'll go into the lobby and visit. We would have come to your home, but Pa has such a short time to get his business settled here, and see those he must see. Pa thought it best to give you the time it would take going to and from your house."

Mistah Abe took me by the arm like I was the Queen of Sheba and help me up those steps. Everyone in that hotel lobby gape. So Mistah Abe took me to each man and a few woman there, seated in a kind of circle, and introduced me as a very fine colored lady who have lived in the Lincolumn home for two years. I notice he didn't say servant or wash-woman.

Then Mastah Robert stand up and say, "And this is my best friend, Billie Vance."

Mistah Abe ask 'bout my Henry and each one of my younguns. Said he'd just love to see them all, but didn't have the time to do so. I ask him 'bout Willie, Taddie, and de Missy.

He say, "Willie and Taddie coaxed to come along, but Mother, who is the busiest woman this side of Washington, couldn't manage to get them ready, and I suspect she needed them for company."

Several men come up and shook hands with Mistah Abe. Gratslated him. He only say a few words to each, 'til he got through visiting with us. The men what he was there in Danville to see come in.

Some of them have gone out, then come back in like they was anxious for Mistah Abe to be with them. But Mistah Abe was always a poke easy. He told them men to stay right there, he'd be with them shortly.

Then he say to Billie, "Bill, I have only one desire before I go back to Springfield, and that is to hear you sing again." Then he say to the man behind that desk, "Would you mind if Bill is willing, for him to sing for us? According to my opinion, Bill has one of the most beautiful voices God ever gave to anyone."

Billie never was skeered to sing. He got out of that chair in a shake. Billie was always quick about every thing. He didn't wait to hear what Mistah Abe want to hear. He just up and sang a new song he learn since coming to Danville. That was the "Mocking Bird Song" [*Listen to the Mocking Bird*]. And he whistle too, like the bird, all through that song when he wasn't singing the words. You couldn't hear a pin drop, as they say. All those folks just couldn't believe it. They was spell 'boun.

Then he knowed Mistah Abe like "Ah's on mah road to Glory now" [*I'm on My Road to Glory Now*]. Before they quit clapping for the "Mocking Bird," he start singing "Ah's on mah road," making all the jesters, as he learned in church.

When he was done, he quick as a dart sang another song Mistah Abe love. It was a church song. I just cain't recomemba the name, but they all clap, some laugh, and some cry. Mistah Abe and Mastah Robert, too.

Mistah Abe hold up his hand, wipe his eyes, and say, kinda perkin' up, "Am I not right when I said Bill has a most beautiful God-given voice? And I know Bill will use it to glorify God, and set all he meets on the Road to Glory Now. But maybe we're all on our road to glory. God grant this scourge will pass away" [*obviously meaning slavery and secession*].

From that on, Billie was call to sing 'most anywhere.

Mistah Abe give Billie some money. I don't recomemba how much. He give me a basket of fruit and a bag of candy, and from his grip what he open, he have toys and presents for all [*Mariah's children*].

He and Mastah Robert shook our hands, even held our hands, and both them and we cried. I just couldn't help, 'cause I knowed deep down, Mistah Abe was going out into this wicked country to be crucified as Christ was, for the colored folks to be free.

After that meeting, from that on, I have all the work from the rich and fine folks I could do. That was the very last time I saw Mistah Abe.

'Bout going to Washin'ton, I never did go, but my Ellen, her go, for to get Mistah Abe to let her man come home. Her didn't want to see Missus Lincolumn. My Ellen was always skeered of de Missy. So de Missy couldn't have refuse to see Ellen or me, 'cause I wasn't there. But I bet her would a want to see me, have I been there.

As afore, ah's tole you, Mastah Robert allus come to see us'n, when in Danville. You'n know, peoples will tell da Gawd-awfulles' lies 'bout dose poor Lincolumns.

[*Billie Vance must have known "Listen to the Mocking Bird" was one of Abraham Lincoln's favorite songs. It was based upon a poem by Septimus Winner, who also wrote music for it. The song was published in 1856 under the pseudonym "Alice Hawthorne." He credited the song's cheerful tune to a little African-American boy, Richard Milburn, whom he had heard whistling it.*

The song was very popular during the Civil War, and people danced to it on the White House lawn when news came of Lee's surrender. It continued to be popular throughout the nineteenth century.

The song seemed to have special meaning to Abraham Lincoln. The "Hallie" in the verse may have reminded him of his beloved stepmother, whose pet name was Sally. Or it may have been a hymn to the life he was leaving when he moved to Washington, reminding him of his carefree boyhood days along Knob Creek, Kentucky, where he roamed the woods barefoot, and of the loss of his loved ones buried there and on other knobs and under other trees.]

LISTEN TO THE MOCKING BIRD

I'm dreaming now of Hallie, sweet Hallie, sweet Hallie,
I'm dreaming now of Hallie,
For the thought of her is one that never dies.
She's sleeping in the valley, the valley, the valley,
She's sleeping in the valley,
And the mocking bird is singing where she lies.

Listen to the mocking bird, Listen to the mocking bird,
The mocking bird is singing o'er her grave;
Listen to the mocking bird, Listen to the mocking bird,
Still singing where the weeping willows wave.

Ah! well I yet remember, remember, remember,
Ah! well I yet remember,
When we gathered in the cotton side by side.
'Twas in the mild September, September, September,
'Twas in the mild September,
And the mocking bird is singing far and wide.

Listen to the mocking bird, Listen to the mocking bird,
The mocking bird is singing o'er her grave;
Listen to the mocking bird, Listen to the mocking bird,
Still singing where the weeping willows wave.

AFTERWORD

The Way It Was

BY WALTER OLEKSY

LINCOLN MADE A FAREWELL VISIT ON JANUARY 31, 1861, TO HIS STEPMOTHER, Sarah, then living with her daughter, Mrs. Matilda Johnston Hall Moore, in Charleston, Illinois. Four days later, the Confederate States of America was formed, after South Carolina, Georgia, Florida, Alabama, Louisiana, and Mississippi seceded from the Union. Jefferson Davis was then elected President of the Confederacy.

A cold drizzle fell over Springfield on the morning of February 11, when President-elect Lincoln and his seventeen-year-old son, Robert, reached the Great Northern Railway station to catch the eight o'clock train to Washington. A thousand well-wishers gathered to say goodbye and bid good luck to their neighbor. Fear of a plot on Lincoln's life had prompted Mary and the two younger boys, ten-year-old Willie, and eight-year-old Tad, to take a later train that evening.

Standing on the platform of his special car hitched to the train, Lincoln removed his hat and spoke these words:

"My friends, no one, not in my situation, can appreciate my feeling of sadness at this parting. To this place, and the kindness of these people I owe everything. Here I have lived a quarter of a century, and have passed from a young to an old man. Here my children have been born, and one is buried. I now leave, not knowing when, or whether ever, I may return, with a task before me greater than that which rested upon Washington.

"Without the assistance of that Divine Being who ever attended him, I cannot succeed. With that assistance I cannot fail. Trusting in Him who can go with me, and remain with you and be everywhere for good, let us confidently hope that all will yet be well. To His care commending you, as I hope in your prayers you will commend me, I bid you an affectionate farewell."

Carl Sandburg wrote in *Abraham Lincoln, The Prairie Years*: "Bells rang, there was a grinding of wheels, and the train moved, and carried Lincoln away from Springfield. The tears were not yet dry on some faces when the train had faded into the gray to the east."

Some said Lincoln shed tears too, but one said, "He had a face with dry tears. He was a man who often had dry tears."

Sandburg also wrote: "A queer dream or illusion had haunted Lincoln at times through the winter [*of 1860*]. On the evening of his election, he had thrown himself on one of the haircloth sofas at home, just after the first telegrams of November 6 had told him he was elected President, and looking into a bureau mirror across the room he saw himself full-length, but with two faces.

"It bothered him; he got up; the illusion vanished; but when he lay down again there in the glass again were two faces, one paler than the other. He got up again, mixed in the election excitement, forgot about it; but it came back, and haunted him. He told his wife about it; she worried too.

"A few days later he tried it once more and the illusion of the two faces again registered to his eyes. But that was the last; the ghost since then wouldn't come back, he told his wife, who said it was a sign he would be elected to a second term, and the death pallor of one face meant he wouldn't live through his second term."

The night before leaving Springfield, Lincoln sat in his office with William Herndon and reminisced about their sixteen-year partnership. As they parted, Lincoln looked up at the "Lincoln & Herndon" sign over the door outside.

"Let it hang there undisturbed," he said. "Give our clients to understand that the election of a President makes no change in the firm of Lincoln and Herndon. If I live I'm coming back some time, and then we'll go right on practicing law as if nothing had ever happened." The two shook hands.

Lincoln was inaugurated the sixteenth President of the United States on March 4, 1861.

The Civil War began on April 12, 1861, when Fort Sumter, South Carolina, was attacked by the Confederacy.

Willie, the Lincolns' third son, died in the White House on February 20, 1862, at the age of twelve.

Lee surrendered to Grant at Appomattox Court House, Virginia, on April 9, 1865. The Civil War, the bloodiest war in American history, was over.

Five days later, Lincoln was shot by actor John Wilkes Booth in Ford's Theater. The next day, April 15, 1865, the President was dead.

After services in the White House and the rotunda of the United States Capitol, the Lincoln funeral train, draped in black, wreathed with flowers, and bearing his portrait, carried his body sixteen hundred miles from Washington to Springfield so citizens could pay their respects. Crowds gathered at cities and towns along the route to weep for the man who had saved the Union.

Mariah Vance did not see the funeral train, but Adah Sutton said that her mother saw it during one of its stops in Indiana. The train reached Springfield on May 3, 1865, and Lincoln was buried on the following day in Oak Ridge Cemetery.

On July 15, 1871, Lincoln's youngest son, Tad, died in Chicago at the age of eighteen. Only Lincoln's widow and eldest son, Robert, survived him.

During the Civil War, Robert Lincoln served on General Ulysses S. Grant's staff. After the war he studied law, and like his father became a corporation lawyer, chiefly serving railroad interests. He was Secretary of War (1881-1885) and then Minister to Great Britain (1889-1893). He went back to private life and became president of the Pullman Company (1897-1911). He never ran for public office.

Robert Lincoln told of an unusual incident in his life to Dr. Charles A. Moore, head of the manuscript department of the Library of Congress. He said: "During the Civil War, I was a student at Harvard, and on a holiday, while waiting for an assignment of a berth on a train at Jersey City, I was leaning against a car when suddenly it started and I was thrown off balance. Just when I was about to fall under the moving train, a strange man grabbed me and pulled me on the train. I discovered soon afterward that my rescuer was Edwin Booth. It certainly was a strange coincidence in view of later events." [*John Wilkes Booth, brother of Edwin, later assassinated Robert's father.*]

Robert was not present at his father's assassination. He had been home from college and invited to join his parents at Ford's Theatre, but declined. Later he said he regretted it all his life.

By coincidence, however, he witnessed the fatal shooting of two other Presidents. He was in the Washington railroad station on July 2, 1881, to witness the killing of President James A. Garfield. He was also nearby when an assassin fired two bullets that killed President William McKinley at the Pan-American Exposition at Buffalo, New York, on September 6, 1901.

Robert refused to capitalize on his father's name. According to historian Mark E. Neely Jr., in addition to having a repugnance for public life, he never desired public office.

In 1868, Robert Lincoln married Mary Harlan, daughter of Senator James Harlan of Iowa, but it was a difficult marriage. She was both reclusive and neurasthenic (someone suffering from nervous debility and exhaustion from overwork or prolonged mental strain).

After retiring from the Pullman Company in Chicago in 1911 on account of his health, Robert moved to Washington, D.C., where he remained almost unknown. At a summer home, "Hildene" at Manchester, Vermont, he found seclusion and enjoyed playing golf. He also was an amateur astronomer and enjoyed solving algebraic problems.

Robert Lincoln lived long enough to attend the dedication of the Lincoln Memorial in Washington in 1922. He died four years later on July 26, 1926, at the age of eighty-three and was buried in Arlington National Cemetery.

Mary Harlan Lincoln's life was a long but unhappy one. Born in 1847, she died in 1937 at the age of ninety.

Robert and Mary Harlan Lincoln had three children. Their first-born was a daughter, Mary Lincoln, named after her grandmother but nicknamed "Mamie," born in 1869. She married Charles Isham in 1891 and they had one child, a son, Lincoln Isham, who was born in 1892 and died in 1971 without having any children.

The Robert Lincolns' second child, Abraham Lincoln II, nicknamed "Jack," was born in 1873. He died in 1890 of blood poisoning from an infected carbuncle at the age of seventeen.

The third child, Jessie, was born in 1875. Her father disapproved of her choice of husband, a college football player name Warren Beckwith, so she eloped with him in 1897. They had two children. A daughter, Mary Lincoln Beckwith, nicknamed "Peggie," was born in 1898 and died in 1975 without having married. A son, Robert Todd Lincoln Beckwith, born in 1904, was married several times but had no children. When he died on Christmas Eve, 1985, the Lincoln line died out with him.

Abraham Lincoln's papers, mostly letters and speeches, remained in Robert Lincoln's possession until near the end of his life, when he deposited them in the Library of Congress to be sealed for twenty-one years after his death. The papers were opened on July 26, 1947, before a group of Lincoln scholars but the event was anticlimactic. "It was a scholar's collection," says Neely. "There was no scent of [*scandal*] in the papers. Scholars have since put the papers to good use, but the collection is far from exhausted."

The Robert Lincolns owned three homes. The one in Chicago has been converted into a parking lot. The second, in Washington, D.C., is now owned by the Ben Bradlees. Bradlee is famous as the former editor of the *Washington Post* and his role in uncovering the Watergate scandal. His wife, Sally Ann Quinn, is a well-known writer and author.

The third home, a 24-room Georgian mansion, is located in Manchester, Vermont. It is registered as an Historic Home and tours of the house and grounds are conducted from mid-May to October 31. The home is run by a Board of Trustees and the curator is Albert Jerman.

Mary Todd Lincoln had a long history of mental instability. Tad's death apparently unsettled her mind, already affected by the shock of witnessing Lincoln's assassination.

To help his mother get proper treatment, Robert made an attempt to have her put into a mental hospital. He finally succeeded. Ten years after his father's death, he hired Dr. Robert Isham, a physician and father of his law partner, Edward Isham, to testify on his behalf at a hearing to have his mother committed. Dr. Isham told the judge that in his opinion Mary Lincoln was suffering from delusions, was insane and unable to control her own affairs.

On the strength of Dr. Isham's testimony, a jury declared Mary Lincoln to be insane. She was sentenced to an indefinite term in a mental hospital and sent to a private institution at Batavia, Illinois.

During the following year, Mary held a number of press conferences at the hospital, accusing Robert of having her locked up so he could steal her money, and of colluding with other businessmen to steal money from the public through shady deals, none of which was true. In order to keep her quiet, Robert allowed a second hearing. His mother would be declared sane if she agreed not to make false accusations against him. She agreed and was subsequently released.

Mary was to stay with her sister Elizabeth Edwards in Springfield. For a time she traveled abroad and fulfilled a desire to live in France. She later returned to America and again lived with the Edwards family. On July 16, 1882, at the age of sixty-four, Mary Todd Lincoln died in her sister's home, where she and the President had been married. She is buried in the Lincoln Tomb in Springfield with her husband and three of their four sons.

The probate court of Cook County, Illinois, Circuit Court, contains records from Mary Lincoln's commitment trial in 1875. Among the displays for that trial are copies of prescriptions for paregoric that she had filled at pharmacies in downtown Chicago, after the President's death.

Mental illness ran in the Todd family. Elizabeth wrote her nephew Robert Lincoln after the jury committed his mother saying she had never noticed insanity in the family until her daughter Julie was born. She said the girl was so flighty and crazy at times, "we had to keep her locked up." Elizabeth's son Albert later said his daughter Georgia died in an insane asylum.

In 1870, when Mary had a physical examination to justify a request for increased pension funds from Congress, it was learned that she was a diabetic. This may account for the large quantities of sugar she purchased over the years to make candy and cakes.

Addiction to an opium-based drug, the large consumption of caffeine-heavy coffee and tea, and heavy use of sugar no doubt affected her adversely. Spokespersons for the American Medical Association and the American Diabetes Association conclude generously that the combination's effect on Mrs. Lincoln "could not be good."

Paregoric, in small doses, is still prescribed today for people suffering severe cases of diarrhea or infections of the bowel wall. Too much paregoric can become addictive. Signs of overdose include seizures, confusion, severe nervousness, dizziness, and weakness. Today, patients purchasing paregoric must sign a narcotics registry book.

Mary Lincoln was probably a diabetic years before the doctors discovered it. Left untreated, her emotional condition indicates she may have been suffering from hypoglycemia. Hypoglycemic diabetics have been mistaken for intoxicated people because of clouded consciousness, slurred speech, and abusive behavior.

Mary Lincoln was an unwitting victim of the side-effects of stimulants and relaxants. When not ailing from an overdose of paregoric, she may have been sick or ill-tempered because of drug withdrawal, a malady unknown at the time.

Lincoln, the children, and Mariah Vance suffered because of Mary's addictions. Lincoln suspected there was a link between paregoric and his wife's frequent illnesses and tantrums. But during difficult periods he was obliged to encourage her to take paregoric to settle her down. At other times, he hid or broke the bottles containing the drug but to no avail: Mary was always able to buy more.

While living at the Edwards home after her release from the mental hospital, Mary Lincoln's eccentricities were apparent to Mary Edwards Brown, granddaughter of Elizabeth Edwards. Mrs. Brown remembered that as a teenager she helped take care of her great-aunt Mary. In an interview with Dorothy Meserve Kunhardt, published in *Life* magazine in February 1959, Mrs. Brown, then ninety-three, spoke of the period before Robert had his mother committed: "She did queer things like getting into the elevator in a hotel when she was undressed. She thought it was the lavatory."

According to Mrs. Brown, Mary wrote letters to wealthy men saying she was poor and living in despicable circumstances. In truth, Lincoln had left her a considerable amount of money.

Lincoln frequently invested in real estate during his lawyer years in Springfield. He saved or invested his Presidential salary and left a net estate of $110,296.80 to his widow and two surviving sons. In addition to giving her a gift of $15,000, Congress granted Mrs. Lincoln an annual pension of $3,000 in 1870, which increased to $5,000 in 1882. (Today, the $110,296 would be equivalent to $1,006,260; $5,000 to $72,551; and $15,000 to $217,655).

Mary Lincoln was not correct in saying Ann Rutledge was "common." The Rutledge family, which had come from South Carolina, had members who served in the Revolutionary War and one Rutledge reportedly was a signer of the Declaration of Independence. Others in the family had achieved high position in society, and Ann's father, a Southern gentleman who owned a respectable inn in New Salem, was a prominent landowner, businessman, and a distinguished member of the community.

Mariah Vance tells us that Mary Lincoln was not only jealous of her husband's early love for Ann Rutledge, but also resented the role the young woman had played in getting her husband's legal career started. Historians have noted that Lincoln had a certain amount of ambition, but it wasn't strong enough to have led him to high office. If Ann Rutledge encouraged Abraham Lincoln to become a lawyer, Mary might have taken comfort in knowing it was she who spurred him on to achieve the political heights. But Mary saw herself as the person who molded his success, and she didn't want to share that credit with anyone. Dr. Wayne C. Temple, a Lincoln scholar, says, "Mary would pitch a fit if he even talked to another woman, let alone speak of a former 'lover' or whatever Ann may have been. In Washington, Lincoln would even ask Mary which women at a reception he could talk to!

"Once, he rode his horse at an army review close to a general's young wife and had a casual conversation with her. Mary had a fit, threw a tantrum, and departed back to Washington. She embarrassed President Lincoln to no end over nothing, and did it in public at that."

Lincoln's marriage may not have been perfect, but he wrote his Kentucky friend Joshua Speed that his father used to say, "If you make a bad bargain, hug it all the tighter."

Two of Mary Lincoln's biographers, Ruth Painter Randall and Jean H. Baker, do not believe the Abraham Lincoln–Ann Rutledge romance. They criticized William Herndon and said he told of the romance only because he and Mary Lincoln disliked each other, and he knew it would infuriate her.

Without witnesses to substantiate Herndon's claims, Mary's biographers didn't believe his story of the New Salem romance. However, they did not know of Mariah Vance's reports or what Mary told her or what she overheard the Lincolns say to each other regarding Miss Rutledge.

Lloyd Ostendorf and other historians have done some further research and have produced additional evidence to support Mariah's contention that the Lincoln-Rutledge romance was, in fact, real. Several significant writings from people of the times are herein quoted.

Dr. William Jayne published his personal reminiscences in 1907 of "facts which were known to him" as a personal friend of Lincoln's. He wrote: "Whenever Mrs. Hill of New Salem heard any remarks about Lincoln and Ann Rutledge, she would tell of her recollections at a quilting bee at Salem. Lincoln was sitting next to Ann, as the girl was industriously using her [*knitting or sewing*] needle, Abraham was softly whispering in her ear, and Mrs. Hill was wont to say [*of*] Ann, 'her heart throbbed quicker and her soul thrilled with a joy as old as the world itself.'"

Harvey Lee Ross was a close personal friend of young Abraham Lincoln. Ross had the mail run in the area and regularly brought the mail to New Salem. He came to know Lincoln on his frequent visits to the New Salem Post Office when Lincoln was postmaster in the village. Ross and Lincoln also ate at the same table and slept in the same loft of the Rutledge Tavern.

In his recollections printed in the weekly *Fulton Democrat* at Lewiston, Illinois, in 1896, Ross wrote:

> There are probably few men now living who knew Mr. Lincoln better than I did in the days of his obscurity. . . . I put up at the log tavern where Mr. Lincoln boarded, and we partook of the corn-bread, bacon and eggs which were our common fare, at the same table.
>
> The Rutledge tavern was a hewed log house, two stories high, with four rooms above and four below. It had two chimneys with large fireplaces and not a stove in the house.
>
> The proprietor was James Rutledge, a man of more than ordinary ability, and, with his wife, remarkably kind and hospitable. They had a large family of eight or nine children, and among them was their daughter, Ann, celebrated in song and story as Lincoln's sweetheart.
>
> She was two or three years younger than Lincoln, of about medium size, weighing some 125 pounds. She was very handsome and attractive, as well as industrious and sweet-spirited. I seldom saw her when she was not engaged in some occupation —knitting, sewing, waiting on table, etc. I think she did the sewing for the entire family.
>
> Lincoln was boarding at the tavern and fell deeply in love with Ann, and she was no less in love with him. They were engaged to be married, but they had been putting off the wed-

ding for a while, as he wanted to accumulate a little more property and she wanted to go longer to school.

Before the time came when they were to be married, Miss Ann was taken down with typhoid fever and lay desperately ill. Lincoln was an anxious and constant watcher at her bedside. The sickness ended in her death, and young Lincoln was heartbroken and prostrated.

The histories have not exaggerated his pitiful grief. For many days he was not able to attend to business. I believe his very soul was wrapped up in that lovely girl. It was his first love —the holiest thing in life—the love that cannot die.

The deepest gloom and melancholy settled over his mind.

He would often say to his friends: "My heart is buried in the grave with that dear girl." He would often go and sit by her grave and read a little pocket testament he carried with him. . . .

One stormy winter's night he was at a friend's house, and as the sleet and rain came down on the roof, he sat with bowed head and the tears trickled down his face. His friend begged him to control his sorrow.

"I cannot," he moaned, "while the storm and darkness are on her grave." His friends did everything that kindness could suggest, but in vain, to soothe his sorrow.

Since the Lincoln-Rutledge romance plays such a significant part in the Mariah Vance reminiscences, we include Rutledge family correspondence that strongly supports her testimony on this matter.

Mary Lincoln scholars who downplayed the romance seemed to have overlooked the fact that Ann Rutledge's mother lived to the age of ninety-one, and if anyone knew firsthand of her daughter's romantic emotions, her mother would. She spoke often about the Lincoln-Rutledge romance with members of her family, unaware that any controversy about it would arise later.

Ann's cousin and playmate, McGrady Rutledge, is quoted as saying that he "always insisted that theirs was a genuine love affair upon Ann's part as well as Lincoln's."

From two grandsons of Ann Rutledge's mother, Mary Ann Miller Rutledge (1781–1878), come little-known testimonials to justify belief in the romance. They are in the form of letters written in 1929 by A. M. Prewitt and

Will S. Prewitt to an Albany, New York, collector of Lincoln memorabilia, John E. Boos.

A. M. Prewitt said his mother, Nancy Rutledge Prewitt, "was fourteen years old at the time of Ann's death in 1835 and she distinctly remembered the courtship. She remembered the look of inexpressible sadness on Mr. Lincoln's face as he stood in the door looking at the dying girl he loved so tenderly. This was at the close of some two hours at her bedside." (From a letter signed by A. M. Prewitt, dated January 14, 1929.)

Another grandson, Will S. Prewitt, also wrote to John Boos in 1929 that he was a cousin of Edward J. Rutledge, and told of the love between Lincoln and Miss Rutledge:

> In reply to your letter of February 1, 1929: Mary Ann Rutledge, mother of Ann Rutledge, was my maternal grandmother. She lived in our home and the home of my uncle John Rutledge from my earliest recollection, dividing her time, and died in our home December 26, 1878, in Birmingham, Iowa.
>
> Scores of times I have heard her tell of the engagement between Lincoln and her daughter Ann. Had I not been in such a hurry usually to get out and coast from the edge of our porch over the top of the yard fence, down the hill to the "branch," I might have acquired information and made a record of it which would now be very valuable for historical purposes.

Mentor Graham, a teacher in New Salem, is quoted as saying: "Lincoln and she were engaged. Lincoln told me so. She intimated to me the same."

One of the most respected historians, Dr. John Y. Simon, professor of history at Southern Illinois University–Carbondale, wrote a convincing address in 1988 in support of the Lincoln-Rutledge romance. His paper concluded: "Ann Rutledge. . . . simply will not go away. Available evidence overwhelmingly indicates that Lincoln so loved Ann that her death plunged him into morbid depression. More than a century and a half after her death, when significant new evidence cannot be expected, she should take her proper place in Lincoln biography."

Dr. William Jayne wrote in 1907:

> Isaac Cogdal tells of his interview with Lincoln. In December 1860, after his election as president, Cogdal called to

see him. He requested his old friend from Salem to wait until his callers from a distance went to their hotels, so that he might inquire about his old friends in Menard County.

All visitors having retired, they both drew their chairs close to the fire. There in the quiet twilight Lincoln inquired after his old Salem friends, their sons and daughters, when and whom they had married and how they had prospered. When he had told Lincoln all, he said, "Mr. Lincoln, I would like to ask you one question." He promptly replied, "Well, Isaac, if it is a fair question, I will answer it."

"What is the truth about you and Ann Rutledge?" Cogdal asked.

Lincoln replied, "Isaac, I dearly loved the girl, and I never to this day hear the name Rutledge called without fond memories of those long past days."

Dr. Wayne Temple tells us that Ann's first suitor, John McNeil, who left New Salem after they became engaged and remained in the East for a long time, did come back. "He returned in 1835, shortly after Ann's death. She and her father died on a farm owned by McNeil. So, they must have been engaged for the Rutledges to move out to a farm owned by McNeil."

Evidence attests that Ann and McNeil had been engaged. Did her feelings toward him change in his long absence? Did she later fall in love with Lincoln?

Mariah Vance's recollections confirm the place Ann Rutledge held in Lincoln's heart, and also the degree of Mary's jealousy of her role in Lincoln's life.

Ruth Painter Randall believed none of it. In her biography of Mary Lincoln she wrote, "Mary had never heard of Ann Rutledge." She quoted from a letter Mary wrote to Judge David Davis, who had administered Lincoln's estate and approved the sanity trial for her, asking him to see Herndon and "direct his wandering mind to the falseness of certain of his statements in his book.": "Each and every one has had a little romance in their early days —but as my husband was truth itself, and as he always assured me, he had cared for no one but myself, I shall assuredly remain firm in my conviction that Ann Rutledge is a myth—for in all his confidential communications, such a romantic name was never breathed."

Mariah Vance reveals the frequency and degree of Mary Lincoln's "irresponsible moments." She explains that they had a great deal to do with Mary's reliance on the drug paregoric. In addition, the editors (Oleksy and Ostendorf) found that purchases from stores in Springfield verify her heavy use of sugar, caffeine, and sometimes brandy.

Mary's excitability was enhanced by these elements. Add to this her obsession to be First Lady, her anger at Stephen Douglas for rejecting her, and her jealousy of the influence Ann Rutledge had on her husband's heart and career, and there are enough reasons for her violent outbursts against Lincoln, her servants, and William Herndon. Herndon may have gotten more of it right than historians have been willing to admit.

The Lincoln marriage may not have been as "happy" as historians have previously believed. Abraham and Mary were opposites in many ways, come together in marriage by a series of circumstances that Mariah reveals in her reminiscences. The match was not perfect, but for their own reasons and in their own sometimes difficult ways, each tried to make their marriage work. They did stay together.

Mariah says Mary told her she "tricked" Lincoln into marrying her, partly on the rebound after being rejected by Stephen Douglas and also because she saw the tall, homely young lawyer and state legislator as Presidential material who could help her realize her dream of being First Lady. According to Mariah, Mary later came to love her husband, but felt he hated her because he knew why she had married him. Mariah tells us also that Lincoln often displayed affection toward Mary.

Elizabeth Keckley, Mary Lincoln's Black dressmaker and closest friend in the White House, held very similar beliefs to Mariah Vance's concerning Mary's relationship with her husband. "Madam Elizabeth," as President Lincoln called her, wrote in 1868 about their marriage rifts:

"We are indifferent to those we do not love, and certainly the President was not indifferent to his wife. She often wounded him in unguarded moments, but calm reflection never failed to bring regret."

Lincoln is quoted as once saying he had "a tendency to melancholy," but added, "Let it be observed [*melancholy*] is a misfortune, not a fault."

Lincoln's profound depression once led him to attempt suicide with a knife. He was careful to wield it in the presence of people who would take it away from him.

Lincoln tended to live on his day-to-day human contacts. He loved to laugh and indulge in humorous stories, turning to humor and work to lift his spirits. "In case my mind were not exactly right," he told Joshua Speed, "I would immediately engage in some business."

Some Lincoln writers say his tendency toward depression and occasional preoccupation with death was fatalism, a doctrine to which he was attracted at various times. In 1864 he said, "I claim not to have controlled events, but confess plainly that events have controlled me."

Concerns regarding his dreams also persisted throughout his life. He wrote Mary in 1863, "Think you better put Tad's pistol away. I had an ugly dream about him." At times before receiving good news from his generals during the Civil War, he had a recurring dream of sailing on a ship near mysterious shores.

It has been reported here previously that he had the same dream the night before his son Willie died and again the night before his assassination. Also, shortly before his assassination he described a dream in which he saw his own corpse laid out in the White House.

Outside of occasional colds or flu, Lincoln's health was generally good. He escaped serious illness except for a mild form of smallpox after returning from delivering the Gettysburg Address on November 19, 1863. He did not smoke and seldom drank alcoholic beverages, although a physician prescribed wine or champagne for him at the White House. He did not chew tobacco and did everything in moderation, including eating.

When he was President, witnesses claimed he could still chop wood vigorously and occasionally enjoyed showing off his skill with an ax. He would also demonstrate arm strength by gripping the end of an ax helve and holding it out at arm's length. After his death, observers said his body had not an ounce of fat. He was all bone, muscle, and sinew.

Despite this, some doctors have suggested that Lincoln may have suffered from Marfan's syndrome, an inherited disorder. Symptoms include long thin extremities, high arched palate, chest and spine deformities, poor muscle tone, and deformed ears.

Jerold M. Lowenstein, professor of medicine at the University of California at San Francisco, wrote in *Discover* magazine in 1991: "What would Lincoln himself, the most humorous as well as the greatest of all our presidents, make of all the fuss? [*of efforts to study his DNA to determine if he had Marfan's syndrome.*] He would no doubt smile to think that people in the 1990s are as keen to find his hereditary defects as people in the 1860s were to find his political ones. The thought that a meddlesome yet worshipful posterity wants him back, a mere six score and six years after his death, might get a genuine laugh."

Regarding Adah Sutton's original handwritten manuscript recording Mariah Vance's reminiscences, she wrote three drafts of the first chapter and two drafts of about half of the remaining chapters. They are almost identical and all were transcribed from her original notes. A combination of all her drafts is included in this book.

I found that comparing the drafts was essential in preparing this manuscript, from the standpoints of accuracy and completeness. Occasionally, I could not read some words in a particular chapter but found them more clearly written in Miss Sutton's second draft.

A few Lincoln scholars who doubt the credibility of some parts of Mariah Vance's oral history nevertheless say it reads like a Prairie *Upstairs, Downstairs* and that some historians, "will consider them to be the Lincoln *Dead Sea Scrolls.*"

To those who may question the authenticity of Mariah Vance's oral history of the Lincolns as recorded by Adah Sutton, the answer may be found in James Agee's book, *Let Us Now Praise Famous Men.*

He stated that the storyteller and the person taking down the stories share a special kind of communication that leans toward reporting the truth. Together, they arrive at "the way it was."

It was an honor to be part of this historic project.

Mariah Vance is seen carrying her twelfth and last child in this 1864 tintype. Seated at her right is daughter Julia Vance Patterson, age 16, wearing her first long dress.

Below is a copy of the marriage certificate of Henry Vance and Mariah Bartlett dated January 20, 1842. Mariah was 23 years old.

STATE OF ILLINOIS ⎱ ss.
County of Sangamon ⎰

I, Maralee I. Lindley, Clerk of said County, in the State aforesaid, do hereby certify the foregoing to be a true, perfect and complete copy of

Marriage of Henry Vance and Mariah Bartlett

IN TESTIMONY WHEREOF, I have hereunto set my hand and affixed the seal of said County, at my office in Springfield, this *18th* day of *August* A.D. 19 *92*

Maralee I. Lindley Clerk.

Co. Clk. Form No. 48

This daguerreotype of Abraham Lincoln was taken in 1846, four years before Mariah Vance started working at the Lincoln home in Springfield, Illinois. Original photo in the Library of Congress.

Mary Todd Lincoln was an excellent seamstress who frequently made her own clothes. In this 1846 photograph, in a beautiful dress ostensibly made by her, she comes off as a young, vital and attractive housewife. Original photo in the Library of Congress.

Top l., Thomas, Abraham Lincoln's father, as he appeared in 1850. *Top r.,* idealized painting of Nancy Hanks Lincoln as she may have appeared in 1817. Hanks family commissioned Lloyd Ostendorf to paint portrait; it is displayed in the Lincoln Boyhood National Park, Lincoln City, Indiana. *Right,* Lincoln's beloved stepmother, Sarah Bush Lincoln died in 1869.

Top, 1836 painting of Mary's father, Robert S. Todd. Print courtesy William H. Townsend collection, Lexington, KY. *Top l.,* Emilie Todd, Mary's favorite sister, taken in Springfield in 1855. *Top r.,* Mary Lincoln's eldest sister, Elisabeth Todd Edwards. The original is in Illinois State Historical Society.

Dr. Wm. Wallace, husband of Frances Todd, Mary Lincoln's sister, shown in Civil War uniform of medical officer. *Above,* Ninian W. Edwards, nicknamed "Uncle Ninie," husband of Elisabeth Todd Edwards, Mrs. Lincoln's sister. *Rt.,* tintype of Frances Todd Wallace.

Previously unpublished 1859 photo of Stephen A. Douglas, the "little giant," the Democratic Party's nominee for president.

An 1859 photo of Abraham Lincoln, the first standard bearer of the newly formed Republican party. A year later he was president.

Above left, William H. Herndon who was Mayor of Springfield, IL, 1854-55 after he had been Lincoln's law partner and subsequently his biographer. Lincoln said, "Billie wants to be my man Friday. He is a bad enough friend at times, I can't afford to make an enemy of him." *Above right,* heretofore unpublished photograph of an older Herndon in 1871.

Left, tintype of Ann Rutledge look-alike. This photo of an unknown young girl Lincoln bought in a shop while riding the circuit. He told Mary it reminded him of his New Salem girlfriend who had been a great inspiration to him.

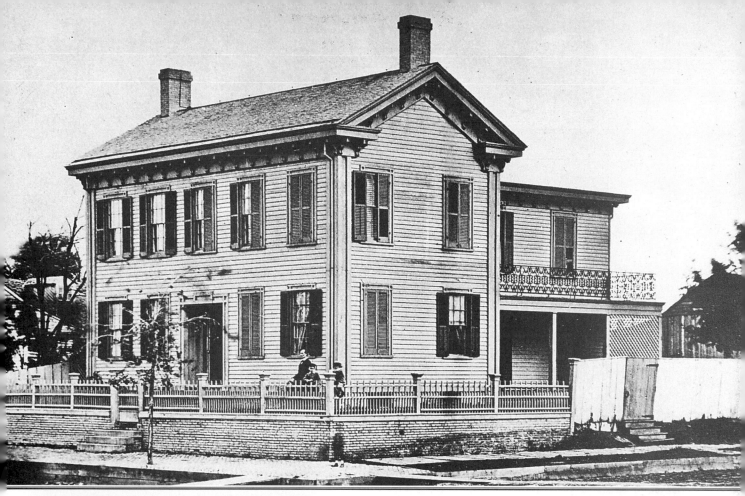

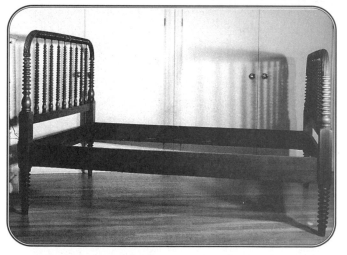

Top, picture of Lincoln and sons Willie and Tad in front of Springfield home. *Left*, Mary Lincoln, Willie and Tad on way to Washington. *Right*, golden walnut spool bed Mariah saved from Lincoln home.

Right, previously unpublished photo of Lincoln's eldest son, Robert, 1858. *Below, left,* ambrotype of Thomas "Tad" Lincoln, photographed about 1859. *Below, right,* previously unpublished photo of William Wallace Lincoln.

Opposite: Top left, cabinet photo of Robert Lincoln. *Far right,* his daughter Mary, *Below, left,* son Abe Lincoln II, *Below, right,* son Abe "Jack" Lincoln whose untimely death in 1890 ended direct male line of Lincoln family.

ROARING RALLY

WEEKLY NEWS.

DANVILLE, ILL., - NOV. 5, 1896

W. R. JEWELL, EDITOR

THOUSANDS OF CHEERING REPUBLICANS.

The Largest Procession That Ever Moved Through the Streets of Danville.

The rain of the night of the 29th created fear of a gloomy wet day for the grand republican rally in this city. The morning opened cloudy, but cooler and sharp southwest wind. The city was soon gaily decorated with national colors and gold and the people began to pour in early from all directions and by 10 a. m the streets were crowded and the ruil badges shone everywhere.

Lincoln Arrives.

At 10:30 a. m. Mr. Lincoln and Out I Carr arrived off the Cairo division of the Big Four, and were met by Hon. J. G. Cannon and other members of the reception committee and conducted to the Ætna house

---

The Poetone Glee club is a hummer. Our people cheered them until the people got hoarse. Come again, boys.

The popocratic committee took advantage of a republican crowd to throw their literature into vehicles. Most of it was promptly thrown out.

HON. ROBERT T. LINCOLN.

Our citizens were very much gratified with the visit of Hon. Robert T. Lincoln, and many of them had the pleasure of shaking his hand. The deep love and tender veneration for his father, who practiced law at the Danville bar, inclined them to love and want to see his son.

Now they love the son for his own sake. Mr. Lincoln in physique does not remind one of his father. But his modest, retiring manner is much like that of his father; also his keen sense of humor; he relishes a good joke or story and tells them well, as those know who were with him here. The following which he told is as good as the best:

Excerpts of Danville Weekly News of November 6, 1896 which heralds presence and speech of Hon. Robert T. Lincoln, at a Republican rally. Before speech he took the time to visit his beloved Mariah Vance.

President Warren Harding, Robert Todd Lincoln and Speaker of the House Joseph G. Cannon at dedication of the Lincoln Memorial in Washington, D.C. in 1922. Photo courtesy of Vermilion County Museum Society of Danville, IL.

Robert Lincoln Misunderstood, Cannon Asserts

Viewed by Some as 'Sort of Hermit' Because He Avoided Notice and Abhorred Politics

Pays Tribute to Ability

Efficient as Cabinet Member, Lovable as a Man, Former Speaker Found

Special to the Herald Tribune

DANVILLE, Ill., July 26.—"Uncle Joe" Cannon, former Speaker of the House of Representatives, had not heard of the death of Robert Todd Lincoln, until this evening, when he was asked for an expression.

"Mr. Lincoln's death removes one of the most misunderstood citizens of the country," he said. "The public, I do not suppose, ever will come to regard the man at his true worth. His position in the world was unique because of his birth. Able, well educated and trained for his life work, he was constantly under the shadow of the great immortal Lincoln. Despite his handicap in life of being the son of a great man he made enviable places in politics, which, however, he abhorred in his later years; in diplomacy and as the directing head of one of America's big industries. But the fact that he was the son of Lincoln was always mentioned about him sooner or later.

"I first met Mr. Lincoln in Washington shortly after I was elected to Congress in the fall of 1872 and while he was a polished gentleman and wholly different in views, actions and physique from his father. I got the early impression of him that thousands of others had. Later, as I learned him, I loved him. He was intensely patriotic and accepted political posts at great sacrifices to his fortune, which in those days was not any too great. As Secretary of War under Garfield and Arthur, at which time I was the head of the Appropriations Committee, I found that he was extremely efficient and well informed upon the affairs and his duties as a Cabinet officer.

"Mr. Lincoln has been accused of being a sort of hermit and was very little seen in public in later years, but this was because of his abhorrence of things political, and the fact that he was being eternally pointed out as 'Abe Lincoln's son.' Mr. Lincoln shortly after his election to the head of the Pullman Palace Car Company, after the death of its founder in 1897, was prevailed upon to make political speeches in the campaign of 1900, the year McKinley and Roosevelt were candidates. It required a lot of persuasion to get him to come out into public and only when it was shown that the success of the Republican party was not assured did he consent.

"One of the few speeches that he made was in my home town. An incident that illustrates the private side of the man came up there. It was the last and biggest rally of the year, the climax of the campaign. Mr. Lincoln arrived as quietly and unostentatiously as he could during the morning hours and registered at one of the leading hotels. A reception was started and then because of complaining of being fatigued, Mr. Lincoln was excused. Several hours afterward when we thought he had rested long enough we sent to his room. The door was locked. No one responded to repeated knocks of the bell boy. Half-fright-ened, we went to the room fearing that something had befallen him. A chambermaid soon opened the door, but the room was empty. Lincoln's baggage was there, however, and we started to hunt for him but without avail.

"Then we did what few Republicans are supposed to do—we consulted a Democratic editor. He was born in Springfield and was quite a bit of a boy before the Lincolns left there for Washington. He had not seen him but he put us wise, and we soon found him. Lincoln, the orator of the day, was found in the north part of the city at the home of an aged negress, Mrs. Maria Vance, enjoying one of the finest meals of corn pone and bacon you ever tasted.

"Mrs. Vance had been cook before the war in the Lincoln household at Springfield and nurse part of the time for young Robert Todd. Lincoln had heard that the woman was still living there and hunted her up. They had spent several hours together. We hustled him away and to the park, where a great and impatient crowd awaited him. No sooner was his task over than Lincoln returned to the Vance home, humble as it was, and enjoyed more hours of talk with the aged woman, until it was near departure time of his train. That was the last political speech he ever delivered. From that day until her death 'Mammy' Vance received a substantial check each month from Chicago."

An interview with former Speaker of the House, Joe Cannon, to pay tribute to Robert Lincoln upon his death in 1926 mentions Mariah Vance in the third column.

SATURDAY, DECEMBER 24, 1904. THREE EDITIONS DAILY. PRICE TWO CENT

DEATH CLAIMS MARIAH VANCE

AGED COLORED WOMAN YIELDS TO PARALYSIS AFTER A WEEK'S SUFFERING.

LIVED IN LINCOLN'S FAMILY

Deceased Was More Than 105 Years Of Age And Known To Many In This Community.

Mariah Vance, the aged colored woman so well known to many in the city and who was the oldest colored woman in the county and perhaps in the state, is dead at the home of her son, Cornelius Vance, North Robinson street. The summons came yesterday afternoon about 4 o'clock. The three children who survive were at her bed-side. Deceased was 106 years of age.

The condition of Mrs. Vance has been serious since she suffered the stroke of paralysis a week ago. After that she was entirely helpless as to her left side and though every possible care was given her she grew weaker steadily until she passed away.

Mrs. Vance was born in slavery and her early life was of course spent in the south. After the war she came north and for years was in the family of Abraham Lincoln. She came to Danville about forty years ago and from then to the time of her death lived in this city. In all her life it is said she never suffered a severe illness until the one that resulted in her death. It will be recalled that when death. It will be recalled that when Mrs. Vance was 90 years of age she began to learn reading and regardless of her age accomplished the task.

No colored woman in Danville was so widely known as the deceased and not one held in higher regard She was a good woman and faithful member of the colored Baptist church Mrs. Vance will be missed by many in this city.

She is survived by three children John, Cornelius and Rosa. The funeral arrangements have not been made.

Top left, pencil portrait of Mariah Vance by Lloyd Ostendorf drawn in 1956 based on description by Adah Sutton. *Top right,* tombstone, erected by Ward Hill Lamon Civil War Round Table marks Mariah Vance grave in Danville. *Above,* Lloyd Ostendorf puts flowers on grave Aug. 12, 1964.

Left, the Danville Commercial News, Dec. 24, 1904, features front page story on the death of Mariah Vance.

Far left, photo of Mariah Vance's eldest daughter, Ellen, circa 1861. She learned to read as a child watching Robert Lincoln teach Billie Vance. *Left,* Julia Vance Patterson, the only one of Mariah Vance's children Adah Sutton met during interviews. *Below,* Federal Census 1850 and 1860 of Sangamon County, Illinois, showing the presence of the Vance family.

1850 Population Census

and

1850 Mortality Schedule

SANGAMON COUNTY, ILLINOIS

368/378
VANCE, Henry   33 M (B) Oh
  Maria   28 F (B) Il
  Wm.   8 M (B) Il
  Ellen   7 F (B) Il
  Catharine   6 F (B) Il
  Phebe   4 F (B) Il
  Julia   9/12 F (B) Il

FERERAL CENSUS 1860

of

SANGAMON COUNTY, ILLINOIS

4??/45?
  Henry Vance   53 " B   Laborer
  Maria   "   35 F "
  William   "   18 M "   Laborer
  Ellen   "   16 F "

           Date 31 June   Page No. 67
  Catherine Vance   14 F B
  Julia   "   10 " "
  Narcissa   "   8 " "
  Rosa   "   5 " "

  John Vance   4 M B
  Cornelius "   3 " "
  Walter   "   4/12 " "
478/458
  Polly Thomas   60 F M
  Dinah Posey   89 " "
479/459

A page out of the Literary Digest story on Aug. 14, 1926 which pays tribute to Robert Lincoln. It repeats story of his visit to Mariah Vance in Danville in 1896.

great statues of him made by Augustus Saint Gaudens and that which I have good reason to expect in the Lincoln Memorial, now being modeled by Daniel Chester French. That my father should be represented in those two great cities by such a work as that of which I am writing to you would be a cause of sorrow to me personally, the greatness of which I will not attempt to describe."

The Lincoln Memorial in Washington, reports Mr. White, was a crowning joy to Robert T. Lincoln. A resident of Washington during cold weather, he watched each step of the progress in the building of the memorial. Former Representative John Dwight, of Tompkins County, New York, was the Republican House whip while the enabling legislation was under way, and, continues the report:

When the appropriation finally was passed under the energetic management of Mr. Dwight, Mr. Lincoln called on him one day and, handing him a manuscript, said that it was the original of President Lincoln's address to the great throng which greeted him on the night of his second election in 1864. "I know of no one more entitled to some memento of my father than yourself," he said. Mr. Dwight was taken utterly by surprize. He since has kept the manuscript in a safe-deposit box.

Robert Lincoln's sense of respect for his own was shown when he caused a headstone to be erected over the grave of his grandfather, Thomas Lincoln, a mile and a half west of the village of Farmington, Illinois.

When the citizens of Springfield moved to make the Lincoln house in Springfield a national shrine Robert T. Lincoln aided in every way he could.

He had an easier start in life than his illustrious father, who left an estate of about $110,000 to be divided among Robert, his mother, Mary Todd Lincoln, and his younger brother, Tad.

President Lincoln gave his son Robert a sharp lesson in political amenities. Col. H. C. Huidekoper, who was in Harvard during the early part of the Civil War and who knew Robert Lincoln while a student there, tells of a fight for the Cambridge post-office in which the friends of a particular candidate succeeded in interesting more or less the President's son. At the earnest solicitation of these friends Robert wrote a letter to his father, who replied:

"If you do not attend to your studies and let matters such as you write about alone I will take you away from college."

Robert wisely preserved this letter and made good use of it. When after that any one attempted to secure his influence in favor of any candidate, Robert produced the letter and it proved to be an effective protection.

"Mr. Lincoln's death removes one of the most misunderstood citizens of the country," says "Uncle Joe" Cannon, former Speaker of the House of Representatives, as quoted in a dispatch from Danville, Illinois, to the New York *Herald Tribune*.

"Uncle Joe," a close friend of Mr. Lincoln's for a number of years and now himself over ninety, presents this keen analysis and appreciation:

"Robert Lincoln's position in the world was unique because of his birth. Able, well educated and trained for his life work, he was constantly under the shadow of the great immortal Lincoln. Despite his handicap in life of being the son of a great man he made enviable places in politics, which, however, he abhorred in his later years; in diplomacy and as the directing

International Newsreel photograph

THE COUNTRY GENTLEMAN

After resigning from the presidency of the Pullman Company, Mr. Lincoln divided his time between his country estate in New Hampshire and Washington. He was one of the notable figures of the capital, and a notable golfer at his country home.

from his father, I got the early impression of him that thousands of others had. Later, as I learned him I loved him. He was intensely patriotic and accepted political posts at great sacrifices to his fortune which in those days was not any too great. As Secretary of War under Garfield and Arthur, at which time I was the head of the Appropriations Committee, I found that he was extremely efficient and well informed upon the armies and his duties as a Cabinet officer.

"Mr. Lincoln has been accused of being a sort of hermit and was very little seen in public in latter years, but this was because of his abhorrence of things political, and the fact that he was being eternally pointed out as 'Abe Lincoln's son.' Mr. Lincoln, shortly after his election to the head of the Pullman Palace Car Company, after the death of its founder in 1897, was prevailed upon to make political speeches in the campaign of 1900, the year McKinley and Roosevelt were candidates. It required a lot of persuasion to get him to come out in public and only when it was shown that the success of the Republican party was not assured did he consent.

"One of the few speeches that he made was in my home town. An incident that illustrates the private side of the man came up there. It was the last and biggest rally of the year, the climax of the campaign. Mr. Lincoln arrived as quietly and unostentatiously as he could during the morning hours and registered at one of the leading hotels. A reception was started and then, because of complaining of being fatigued, Mr. Lincoln was excused. Several hours afterward when we thought he had rested long enough we sent to his room. The door was locked. No one responded to repeated knocks of the bell-boy. Half-frightened, we went to the room fearing that something had befallen him. A chambermaid soon opened the door, but the room was empty. Lincoln's baggage was there, however, and we started to hunt for him but without avail.

"Then we did what few Republicans are supposed to do—we consulted a Democratic editor. He was born in Springfield and was quite a bit of a boy before the Lincolns left there for Washington. He had not seen him but he put us wise, and we soon found him. Lincoln, the orator of the day, was found in the north part of the city at the home of an aged negress, Mrs. Maria Vance, enjoying one of the finest meals of corn pone and bacon you ever tasted.

"Mrs. Vance had been cook before the war in the Lincoln household at Springfield and nurse part of the time for young Robert Todd. Lincoln had heard that the woman was still living there and hunted her up. They had spent several hours together. We hustled him away and to the park, where a great and impatient crowd awaited him. No sooner was his task over than Lincoln returned to the Vance home, humble as it was, and enjoyed more hours of talk with the aged woman, until it was near time for his train. From that day until her death 'Mammy' Vance received a substantial check each month from Chicago."

One of the most interesting details emphasized by the death of Robert Lincoln is the fact that "there are as many as ten thousand letters written to and by the martyred President that have never been examined by historians." According to the arrangements made by the son and executor of President Lincoln, these documents must remain for twenty-one years under lock and key. While there are some complaints of unfairness at this arrangement, considering the importance of

VOLUME TWO

FACSIMILE EDITION
OF ADAH SUTTON'S COMPLETE
HANDWRITTEN MANUSCRIPT
TRANSCRIBED FROM THE WORDS
OF MARIAH VANCE

Preface — — — —

No doubt the readers of this book "The Reminiscences of Mariah Vance", who without this explanation, will wonder how I came into possession of these facts. Why they were never retold in a period of over fifty years. Especially since some of these facts are quite revealing and enlightening.

I am making every effort to conscientiously repeat word for word the stories, as told to me, by this highly respected and greatly loved colored servant of the Lincolns. She served in their home at intervals from 1850 until 1858., and continuously from 1858 until after Abraham Lincoln was elected the 16th Pres. of the U.S.

The greatest task in the retelling of these facts has been to change Mrs. Vances negro dialect into Mr Lincolns own words where and when he converses. A. Lincolns character of words is not easy to come by. He was truly an individual. His words were expression of beauty and symmetry. They flowed freely from a truthful, pure heart and mind. Though I feel sure of this, Ive caught and expressed his exact meaning from here strange wording. Though it has been a staggering task. To leave all these accounts in her negro dialect would have become monotonous to the reader. I can only trust that the readers of "Mr Abe and Aunt Mariah will enjoy and appreciate her stories as I did. Outside of the joy, I witnessed, that it gave this lovely Christian, colored woman, as she again lived and cherished the life as a servant in the Lincoln home, I laughed with her and sometimes cried. Im not ashamed to admit.

I feel duty bound to go back to the turn of this century. Will relate each step from there, so you will not fail to understand the whys and wherefores. The final garlanding and ultimate compiling of these stories in manuscript form.

I was just out of the Attica, Indiana high school, a period in each young life if not carefully planned, be-fore-hand, in which teen-agers are at sea, as to how to employ their time. In July of that year my brother-in-law turned over his interests in The Le Claire Brick and Tile Plant, to his father and brothers. He wanted to embark in a new venture, the manufacture of Concrete blocks. As Danville, Ills., a highly industrial city, seemed to him the right location in which to start, he moved his family (my sister and their baby daughter) there. At the last minute I was asked to go with them. To stay until my sister become adjusted to her new home and surroundings. I was quite happy over their decision to include me.

Trough church and social contacts it wasn't difficult to meet and become acquainted. Nor in this city was it difficult to find employment. I sought and found employment as a bookkeeper and cashier in a shoe store. As fall days shortened and it became quite dark at closing time; we realized it wasn't too safe to walk unescorted from the car line stop to their suburban home. My sister that I should give up

2. my work. I was reluctant to do so, as earning a salary was a new and entirely welcome experience. So the only sensible thing to do was to get a room close to my work. About that time the daughter of the apartment owner where we were living, married. She offered me a room in her new home on the North Vermillion car line. This was not far from the business district. I was happy to accept. It ment not only being with someone I knew but very pleasantly located. This too with being offered a much better position opened a new era of life for me. I liked this complete change as my new responsibilities made me feel quite grown up. No longer dependent on others, I could now return to Attica on week ends (via Wabash R.R.) visit with home folks, then return to Danville for Sunday church assignments. However the advents of winter weather finally made the trips home difficult and sometimes a real hardship. Curtailing these visits home not only ment I would having to control my homesickness, but finding some-one to do my laundry. For with only a sleeping room such work as I did for myself when at home would be prohibitive.

I shopped around from one unsatisfactory wash woman to another. As spring come I was told of a little colored woman (Mariah Vance, and her daughter Julia) whom did such very nice laundry. Finding the address of these two was such a short walking distance from my address, I hastened over to interview them.

On entering their home the view of the interior was so neat and clean one could only conclude their work would be satisfactory. The elderly lady who admitted me, very graciously apologized for having to make me wait, as she had to finish waiting on her daughter "Who wak, as she said, ah littah undah dah weathah". I couldn't help but form a different opinion of the colored race, than I had been led to believe, if this Mrs. Vance was not an exceedingly rare representation of her race.

When she returned to the room I told her of my experiences trying to find a good laundress, I can see her yet, standing there looking straight at me, with hands on waist crossed in front saying, "Wal honey chile, Ef ah wak good 'nough fah dah Missy Lincolum ah shuh ahd be good 'nough fah mose any one. Dat woman wah shuh ticklah." I'll admit this Missy Lincolums didn't register with me. However as their work had been highly praised, I left my bundle wash, as it was called with her. I returned every two week there after, and never failed to complement her on her splendid work. Often she repeated "Ah wak mose good 'nough fah anyone ef good 'nough for Missy Lincolum."

The first time I saw Julia she came out in the yard where "Aunt Mariah (as she chose to be called) and I stood talking. Julia looked very frail and ill. However there was something in her bearing that emphasized her good breeding. With a gentle kind voice she called

3. a very beautiful, light colored young lady who was skipping rope on the side walk. This child was Julia's grand-daughter visiting from Crawfordsville, Indiana. She promptly came running and singing with a clear rich quality — unusual to-day even in highly trained voices. Her name was Ena Johnson (who later married Gene Jackson) an accomplished harpist on the Lyceum circuit. This fact was verified by programmes still in existence, and by the Poston and Barnhill families from Crawfordsville now living here. They stated that Gene Jackson also was a musician. Being both a cornelist and violinist. Ena and Gene (after moving to Danville) entertained for weddings, receptions, etc.

Aunt Mariah continued to talk about the "Lincolnmng. I lent, at first, almost a deaf ear for it gave her great pleasure & could see to relate incidents in her early experiences. Finally I questioned her about these Lincolumns. She seemed greatly surprised to learn that I didn't know anything about these Lincolumns, saying "Ah's bewildderah'd ovah yoah Ah's nevah befoah heah howdy oh soul what wondahs 'bout Abe Lincolumns or dah missy Dahlin didn yoah all evah know'd Abe wah da 16 president ob dah United States, But ah's oldah' dan yoah all an ah's done speak good, white folks talk. I 'spose yoah didn undastan. Ah loves ta tell ob mah life wid dah gran good folks ah work fah, wen ah wah young. Mah kin folks wah sick an tied ob deese Lincolumn's hapnins.

From that on I lent a listening ear. Even looked forward to her stories. Particularly the amusing ones. Then became quite interested in events Phistorical. Tying them with incident my father had related. His meeting Abraham Lincoln at one time during his service in the Civil War — my mother also told of aiding on a spring-wagon from Oxford Indiana to Lafayette, with a crowd, who stood along the railroad track waiting for hours for the arrival of the Lincoln funeral train. She remembered every detail so vividly for she was her only 15 yr old.

Finally becoming to deeply interested in Mrs Vances stories I thought it would be nice to take these stories and incidents down to retell to my parents. She willing repeated the ones she had already told which I jotted down on any bit of paper available. She was very happy to find someone to listen. Shefut new life and meaning in the telling. Vividly portraying with picturesque zest, gestures and negro dialect these reminiscences. Laughing, joyously. Giving expression by a shudder as she called forth some dangerous or revolting incident or great tears would flow from her soulful eyes at some sad memory. She was never without a pipe. Sometime a corn cob pipe and often a clay pipe with a little knob under the bowl, which she always held the pipe in place by. Shifting or removing it as she talked. When the weather was clement we would sit together on her front

& step. When stormy or chilly by her fire in front room or spotlessly clean kitchen, where I was served corn pone when convenient for her, the same kind of corn pone she made for the Lincolns. I'm so proud to relate. Then too she served the same fare to "Masliff Robert (as she still called him) on his many visits. Sat at the same table and ate from the same plate used by Robert Lincoln, so this lovely colored woman told me.

I had tryed to espacially glean from her picturesque speech bits of her true meaning regardless of expressions of looks or actions but back of it all shone forth the great love she bore for the entire family. Never antagonism or effort to smear their reputation. Just plain truths, simply told of sometimes in plainer english than I would have used.

These scraps of various shapes, kinds and sizes of paper which note of her reminiscences were jotted down on grew into a sizable paste board box full over a period of four years. Never were her stories ever told in sequence, just as they came to her mind. Being young the thought never once occured to me to put them in book form. Often we were not able to talk for only a few minutes, for Julia's illness became serious. "Aunt Mariah" had to take care of her. Do all the washings alone and have the Baltist fellowship once every week. In her home the Baltist church was born. After her death this meeting was continued in her son Cornelius Vance's home. There the plans for the church were made and finansed,

No one but "Aunt Mariah" with such fine feelings and perceptions of rightousness could have carried on. When Julia died that year of 1900, she said to me "Julia mah beloved baby when ah's wen to work fah dat Cincolumns is now in Heaben wid all dose Lincolumns." Reft my Robert. No tears jist that supreme confidence and gladness that Julia was free from earthly cares and physical sufferings. She said "No matter what befalls me Jesus doeth all things well." Until her own passing she carried on nearly to the last with that same stoicism. In January of 1904 her first born, her dearly beloved Billie died. During this last illness altho' she was past 80 years old and growing quite feeble she cared for him, and called it "Putting her shoulders to the wheel." That until after he was gone did she seem to lag, I could see at each visit she was failing. Though she didn't complain she continued to tell of the Lincolns until on Dec. 24th 1904 she passed on as peacefully as she had lived. She left an heritage greater than money. Her stories were put away but prized as a treasure given to me by this wonderful little woman.

I took various office positions. In 1912 my dear father passed on suddenly. Mother would then be alone for her other children were married. I felt it my duty to stay at home with her. To continue with office work and keep house as well ment neglecting one or the other. But it was necessary to do something that would add to our income, but nothing I tried seemed too profitable. It was suggested I buy and sell antiques. I started with a small investment. As I sold I re-invested. I found it a dignified interesting occupation. My mother loved it, for it brot into our home, cultured, refined and educated people. The work was fascinating also. Always learning of makers of furniture, glass, china and art. From literature I learned of authors of rare books and the histories of them and great painters of fine art. Expert knowledge of types and patterns of primatives. Especially enjoying biographies of statesmen, something I never enjoyed in school.

Occasionally I sold bits of glass, china, furniture or jewelry which I had purchased from Aunt Mariah after Billies death from what she called "plunda" from the Lincoln home - Both thrown away by them during her four years service there and when they rid out all excess when preparing to go to Washington in 1860. But I always held on to the photographs of Lincolns family, friends and relatives. They seemed to belong to the stories she told. Quite often I showed them to clients interested in historical items. One professor from Illinois University suggested I get in touch with Louis A. Warren, Director of Lincoln Life Assn. of Ft. Wayne, Indiana. Said that he might be able to help me put the stories (I told him of) in book form. That was either in 1937 or 1938. Dr. Warren was very encouraging. We exchanged a few letters. In one he expressed sincere conviction they should be put in book form for posterity and was willing to co-laborate with me.

About that time my mother became very ill. She needed constant care from the fall of that year until late spring the following year. I put the idea of writing completely out of my mind. Word travels fast and I must here state that there were a number of people offered help with such a book about that same time. Mrs. Dr. Horner of Washington D.C. Pres. of Amer. Pen Women, and a sponser of New Salem. Her aunt having resided in New Salem at the time of the Ann Rutledge, a Lincoln association. Dr. John Wesley Hill, Washington, D.C at which time he was Chancelor of Lincoln Memorial University. But the undertaking, so foreign to my ability was too great to even think of with my responsibilities.

My mother passed on in 1947 by then the having of these notes had completely faded from my mind. Then in 1954 or 1955 I was scanning through and checking advertisement in "Hobbies Magazine" when my attention seemed to center on an insertion by Lloyd Ostendorf of Dayton, Ohio calling for Lincoln original photographs. After some correspondence I sent the entire collection I had to him. He took them to various cities where there were large collections of Lincoln pictures, Springfield Ill., New York City, Detroit, Ft. Wayne, Cumberland Gap University, (LINCOLN MEMORIAL U.) as well as trying to identify as many as possible for me from his own fine collection.

6. Those, he didn't purchase at a very, very fair price
after identification he returned with notes attached to
each with with suggestions. In nothing was he anyway
but trustworthy. He later stopped over here when returning
from a trip to Chicago where he attended the dedication
of a Lincoln statue in the new Lincoln square, which
his illustration of same had been awarded the honor
of being used as a design for same. We talked at that
short visit of his about the possibilities of a book from
the notes I had taken. About the same time Mr Joe
Barnhart of Danville Ills. a Lincoln historian and writer
(resident of Home where Lincoln addressed a political audience
on south portico of former Dr — home) encouraged me to
write. Mrs Ramme of Terre Haute Ind, a Lincoln scholar,
Mr Fay custodian of Lincoln tomb and his son, who was an
artist and many others had tentatively built my courage. But
Mr Oslendorf gave concrete evidence of his willingness to see
the book a reality. Said he would correct and edit it for me.
I was, in a way, convinced I might be able to re-assemble my
notes. Having done systematic office work, I was schooled to
go about it in an orderly way. However it was a stupendous
task to commence and expect to carry through. I went over every
note carefully. Many were badly worn, brittle and writing
so erased that they were not legible. These I destroyed.
First I pasted on large sheets of paper. Re arranging as best
I could in sequence and according to sites of historical facts
which she often mentioned. When I at last started to write I
had to look over the entire number of sheets of paper to make
sure I hadn't left out at the proper place any note that should
be used. At each time I used a note I underlined it with red
pencil. I had no literary ability and was concious I could never
add as I went along, my own deductions. Nor did I mention at
any times traditional stories, even though some of her stories
verified facts about traditional. This book conciencious, exacting
confining labor. Nerve wracking in the extreme sometimes. But
rewarding for an accomplishment, which, mariah Vance and the Lincolns
would if they could see and knew that it was a labor of love, would
thank me, and those who so graciously helped me.
    Aunt mariah could not say Abraham or Lincoln correctly. Altho
mr. Lincoln never wished to be called Abraham & I sense the
name Abe was too familiar, it was decided by Mrs Lincoln
that since mrs Vance always had called him Mr Abe, she
could continue so doing, well as continue to call her "missy"
However she said it was a complement from Mr Lincoln if her
permitted her to do so; Thus it was in her telling that she
used these terms, making her stories come to life after a period
of forty years, by using mr. Abe, Dah missy, mastah Bobbie or
Robert Willie Taddie and their term for her Aunt mariah

All of which adds up to the love and esteem IN WHICH the Lincolns held this beloved servant.

Even until her last days Robert Lincoln visited her. In 1893 after returning from England (where he was U S minister) he stopped over in Danville, on his way from Chicago to Springfield to visit with her, perhaps too he longed to recapture some of his early home life and incidently and eat some of his early home cooking. I feel sure Robert Lincoln appreciated Aunt Mariah's sterling qualities and trustworthyness far more than anyone else did, And there is no doubt from all I have read by various authors concerning him, that Mrs. Vance was aware of Robert Lincolns genuine fine character from childhood more than anyone. Understanding what others even his father and mother thought of seemingly, as a complex life. At least never fathomed as Mariah did. She once said, "Hen wah so quiet an serious, Nevah intahfeahin wid anyones life. Hisl wah so kind an hepful to mah chillan and precitate evah kindness what wah givn. Hen wah backard. Didn wan no uns ta glorfy him couse oh his pa. Dat man love mah Billie mose as a brothah, nevah nevah did hen fohget Aunt Mariah thro' her worstest times. Hen wah ah very true christian foh hen nevah let his left hand know what his right hand doith." No one knew from him that on his visits to her he provides some for her future. That he paid Julia and Billies doctor bills and funeral expenses. It must be recognized by all my readers, as I come to recognize that he never would have given her more than a passing thought had he not admired and respected her very highly for her fine worth. She not only "Put her shoulder to the wheel" as she said, by which she helped herself and hers, but neighbors testify of her charity giving of her feeble strength to help.

By far one of the most, if not the most rewarding outcome by the release of these articles has been the genuine interest shown in the progress of this book. Not only Lincoln students and scholars have encouraged and offered willingly to help, but friends in general. I have also made new friends, sincerely interested in what I have endevored to do. Besides those I have already mentioned I extend my sincere thanks to the Personal a Springfield library where I did research - micro-film operator at Federal building in Danville (copies of Commercial News, Ben Thomas author of Lincoln articles and books, Fanny Earnest Champaign Ills. a colored lady who at one time lived in the Vance home Mr & Mrs Gene Jackson and Mrs Jackson's father who furnished programes and photos Recorder of Danville court house at Danville, for the Vance records as, also the caretaker at Crown Hill cemetery. Dr Maris of Attica who explained effects of the drug paregoric. My neice Mrs John Weaver Frey, Washington D C spent 3 hours at archives scanning micro-film, verifying records else in my possession. The following Attica folks who furnished transportation so I could do research - Mr & Mrs Chester Cooper, Mrs Laura Cook and Mrs Ara Stanfield. Not forgetting the well wishers to which I extend thanks

Without the help of "Mr Ottendorf I must repeat here that I might never have found a way to give this book to the public. It was his confidence and ability, his patience (for no doubt I have been very trying) that made me feel I would ultimately finish.

In ending I have confidence that many scholars will conclude by comparison, that this books, has verified some traditions as facts. Stated new facts and separated legend from facts ̶ Sincerely thanking all for reading   I am

Humbly & Gratefully Yours

Adah Lilas Suttow.

ATTICA, INDIANA
APRIL 12 1960.

Mariah Meets the Lincolns.

After a bad storm in April of 1850, about four o'clock in the afternoon; Henry the kids and ah was setting out front war we live in Washington street near Jackson. He was watching the comings and goings of a rainbow which showed up after the storm in the east sky.

Henry fussed cause he thought it foolish like, for me to tellem de youngins 'bout Noah and de flood. It did be a long drawn out tale. Ah war 'bout winding it up. Telling ho how the rainbow was to remind us of Gods covenant. That never again, no sir, Dar would never be a nother flood. Ah tryin to larn them dat de flood had to come. It or somefeen else had a come Cause people war so wicked.

My Henry tol me to keep my clap shut, we war going to hab company Henry had watched a tall man, headed our way. Coming down Jackson. I never once sat eyes on him until up he stepped, and turned square in our front yard. It war Mr Abe Lincoln. We all knowed him. We all knowed he war a good man. We'd hearn tell stories about him That he war a friend of colored folks, jiest as how he war a friend of white folks. My Henry spoke to him right friendly He liked Mr Lincoln. But not most white folks. He and his folks had been slaves. He never knew his real pappy. He done got de name of Vance from a slave holder who owned his mammy when he war barn. His father had been sold off to another slave holder. But my man & his'n mammy got north thro the unner ground.

Now me I war never a slave. My kin folks lived jiest cross the Ohio from Kaintucky. We'es often wandered down to the banks of de ribber to play. Well now I jiest don't member how many of usn there war. I only know dat while we played a big boat sailed up to de bank. Some mean white men got out of dat boat an drove de older ones of usn away. Ah war so young I don't rightly member, so as how Ah caint tell it all. They'll tell Ah an a brother ran an hid. It war are older brother Neal. Come up in time to save me. Neal war not so big 'cause as he done run with me, he letin me fall on a stump. Ah war too heavy for him. See dat white scar on my shin? must have struck mah shin bone parful lick. Yas sar e-Ah'll carry dat mark to mah burying. It are de only white about me. Ah's jiest plain black cow She she laughed showing her pink tongue in her toothless mouth

But Ah's right proud ah's real black. Had ah black pappy and black mammy, african black with good red blood and white hearts

Mammy grieved a heap over loosin her chilin. Lawdy goodness it war no use trying to spunk her up. Poor pappy he'd go putterin around out of her way. She paid no mind to any ting in dat Goodforsaken wilderness, but tryen to do what war needful for mammy. She'd fix a pot full of possum. But de possum war tasteless to mammy. Poppy'd say. Et haint rightful dat you young'n should starve. So mens et a gorge of possum.

A traveling parson come along and set up a camp in dat wilderness. Mammy and poppy gres to de camp meeten. Dey done got the Love of God in der hearts. Ah's sheer poppy would hab bust clean out of dat meeting, but he see as how mammy was gettin happy, so he got up grit an stayed. He didn't dast go. He'd he ah plumb fool not to see de home war going to be right as not again. Youse can see ah war raised a christian woman.

After de meetin we done went farther north and west. Wound up in Illinois somewhar close to Springfield. Dats whar I met my Henry. Ah war jist a skit of ah gal when we got hitched. Five youngruns in eight years war born to usn by the time we set foot in Springfield in 1850. We didnt have much but young uns an old wagon, a cart an a wee bit a plunder.

We hardly got settled in our hut, until folks, good folks they be wanted my man to haul wood and do chores. Et war so cold in dat hut, et froze ice water bucket an outside in our cistern. He picked 'bout de Gawd awfulist time to move my man said we picked the Gawd awfulist time to move. We jist had to go whar we could find work or plum starve. I got scrubbens and washings from folks. We got hitched up on food stuff and some warmer togs. The lep young uns stayed in so didnt need shoes. Rent was only 75 cts. a week.

That spring it had rained a deal. Spacially April. Ah warn't asked to work a heap. De mud in streets war black an sticky and worsern black whar he cows roamed and pig wallerd. Guen folks figer'd better leave well enough alone, while rain kept up. Rather than have de muck in dar homes.

Ah war speclatin on getting most somethin to do, after the rainbow promised no more floods; an war about to tell my Henry, when Ah hear'n mr. Abe say after greetings. I'll come right to the point mrs. Vance. I believe you are the lady who did cleanin in our office awhile back. Anyone who would clean those windows so you could see through. Really clean scrub that floor, straighten up and make that office smell fresh, is the kind of woman we'd like to do our washing and other household chores.

I'd like most, for you to come in the morning. I'm going out of town in the circuit for a spell. Mrs Lincoln will be alone with our boy, Robert, now to make a long story short. my wife is not well. We just lost our little boy, our Precious Eddie. Mrs Lincoln has lost other relatives she loved and her heart is greived. Besides we think she is with child. She has morning sickness, besides bad pains in her head. If youll say you will come, I'd he powerful much obliged.

But mah husband right pertnent spoke up. "mr. Lincoln I caint no how find fault wid any your doins or how you done treat folks. But I don't want my woman screamed at an chased us off the place like your woman tha done did other workin womenfolks, so Abe hear en tell. Now my Mariah is a mild woman. Aus Ah's got a shield her and take her part. She might talk back a bit but Ah's feared she'd nevva fight a she cat. Ah's not wanted to hurt your feelens Mr. Lincoln, but I caint bide by sich like as day say bout dat woman of you ens.

Mr. Abe stood right still, right thar, as if rooted to dat air ground you could jist see dat man had a worls of troubble. After a spell he said, Perhaps what you have heard is partly true, but you know when a ball starts to rollin in the mud it gathers more mud.

Now Mrs Vance, what do you earn? When you wash, do you work by the piece, by the hour, day, or by the week? I know with a very sick woman to work for it is going to be quite a trial. But if you'll try to understand my nieces, I think you'll learn to like her. And I think she'll like you. Sometimes it's all in getting acquainted. I'm not a saint, I know I have ways which jar on Mrs. Lincoln. Whatever you've been earning I'll be glad to pay you more, because you'll have more trial than most places you'll work at this time.

Wal Ah says to Mr. Abe. Since my Henry is not working now, wont need the mule and cart, he air can stay with the older younguns. If'n he says so. Can take the two wee ones. If'n you has a place to tuck em in while ah works. Well says Mr. Abe I'll be much obliged, and I'll find a place for the children. My youngest Julia was thirteen an Ah had to take her. Ah could put her to nap, but when she done woke up, if'en she had no company would cry. That's bout the ornerist thing for me to put up with when workin. A cryin young-un

My Henry said. For sure Mr. Lincoln, first this onst an no more if'en your woman bussed my woman. Mr. Abe says. Now Henry and Mrs. Vance I'm ever so grateful to you. I feel relieved to leave my home in a good woman's hands. He gave the chil'n some stick candy. Tole my man hed get him all the work he could. Said "I'll have the water pumped and the boiler on early you won't have to rush too much, not so much that you'll have to neglect your own family". At that he sauntered around the corner.

Wal ah got to Mr. Abe's about 7 o'clock. The next mornin Shur enough thar war Mr. Abe pokin wood (from a stack he had cut and piled in the yard) under de boiler. De lid of dat old battered boiler war bouncin up an down, like it had a hid foot. The wood wash tub war on de stool in de back yard. There war soft soap and wash board. A new fangled contraption then De clothes war all in a pile on the floor of a shed. Ah tucked mah sleepin younguns in a corner of the shed, and asked Mr. Abe if he done have his en breakfast. He said All ah care for, but there's a mess in here I fear I caint tackle.

Ah went into a nice ~~large~~ kitchen. In dat kitchen war a big fire place, a large table, a small work table ~~&~~ a corner cupboard ~~The~~ dishes pans and scraps of food were every whar stacked. Ah figured while there war plenty of hot water Ah'd be mighty smart to clean up the soil around about, fore starting washing. Ah'd hardly started stacking dishes an brushen up afore I heard some body coming down de stairs. It war a boy about seven years old. For de life of me I never sot eyes on sich a sober looking boy. Proud looking ~~he~~ war to. I felt a little quee- roun sich a boy. So different from Mr. Abe's sad deep set patient eyes. But ~~the~~ boy war Robert, and how I loved him right off, He done smiled such a friendly smile, that skur as were sittin her on dis door step, washed off ~~that~~ dat sober proud look right away. He said – Aren't I deserving of any breakfast, I says Land a goodness Honey chilo you'se 'serving of all de breakfast you little fat belly can hold. I'd cook all day an all night to feed sich a dear sweet little man boy what he likes best. But don't rub dat smile off. Dats worth heap of shining gold. Robert laughed, Really laughed out loud. He war a very still boy and most awful serious.

Mr Abe says "Robert this is our new help Mrs. Vance, I'm about to leave now and I'r going to put you in charge. I want you to help all you can, Your mother is not well you know. So be helpful and comforting.

Ah finished with Robert's breakfast an de kitchen and went out to my wash. I was sorten the clothes in the shed, when what should step right up to dat door but ~~the~~ most prettiest woman ah's ever laid eyes on. I says Howde missy. She paid no heed to mah Howde. Jus walked over to de corner whar my young ens war tucked in and said "What's this, and gave a terrible jerk on Julia's foot. Julia woke with a Loud split-en ear yelp. The missy screamed "Get those yelling, dirty, niger brats out a here" Get em out of here I say, right away, Ah's about to oblige her. when Mr. Abe comes in. Sweet like he says, say she. "Mother this is Mrs. Vance the lady who is going to do the washings and hep while I am away." Says the missy "Well what can she do with them whelps screaming My head, my head. mother, mother you know full well what you'd do if a cyclone came up, sudden like, and jerked you out of bed. You'd do more than yelp. You'd raise the neighborhood and after you got them raise you'd swear that cyclone that did it, was possessed by a demon." Mr. Abe had a powerful bad time with her. He turned to me an says, Says he Mrs Vance I done tole you Mrs Lincoln is a sick woman. Please pay no attention to what she has said. Just go on with your work and I'll make mother comfortable. Mrs Vance she's a good woman but so sick and troubled. Ah thought right there an then. Ah don't

see no good only pretty to look at. She's a she devil and she
aught to have 'em troubles for how she troubles Mr. Abe. Even
dat poor little Robert ran to de barn like he war a flip jack.
I settled Julia wid my suckin and gave the other young un
a cracklin I'd swept from the table. The washing was big and
hard. I shur know'd it warn't a weeks wash.

Robert kind a timid like came back bring in a kitten and
a ball. He played in dat shed wid my two uns the rest of
dat blessed morning. He was be in helpful. His pape had
told him to be. Ah'est figgered he missed his little brother who
had jest died. He tole my chilluns it was Eddies kitten and ball.

When Mr. Abe lead de missy away, Ah heard him say
can't I jest for once leave here with a happy thought of you.
Why do you always send me away to worry. She replied
"If you were half as smart as I once thot you were, you
wouldn't have to go wandering over the country, leaving us to
get along the best we can with low life help. You would
stay at home like my people do, and make a desent living."
He says then, "Well Mary maybe we both made a mistake. And
I declare I don't know which one made the worst mistake. But
I'll do my best as I see it. I get you something to quiet you
and then must be on my way—I don't want to keep the
others waiting. He poured something out of a glass jug and
handed it to the missy. Since then Ah learned it war perigoric.
He took her up stairs and put her to bed.

Ah had finished hanging the wash. Some war dry and Ah war
folden them. He says Mrs. Vance your work is done
right fine. The clothes are so clean mother is going to be
happy with them. I am glad you stayed. You must have
an understanding head and heart. Mrs Lincoln is always
ashamed after she has one of these spells. I want you to come
once a week if you can I don't think Henry will object when
you explain to him. Ah know'd my Henry a heap more'n Mr Abe
know'd him. Weins needed dat money. Mr Abe paid me 50¢ after.

He packed the rest of his belongins in a bag. Came out
to the clothes basket an sarched out some clean bandanas
and socks—Carried in the basket filled and packed down hard
with clean clothes Ah finished taking from line—Put some
paper in his tall hat—Took Robert on his knees kissed and
held him close—I declare I remember if twar yisterda the big
tears dat rolled down an splashed. Dat man war a man of
God and he were crusified every day. He said good bye again
and thanked God for your help agin and slumped away to the barn
to hitch back.

Ah pitched in an finished straighning de house. Sat Roberts dinner on kitchen table
sent food up to the missy. When I came back with mule hitched to cart
out came Robert carrying Julia and leading Phebe. God like he said

Good-Bye an went back to de barn carry'n the kitten. Such a lonesome little tike. A knows right there and then dat Robert war born to trouble. Having such an ailing mother But if he lived thro' it, some day he would be a great, good man like his father ~ good as to looks like 'n his mother.

~~The~~ week hadnt passed when one afternoon I sees a small boy chasing all out of breath right in to our yard. Flashes of lightning an week tunder war coming out of the sky.

But that is another story

How my heart plum melted for that poor little mastah Robert, He war so lonesome like, an good an kind. And I tole my Gawd right there an then ah'd have to go back to that he deviled house for that poor little boys sake.

De week ob my fust wash day at Mrs Ailis, hadn't passed, when one aftnoon 'bout four, Ah sees a small boy chasin all out a wins, right in on ma's front yard. Flashes a lightnin an week liky tunder war comin down out ob de sky. Et war dat poor spunky Bobbie callin out, Mrs Vance Mrs Vance come quick my ma is in torment.

Ah got him quietin a spell. What air yous'e mean yous'e ma is in torment. Tho' ah just wants hows to say, Her's gettin hern'. jus due from Almighty God on hern'. But shur as der is dat Lord in Heaven when Ah looked at dat poor skeered baby boy Ah says to masef, Lut you infernal evel, devil thinkin an gentle down. Den Ah says, war ailin you ma?

Ah, Mrs Vance do come. I've asked everyone I know and it's no good, No one wants to help her, One woman says to me. Let her die an go to hell. They hate her! They hate her an they hate me! She's afraid of this thunder and lightning. She's got her head covered and screamin for help. Pa's gone and Ah all ma has. You heard pa say so.

Mr Henry settin thar says, Mariah think as how you'd betta go? Ah'll mind de brats a spell. Bobbie's eyes done lit up lak one ob dose new fangle oil lamps. When he spied our Billy. Billie war bout de size of Bobbie. Dey took to de wed'er bout as how two monkey in a cocanut tree Bobbie forgot he war in a shake to hep his ma. But ah did no fiddlin, Ah wants to get goin an get back fore de storm broke. Not a fam'ly ting would gentle those boys down. So ah says, Bobbie should ah take Billie along in de cart wid us'n? He war so pleasured he had a attack of chuckles right off. Right der an den Ah knowed mah black Billie an dat blessed little white Bobbie war goin to be everlastin, fast friens. De'uns loaded aheeves in de cart, an you should a saw how, away dat mule shoved along, wid each clap of tunda. De boys yelled an laughed wid heeps of spirit. De tunder got louder an de mule got fasta Ah shur believe Bobbie war more joyful dan he'd ever been afore in his'n onhappy little lonisome little life.

Bout haf way der. We'd gone bout 3 or 4 blocks out jumps a pack ob rascals to try to stop dat mule. You'd nebber knowed wat dat darn fool mule were bout to do, until he doed it. He pushed rite smack thro' dat mot. An did dey scamper a spell. Den dey got der haids togetha an give chase wid mud balls an screamins at poor little 'bused Bobbie. "Ole rail splitin Abe's boobie is a niger lover. Dem catched up wid us'n an grabbed dat cart in de rear an pulls back hard, Ah pulls as hard on de straps. An dat mule seem to hab hoss sense for onest. He slow'd'n down. Ah knowd my Billie and Bobbe war in no match for'n dat mess ob heathens. Day war de debils own. My Billie wood hab gotten out of'n dat cart quicker dan a cat could catch a rat, but ah grabs him by de seat of his'n pants wile he war going ober de end an holled 'kin back. He called den white trash a Lowd condemned awful name. Quick as flash ah gibe him a lick ober his'n deflies blasphemin mouth an knowd he'd been mis'n round wid dem white trash on Juckson street. Ah gibber him nother lick for good measure an warn him, ef'n I ever coutch him wid any dem white on Juckson street Ah gib him wors'n blister'n dan Shadrack, Meshack an Obidnego wood a got if'n God hadn't rescude dem from de fiery furnace. But all dat talk of mine to dem young'ins went plum thro' both der ears. Ah swar ah hardly got mah speech out ob mah mouth

Aen Billie howld mammy, mammy here'ns pappy's' black snake,' Git
et to em. Dem blasted white trash war'n crawlin in de back end ob
mah cart. Jist as ah grab dat God bless'd black snake whip, un reach'd
et'at dem, God sent a turble streak ob lightin an a clap ob tunder,
dat most offsot us'n, wen de mule gibben notha lunge. We'n all
screamed un dat mess ob rascals done must hab thot dey'd war struck
by dat lightin. Ah sware "War Hose" couldn hab catched dem, Dey shear
didn molest us'n no more.

But Oh mah God in Heaben wen we done got to de missy, et war wors'n
dan all de messes ah war eber in, in mah whole born days. Thar war de
missy laid up on de ole black sofy, her'n feet twitch'n an kickn. Her'ns
haid covered wid a quilt an spew all ober de floar. Ah says to little Bobbie
run for de docta, run, run you scamps run. But dem mah Billie allers
snoop'n round, says Mammy, mammy look at her'n, Der haint no need
for de docta. She'n peep'n. Her'n play'n possum, lak grandpappy pet possum.
Just git dat black snake un gib her'n a good wallop'n an her'll forgit et
air blow'n outside or dat its goin to blow dis awful hell hole up. As
quick as dat lightin done boys ran out. Ah couldn catch dem. No sir,
afore ah uncover'd her'n haid or hole her'n feet from der jerk'n an
twitch'n, back dey come, wid dat black snake. Billie come bust'n in de
door screech'n, Wallup dat she debil good mammy, an her'n'll stop skeer'n
folk out ob der wits.

Bobbie look'd skeer'd. Poor dear sweet little Bobbie. Dat angel chile hab
nebba hein round any sick as mah Billie. Maybe Ah art'n to done et
but Ah right der an den gab him a cut wid dat black snake. He'n git
out a howl wors'n dat tunder.

Up jump'd de missy. Har down an all tangle up. Face covered wid her.
Der war no angel pretty bout her'n now. Ah says, please missy done
upset yourse self. Ah's come to protect you'ns. Dis storm boun to be
ober soon. Mah Henry allahs say, De hard'n de storm de quick'a its ober.
But Lawd Gawd her'n war'nt jump'n bout de storm, her'n war
har full'n mad cause I wallop'd my Billie, Her'n says to me
Haven't you even got niger sense. Billie only told the truth. This
is a hell hole. And I've made it so, If any one need to be beat, I need
it. But no one needs cruelty and I won't lay still, no matter how
I feel and see it practiced in my house.

Bobbie done run to his'n ma and cried. Oh ma, Don't scold Mrs. Vance.
She is a good understanding woman in her heart and head. I heard pa
tell her so. Yes Oh yes say the missy. It was good of her to come over
here in this storm, to be here to protect me. Leave her home and family.
I shouldn't have had you go for her. But I was so sick and afraid.

Wal Ah just tole her, Her'd hab to git more love in her'n heart, for
mah good book says, Love casts out fear. Wal her'n say. If Love casts
out fear Mariah, Love will cast out whippings too. Ah did'n want to
arguefy wid her'n, but mah teach'n nebber say any ting bout whippings.

Dey storm just as mah Henry say. Did'n last long.

Ah got a basin a watah for de missy to wash her'n face. Ah ask ef her'n
wood want as how Ah should clean out a clutta ob parcels all round

3. on de floor: Da you'ns know what her'n up an say. why mariah those are little dresses I've made for your baby Julia, from our darling little Eddies clothes. I was so very sorry I disturbed baby Julia's sleep. I do so many wrong things when I have these headaches. Wal yes, ah say to her'n. You'se a vera sick woman. But youse should'n carry on so, wid dat baby youse got to hab born. An bless youse pretty heart youse didn't ought mak black young un any dresses. I've'uns didn't see a strange woman soon enough but thar her'n stood right smack in de door. De missy spoken right up to her'n. Nice time for you to be coming Lig. Den dis Lig spew de spew on de carpet an her'n acted all upset. Went over to de missy an say. Mary baby why didn't Bobbie tell me. Even though I've been swamped with work and must give a party, would have dropped everything and come right over. De missy say. Well you know how afraid I am when it storms and that Mr Lincoln is away. All you think about is clean, clean, clean that big house and cook, cook, cook for parties. Wal Mary, Lig say, If you'd think less of sewing up all the good in the county to outshine everyone else in dress (looking at the material strewn around) and learn more about cooking and providing the right nourishing food for your family, you would have a happier an healthier family an home. De missy huffed up right smart bout dat. Now Lil-(wan her'n war mad her'n called dis Lig. Lil) If its any of your nosey business, I'm just making a few little dresses for this fine colored woman's child. Lil right smart up an say. Since when have you become so patronizing to colored folks. But its time you're thinking of someone besides yourself. Wal say de missy wid her'n hans on her'n hips an does pretty eyes turned into a cyclone, but still lookin strait at dis Lil, like her'n puled de earth. Mariah came to me when you wouldn't, and you know Lil I would'nt send for you or anyone else unless I needed them. Dis missy shur had a worl of spunk. Den her'n say in de sweetest voice God almighty eber put in a human bein. This is my sister Elizabeth Mariah- Mrs Edwards this is Mrs Henry Vance. She came to help us out last monday Lib. She is a good, clean, honest woman. Rite quick like Elizabeth spoke out. Well Mary you need some one an I hope you dont take any tantrums with this Mariah an run her off. An couldn't bear to hear ant sick woman, to any more like dat, so ah say, Wid her'n fired up like her'n is. Her'n's a mighty sick woman, wid all her'n otha complaints. I know, I know, says Mrs Edwards. But there isn't anything wrong with her that good come sense won't help some. Mince, Father and I have humored un spoiled her, because she demanded it. An now her servants, Bobbie and Mr Lincoln espacially, has to take the brunt of all our foolishness. Abraham takes it or gets out, many times he gets out so mary can have her way. I hope once in her life she has common sense enough to keep a good servant. All her othea servants just couldnt take it, so they got out an stayed out. Dat war all sweet talk bout me., but poor missy her'n spilled ober a bucket ob tears, cryin her poor, poor sick heart out. Lil softn'd like puppy's cotton balls, an as shur as Good made little apples, her'n went ober to de missy, kissed her'n, wiped up her'n tears wid her'n silk hanchiff, an cried a little her'n self.

Lawd a goodness I nebba onst sot eyes on sich carry'n on. A begin mad at one an tuther one minute an next minute, lov'n an kiss'n like's turtle doves. Maybe dat good raisin'. I or, Ah an my Henry a little bit of fight, to git to make up seems powful good. But two kin Ah jus caint see who eber that dat war even good sense. My poppy would hab gibben us'n a larnin we'ns memba wid his harness strap. Der wood be no needin's for kiss'n an make'n up. We'ns das n't nebber fuss an fume in us'ns home. I speck day'd betta kiss an smooch fust, den der wood'n be no fume'n and fight'n lak wild cats. But for ten years Ah saw such doin's. But day always parted friens in happy like. Not wid Mr. Abe. Bout time he'n got his'n tank ful of sich foolishness he'n jest up an walkes off. An waites until de fire cool off. Not dat ah could allahs bide by dat. But dat man war a man of God. He'ns jest plenty fumin aroun enough to take his'n own part. So dar war no need to kiss an make up.

Ah, hardly could hep bawlin mah self. But et war soon ober an Mrs. Edwards went home, I say. I she'd come every day or send her husband to find out if Mary needed anything that they could do or bring. When aut Elizbeth left, de missy say, Elizabeth is very dear to me and I love her very much, but she has always tried to direct my life as she wants it. She would resent it if I meddled in her affairs. Elizabeth has been so kind through the years, that perhaps I should look over her few faults. But I have both the Todd an Parkes southern temper, which I was never persuaded to try to control. Oh I've so many evil stays. An gain her'n start to cry. Ah say to her'n You're not evil, you're jest sech a sick woman in you'se head. An you'se should'n be 'bout tir'n you'sef makin dese dresses for mah Julia. I'se ween'n her. I should have a spell back. But her'n war so puny, an de oder chillun needed all de vitals we'ns could get ah hans on. We'ns war so hard up. Milk sickness war goin roun colrah an ah war fear'd

Dese dresses air most to fkeil dul for poor colored folks. maybe you'se could let some you'se rich folks hab dem. Right den an dere I made a horbal mistake. Ah caint see why as how, ah caint leave well nough 'lone, an keep mah big mouf clamp'd as mah man say ah should. For de missy raily wanta make up wid un'ns, becaise her'n pull Julia's laig, an made her'n howl. Her'n say, Oh Mariah, wont you use them. Maybe I can change them some and they would be more like play dresses. They are made of good strong material and colors that won't show soil easily. I have so many more. But if you feel you don't want Julia to wear little Angel Eddie's clothes I'll put them back in the chest. Der war a lot of love stiches in dem close. Her'n had put a lot more in to make up to Julia. So ah says, why'n bless you good Christian heart missy, Ah sees you hab powerful lot of idees bout dress'n little girls dat are rite good. If'n you'se nebber hab any of you'se own. Ah jesta plain black nigger an haint got a heap of sense bot close. Mah Henry's goin hab to change his'n mind bout you. Ah clamped mah hen over mah mouf fasta dan dat lightnin. For shur nuff ah let de cat out of de bag.

But jest den in bounces Billie an Bobbie wid two etra kittins. Rite den an saw if ah nebber done did nothin tirg. Ah hab to git dat Billie of mine out ob dat clean house ob de missy befor all holla broke loose. Dat house war so clean et glisten like. Onla a wee litta 'room whar hern hab been stichew an de wet spot whar mrs Edwards hab clean up de floor.

Robert said, Billie you can have the kittens or you can give them to Phebe an Julia looking at his mother's frown, he said, Ma dont like cats Pa he'd bring all the cats and dogs and other animals he found on the circuit. One time he brought us a white rat. It in oul pocket and a turtle in the other. He had put candy in each pocket for them. But the rat ate a hole in his pocket and was about out, when he got home and the turtle snapped his finger as he took it out of his pocket. It's the only time I ever heard Pa howl. Afterwards he laughed about as loud as he howled.

Dis put de missy in mind of a story me Abe tole. A Parson was giving a toast to the really good things in life. He said, Parsons are preaching for them, Lawyers are pleading for them, Doctors are prescribing for them, authors are writing for them, Soldiers are fighting for them, but only a few are enjoying them. may we never forget that vice stings us, even in our pleasures but virtue consoles us even in our pain. At which one of the congregation replied, He makes no friends who never made a foe. So mr Lincoln says he them bit an snap. mother can have a pair of white ear muff and I'll have my turtle soup. You see says the missy your pa befriended a rat who chewed up his coat an a turtle that bit him after he gave them candy, but he still felt well feed. Bobbie shur nuff like de story, but mah will Billie say. De dirty bums 'he'd cram dat candy down der dirty necks an grab em by de tail an beat der brains out for not swallowing it. Dat speech didn't to much like, please de missy. But Bobbie jumps up an down an laugh an throw en his n Rat in de air Ah know de missy war gwine to quiet n down. But Just she say, take dem cats out an come right back in Ah goin to need you Bobbie. Wen dey came in. She says, as sweet as an angel. Dat woman hab must y'in turned back to de prettiest woman ah most ever seed. Ah dont know as how she did it so quick. But hern took de boys careful like by de arm an tole them to sot there, an if dey be quiet dey could hab some cakes with roesins. Billie hardly got sot till he no screamed for cookies, but Bobbie war a little gentleman. missy brot de cookies from de cooky jar an wen dey war et up, hern brushed up de crums rite quick.

Den say, Boys stan up, Billie war a wee bit higher and Bobbie war heeps fatter. Den hern says. Bobbie go up to your room and bring me your waists and pantaloons and waist coats. Billie started to follow, but she grabbed him by the sleeve (what war so dirty Ah war asham). Now de missy say, You sit right there and be quiet, if you can for a little while. Fore Robert says. Ah'll strap you n if you n dont. Ah habn't yet larned de lesson de missy wood n bide by cruelty. Oh no you wont, she says, I run this house an you're going to do as I say. Do you understand that mariah. Billie yelled loud as tunder. Get it to her n missy said both barrels. Dat pleasured de missy an as black an dirty as he war. Ah thot shur she war going to kiss him. From dat very Good blessed day on her loved mah Bobbie Boy. an her n war tooth an toe nail for her n. Ah still that Ah'd strap he n s when Ah got home.

Ah jist caint figger how dat woman as sick as her n war wen Ah left her on wash day, an as sick as her n war de lightnin day, could in betwixed, done such loads of work. On wash day, ah'd oula washed an straighten up a speck, but dor war nary a speck of soil on a form ting as big as a fly speck. Her n war a fine house kapa. Sides de house as clean as de driven snow. Her n hab plant flowers, onons, littace, peas an lans Ah done know as how wha all in groun det mr Abe hab dug up. Her n pretty dimple hans war all scard an dat dirt groun in what dat lie soap hab made cracks. Ah tole de missy her n should n ben

over in her'n condishune, Herie says. I would like to know who else would
Mr. Lincoln is too tall to bend. He's bent so much already carrying the boys
straddle of his neck, bless them. An playing piggy back. Then he carries
the world on his shoulders

Nal her'n tole Billie to put on some of Bobbie's close. Billie grabbed de bunch an
when racin to de shed. Ah got der wid a towl missy, hand now an brush he'ns up
a bit Ah swar wen you'ns can see dirt on a black nigga, days dirta. Ah gotten
ona de worsin off'n. Ah had a fight wid he'ns to huze a ruffl'd he dubb'd
waist'n pantaloons butto'n at de nees. But ah led him in to de missy by de ear
He'ns screemed bloody murda. Ah made he'ns march rite in to de missy, scream
uh done wan dese sissy ruffly duds, At which Robert spoke up an said, You see
ma that's why they make fun of me and call me sissy.

We'll see about some of the rest. She picked up the plainer stout ones, and put
them in a stack on a chair where the clothes for Julia were laying. She thanked
mariah for coming, said Mr Lincoln would pay her when she came to wash again
Laway missy Ah would'n take no pay, afta you gibben us'n all des duds, Bless you Bless you
so much. You're very welcome mariah and bring Billie again. Bobbie and I would love to
Now mariah I believe you need not come only every two weeks, since Mr Lincoln
is not at home. I will wash out the few things we really need, I'm trying to get
someone to stay at night, It's so lonely, maybe one of Bobbie's friends, or perhaps
an irish girl I've heard of. She can get breakfast, then clear the dishes before she
leaves in the morning. That will give me a chance to catch up on my sewing. Since
my father died last July and grandmother Parkes this January we've been in
Lexington looking after affairs or here caring for our dear little Eddie during his sickness
and death. We've grieved so. I neglected so much too. Mariah you and Billie have been who
I needed all along. I feel I'm back home once again with mammy Sally and all the
picks-a-ninnies. At that Bobbie spoke up, Oh ma can we call mrs - once - mammy
mariah? Ah done kno why, but dat jus did'n seem rite. Ah says, Ah's mammy to
mah young'ns, but ah war nebbar mammy to no white. Ah asked him a sheered. How
ola he'ns you'ns Mrs Lincolmn? Her'n say, I'm 32 mariah. How old are you? Well
ah 28 de very nex month in July. Dat war in June den. An ah's no ways ole enough
for you'ns to call mammy. All right Mariah. Maybe you wouldn't object if Bobbie
calls you Aunt mariah. Would you like that? Dat war so blessed, bein called Aunt to
a little white boy like'n Bobbie You'se a heufel good woman Mrs Lincolmn. She says
I hanks mariah, If its hard for you to say Lincoln you can continue to call me missy, as
I heard you call me to Billie. But Billie you can call me missy too. It'll sound so sweet
Ah tole her'n ah'd pay her'n in works, for de young uns duds, her'n gibben me, Her'n
jus shew me off. Tole Billie to git in bottom of cart an spread all de close ober his'n, So
de white trash could'n see he'ns on de way home.

Nah Henry start'd to raise de very debbl wen Ah war unhitch'n dat Mule Maud. Ah
went in. He'ns war worn out wid does four ah left wid him. Den he'ns spied dat stack of
finery. He'ns dug in dat stack for some shirts for his'n self, dat Mr Abe war tired of. Ah
says, ah guess Mr Abe wears de tails off'n his'n own shirts. _ Mai like Henry says,
Did'n you'n bring any grub? We'n starved. Lawd dat Henry war de gruy'n is man
alive, an ah tole him to shot he'ns fool ish hog ish ness. Ah'd fix him some flap jacks.
He'ns loved flap jacks. Ah tole him'ns all bout he'ns truble wid de white trash rascals.
Ah know'd dat big mouf'd Billie wood spill de beans, if'n Ah did'n tell.

Lawd hab mercy on ah souls. Does white devils haint worth'n hog tien an kill'n. But
dat's what dey'l do to us'ns. Every las black crow of us'n, if day catch us. Dey done a heap
more for less. Jes for walk'n in de street, when day get a mean streak, day string de
black man up an laugh wid his dy'n jerk. We'ns jist hab to stay unda cober. Ah jest
tole mah Henry to slimma down, Ah war'n go'n back to Mr. Abe's for 2 weeks on de
stink would all be blown way by den, maybe Mr Abe would be home by den, an if'n
any ones could fix tings dat Mr. Abe could. He war a smart man. So mah man quiet'n
down a spell. But you'ns know Ah's telling de truth. Henry war sheer'd a spell for a plum
week. But Ah did all de pray'n Ah could think of. Ah promised God Almighty eberything.

Mr. Abe Cure Billie Lee

Ah got onah to da missy around six ta do a 2 weeks wash. War war da fire ready ta light unda da biler an da biler filled wid wata. Ah went in da shed an da clothes war sorted. Da tubs war on da bench, da lye soap an board te. All ah had a do war wrench da clothes in cold clear wata. Wile the biler done got hot, fa hot suds ta wash with.

Ah had walked ober Des hair yar, da spring weather war so beautiful. Da flowers war up an still some bloomin. Ah found ah war couched as well as da missy (ah done weened Julie in da nick ob time) Jus know'd ah bette walk an keep movee ta keep well fa da next kid

Bout seben as ah war hangin up da white clothes Bobbie rushed out ob da house an done look fa a neighbor whar a boy frew lived. Lak da little genman he war he called Howdy do Aunt Mariah. Dat Aunt Mariah made mah rite smart happy.

Ah finished da colored ones. Emptied up aroun an taking down da fust ones dried, when ah seed a red hedd gal leave. Her'n war young, maybe goin ta school. Her'n name war Laurie.

Da missy had done tole me Bobbie's eyes war still week a little, on certain yet, aftasan opration on his'n eye by her'n sister Francis' man an a German doctor. That Bobbie had gone to school some, but she had taught him to read and write and some numbers, oh yes and a little french. He didn't like french, but jus guess her'n crammed it down him. The children at school had tormented him about his eyes, so they still was undecided whether to start him in school in the fall.

Wal when ah carriedin da folded clothes ah saw dat Laurie had straitin up a bit. Da missy heard me an called, Air dat you Mariah? Ah axed her'n how war her'n. Her'n says I've been too busy Mariah to think of myself. I've made curtains for the entire house. Made clothes for Robert, if he goes to school this fall and clothes for the new baby that is coming. Hope it is a girl. Mr. Lincoln and I would both love to have a girl. Wal Ah ups an say ahs wanten mine'll be a boy.

Wat dat da missy say?

Why Mariah why didn't you tell me you were expecting a child too.

Wal ah say, because ah didn know ah was cauteched. Wuldn tell as how as long as Julia war nursin. But since her'n air weened it thowed up. Ah do hope et air a boy. Billie raise da roof efin notha gal shows up.

Ellen da olest, her'n bats aroun. Guess its jus his'n way of sayin her'n wish her'n war a boy. That makes me think Mariah. Why

2. didn't you bring Billie? I've fixed over the clothes he called sissy. You must bring him the next time. Maybe Robert will stay home awhile if Billie is here to play with. I never know where he is or what's he doing when his father is away and that's most of the time.

I haven't heard a word from Mr. Lincoln. I wouldn't blam him if he never wrote, or even if he never come home the way I cut up.

Wal now ah say missy ya jes done no as how hen's kind outa be nurered. Wal herin say - Does anyone? I've tried every trick. If at the end of each trick, it just doesn't work I get discouraged and blow up.

He just doesn't love me and there is no other way to reach him. Oh now, ah say, Back up missy. Dat man jes love do whole worl at that herin say, ou herin hab me stumped - Ah don't want him to love me like he loves the whole world. I want him to love just me as any man should love his wife.

Ah shur could think ob oula one thing a say afta ah pondered an considered. Wal dat man, dat Mistah Abe ain't a man ob God an ah good preacha say - God is Love.

Herin sent me home saying - Take care of yourself Mariah, you're the only one I have to depend upon. Come in two weeks and bring Billie.

Ah went home wid a down cass spirit. Everyone thought herin war a bad, bad woman. Herin war oula a badla mixed up woman. Ah woman who'n didn unerstan herin man, or herin man unerslan herin.

Et war now June wen ah went back in 2 weeks. Ah took mah Billie wid me. Mistah Abe war thar dis time. Hin war so pooh an holla eyed, look as how hen's hab nary a thing ta eat all month.

Hen's hab all for da wash ready, an a heap of wood cut. Ah swor ah knowd hen nevah seen me. Ah call out morin Mistah Abe. Hen spied mah Billie. Ah do believ hen thot et war Billie sayin morin Mistah Abe. Hen perked up by littles. Billie's lak his mammy nevah could kape hisn fly trap shut. Calls hey there - Are you'ns dea. Wars Bobbie? Mistah Abe say nary a word, jest pointed up stairs. Billie knowd none ob dis hair sign talk. Hin took an ole sock ball out ob hen's pocket an socked it up on da house whar Mistah Abe hab pointed. Dat shur woke him up some. Whan et bounced off da house hen cautched da ball an throws et back ta Billie. Billie slammed it back an thet got dar guaintance started. Dey keep movin by littles down closa ta da barn. Ah figered Mistah Abe waned to get out ob mah wey an far nough wey, so dat ball wouldn strike da house gain. Dey keep up dat play 'til Ah war near done mah wash, an et war a hard one, Mistah Abe hab brot home

3 a heep ah dirty clothes. Smell'd bad lak hen's hab a fever an fagot ta taken dem off whan hen went ta bed.

Finely da got tuckered out throwin an cautchin. Mistah Abe an Billie sait down on da wood pile. Billie squirmed roun an finely went afta da lice hen coutched in dat black wool of hen.

Guest hen done got dem stirred up, playn wat mistah Abe calls a fast game ob han - ball. Dat man shur loved ta play dat han ball.

Mistah Abe noticed Billie scratchin. Said "mariah what's Bill digging up there for."

Mistah Abe ah swar ef hen cautched dem agin, playn wid da bad set nex reins. Ah'el nera knowd what a do wid hens. Ah allus tell mah youngins ta sta way from dem white trash.

Mr Lincoln caught Bill and cracked a big louse with his fingers. Said - Mariah I know the very fellow who can get rid of these lice in a hurry, if you'll let me take Bill to him - Aunt mariah consented. So mr Lincoln took Bill to his barber. He brought back a shaved - headed, bald boy.

At first mariah didn't know her own son. Said I who dat ope? when she recognized him as Billie she said - Ah got so all fired mad ah nearly left da Lincolum's den an dare for ebba -

Ah hab no ide mistah Abe wood done get hen's haid shaved. Et took a plum year growin hen's wool back. Da colored folks en dose days war proud ob der wool. Ah war worried til et began ta grow back. Straighta but still wool.

Hal mariah say mistah Abe - I cant say Im surprised that you love those kinks, after seeing my unruly black wig. At least kinks stay where you put them.

mariah raved again. Ah's most bout ta gib hen notha puneshment. A litta peach ile as youns say mistah Abe. But spect hen's hab most nough. Lousy an a bald pate, fer gettin too thick wid dem white trash.

Well said mr Lincoln hin white trash. Now look har ah says, mistah Abe youns done bout nough awready widout tellin, ahs workin fa white trash.

Lincoln laughed and laughed -
Ah war bout ta pick up mah youngin an leave. But Mrs Lincoln stopped laughing and said
Well mariah, if mother can stand me you should be able to - and if my son gets lice I'll have his head shaved.
But as for white trash - I was called white trash and I must admit some of my folks were a little trashy. If they'd all met a mary Todd to put up with them and love them, maybe they'd tried to match her trying

As I did

now mariah, when you go home give those white trash neighbors a little kindness, if you cant love them, With your big, kind heart I believe you can help to make them over to be as fine as your own family are. Remember there is only one power love. For God is love

At that he took from his long coat pocket a sack of licorice sticks and passed them around,

mariah said - Ah stayed an shur am shamed I cut up so. Ah heard steps in time ta push Billie's sock cap down tight ober hen's bald haid. mistah Abe, Billie an ah all laughed. Da missy got specious an say, So you can find pleasure with someone, or something outside your family. Wal dat talk took men's all by sprize. Ah sobered up - mistah Robbie grab Billie an rushd fa da barn an mistah Abe looked black. Ah nebba saw such a down cass black look. As hen left wid da missy ah heard hen's say. Now mother dont get upset again, I had to take Billie to the barber to get his wool cut. It was full of lice, Guess Aunt mariah was ashamed of Billie's bald pate and pushed his cap down so tight it covered his eyes. Thats why Billie stumbled and almost fell when Robert grabbed him and rushed away. Is there any harm in laughing at that.

Da missy raised da paregoric bottle an drunk from it. Ah know'd dat bottle war a plum gallon. mistah Abe said, mother, mother I wish you wouldn't. I suppose this means another day of stupor. If you would only try to control yourself for the child coming. If for no other reason. Da missy say - Little you care about me or the one we have., Leaving us month at a time without a word and when you do come, with your hideous appearance and filthy clothes. How could you expect me to appreciate your return and fawn over you. Even the sight of you is repulsive.

So get out, get out I say. Hen got out an drug hen's feet ta da barn whar da boys war. Ah hearn Bobbie say - Pa ah want my head shaved like Billie. Now, now, Say mistah Abe. Not now. But if you get lice. Off that beautiful hair comes. I'm going to get lice screamed Bobbie. Well Robert said his pa if you do I might give you a little peach oil before the shave. Ah gee pa you never do what I want. You said you would take me to the woods sometime, but you never have, And I dont think you ever intended to. I want to see the flowers and the giant trees, like you said you had split. I want to climb one of the giant trees and do what you used to do when a boy. I just know thats what has made you so big and strong and good. I dont like to hear the boys say mean things about you splitting rails As if it were a disgrace. Oh cant we go. Cant we.

5. Ah guess that war too much fa mistah Abe. Hen took mastah Bobbie by da hand, picked up da ax an dey started off.

Billie tormened mah ta go along wid dem. Ah hab ta box hen ta get hen to shut up.

Ah finished carryin in da wash. Straighten up a little aroun. Sifted some grub on da table, an went back home wid Billie. All da way back ah war pourrin wat ah wood say wen mah Henry saw Billie's shaved haid. Ah tole Billie hen shur mus hope hen's cap on in da house whan wen's got home. But da firstes thing hen done did war ta sling dat cap cross da room. Et war no time 'til Henry calls come har Billie. Wen Billie come har, mah Henry grabbed hen an 'fore ah could even think had dat boy cross hen's knees, Henry war short from hen's belly ta hen's knees. So all ah could do war to grab Henry by da feet an yank. Down slid Billie ta da floor an den maid a dash fa da door. Ah grabbed Billie by da collar. Ah hearn da buttons snap snap snap off an Billie war out dat door lak greased lightnin, wid ma holdin his coat. dat bust off ob hem. Dat nigger man a mine war so mad hen's eyes pop out an hen's mug scbowl up as big as a new red moon. He war dat mad. A swarin somethin God awful. Hen wood bust out dat door an afta Billie, but ah stood wid mah back gin dat shack door an hen knowd ah'd takin mah stan. Ah say now youn big black ignorin coon, youn back rite back ta dat cheer or ah'll dent youn's ole dum haid wid dis poka. Now youn's lisin ta mah. Ah Billie cautched lice from dees poor white trash hen's been playin around wid. Mistah Abe took hen's up ta da babba an hab hen's haid shaved. Ah war mad wen ah saw dat fine crop of wool gone. But et air gone, so air da lice. An ah say How youn's goin ta put dem back ah say. Not by scorchn dat poor boys bottom. All mah man cauld say war. Dat long leg jack-ass scare-crow. Dat ugla lantern jawed jack-ass. Ah waited 'til hen run down abusin mistah Abe, den ah made et clear, Billie had hen's punishment nough now. Ah let on et war settled an wend 'bout gettn da vitals on da store. Ah made Billie wash da dun off'n hen's hans hen got in mr Abe's barn. Made hen sew da buttons on dat popped off, fore ah give hen any sow belly an beans an corn paul. Dat seemed ta please mah Henry. He still growld roun once now an den but disstifered off as Billie's hare growd out.

Billie larned a heap before dat wool growd. Da lice neber hung roun hen's any more Cause hen's quit hangn aroun whar he could cautch dem.

Ah caint zackley recomemba ef et war da nex two weeks afta Mr. Abe, an Billie's har off fah lise or not but somewhars near dat time. But wen ah went to do da wash da doors war locked. No watah out an no clothes in da shed.

Ah war plum skeered. Ah thot da Missy might hab took too much paregoric, an done laid up dar daid.

Ah war poundin on da door an ringen mah hands, an praying God to hab mercy on dat poor critta Missy's soul, wen Bobbie open up dat vera same door ah war poundin an say — "Boo Aunt Mariah." Ah jumped as high as da door knob, Ah almos fell in dat door. Ah shouted Glora Hal lulah, Glory hal lulah. Dat Bobbie nigh split heis fat little sides laughen.

Ah giben dat young towment a spank on hisn rump, an say, Wars da Missy? Whats da fault wid herin now? nothing wrong with her Aunt Mariah. She had folks in after church yesterday. The Preachers, his wife, Aunt Lizbeth and uncle Jinnie, uncle Wallace and Aunt Francie and some of the children. They had dinner with us an stayed for supper. The preacher and his wife went home. But our folks stayed. Played chess and some other games until late. She's sleeping this morning to make up for sleep she lost last night.

Ma, said "Go let Aunt Mariah in before she breaks the door down, The neighbors will tell I've been beating you and your father to death. Hurry Robert before I have another spell".

She tries to scare me, but I'm used to ma's spells. Aunt Mariah you'll get used to them too. Pa says "She's still just a little girl who has never grown up." But I wish she would grow up or I would. I effect if I was grown up I'd put her across my knees as your Henry does Billie. Suspect Pa feels like it sometime Now, now I says to dat. You'ns mammy ais a porofull sick woman, an you'ns Pa knows it. He wouldn—think of molessing young ma. Herin needs love an care da worsest way. Don't you'ns neva neva say unkind things about herin or to he. Aunt Mariah I don't dare say them to her. Den hein stopped right dar an den, cause ah pointed mah finga at him an says shew, Hein skipped out da door, den comes back an say. "I almost forgot Aunt Mariah, ma said, there would be no washing. She did it Friday and ironed Saturday. She wants you to clean the kitchen and get dinner Said, Use up what you can of the left overs"

Ah war dat woman war da mostest, savin on vitals ah eber seed Only when herin hab company. Da floor war dried. Ah scrubbed da water kitchen floor til et war white as sand. Ah had to hab a hot fire to wash da dishes. Dar war stacks of dem dishes Ah stood on some ole clean hemp socks in da corner of da kitchen while Ah washed da dishes an da floor dried.

Ah made dinna of corn bread, chicken cut in little pieces and heat wid da left over sop. Da call dat some big name now—frigaree (fricassee). It war jus warm over chicken, but da missy wen hern smelled it an comb down to eat said, "Why mariah with da left over vitals, desert and that fine smelling chicken gravy over corn bread, it really tastes better to me than our Sunday dinner.

And this drink Aunt Mariah, what can it be, its delicious, Hal. Ah jes tole da missy — Ah couldn't find any wine about fa pairs Da bottles layin round war plum empty, so ah jes parched some corn, rolled et down fine wid da rollin pin an den biled et in wata. Ah an mah man an chillun lak et. Bobbie drank two cups of it. He said Ma can't we drink this every day, maybe I'll git stout like Billie. Da missy done didn ansa Ah see eben ef hern did lak et, to hern et war black folks or poor white trash drinkin.

Ah hab put da tin cup full ob wilted wild flowas in da centa of da table. Da missy spied dem, an said, I'm glad you didn't throw these flowers away Aunt mariah. Robert brought them home from the woods last monday, where his father took him, as he had promised so often to do sometime. Robert and Mr Lincoln must have had a grand trip. Neither one could stop talking about it. It brot back so many memories to Mr Lincoln of his early life. Which he always seemed so reluctant to talk to me about. Though he reviewed in detail to Robert. Im sure Robert's new impressions of his father as a woodshoper or rail splitter will never again give him shame. He has been taunted by that in school what little he attended last year.

Now he has two battles fought — His eyes and his fathers menial beginning — Now he looks at his father as a mighty oak, a man who has grown unsuppressed by the all protecting hand of almighty God.

I heard Mr Lincoln say to him, Son I did split rails. But no rail is going to stop me and dont let it ever stop you. Whether splitting rails or doing any other honest labor, has its purpose in Gods plan. So spurs you on by first providing growth of body and inny muscles. As the body builds the mind will build honest thots, deeds and finally achievements. Honest labor goes into making honest men. always remember that Bob and you'll never be hurt.

Robert on his own initiative gathered these flowers for me. That is one way Robert is like me. He loves every little tiny blossom. Even weed flowers, are beautiful and precious to him. So I'm making these flowers, this bunch of love, last as long as I can. Its his first full bouquet to me.

Im glad he's like what's best in me, if only a little. So like the Todds in body too. But what pleases me most he's so like his father "sensible and honest. Mr Lincoln brings me to task so often about the little fibs I tell. He calls them fibs, but sometimes they have gained the proportion of a black lie. It seems it has grown on me since childhood. My dear, dear father called them fairy tales and laughed at them.

Mr. Lincoln once said Mary dear I want you and my family to have all the good things I can provide. Don't think you have to fib to me. I'm so often embarrassed by bills poked at me, which you claim you have not run or have paid. He patted me once and said, Mary if you have to fib, do make it such a whopper I can't catch you in it." He's never been unkind to me. Since little Eddie went away he's gone out of his way to try to please me. But I know as God knows it isn't because he loves me.

Ah, was afraid to let hern get too deep in dat subjec so ah says What was you gwine to tells me about dere trip to da woods?

Oh yes. They brot back slippery elm, bee bread an robbed a tree of honey. Mr Lincoln smoked them out by burning both of his socks on a long pole. That was a good excuse for getting rid of his socks. He just doesn't like to wear them even in winter.

You should have seen Robert when he and his father first came home. Robert was honey from his chin down. It was a picture I shall never forget. He was so smeared and bee drabbled, but so happy. I believe his father was the happiest I have ever seen him. That trip will bind them closely. Closer than anything else. They've found a common bond that will last.

I pray God that Mr. Lincoln and I could find a mutual tie. I think we have both tried. But our foundations to begin with were so different so insecure. And our perspectives have grown farther and farther apart. I've even been afraid since Eddie went away that Robert will be taken, as a punishment for my gross sins. I've even thought I should take my life so I would not bring another one in the world to suffer for my sins.

Now, now prays. Look rite here Messy. You stop dat rotten kind of talk. You'n was brot here to replenish da earth. Now as ah know or anyone know how as dar chillen will do or hab a suffer. You'n suffer for you'n own wrong. So as if'n you'n knows you'n so wrong its time to get right with God. Stop dat stubbornness an pride an if you'n cant kneel, bow- to da almighty.

But Mariah. If I should live to be a thousand years old I can never repay Mr. Lincoln. He's has been the kindest father an husband in the world, and I'm the meanest, most exacting and demanding. Even when I know I should keep still and keep my hand off. Not ever try to make him over. He's so perfect in his way, which is right

Ah didn't wan a say too much, cause ah sees kern waned to talk sometings out. Ah just had to tell kern tho' what mah poppy used to say. Hein war igorant but he'd ast us_"Cant youse brats see youns onery? When we'ns say yes. Hen say no one's ever quit dat oriness until day saw see et."

Well Ah's tried so hod da Missy says

Ah say—ah believe if youns humble youns sef before da Lord, he'd hep youns out ob dis hell youns in. Now ah don't tink youns bad. Only to youns sef. Jus humble youns sef unto da Lord.

no mariah I just can't humble myself.

Ah just don't see ah says wha makes folks so gishdurn proud. It's all flesh, bone an blood an alls born without sense an all die an den no sense. Ef youns proud of youns poppy's money. Whar es et now? Ah says. Ef youse proud of youns looks, youns only looks pretty when youse good now. Looks fade lak Mastah Bobbie flowers. Ef youns proud of youse french, who in dis neck of da woods understand a durn word of et. Ef you think youns goin to get to da White House, who's want youns there da way you parform. You'd betta ah specks, just settle down to Mistah Abe's ways—Ef da Lord wants an needs Mr. Abe in da White House you can bet you chimney he'll get dar. You'd just betta pend on God an quit goin's naggen. You jus beta try or youns wind up allays drinkin dat pizen paregoric.

Well mariah I believe you are serious and honest. If paregoric were poison, the whole Todd Family would have been dead years ago. Some never born. We were raised on it.

Well ah says it are lak da debil. Et does its work slow an sneakin. Jes youns lisen to Mr. Abe an stop dat. Et are worin him most awful. Mr. Abe air 'fraid while hein's gone youns wal kill youns sef or set youns sef crazy. Or maybe give some to Mastah Bobbie. You jus betta quit pendin on dat such lak, an fend on God. Dat ole paregoric is da debil are hein's shur got ya hooked.

First mariah. Tell me has Mr. Lincoln expressed his concern ⌐to you⌐

No ah says, Ah heard him's complainin, bout it to you ah warn't lisven Ah jus couldn hep hearn. Rite den ah new as how hein come home so little, fo fear of offsettin youns wase hein did done come, or wat might happen to youns wile hein war away. Dat why hein comes home all bed draggled an lookin starved an nigh out ob hein's haid. Cain't youns use some common sense as Missy Edard's says an see et.

Well mariah all you say may be true, but he hates me. I can see it in the shy looks he gives me. When he takes time if ever to look at all. I think he never did love me. He loved some finnmon girl

5 in New-Salem, and he loves that common cheap drunk Herndon
who he has in his office

Wal ah doin' know as how bout dat girl (Ritedew ah did'n know)
But ah jus up an say, Wal missy tho feah'd youn's'll get hot
if Ah says what ah think bout dat cheap drunk Herndon
But Ah's jest got dis in mah haid an ahs got to say it fa youn's
own good, Hen out an out gits good an drunk on cheap rot gut
Den its ober wid. You snow youn'sef unda wid fine wine an
paregoric, way to ofen fa youn's own folks to put up from you or
fa da good of youn's sef. Youn's got a bad bad habit. A
real bad habit fa a good woman lak youn'sis. Youn's betta
pray fa da good God to rut out dat ole debil. For dat debil
pull youn's clean down to Hell. an eben take Masteh Bobbie wid youn's

Mariah I should be terribly vexed by that speach, if I thot you
knew what you are talking about. I know I asked youn's help
and youn've done the best you can

As for giving Robert either wine or paregoric, he'd scream his head
off if I attempted it. When his eye hurt so badly and I tried to
ease the pain the only way I knew. The smell of the sickened him   [paregoric]
He's his father's true son.

(Doctor Mario when I called him gave me this information about
PAREGORIC --- CAMPHORATE-TINCTURE -OF- OPIUM_FLAVORED-BY-AROMATIC.
IT'S -VARIOUS - SUBSTANCES -HELP-IN-SOLUTION -BY 10 % ALCOHOL. IS-A-NARCOTIC.
ONCE-USED-TO-CONSOLE-SOOTHE-MITIGATE -OR-ASSUAGING-PAIN-OR-DISTRESS.
IF-USED-IN-LARGE-DOSES-OR-FREQUENTLY -CAUSES-ADDICTION, AN
INTEMPORATE-HABIT. ONCE-THIS-HABIT-IS-FORMED-IS-NO-LONGER-MERCIFUL
CAN-CAUSE-INSANITY-OR-EVEN-DEATH.
(He went on to say, Had the Todd's and other cultured families in
those early days, have known the effects of promiscuous using of
paregoric would have held their hands up in Holy Horror.)
But Mariah my trouble dates back to my school days. You cain't
know of the thots that were instilled in my mind, quite innocently by
wonderful friends. Nor of the battles I have had, trying to attain my
ideals or ambitions. No doubt now obsessions

My early loves were ideals, My father an ambitious emproud politician
Henry Clay a learned politician, who accomplished at least a part of his
ambitions, Cassius Clay a pure political reformer, who would fight
unto death for his ideals. Political views and dreams of the
White House were instilled in my mind by these men, whom I esteemed
as perfect ideals to listen to.

My studies were secretly for the ultimate purpose of someday fit
perfecting me to become the first lady of America. Not alone for
the social distinction. At heart I had become a politician. I thought
that someday I might be an indirect means of accomplishing my
father's, Henry Clays and Cassius political hopes. I would have married
tottery old Henry Clay, because he seemed a potential candidate for President
of the United States

& my love for Henry Clay was ~~paternal~~ like a child for a parent. At that early age, I didnot distinguish the difference one felt for a parent and a husband.

I had lovers in Lexington whom I could have married. Inthe final annalyzies, they did not fit in with my plans.

Years later, I met a man who in every way met my needs & Even # fell in love with him. When I felt sure he loved me I was overjoyed. For he was young, immasulately attired at all times. Was my social equal, polished, cultural and edusated. He had gained a political summit. A step only to becoming president. (Stephen Arnold Douglas)

I found in all his political veiws we clashed. I tried to sway him to my way of thinking. Even became quite nasty with him at times. But he could not be swayed. He had as I his course mapped out, Even though I tried to convince him his tatt licks were unscupulous and brutal. But still I loved him

He became tired and disgusted with my nagging and bickering. He turned me down. Not abruptly, that sould have been kind. It was not kind. I was deeply hurt. I knew crawling to him would never make him reconsider me. Would only enhaunce his conseit I was young and proud and would let no one know that we had been more than just good friends.

I decided to show him I could find a lover who was his political equal. Even could see from my points of veiws

Fate or whatever one might call it played in my hands. On my first trip to Springfield I had seen a Mr. Lincoln who a cousin of mine told me was very bright and would go far in the legal profession. On my second trip to Springfield, one night while attending a highly social dance I was introducted to this Mr. Lincoln by my cousin who had brot him. We dansed at that time to my music now to his

For years I held that love for Mr. Douglas in my mind. But to twart yaut maneuver him was my way of trying to impress him that as far as love for him was concerned, he was completely out of my mind. So I went about using Mr. Lincoln to this end. He was so gentle and plyable Spineless I called it. I actually thought he was in love with me. Until one time I received an annonymous letter, telling me, that Mr. Lincoln was and would always be in love with a girl at New Salem (Ann Rutledge). She had started him on his legal and political career. I think she was just a common house servant. I didn't pay too much attention to the letter then altho' now I know I had a twinge of jealousy.

I planned how I would win his love no matter who was hurt by it. No one will ever know how unfair I was to Mr. Lincoln but myself. I was always comparing his awkward ungamly ways and mannerisms with Mr Douglas' suaveness. At times I had such a repulsion for him. It was hard for me to carry on my deception. I used every art given me. Even caressed him. At last I got a marriage proposel from him. I assepted and we were engaged and the date set for the marriage. I felt now he was clay in my hands. By careful tacties I could still avenge mr Douglas. Possibly reach the White House before he could for I had learned that Mr. Lincoln was a skilful, honest lawyer with ambition also political views much like mine.

When I approached him about his love for this girl, he didn't deny. He only asked that we would not dwell on it. I was continually trying to change him subtly, but I believe he sensed it and resented it. I will always believe that my continual probing resulted in mr. Lincoln breaking our engagement.

Deep down Springfield people knew even tho' mr. Lincoln tried to leave the impression, that he was the one who was turned down. His only regret was for hurting me.

Later it was proven to me. Box two men had not wanted me.

Yes I was hurt, but only my pride in my mind. Now not wanted by I turned this over and over in my mind. I made a vow he would crawl this uncouth, ill-bred creature. I made a vow he would crawl to me.

Oh I know Mariah you will never again think of me as a good woman, just a scheming wicked woman. I tried every approach. Using all my friends. At last I cornered him. I made it plain to him that he had to reconsider me if he was at all honorable. I cried not from shame or remorse, but because men can't stand tears. Only his great good heart responded in sympathy. He begged to be forgiven for the wrong he had done.

After our marriage, often I would feel I couldn't bear him another minute in my sight. I'll not repeat all the cruel things I said and did.

Then Robert came. My father came to our apartment in that terrible rooming house. I was ashamed for my father, the epithet in my heart of all good, to see me living in such a place with such a man. But the minute my father saw and talked to mr. Lincoln I knew, had he not told me later, that he was deeply impressed by his wit, intelligence goodness and honesty. As I loved my father so dearly, and never that of him as anything but right, I began to turn his new points over in my mind and accept them. But the paramount thought even then was that by scheming and driving I might after all, succeed in reaching Washington.

We did go to Washington, after little Eddie was born. Mr. Lincoln was elected to congress. I bought and sewed clothes for myself and 2 boys for weeks. I was going to be a social leader in Washington a grand success. You'll never know how dis-illusioned I was to learn that a congresswoman, simple because he had reached the U. S capital, was not always eligible and accepted in exclusive circles. We didn't even live in a home by ourselves. Again had only quarters in a cheap rooming house. Oh yes I again heaped abuse on Mr. Lincoln.

I did not stay in Washington too long. I was as glad to leave as I was to go there. The children and I returned to my father home in Lexington. When mr. Lincoln finally came to Lexington, it was plain to see what good—clothes, quiet, and a highly intellectual environment could do for him. It was right at that time I am sure he saw me in my true light, a shrew. My father even noticed the change in him.

It was then I took new hope that after all I might yet become mistress

I was doomed for another dis illusionment, for Mr. Lincoln after several reverses, decided he was positively getting out of politics. He went back riding the circuit. What little time he was at home I treated him in an exacting unbearable way.

Right dar an den dat woman broke down an cried. Dat poor little soul sick woman. Ah said, now, now don't youns cry youns blessed little heart out. Mr. Abe neber in des born worl hab put dat—Love am forebber ("Love is Eternal") in dat ring on youns hand if hen hadn't loved youns. "Oh Mariah, thats' just it—~~He hadn't he~~ He loved me for what I had tricked him into beleiving I was. I never loved him then, but I know I do now with all my heart. But he hates me, he hates me, he hates me.

Youns wrong missy. Hen don't hate. His plumb scared of youns. Ah can think of outa one ting. Youns can start right now, making youns sef back in da kind ob parson hen's that hens was getting hitched to. Jes quit dat paregoric, so youns got some sense in youns haid to think.

But Mariah those head aches.

Wal missy get happy an youns woun't hab head aches.

Jest den Mastah Bobbie dashed in for more corn coffee. Da pot war dry, onla da grouns war in da pot. Hen scroped dem out, put a load of sugar on an ate eber last bit of dem.

Ah'd listened quite a spell to da missy, an as mah Henry an youngsens war waiten for dar grub der at home—Ah pulled mahsef away.

Hern said—Well Mr. Lincoln will be home in July awhile, before going to Chicago on business (railroad). I expect he will bring home quite a few badly soiled clothes as usual. When youns come then bring Billie to keep Robert company.

Dat Mastah Bobbie throws hens hat in da air and yelped out loud nough to split youns ears. Harrah for the Fourth of July, Cristopher Uye and Geo Washington cherry pie—Oh I forgot, Washington can't have no cherry pie! He cut the cherry tree down with his little hatchet.

You see what I mean Aunt Mariah—I'll ship those 2 boys on to the barn, out of our way—They play so nice together—Don't fight.

Maybe I can take some of your advise Mariah. I feel better since talking my thoughts out with you. I was back with Mammy Sally. Take care of yourself for the Lincolns need you.

Ah stopped to get some grub an ~~sher~~ nough, made tracks for home,

Robert and Bill Go Fishing

Ah reached da Lincolumns 'bout same time as afore, at twixt 6 an 7.

Ah unhitched Maud. Ah started to da shed but turned 'round in da nick of time to catch Billie spittin out a cood of 'bacca. Ah boxed hen's mouf good an hard. Hen yelped an brot Mr. Abe on da run. Mr. Abe say to Billie "Whats got you this time, a horse fly?" Ah speaks rite up, "No Mr. Abe, ah boxed Billie for chewin 'bacca. Now, Now Aunt Mariah - Bill surely had his mouth too full of licorice candy so spit part of it out. Ah points to do ground an say, See da cood at youn's big toe. Ah hadn' notice hen war bare foot, ontil den. Dot man hab da most awfules feet ah eba see. Sides hein 2 times as big, as da awta be. Day hab bumps all oba. Hen see usin lookin. He say "Whin barefooted I feel more at home Aunt Mariah. But, what we going to do about Bill chewing tobacca. That would be bad if he taught Robert that. You know Robert thinks the sun wouldn't rise if Bill weren't on earth." Jus den Billie heaved up. It war Billie's fust chew ob 'bacca. Mr. Abe laughed an laughed. "Guess that ends it, he said. He won't ever need to be afraid he'll teach Robert that bad habit.

Da missy learn da nosses, done come a tearin. Wat a sight dat poor missy war. Hen hab been doin da wash, an Mr. Abe hab been hangin' out da clothes. Wal ah swar, ah say, Hair ah comes oba wid Billie, as youn say ah youn don't need wen. Well da missy say. I declare Mariah when I told you to come on the fourth of July I thought to-day was the 4th. I found out yesterday that to-day is only July the first. (The preacher mentioned yesterday, in his sermon, about the celebrating of Independence Day coming this Thursday) So I felt sure you wouldn't come until Thursday. However, Mariah the washing is only started as you can see. Mr. Lincoln has hung them on the line as best he could." Youn's should a saw dose close. Et war da mostest mixed up mess you'd eba seed. Da missy winked at me an shook'd hern haid jus' in time: so as I kep ma big mouth shut

Mr. Abe warn't fooled. He's goes way grinnin.

Ah took ma slat bonnet off — Roll up ma sleeves an hab da white ones on da line, in short orda. Ah straitin out dose on da line, what Mr. Abe hab hung. Day wouldn' hab dried in a week.

Da missy say—"I'll go in now and clean the house. Then clean myself as Elizabeth is coming to go with me to German's gallery. Elizabeth insists that I should have my photograph taken, before I get any larger. Dear, good Elizabeth, I know that she thinks I may die—I was torn when Eddie was born, and haven't been exactly in physical condition since carrying this child.

"Mariah will you find Robert, Robert was going with us to the gallery, and when you finish with the laundry will you straighten the kitchen and fix our dinners. We have left overs again, and so make corn coffee. Robert has never quit talking about it and begging me to learn to make it. He has his father in the notion for some corn coffee too—Mr. Lincoln said he never had any other drink, but it, and water when he lived in his fathers home. I'd burn the corn if I tried to parch it.

"Rev. Smith and wife came home with us after the services yesterday. Lauri wanted to-day off so she helped prepare dinner and helped serve. But after dinner refused to wash the dinner dishes and cooking utensils, since she had an afternoon engaged—ment with a gentleman friend to go for a buggy ride. I swear if it wasn't for being alone at nights I'd dismiss her. Unless I watch everything she does I have it to do over. I could get Howard Powell, Robert's friend. If we needed help in the night he could go with Robert to get whom or what we might need. You couldn't awaken Lauri if a cyclone struck. Still she's always here, at least during part of the nights, while Howard can't always come. His folks are talking now of moving."

"Well molly you think of everything" he' say, Mr. Abe. De missy answered him right sharp. "Yes an I'm still wandering what made Billee sick and yelling, out at the barn. Ah ought a hab ma big mouf smash'd lak ah smash'd Billie's"— Ah tole de missy 'bout Billie chewin bacca, an dat, dat wale dat swallow'd Jonah, mary heaved up dry worste when he took da notion to git rid of Jonah.

Da missy an Mr. Abe cut loose da most awfa laughs ah'd eva hurd 'bout dat house. Her'n choked on dat laugh so's hard Mr. Abe (as shure as ah's sittin har on dis door-step wid you) beat her on da back ta make her stop chokin so hard ah thot shure her'n would break her'n back, fore she stop chokin, ah thot da war boaf goin plum daff 'caus ah couldn't see a thing ta laugh bout. Ah's just tellin da plain gospel truth 'bout Jonah an da whale — when day stop laughin an screamin, ah said, Glory Hal Lula, Praise da Lod, you'ns haint daid, Lod started dem up gin. Day mus hab haid somepin ta make dem powerful happy 'fore I come. Maybe she jis sided ta get happy, as ah tole her to, an dat woof drive da haid-aches way.

Mr. Abe picks up hisn sef an mossies ta da front hall, Props hen's sef gin a char back, pulls up hisn knees an settles down a read. Mus hab been notha Artemus he war readin, fore hen kep da house noisy wid his loud laughs.

Da missy got her'n sef dress'd, an sot down wid her'n sewin an waited fa Lisbeth.

Ah went to da barn fa ta hitch maud an dar war dat bless'd Masta Bobbie, teachin mah Billie schoolin.

When wens reach'd home Billie war as proud as a strutin cock. Hen knou'd lettas an numbers. How Masta Bobbie eva got hen to sot long 'nough ahll be blessed if ah ever knou'd. Mah Henry war as proud of Billie's larnen, as Lucifer, as da good book say.

Fore we'n left Mr. Abe comes out an say "Mariah has Mrs Lincoln paid you for these weeks you've worked? Ah say, Yes sah, Mr. Abe da missy hab mor'n pay me. You'ns can see fa you'ns sef. Billie's nise pantaloons an shirts an she dress mah Julia like her'n belong to Pharoah da King mariah that isn't pay, that's a gift. An do you'ns know wat dat Mr. Abe do. Hen toked a big ten dolla out of hen's pants pocket an gib et ta me. My eyes watakin an spilled oba. Ah war dat boaf sad an happy. Ah nebba hab dat much dough all atwanst in ma hole life. Ef hen hab let me ah'd got down on mah knees an washed does dirty feet oh hen's wid mah wool. Lake da woman mara maglene wash Jesus feet

Mr. Abe say, I'm leaving for Chicago on the fourth mariah. I have business there. Will also attend the United States District Court meeting. I believe Mrs Lincoln will be looking for you and Bill then.

As sone as we'ns reached, Kate ah'd put aur grub on da table. We'd hardla got start'd eat'n, when Billie began to beg hih pappy to go fish'n. Henry war kind'a tucker'd from tend'n da younguns, whal ah are Billie war gone. Right sharp mah man say no. no meat no wen Henry say't. But he war so all fired proud ob Billie larn'n lettas an numbers hein say. maybe to-mor. Wal Billie say, Dat's zackla wen ah waned to go. To-mar to da ribba. Henry say, Ef you'ns tink ah's bout to walk 6 miles to hold a string in da wata you'ns plain dum. Wal ah spoke up an say wal if you'ns don't you'ns plumb lazy. You'ns shur can do dat much for you'ns boy wat's guin ta be edicated

Billie drow'd hein sock cap like allows. Den sot down an made all da lettas an numbas Mastah Bobbie hab tell'n hein how. Hein's kept sing'n ova an ova 'morrow at eight.

Ah fixed dem a packet of corn bread an sow meat. Mah Henry made fish poles an fin hooks for aur Billie. Den dug some squirm'n worms. Ah war glad wen day war gone. Henry war allays in mah way wen ah war work'n ta home. Hein could be da mose aggervatin man, wen ah waned ta clean. An Billie war allaws fighting wid da girls, or ah war fear'd, whar he war, ef out of mah sight.

Day come home as da sun war 'bout ta go down, an does you'ns know, day hab a string of fish. 'Bout 8 ar 10 nice fat fish. Day war boof tired aut, but sot right down an cleaned dem fish.

Ah made a pile of griddle cakes an fried some ob does fish right off. Day war so hungry an da fish war so good, we'ns like ta bust'd eatin dem.

Den Billie up an say. Ah bet Mr. Abe an his Bob wish day had some of da fish day gibben to us'n. Mah Henry look down dat flat nose of hisn. Ah say now Billie wat you'n been up ta? How come Mr. Abe an Bobbie war fish'n dar 'cis you'ns? No wonda you'ns know'd jus wen ta start des morn'n. Ah says "Ole man ah you'n guin ta sot dar lak a bump on a notty log an let hein's lead us'ns an da Lneoleums roun by da nose. Ah, bet my best shimmey, Mr Abe saw thro' Billie's plots, if a knot haid lak you'n could'a. Seens you'ns an dat scarecrow, as you'n calls Mr. Abe, musta made up Wal da Good Book say, "A little chile shall lead them" Wal mah Henry say. Ef you'ns stop dat dam preach'n, dat ah get so fernal tard of hearin, ah'll let youns knows, a blind ma could a saw twat dose two scamps done did, an how day put da hooks in usin, 'fore we'n put da hooks in de fish. Just wen we'n got to da ribber, Billie wanted to climb a tree. Ah say go haid, Hisn clum clean to da top an look 'roun an roun. Den come down slow all tuckered. Hein got hein's wind 'bout five or ten minutes afta dat. Den put boof two fingas in hein's mouf an whistled sich a god awful loud blow, bout scared meh stiff. Ah, said, Billie if youns dare do dat 'gin, ah'll break dose fingas plum off, so youns caint scare hell out a meh 'gin. But jus den not so far off was a whistle, not so loud as Billie's blast. At dat ah new ef et warn't a bird answering — Something war up. Ah, say, Billie youn's blow 'gin. Billie rite way blow. 'Fore dat blow got 2 feet 'way, youn's nerva heard such a ear splitin noise in youns born day. Dat Mr. Abe knew as well as ah what war up, an hen done hab answer.

Wen we'n met, Mr. Abe put out hisn big han to shake hans, an laughed but say nary a word. Ah thot, if Mr. Abe can keep hein's fly trap shut, so can ah. We'n's went rite down ta da Sangamon an start fishin, war warn't any talk. Mr. Abe an hen's Bobbie got da first fish an kep gettin more'n. But dayn shur hab a good long fish pole, an cooked bait wid meat cotton, corn meal an sweet, oil —

Mr. Abe say he hab some portan work, an mus go. Hein took Bobbie by da hand. Bobbie want a stay, but Mr Abe say "Let's give Mr. Vance (just lak ah war a gentman an Bill asse fish. Den hein wish usn Good Luck.

Dat Mr. Abe sure taught me ah lesson. Hein didn't fus at or whip Bobbie. Hein hab sense 'nough not ta spoil da day for usn, or scare da fish by hautin an rarein. Ah took a nap 'fore we'n's come way.

Den mah Henry say, "Wal, Ole woman what youns goin ta do 'bout it? Is youns ole man got brains or haint he?" Ah say Da best ting Mr. Abe taught youn's, as he say "A still tongue make a wise haid. Mah Henry's lak an ole woman, hab to hab da las ward. He say, "Spose you take some dat larnin too.

A new Tantrum Etc — JULY, 4, 1850

Ah dressed mah sef in mah best duds. Dressed Billie in hen best. Pinned a wee flag on hen sock cap an walked ovah ta Mr. Abe's on da Fourth of July 1850. Hen wen's got dar ah foun Mr. Abe hab hitch Buck ta a new buggy. Da missy war dress up pretty and war dress' Bobbie in a little Lord Fauntroy, hen call it dat. Bobbie twis an squirm dis way an dat. Hen wen no such close. Da missy held hen tight as bees wax, an got hen rigged up for da cel'bration.

Ah felt plum silly when hen say, Why Mariah, what did you and Billie come over to-day for. There is no work to do to-day. You know you only come on Mondays every two weeks. Ah back'd way, Hen looked cross as old satan. Ah done thot maybe hen air crazy as some folks say. But ah pondered and consider'd in mah heart, maybe et air da weather. Maybe Bobbie twisin an squirmin, or hen carryin a kid in hen. Maybe somethin' gin 'bout Mr. Abe. Ah said at las, mutta he men,.. Dat heffed ole Mariah up. Wal ah say to da missy, Haint dis da Fourth of July or haint et? You'n done said, Come da Fourth of July, an hair ah air,— Mariah, listen to me: say da missy, Haint you'n got a lick of brains in dat black skull of you'n. You'n so all fired dum. A two year old would know better. I told you Monday & thot Monday was Fourth of July until the minister reminded me of my mistake. Surely any servant, espacially a black one, would have sense enough to know we don't include them at any time or place in our social life, yet you come over here dressed, thinking we would think you our equal.

Just then Mr. Abe come down da stairs wid hen valise. Bobbie grabbed Billie's hand an started to run to da barn but Mr. Abe call to dem, Just hold your horses right there boys and not so fast about getting away. Just trot right back here. And pointed to a spot where he wanted them to halt, I've a crow to pick with you two boys and I want to pick it before your two mothers. When you two little rascals put for the barn it isn't all for reading, writing and arithmetic. Understand this first I want you two to be good friends. I'm more than glad Bill wants to learn and Robert is willing to teach him what he has already learned and its fresh in his mind. I want you two to have all the fun life holds for you, unless that includes trickery and scheming, as you two pulled over on Mr Vance and I about a fishing party for four.

Bobbie speaked rite up lak a little gentman an say Pa, Billie didn't trick or scheme. He wanted so very much to go with us to the woods the other day, but you didn't insist and Aunt Mariah wouldn't let him. She told him he should know his place with white folks. Pa, why if one is white and the other darker, what makes the difference? Then das missy was going to put in, but Mr Abe held up his hand to make her'n keep her'n mouff shet, Well sou let's forget the white and black right now and continue with your explanation concerning our fishing episode. Bobbie den went on. I told him I was going to try to get you to take me fishing. That was while I was teaching him numbers and letters. He was writing down and I was waiting until he got through copying the 26 letters and 10 figures which I had set down for him to learn from. Well Billie jumped up and he almost cried that he wanted his pappy to take him fishing also. I told him if his pappy knew how hard he was trying to learn, maybe he would take him. Well he said, "If I can get him to go, maybe we can meet you and your pa at the river". So I said, if we could both start about the same time, maybe eight o'slock to-morrow we might get there at the same time. But I knew pa your legs were longer than Mr Vance's legs even if you do walk dragging them and I knew Billie's pappy was mad at you Pa for having Billie's hair cut. So that were two problem which presented problems. I don't know what Billie done or said when he reached home, but the last problem must have been worked out satisfactorly. for when we met at the river Mr Vance seemed to like you Pa.

Billie said, maybe we would reach the river at different places. I said, He could whistle if he didn't see me, and I would answer his whistle that was all there was to it. Now where do you find a scheme or a trick.

Wal say Mr Abe. I want you two boys to be good friends always, but I was beginning to think you were bad for each other. I see now how wrong I was and apologize. Whats apologize put in Billie. Well thats one way of saying Im sorry. But it wouldn't have been too hard for Robert and you Bill to have put confidence in your pappy and I. Whats confidence say Billie. That Billie of mine want to know everting say Abe. That word was a little to big a jaw breaker. But it means both you and Robert could have told your pappy and I your plans to meet. Wal sir dat Billie of mine speak right smack us

Dat warnt Bobbies fault. I knew my pappy war mad at you on count of mah hair, for he called you a scarecrow. Mr. Abe let loose a big laugh. Thats what I am Bill. But Bill you did scheme a little didnt you. Billie say. I thought of course he wouldnt go or if he did go he'd sock hell out of you. Mr. Abe lak to bus hens very sides laughing, but wound up saying. Thanke Bill you're a real protector. But always remember Bill to try kindness before you try your fists.

Da missy couldn't hold in any longer, she war so mad hern fairly shook. But sent the two boys to da barn, as does two Lincolumns, don't quarl afore Bobbie. Den she let loose. Lookin rite at meins says, "I don't want Robert to associate with the like of Billie, that scheming little trickster. The barns the place for them where no one can see them to-gether.

Now Mr. Lincoln, you big baboon. I'm ashamed I'm your wife or who do you think I am that you can't confide in me your doubt and fears concerning Roberts welfare. Or and I nothing to you or Robert in your point of veiw. Whose opinions and mothers love doesn't count. Mr. Abe looked black and his bad eye shot up to the left han curna. Mary, mary cant you see I tried to shield you. I didn't want to worry you. The time to judge is after all parties meet, discuss and defend as in a court.

I heard what you said to mariah, mary. I told her to come. I wanted to discuss other angles of her employment, with both of you, but this fishing episode came up and I felt that that should be cleared away first. Mariah I am sure you can find it in your good christian heart to forgive. Mrs Lincoln is not just herself these days.

Den da missy blurts out Who could be themselves around a glum monstrosity. I wish I were dead, I wish I had died with little Eddie. I wish I could die with this one I'm carrying. Mr. Abe say, now now mother quiet yourself. I'm going to Chicago in a little while. I'll take you and Robert with your picnic lunch to the fair grounds. Da missy say. You can relieve your mind right now, my Lord and master, of your responsibility to a wife and your child. I'd see you in Glory before I'd go one step with you. Now get out. Go to Chicago, I'm not in the right shape to go with you. Billies pappy is right you long legged awkward scarecrow. If Robert and I go we can walk

Ah wanded to run — Ah wanta ta grab Billie an nevva go back ta dat hell hole. Ah wanta pray for da both of dem. Herin war sick both soul an body. Mr. Abe war 'bout ta da end of da rope wid da missy. Ah swar ah'd ratha live in da hovel mah man an ah had, dan in dat fine home on 8 th.

Mr. Abe unhitched Buck. Hein took hern at hern word. He took Robert by da han an starta for da front an hein's valise. Ah sided ta go da front way home, cause ah war wid mah bes close on. So took Billie by da han. Wein's got to da corna in time to see Mr. Abe kiss Bobbie good-bye. Da missy say nary a word. Her eyes war kid as hern stood on da front. Mr. Abe nary even wave. Ah thot, what air goin become of dat blessed Bobbie — Bobbie say good-bye Aunt Mariah — Good-bye Billie

Ah went home, an tole da hole story, ceptin what da missy say to min. Hein say, Dares nothin wrong wid dat woman ceptin what a darn good beatin would settle. Kid or no kid in hern, Ah'd cook her goose so dam brown, a hawk wouldn't touch it. Den ah'd make her eat it carron an all. Ah didn want a say too much. Ah war all upset an felt a bit squirmish in mah stomach. Walkin ovva an back from Mr Abes, wid out settin a bit had got way wid me. Dat nite Ah thot ah'd die. Ah war dat pained. Ah lost mah chile I had in me.

Henry war skeer'd. He ran fa da colored preacha's wife and her's took good care of min. But ah didn mend as quick as when ah had mah younguns. So ah war still in bed wen Bobbie come tearin in 'bout 3 days lata. Sayin his ma was sick an would I come. Poor Bobbie look'd scared an hurt wen hein seed me. Guess ah war a coon 3 shades lighter than when he seed me las. Ah, sended Ellin, da olda girl. But ah really needed hern. Hern didn stay long. Da missy send her back wid a kittle of soup, beef soup, noodles an lots of good veg tables, a suck of meal an a whole dolla. Dat poor missy hab robbed dem sefs of dair dinnah, as sick as hern were for wein's.

Dat done put da screws in mah man. He say, maybe dat poor ting needed lovin, sted of beatin an ole Abe hab forgot if hein eva new how ta love. But hein's right dare say, its bess to kepe usn's noses out ob dare fairs, wein's hab enuff ta sweep our own back yard.

Da missy sew ovva eva day someting. Fruit mosely. Onst 3 or 4 kinds of vitals an fancy stuff. Hein'd hab a party. A lot of folks been dare, an brot in stuff. Bobbie say what warnt wash'd an notha dolla.

Ellen hab tole her ahd loss mah chile – As soon as ah war able ah hitched maud an go oba, mosly ta take her'n pans an dishes. Ah war 'sprized wen ah got dare ta fine her'n up an in sech good spirits. Someone hab took her'n a message dat Mr. Abe had been sleated to speak da services (eulogy) in Chicago for Henry Clay who hab died 'bout den.

Her'n wen clean owah board 'bout what an honor dat war. Said, Henry Clay war fuust afta her'n fatha next to God. Now no more babboon or monstrosy, but a fine high minded man. But ah allas new Mr. Abe was a man of God.

Ah war to return, if ah felt able on reglar wash day. Dare wood oula be a small wash cause Mr. Abe would not be home yet, an her'n washed out da party tings. Ah nevva took Billey next time, an ah didn see da missy or Bobbie 'bout. She fire an all war ready. Wen ah war done an close in, ah see no dishes or kitchen ta clean. Bobbie cautched up wid men 'fore ah retched da barn, an say Ma waned me. Said, her'n owed me an 'pology.

Mariah, I owe you an apology. I'm deeply sorry in my heart for the unjust things I said to you. If I was the cause even indirectly of you losing your child, I know God will punish me. I just can't seem to learn that I'm only punishing myself when I'm trying to punish some one else.

I was so put out, I wanted to go to Chicago with Mr. Lincoln. At the last minute I had a little upset physical condition, so he decided, the trip would not be good for me. But Mariah I never receive the least attention from him unless I approach him first. You could have seen when he left he kissed Robert over and over but never even waved at me. Ah laughed an said, Wal missy maybe her'n hot you'ns think it war a babboon wavin at you'ns. Her'n really smiled a wee bit. Ah tried to tell you'ns honey cauth's more flies dan vineya. Den da missy say, Only God knows how this will end. All he thinks is the circuit. Any trip to get away from me. I believe if he felt justified he'd take Robert and leave for good. The only hope I have is that I love him so desparately, that that love will find a way to keep him with me and cleanse my heart.

Well dat trip to wash war so much for men's. Ah didn go back fun dat fall. Ah doan know how she'n and Mr. Abe made out. She'n tole my Ellen ah had spoild her'n so with my fine wash. Her'n would wash herself afore lettin ans any one wash for her'ns now.

Ah dressed mah sef in mah best duds Dressed Billie in hisn best Pinned a little flag on his sock cap and walked ovah to mr. Abes on da Fourth of July 1850 -

Wen wens got dar ah foun mr. Abe had hitched Buck to a new buggy Da missy war dressed up pretty and war dressin Bobbie in a little lord fountroy as she called. Hintwis an squirm. Hin want no such close, but shinheld him tight as bees wax, an got him rigged up for da celbration.

Ah felt plum silly when hern say. Why Mariah, what did you and Billie come over today fer. There is no work to do to-day. You know you only come on mondays every two weeks. Ah backed way. Hern look'd cross as old satan. Ah done that maybe hern air crazy as some folks say. But ah pondered an considerd an said, in mah heart, maybe et air da weatha, Bobbie squirmin, hern carryn a kid in hern, somethen gin bout mr. Abe, or if men - Dat huffed men up. Wal I say to da missy. Haint dis da Fourth of July or haint it - youn done said "Come da fourth of July - an hare ah air. mariah, listen to me say da missy, Havent you got a lick of brains in that black skull of yours. You are so all fired dum. A two year old would know better I told you monday, that monday was the fourth of July until the minister reminded me of my mistake. Surely any servant, espasially a black one would have sense enough to know we dont include them at any time or place in our social life.

Just then mr. Abe come down da stairs with his valise and Bobbie grabbed Billies hand and started to run to da barn, but mr. Abe called. Just hold your horses there boys, not so fast. Now you trot right back here and pointed to a spot where he wanted them to halt. I've got a crow to pick with you two boys and I want to pick it before your two mothers. When you two little rascals put for the barn it isn't all for reading, writeing and arithmatic. understand this first. I want you two to be good friends. I'm more than glad Bill wants to learn and Bob is willing to teach him what he can. And I want you to have all the fun life can holds for you, unless it includes trickery and ~~skeaming~~, as you two pulled on Mr. Vance and I. Billie spoke right up like a little gentman, an say. Pa, Billie didn't trick, or scheme. He wanted so very much to go with us to the woods the other day, but you didn't insist or Aunt Mariah wouldn't let him. She told him he should know his place with white folks. Pa why if one is white, and the other dark, what makes the difference? I tols him I was going to try to get you to take me fishing. Dis was while I was teaching him numbers and letters, He was writing down, and I was waiting until he got thro' copying the 26 letters and 10 figures which I had set down for him to copy. Well Billie jumped up, and he almost cried he wanted his pappy to take him fishing also. I tols him if his pappy knew how hard he was trying to learn he would take him. Well he said, if I can get him to go maybe we can meet you and your pa, at the river. So I said if we could both start about the same time, maybe eight o'clock we would git there at the same time. Billie's pappy was mad at your pa for having Billie's hair cut, so that presented a problem. I don't know what Billie done, but, that problem must have been worked. When he met you at the river he seemed to like your pa. Billie said, maybe we would reach the river at different places, I saed, he could whistle if he didn't see me, and I would answer. That was all there was to it. Now where do you find a scheme or a trick?

Wal say Mr. Abe. I want you boys to be good friends always. I was beginning to think you were bad for each other, but I see now how wrong I was, and apologize. Whats apologize, put in Billie. Well that one way of saying Im sorry. But it wouldn't have been too hard for Robert or you to put confidence in your pappy and I. Whats confidence say Billie. That Billie of mine wants to know everything. Well both you or Bob could have told you pappy and I your plans to meet.

Wal sir dat Billie of mine spoke right smack up and say. Dat warn't Bobbies fault I knew my pappy was mad at you on count of mah hair, for he called you a scarecrow. Wal say Mr. Abe, an let loose a big laugh. Thats what I am. But Billie, you did scheme a little, didn't you? Dat Missy couldn't keep still any longer

She war so mad she fairly shook - saying, You two go to the barn I don't want Robert to associate with the likes of Billie, & he barns the place for them where no one can see them to-gether. Now Mr. Lincoln you big babboon. Who do you think I am Your wife, who you should have told about your doubts and fears about Robert or someone nothing to you, whose opinions and mother love doesn't count. Mr. Abe looked black and his had edge Shot up to the left hand corner. Mary, Mary can't you see I tried to shield you. I didn't want to worry you. As in a court, the time to judge is when all parties can meet, discuss and defend.

I heard what you said to Mariah - I told her to come. I wanted to discuss other angles of her employment too and with you, but this fishing episode came up and I felt that must come first. Mariah you can find it in your heart I am sure to forgive. Mrs. Lincoln is not just herself these days. Who could be themselves around a glum monstrosity. I wish I were dead. I wish I had died with little Eddie. I wish I would die with this one I'm carrying - Mr. Abe say, now now mother, quiet yourself. I'm going to Chicago in a little while. I'll take you and Robert with your picnic lunch to the fair grounds. & a missy say, You can relieve your mind right now of your responsibility to wife and child. I'll see you in glory before I'll let you go one step with me. Now get out & go to Chicago. I'm not in the right shape to go with you. Billie poppy is right you scarecrow, what shape do you think you're in. If Robert and I go now, we can walk. Ah wanted to run. Ah wanted to grab Billie an never go back to dat hell hole. Ah wanted to pray for 'em both of dem. Her'n was sick boaf soul an body. Mr. Abe war about at da end of da rope wid her'n. Ah swar ah'd rath a life in da hovel my man an ah had, dan in dat fine home on 8th. Mr. Abe unhitched Buck. He took her'n at her'n word. He took Robert by-da han an started for da front an his valise. Ah decided to go da front way home, as ah war all wid my best close on, so took Billie by da han, and got to de corner, in time to see Mr. Abe kiss Bobbie good bye. Da missy say nary a word. Her eyes war red as she stood on da front. Mr. Abe didn't even wave. Oh what is goin become of dot blessed Bobbie, who say, Good Bye Aunt Mariah good bye Billie

Ah went home an tole the whole story 'ceptin' what da missy had said ta me, to mah maw. Her say, Dare nothin' wrong wid dat woman ceptin what a darn good beatin' would settle. Kid or no kid in her I'd cook her goose, so dam brown a hawk would touch it an make her eat it. Ah didn' want a say too much, ah war all upset an felt a little squirmish in mah stomach. Walking over an back from Mis Abe's without settin' a bit had got away wid me. Dat night ah thot ah'd die, ah war dat pained. Ah lost mah chile ah had in me.

Henry war skeered. He ran for da colored preacha wife an their took good care ah men. But ah didn' mend as quick as when ah had my youngns. So ah war still in bed wen Bobbie come tearing in about 3 days later saying his ma war sick an would Ah come. Poor Bobbie look'd scared an hurt wen he seed me. Guess ah war a cou 3 shades lighter. I sent altho' I'd been da olde. Ah really need him. Him didn't stay long but come back with a kittle of beaf an soup, a sack a meal an a hole dolla. Dat poor missy had robbed dem selfs of dair dinnah, as sick as him war for usin—

Dat done put da screws in mah maw. He said, maybe dat poor ting needed lovein sted of beaten and ole Abe had forgotten if hen eva knew how ta love. But hen said its bess to kepe our'n noses out ta dare 'fairs, we had nuff to sweep our own back yards.

Da missy sent over eva day someting. Fruit mosely. Once two or three kinds of petals an fancy stuff—Hern hab a party. A lot of folks hab been dar—Some hab brot in stuff Bobbie said, what warnt touched—An hern sent notha dolla. had tole her ah'd lost mah chile.

As soon as ah war able ah hitch up Maud an go over—mosly to take her pans and dishes back. Ah war s'prised wen ah got dare ta see hern up an in sech good spirits. Someone hab been dare an tole her or took hern a messy dat Mr. Abe had been selected to speak da services (eulogy) in Chicago for I Henry Clay who hab died 'bout den. Hern went clean over board 'bout what an honor dat war. She war dat proud, dat hern man would be so honored. Said, I Henry Clay war to hern next to God, But hen were now, no more babboon or monstrosy, but what ah allus knew a man of God.

When mr. Abe comes home from Chicago he-ns mus ta
got right on da airsuit. Da missy sends Bobbie ober
for me-ins to come quick. Ah jus could'n go. Mah
Henry war out wid da mule. Billie war wid he-ns, an
ah war done head over heals den at home. Ah hated et da
worse way on count ob maatah Robert. Ah swar da boy
look'hurt ah glum ab hisn, fa done did' bout da mose ob
da time. We-ns need da work da worse kine. Times war bad
an winta war come-in on to pre-pare fa. Da fruit we-ns
hab war mosely wild fruit. Mah man hab clean out some
attics an lighten caves. He brot home a heap a plunda.
Mong it war ah pile ob light-n jars. Day war top heavy.
Hab big gobs of glass on da top. But ah cleaned dem up.
Mose of dem held plum a half gallon. Ah canned fruit an
some vegabals out of our garden. Tied da tops shut wid
pieces of muslin ah-d wash. Den cover ober wid way ta seal
all oh da air out. Den ah fill da crocks. Henry got wid da
plunda, wid cabbage, kraut an made some cida vinger an
cida. Ah figered wid da fish mah maw an Billie wood catch
da possum, coons, wile turkey, bare an wile hog, we-ns could
live. All we-ns need buy war meal, a few duds, an pay da
rent on da shack.

We-ns didn need much duds. Cause da missy hab gibben us-ns
stacks of closes. Sides close Henry brot home fromh attics.
mistah Abe hab help Henry by gib-en he-ns ah good name to
any one dat need work done. Dose mak sure had time. Dar
war ah few ah work fa, fore ah went to da Lincolnmus. Ah
could'n put da Lincolnmus fust. Den ah still did-n lak da
slack da missy gave me-ns on da fourth of July. Ah lak to
forgive even to 7 times 70, but da missy pile up da huet ta 70×70.
'Bout 2 o'clock dat same afta noon - poor little Bobbie comes
back. "Oh, Aunt Mariah", he'ns say, "won't you come? Ma needs
you so much. She is giving a party - Louiri got out of patience
and left. Aunt Lisbeth can't come, until time for the party. She
has her hands full in her own home. Ma has sent for almost
a dozen. They say, "I wouldn't work for her if she gave me a
million. She's too mean or bossy. Let her go down to Kentucky
an get her a nigah, she can flog. Won't you come Aunt Mariah?
mah heart was plum broke for dat little tike, but ah jus
could'n go

Afta hard work ah sent mah ole-est gal Ellen, tho' ah need her-n to run errans an tend Julia. Ellen put up ah howl, her-n shuh did-n wan a go.

Ellen war ah pretty light colored gal, an wen slick up wah fit-n ta be ah queen's maid. Her-n hab spunk an pride. Ah tried ta teach mah chilluns et war ah black sin ta be prouder. Ah sometime wonda ef some white mastah's blood did-n run in mah chilluns. Et mus ta been on mah side, cause Henry war black as night wid ah flat spread nose. Her-n mouf turn wrong side out. An he-ns wool wah so matted ah could-n comb et out wid mistah Abes comb. He-ns use on Buck's tail an mane.

Ellen did-n come back til wah gittn dark. Her-n stil nary lak da missy. Say da missy shuh war a slave driva. But rite dare ah stole her-n, ah speck fore her-n died she-n hab ta do lot a hard work. Trouba war ah nevva put much on mah chilluns shouldas ta carry.

Ah'd nevva been ah slave, an my poppy an mammy let usin putta an play. We-uns wah puttan an play'n on da Ohio, when dose white men, drag mammy an poppy's chillun off in dab boat. Ah hab ah easy chile life. When ah tole mistah Abe say. "Mariah you had an easier more sure free life than I. Perhaps was far better cared for than I.

Even to-day there are many more colored folks than white people, even the slave holders who have a happier life. They do not strive for things as white people do, I believe their spiritual values are higher. They only strive and want above all else happiness. Happiness comes from only one thing a clean mind. A mind lacking jealousy, greed and hate. A heart of love.

You have much to be thankful for to God. You wasn't a slave. Had fine christian parents, who taught you their christian way, and wanted above all else to make you happy. I shall endavour to give my childeen all I can, both of this world's goods and happiness. Then in later life, with a foundation of love, they can more easily judge their fellow man and cope with the vicissitudes.

Ellen say, whan her-n fust went a work fa da missy, da missy put her-n ta wipe-n dishes. Da fust ting her-n do war ta drap a lassa of fine china. What da missy nevva use fa common. Ellen grab her-n bonnet, an wah 'bout ta run ta home. Da missy say, 'Why Ellen that was only an accident. You are just nervous. You didn't do it on purpose. So come right back and finish these dishes. Ellen stay'd skeer'd stiff all da time fa fear she-n would drap and break more ob dose thin, posy'd dishes trim in gold. Da missy hab some heavy ones wid blue pictures on, dat her'n gib ta me later. Ellen den hab to polish silva. Some war heavy. Too heavy fa Ellen ta lift. Her'n war not seven den. Her'n help lay da table. Did dustin up stairs an down. Her'n come home luggin ah big basket wid someting ob all da fine vitals, da fine salads, jelly cakes, fruits, an a big ham bone, fa us'n. Lots of good meat on it yet. Ah knows mah Ellen war tireda dan her-n eva been in her-n life. Da onla way she-n war happy, war cause her'n hab da fust dolla in her'n life. But ah say rite dare an den ah'd nevva sen her-n ah gin. Ah's go fust ef et kill me-n.

Seberal girls work fa da missy fore little Willie war born. Ah declar ef ah hab ta 'pend on some un ta do mah work ah would'n be so fin-a-ky. Ah could'n get mah Ellen ta go back, evva hab ah waned her-n to. She-n war plum skeerd of da missy.

Et warn't onla ah week or so 'til Willie war born. Just part ob December. An da missy war-n so well for nigh a mouth. Dr. Wallace dat war her'n brotha-in-law, (her'n sista Nancy husband), waned her-n ta be quiet. Her'n war-ed ta get out an go to da parties go in on, but he-n put his-n foot down. Ah don know ob any one dat could make her-n behave, but Dr. Wallace. She'n even named da baby William Wallace fa he-n.

Mah Billie thot da William war fa he-n's. I tole he-n to come off'n da high hoss, da he-n war gist get'n too big fa he'n breeches. Dat da missy would'n name one ob her-n precious litta ones afta ah black coon. Eben ef day done did lak he-n ah heep.

At Christmas har come dat blessed Bobbie wid presents fa all ob us-n. A lot of close. Da dresses fa me war to high flutin. Some of her'n. Afta da missy dropped dat precious baby Willie out ob her-n. Da dresses war too out ob shape an too big. Henry got shirts an bandanas, an Ellen ah right pretty hood. Den I toys fa da res of da kids an candy. Store candy. Her'n war-n up until New Year's or later. Ah for git, her'n send 2 silva dollars.

Bobbie stay ah long time. Her'n war shur larnin at school. Ah done rememba ef et war Mr Estabooks (Estabrooks) school yit or not. He-n sat right down at we-uns kitch-on table an larned Billie an Ellen what he-n hab larned. Mah Ellen

larned fasta dan mah Billie. Billie did done put letta
to getha an made words. Bobbie came back afta that evva
few days. Mah young un larned to read an count. Mah
Henry nevva couthedow, but dare an dew aho wen ah got
mah learnin

Eber time Bobbie came he-n bring fittals, chesnuts an
toffy. Aftook da dishes an pans back afta Christmas. Ah
wan ed to see dat blessed little new baby William Wallace
Day allas call him Willie. It war nevva William, Billie
or Bill. Mr Abe allas called mah Billie, Bill. No one else
evva did call him dat until da day him died

Ah nevva knew da little angel Eddie. But da say dat
Willie war da spit-n image of Eddie. I learned why da hab
sent Bobbie ober so offen. Day wanted to git him out of
da house so he-n would-n destarb da baby or da missy

Ah waned to tell em day war makin a mistake, but
her-n war not fit ta talk to. Caze her-n mind war sot.
Her-n run dat poor little Bobbie out eber time he-n comes
near. He-n tip-toe roun lak ah little mouse.

Da missy tole me her'n got cautched while visiton in
Kentucky. Her-n come home afta Mr. Abe had bout ah
mouth afore. Dr Wallace said, "Mary you are so
nervous, the trip has been difficult for you. Unless you
relax complete you may experience nausea, may even
loose your child. I want you to go to bed and rest completely."
Ah tink that war bout da time ah fust wen to da
Lincolumn ta work. Ah nevva saw notha pa-fom as
her-n did when her'n carried dis Willie. If old woman's
stories war truth, dat baby Willie would hab been
ah screemin little chil. He-n did done hole his'n breath.
Mr. Abe say, "We'll have to heff him ofer that someway, for
with him holding his breath, like I have to hold my tongue
and Robert has to tip toe, the neighbours will think
the Lincolns have moved out.

I put da pan an otha tings Bobbie hab brot our-n
presentson, whar day belonged. Ah wash da baby Willie
fa da missy. Straghtn doun some to. Dat gals day now
hab war not so bad but hab her-n hans ful try-n ta
please da missy

Ah aidnt stay only ah speck dare. Her-n tole me-n ef
ah felt able ah could come ow reglar wash day, for dare
wood be ah litta wash her-n would not trust to da maid.
Ah did-n take Billie nex time, an ah did-n pet da missy
or Bobbie bout. Da fire an all war ready bef ave-ns had-n

been so bad up Ah would'n hab gone., but ah war
glad afta wods ah did, Her'n war ah sick woman in
bed, by da doctas ordas,

Wen ah went in afta da close war dry an fold; dar
war no dishes or kitchen to clean. Bobbie catched up wid
me fore ah ritched da barn, an said, "Ma wants you Aunt
mariah" Ah did-n much wan-a see her-n agin an
ah wan-a git home. Dar war so much a home ta do
these winta days. Ah war 'fraid us-n might a had
words yet. Wen dat would finish us fa good. Et would
be an awful ting of I rebuke a sick woman. Some way
ah did-n feel so good 'twards dat woman. Ah prayed da
Good God ta take dat aufa sin ob hate out ob mah heart
but he-n hab-n done clean-d mah heart yet, eben wid
all da Christmas Bobbie brot.

Ah wen up stairs to war her-n war. Her'n started
right in. Dat poor ting war more struck-n wid her misdeeds ta me-n dan ah eber thought dat proud woman
could be. Her'n say: "Mariah, I owe you an apology, I
know I have hurt you deeply an so unjustly. I am sorry
for what I said to you on the fourth of July. And I sense
either Billie or you haven't gotten over it. Can't you
find it in your heart to forgive me. I just couldn't think
of starting a New Year without making an effort to
get your good thots towards me, again. Ah de'clar ah
wilted plum down lak da litta snow man Bobbie hab made.

Ah almose thot ah war da sinna 'stead of da missy fa
da sin ob hate in mah heart. May be it war not hate,
maybe ah war jus proud. Ah done know what ob da
two ah da worse: Ah war-n pracsin wha ah preached
Ah tole mah young un da worse sins war ta be proud.
an ta hate, an ah done did bofe of dem.
Ah tole da missy Ah would forgive her so ah to could
start da new years right

Da missy go on: "If I was the cause, even indirectly of you
losing your child, I know God will punish me. I just can't
seem to learn in time that I'll be punished, and I've have
been for the guilty conscience that has been mine sense
I was so rude to you and Billie.

I was terribly upset that day I had planned and had
wanted so very much to go to Chicago with Mr. Lincoln.
At the last minute I had a little up set physical condition
Mr. Lincoln decided the trip would not be too good for me;

But that isn't all - I never receive the least attention from him, unless I approach him first. You saw how when he left, he kissed Robert over and over, but he didn't even wave good-bye to me.

Ah laughed an sayd, "Maybe he-n thot you-n think it war ah baboon wave'n at you-n." Da missy really smiled a wee bit. Ah's tried to tell ya Honey catches more flies dan vin-gar.

Mariah - God only knows how this will end. All he thinks about is the circuit or some other trip, Anything to be away from me. I've so often thot before Willie came, that if he felt justified in leaving he would take Robert and leave for good. Now that Willie has replaced Eddie or at least has soften the blow of Dear Little Eddie's going, he may come home oftener and find more happiness here

My only hope, so far as I am concerned is that my deep love for him will find a way to save our marriage. Ah jis war-n able to go back 'gain til almost spring. Ah done know how her-n an Mistah Abe made out. But her-n tole mah Ellen fore ah made dis las trip, dat ah hab spoil her so wid mah fine wash, her'n would do it, afore jis anyone else.

Bobbie comb ober offen. Eber time mah chillun larned something from hers. Sometime her-n brung ah few duds fa ta wash by han. Folks sayd dat Bobbie war mean to Eddie an now war mean to Willie. Ah know dat war not so. Ef any ting Bobbie war shoved off an out, so as he-n wouldn disturb

Ah know Mr. Abe seed it dat air way too. Et war air turble mistake. Not intenshon at all. Ah do know Bobbie wared ta hold Willie one day, said, he-n didn know how. Dat war no excuse. Day should hab teach he-n how. Otha chillun could come in an play 'round Willie but not Bobbie - Ah's not zadgeraton. Dat Bobbie war ah little lonesome boy whan at home, unles Mr Abe war thar. Ah think Mr. Abe should hab come offen war on Bobbie's 'count. Mr Abe war ah turble busy man and folks sayd 'twar makin heaps of money now. Ah knows day sent me-ne money all dat winta.

All Well That Ends Well.
===

Dat winter war long, but pass quick lak, et seem. Henry hab lot ob haul-n fa stove wood. He-n haul da Lincolumn 'bout 8 or 10 cords. Da poles Mr. Abe chop he-n sef. People nevva fagot Mr. Abe war ah wood choppa. Ah allas wonda wat war so strange 'bout dat? Bobbie comb home one day in da spring, complain-n dat da boys war now mak-n fun oh he-n pa couse he-n war ah wood choppa. Et use ta be Bobbie's eyes, day made fun ob. Now et war he-n pa wood-choppan. Da missy say da Estabrook (Estabrook's) school should hane better control over their pupils. She told Bobbie to tell them his father had had eight years in the State Legislature, Was in Congress of the United States for a term. Fa a successful lawyer. And someday would be President of the United States. So, if wood-chopping started all dat, maybe some of their fathers should go to the woods. Could be it would make something of them. Ah tells yar, her-n war mad. But dat did-n stop Bobbies hurt a bit. He-n jist nevva got ova folks throw-n up tings 'bout his-n pa an ma ta him. He-n hab sech ah tenda heart, an would nevva say tings tit fa tat to dem who-n tamenta he-n. Nevva da worl ova could your-n fine ah fina man dan Bobbie turn out ta be. He-n war-n stuck up. He-n comb-ta mah house whan eba in Danville an he-n allas ate corn pone at mah table. Onst he-n brot he-n litta girl Mary Todd Lincolumn, as he-n war going ta see his-n motha, wha war ah very sick woman at Aunt Lisbeth in Springfield. That war afta Mr. Abe war 'sassinata. He brot me-n litta Abraham (Jack) picha. Et war in dat picha-book you-n hot of me-n.

After day tease Bobbie 'bout his-n pa be-n ah wood-choppa, dat day he-n pa comb home, took da poor litta hurt boy by da han an say "Son I'm not ashamed of any honest labor I ever did, or am I ashamed I am a son of a common, illiterate, hard working father. That has been stepping stones ta the better life I now enjoy, so far education and material gain is concerned. Yes son I split rails. Though no rail is ever going to stop me. So let's us let them rail on. Our pioneers have been spurred on by rebuff and criticism until they acheived. Some have accomplished great things. While others have just become honest men. Their honest thoughts and deeds have produced this progressive America. Son, just push all that teasing that those youngsters are up to, to the back of your mind. Just feel sorry for them that they are using their precious time, and their God given power to think, so foolishly. They are the losers— Not you Robert. I can't wish harm for them. Nor you must not. The bible says son, 'The bread that is cast on the waters come back' they may reap someday. The humiliation they are trying now to afflict you with. They may then think.

Never let anyone show you they are master over you. If they start you to worrying they are masters in a wrong way. They are really below you, for they are not good to listen to.

I want your child hood and in fact your entire life to be happy above all else. Without the foundation of a happy childhood you have a poor chance for a happy out look in later life.

I want to tell you about the engineer on the train I last road to Chicago. A big hog and a litter of pigs were on the track. He stopped the train, dismounted and by throwing some food from his lunch pail, far off the track, succeeded then in driving the mother hog to the food. Most of the litter followed. The little straglers we helped him pick up and also remove from the track. He quickly hollered "All aboard." The bell rang, the whistle blew. We sclambled back in and were on our way again. Not one of those swine could think of us as anything but friends.

It might be a good idea to shame them. Or perhaps make friends of them, by doing each one a kindness. Never say rude things to them and put yourself on their lower level. Still fly off now. You try it.

Pa I just can't see where the engineer getting the hog and pigs off the track, applies to what the boys say to me about you and ma. If I'd call them hogs and pigs that would be rude, wouldn't it? Mr. Abe laughed. Son, I ment to emphasize the fact that the engineer didn't rudely plow those swine off the track with the engine cow-catcher. If he had plowed into them he may have de-railed the train, perhaps thus injuring the passengers on board the train. Or otherwise costing a large amount to have the train or tracks repaired. He no-doubt would have killed most of the swine. This would mean a loss to the farmer who owned them, and could ill afford to loose them. You see son, though it delayed our trip a little, that engineer's gentle thought, level head, and kindness, paid off. So will it pay you Robert, to deal with these boys, and all difficulties, with careful thought and kindness. If it can't be done that way, then they are not worth an effort, so steer clear of them as much as you can. If they see it isn't bothering you, they may cease. That has been my experience, so often. In other words "If you can't cure, you can learn to endure."

Yuhknows wat. Ah belive wat Mr. Abe preached in to Bobbie's head help ah heap. Cause rite way Bobbie hab some boy friens he-n nebva hab afore. He-n was mow cheeful lak, an happy, fo ah spell. But ah did done wanda afta all wich vice he n done took. Wat ob his-n pa or his-n ma? Ah allus thot dat et war good dat dey did-n give dare vice fore each otha. Day war bof of dem so difermet. Could hab end in ah rumpus tween dem.

It was, ah tink, ah may be mistak 'bout da time, Eesta vacation fo Bobbie, an mr. Abe war goin out on da circuit. Mr. Abe wen in, pick litta Willie out he-n crib, in da room off da parla. Da missy hab made ah

3. nursera dare. Day hab ah ole fashion crib. Look lak ah hollow-out log. Cut wid ah hood at da haid an ah set ob rockas on da bottom. Da missy hab et all flub-dub up. Dat Willie war jest lak ah pitcha. He'n war dress lak ah dress mah girl babies, maybe da missy wan ah girl so bad, war why he'n dress et dat way. He'n dress Bobbie wid flub-dub an ruffles 'til he'n fa onst got he'n dauda up.

Mr. Abe walk 'roun 'bout da house, cartin Willie on his-n shouldas, as young as he'n war. He'n kiss Willie an fa da first time since ah know dem; kiss da missy.

Bobbie walk ta da barn wid he'n pa 'til he'n hitch Buck. Den come runnan back fa his-n pa stove pipe hat. He'n carra et wid da top down, so ta not spill out Mr. Abe's poppas. Dat's da onla time ah evva did know ob he'n leavan his'n hat. Mus ah hab ah heap ob someting on his-n mind ta fargit dat hat.

Da missy war so happy dat morn-n, her-n did-n act natura. Ah tink dat blessed Willie war a blessom

Ah wen ebba two week an war nothan new. Ah did-n hep at partas, cause, her-n hab ah Irish maid 'gin. An her-n hab partas all da time. Et shud hab bin hard for her-n. Da missy hab sech ah time. Hab ta be en bed afore an afta dat blessed Willie Wallace born. But her-n jest hab partas on da brain, an ah knew would be ob no 'count to tell her'n et war not so good fa her-n.

Onst da missy say, "At least my guests won't have to wade through cow and hog tracks to get to my parties. Thus ruining my carpets at last the town board have decided, it's high time, that the owners of stock, must keep them pinned up securely, so they will no longer run the streets.

Ah thot she-n should go plow, 'bout using so much money ta hab partas. Ah heard Mr. Abe say ta da missy. "Outside of being retained by the Alton and Sangamon Railroad my business is slow. We now have this little account in Jack Bunns new bank I can't permit any with drawals. With a new baby and all expenses relative to his birth, a sizable hole has been made in our checking account. Please many an dissipate our deposits drawing interests. If you run out Billie (Herndon) will supply you with my share of our receipts here. Da vera name of Herndon made her-n blow up. "If you'd use any judgements you'd send that lazy Herndon out on the circuit, at least half the time, You're so determined to share half with him. Then spend more time in your office, as all big lawyers do. And incidently more time with your family. We miss you so. Then too you have two sons again to guide at least share part the responsibility with me. He'n say. Well mother I know I have an equal responsibility with you. And I'm trying my best to assume it. We have I hope, a long life ahead of us. And we must both be more patient

4. Afta dat xings gun to cool down fa ah spell. Nen Mr Abe lef
   sin, ta go on circuit, ah that ebu ting war rite 'tween dem.
Her hardla got way wid Buck 'til her-n gin da plan-n fa
partas. Her-n say ta me-n, "Mariah I just must get out some
from now on. I must make mor friends. At least from
now on I must return to my place in society. I've icelated myself
ands have withdrawn myself too long already. People will forget there
is a Lincoln family in Springfield. Since the Slave question has
been quieted down, Mr. Lincoln wants no part in politics. I'm
sorry for that because it gave him prestige. The Todds have alway
enjoyed social distinction. I'm determined the Lincoln family will
not lag behind."
   Dat missey hab one parta afta 'notha. Her-n eben took ah parta
ta ah show, an den bring dem home an feed 'em. Mr Abe didn
comb home fa eight or nine weeks, wid out ah word from he-n.
Her-n hab use up da check 'count, hab run bills at da grocra
da goods stoas, an eben say her-n would hab ta let mah pay go
'til Mr. Abe comb back.
   At las her-n hab ta go ta Mr. Abes offices ta get Mr Abe's share ob
wat Mr. Herndon (dat man wat she-n hate) hab save fa he-n.
Her-n would hab use all dat, but Mr. Abe comb back da vera ney
day. Jest tink use all dat air mon-a on partas fa folks wha say all
sots ob mean xings, bout her-n. Sech as one her-n allus 'clude in
her-n 'ciety tole me, "Mrs Lincoln entertains more lavishly than
any of us. All of us could better afford such expense than she.
2. be honest there isn't one of the girls who gives a fidlers dam for her.
   Nen Mr. Abe comb home. Her-n war delitea wid da $200°° he-n
put in her-n lap, but not wid he-n. Da missey would-n let he-n
kiss her-n foot eben if he-n hab wan-a ta. Her-n war mad cause
he-n sta 'way so long. Smarta 'cause her-n hab ta go ta dat Billie
(Herndon) fa mon-a. Dat filtha man an dat filtha office.
   Ah hear her-n say, "What kind of clients would go to such a filthy
office and be interveiwed by that filthy character. Yet you would
have your wife be humiliated, before you would get a partner, who is
gracious at least. Who would see to it that his office was not offinsive.
But you deliberately make it necessary, by staying away almost 2½ mor
Other lawyers on the circuit, appreciate their family. If and when it
isn't possible to come home, they write, showing their love & concern.
Robert wonders why you stay away. You should know all I've endured
this last year by grief and sickness. Or hasn't it concerned you in the least.
   Mr. Abe say, "Molly, I'm sorry if you ran short of money. I thought
our checking account was sufficient. I'm truly sorry you had to
bother Billie Herndon." At dat her-n farela tore da roof off. Her-n
rund at he-n wid da butcha knife. Ah got out ob da house. Guess
her-n scream worse dan a pantha. Mr. Abe grab her-n han, an
took da knife way. Dat war da worse wile-cat spell ah ivva saw.
He-n din sat her-n down en ah chair. He-n say, "Molly kid you run eny"

5. bills? Her-n lie an say, "No." Well he-n say, "maybe the money did run short. I don't feel too surprized now. I want you and the boys to have all the comforts of life. Since your indisposition for a year, besides your change of figure you did need clothes." Dat man git her-n eber chance to tell he-n, how her-n hab spent so much money - Her-n only look black-a an black-a. An held on ta dat mon-a Da 200°° from Mr. Abe an he-ns share at da office

Finela he-n lef da house. But war-nt gone long. Ah could tell he-n was dreadful disturb. He-n wen rite in da back room of da parla whar da missy was. Wen he-n get not up he-n talk squeaka lak an lik he-n war choked. Ah couldn hep but heah he-n say: "Mary little did I think that my wife was both a liar and a cheat. I've tried to tell you that I can't tolerate an habitual liar, I'm afraid I'll have to call you that. I've overlooked occasional fibs and I've put up with your senseless tantrums, your incessant false fronts. But with that I've found out you are a cheap little cheat! Ah tells you-n he-n must ob-hab all dat stored up for ah long time. Cause he-n laid it on lak he-n was 'sploden You've charged bills everyplace you can. When I found you owed so much at the grocery, I that I should go the rounds of the stores. You must have fed half of Springfield on finefoods. But we've always sat down to the plainest of fare. Since you said you wanted to economize. For what to feed or rather spludge on what you've robbed your family of, I can't object to dry goods, but why rolls and rolls. What do you do with it. Don't answer me, I can expect another lie. But the worst is so little I'm ashamed almost to face the good people of Springfield. At the drug store you took out bottles of perfume - broke the seal, used what you wanted. Then took the bottles back, saying, that they were poor quality. It's common talk among the hundreds you entertained while I was gone about this one act, besides your extravagance. Now Molly hand me that money so I can go down town and try to settle up. It may not be enough but I'll try to make it stretch as far as I can."

She-n thow dat mona at he-n an say "Take your pinch-pennies and git out. I wish I had never layed eyes on you, you homely uncouth brute. I wish I had married in my circle - Elizabeth warned me. I wish I had married Steven Douglas." Mr Abe say. I wish you had to. But I said, "until death do we part." maybe this is death? - It's worse. I must say this since you brot up the subject of Steven Douglas. There's one reason you didn't marry him. He was smart enough to learn soon enough what it has taken me nearly ten years of sad experience to learn. You are a spit-fire, a cheat and a liar. Ah did-n prove of all he-n said. Ah really felt sorry fo da missy foonst. Ah still 'lieve her-n love him. E, was into ah mad cat fit, ah notha tan-trum. Wen her-n call he-n want But Mr Abe war in ernes an her-n knew it. But her-n vows wi wid da las word. "I'll have grand-mother Parker's and my father's estate. And when they are settled I'll penny pinch with you no more I'll take my sons and git out. Ah reala done tink he-n heard. An ah done tink den he-n would care only for Robert an Willie. He'n lef da house an wen to da barn. Dare Bobbie was t' play-n wid ah bunch ob his-n new friens. Day hab ah theta wid bexes fa seats an covvas from da house fa stage curtain. Bobbie jump up an down wen he-n see his-n pa, "Oh pa I told the boys you would take us to the woods and show us how to chop trees down like you did in Indiana." Den boys all gatha roun an say "Will you Mr. Lincoln? Bob said you took him once and he climbed trees. Then he told us about your fishing trip to the river." Ah wanda if he-n tole dem 'bout mah, Billie an mah, Henry go-n fishing too. Ah 'speck he-n did. Bobbie war not proud. He-n nevva mis-treat Billie, cause day call his-n an he-n niga lovas. Da Abe say "Nows as good ah time as any to take you boys to the woods. You boys run home an tell your mothers where I am taking you, if, they have no objections. Robert you go in and tell your mother."

But God ah mighta. Dey nevva went ta da woods. Bobbie comb ah runnen ta me-n an say, "Mas laying on the bed with her head hanging over to the floor, and baby Willie just look awful." Ah push he-n an say, "Get you-n pa quick." Mr. Abe mus-ob take oula two steps to da house, an tore he-n shirt to get in ta whar da missy war. Her-n hab taken ah big swig ob paregoric, an den let Willie nurse. Mr. Abe shook her-n an shook hey-n, but she-n did-n budge. Then he-n pick up baby Willie who-n mite hab jist ah natural sleep. But Mr. Abe thought maybe her-n hab gib him some paregoric to. He-n rush Bobbie off ta git Aunt Lisbeth an Dr. Wallace. I ole Bobbie not ah tell anyone, but dose two.

Dr. Wallace comb in three shakes, as did Aunt Lisbeth. Dr. Wallace knowd at onst wha ah do. He-n hab had some ob dat same an his-n own home. He-n tole Lizbeth ta make some black coffee. Dar war n ah form ting in dat house. Da coffee an ever ting hab been goble up by her-n partas. Mr. Abe hurra ta da peoples who-n wrote da papa dare, Ah missy Francis. An her-n gave Mr. Abe ah pot ah cole coffee, wat we-n put on da stove an git it hot. Dr. Wallace tasta it, made et weak lak an gabe ah litta at ah time, wid ah spoon ta Willie. Dr. Wallace say "I hate to give this awful stuff to a baby so young. But its 'about all I can do until he awakens. Then I can see if he's had any paregoric given to him." Mr. Abe hab shoo Bobbie out afore Dr. Wallace came. so he-n would-n hear wat war said, so he-n could-n tell da boys. But he-n tole he-n ta tell da boys he-n's ma war sick an day would go notha time.

Dr. Wallace say. The child could not have nursed that from mary. It has been too short a time for it to take effect. She has given him a little perhaps. But I wish she wouldn't. He has been such a fine healthy baby. Mary has been under a heavy mental strain to have done this. He-n gib her-n some black thick look-n stuff. Tole Mr. Lincolumn ta "Take her arm Mr. Lincoln and I'll take the other arm and walk her." Her-n haid lolled from one side ta da otha. Her-n war a plum awful site. Dr. Wallace say, "She'll become sick an both the

? medicine and the paregoric will come up. Sure et did.
'Lisbeth clean eber ting an say "Poor baby, poor baby you
were awfully sick. Now you'll be all right" But her warn't
nor war Willie fa ah numba ob days. Dr. Wallace watch'em
fa a numba ob days vera careful.

All dis cause Mr. Abe cautched her'n en ah lie an cheat en.
Ah never did see such ah fernal mess as dose Lincolumns could
git dem self en. Ah war gitt'n out ob dat house as far as ah could git
Mr. Abe hab grab da paregoric, bus da battle wid da ay an beera
all in a hole he-n dug. Ah made up mah mine ah never 'plane 'bout'n
folks gin. Ah straighten da kitchen an war on mah way ta hitch
maud an git fa home, when da blessed Bobbie comb tearen up
from da barn, an say, Aunt Mariah bring the meat cleaver and
come to the barn quick. Pa got caught in the trapeye, he hung far
us, when he was trying to show us how to skin the cat! Aunt
Mariah hurry hurry He-is all tangled up in a knot." Ah
could'n move, Ah jis hab ta stan dare still an hole mah sides
Ah 'bout buss laugh-n. Bobbie rush in, git da meat cleaver an
bus out gin, He-n grab mah han an say, "Run Aunt Mariah,
run quick."

When ah git out dare, dare war Mr. Abe hang'n ba da feet an
haid, all tangle up, in dat trapshun, he-n hab fix fa da boys. Day
hab comb back ta go ta da woods, Mr. Abe war gitt'n dem settle
'bout not guin ta da wood. An he-n war wan-n dem ta sta out
da house, an not run en dat mess. He-n war laugh'n at da top ob
his-n voice. Ah war split'n mah sides, an da boys all but poor
Bobbie (He-n had da day lights skeer out ob he-n two times dat day)
war yellow an jump'n 'roun lack wild injins. Mr. Abe got ah
litta settal ah say "Ah jist cant hold on much longer, I'm
mighty uncomfortable, He'n war high up. He-n say "Aunt Mariah
just chop dat rope up close to the plank it is tied to, and let me
drop." Ah swar ah war so weak fa laugh'n, ah could harla raise
dat meat cleava ta chop. But wen ah gib et ah soun whack,
down Mr. Abe fell. Ah skeered he-n would ah break he-n back
or neck But do ya know what He-n landa rite smack on
his'n fiit, lack da cat he love

Ah put fa home, an Mr. Abe put fa da office. He-n tole da boys
Boys don't go to the house. Be good boys and I'll take you to the
wood the next time I come home from the circuit".
When ah reach home ah never tole mah man 'bout dat fracus
at da Lincolumns, Ah tole he-n 'bout Mr. Abe's trapshun an ah
that dat fat belly of his-n would wiggle plum off he-n laugh so ho.
Ah war glad ah did'n take Billie Billie would hab spill da
beans hab he heard da fracus of da missy an Mr. Abe. But he
war mad he-n war-n thar to see Mr. Abe'formance,

after da fight 'tween da Lincolumns. Mr Abe mus hab sided to stay home ef spell. Henry war work-n down town whar day war tear-n down old ram shacks an build on new brick build-ns some 3 stores high or nigh 'bout, Henry saw he-n almos eber day. One morn-n Mr Abe came out his office as Henry war start-n ta work. mah Henry say, et war da talk he-n do more any ting to get way from da missy - Now Ah say, Mr Abe hab ah lot on his-n mine - He-n make he-n live wid his-n mine, an he hab ta be war he can tuck ah dis out. my Henry say. You dum as an ox mariah. Why dat man is on da street mos of he-ns time. Crack-n stories. An ah ket he-n hab ah bunch in he-ns office tel 2 or 3 in da morn-n just raisn hell an laugh'n. Till war too late ta go home. Dat would be tough afta so much fun; afta each ah dam good time, ta go home ta da hellfire he-ns got fa ah wife-- Ah might ah 'lieve dat ef Bobbie had-n comb orra an say "ma has been sick again with headaches. She doesn't want me around with the boys making noises, so she sent me over ta play with Billie."

Dat please da hole bunch of my young-n. Ah ast he-n, How war baby Willie. He-n say, Ah Willie he fine. Only once he had colic. I wanted to hold him, but they are afraid I would let him drop. I'm almost ten. And ma still thinks of me as a baby- Ah say I told you horses Bobbie. You-n war born in 1843 an dis is onie 1851. Well any way he-n say. Am tak'n latin and pas studying with me. He ast Billie if he-n would lak ta study some latin. So ahd ratha learn how ta spell an read. mah kids all jossed in an say, Day wan ah learn how ta count an put letta tagetha so day could read. So God bless dere litta harts day all sot on da floor an had school. Ah could't git wha Henry say about Mistah Abe an da talk of da town. Well Ah know-n people talk. Ah know da talk about da missy ta me. But Ahs sprised da talk 'bout Mr. Abe. Ah felt lock ah should go ta his-n office an tellin him, He-n should be ta home wid dat poor woman an dat blessed Willie. Aula Henry tole me so offen ta keep mah nose out of dare hussess. Ah new dare war some tuf in Mr. Abe hare-n hell at home. An ma be no humanss can hold dare tongue fa eba. But ah swar Mr. Abe tole her-n all he-n hab store up in his hied 'bout her. An he-n did-n choke off his cause da really war no less. Still ah tinks Da missy serves ta be forgiven. For here-I so mixed up. An ah 'lieve her-n do love da man an is near dyin cause she tinks he-n done care fo her. But he-n say 'til death do we-n part. So ah tinks he-n wal stay wid her til death. An maybe day 'l patch it up. Ah-m goin ta tell mah man ta keep his lip button 'bout boaf dem. Cause day wich us ah friens an help us. An Bobbie are gibben he-n education to us-n. Ah learn-n ta read an count

Ah send mah Billie up ta da town to tell Henry ta bring home some corn.

for hominy an ta make harsh corn. He-n had Maud and da cart
Bobbie wen ah long. Dey did-n stop wid Henry long, dey went an ta
town an ran outa Mr. Abe. Day soax he-n ta take dem fish-n. It so
war a nice day, but he-n say "Ah have some important word ta do. Stop
to-day, maybe to-morrow." But right way he want a ta know why
Bobbie war down town wid Billie". Bobbie say "Ma sent me over to play
with Billie cause she wanted the house quiet. She didn't want it over run wid
boys all day. She wanted Willie to sleep as he did'nt rest last night — s'len when
I was playing with Billie, Aunt Mariah wanted him to come down here to see
his pappy, so as, to bring home some corn for hominy an fresh." "That sounds all
first straight" say Mr. Abe. "Now here is a nickle, here go and get you some
candy. And get off the street it's so tore up, from the building going on." "Well"
say Bobbie "Hows it come you are on the street instead of in your office"
"You must learn Robert, that men can do a great many things little boys
can't. But to get to the point son I have business on the street. Billie wid
his big mouth say, "Stan-n roun crack-n jokes wid da bums"? Listen
Bill. "That crackin jobs as you call it, or telling stories as the truth of the
matter is. I must be friendly with all people. That's my way of being
friendly. And in a way if I make friends I may get their business
if they like me, they'll come to me. There's too many lawyers round these
parts to neglect all you can do to get your share of the business. I do the
some thing on the circuit and in court, I make friends and I like friends.
Always remember boys, you can't buy friends, you have to merit them.
People will be more apt to be your friend if you make them happy than
if you make them angry — But as I said I like friends. Until I came to
Illinois I was never in a position to make many friends. The country
where our family lived was sparsely inhabited. It was a bleak
wooded and desolate country. I often longed for companionship that I
could talk with and learn from. Especially discuss the learning you
get from books. Don't misjudge me boys. Always remember you can
learn from everyone. Even the lowliest. If not any thing else. Good
common sense often. My father nor mothers, didn't have book
learning. But each in their way, had good common sense. Did the
best their meagre education permitted. And above all were happy.
Bobbie spoke up an say "Pa then why don't you act happy at home? "Well
son maybe I don't act all I feel but you, I must think out how to plead a
case or meet obligations. At home when away from the hub-bub of
the public I can concentrate and plan. Maybe I haven't spent enough
time with you Robert. We'll go fishing to-morrow. I'll ask
your pappy to go fishing with us.

Bobbie he-n stay for dinna, ay
put off home. H'an mah man
come fa his dinna — Billie lak
allas popped off. About ebber ting
Wal old Abe Lincolumn can
da hell de he-n think ah can fish an work at da same time.
why can't hims go on Sunday, ef'n he-n wont for me'n ta go
'ishing. Jus cause he-n knows ah cant go. Cantcha a white lawer

I turned the sar-jarly to
myself to think things out, you see
the habits you form when young
are almost impossible to break
go fish-n wid you-ns, but how

goin any whar wid ah niggs — Specly one who-n got hitched
ta ah white high 'ciety woman lak Mrs. Lincolumns. Billie
say, dat ole woman did'n wan Mammy an me ta go wid
her-n on da Fourth of July, ah hursh thin up the Bay-n —
Nal we-n did-n want ah go. So we-ns knew, But Billy
stuck up fa Mistah Abe the say'n Nal we-ns war fish-n
'getha an he-n walk plum home wid us-n. But mah Henry
hab hardly got 'way when dat Blessed Bobbie came tear-nt
back an hollar. Oh Billie, what you
think the whole gang is going fishing with us. Billie
look down his-n nose Who's da gang. Bobbie ups, an say
The bunch of boys I play with now. told them you
could whistle like all the birds. An was a peck of fun,
they all want you. You come over in the morning
early. We'll fix picknick lunch for you two, so don't stop
for that. He can go can't he Aunt Mariah —

Whan da gang all got ta da Lincolumns, da missy say
Dhat Bobbie of mine, will some day be a diplomat or an
embassadore. An shure enough what da missy say,
come true.

Day all wen ta da woods. An Billie dave make all dem boys
he-n frien. Some dark boys war da one what ah hab ta cut wid
da black snake to get dem to leave us-n alone dat time in de
cart. Bobbie made frien wid dem. Den he-n fix et so Billie frien
wid Mr. Abe lost mah Billie home fust. Bobbie lak ah little
gen man dressed dem all ta me-n. Jus lak ah war da grandest
lady in de lan. Den he-n tole me his-n mammy wouldn't
want me for a while — did'n go back til in Novemba
Da missy did da wash and house an all he-n sewing
twixt da time Ah work las an time ah went back
when Mistah Abe comb en from da circuit fa da winta
Herin war mak'n up fa da part herin spend so much
money on an herin sheir looked lak a work woman.

Ah work fa otha folks. some dark folks gave da Lincolumns
fits. Day say da missy want Mistah Abe ta wear ah baus ob crape
round his-n hat wan she-n pa died. Dat war showing no grief an
no respect fa he-ns pa. He-n say pa war nevva in Springfield an
day'd tink ah war mornin for one ah mah cats. He-n say Ah
did done all ah could fa him when he war wid us-n. Ah left money
wid mah when ah war doe lass, fa what might happen ta mah
ungpa. An ma promise ta keep it fa dat. Ah know her-n would'n
spend a penny fa any ting else her-n so honest. If-n ah had gone
back wan pa war here, brotha John an Ah would ah hab to fight et
out an dat would hab hurt pa more than wat pleasure mah visit
would ah been ta he-n, so ah stay away. Dat John ah shifless thrift.

Mr, Abe war walk-n da flo whan ah got back dare in November. He'n war talk-n ta he-self or' praps little Willie. He-n war wid Willie in he-ns arms. He-n pay no tention when ah say, Good morn Mistah Abe. Directly da missy comb an took little Willie from he-ns. He'n woke up ah speak an say, "Do you know mother, I can remember my little brother, some what. My Pa called him "Jim Tom Tinker". I belive Ive figured out who our baby looks like besides little Eddie. It was my darling little brother, buried back near our last home in Kentucky. Mother took sister Sarah and I to his grave before we moved to Indiana. Pa left us in Kentucky while he found a place in Indiana where we could locate. Mother knelt down at his grave. She had sister and I kneel too. She told us to bow our heads and she prayed. She asked God to be near him, so he wouldn't be lonely after we were gone. Pa was religious too, but not the kneeling kind. Da missy say noting, but walk 'way wid Willie cry'n fa his titty. Dat woman war as full of milk it a run from her a all da time most. She helps Mr. Abe You had write to John now and relieve your mind of all you have on it, maybe then you can get about some other business pending. Perhaps I should mother, he replied, if I don't, he'll deprive mother of her home, and then write me for a Christmas present of a few hundred, for relieving her.

It was sometime in da las of November, an Willie's birfda war in Desemba. He-n wood be one year an da missy war plan-n ah party fo he-n. After mah work ah wasn't due, da missy ast me to go up stairs an straighten. Wen ah got up dar was Mr. Abe sot right on da floor his knees drug up most to his chin af readin. Maybe Shackspar for he war mosh'n lak ah act in ah show. He'n allas read out loud. Once say he larned dat in da blab school. Da kids all blab at once so da teacha know days not fudgin. Well ah took da broom and say Mr Abe all have to sweep you out. He'n sot fa a spell but when ah nudge he'n wid da broom, he mossed out to da stair. He'n sprawled on da three top step. En ah little ah heard da missy screem at he'n saying. Caint you move. I bell give you'n til ah count three, den if you'n don't move I grab ah bunch oh dat black hair and fall you down da steps.

Mr. Abe look up an say. Dat puts me in mind of an experience I had in Indiana— I was on my way to the home of a friend who had lend me a book to read. I was busily reading some line I wanted to be sure I had committed to memo. as I walked. I was paying little attention to where I was walking until reminded by falling head first over a billy-goat eating the long grass in the road. I landed in a mud hole. I was

leaning over to retrieve the book that went in the mud with
me when Mr. Billie Goat having a vindictive disposition
decided that my posterior was in just the right position to
retaliate for the way I had disturbed him — My second header
seemed to strike him as a game he liked. After a few turns
he put his head down an made another lunge. But I
was ready for Mr Goat I stepped to one side — Grabbed
his whiskers and after tussling for awhile swung him
over my shoulder an he landed head first in the mud
hole. He picked himself up, decided that game of leap frog
was not for him. De missy say — You wouldn't dare
She say any one who takes a dare kills a horse an eats it
raw. At that he got up. Turn around. Put one ov his big
feet on da top step, Layed da missy over his'n knee
an spanked her bottom. Hern came in to whar ah
was workin as pleased as a pet kitten — Ah swar
you never could side tow dose folks would wine up an
have argufiging. Hern were done stair laughing fit to kill
An herin smiling, an singin at herin work — Ah guess
say patched it up bout da cheating an lying business —
Altho' da missy tole me later dat Mr. Abram would
never temporize with evil, least of all morals that might
lead to crime,

Mr Abe wen out on dat circuit dat fall in good spirits an
promise da missy to come back soon 'f he'n could. But Ah swar
dat circuit kept he'm as allway away da full time. Da missy was hevilish ma
an hurt too. Said Mrs Lincoln knew they condition. How she had more
while carrying Willie. 'I the care of two instead of one an doing
her own work besides. Because she either can't git a full time nurse
or maid or they are worse than if she did her own work. Thanks
God Bobbie is in school part of the time. Bobbie loves to play wid
Willie. Especially now since Willie walks and talks some. But
Bobbie is seven years older than baby Willie and I always afraid
he will hurt that darling child who took the place soon soon after
precious Eddie was taken. Robert dont mean to be rough, but he
has played with some pretty rough boys and has learned from them
Then too he tries to emulate his father. or perhaps surpass entertain
Willie, such as piggy back, then jumping with him on his shoulders. He
takes him by one hand and whirl him around in a circle. And the
last time I caught him trying to teach Willie to slid down the
banister. Its all in play. I had to reprimand Robert. I wanted him to
understand the danger to baby Willie's life and limbs. And incidents
that he's not as grown up as he thinks he is. Mr Lincoln say
if I kept on picking at Robert, he'd eventually resent it keenly.
Either by withdrawing from all of us. and seeking the company who
may mislead him. Or withdrawing into his shell, thereby becoming
a stranger to us, backward and unnecessarily quiet in his
childish way of self-expression. That he loves Willie. I say
be a companion. He need Willie. Willie need him. If you now
Robert to stay young, to play with the baby brother is a good way
Not force Frensh and subjects too old for him on him. You'll even
cause Willie to fear Robert with your constant raving. I don't want
my sons to dislike or fear each other. If Robert can't play with Willie
Willie will seem a pest and intrusion into his young life. So
mariah you see how we conflict. He doesn't seem to realize my
side. He's utterly without fear, while I fear my shadow. Specially
the house at night when alone. Every little noise is a torture. Some
times I'm sure its a robber breaking in to cut our throats an
even as bad carry my babies away. I say babies because Eddie
is always with me still. Ah know people say she screams out
the windows in the night she is being robbed. Once the sheriff
who lived close came and searched the house but found no one.
She swore he ran out as the sheriff came in. Day said boys
did play jokes on her sometimes cause da knew he'n was afraid
me. when she was crying because she was afraid to go upstairs
in there country home in Lexington in the dark. Her stepmother
said She had the devil in her. Then my father took me in his

arm an said I'll go up stairs with you, so you can get these is nothing to fear. And I was so glad my mother. She was all my step-mother had much to contend with, especially her 8 step-children, as Grandmother Parker would bemean her when we ran to her with our childish complaints and problems. I believe my father had in his mind, that, as the reason he sent me to boarding school. Bless my good, kind father, He never complained but did the best for all that he could. He dearly loved my step-mother, but he loved all his children, but I know he humored me the most. Maybe it was because I was like my mother. Maybe it was because I clung so to him. And maybe because I never resented my step mother, or as Abram says was picky unish with her. She was a ghly cultured, beautiful attractive woman, but her children all showed the good stock that was in them. my choice of all of them, is a beauty. Sometime before too long she will come to visit us.

But speaking bout Pak ah remamba onst dat fall fore me been on da circuit an hein war wirth Sallie in her. A big storm came up. Ah looked out da winda an daswash herin down da road walk towad home, Hen bust in da door jus lak dare war no door dare. Da missy hal put round da windows whar herin war an ah put down to res up stairs when Da missy hal lay down on da cot in da back fachla an cah up in ah kout wid a coverah over her-n head. say. she that Herin war home alone. He-n found herin an began to talk da roughes talk ah tha did heah from he-n. Said Now haint you got narry else a to but lay roun with you cooked in the cibers.

Lord how dat woman got up like a wirl wind an screamed Abraham Lincoln, don't you ever speak to me again as if you were addressing a woman of the street. Now jet and go back to that class of luds you've been associatin. Hin picks herin up in hin arms and help her so close her couldn breath or talk. As soon as he let loose ah litta, she beginned poundin dat man. How herin laughed an laughed worha had hen gone crazy too. Till he-n said, Purdear that the way Id rather be free of the two evil. He kissed da back of her neck an din herin face, an put off down town. Herin war still mad too mad to know it war lightnung an tundering out doas. As da storm quiet down herin quieted

...she asked Mr. Abe if he's believed in visions and what church...

"I remember going to a camp-meeting in Kentucky. I was a little tike. We drove several miles with folks who picked up my mother, sister Sarah and myself, then on down a few miles they took on some of our neighbors. Dennis was bent on going, but he hadn't finished the work laid out to him. He was punished by having to stay home. He liked this, and hit the road, getting there about 2 hours after our load. And it was a load for a cart not much bigger than yours, Mariah, and an old broken down horse. Part of the way we got out and walked to relieve that poor nag, when the going got rough. There was preaching. Immersion was novel in those parts, so much so, that many from a distance were incited to come. There were houses of worship, but few parsons. The churches, such as they were, and "gospel droners", such as those professing to be preachers were. I remember I was more impressed by the droning that Sutton Lane (I believe that was the Baptist preacher's name) gave those who repented after being enchanted by his exhortations. They testified after swooning that they were delivered by a vision, a dream, an uncommon appearance of light. Some by spoken voice to them. "Thy sins are forgiven thee", by seeing the Savior with their natural eyes, all of whom were received into full fellowship. Knowing no better way, I, as did my mother, considered this to be the work of God. I still believe a part of what those people testified too, because visions are not uncommon to me.

Nor were they uncommon to that blessed mother of mine. Until her death, she was a devoted Christian. She often spoke of things that would happen. Even foretold her early death. Once I heard her tell my father, when she I was in seemingly good health. That was in Indiana a number of years after the Babtist Camp meeting in Kentucky. Jest when she would die, and asked him to marry some good Christian woman to care for him and their children. I believe that promise he made her, was sincere. He could have married a short while after my angel mother was loved away on that knob, but he waited a respectable time and brought to us a good woman. No better woman ever lived than our mother Sarah. To her I owe a debt of gratitude that can never be paid in acts of appreciation, outside of help financially. I often worry because I can't give her more."

"Wal I says to Mr, Abe, Dew you air a Babtist? Ve den say. Mariah, I can't remember we know too much about the doctrines of any church. I believe though, since my dear mother and step-mother were both good woman, and were Babtists and taught me nothing, but good, I'd join the Babtists, if any church. But I've ideas of my own. I pray God they are not false ideas. They have a way of directing me. And if I'm in doubt (Mrs Lincoln and I both agree on this) since, our Dear Eddie death, we go to three good women who are in touch with the spirit world and can straighten us out. This Mrs Lincoln and I do find comfort in." Now you know messy

Ada the Pickers of docs & the fortune tellers as call
'em as in date box of stuff, you done lot of much.

This is a copy of a story I feel I must include
I have the pictures she spoke of. From my own
experience going to seances with groups for fun
they fit my idea of the general impression I got of
all the mediums.

I think I sent this picture to you once — Do
you remember? If not will mail you

Believe it or not, I had another accident — A boy
who lives across street, threw a stone at another boy —
It struck foot of lady who was talking to he in front of
my home, bounced and struck my left eye frame. Bent
frame and lense fell out as my glasses struck ground.
They have been inexpertly repaired, so not so good
However I am on two more stories and think can send
soon. I do want this over with, so you can feel relieved.
I want so much to go to the Indiana Trek starting
Oct 22. A build up for the 150th anniversary in 1959.
In letting this range as I copied it, I am not
keeping a copy. So you may return it, or make a copy
for yourself if you wish. — Dont consider this a
letter, am in such a hurry —
                    Sincere Good Wishes   Ada Sutton

Ah jus good-n think mistah Abe an da missy coud go ta dees cheats. Ah say ta mistah Abe. Do you-ns pray 'em? He-n say "Why Aunt Mariah, of course we pray them." Ah say, Ah jest cant 'lieve you-ns put 'em fore ah good parson. Mariah he-n say "I believe in God, as I know you do. I believe in Christ as I know you do, I believe God created all that was created. I believe he spoke the word and all was created good. I believe God is love - that universal love is all, since God is all in all. This because I believe thoroughly in the bible. And that same bible says, God is spirit. So if all things created in his image and likeness, as the bible says, and I believe that also to be a main truth, then, he too was spirit. Then we are spirit. We could go on and on an say the birds of the air fish of the sea etc etc were spirit.

Christ was crucified, returned and ascended into heaven. Christ said, we could do even greater things than he did. If that is so, and I believe it is, for the world has only begin to touch the hem of his garment though faithful prayer then, Why couldnt we, or our loved ones return after the state called death.

Hell ah says mistah Abe, Da blessed Christ didn hab to return cause 3 ole cheats call him back. So if da dead do come back, da can do da same as Christ if da are like he-ns, ah spirit. Ah know you an da missy need comfort. If you-ns little Eddie air in heaben, why would youns want hem ta come back to dis bad worl? Doue you-n think, dat is selfish? Cant you-n fine comfot in known hems out ob all dis wicket worl? Or Christ habn come back since he-n when up to heaben. He-n war right here when he-n return from da tomt. He-n waned ta talk ta hisn 'siples. Cant youns fine comfot in kno-n God does all tings well? Christ says, Dees little ones, For ob sich is da kingdom of Heaben.

Ah believe ah do mistah Abe good. He-n say "I'll think an think hard about what you have said I want to think right. maybe I've missed an emportant point some place, Ah say, Ah jus pray an ah believe an ah know God hears an will ansd. Da mistah say, "Mariah Im ashamed to say. "Your way of the Christ cross is so new to me. You are a good, devout, wise christian, maybe your coming into our home has been a wonderful blessing besides the good work you have done for us — Sometimes I have believed little Eddie was taken to lead me to study, to see and to be redeemed. For a little child shall lead them. That could he in death the same as in life."

"The minister who preached little Eddie's funeral has helped to open my eyes. I now have a book this minister wrote "The Christian Defense" and I'm trying hard to believe it. It seems so hard to believe we had to sacrifice a precious child in order to gain insight into the devine road of life and to life eternal. The way so says the bible is straight and narrow. Maybe we are trying to take the easy way, but I'll assure you Aunt Mariah it would be a cross I couldn't for-give my self for, if I disturbed that angel baby, so that he could shoulder my cross. It would indeed be a dear price of conscience, to pay for a momentary comfort.

Ah done know if'n da missy ever gave up da fortune tellers, but ah hearn dat Mr. Abe had a time wid her — n after Willie died in da White house, for her'n hab fortune tellers daze. Mistah Abe thot her-n war goin crazy. Da missy grieved ober eber ting too much. She war ah good woman but powful odd.

Da next time ah war back ta da Lincolumns ah hab ta take Billie &
da crow. Dat crow war unda mah feet an in mose eba ting in
own shack. He'n daren let et loose. Wen Billie did take it out he
hab ta hole fas ta et. Et cow cow so, da white-trash could put
Billie en da jug or worse still string he-n up. But ah 'lare those
white-trash hab simma down some, since da foun out Billie now
hab high-flutin white friens. An mah Henry plum 'simma afta
he'n saw da respec da Lincolumns and dare friens, show Billie
an he'n mammy.

Mah man's boss on da build'n tear'n up, war say'n some
mighta mean tings 'bout da Lincolumns one day. Henry knows
ta keep he'n job he'n hab to keep he'n mouf shet an keep he'n
fists ta his'n sef. Et war all he-n could do. Dat man comb home
madda dan ah poked hornet. Ah hab da chance ta tell he'n now
he'n know'd how et sound wen he'n pop off bout someting dat he'n
onla 'spect an hab no sense in he'n blabban.

Dat man of my'n say, when his'n young'ns git edicaton from
Bobbie, dale know how ta hep all da poor niggahs wah's bein' lashed
an driven. He'n wish Mr. Abe would get back en poltics an go ta
Baston gin. Dis time maybe he'n could put some sense in dem
dedalators heads an day see, black an wool am no diffament than
red-heads an frackles. Ignowance am ignowance. An da
worstest ignowance es ta tink God made ah diffamence en
our-n soals. Ah war so happy ta heah mah Henry say God, for
he-n allas say he'n didn go in fa dat religous stiffness much.

Et war ah litta late dat morn twixt Billie birthday an
Christmas, wen got ober ta mah wash. He'n hab ta walk,
couse pappy war haulin an et war cold. Ah wash in da shed.
Eber ting war ready. Mr Abe hab made da watta hot out dose din
carried it in. Ah hab ta bile da clothes out dose. Wen ah got
done Mr Abe build up more fire fa da hog he'n war killin. He'n
kill two chickens, an pick dem afta scaldin. Ah dress dem.
Ah dunna know dose chicks war fa until wen started home.
Day givin us'n a lot of dat hog too.

Bobbie an Billie stay in da shed, couse et war too cold in da
barn. Da manage to keep quiet 'til ah wen ta da kitchen to clean
dat while da close dry. Da frozedry.

Da missy hab knitted an pair ob mittens for each of mah chillun
an me'n. Dat took a lot of knitten. An day bot a pair hose hid gloves
lined wid wool fa Henry. Does new wool yarn mitten shur kep
mah hans wam wen ah took down da close.

Billie didn gett much larn from Bobbie. Da crow got da larn
mah Henry done did ah good job larn'n dat crow. Does boys say
stop so offen, dat crow larn to say stop, stop, stop— Bobbie laff til he'n
cry. He'n beg his'n mah to let he'n have da boys come ta hear. But he'n say

Da next time ah war back ta da Rinerlumens ah hab ta take Billie's aa crow. Dat crow war unda mah feet an in mose eba ting in owr shack. It s'n daren let et loose. When Billie did take et out he'n hab ta hole frae ta et. Et caw caw, so, da white-trash could put Billie in da jug or worse still dan dat, string he'n up.

But ah clare dose white-trash hab simma down some, since da faum out Billie now hab, high flutin white frens. An mah Honey plum simma, afta he'n saw an respec da Rinerlumsw in dwie frens, how Billie an Billie's mammony

2, notha day.

Ah stir up a batch of fresh cracklin bread with fresh chops
an gravy sop for dare dinna. Ah wan a put off fa home to
get mah Henry someting hot, so day couldn coax men to stay.
Bobbie coax me in to lit Billie stay, but da missy put her'n foot
down. Her'n say if Billie stay, da rest of da gang will get here
someway an dis house will be ovva run with boys. Some
warm day wan youin can all go ta da barn. Any way her'n say
Bobbie you have to practice your recitation, which you are on
the programme to give Christmas Eve, at church. Bobbie say "Oh
shoot ma". But her'n got no fatha, Da missy say. Bobbie go up stairs.

Mr. Abe say, Well Billie since you cain't keep the crow and
it's about to become a bone of contention here- I've made a cage
for it. Maybe when it learns this is its home, when it becomes
more tame, it will not go far when let out. It will easily find
it way back here to its friends and food. I've always loved a
parrot. I saw a cook-a-too at a circus. It could talk better
than a parrot. But I like this crow, maybe I can talk to it once
in awhile, instead of talking to myself. It just might be able
to prompt me on some of my pleas, I practice, when it learns to talk
better, I ken he laughed.

As he'n war 'bout ta go out dat door, dat lire crow, right up an flew
on his'n shoulda. Mr. Abe patted it an brush down its feathas, as
it saw, cawd. Din Billie hole out he'n arm an da crow flew
to et. Bobbie comb back down stairs. He'n war ah litta scared
when he'n turn comb, Dat crow done act just lak it war gwine
ta fly at he-n's face, Stead it lit on he'n's head, Bobbie laugh so
loud an long, dis is no lie, dat black crow laugh too.

Mr. Abe say, I hate to cage that bird - But these six cats, especially
the black tom, will have to be tame a little more, as well as the
crow. The crow may come up missing its wings and tail and
the tom may have this eyes picked out. If anything should
happen to the little kittens, I know Mr. Crow would have to go
back to the woods. Mrs Lincoln doesn't care too much for the
noise of the crow, since Willie the precious little rascal is here
and mustn't be disturbed, Since a cat jumped into the crib with
Willie, she keeps them out in the shed or barn. I suppose the shed
is where Jim will have to go.

Our little white rat that I brot home at one time, in my pocket
(Remember it nibbled a hole in my pocket) had to be caged. You know
cats like rat meat and don't go slow on eating birds.

Our turtle has hibernated somewhere, perhaps just for the winter
I had it tied in the barn. Part of the rope is still there. Mr turtle
may be miles away to the south where the weather is warmer
Turtles know what they want and go after it. Slow but sure. I'd
love to know their minds. Maybe they thinks better thots than we
maybe some day, who knows, they will rule man instead of man ruling

3. Take that crow et can talk our talk, so we can understand. Can we talk their language? No. They wouldn't recognize what we were trying. Nor would we know how to go about trying. Can any living thing but a bird fly — Some birds such as duck can fly and swim too. I've often wondered when seeing birds flying if man will ever attain their height. Maybe mechanically. A balloon is not the answer. Maybe breath control. The bible says "The last shall be first and the first last" maybe we, as mighty as some really believe they are, are only the last.

The nearest I ever knew anyone coming to understanding all creatures, especially birds is Billie. Billie answer them and they answer him. Maybe I'm given Billie too much credit for understanding — It's that God given talent of the finer shadings of tone that he can execute, perhaps. Billie will be a fine man. God must have loved Billie greatly to have given him these greatest of talents and Billie is using them. The bible say "If you don't use your talents they are taken away.

Bobbie spoke up an say, What's my talents pa? Well Robert you are a very sincere, kind, lovable boy. You make friends whom are worth while. You love friends and you keep them. Didn't your ma say, "Someday our Robert is going to be a statesman an ambassador or diplomat? Why? Because you smooth out the hurts, that might develop into worse hurts among your friends, and with you. I said just to show you what I means. Den mah Billie dat awful blab out, up an say. Mah poppy war mad as heck tore Mr Abe an da missy til he'n foun you'n war not stuck up. He'n fight hell out of da bums he'n could ef da got lippy 'bout youns. He'n mad at he'n boss fa talk'n 'bout da Lincolnmus, He war 'fraid to fight da boss, cause he'n loose he'n job. But ah bet someting awful will happen to dat boss, fa saying lies 'bout you'ns. Ah finely grab Billie by da arm an marched he-n home. Ah preached to he'n all da way 'bout being ah tattle tale —

He'n got home fore Henry. Da kids war all hungry — Ah made corn cakes an cooked dose chickens, He'n had a meal as fine as anyone Christmas dinna. Dat chicken wid chicken sop an some flub-dub food from Willie's birthday parta, was licked up clean by we'n seven.

It war in January 1852 fore Ah went back to wash. Da Lincolnmus war in a funk 'bout grandma Parka's state. Something 'bout a law suit connection wid two colored peple dat hab ah high edication an den war ship off to Africa. Da otha war 'bout da missys step-motha gettin too much. He'n step-sons, da missys brothas war makin trouble. Mr. Abe war in

you make friends with your friends and Billie.

ti da middle of all dis. as he'n war lawin for da missy.
Aunt Lisbeth an Aunt Francey. Et war all so mixed. ah
couldn get much sense. But Mr. Abe war going to Lexington
But he'n wen on da circuit as usual dat spring. An wen dar
to Lexington in da summa

There warn't to much 'citement ob any kind dat ah could tell
Only da missy raven fust 'bout one den 'notha ob her'n folks.
Mr. Abe say its no use crossn ah stream fore you'n get to et.
Well ah hearn da missy say If you could see beyond you nose
you would know we are in the middle of a big puddle now.
Her'n tried her'n best to keep Mr Abe off do circuit. She said
Hen make more all 'round setlin dese 'states. But he'n knew
dare war too many to get dat state money, fa anyone ta get rich
offen et. Cause her'n pa owed money dat hab ta come out fust.
Ah didn know much dat wen on dat summa as da missy done
did her'n own work an wash.

Her'n war all work up dat fall. Such fussin ober ah litta
dab ob money by brothas an sistas. Day war all smart nuff
an could get out an make more dan day got, in less time dan
et took ta fuss 'bout et. Ah hear'n Mr Abe say, I wouldn't
drag out all the family skeletons for people to snicker and
gossip about for all you all will get collectively. But he'n
war da lawyer an hab ta do as she'n said, EA war da money
her'n say her'n would get out, when da states war settled an
take da boys. Her'n said dat when her'n war mad. Dat woman
would come slippin back, Cause dat money wouldn keep her'n
in ah shack fa long.

Not long afta Mr. Abe come back from da circuit dat spring
Dare frien Henry Clay died. My but da missy war grieved.
Her'n tole of what ah fine man he'n war, An 'bout he'n son
who war bitta gin slavery. Her'n say, "Mr Lincoln was selected
to eulogize Mr. Clay. It war in da state house or some otha
big buildin in Springfield (July 6, 1852) Her'n brag an brag
'bout what a big honna dat war. Henry Clay war fust afta
her'n fatha next ta God. Her'n say when young "I dreamed
and planned to marry Henry Clay. Because Henry Clay would
be President of the United States someday. Then I would be the
first lady of the land. I little knew then that love entered
into marriage, my love or rather great respect, I entertained
for him, was as one would love a kind, good and indulgent grand
father. He was in our home so much, always discussing politics an
goverment Or we in his home (Ashland) The Whigs have lost another
fine an strong supporter. Webster - Mr. Abe talked a lot about dem.

Hen got hold of ah new book "Uncle Tom's Cabin" dat year. Ah
wan ah stay an hear her'n read et plum thro'. Her'n read so loud

5. ah could undastan'. But ah hab ta go home. Hern war terrible, work up ober dat story an' sed, "maybe someday I can take a crack at slavery and when I do I will make it count, if I cant bust it completely up. He say Iّm glad for the 'Underground Railroad. This system has been in operation for at least two years. It has stations at regular intervals. Already many thousands have been brought north and are now living as free people. The main route is from Richmond to Philadelphia. They are even coming through in coffin boxes. He said of Filmore, who was made president after Taylors death. "I like Filmore as a man but he has lost prestige by signing the Fugitive Slave law. The north doesn't want slave owner invading the north. Seizing any colored person they said was theirs, then without process of law, draw them back south into servitude. Many free negros whom were always free and had always lived in the north were virtually kid-naped

✕ Ah didn' tell Mr. Abe, but mah Henry war shur skeered stiff. Mr. and Mrs. Lincolumn' talked of all da new tings what hab happen since ah wera ta work fa dem in 1850. Ah may not allas get da date rite now, since et is gettin hard fa me ta recomemba dem. But ah do 'memba dem talk'n ah lot 'bout ah beauful an fine singa from Sweden. Hern name war Jennie. Hern hab travel in ah private railroad coach. Hern visit da White House an da Filmores.

Dere war yacht races. America won da prize from ah bunch of English yachts. Ah bet dat made dem English mad as blazes.

Eba time da would talk 'bout boats or railroads da missy would plan ta travel somewhar. When da talk 'bout da trans-'lantic steama crossing da 'lantic in 10 days, hern war going ta git ready fa a trip ta France. Ah swear ah neva seed such ah mixed woman. 'Stead hern got cautched 'gin. Et war shur guin ta be a girl dis time hern. Dat fall da missy tole me'n, dat Mr. Abe hab been sulken or y somethin strange. Would'n talk ta hern or stay home, afta com'n home from circuit last of June. 'Til hern cautched hern wid mornin sickness in August. She said then he was ashamed and has been more like himself. I tried everythin I could think of to try to draw him out of this mood. Talked to him about this same book he is now reading "Uncle Tom's Cabin. But he acted always as if he didn't hear me.

Mariah we've had so many fights. I now sometimes doubt my sanity. I really threw a stick of wood at him and hit him. Ah that ta maksef maybe Mr. Abe didn' really love dat poor woman. But den how could he da way hern carried on,

6. Ef he'n talk he'n war wrong an ef he'n de'dn talk he'n war wrong. Maybe what da say den war true. He'n hab so much hell at home he'n hated ta go home. But he'n tole Bobbie he'n like ta be alone. Alone wid he'n thots ta think tings out. Ah jus offen wonda, as smart a woman as he'n war an as hard as he'n work ta give he'n all he'n war raised ta. Why in da born worl why he'n didn simma down. Let he'n boss he'n house an he'n 'ciety and let Mr Abe take care ob his'n business. But no da missy hab ta boss et all. Mr Abe war his'n own boss too many yeas ta be bossed by what da now call petticoat govament. Mah man say wen two head strong bosses gets 'gether, one fromd da noth and da udda fromd da soth et jus hab ta be ah fight ta settle et.

Mr Abe wen out on dat circuit dat fall in good spirits an promise da
missy to come back soon as he could. But ah swar' da circuit kept dat
man, as always, da full time.

Da missy war devilish mad an hurt too. Said. Mr Lincoln knew my
condition. How I suffered while carrying Willie. The care of two
instead of one, and doing my own work besides. I can't get a full
timenurse or maid, an they are worse than if I did my own work.
I thank God Bobbie is in school part of the time. He loves to
play with Willie. Especially now since Willie walks an talks
some. Willie has learned faster than either Robert or precious
Eddie. I believe he will be very bright. Robert is seven years
older than baby Willie, I'm always afraid he will hurt the darlin'
child, who took the place of our little Eddie so soon after Eddie
was taken. Robert don't mean to be rough. He has played with some
very rough boys and has learned from them. Then too he tries
to emulate his father, or perhaps surpass his father's stunts of
entertaining children. I believe Mr Lincoln had so few play boyz
with other children when he was a child, he is fulfilling that
longing now. At times he acts so like a child. Robert tries
to imitate his father in games such, a piggy back. Then he
jumps with him on his shoulders. Something I've never seen
Mr. Lincoln do. He takes him by one hand and whirls him around
in a circle. The last time I caught him trying to teach Willie
how to slide down the stair's bannister. It's all in play, but I
just had to reprimand Robert. I wanted him to understand the
danger to baby Willie's life and limbs. Incidently also, that he isn't
as grown up as he thinks he is.

Mr. Lincoln says if I keep on picking at Robert, he'd eventually
keenly resent it. Either by withdrawing from me. Then seeking the
company who may mislead him. Or perhaps withdrawing into his
shell, thereby becoming as a stranger, maybe backward and
unnecessarily quiet. That is Robert's way of self-expression. That
he loves Willie. Wants Willie to be a companion. He need
Willie and Willie needs him. If you want Robert to stay young.
Playing with his baby brother is a good way. Not force French
and subjects too old for him to grasp. You'll eventually cause Willie
to fear Robert by your constant raving. I don't want my sons to
dislike or of all wrong thots, to fear each other. If Robert can't play
with Willie. Willie will seem a pest and intrusion in his young life.
I told him if he was more capable than I, of directing our children
Perhaps he'd better quit the circuit. Settle down like a husband and

2 father should. Get rid of Billie Herndon. Clean up his office. Get respectable office furnishing, and assert himself as he should, as a first class, respectable lawyer.

Mariah you see how we conflict. He doesn't seem to realize my feelings, or how I am so continually embarrassed. The fear I so suffer, alone so much. He seems utterly without fear. I fear my shadow. I walk the house at night when without someone to stay with the children and me. Every little noise is a torture. I have even feared my shadow. The shadow has made me really believe, that a robber has broken in to cut our throats or worse carry our babies away. I say babies because Eddie is still with me. I've even screamed out the window in the night, that were being robbed. That a cut-throat is after us. Once the constable (who lived close) came. He searched the house but found no one. Another time the sheriff (who lived only a stones throw) came. He told me I had the night-mare. That the neighbours were complaining about my continual disturbance in the night. I swore to him, that the intruder ran out as he came in. He said poppy-cock. See how I'm ridiculed.

Day said, boys did play jokes on her'n sometimes, cause dey known her'n war fraid. Ah tole her'n Da Bible say, Fear are uns worst enmay. Her'n told me 'bout when her'n war a chile. Dat when her'd war cryin' cause her'n war fraid to go upstaars in da dark, in dare country home in Lexington Her'n step-mother said, Dat was da devil in her'n. My father took me in his arms and said, I'll go up stairs with you. You can see there is nothing to fear my bably-love. He said, I was so like my mother. She was always so afraid. Now don't misunderstand me Mariah. My step-mother had much to contend with. Her step-children were a problem. If any little thing went wrong, we would run to our Grand-mother Parker, who resented her taking our own mother's, her daughter's place. She demeaned this good woman, who was trying to do her best, by both her brood and my father's first children. After Grandmother's thorough, lashing her. I and our childish complaints, often unjust, became problems unsolved.

I believe, that was one reason my father sent me to boarding school. Bless my gentle kind father. He dearly loved my step mother. She was a highly cultured, beautiful, attractive woman. Her children all show the good stock that was in them. Emilie, my choice, is a beauty. Maybe because she is so beautiful. I've always loved the beautiful. Sometime before long I want this little sister to come to visit us. My father so loved all his children I know he humored me the most. Maybe cause he and I had

3 much in common I clung to him so. maybe because I was so like my mother. Or perhaps that I never resented my step-mother. maybe as Abram says I was never picky-unish with her

After my mother's death, mammy Sally seemed closer We'had Aunt Ann with us. my father needed companionship and a wife and I was glad he married a woman we could never be ashamed of.

But 'bout leah, ah memba onst dat fo'lore Mr. Abe wen on de circuit, an herin war with Taddie in herin, Ah big stom comb up Ah looks out da winda an dar war Mr Abe terrin down de road walk towards home. Hin bust in da dooh lak da war no dooh dah. Da missy hat put down da windows wha herin war an ah put down in res up stairs an down. Da missy hat lay down on de cot in de back fahla, all roll up in ah kvit wid ah covva ovva herin haid. Mr. Abe thot herin war home alone. He foun herin an begin ta talk da roughes talk ah eba did heah from he'n Woll haint you got marry else a do with you haid socket in the rivers. Lord how dat woman got up lak ah wirl-wind an scream. Abraham Lincoln, don't you ever speak to me again as if you were addressing a woman of the streets. Now get out and go back to that class of loose women you're been associating with Hin picked herin up in hers arms an held herin so close herin culdn' breath or talk. As soon as hen let hold of herin ah little 'a woman begin poundin dat man How herin did laugh an laugh. Ah wonda Had hen gone out he'n ming too. Wen hen said Puss dear thats the way I'd rather see you of the two evils Hin kissed da back of herin neck an den herin face, an put off town town.

Herin war still mad, too mad ta know et war lightnin an tundin ut doas. As da storm quiet down herin quiet down Herin say Please mariah don't ever tell anyone Mr Lincoln talked that way to me. He know that I so dislike incorrect grammer from him, let alone dicrespeatful. I wonder why he takes such an ill time to approach me that way- He know it make me curioes

Well ah says, missy dat easy to splain, ur haint you'n got da reason in yuu haid now ta do dat. Hin wants fa ta make you'n so mad you'n would faget da storm. Ya see hin did it too, Well Ile think that over, and Ile promise Ile never let him curb me again in that way She wen back to da back parlor picked up Willie who was fussy and took him out to see da beautiful rainbow coming up east a de Lincoln's in ah clear sky - Ah say dar is so much ta be happy for Den should all tink of as ah why fta rain - Da air am so

4 sweet an fresh. Eber ting is so wash clean, and dat promise God gib'n us'n wid da Rainbo.

First dat spring wen Mr. Abe comb home from da circuit he war so glum he'n look like a storm cloud fa shur. Afta ah while ah coutched on et war 'bout da Todd state. Hen say hed spent moh time an worry ober dat state, dan any case he'n hab. Now day wrote a letta say'n hen owed da state. Hen knew which war at da bottom ob it. Dat war Levi. Jus fa spite. Da missy say · Did you answer the charge. Hen say · That letter was forwarded me. I answered it (from Danville.) As for collecting an keeping any money belonging to a firm your father was connected with, is without question a cooked up lie. The only money I ever received from your father was $50.00 in 1847. I did collect, but as you well know your father gave us. That was his own personal affair. I still say Levi and George have no self-respect or shame. I wish I could wash my hands of the whole thing. Ninian Edwards wouldn't have wasted his time with it. However Ninian and I had to enter suit against Levi. This was the upshat of this attachment of $50.00 against us. Now its up to them to prove it and they will never find, by any man or firm, a claim against me.

Dat same spring ah think et war da first part of April. Bobbie rush in our shack an say. Mah wanna you'n Aunt Mariah. Hern awful sick. Ah have ta hurry ta catch fa at da office fore he-n go out on da circuit. Ma say to tell him too ta hurry. By da time we got dare Dr. Wallace and Aunt Lisbeth war out han. Da litta big head baby didn sqall lak mah baby's when da docta turned dem up an spank dar bottoms. Dr. Wallace turn 'round to Lisbeth an shook he-n head. Mr Abe wen up ta da bed. Hen see da baby hab a large head. He joke an call hen Tadpole. Mrs Lincoln get ah litta 'cited an say Oh my. Oh my is my baby deformed. No said Dr. Wallace. Het a fine baby a really beautiful child an you'n know, Taddie as day nix name hen fo Thos, hen real name, was alway dace best lookin. Mrs. Lincoln say his name will be Thomas for Mr Lincoln's father. He should be honored for giving to us such a fine husband and father as Abram. Mr Lincolum say. Ah shuck mother you wouldn't be a soft soaping me. He was ah wee bit boared.

Ah helped out what ah could. Lisbeth greased da baby an dress it, an bossed me. Ah think of all da ladies ah ever worked 'round Aunt Lisbeth knew da most about mangine and war da kindest. Hern did every ting in et's time. Never wanted ta do too many tings all at once as de missy. She war nevva bossy, extravgent and war a fine cook. Mr Abe sot in da kitchen wen

5. wen war getting da meal. She seemed overjoy with that new baby boy—
Lisbeth had me ta make da corn bread wid meat cracklin in it. She bragged
on my good baking an cookin. Ah took somethings home to wash. Ah was due
ta have mah nex baby, anotha girl Narcissas. Ah didn show. Ah was so thin
at all times any way, no one ever knowed, an ah felt fine dis time so as how
ah didn tell. Altogeba ah had eleven, an dar war not as much fuss ova
dozens ober does eleven, as ober dis one Taddie. Wen ah, wen back da nex
time an tole her ah had Narcissas. That woman da missy 'bout called men ah
liar. Her say, Mariah how on earth did you carry that child without me
knowing. Of course you hadn't been here for some time, until Taddie was born.
But I'm hardly up and around, while you are out working. An ah wen on
wid my work, carryin my baby wid me as I did all da res. Sometimes ah
hated ta leave mah Rome. Specially of any war not well—Hebe war always
my weak one. Setting an coughed a heap. Da chillen war all good to her.
Ah had good, happy chillen; so ah warn't 'fraid ta leave them. Et war only
dat da hab a rite ta a motha all da time. But mah Henry couldn make
'nough to feed an keep that hole kitten-posy.

Lisbeth tole me dat Mary didn know at first thar war a fault wid
Taddie. She thot da runnen of da milk ober her'n wen Taddie sucked was
'cause her'n war so full—Wen her'n found out dat milk war comin in
Taddie's mouf an runnen out he'n nose, Lisbeth say was thought
Mary war givin into notha of her'n spell—Dr Wallace said fa her'n
not to worry 'bout dat—Her'n war gettin plenty wid out whit run
out. But he'n speks dare were thousands luk that—He said, speck
not fa shore. Dat ease her'n a litta. Her'n finial found a way
ta turn dat baby so da milk stayed in her'n. Mr. Abe said right
way Dr Wallace assured us when Taddie is weaned, that condition
will clear up. But dat war a long time. Cause da missy put
ever ting on her, litters an lamp black. But if her'n war sat
some whar what he could pull he'n self up. He'd tug at her. Dat chile
war so long walkin an talkin, ever one say he'n nevva would.
Mr. Abe say Mariah I don't have to ask you not to discuss Taddie
with anyone. Sile make et hard on Taddie in later life and Mrs
Lincoln. She already is beginning to borrow-trouble. But dat news
leaked jus da same. Ah no dis, da Lincolumas had a lot ob neighbors,
but only to speak ta, wen out some whar. But da missy say—
She didn't encourage neighbors to run in an out at their
pleasure. I don't go into their homes unless asked. When I went to
the Ward School in Lexington and later in Mme Montelle they
were very strict, about our social relations, as well as our studies—
Perhaps that is why I'm such a hard person to work for. Besides
I only have and only want callers when I invite them—There is gossip,
more than enough in this town without calling for more. Maybe
they don't like me, because I hold my self aloof. I want to be friends
to people. I have a few very close friends. Mrs Francis. No better

friend could be found, even if she is a little nosey. If it hadn't been for that dear woman and her husband, I doubt if Mr Lincoln and I would now be man and wife. Then there is the Presbyterian minister's wife Mary Black who married a very true friend of Mr Lincoln's Henry Remann. She is now a widow. Oh dear, I really should go to see her. She has had so heavy a load to carry. Shortly after her husband died a baby boy was born. He wasn't a year old when I took him to a photo gallery and had a picture taken of him. Elizabeth had a picture taken of one of marys daughters at the same time. I dressed Henry. Mary named him for his father and the little girls name was mary. She couldn't have been over three years old. I liked her as did Elizabeth. But Mr Lincoln like the older one. Guess because she wasn't so shy and he would be more at ease with her. marys picture was so natural but poor little Henry looked more like a shadow than a picture. Parts were so blurred Perhaps he may have moved or was dressed too fairy like to take good. mary declared it was a sign he was now crossing into the spirit world to be with his father. She had so much trouble and grief while carrying him. She really that he would not live or would not be right But he is now a fine healthy, sturdy boy. A little unruly. But at his age almost four now, one can expect a problem. I think mary is about seven now. A very pretty girl. I have other good neighbors. But if I let one come the rest would be antagonistic if I didn't let them come also.

Mah Henry don't want da white or da colored in ah parts to come in. Hen say we bofe work too hard to be molest by dem.

About da time ah war back dare to work again war in 1854. Ah know dat cause dare war quite a stir 'bout dat time. Henry comb home one day all excite. Hen say da Black Flag will be afta usin. Lets get our's duds an tings pack an get noth. Days goin teal da missue Comfrige [missouri Compromise] an dats goin ta let da noth hab slaves. Maybe we'ns can get ta Canda. Marilh you'ns nerva been ah slave now you'ns chillums, but ah had an of da kolah me'ns dare flog me'ns mos ta death - an maybe da rest of our'ns folks.

Ah quiet Henry cause Mr Abe hab comb home in June cited so Dat dirty rat ol Douglas is stir'n up a mess dats gwin ta be hard to settle. An only for political favors. Outside of that I can't understand why he would do such a thing. Just den da missy comb in an say - Why Abram I never heard you call anyone a name before. I do believe you are jealous of Stephen. Mr. Abe say, You should know how I deplore slavery. He's using his position as Senator to champion the Kansas Nebraska bill in order to repeal the 1850 missouri Compromise. These squatters rights are just a prelude to moving slavery little by little farther into the north. He declares this the way to settle the north-south controversy peacefully. He's only courting the southern votes in order to be re-elected senator. Already there has been blood shed in Kansas between pro-slavery and anti-slavery. mark what I say mary, I will kill that killer! Afta that bust out of his. Mr Abe began to write notes an write notes dat he almos fill dat place his of he'ns. One time whan ah war dare. Mr Abe an da missy had does note all spreed out an da table in da big kitchen. Little war squallin hens head off when ah comb in dat room from out whar ah had been washin. Ah tol he'n "Boss" [da [THE] cow] war full an should be milk. He'n

7. didn' hear Daddie or mein. Willie comb rompin' thru' da house
grab Mr. Abe's coat tail an' screamed fa Mr. Abe to play
wid da two. Et war ah nice day an' dose kids. need da
outside. Bobbie warn' there. But et wouldn' made aform
diffarence, because Daddie always bit Bobbie when heh comb
near. Once Daddie had a big welt on he'is an' da missy
claim Bobbie hab bit him or pinched he-n. Ah sarched an'
found a great big bed-bug in Daddie' crib. As clean as da
missy whar ah declare ah don't know whar it comb from.
When herin asted mein, ah hadn' bein dare fa months, Ah war
right smart mad an' war goin home an' nevva coin' back.
Den she'n cuse Mr. Abe, bringin it from one ob da dirty taverns
hein lodge in on da circuit. Mr. Abe say well mother, if litta
Daddie nevva gets anything worse than a 'bed-bug bite, he'll
come out in tip-top shape. I've had worse bits from various tongues.
Willie pulling, an' Daddie biting, Mr. Abe let loose, after da missy
scream fa Mr. Abe to do something about quieting them. Hein put
all da notes in he'n hat. Herin wanted him to leave them on
the table and let her arrange them. But he stooped devilish put a boy
under each arm like day war sacks of meal and went out wid dem.
    Da missy say "well Mariah, we'll need the table in a little while"
anyway for dinner. I'll need you a little while longer to-day
because I must clean the rubbish out of this house. I'll plan
on a maid this summer. There's a colored girl, Eliza, I'm
sure I can get. Francis found her. And I do need an all
time girl now. I wish I could have you all the time. But
your family needs you, since Phebe is so ill, and the new
baby Narissas has added another one to your already heavy load.
    Herin got thro dinna early. Den herin begin to pile things
dat hab to go up stairs. Pick up what war strewn 'round
by da boys an' Mr. Abe. Sweep hear an' dare into a cleanin'
pan. While I folded da close, wash da dishes, an' straighten up
da back part, inside an' out. When herin comb down stairs from
fixin beds, she had emptied draws of a lot of plunda. Dresses
shoes, bottles. of all kind an' some jewelry herin hab mended an'
et didn't suit her. Herin said, "Mariah pick out anything you want
and I'll have Mr. Lincoln to take the rest out an' burn."
    Just then Mr. Abe came in, Ah was pullin down ma
sleeves. Ah'd roll dem up to keep dem out da wash. You might.
tink dat man didn't see rings da way he'n went 'roun wid hisn
head down. But hein spied da long slit in ma sleeve. Da missy.
had handed me da pair of ear rings with white heads on (cameo)
da bress pin to match. Mr. Abe say, mother I expect Mariah
could make better use of a new dress. She looked up as he put one
of his long finger is the slit in my sleeve an' torn it clean down.
Da next day or so, she'n send Bobbie over with 2 new more calico dresses

Lincoln First Tiff with Douglas — Or Back in Politics to
Prevent the Extention of Slavery Farther North

Et seem ah jus couldn' get 'way from dose Lincolumns or da
Lincolumn's get rid ob mein's. Dat Eliza onla stay two or three
weeks, den da missy send fa Mariah.

Phebe war getin worst an worst. Wid Nacissas ah hab two babies to
carry ta mah work. Ah work fa some Docta's family. One Docta say et
are T. B. ob da bowels. Phebe, da poor litta chile war passin' blood en
habin hemrige too. So dis Dr Henry say hen could do nothin', but sometin' ta quiet. 'Nothin' Docta Dr Elias Merryman say, et war da lungs
ahtogetha en et war cotchen. Ah quitedat place, 'cause ah couldn' keep
Phebe close 'nuff ta watch. Da say ta takphenin ta da attic. So wen
Mr. Abe comb fa mein ah wen back.

Da missy war plum flusta when ah got dare. Mr. Douglas hab
make ah speech in da Hall of Repsentas. Mr. Abe war givin ta 'gin
hisn killin ob da hilla dat day. Hein war near cryin. Say'd Mariah
ah feel lak kissin youins — I can't imagine why Eliza left I liked her
so much. She was such a neat, nice little girl. Did just as I told
her. I worked rite along with her. I have so much to do. Mr. Lincoln
is back in Politics. Thank God. He may stay at home more now. Altho'
he has done so well since Taddie came. Mr. Lincoln was back in
three weeks after April 4th when Taddie came. We have had several
very companionable talks. I believe we understand each other now.
We both love Taddie so much.

I'm trying to prepare his clothes for him to wear to-day. He will give
an address in the "Hall of Representatives" where Douglas spoke yesterday.
It's an answer to Stephen Douglas on the Kansas, Nebraska bill and
the Missouri Compromise which Douglas has backed.

I want a driver for our new carriage. Mr. Lincoln insists he
will drive it. Our estates are now settled and I can have some
freedom now; spending money.

I would love to have kept Eliza. She made no explanation why she
was leaving. I tried not to work her too hard. I've been called a
slave driver so often by the careless Irish, whom I have put up with.
Eliza reminded me so very much, of mammy Sallies little girl, Judy.

Ah know'd nigh wat Eliza left bout. But mah Henry hab say, Keep
quiet Mariah. We'ns all getin tings en shape ta move wen da time es
rite, so mus keep et ah secret. Day mus not fine out. Day wood move
in on usins an drag usins all back south. 'Spec Eliza's folks war
movin fore any trouble 'gins. We'ns colored, down by da Afican church
war da colored folks live, hab 'cuss'd et. Day first plan ta move ta
da unda-groun in Injiana. Dare war swamp dare. Et war close nigh en
Injun mouna. Some Shawnee Injuns wat hab marry some black,
wood hep usins. Mah Henry thot up north in Illinois, way hen could
get work in da coal mines, wood be betta wid ourn big fambly. Ah

lak ta talk et oba wid mr. Abe, Henry say, No. Jus as sher
as God made litta green apples, ef it got roun, wen's ware dead nigas.
Wen's hab all plan ta fight, even ef wen's war kill.

Wen's all wood ah lak ta kill dat Stephen Douglas, but ah
preacha say Don't stat ah now, Ef youns do, ah cause is lost. Let
all da colord folks pray fa 'tection, from da oula 'tection, Da God
see an will ef wen's believe. Ah tell ya, ah back-slid ah heap, but
war still prayin, Ah pray, an pray fa Phebe den too. But ah guess God
gibs an God take 'way. God take mose all mah chilluns now (1902).

Ah wen ta da kitchen, Mr Abe wen ta da parla wid hen's payfas
out of hen's hat. An da missy take litta Phebe in 'hen arms an
carry hen up stais. Hen say "Mariah, I'll take Phebe with me. You
watch Narcissas." Dose two babies war booth sleep. "When you finish the
kitchen, wash out the diapers that Taddie mussed. Then go into the
back parlor, straighten and dust."

Ah war through in three shakes an rund into da parla, just
en time ta get ah hard punch en da eye, fromb Mr. Abe's fist.
Hen war standin fore ah long lookin glass pracsin speech makin.
Hen war so erness, makin jestas, hen didn see men 'til ah screamed.
Dat scaird hen plum out ob hen's speech. What he war jus sayin
If ah colord man, am ah man den, and dens when hen struck
Da missy comb running, Narcissas gin squalin. An ah say "youns
great big galoot! Youns, but mah eye mose out. Hen still dinna
unda stan, When hen did, hen laugh an laugh. Hen near bus
booth hen's spendes laughin. Dat made da missy mad as blazes.
Hen say "Don't stand there like a laughing idiot, Do something for
mariah! Get Dr. Wallace." Hen love dat Dr Wallace since hen
coax her not to hab ah'mid-wif for Taddie to be born by, an get
her Dr. Wllgemuth. But Mr. Abe didn stop laughin Hen say, "Ahd
hate to think how I'd look if they hadnt turned up so much for
hands and feet." Da missy pick up Narcissas an walk da flow wid
hen. Mr Abe finela go to da shed an breng a piece ob fat meat
fa meuns ta tie on mah eye. Dis nary please da missy Hen say
Get out an get Dr. Wallace. When da docta comb hen say Brother
Abraham done the best anyone can do Mariah But who are you
going to tell Henry youns been in a fight with?"

Da missy say, "Don't tease Mariah, William. Mariah has this to
add now to her already heavy burden. She has a very sick child
upstairs. I want you to see her. Do what you think is best for the
little one." Hens wen up stas an comb down wid hen in hen arm.
Hen feel hen pulse. Push down on hen fings nails. Famin her noze
to see if it war pinch, an den say "Mary, Why on earth havent you drawn
my attention to this child before." Hen say, "Well Dr. William, this is
the second time I have seen this child in almost four years. It was
only a few weeks ago, when I learned that the child was not well. Then
all mariah said was, that Phebe has always been funy and coughed.
Is it serious?" Den Dr. William Wallace first look at da missy den at men
an say. Mariah do you want to know the truth? Ah tole hen's ah

ahreada know'd da truth. Mah Phebe war goin ta heaben. Hen looke straight at men's an *ask*. Have you had any medical care for her. Ah say Dr Anson Henry tole me'in ta make some hoar-houn tea, He gave you no medisine? No. Hen didn want ah botha wid black folks. Hen say – What a shame, what a shame. Some of these doctors can't see. There is no differenc between black or white. Just the color of pigments in the epidermis is different. In most cases now that differens is slight. Ah say, maybe dat docta didn want ah fool wid out getin ah heap of money. By the God's hen say. Can it be any doctor can be that mercinary? A life is a life, whether it be saved by a vetinary or an M.D. That is our responsibilty. A tithe to God, if one will think to put it that way. Mariah does the child eat? Ah tole Docta Wallace; a litta, such as men's hab. I'll give you a litta medicine It may give her an appetite. Get a soup-bone. After it is well cooked, Skim off the grease. Take out the bone and cook some barley in the skimmed broth to a consistancy of a gruel. Don't begin with too much water, but don't add more water after the meat starts to boil – Cold water Mariah. Hot water will keep the strength of the meat from the soup. Just enough salt to keep it from tasting flat. I had to teach Frances to cook. These southern belles are good tasters, but are the world's worst cooks. Have you given the child plenty of milk? Ah tole Docta Wallace mah Henry milk own's cow til it wen dry. Den dat poor bossy, hab getin thinna an thinna en cough too, din done lay down ah die. Sinse den wen's hab skin milk from whar ah works. Do's younguns ob own's lobed skin-milk, spacily wen et clabba. Den day eat et wid a litta suga an break up corn-bread in et. Wall say da docta How are your other children? If they are like this new baby of yours, you have nothing to give you anfiety about them. Ah spoke rite up, Ah do da bess ah can, Ah habn much time fa worra. Ah preacha say, Hens should weep at ah birth an rejoice at ah death. So if God wants mah litta Phebe en hen colored heaben, I'll jus go on getin da res ab dem en ah shape, ta be wid her'n when God calls dem. Up spoke dat docta, "Mariah, you are ah brave, good God loving woman. Don't hesitate at any time you need me. Bring any or all of them to me. I have a country route to make every day. Unless a call comes from the country at night, that is urgent, I'm at home or at my office. Ah thanke Dr Wm.

Ah could see da missy war narvos, Mariah hen say, "Now that the children are resting, let's get this house in order. I declare I send my children away for Liz to take care of, so they won't interfere with my work. I still have the meal for our party this evening to prepare. There's more commotion, than my children would have caused." Wal say, Dr Wallace, I want to know who called me here? And who sent for Mariah. You an Francis are the least respectfully of anyone's feeling or wishes, I ever en countered. Ninian Edwards has taught Elizabeth that all aristocrats didn't come from Lexington. That the most aristocratic are the most tolerant. I want to know, Mary. Did you ever in your life consider anyone's wishes or feelings before your own? Ah spoke right up fa dat poor missy. Dr Wallace yo'uns air awfa kind. But no kinda dan da missy. Dis dress, ah frok on de missy made out ob new calco an gib ta merins. Den huf gil usin's so much fine food. Mak Henry say. Weuns all done got a Rich man's aptite on ah poor man's pay. Da docta laugh an say, — let me know about Phebe, will you, Mariah? And be sure the next time you catch, brother Abraham, propt against the wall in one of his dense moods—Sock him a good one in the eye.

Abraham make that answer to Douglas a scorcher. Mr Abe laugh I wish I could. When mariah screamed it scared all the speech out of me. Just remember say da docta, These poor colored folks need all the help you can give them. Try to meet, if not do a better job than Cassius Clay did. Id suggest you scare them into thinking that the black man will prevail some-day. Dak mah Billie ah ast, Dat is prevail? Well mariah the way I've used it. They, the colored, will rule over the white man. Ah Clare, dat doota didn know. Dat's what got usin in dis mess in da fust place. De prosha say—King Pharoah was ah black man an he'n made slaves ob da white, Turn 'bouts fair play. Is wha wins ah slaves. Docta up an say, If the white now, think they are so much better, why don't they do different than they did way back in the black man's rule. Why don't they start a new era. A new thought, as our constitution says all men are created equal. Are to be given equal rights to life, love and the pursuit of happiness. But mr. Abe speaks up. That eternal cycle. The earth is round and never ceases to go round. The moon the sun and altho' no one knows even the twinkling stars may be round. We know they travel. Or are visable at different time in different places. Oh that master mind, how marvelous. We the little minds who can do likewise. At least are here to continue the plan. Seed, bloom grow into mighty plants animals and man. To enjoy to the fullest. To have dominion oah; Not to destroy this cycle. Yet the mighty, who so wrong, stoop to such little views that leads to little deeds. Da preacha say dat Christ wenten 'mong dem black men an larnd ah lot fromb dem, dat he'n couldn larn fromb da jew, what was he'n own folks. Dey just that 'bout money. Dey made da house of God a den of thieves. But he'n upset dare apple-cart. He'n threw da money changas out ob da temple. Dat why day didn lak he'n. Da say all manna ob evil 'bout he'n. Dat why da nail he'n ta da cross. Day still think money da onla powah. Rite heah Mr Abe had he'n say, "All Christ said made good sense. Even a child could understand. Yet he was crucified. I think we should all do as the Catholics do—Dat the cross, as an emblem of his suffering to show us the right way— The easy way—to live and have without suffering, with cheating, lying or in any way abusing our fellow-man, which would put our minds at peace. No strife; No fear; An all encircling love, he taught. But about the jews, there are

Da missy say. I'll teach both you men something if you don't leave mariah free to get her work done. Da docta snap back. Mariah is doing more work, while listening, than you are. But brother Abraham; try to squelch that little Giant. Do as good a job if you cant do better than Cassius. If he gets up to oppose you, I'll be there all right; You reach out with one of your long arms and push him back in his seat. Thats what Cassius would do, or maybe use his bowie-knife.

5 Dat make meds-think ah war at da Lincolumns when dat Cassius, da son of da missy's Henry Clay, spoke in da grove, Da woulda let hens speak in any public buildn. Cause da say he war a radical. Mr. Abe went ta dat grove an lisin ta hen's speach makin fa 2 hours. In da hot sun beatn on da groun fa 2 hours Da missy hab sent for dis Cassy ta eat wid a numba of hen's friens dat evening. Hern want Mr. Abe to know Cassy, hern say, Want dem to get quainted, so both would know just what da ober stood fa. Dis mistah Clay hat notice Mr. Abe on da groun. Hin war glad hen say ta learn who hen war an jus why his fine friend Mary Todd hab sells hen of all her loovas. Ah decla da way hin look at da missy and hern look at dat man, you'd tink da war loovas, Ef ah didn knowd hern war so bad in love wid Mr. Abe now. Eben doe dat men war ah Kentuck, hen hate slavery worse iben dan Mr. Abe. But dis what make men tink Mr. Abe hab ah big job on hen hans ta beat da Cassy speach.

Da Lincolumns took da carriage 'way in time ta pick up a few friens. Dat Julia Jayne an hern husban Lyman Trumbull den notha I faget. Mr. Abe war all slick up. A nice white shirt da missy hab made ir stock dat war strait when he'n left Boots shine an close clean an press out smooth, an hair watah down lak it hab been plaste to hen's haid.

Lisbeth warin goin ta da speach makin, Hern comb wid da three 'bout time ah hab all mah work done. Hern say mah bake chicken an sage dressn smell good 'nough ta sample. But hern didn. Hern younga boy Charley comb long ta play wid Bobbie Willie Wallace an Taddie hern put ta bed up stairs. And told them if they would take a good long nap, they could stay up for the party that evening. Bobbie wan ta know whar war Billie Ah said. Billie are now 12 years old. Hern keep im in wood cause pappy am so busy haulin, Sometime Billie then help pappy, Bobbie. Ah shoot, Charlie an I cant have fun without Billie But dayin wen out ta da shed an da fust ting ah knowd, Jim Crow made dem heaps of fun

Lisbeth nevva notice mah eye. Ah'd take da meat off. Ah hat ta see what ah war doin wid both eyes. Hern hab such good manna any way. Hern nevva stare you in da eye lak youin war lyin. Lak some white folks do.

Ah hep hern aroun a spell 'til fust ting ah knowd all da Lincolns an friens comb in. Mr. Lincolumn war happy. Talkin, tellin stories an joken wid all dare friens – Day war gratulatin Mr. Abe on hern wonderful speach makin Et war gran, Et war da bess in da worl. Hern hab Dougie obey a limb. But Mr. Abe say, Lets wait until this is all over. The little giant isn't goin to let it stop at this. I'll admit he had me sweatin. Da missy say, Abram Ah so humiliated and ashamed of you I could cry myself sick. The work I went to to make you appear genteel and you got up there with no coat on. Your shirt sweat out – Raked your hans there your hair And even lose your stock off right on that platform. But it was crushed and under your ear anyway – An the mud in your boots. Look as if youd tromped through a hog pen. Well, mother I knew if I waited until after the meeting, it might be too late to round up some the things I knew Mariah should have for Phebe. Here's part of it, Mariah. He pulled out of his big pocket a sack of barley. A big sack of candy 's for da chillun. A Jinnie Lynn doll fo Phebe, a ratla fo narcissas an a out ob 'bacca fo mah man. Den hen say, "Robert, Charley an I will take you home. We'll go past the butchers fur your soup-bone." Ah rap narcissas an Phebe. Ah held Phebe. An Bobbie ride in da back seat wid narcissas. Charley war about ta get in da front wid Mr. Abe when Dr. Wm. says "If you're taking Mariah home, I may as well go along and see if there is anything I can do for the rest of her children." While Mr. Abe war afta da soup-bone, da docta goes in da grocery and wen hen comb out, hen say "Here, Mariah is a sack of prunes for you." Dar war bout ten pound an in a pappa war six loaves of good yeast bread, day'd jus been bake. Still stuck tagetha in squares and warm yet. When your getting supper, cut a slice an put it in the oven to dry out for Phebe to eat with her milk. Den hen han me a bran new tin bucket wid two gallon ob milk. Ah war so happy ah rite dare an den bawled. Bobbie notice he hab anotha package an say, "What's that?" Dr. Wallace grin an say. "Dat mine." Well Bobbie say "What is it." "All right little snoop, I hab crackers an a wedge of Swiss cheese." Well Bobbie say, "Aren't you coming tu mothers party? Oh yes. You bet I am. That cooking your Aunt Elizabeth and Aunt Mariah did smelled too good for me to miss — I eat cheese an crakers, when I have calls and have to miss my meals."

Den mr Abe an da docta got 'way, mah Henry comb in. He hab a big wooden box in hen cart an brot 4 or 5 big hemp sack around ta da back of ah shack. Da docta splain bout da chillun. Tole Henry hen hab a fine family of healthy chillun. But Phebe would need close tention an hen would come back if culled. Mr. Abe had spied da sacks an box an ask mah Henry, if he war fixin ta move? Henry look sheepish but look cross ta me. Mr Abe say "Those sacks look like the ones we packed our plunder in when we came to Illinois." Henry call Mr. Abe ta da back an done tole him hens plan. I'n shur that ah'd spill da beans. Den Mr. Abe comb back ta get in his buggy hen look worried. He say "Ah heard him," "Don't do that Henry. It's a foolish move. Dissourage the rest."

Hen pay me mah wage an say, "Here, mariah, you may need this." He gib me ins anotha $5⁰⁰. Den da docta say "Take this too,— It wont strap me and you may need it soon." Ah did need it. Mah Phebe in a few days, jus wen ta sleep wid Jennie Lynd in hern arms, wid a happy smile on her little peeka, pale face, an wake up in heaben. Da onlest time da missy ever war in mah house was ta bring da clothes Phebe war laid ta rest in. Hern cried when hern saw my face litta Phebe, almost white, wid dat doll in hern arms. Da dress an fluff litta petta coals. Du ribbon in her hair, an litta mocasin de missy done nit. Made mah Phebe look lake a litta princess of fairylan. Hern war bury in da poor lots of da grave — jack whar Mr. Abe war first layed wen da brot hen back from Washington.

Mah & Henry couldn' get ovva da pickle, hen that. Hen hab got
usin in by tellin ta Mr. Abe, all weuns black, hab plan. Hen
say eber'body war talkin' 'bout how Mr. Abe hab lam bash'd
Stephen Douglas. An da help, he war trying ta gib da black man.
But da black man mose say et's bess ta get out. Mr. Abe
say nary a word 'bout usin moving. Cause ef hen hab, dare
would hab been talk, an Henry wood a heard it. Mistah hab
tole mah & Henry ef dare war any movement he'd get it to Henry
rite way. He say, "Springfield is full of people who once lived
in the South. Highly educated and good christian people, who
hate slavery — Until Nebraska and Kansas are invaded by
the slave trade, which will never happen. No one will start
the slave traffic in Illinois. What I would like to see and
I thoroughly believe will happen in time. Is — I or the north and
south to come to a reasonable agreement. And gradually free
all slaves — Perhaps for a price — But free them. And I'll
continue to free the slaves, until the last breath is gone from
my body.

Ah tole all da folks about da missy comin' wid da dress she'n made
and layin mah Phebe way in. Wid da litta doll baby Mr. Abe 'bout en she
held in hern arm when God took her. Dose folks, ah work fa war
sure astonish. But some of dem say day knew she did. Cause day
watch her in hern fine carriage, whar she'n go to — Ah tole 'em all
'bout what Mr. Abe and Dr Wallace did. Ah luik right dare, an
den, day gin ah get shamed, how day hab talk 'bout da Ancolumns.
Day all gin gibben usin good stuff, stead cast off skim milk, an
day bones da that weuns could eat. I rey our dog got all giden bones
That hen couldn' eat, hen bury for a slim eaten day.

Dere war a lot moah speech makin. Day say my Abe warned
dat Douglas, so, hen ran out ol someting ta say, keys repeaten
what hen hab already spout off. Right dere an den is when ah think
an so did mah Henry. Is when Mr Ancolumns stated for da white House
fa President. Da missy war so full of joy, hen nearly bust! Hen ride roun in dat fine
carriage wid a driva. People war green, some whar, 'cause day war so
jealous. Hern didn' bothe 'bout taken dem. Hern war da same 'bout dat
as hern war about folks foppin in at any time at hern home. When Hern
want dem, Hern ask dem. An hern ask dem ta partas, Partas, partes,
partes. Special afta little Sister, Emilie come.

Mr Abe win out on da circuit. But wen ta Chicap an otha place,
too. Hen now hab a big job wid da big railroad. About rite ways
Day gibben hen a pile of money 'bout 200 or 300 fore hen even started
ta work far dem. Ah do believe da Lord prospa dose folks cause da

war on da colored folks side.

Mr. Lincolum say, "one got to" be comfatable as no speech comes. Ef ah hab tight collar or tight boots, specially, dat all ah can tink 'bout 'til ah's easy lak. Hin say wool socks mak hein feet bairn an sweat. Hin never will get use ta dem. Dat makes me tink one time, when da missy was goin te have a parta. All da good tings ta eat war on da big table in dat nice big kitchen. Hein hab fore hein seein it, by cutin et up in fitta cubby hole.

Bivis hein call, "Abe da wood-choppa," hein war call "sockless Abe." Ah know hein never wore socks, only wen made ta, by da missy. Hein make such nice Britten. An took special care maken Mr. Alex Socks. Dis day in da handy of da parta, ah was about to carry some of da fancy fook en da soups, when da guests come. Wen Mr. Abe comb round da all da lak ol. Mr. Abe wie da raggadis, mose falorn begga ah eba eba did all da lak ol. Mr. Abe say "Mariah, you see that this traveler gets something good an hot to eat." Hin set down by dis tramp an nibble as da tramp ate some of da good. Mr. Abe say ta said fook ah tink word he hes fa ah poor staved man. Mr. Abe say ta him, "is yours warm?" Hein look down at dat tramps feet an say. "look lak yours toes ice out." Den hin begin ta tell what hein pa did ta keep hein feet warm.

We were very poor an had no money to buy wool to be woven into yarn. Therefore no yarn to be knit into socks. My pa discovered that paper could be wrapped around his feet. This paper used instead of socks and was a greater protection from cold than wool. Wool made his feet sweat. And when the feet are damp of course will freeze much easier. Wait a minute, I think I can find you some socks I am not wearing. Then he pulled his pants legs up high enough so the tramp could see his bare legs and a bit of paper that had slipped up to the top of his boot. Aen Mr. Abe had started fa ta find dose socks, dat tramp push hein chair back. Hein praise and praise dat good man an thank meins. Ah think ah should say someting. So ah say, yes, Mr. Lincolum is a very obligen an good man, when ah say Mr. Lincolum dat kum grah hein hat, an rush ta da door, dat waitin fa Mr. Abe an hein socks. Hein didn't get out tho for da missy comb in all dress fa da parta. Hein say Mariah what was that dspirit doing in my house. Hein spied da dishes dirty on da table an was so mad hein like ta bust hein bussel off. Don't you ever let such a character in our home again. The affrontery of you setting such as he down at our table to dine. Well ah spunk up an say. Just keep yours petticoat on. Mr. Abe brot hein here an Mr. Abe set down an eat wid him. Just then Mr. Abe step in holdin a pair ah socks in each han. Da missy put hein hand on her hips an fierce hein wid dose mad eyes of hein. "Abraham Lincoln," hein say, "explain this new insult from you. Is this the class you associate with? But over my dead body its the last of this kind you'll bring ta my home. No wonder you have no refinement. Sprawling around on the floor. Eating in your shirt sleeves. Wiping your mouth on your sleeves. And raking food from meat plate or food bowls on your plate with your knife. No wonder these social blunders that humiliate me fore my friends. Hein let her spout on. Den she spied the socks he was holding. Hein didn't give hein time ta jump off straddle of hein boot dat. Hein say, Mariah, where is my culprit friend. Hein hah heard da missy call da him a "culprit." Hin flew da coop when ah jus said Mr. Lincolum an obligin an ah good man, den on went fa dat door lak

3 hein war chase by da debil. Mr. Lincoln laugh and laugh, split to kill. Da more hein laugh da madda da Missy got. Hein pranced dat kitchen lak ah wild woman. Finely Mr. Abe held up da socks fore hein very eyes, an say. When you cool down Molly, you can ask me 'bout dese sock. Hein threw back hein haid an scream at hen. Take dem back whar da belong. Ah knows 'bout dem, little do you care how much I work so you can live less like a freak. I spend hours knitting, so you'll have nice wool socks an live like a gentleman. But no, you wrap your feet in paper, and give decent clothing to your indecent friends.

"Well mother, I'll admit that the case in question, looks black against me. If you'll come down off your high-horse, maybe the case will prove less formidable. Really Mary you do look pretty, all strung around about with flowers. If you'd manage to smile, maybe I could manage to like you." Da more hein tease da worsen hein carry on. Finely hein say. "Mother you've got yourself in a fine fix to receive your guests. You've pranced your hoops and bussell over to your left side and the posies are falling out of your hair. Now straighten yourself and listen to what I have to say before you go any farther.

I did know that man and he is a bum, and a culprit. Once when I made a speech in Vandalia, he was a successful lawyer. I went before my audience perhaps as disreputable looking to him, as he is to you to-day. He looked at me as though I was an intruder in their midst. Through the years that have intervened, he had come down considerably from his lofty false airs. A social drink, finally developed the drunk and dirtiest he now is. His lovely home life, good practice and respectable friends are no more. Yes, Mary he is a culprit. Petty larceny, etc. A vagrant. I knew he didn't know me. But, perhaps he has learned of me getting this lucrative railroad job. That is no doubt, why he ran when Mariah mentioned my name. He couldn't face a man he had once shunned and sneared at. I'm sorry he didn't get the socks. His toes were cold and he looked cold. I hope the little he ate did him some good. If it hadn't took me so long to find those sock I'd made it back before Mariah gave me away." Guess I hid them so good I couldn't find them, I'll try to do better next time." Mrs Lincoln snatched them socks and put dem nice wool socks in da kitchen stove fire. Mr Abe say," Why mother, your only making yourself more work. You'll knit more for me.

Or will I have to continue wearing my "everlasting socks". Dats what hein call his bare legs wen dare war no pappa around to wrap his feet in. Hen say. that would be another relieve to you and Mariah. Never a whole to darn, and best of all, Mariah will be relieved of washing them, That a job after I've warm them an my vile feet."

Mrs Lincolnnnn, war still mad an say," I never want another tramp in this house." But Mr Abe spoke up pretty quick lak." If you would think of anything but your own wishes, and be a little more human, you might see that no one should be turned away hungry. Espaially a day like this, there is plenty for half the town, yet you begrudge a small morsel to this poor unfortunate. Mrs Lincoln maybe as you have said many times. it is encouraging these beggars to raid us when coming to Town. Encouraging this easy way out of work and thrift. Encourting others of them. slothful. But my intention are good and my conscience is clear.

I pray God my boys will never be cold, hungry or ill clothed. We have tried to set an example of clean and dicent living before them. We have

4 given them loving care and protection. But who knows the course of
human events. God grant they shall never have to ask for food or shelter
as I have had to do. But if that day should come, I don't want them to feel that
the sins of the parents have been visited upon the children? But begging is
honorable, rather than stealing. When our family traveled from Indiana to
Illinois. Though we brat along some food.. At various stops along the way
those kind hearted Hoosiers, gave us food and shelter. Each time I live that
trip over. I ask God to bless them and prosper them. Sure we were not
bums. But it never hurts anyone to lend a helping hand."

"Und as yourns know. De missy nevva, nevva turn away notha begga.
As I ask Mr Abe now dat he war gettin long fore an hat ah
nice family did he, eber long for earlier days in Kentucky an
Indiana. "Yes Mariah, I hardly believe there is a person living who
hasn't wanted to be a child again.. Their childhood may have
been devoid of luxurie's, even very frugal. Luxuries weigh us down
Any material does.. The more one has, the more cares. As for
the three states, I find the people very much the same. Altho I
was only 7 years old when I left Kentucky. I got my sprouting
start there. I learned to love every one and everything under
God's blue sky and all above in God's blue sky— I got my first
taste for learning, for work and play— more play than learning
or work. my mother could read a little and when not busy she
read the bible to sister and I. She could sew. And did make a
quilt by littles from patches she gleaned from her early dresses
and her aunt's dresses. Her aunt raised her. She weaved when she
could find material necessary to make up the skeins. I could
weave and in later years helped my step-mother weave and wind..
I was born under a quilt she made. Oh yes, I was born under
a buffalo rug covering. But to pretty it up. A quilt was throwy
over the buffalo rug. Mother gave this quilt pattern to the neighbour
who was so good to us. during our home in Kentucky. Their
names were Mr and Mrs Abraham Enslow." Ah say, Den
dats' hour dat big name Abraham war hung on you. "Yes, say
Mr. Abe, partly. And partly for Abraham Lincoln an ancestor. I've
always, been called Abe. Outside of Abe being shorter I can't
see its any improvement. Abe seems too familiar. And familiarity
breeds contempt. my home is Kentucky will ever be dear to me
As will my home in Indiana. Under God's blue sky there never
were kinder, more accomodating and generous folks than the
Hoosiers. I've often wondered why pa had to take it in his head to
leave Indiana. And guess he was struck with wanderlust. Guess
I took that attribute from pa. I love to wander. I've enjoyed every
minute of my circuit riding. And I've relived my Kentucky
and Indiana life on my fishing trips with Robert, Bill and the
boys. I'm a boy again. I now understand much better the way
of creation. The never varying plan of the universe. A continuous
cycle of rotation. Once I was lead to believe by reading the wrong

5 books, and not sticking to the most worth while book ever written, that science explained all. But Marioh, by your unshakeable faith and your Christ like mind you have lifted me out of believing only in material values. Now I know without the spiritual, or easier to understand mind values are back of all material or scientific things. Those things would not function. For thought or spiritual, whichever you choose to call it is the power, that operates the universe. I'll never be side-tracted again. For I know the spirit is the ruling power and principal and no material can explain it. But the spiritual can explain the material. There is still a creative principal we should all strive for. Christ said "You can even do greater things." He multiplied the loaves and the fishes. He made wine from water - he healed and lifted the dead. He did this by faith alone. in the father, God creative principal - This he tried to teach. But was lead to "rebuke" the ye of little faith.

When I reached Illinois I was 21. Then labor of a different sort, began and what spiritual values I had gained, was pushed to the back ground for material gains. Maybe it was a poor swap. And maybe it will prove to be just what an Almighty God knew was best for me. I've enjoyed my life here. I've had material help I never had in Indiana. Altho' in the location in which I've lived in Indiana gave us the best it had to give. At least I grew strong and was isolated from detrimental environments. I believe I can credit Indiana with giving me the basic for clean, thinking therefore clean living. The folks there were kind, clean, and honest as were my father, mother, and step-mother. There those traits were instilled in my make-up. So much so that it amounts to almost a hate of the reversal. In court I deal with cases so revolting sometimes. Cases that only the blood thirsty for social, political or material gains could perpetrate. I often wonder if I wasn't lead to the courts to test my strength of character.

I often review my life in New Salem. Especially my association with one person, a young girl some five years younger than me. We often talked about the new beginning, after coming to Illinois about what was the best thing for me to start out in, as a trade or profession. I had made some bad business ventures. After I had made a political stump speech, the New Salem people liked. She encouraged me to study laws. Had I not had great respect for her, for her sincerity interest in me and her intelligent judgement, I would never be where I am to-day. When God seen fit to take her for awhile, the bottom seem to drop out of everything. Only knowing that I wanted to do what she wished and planned, forged me on.

6. I have set - backs and discouragements, but I've never doubted that I was lead by her (Ann Rutledge) right advise and warm encouragement. She seemed more anxious for me than I was for myself. Even her memory brings forth my grateful thanks. By her help I went to the ligislature in 1834. She died in 1835"

Da missy hab listen, but guess her'n hab all her'n wanted to hear. I'll her'n say, "Let that dead girl rest. You've got a wife and family that wife who has sacrificed and still sacrificing for you. But what thanks or appreciation do I get. Even the little things you could do to show me you value my efforts, you shrug off. I never even mention. But this common kitchen servant you flaunt in my face."

Her'n say not noth'a word, but took his stove pipe hat and old gray shawl down from da hall tree and started fa town. Dat woman war so mad her'n eyes flash fire. "Now you'll see, Mariah, now you'll see. Is he still such a God-man to you?" Ah say "Ef mah Henry hab said such as Mr. Abe say Abe praise God him war on da right track. No different who or what put man on dat track. Ah don't wan a hurt you'n but dat man is workin an gibben you all da good clothes an what else you'n want. Ah heard him say, You'n knows what you want, so go and get it. I wouldn't know how to select thing-a-mah-gigs fa you'n. Him don't drink or smoke or curse or blaspheme. Him dotes nan you'n. An him goin ta be a big blessing to you'n and you'n boys. Ah'd simma if ah war you. An if you'n cant stan what him say. Why don you'n just walk away until you'ns cool off. Dat's what him did just now. Him don't starts fights, an him don't let you finish them. Now my Henry wouldn walk off. He'd finish dat fight if I started one, or slap me down. What ah knowd an didn say war dat her'n war jealous, mean jealous of her'n man. Ah felt sorry fa her'n. Her'n war a good woman in so many ways. But just couldn't get on da right track to be happy or make her'n folks happy.

Da fall or winta little sista Emilie came. Da missy sew an sew for her an make pretty hats for her'n. Dat child lady didn hab too many clothes when her'n camb. Her'n make Emilie fine dresses an crochet nice gloves ta go wid each dress. Her'n would hire a drive for 25 cents to drive dem through town ta show dis leета sista off. Her'n war shur dat dis pretty sista would fine a rich husband in Springfield. Day went ta partas and had partas. Da whole kitten foosy of dem tried ta get Emilie married. Mr. Abe like dis Emilie an didn stay away so long while her'n war there. Her'n say brother Lincolumn war an ideal husband an father, but

7. there war no more as good or as smart loose in Springfield so in about 4 months or so in 1855 hern wen back to Lexington. When da missy war building a bigga up-stairs and a littera kitchen down stairs, while Mr. Abe war on circuit in 1856 her heard from Emilee and shen had married.

Bobbie war bout 13 now an war quite a nice quite boy. But jest as Mr. Abe say Robert & Willie and Taddie would grow apart. Willie was five and Taddie three and such mischevious little fest youn nevva saw. Da missy say One reason she changed the upstair was so Robert would have his own room away from those precious little torments. Taddie never lets Robert alone when he is at home. Robert really is not a student and needs all the privacy he can get to study. I think a change of school will create new interests for him. He really is studious if not a student.

When Mr. Abe comb home and found da house all change hen pretend et war some one elses home. But ah could see hen war happy bout it. Hen like his new bed. Et war big and long. Long nough so hisn feet didnt hang oher da foot board. Hern spent herr money an went in debt ober 500 00 for decorations and furniture. Mr. Abe paid an said nary a word. Hern didn lie bout her debts dis time. So hern did have ta take anotha tantram an perri goric fordsin ta Mr. Abe.

Mr. Abe war growin bigga and bigga in Springfield an all round da country whar hen made speeches. Ah hearin dem say Mr. Lincoln is now in politics up to his neck. While da missy still road round in her carriage wid ah dairva, Sewed, sewed, sewed, clean clean clean, Go to shows wid da chillun, Give partes and go to partes. Eben afta litta sister go hern keep da up. Mr. Abe twixt ridin circuit, goin to Chicago - Speech makin saw litta of hisn home. When hen got home, hen had so much ta tink bout war fromb him. Hen hardly knew he war there. Sept when does two Willie an Taddie stuck hin with da missy's hat pin or trip him, when he war walkin or made mud ball an pasted him wid dem or bout a million oda tings den hen would wake up. Take dem for a walk, Play piggy back or sumbos salt. Hen would sit a da table an not eat or talk ta anyone. One day da missy fill a tea-spoon of salt an say, hear

F. Mr. Linsolumn, taste this, you may like it. You don't like anything else I prepare. Like a child opening its mouth to grab its titty he open his mouth and she put da spoon of salt in. As always he said nary a word, wen to da back door, spit it out an started on more paper writen. Willie tormented him asking, why his pa didn eat. Why say, Mr Abe "Didn I eat?" Den hen say, "Mariah, are weuns out of meal? Ah say, Ah'll look an see." It hot war thar war stale. So ah say I'll go by da mill an get some in da morning. Ah war goin back da nex day to help clean.

Ah war returnin from da mill close around Springfiel. Ah hab dat meal in mah cart. All ta once dat ngilly mule bucked. Ah crack et wid mah black snake an do 'bout eber ting ta get et started. Ah eben got out an tried ta coax et. Mr. Abe came along an say ah that maybe you would forget to bring the meal. So it was on my way to the mill. Back in Kentucky and Indiana that was one of my chores, either grinding the corn for meal, or going for it to the mill. Den all at once hen see ah hab da meal and dat dat onery mule war bucking. Well so Mr. mule is hungry say Mr. Abe. We'll fix that. He turned dat cart around so maud war facing da cart. Ah thought has dat man plum loss his senses. He say, She smell the corn meal and start, reaching for it. Sheer nuff da dash her made wid weuns in da cart like ta upset da cart. Ah scream. Let loose ob de line and waving wid bolh hans in da air. Ah speak dat sight would air made ol dog laugh. Skacely Mr Abe dashin afta dat mule. But wid hen's long legs hen caught da mule. Hen gib mule a litta meal from hen han. Dat stop da chase. Hen turn dat mule around lak hen sheer should hab left herin in da first place. Took a candy bag from hen's pocket. Fill it wid meal. Tied it unda dat stubborn mules nose and herin ran after dat bag of meal right under her fool nose so fast ah could hardly guide herin or stay in da cart. Mr Abe followed laughing eber step an manage ta reach home when maud did. An what a God fa sheer blessing. Ah war near tuckered, see sawing on dose lines.

MULE

Early one morning wen ah reach da Lincolumns ta do dare wash an some work. Da table war cleared an pappas from Mr. Abe's store pipe hat war pile high on da centa ob da table. Hern would take a pappa an write down. Den hern would do da same. Some war clip from pappas all ober da Unite State. Once hern cuss da newspappa 'cause hern took so much time readin dem. Now hern read all dem an cut, cut, cut from dem.

Den Mr. Abe would take da stack from hern and hisn writin an read, ober all. Hern would say 'bout dis an dat. This cannot be. This man's convictions. Or it's a political maneuver to get votes. I'll jot down only the nibs of the points I wish to make. God will place on my lips the words to speak on each point. If I wrote out a hundred addresses I'd never speak them as I wrote them. So thats no good go. I heard all I wanted to hear of that when I was in Congress in 1847-1849.

Political scoundrels gained support of other scoundrels by twisting an issue. I'll tell you Molly there are more scoundrels in politics, espacially on the slavery issue than there are in the penatentaries. Oh Abram hern say. You are a radical on that one subject. Hern say. Yes mother, I'm a radical in the same way Cassius Clay is. I'll dare to do right and be true to my convictions. Even in the face of ridicule and failure. Even death if that must come.

Mr. Abe run fa da senate against Steven Douglas, or so da missy 'clared he would in 1855. In da primary da call it. Mr. Lincoln an Julia Jayne husband Lyman Trumball were bofe on da ballot. At dat time da legislater select da ones ta run fa senator.

Mr. Abe win at first. Den on da res of da ballots hern slip a bit. 'Til hern tinks best ta give hisn votes ta Trumball who war lected. Da missy wid out any sense at all, hate dat frem Julia Jayne from dat on. An hern so mad at Mr. Lincolumn, hern rave on rant. Gets headaches. Take peri-goric. Dese tantrums of hern got worse stid of betta. Hern act more out of hern head more lak a crazy person. Ta days hern not clean up, not eben comb hern hare; All jus cause hern thot day shur war goin to da White House gin an finish Steven Douglas foreba.

Hern wouldn go to da door ef any one came, or wouldn go out eben in hern carriage, an no partas; Hern carry on dis way more dan a month. Hern neglect da chilluns; til Willie an Eddie

2. near pie. Dr Wallace work night an day to save them
mr. Abe war in Chicago on business Da missy send word
to Mr Lincolumns. When hen comb home shen blame him
cause hern hab so much wid da care of dose boys 'low. Hern
couldn handle et.

Dat's da fust time ah eba felt lak chipin in rite dare an say
what ah knew whar so. It war jus cause dat woman couldn
go to Washington 'gin. An maybe Jayne Trumball would get ta go.
Ah do believ dat woman's jealous thots war da very debil in hern.
Hern sista Lisbeth fotonse didn fret hern. Or Lisbeth warn't
eben disturb cause Mr. Abe warnt chosen. Da Edwards hab a
big parta ready fa Mr Lincolumn dat night ob da selection.
Day thot shur hen war goin ta be choose. Et didn botha dem at
all 'cause da parta hab ta be call off.

Mrs Lincolumn didn give nary ah parta or go ta partas fa
weeks. Hern say, Shen war too humilitate. Mr. Abe wen back
to da circuit, an ta what otha business hern hab Dn hen say,
Hen work an pray, day an night, fa da colored people. Hen would
help free dem or die in da attempt (Hen say right, Only hen
free dem an die too). Hen knew someway, somehow, someday
God would leberate them. Ah don't 'lieve hen's heart war on
law or politics afta that. Hen say once, That humans were held
in bondage, abused and not permitted to rise above servitude
made him miserable, Dat man war so sad hen hardly hab a smile
fa hisn litta boys.

One rainy day wen hern got oba hern huff 'bout sometings
(Dat woman hab sent out invitation a week afore fa a parta
fa da boys.) hern hab a parta. Da mothas could come ta sew
fa da church mishnary. Hern put all da boys play tingo in
da shed. Hern hab da barn clean an fix wid a stage an seats.
Afta da sewin' da missy serve what hab hen greed on by da
business ob da circle. Just 2 tings cakes an fruit, an course
coffee or whot da want a drink.

Hern fix cakes an candy 'an lemonade in da shed fa
da boys. Emilie habn't gone home yit an hern hep serve.
Et shur war ah nasty day, an da missy say, hern speck most
of dem wouldn't come. Hern put ah piece ob carpet out fa dem te
wipe dare shoes on. An as litta sista Emilie an da missy receive
dem, day put dare wet brellas an wraps on da new hall tree, what
finely got dare from hern pas state.

Da sewing war oba, as well as da gossip 'bout dose who warn't dare.
Den da sewing 'gin. When in march Willie an dat whole

3 kitten posey oh boys. Each one hab an anmal. Willie first let down da white rat on da floor. Da women gin ta pu+ up dare feet an scream. Some eben stood on dare chair. Den up steps a boy wid a turtle, some kittens comb nex+. Ah whole slew ob chicks one fromb each boy, a hop-toad, a big bull frog crokin fa ta go back ta water, an ole hen, Jim Crow dat repeat ober an ober "Get out ya brems". Da boys hab taught him. At las some boys let down onda flo da big tom-cat. Da screamin scceere, dot black heb'l an ah nebber, nebba seed sich racin roun in ah house in mah born days. Day womans put fa do door, grab dare brellas an coats as day daparted. An day scream at dare kids ta come or day would beat da day lights out of dem. Emilie laugh until she cried. Ah bust mah sides an da missy war gin humilitate.

Herin grab Willie an scream. Why did you do such a thing to me? It war always me. Lita Faddie lak i+ so much hin roll an roll on da floor an clap hen's litta hans. Ah bet dat war da best parta dose boys eba hab. Da missy kept repeatin, Why did you do i+? Finely Willie say. The boys got tired of all but Jim-Crow. So we decided to hane a circus parade, an let the animals act. We wanted the ladies and our mas to see our show. I was to bring in the chariot driven by the white rat. Each animal was to have an act, but they acted better than we taught them. Jim Crow was the clown. He was ta say "Get out you brems". Just as the circus clown said, in the circus you took us to. You remember that, Don't you, me? Da missy didn' answer. Herin war so mad. Den Willie say Well pa will laugh. He don't like a gang of woman here all the time anyway. Herin eyes spot fire, an hein yell, William Wallace, Did your father say that? Willie war smart she grin, an say, No ma, but no cow tell when pa doesn't like anything. He's sad an quiet. But I bet he'll like our circus.

Shur nuff when mr. Abe comb home an mrs. Lincolumn tole hin all bout da fracus da boys hab raise. Mr. Abe in hisn high-pitch voice scream. Good. Hen den, all talk at once tellin bout it. Emilie who hab been double ober laughin bust out an say. Brother Abrom you missed the biggest show of your life. Why cant we have another party soon when you are home and have the boys put on their circus parade. Da laugh so loud an long. Da missy really scream an pull hern hare. Hein paid no 'tention to hern rantin. Hein war shur happy gin fa ah while. He say Litta sista I do beliere I like you better than ever. Im in on that party, if I have to miss the circuit. Ill never again tell a story that tops that one.

Da missy rush up stairs. Ah don't tink her war so sorry wen Emilie went home.

For days afta dat. Mr. Abe would bust out laughin if Willie or Taddie war near. Da would almos alway say Pa wen can wen's hab da circus. He'n would pat an hug them. Dew day would run fa some da anmals. Da chicks, white rat an Jim Crow climb oba dat man, wid dose two boys pestering pestering eben when he'n read. He would jine in da fun wid dem onst in awhile.

Wen masta Robert comb home from school, the boys tole he'n bout da circus parade day hab. Bobbie couldn hep but laugh. Tho' he'n knew what torments those boys were. Bobbie couldn call he'n life he'n own. If he'n complain da missy would scold he'n an say "You had freedom, why are you always complaining about the fun these boys have. But Bobbie nerva hab such freedom.

Robert loved his mother. He was so kind and thotful and good. An so sensitive he'n sef. He'n felt sorry fa he'n poor ma. Robert always put he'n arm around him inch an comfort he'n, if anyone took sides against he'n. He'n try ta smooth oba da hurt places.

Ah tink all da boys lak dare pa da most. Day nerva stop to tink, dare pa could presate dem more, cause he'n war not wid dem much. But dare ma sewed, cooked, sometime wash, nursed dem, kept a nice home far 'dem, kept dem clean took dem to shows an church an welcome dare frens. Eben ef he'n warn't much fun. He'n nerva buese dem an did da bes in da world fa dem, as well as hersef as he'n see it. Ah tink Bobbie knowd more dan he'n let on. Ah tink he'n knowd he'n ma war a sick woman in her mind.

Once wen masta Robert war on he'n way to see he'n ma. who war den sick at Aunt Lisbeth's in Springfield. He'n stop in Danville, Ills to see men. Ah don't tink he'n eba went through Danville widout stopn at 812 Oak Str. Dat war our home close to da Big Four track as it is now (1902). He'n talk a heap bout he'n pa. Say, "Ill never believe that pa was ever any happier than after he signed the Emassipation Proclamation, He'n tell— One time on a trip from school to see the folks at the White House I happened in pa's room unexpectedly. Pa was kneeling, praying exziestly to be directed arlght. The north were beseiging him to free the slaves so they could fight. The officers especially Stanton (Sec of War) said he was so slow he was ruining the country. But pa said, I trust

a mightier guide than mortal man, the emancipation
will be signed. But when it is, God will direct my hand
that holds the pen. He suffered for the fallen soldiers of
the south as much as for those of the north who were
injured or were killed. He excused the rash abuse
heaped on him. Once he said, "Father forgive them."
He died many deaths before Booth killed him. I firmly
believe, Masta Robert said, If there is a heaven such as
is written, that God could choose pa to sit on his left as
Christ is chosen to sit at his right.

Maha a good woman. She did much to smooth away
pas primitive habits. But she or anyone could never for
one second influence pa, if he didn't think they were right.
He would often say God would act in his own good
season. He never took credit for a thing. It was always
God. He never intentionally hurt another's feelings. I wish
I was like him.

Masta Robert was always a good boy. So tenda an easy hurt.
He'n put ah brave front on afore men, but ah saw he'n cry
'til would break youn's heart about da passing to God of
he'n brothas, his son Abraham Jr, his'n pa an da shape he'n
ma war in. Ah done think ah eba hea'n Bobbie cry when ah
work in dar'n home in Springfiels. Et war da years dat
make he'n sad. He'n say Garfiels an McKinley both kill, an
he'n cry fa both dem. Maybe day brot back Mr. Abe ta him.
He'n war tenda heart ta animals. Eben wen 16 or 17, wen
Willie an Taddie abuse da birds an animals all obs dare home
Masta Robert would pet an eben kiss dose poor abuse creture.

Often wen he'n's ma war upset, he'n would put his'n arm 'roun
her an pet her. Mr. Abe nevva' courage he'n in he'n tantrums.
Dose lass two years ah work right steady at dare home. Ah
hear Mr. Abe say. Motha youn's make youn self sick. Or,
cant youn be more siderate. He'd more often leave, but
sometimes kiss he'n good-bye. Da minute Mr. Abe war out da
house dat woman would settle down an be he'n sef. Less he'n
took a notion ta take peri-goric an go ta bed.

All da talking Mr. Abe, Dr Wallace, Liebeth an ah'd gib he'n
did'n do no good. He'n love da peri-goric. Once wen da missy
say youn's mouth is black all 'roun wid da licorice youn's
fo eba chaw'n. Youn's mouth is ugly nuff wid out dat. Dat
man hab da prettie's teeth ah eba saw. But da did get black wen
he'n chaw licorice. He'n say, Well mother I like licorice lik

6 you like peri-goric. The difference is in the effects. Licorice, if it be a vice, will not injure me or anyone else. But someday, unless you stop, it will destroy you.

Wen Dr. Wallace war doctorin da boys hen say to da missy. Now you listen ta me Marne, If you give another of that dam stuff to these children she through. Do you want to kill these two also. Ah war plum shock. If I knew where you get it I'd take the law if I had to, to stop it. Abraham has done the best he can. Gurgle it if you must, though I swear by the Eternal God, I'll not stand by and watch you ruining your own sons. Day didn' say peri-goric. But ah say to mahsef. What else air it?

Hern war so good, wen eba ting went hern way. Ah mean lak. when Mr. Abe git Stephen Douglas all tangle up in hisn speech makin. But wen Mr. Lincolumns made dat first speach, an stan dore, side dat primp up Douglas, all rumple hare, wid out coat or colla, one gallus an muddy boots, her war humelitate. Den wen Mr. Abe gib hern votes ta dat Trumball, hern war furious an jealous. Wen hen say nice tings of Ann da Salem girl hern war mad an jealous 'gin. Hern got so hern didn' want Mr. Abe to praise anyone, what hern didn' lak, an some of dem she'n did lak, Lak litta Emilie.

Afta da missy fix da house differment, an war busy getn' et all pretty up, ah tink dat woman war happy some. Ah believe Mr. Abe really lak hisn home, betta, an war happy 'bout et fa ah while. Hen nevva say ah word 'bout wat war spent on et. Hen still hab hisn 'spells oh deep tho't. Hen was ask hear an dare, an eba war to speech make. Sometime hen take da missy. Afta hen's answer Stephen Douglas in Springfeild. Hen speech make in Peoria Urbana Quincy Jacksonville an eben Chicago. Dees speechin came from hen's heart 'gainst extend of slavery. Da missy war glad hen war back in polites. But Mr. Abe say "If its a means to an ending in right I must go back. But I'll be on the side and with the issues I think are right. The ending in question is the recognition of our constitution. The main issue involved is - That all men are created equal. The extention of slavery is flaunting disloyalty in the faces of free loving peoples. Slavery as it exist is so wrong and we in this republic are taunted as hypocrites. That for economic reasons alone of self-interest, we would sacrifice human souls and bodies, in dastarly, brutal acts. Acts against fundamental principals of civil liberty

1.

Another Rift

I addie must hab been most five an Willie most seben. Wen ah comb ta work dat mornin, et war pretty cold. Mix. Abe war out speech-makin or maybe au circuit ah jus done rightly memba. But dis time ah hab ta build da fire ta heat mah watah. Dat wardsheer ah surprise as da watah war always hot fa men. Da clothes before dis time, sorted an eba ting ready. Ah didn' see ah soul 'round. Ah counted mah fingas to be shur et war da right day of da right week. Ah hab left Narcissas an Rosa mah las girl at home, an brot my wee chile, dis one a boy John. Hen war such a litta sleepy head ah nevva hab trouble wid hin. 'Cause ah made da fire in da kitchen, ah hab ta carry da watta out ta da shed, whar ah wash. Wen ah air busy ah nevva stop 'til ah's done.

Dis mornin ah smell smoke. Ah look up au see da smoke comen fromb da kitchen door. Ah says, Holy God da Lincolumn's house es burnin down. Ah dash in da kitchen au dare stood I addie au Willie in dare night clothes, each wid ah soap bubble pipe en hens mouf. But no soap bubbles. Day hab torn papah au dry corn silks in dare pipes. Day hab start dare pipes wid mah kitchen fire. Ah scream at dem dat day would sot da house on fire. But day paid no heed, au each spit some black spit in da fire. Dat skeer me, until ah foun out et war licorice juice, da war spitten out, tendin et war 'bacca juice.

Ah say, Whars your Mak? Willie say, Don't you dare wake Mak. Aint Mariah. She was up late with guests and wishes to sleep this morning. We are the men of the house. Ah say, Youns not men youns two bums. Smokin au spitten au skeerin de day-lights out of men wid da smoke au black spit. Day bofh laugh aloud. Youns pa is ah man au he don't smoke au chew 'bacca. Well say Willie. Maks guests are the cream of Springfield. They smoke, au chew because we saw them last night.

2. Ah up an say; Whin do youns tink air da bes man in da worl? Both say pa is. Well ah ask. Who would youns rathe be youns pa, or one ah dees 'bacca chewin an smokin men? Daddie threw his pipe an wad of bacca from her's mouth in da stove, an scream, Papa da. Now get out an leave us alone, say Willie.

Da missy comb tearin' in. Her'n hab an idea ah war da cause oh da bedlum. But Daddie gave it 'way. Her'n grab Willie's pipe what Willie war holdin' hind of her's, an say, ef youns tell ma, ah'll hit you Aunt Mariah, wid Willie's pipe. Daddie didn talk as plain as dad cause her couldn'.

Da missy, allus seem ta fava Willie — Her'n say, Willie precious, tell mother what you and Daddie were doing? Willie war smart an her'n say meek like. We were only playing. But how playing, say da missy. Tell me about the pipe and this smoke. Give me the pipe Daddie. Her'n held et back of her'n fa a spell, den finely shove et at her'n. Da missy, look at it, smell it an say. Come to mother boys, Daddie step up bold like, but Willie hung his'n head an went slow like. Now boys, her'n say, I know you were playing, but this is an order from mother — No more such playing. But mother Willie say, Those men at your party, last night smoked and chewed and you didn't tell them to stop. Why should they have more privileges in our home than we have? Her'n say, Men can choose or can limit themselves when it comes to vices. But little boys must be guided or directed by parents who love them. Your father would not do, what he would not have his boys do. You know he would not have you pattern after men who are careless about their habits. Don't you want to please your dear father? Day look of dem of course day day do. No spankin, no scoldin — Dats da way mo' Libe an da missy manage dose boys. Ah neva did see da like. In dose boys oven back to dare, makin soap bubbles wid out notha ward.

As allus afta partas, ah hab stacks ob dishes, an da house ta hep clean. Now dat da missy war up, ah knew ah'd nevva get 'way 'til da las speck ob dirt war out ob da house. Ah hurried wid mah wash cause et war ah big one. Hem mus ah strip da beds ob covalets an chars ob tiddies an da windows of curtains an sash curtains. Dare war ah lot ob cleanin' rags, sides da reglar tings. Hem tell da boys ta play en da yard an not git en Aunt Mariah's way. But mercy 'lins, dose boys wen fromb one ting to 'notha so fast, day kept me'n yelpin' at dem ta keep fromb trompin' dem down. Day allus skeer me'n wen day clumb da wood pile. Shur et hab poles at da ends, but da stack war so high an day clumb ta da top. Willie allus drug Taddie up. Ef dose poles hab busted an start da wood ta role, dose boys could ah been mashed pleumb flat as spanked tatters, wid dat wood. Somb ob da chunks war big an heavy. All mah kids seems ah how nevva got into so much divelment as dose two. Ah nevva know why ah worried so much 'bout does litta scamps. Dare mah an fa didn'.

Mah work warn't oba 'til time fa dinna. So ah hab ta fix mwah left-obas, as allus afta partas. Hem let me'n bring John en. Hem say once, herse didn' lak smelly colored babies. Hem gib me'n powda ta put on afta ah diddies John. Et hep her'n fromb gauldin. Et made dat baby boy smell good too. Da missy gib me'n ah bag ob assifidity ta hang on ah string 'roun hen's neck. Hem boys allus wore dem ta keep 'way seases. John war too litta ta eat, so ah gib her nurse fromb me'n. (Da missy allus say, Aunt Mariah don't say that vulgar word titty, say nurse.) Ah do forgit once in how an den, but fore God ah done mean oh he vulga.

Wen hab hardly start eat'n' wen Mr. Abe comb en by sprize. Ah tink by dare talk her'n hab got ah wire ta comb ta Chicago on somb business or otha.

+ Right way, herin plan ta go long.

Mr Abe war heap happy 'bout somet'ing. But dat change soon nuff. Ef day hab frocuses afore, et warn't ah potchin ta dis one 'fore hen war home long.

He say mother (dis war afta hen hab eat ah bite ar two at da table wid dem) I have something here (Hen reached in hisn pocket an drew out a picture) that you've asked me about so often. Now mother this is not a picture taken of the little girl I knew, and who was very dear to me in New Salem. However it couldn't look much more like her if taken of her. I picked it up in a picture gallery to bring home to show you. Hen take dat picha an look an look at et. An da more hern look, da blacka hern look. Ah hope ta die right har on dis spot ef dat woman didn' push her cha back, stan up, slap dat picha down hard on da table an say. You'll never make me believe if you tried to convince me before a tribunal, that a girl who looked like that cared an iota about you. The way she is dressed show she is not a common country girl. Mr Abe say, It's the face, the face of a young innocent angel. Boo-Boo say da missy innocent, when she would go with you, while engaged to marry another. Hern look lak tunda and hern look lak hen war struck by lightning.

Hern grab da picha up an start fa da stove. Hen quick-quicka dan ah eba see hen move, afore, grab her an squeeze da picha out ob hern fingas. Dat woman plumb act wild. Hern scratch at hisn face. Pick up ah fork an ah 'lieve hern would ah dug hisn eyes ou wid et, but Mr Abe grab hern han an got da fork 'way. Den hen sot hern on ah char. Drew notha char out fromb da table an sot squar en front ob hern, an look hern right smack en da eyes, an say, "Woman, how long suffering do you think I am?" Had you destroyed that picture you would have destroyed the symbol of some of the greatest happinesses I've had in my life. Not alone because it is so like a little lady, who tried an' did help me start what I've now accomplished, but it is so like my angel mother. Had you destroyed it you would have destroyed a part of me that can neber be replaced.

5. Something that would be encouragement to go on (every time I looked at the picture) to better things. Could help me live through trials; Could help me live over and over south the greatest happinesses I've had in my life. I would lie to you woman. If you continue these fits of insane contemptableness, I'll promise you and myself before God, you'll just be a mother of my children and no more.

If you try you can stop this silly jealousy that has ruined what could have been a loving disposition. You've let yourself go, unchecked until it has become an obsession. I thought I was marrying a woman who would be a help mate instead of a hindrance. No man can go on and up shouldering such. You can make up your mind."

He started for the door. Then screamed, Ran at her, Throwed her arms round his neck, Tried to drag his head down ta kiss her, or her kiss him. Mr Abe stood lak ah statue. Bore her let loose wid both hans round her neck, Her draw back on him an slap dat man ah God awful slap en da face. Den her ran ta da door, lock et, an tole Mr Lincolumn if her left, her would kill her sef.

Den we hear poundin at da door. Laddie war cryin ta come in. Mr. Abe say, Give me that key or I'll have to take it from you. She threw et on da floor at her feet, when her stoop fa it, her jump on his back an pull his hair an try ta choke her. Her straighten up quick an her sot hard on da floor.

Her opened da door an en rush da boys, who hab been shewed out wen da fracus 'gin. Laddie hab ah big splinta in his foot. Willie hab drug Laddie up on da wood pile 'gin. Mr Abe pull out da splinta, wash da foot put on some turpentine an wrap ah clean rag 'roun. Her kiss da boys an start out 'gin. But 'gin da missy tries ta lock them in. Her push her ta one side an go out. Her goes out too. Grabs his coat tail an hangs on.

Wal dat woman thus hab him, cause Mr Lincolumn war ah public spectal. No one on da outside knew his trouble. Cause her tole no one. Guess her war

6. to shame. Hein come back in

Hein try an try ta talk ta dat man, but guess hein said hisn say an ment eba word of et. Hein sot wid hisn chair 'lean back' gin da wall, wid hisn head down, an hisn arms wrap 'round hisn knees.

John war sleep all thro' da hella-baloo. Ah had ta pass Mr. Abe to go home. Hein say narry ah word. Reach in hisn pocket, take out some money an han et ta men. Ah didn know et war five dollas 'til ah stop at da sto and da sto-keepa hans men da change four dollas an ah quarta. Ah war sure Mr. Abe didn mean ta gib men more dan two dollas, so ah starts back ta da Lincolum. 'Fore ah gits dare ah knowd hein or some bodies else war comen, cause ah sees ah breesh limb of ah tree oba da fence wiglin an ah long stick, stuck thro da bottom oh da fence dat touch da board walk. Eet war Mr. Abe combin wid hisn head down. Dat man nebba would ah comb out ob dat sad look if dat breesh limb hadn knocke hisn hat off an dat long stick got tween hisn legs an stop hem. Dose litta scamps laugh at da top of dare dear litta voices, Mr. Abe reach oba da top ob da fence, put one on one shoulda and one on da otha, an dots da way da war wen ah met dem at da corna ob da street.

Mr. Abe say widout ah smile. Ah taking these two socks of coral to the mill to have them ground into meal. Dose two boys began to wiggle. Taddie say, "no meal, papa da." Da othas all say "po," an "ma." Sometime Maslah Robert say, fatha and matha. Den Taddie gin ta kick wid both feet. Mr. Abe let dem both down. kissed dem. Gave dem each ah love pat an send dem down back home, afta hein tole dem ta be good boys an not forget ta close da gate.

Nevva once did dat man smile gin afta dose boys rund back. Hein say. Aunt Mariah did you forget something? No ah say, Mr. Abe youn made a heap big mistake. Ah stop at da store for some grub an day gib men dess four dollas an ah quarta back. Now ah

I knowd yous done made ah mistake,' 'Cause da five dollus whut youn gib me warnt da two dollus ah spec et war. Wal, Mr Abe say, Youre a very honest woman Aunt Mariah, I made no mistake, I knew the five dollars was all I had in that pocket. When you first came to work for us, all youn ware expected to do was to wash. But youn been ready and willing to take time from your family to help with all the other work. Have you always been paid for this extra work you have done? Ah say, Why Mr. Abe ah'll nevva be able to pay youn fa all da extra youn's gib men. Youn's an Dr Wallace an da missy.

Gifts are gifts, say Mr Abe, and work is work that is only compensated for by pay in dollars and cents. Id would never forgive myself ur expect to gain if I withheld from you what you so rightfully earn. No one will elz know, just how really God-lak, dat man war.

Ah war sad fa da nex two weeks 'bout does Lincolununs. Ah couldn do or say a ting to help dem. But ah guess sum'ting mus ah comb up ta partla straighten tings out, as da missy goes ta Chicago wid Mr. Abe. Herin tell men 'bout da wondaful time dey hab at du shows an herin buys dress goods an more curtain stuff.

Mr. Abe nebba brag 'bout nothin. Hen whip Stephen Douglas pants off. Just by tellin da God's truth in hena speech makin. Hen nebba, nebba taked da credit fa hen smart. Hen say while he war speech makin All I want and all I have are the points I wish to speak on. I sift Stevie Douglas's argument down to the subjects he evades or handles recklessly. I jot down those points and store in my hat. The good Lord God carries me through from there Once Hen tell da missy when hen ask if hen warn't 'fraid hen would make a bobble if hendidn't go over all da points wid hern. Maybe she can suggest something from a political angle, as that is my fort. I've been versed in politics since a child, Henry Clay was a mighty politician and he know all the tricks of the trade. So does Stephen Douglas. You must hold in mind always, that he is a powerful weapon for the slave holders and against any opponent who gets in his path. Abram don't let him play you

Say Mr. Abe Hell mother I am well aware of the fact that you are a real little politician, And I understand perfectly your earnest and abiding faith in politics and your ambitions that have never cooled off However I have faith, if I follow my convictions and the principals of our founding fathers who established this great Republic I can depend upon God to put the right in my mind and voice to speak. He always has when I yields to him

A long time ago I sensed, if I chose God as my prompter, he would fill my mind with the right. Nor would he forsake me in any difficult undertaking To me its not a question of whose, mightier or righter; God or Stephen Douglas. Right is might. I know if at any time my frail mortal mind attempts to trust for might, if it is not right. God will either set me on the right track, by some example or I will fail by failing to recognize his loving care The bible says To trust not to meditate before what ye shall say. For I will give you a mouth to speak wisdom,

Its unexplainable to me as so much has been, espacially since my residence in Illinois Out of a clear time came the thought You are twenty-one, No longer you should depend on anothers orders. I had always felt that I was subject to my father's directin and care. Ill admit I had some fear of this new adventure. Embark-

2ing alone in a new country. Immediately upon my decision to go it alone, I found new helpful friends. Every step until now has been test and try with many trials. But by trust, this mighty power outside of the physical or mortal mind, has directed me. Someday I hope to gain Mariah's faith. The faith "Bigga dan da mustard seed". Her faith, that will remove mountains of trouble for the colored people. If I can through God's help utter one word that will produce a chain of reactions, which will eventually free the black man; I shall never cease to thank God for that one word.

When I started to practice law, I promised God if I found anyone whom I was hired to defend were guilty, I would quit the case. In unexpected ways, that promise which I have kept, has paid off. Many times when it seemed I was about to fail, a true story of some happening in my early life would come to mind. I unhesitantly used them to illustrate a point, that seemed not to come clear how that story really would fit in. Even sometimes the point was not too clear that I wished to make. I'd seem to be treading on thin ice. But I never was let down. The finish of these stories seemed not of my own mind or how they applied. The outcome of the story and points gained were so surprising I often laughed more heartily than anyone else. By steadfastness in this promise to do right as God shows me the right, as I submit to his guidance I know I cannot fail. Christ said, "It is the father in me" and "not my will but thine be done".

Remember how Mariah gave up her little Phebe. How she accepted it and was comforted. Did we do, as she did, with Eddie mother? Da missy, began to get powerful narrow an say, Abram let's not have anymore sermons from you. Once a week at church is enough and the place for that. Lat all I can digest. Let get down to earth and be practical. Sometimes I think you talk like a crazy man. You'n see herin warn ah God - woman. me, Abe war ah God - man.

Hen try ta be patient wid dat woman, an say, mother Ise so often gone over your plans for me with you. You have help me in many practical (as you say) ways. However when it comes to our planning an address, it just doesn't work out. We stood for hours, reciting what I that I would say in defense of a client or a conviction of mine. Those words first didn't come out. New triumphant words came from my lips. Often strange statements. But they never failed to be the right.

3 You remember what was the outcome of one of my rehearsals?
mariah got a black eye. He'd laugh and laugh. Da missy
say now I know you are crazy. Ah tink it war jus lak
Dr Wm Wallace sayd. Dat false aristocracy am Big me an
litta you. Eben God es da litta one.

  Mr. Abe habs all da laugh take out of hin. Dat man as
allus look sad. Hen put on hisn tall hat, shawl an fut off
out dose. It war no use. Eber time hen open hen mouf dat
woman drove a wedge twixt dem fartha an fartha. Hen
talk an talk da men afta Mr. Abe war gone. Ah didn say
nary a word. Ah knowd day war as much defferment as
day an night. An ef ah spouted off, ah'd get mah foot in it up ta
mah neck.

  Hen say It's a wonder Mr Lincoln didn't mention that
common Ann, from the backwoods where he came from. He's
never derectly told me he loved her or that she loved him
He's mentioned her many times. He's even given her credit for
his start in the practice of law. I've so often asked him what
she looked like. Though I suppose she was a straggly, ill
cared for farm girl, He's always said. She's too etherial to describe.
Once I heard Mr. Abe tell da missy - She's the only one who
ever reminded me of my mother; buried back dare in Injiana.
He Said, My mother as I remember her was a gentle christian,
as was Ann. Da missy say whenever he speaks of his
mother or this Ann, he always he comes quiet and sad
afterwards. Won't talk to anyone for a day or two, and wanders
around as if in a doze. It leaves one wondering if its her
mother or this Ann who occupies his mind so completely.

  Wal ah tinks. Maybe ah'd feel hurt too as hen does. But
ah'd shur try ef ah love him ta change mah ways. Be more
lak da ones hen loved, fa dare gentle christian ways. Ah'd try
ta undastan mah man more dan hen do. Et are so plain
ta see when hen got on ah subjec hen, nevva, nevva, got off dat
subjec til hen hab that et out. Hen could hep bofe hen sef
an dat man by stopin blabbin an scoldin an dose wild tantrums.
How hen could seal dat mind of hisn off gainst hen outbursts
beat da world. Hen didn relize et war cousin talk dat, maybe
warnt true. An cousin hen thots dat war bad fa hen. Maybe God
got dose two strange folks to getha to make boaf of dem stronga
But da since made a russel ob it. Ef hen could jus ah been

happy with me. Abe doin someting good 'stid af always watchin herin ta do someting big. Common circuit riden an common frens made herin mad. Ah'd ah wouda, if ah hab'n know herin lak men, 'cause ah remind herin of mammy Sally back in Lexton. Herin lak nalin an war good, spacially ta mah chillun. Eet maybe mammy Sally war an ristocrat coon, cause herin belong ta ristocrats. Mr. Abe belong ta herin. So herin should be a ristocrat. Herin didn want hisin folks or hisin frens 'round, cause da war common no count herin say.

Wen herin hab a parta herin pick da cream oh Springfield. Mr. Abe nary care doe. He warn thar half da time anyhow. Wen herin war, herin act as if day warn dare. Herin go ta da table wid no coat or colla. In herin sock feet if hisin feet huert. Eben widout socks. I lick bones from hisin plate on da table cloth. Drink juice left from da desert out of da sauce dish. Scoot food stuff from da tureen or dry meat platta ta hisin plate. An worse en all, wipe hisin mouth on hisin shirt sleeve. Da missy would act as if herin didn see, would be sweet 'bout it, til da guest leave, den herin would raise tickula hell. Eben mah Henry hab betta table mannahs. But Mr. Abe did jis love ta tease herin. Wen herin finely stop raven. Dat man stop doin. Herin jis couldn' be driven. Wen herin stop drivin fa awhile, dat man would go higha in law an big jobs.

Dose Lincolumns boys mus hab taken dar teasen from dare pa. 'Cause day war da worse teases ah eba saw. Once when da missy hab ah big day time parta, some of da lady brot dare brats 'long, as da missy call dem. Herin say day put herin boys up ta mischief. But Willie an Taddie love mischief betta dan dare toys. Ef dose woman's boys could teach dem two Lincolumns any new tricks, da missy should hab gibben dem one oh da parta prizes.

Mr. Lincolumn hab jus tole dem 'bout always tyeing herin step motha's apron strings ta da slats in a ladda back chair eba time herin could. Til herin finely made hin repair da damage (cause by dis trick.) ta da strings an sometime da apron. Herin tole 'bout holdin a little bare-foot boy up-side down, so's he could walk on hisin step-mas, whitewash ceiling wid herin dirty feet. Cause hisin step-ma made hin wash hisin feet, fore hen track in on herin clean scrub floor. Herin make a funnel from a leak in da log-cabin roof ta a wooden-stave tub. I har hin caught wata, good rain wata, so's hen wouldn hab ta go ta da spring ta carry da wata. One day herin pa rave cause dat spring wata taste jus lak roof rain wata. Herin wen ta da spring ta try ta scour da cause. Wen hen comb back herin clumb in da loft ob dare cabin

5. an foun Mr. Abe's funnel. Da funnel an da fun end rite dare. Cause hen's pa lam hen good. Hen's step-ma took dat boys part, an laugh bout da tracks on da ceilin an da funnel. Mr. Abe nevva war a ting lak hen's pa. Onla hen did lak ta wonda fronb one place ta 'notha. Hen love ta wonda unda da stars at night. Love da woods an do circuit. Hen make extra trip ta Indiana ta his poor maka grave. Hen go to see Dennis Hank and his wife who war Mr. Abe's step sista. Any whar so he war on da go.

Mr. Abe once tell da missy if hen would make one circuit trip with him, she'd enjoy the changes of scenery, the various court proceedings and the fun they had. Or if she would take the boys fishing, she learn ta love nature. Da only nature her love war hen's flowers. Hen say hen got 'nough nature at dare country home in Kentuck. Hen war always fraid out dare. An say, I can't see any sense, in rambling around, when there is so much in this big world to see. Like Niagara Falls, she Liberty Bell. All the cultural of Boston. Then London and Paris. For you (her say to Mr. Abe) if you speak of a trip its California or Oregon. Hen say, I want my boys to learn of the real wonders. Those still in the primitive state as created, never desecrated by man. Should man by his medling change the course of the stars, sun or moon, then the end is near. That, if ever, may be ages from now. The bible says "There will be no seasons, no time and the powers of the heavens will be shaken. This couldn't be by who created them and called them good. It must be by medlin men, men who are prone to heed the wrong instead of the right. In spite of dat man's good ways hen provoke dat woman. If hen's could hab been provoke as much by hen's boys, dat home would hab been worse dan a hell, but hen's couldn see ah fault in hen's boys.

Does boys at da parts, wid dose otha boys dare, tied all da ribbons an sashas dose ladies hab strung from dare hats an dresses ta da back of da chars. Day war lak litta mice, at dare jobs. Da left da streamers loose, but tied da knots tight. When da ladies moved or turned dare head too far. Off pop da hat to one side or da otha. Sometime dare bonnets fell ta da floor. Da streamas from dare necks would choke dem. Some da sashes war full clean off when day got up from dare chars. Dat parte ended wid dose women screamin' at dare kids. Da kids whoopin an laughin. Some da women blamin da otha woman's brats. Mr. Abe fairly role off hen's char laughin 'bout it when told. Hen hug dose litta rascal ta him, as if day war litta angles 'stet of litta torments.

Sin say ~~that~~ I couldn' reprimand them for doing what I so often have wanted to do ~~when in~~ especially in church! When ~~women~~ there in attendance fling themselfies about wiggling their jew-jaws attracting attention to their finery.

Da missy still say it was not her boys at the bottom of it. Da older boys were to blame. But I'm sorry it had to happen in my home. It broke up the party, and was a reflection on my ability as a perfect hostess.

Mah goodness, but dat house war shur purty afta da missy hab it made ober. Herin eben hab wall poppa from Paris. An da mose new orments on da mantle an what-not. A new ~~tango~~ clock. New carpets an curtains on ~~drappery~~ an ~~drappery~~ tie-backs. Ah crystal light froml da ceiling of da front parla wid lots of bangles of glass an candles. An candles on herin mantle.

When herin hab a parta and da table war all set wid herin fine china an crystal. Wid all de mounds of good eatins. Et war wondaful. But ah nevva wood a giv up dat good ole big kitchen an dat nice long table fa all da rest ob da house fixins. When herin hab much company da hab ta set da table in da settin room. Da dinin room herin cut off from da big kitchen shur warn big 'nough.

Herin gib usins da nice kitchen chars. Day war black painted wid bright fruit an flowers on top da black. Da ole bed Mr. Abe say herin out growd an a load of purta litta orments. Some blue chine dishes an almose mah cart full ob pots, pans, ole carpets an ole close.

Mah Henry hep me unload dis plunda in da shed. Herin say some day, maybe we could add ah notha room, made of plank ta da shack. But herin nevva did. Most dat plunda stay in da shed 'til weins move ta Danville. Mah chilluns broke up mose da orments playn wid dem. Weins ware da carpets an close out. But da res ah hab, an ahll sell fa da money ah need. Ahin ole now an day are in da way ta clean.

Since Julia dead, herin chillen an mah chillen don't care for dem or mah stories 'bout dem. Day got tired years ago lisnin ta da kincolumn talk ah guess. Ah get what ah can out of dem. (I bought what she had left of ornaments, china jewelry, books, furniture and pictures.)

I asked Aunt Mariah if she knew why Mr Lincoln left the whig party

Ob ah did hare tell. One time whan Mr Abe wah talkin' polticks. Dis talkin wah wid big folks. Some what comb, what wants get artcals ta put in da poppa. Udas what want job wen he got ta Washington as sentoh.

Wal Mr Abe say "It might surprise you to hear that I was once an Andrew Jackson man. All the Lincolns were Democrats. My father, the Hanks and Johnstons were Democrats.

Ah did have tell, lets see, ah tink it wah Mr. Sam Graves Mr. Graveses litta boy wah Willies playmate afta Eddie died an fore Taddie come ta town. He say not one ob Mr Lincolns no count reltives voted for him. But evan las one ob dem would be afta dat poor Mr. Abe fa money whan he got ta da Whitehouse. Evan las one ob da Lincolums neighbour vote fa him, an day did gin in 1860 fa President. Cause da all say so. Dare wah da constable Abner Watson, Mr. Billington da sawyer, who Mr. Abe sometime hep's fixting, an like ah heap. Wen da wah day county sheriff Chas Arnold what didn like da missy cause da screamin round she did disturb da neighbours who send fa him in da night Wen mr Ben Moore da survaor. Mr. Abe hep dat man too whan he get in ah pinch. Mr. Abe say "Sometimes dat Benj. Moore in his surveying doesn't know where to start an where to stop". Bout all he knew how ta do was drive a stake and drag the line straight. But Mr Abe love his neighbours an all da neighbours sides the Francis, da Trumball an Brownins wah his friens. Some ob da woman folks didn lak da missy too much.

When da Lincolums got in high polticks an make lots ob money from da railroad job, an da missy hab a fine carriage, an wen in big city, high 'ciety. Day all hova 'round ta get an invite. An dats jus' what da missy did, she could show dem "hangers on" as her call dem, how 'aristocrats entatain right. Dat blessed woman wah forgiven. Her look ovva all da mean tings they done did ta her. But her also hab a heap of polticks, an know how to get votes fa Mr. Abe

2. But Mr. Abe wahn't made sentob. Da "Little Giant" as Mr. Douglas wah call, beat him to it. Mr. Abe say, dat if Stephen Douglas fall smack dab in da Sangamon riva, day would pull him out wid his pockets full ob fice.

Mr. Lincolumn say "One thing he didn't like about Mr. Rep. Douglases defense; which should be clear an concise, from moral, Christian or political angles, were side tracked, for nothing more or less than dirty attacks on his opponents. Always laden with nasty insinuations or quite often smears that were heavily laden with untruths."

I stopped Aunt Mariah, because she had failed to tell me why Mr. Lincoln left the "Whig" party. She said, Ah gets so all fired excited whan ah tink ob how Mr. Abe wah abuse by ebba one ob dose newspapas by da Demarats. Nid all dose horrid pichahs. Dose Demarats most ebba one pig heads at dat time, makin fun ob dat smart man; smart nuff ta become President. Ah just git all rattle up. Now whah wah ah? I told her, back where she said, that his father, the Hankss and Johnstons were Democrats.

"Oh yas', said Aunt Mariah, Mr. Abe, say. At the time I turned "Whig" in 1826 (I think that date should be 1832) the uncertainty of the currency was the deciding factor. My friends in New Salem, at that time, were Wm. Jones and Wm. Woods who were strong Clay men. They gave me Clay speeches, which had been written up in newspapers published in Cincinnati. I became a fervent supporter of Clay great principols. I read other papers from Louisville, One called the Journal and another from the number given me by friends called the Telescope. I learned what I read, word for word, so I could repeat correctly. They called me their walking newsboy. But the "Whig" party finally petered out.

From the "Whig" party, this new Republican party has been born. Named for this our Republic, The Republican principols are not wholly unlike the Whigs. It supports in everyway the original constitution of the United States, I feel quite certain this original principoled constitution which was concienciously thought out and prayed over will keep us a United States, as long as the world stands, Should all nations, everywhere, follow its precepts and leadings, of this new party, all men everywhere can eventially become free

3. Those who oppose freedom will become extinct.

Men from the beginning were given the free moral right to choose between right and wrong. Some may choose wrong because they have been deprived of their right to think. Have been mislead. But with strength of character and the power of a good mind, one can seek and find the right road. We need not follow a wrong choice as lack of mental development causes.

"Once my pa said, 'I'd know right from wrong if he were raised in a rat hole'. My father was a good man, but without a developed mind was often mislead. Pa done right as he saw the right. But pa never had even a good start. As for me I had an angel mother and step-mother and wonderfully good friends to guide me aright. Such help as I received from them, helped to develop my mind and overbalanced those who opposed my desires to learn and rise.

Pa opposed me, but he thought he was right. A great many people here in Springfield think Mrs Lincoln and I are not bringing our children up right. The first step in blocking anyones progress, through development of mind, is to not allow them freedom. One should set a good object lesson, for one thing, before their children. Then give the children freedom to learn from the object."

Mr. Lincolumn onla hab two Sundays ta home durin his debate wid Stephen Douglas fah da Senate job. But dose Sundays fromb Friday 'til Monday wah so full with partas by da missy an odas, dare wahn't ah single moment ob rest. Da wah ah heap ob peoples comb ta see Mr. Abe. Day wah all so shur he wood be 'lected.

Wat time Mr. Lincolumn wahn't trabelin from one speach makin place ta da pedah, durin da debate, he hab no time ta take care ob his poar feit. Sides corns an bunions, day wah an ole case ob frozen feet dat botha dose big feit of his. Ah don't tink dat man wood ah comb home dose two Sundays, but it gabe him ah chance ta soak an dacta dose poar feit. W-an he wah home, it wah "a whirl" (as da missy say) ob partas. Sides mah work fa dem, day hab Mary da maid—Ah wah call da servant. But da missy keep Mary so busy, her 'bout fall in her track. Den one day wan us wah goin ta fix fa a big parta cause Mr. Abe war home—Dis wah a boltize

Those who oppose freedom will become extinct.

Men from the beginning were given the free moral right to choose between right and wrong. Some may choose wrong because they have been deprived of their right to think.. Have been mislead. But with strength of character and the power of a good mind, one can seek and find the right road. We need not follow, a wrong choice as mainly lack of mental development causes."

"Once my pa said, 'I'd know right from wrong if he were raised in a rat hole. My father was a good man, but without a developed mind was often mislead. Pa done right as he saw the right. But pa never had even a good start. As for me I had an angel mother and step-mother and wonderfully good friends to guide me aright. Such help as I received from them, helped to develop my mind, and overbalanced those who opposed my desires to learn and rise.

Pa opposed me, but he thought he was right. A great many people here in Springfield think Mrs Lincoln and I are not bringing our children up right. The first step in blocking anyones progress, through development of mind, is to not allow them freedom. One should set a good object lesson, for one thing, before their children. Then give the children freedom to learn from the object"

Mr. Lincolunn oula hab two Sundays ta home durin his debate wid Stephen Douglas fah da Senate job. But dose Sundays fromb Friday til Monday wah so full with partas by da missy an odas, dare wahn't ah single moment ob rest. Da wah ah heap ob peoples comb ta see Mr. Abe. Day wah all so shuar he wood be 'lected.

Wat time Mr. Lincolunn wahn't trabelin from one speach makin place ta da pdah, durin da debate, he hab no time ta take care ob his poar feet. Sides carns an bunions, day wah an ole case ob frozen feet dat botha dose big feet ob his. Ah don't tink dat man wood ah comb home dose two Sundays, but, it gabe him ah chance ta soak an dosta dose poor feet. 'I-an he wah home, it wah "a whirl" (as da missy say) ob partas. Sides mah wark fa dem, day hab Mary da maid - Ah wah call da servant. But da missy keep Mary so busy, her 'bout fall in her track. Den one day wan us wah goin ta fix fa a big parta cause Mr. Abe war home - Dis wah a boltion parta. Mary got plum play out an sick so couldn' come.

Mr. Abe wen up stairs. Ah thot maybe he wah up dare restin his pooh hurnné, achein' feet. Ah hadn' seed him take da foot tub oh watta up. Ah nebba seed ah man wash his feet so much.

Dare wah lots ob work up stairs ah hab ta do afta mah kitchen work. Wen ah got up stairs, dare was Mr. Abe an da two boys rite dare in mah way. Da boys tearin 'round es allus. Mr. Abe wid his two pooh feet in da wata. Mr. Abe call da two boys. Da wen ta dare ba on ah gallop. He say, Keep out ob Aunt, Maricho way. Just then Taddie spy a pickcha he nebba saw 'fore on da tub. Day both squat down ta look at all dose pickchas on dat tin foot tub. Seems day nebba could get 'nough look at dose pickchas.

Mr. Abe carry da wata up stairs fromh da pump in da back yard. Summa or winta, dat man wash his feet in cold wata. When ah first work dare in 1850, Mr. Abe use soft, but wan he make lots of money wid lawin' an da railroad, day hab castill or such lak soap.

On dis day, ob da bigges parta, wen 'bout da hole Springfield wood comb in dare carriages wid dare finnery on, Ah workin so fast ah wah all out ob breath up stair and da missy work lak a nigga shur nuff. On da midst oh all dis hab—huh es comb ah bunch of men down in front. Mrs. Lincoln who wah jes den hangin da table afta dustin an rangin da furniture (Mary wah sick an stay home) hid fa her wah ah sight an couldn' go ta da door. Ah shur wah a mess from top ob my woolly head ta mah flat feet. So Mr. Abe pull his feet out ob da tub, Gib dem a wipe, Put on his carpet—slippas, an as cool as yas please, let dat mob in. Took dare hats, an hung dem on dat hall tree. Lead dem in da parla dat wah oula 'bout half done clean. Say, be seated gentlman. An den day 'gin ta talk.

Dare war da missy cage fa ahfull half hour in da kitchen Mr. Abe call her, den wen ta look fa her ta entaduce ta da gang oh dose men in da parla. 'Spose he found her, but jes said all jokin lak. I suppose Mrs. Lincoln is out messing up something, so she can find something to straighten up. That little woman is the busiest little body in the world. Day all laugh heartily.

Ah wah doin mah best ta keep dose boys quiet up stairs. Ah say, Do dis an do dat ta help. Wen ah say, You pa hab leave dat tub right in mah way, Ah shur starta ah hella—baller. But ah still hidn' stop gabbin' ta dem boys. You pa allus throw

5 da water out da upstairs window. He can throw it far nuff et dont didn drip down on da house. Ah tole da boy ah'd make dem johnny-cakes (dey lak johnny-cakes wid mople syrup) if dey would be quiet an not scatta trash fasta dan ah could clean

Wen dey got too quiet ah hah ta see wat wah up. Shur nuff dose two wah workin' lake litta scamps (dat da wah) pullin' dat foot-tub, so dey soy so it would be out ob mah way. Uh say You es good boys ta hep Aunt Mariah. Day wah whisparin - oh that et wah cause ah ask dem ta be quiet. Rite dare ah say, Dose two litta angels es bein good fo johnny cakes.

In less than a shake, ah heard dat foot-tub tumble down dose stairs. Ah ran ta see. Holly God ah say. Dose boys burst out so loud laughin, wid da noise ob dat tumblin-tub. Mr. Abe an da missy comb tearin.

Mr. Abe, take one look en dat parla. Bouse hisself ta da men an say." I have a little job ta take care of for a second." Da missy wah ringin' her hans. Mr Abe, gentman lak say." Mother its nothing much to worry about. But put his han obba her mouth, fa fear her wood rant an scream. Den he pick up da foot-tub. Put Taddie en it, who stood up and hug his pa round da neck. Led da missy wid his arm round her. He knew dat wah da way ta quiet her if he made ah little love ta her. Dat otha rowdy Willie follow wid his pa an mah an Taddie out ta the shed. Whar Mr Abe lock da boys in wid jim-crow and da otha pets and pests. Kiss da missy and pat her. Her wah fit ta be tied. Den comb back laughin.

Wen he ast da boys why da did et. day say, Well fo. sides hepin Aunt Mariah, by getin dat tub out her way. we 'member you tole us 'bout Niaga Falls an da cat-racks. Dat wat we wah makin da cat-racks. Dat tub wah jes da boat tumsin on da rocks goin oba da falls. Mr Abe say well boys, You got the right idea but in the wrong place. Un as allus. He laugh split ta kill.

But dif stairs wah shur ah big mess ta clean an dry, wid all da file ob oda work. All Mr Abe say wah." Well that's one way of cleaning the stairs and carpet in short order". He nebba left his foot tub watta standin gin. Da missy say," Dat wah notha gample he hah set fa his chillun to follow. Dat stairs

6 git clean fa da parla, but mr Abe hep.

Ah really done tink dose men zackly knew wat all dat runkiss wah' bout. Mr Abe wen back in da parla as cool as ah cucumba. Talk awhile. Comb out from de parla to da hall. Gib dem dare hats froomb dat hatrack. Day wish him luck fa his 'lection to senat. Mr Abe thank dem. Bid dem good day an den close da door afta da full hour of 'citement.

Mr Abe put out ta da shed ta let dose litta rascals out. No whippin', no scoldin', no do dis or do dat. But dare day wah new fangle merry-go-roun. Jim crow wah screamin' ta dem comb back, comb back. Dat crow missed dem. Wen out ob its sight, lak it wah its lost brothas. Mr Lincolum kep dem two out ob da house 'til dinna, playin' han ball, rintey oba, an Lord knows what all. Cause dat man knew da missy, wah fit ta lay down an die, her wah so work up. Et jus' wahn't possible ta leave dose boys out of sight fa a blessed minute.

When Mr Abe did leave ta go ta da office fa ah spell dose boys wah den en da barn playin wid da litta wooden wagon. Dat whole Lincolum fambly love cats. Day hab cats ob all colas an kinds. Litta kitty baby ones nursin dare mammy, cats an big toms. Da missy woodn hab dem en da house. So day hab ta stay in da shed or da barn. Dis day, onla an spick afta Mr. Abe left day decide ta take da mammy cat an some suckin baby kitty fa a trip fa ta see dare brotha Robert, who day thot wah in school dare. Day say dose cats need edication too. Day hitch two toms to da tong ob da wagon. Willie hold dem so day couldn start off til Taddie put da motha cat an babies in. Den Willie start ta lead dose two tom cat. Bout dat time Taddie 'cided day hab betta go fasta or day wouldn get ta school dat day. So he gib dat wagon ah shove from da hind side. He rush an shove da wagon. Da wagon twist an turn an da toms roun. Ah guess dose toms thot da oda one hab 'cided ta fight. Day gin da God awfulles runkus you eba did heah. Taddie rund up ta hold da black tom, while Willie hold da stripe tiga tom cat. Dose wah big cats, an hard ta hold, 'specally when day hab fight in dem

7. In da tussel ta keep dem cats fromb scratchin each otha eyes out of dare head; dem boys got scratch on dare face an arms. Dose cats hiss an his at each otha. An screach an scratch, but dose boys hold on. Finely Taddie say. Willie lits make dem make up. Dat's what pa an ma make us do. So day hole dose toms snoots right up ta each othas snoots ta kiss. But do day kiss? No et's more scratch, screach an claw. Dis wah jus too much. So here dose boys comb screaming ta Aunt Mariah fa help. Ah throw up mah hans in plumb horrah, at da sight of dose boys. Blood all oba dare faces an arms, an close torn. Screamin Aunt Mariah make dose blasted toms make up. Ah took both dose torments by da hans ta da barn. Dose cats hab broke loose da strings fromb da wagon an wah en ah real cat fight. Hissin, spittin, clawin, cryin. Da tiga got da best ob dat fight. Da ole black tom comb up wid ah clowd eye. Ah hab ta git a buggy whip ta seprate dem. Dose boys cried 'cause ah wip dose toms. All thro' dat hell ah baller dat mammy cat an her litta kitten lay en dat wagon bed as content as if daze hab been no cyclone. But cats are da laziest crittas on God's green arth on da dummes. All da knowes ta lay 'roun in folks way to stumble ova.

Ah got dose boys back in da house. Wash dare dear littla dirty bloody face an arms. All da missy eba saw wah da torn clothes an scratches. An dat wah nothin new fa those two boys. Ah swear hab she saw dem fore ah clean dem. We wood hab ta send fa da undataka. Her wah ready ta drop wid dat niagah falls an da hard work on da porta fa dat aftanoon an night.

Why dat woman couldn see what et wah doin ta her is plumb ah mistry. All her tink 'bout wah how day wah goin ta manuvra to get back ta da White House.

1. Wal Mr Abe an da missy hab jus came back ta
Springfield, fromb da las debate at Alton, Illinois. Da
missy wah argufyin' bout some mistake Mr Lincolumn
hab made, dat gave Mr Douglas da best of him. Wal
he say, "mothar, youll see some day that Ive tricked
him into really asserting himself, for what he really is.
He may become the senator, for with his beautiful
and gracious wife and the idol he has made of himself, for
so long, can win. But when the south wakes up he is
a dead pigeon on a presidential ballot. The south is
bound to see, he is really at heart no slaveryman. Even
though the north and south differ on this subject, I
dont condemn them as blind and ignorant. For I
wouldnt honestly know what to do if I was placed in
the south to decide. There are a great many good and
kind slave holders. Better than some whites in the north
are to the whites. And Im convinced that their conviction are as sincere as ours and they are not goin
to like a hippocrit. They will see he has been manuver-
ing for votes from both political parties. That Little
Giant is a wonderful politician, but I believe Ive
tripped him up this time. Another thing Mollie Ill be
better known throughout the country on account of the
publicity given me. You see this association (my name
in debate with a name like Stephan Douglas) with one
already nationally and internationally known as a
power, cannot help but give me some prestige. The
question is bound to arise. Who is this man Lincoln?
As Douglas opponent they will reason. Douglas is too
smart a man to consent to debate with anyone easy to defeat."
Shur nuff even fore Mr Abe wah nominated fa President
he wah ask ta speach make clean through ta da Atlantic
ocean. Ah just cant recomember whar alls or were. But
one wah Coopa Institute. An at da school wah Robert wah goin
in da East. Ah guess dat school didn tink day wah bout
to get much ob ah speach, wen day first saw Mr. Roberts
fatha. Afta he spoke, dat blessed Bobbie wah awful
proud ob his pa. Da want Mr Abe ta speach make more and more

2- Da missy got a letta afta dat from Bobbie tellin' all 'bout his pa's visit an how proud he wah of him an wat a differrence it made wid his class-mates opin of him.

Most time wen Mr. Lincoln hab ta go away, da missy go 'long. Her went ta Ohio. Ah tink Columbus, Dayton an Cincinnati. Day left da boys ta home. I tink dat time Aunt Lisbeth cumb each day. Mary da maid an her brotha George stay at night. Ah go home at night ta fix fa my man Henry an mah chillun fa next day. Ah went back most ebbe day. Willie an Taddie wore us most all out, clean thread I bare worn out. But we dasn't punish dem.

Georgie went to day school an so did Willie wen he want to. If he didn' want to he didn'. Georgie didn go in Willie's class so wah not pestead by Willie durin school. But da two dose two Lincolnum boys made up fa it at night. Ah knowd dat Georgie wah da gladest boy alive, when Mr. Abe's cumb home. Et wah in da fall ob da year. I ore day go day gib some pedas. "Aunt Mariah, do dis an do dat, if dey hab a cold gib dem vinegah tea, Made wid suga, red peppa, vingah an hot watah. No screamin or scoldin da boys. Day say da same ta Mary. Butte Aunt Lisbeth make Taddie keep clean an spruce up while her wah dare. An wen he got too frisky, sent dat scamp ta bed or made him sot on da kitchen char. Her would allus use da kitchen chars cause Taddie kick an squirm so much he hab all da stuffin' pull out ob da letta ones.

Da missy cumb back braggin' bout how "ciety invite dem ta dare mansions en all dose Ohio places. Gineral this on an Doota so an so, an da Mayor ob all da cities. Her kinda got ober da tantrum 'bout Mr. Lincolnum not gettin' 'lected ta da Senate. Dat woman nerva got 'nough 'ciety. Mr. Abe, most say, Mother, you want to go to Washington for no other reason, than to be in the highest spot-light in society in America, Mrs President. While I have only one desire to return to Washington, this time as President, To save the Union. If to save the Union means, saving the colored people and lowly whites from bondage; It shall be twice blessed." Dose two folks wah as fars apart en all day thought an strive fa, as da norf an soth. An da sad an sorful part wah, day nebba, nebba wah any differrent.

Mr. Abe ast day missy afta dat trip effen her that her could settle down for' while 'til he made sum more money? Dat, dat

3. debate bizness wid Stephen Douglas hab 'bout strapped him. Dat wah a hod job. Her did try ta save by stayn' home sewin' tigitha all da lace an material her got while 'way.

Mr. Lincolumn hab lots of work. Lots ob big men in polities frumb all ovva da country cumb ta see him. Ah know dat man nevva want ah be President. He tole one man dat he railly wahn fit fa da job. His step-motha didn want him ta be stha, he done tell da missy. But da missy say "She may be a good woman, but she doesn't know enough ta use good judgement." But mrs Lincolumn, ag him on an on. Da onla rest dat man got wah wen he clam up, an wouldn talk or wen da boys deman ah romp. Ob course dat wah evva time he step in da house. Mr Abe get too busy ta talk to. He still chop wood, milk da cow, feed an ten ta da horses, go on circuit, joke wid da men downtown, an walk in street late at night. Boft 'fore an afta he wah nominate fa President. He done did all dis, most ta he plone an not be pestered. He still hab his trip ta Chicago an speech makin.

Da speechin' would cumb out en da pappa. Wen ah go home mah Henry would hab me or one the younguns read, dess pappa he pick out ob da trash he haul. Mah Henry near hab ah hemrig bout da slams an awful pitchas of Mr. Abe. Et wah ah shame mah man say dose fellows wat make up such blasphem pitchas should be strung up lak da do niggas. Ef niggas write such stuff an draws such hellish pitchas 'bout whites day wood be burn an cut inch by inch. Mr Abe wood onnla laugh. But da missy hab head aches from raven Den take parigoric. Not so much as onst, but too much. An Roberti wood write. His pook baby heart wah broke.

Masta Robert cumb home afta his fa wah nominate. But da pook boy got no peace frumb dose two litta imps. He try ta play wid dem ta keep dem home an content. Wen Bobbie wah playd out an wen ta his room, da follow crawl all ovva him lak daydo dare fa. Write wid his pencil oba clothing. Den scream an fight lak litta demons. Ef dat blessed Bobbie held dare hans, da missy say he wah 'busin' dem. Finely dat pook boy hab ta lock hissef en his room, to get any rest. Den dose scamps would pound on his door.

Masta Robert want ta study up ta go to 'notha school dat fall. He want ta go ta Harvard. He try ta get en onst, but wahn good 'nough. Now wid some instructin' da

4. gave him at Exeter, wid study in da summa ta home
he might succeed, an he did. But wid all da torment
dat boy wen thro', Ah jus can't figga how he done did it.
Dat poor boy rarely wen anywhah. His old friens he
play wid, wen ah litta tike, say he hab da swell head
But warn so. He couldn step out, dat some one ob dose
demacrat kids wouldn make fun ob his pa an ma. Den
tell him how Douglas hab wallup his lyin' pa. An Doug
wood wallup him gin fa President. Day say eben his pa
couldn speak good english. Dat Mrs Lincolumn an his pa
talk nigga talk. Robert knew he didn say words jus
lak his pa an ma say dem. Robert spoke correct. He spent
ah lot of time try'n to get dem to say words so day wood
sound differment, but wah no good. Both Mr. Abe an da
missy did talk lak Kentuck folks, wat day wah.

Mastah Robert spent lots ob his time wid my Billie wen
Billie wah not at work, an ta home dat summa. His ma
an pa wah gone most all da summa, here an dare. Day
would sometime take da boys, sometime jus Taddie.

Uncle ninean couldn bide dem boys. He say, Da wah ruffians
an ruptin his house. Wah ah bad influence for his boys an
grandchillens. Et wah imposble ta keep dem fromb devilment.
Wen dare ma an pa take Taddie or both wid dem, dats 'bout da
onla time any ones hab any peace. Ta entatain dem hab ta
be some devilment, lak makin tick, tack on da window or
punches up thro' da bottom of chars wid darnin needles.
So wen you pull da string da darnin needle would pop up
thro da seat an stick anyone wat sat down on dat seat. Ef
ya pull three time da needle punch punch punch up thro'
dat seat three times, an den dose who got dat good hard
sticking, howl three times.

Ah do believe Mr. Robert enjoy some ob dat (Dust wen da
missy hab a parta fa dose who cumb ta gratulate Mr. Abe
afta he war nominate) since he couldn bide da airs ob some
folks dat cumb callin.

One parta wah at night, an many da maidy hab put da boys
ta bed. She read ta dem 'til her thot day wah sleep. But day
wah play'n possum. When da parta got goin, down day
slip in dare red flannel night clothes wat da missy
make ta keep dem from catchin cold in da head

5. Aut doors day go wid da tick tack on da window. Some da ladies thot et wah spooks frumb da otha worl. an say et wah ah shuer sign ob bad luck. maybe some one dare wah' goin' die. Maybe Mr Lincolemn wouldn' be 'lected. maybe would git "sassinate. Mr. Abe wen out, carry dose two rascals in, an say, Here are our spooks. Da ladies all pull away frumb dem scamps. But as soon as one big fat gal sat down on da char wid da darnin' needle. Pull, pull pull went dat string. Her jump up an scream more dan an indian. Her say debils an hornets wah in dat house. Mr Abe an Bobbie knew but look 'stonish an say 'nothin. Ah could see day wah shakin dare hides off mostly, cause day want ah laugh so bad wid dose boys, what laugh an laugh an role oba. Mr. Abe march out, git a flat roun board, we used on da clabba crocks. Put et on dat char an sot right down on dat board. Da boys didn' know, so pull da string. No punch no stickin' frumb da darin needle. Day thot da fun wah orra, so put ta bed lookin sour, but as meek as litta lambs.

Ah tink Mr. Abe an da missy wah most awful proud ob mastah Robert. He wah quiet, an such ah gentman allus. Wen he pass da gamnation, an day let him en Harvard. Ah tink Robert wah proud of his pa an ma. But nevva nevva proud da show off kind. He tole me oust wen he pass thro Danville, an stop ta visit a little wid us dat, he hab want ta go in da reglar army as a private. He nevva want ta take advantage of his pa being President. Then or nevva in afta life. His pa want fo his ma's sake that he should stay out ob da wah ar take something easy lak an officer. unda Grant. He wah unda Grant, but took dangerous missions. Ah knew mah pa would be critsized, but ma wah fas problems. Her wah fo ah long time bad in her mind, an should Robert be kilt, her wood hab ta be put 'way, as Robert hab ta put her 'way, wen her perform so in Chicago. Robert left his home an stay wid her. Wen he went back home to his beautiful wife, da missy, ran 'round naked en da hotel, wood hab gone out dat way on da street ef not stopped. Her spent money so foolish, dat poor litta Laddie would hab been widout money for an edication. Mastah Robert cried an cried.

6. Cause da 'tatratives say he must put her 'way. His heart wah broken. Den his ma blame him. Say he wantah rob her. What wan he ta do. He couldn' be wid his ma and he couldn' be 'way from her. Lisbeth den wah mad fa 'while, til da missy stay wid her. Lisbeth hab ta put up wid so much of dat foo' mindless woman. Her dark room, with a candle or lamp burnin' dat might be fire. Heap and heaps of trunk full of dresses and stuff ta make dresses. Da woman den 'cuse Lisbeth of stealing her money. Aunt Lisbeth, then hab at las' to ask Robert ta fogive her.

When Mr. Lincolumn wah 'lected President, dare wah 'notha change in that parade, what hab start ta comb ta dare home. Mr. Abe hab ta see so man' poltic men, an dose dat wan him ta git dem jobs in Washington, he hab ta move ta da State House. Da missy couldn' hab dem trampin' in at all hours an her office wasn't big 'nough. Da south wah seceding an Buchanan but dare as stiff as a poka an did nothin'. Mr. Abe needed most awful ta be alone, to tink an write. But no, it hab to be ah hella hallo framb. dat he hab ta face. Den too, dat Herndon, who turn out ta be a no 'count, lyin' & alway. jus' as da missy allus say he way tried eva way to ruin Mr. Abe's business. But fa da good Mr. Abe allus saw en him, he stay friens. Say Billie & Herndon so ah had 'nough friend at times; I can't 'ford ta make an enmay ob him. What Billie wants is ta be my man Friday. An he laughed. He'd allus smooth tings over fa dat man. Ah tink he always knew how he would end if contraried. So he say wen he left dare office fa da las' time "Leave dat sign Lincolun an Herndon. I'll be back an' well continue to-getha." But that nevva stop Herndon. Even afta Mr. Abe wah 'passinate he wrote mean lies 'bout da missy an then some 'bout Mr. Abe. Robert say he try to hab Herndon take back what he told in a speach an' wrote in ah book. But it hab gone too far. Too many wan ah believe bad enstead ob good. 'Specially 'bout da missy. Mastah Robert wah plumb crush. Da dirt day blame on Mr. Abe. at dare office wah not Mr. Abe's fault. Truth is da Lincolumn sent me ta da office ta clean, many time. Ah would go, but could ah get in? No. Cause dat Herndon wah lock in dare stone drunk. Yah could eben smell him in da hall. Onst ah went jus as he wah comin' out. He say Yah can't go in. Ah's lockin up ta leave. So you see who wah de cause ob dat dirt he done blame on Mr. Abe. Wen da truth air, as shuer

7. as God es. wah all Herndon dirt.

Da missy plead an plead ta get rid ob dat man, dat derty bum, ta get ah nice boy lak one hab come to da home to eat sometime, Mr. Abe say Herndon wah smart an could help him. Mr. Abe done all he could ta lift dat man out ob da gutta. Den yah see how he pay back. He tell jes' nough truth ta make et all soun lak truth, Mr Robert say. Dat onry man pay fa et. He died in pay's. We got da book he wrote, we read da lies an lies, an got so all fire mad we burn et up.

Dare wah ah bunch cumb ta notify Mr. Lincolum dat he wah 'lected President. Da boys wah all dress up fa da 'cassion. Da shook hans as dose gentman cumb thro' da gate Mr. Abe met dem an entaduce dem, as day enta da parla ta da missy, all dress up waitin dare.

Her plan ah litta parta fa dose who stay dat night. Her tole da boys, ef day stay clean. wat her would git dem as pay. Day go up stairs ta dare room an wah as still as litta mice Ah say! Day can be good litta angls ef day get what day want fa bein good.

Well da hab chicken an some fancy fixins, Mary da moid wait on da table. Ah allus keep tung goin in da kitchen. On parta ah could hardly turn roun en et. Da missy hab et cut up so, Dat nice big kitchen hab ta go fak Bath room, an dinin room. When da boys cumb en at last ta be seated at da table. Dare day wah wid ravel out sock yarn, pasted an tied all ob dare faces fa whiskers. Dare ma hab call dem litta men so uffen, day 'cided ta look lak dare pa an hab whiskers, what he hab grown. Mr. Abe grown dem cause ah litta girl done wrote him he wood look betta if he would done grow dem whiskers. An maybe day would hep him ta git lected President.

Mr. Abe wah allus proud wen his boys want ah be lak him, an et please him powerful, dees whiskered sons. Day missy wah shook but wouldn scold dem fora company. So dare day sat eatin chicken an soup wid dem black sock yarn whiskers full of drippin. Ah thought wen ah saw dem (Mary come out in da kitchen chokin' up an laughin) God in heaben what does litta imps ob da debil goin ta do next ta embarass da missy. But Mr. Abe laugh an laugh about it an day fix him, for he got out of commettin myself to those men. Thanks ta Willie an Taddie." Da missy say as she cut off dose whiskers. You dont deserve all I was going to do for you. And until ya learn to behave, you while hab to be left out of parties, given for your father". But ah notice Mr. Abe edge dem in, eber place he could whar dare wah a parta.

Billie Sings For Mayor Sutton
Sometime in 1856 to 1860

Mr. Abe loved mah Billie's singin'. Ah neva did no ob anotha kid who-n could sing ah tune clean thro' lak grown ups, an' neva miss one single soun' lak mah Billie could whan he-n war onla 2 yars ole. He-n could whisle lak all da birds. An' evens get dem to flay to he-n whan he-n war five.

Da missy say "God war good to our Billie." She-n hab ah litta spinet. Her-n would play, but mah boy say'd she-n couldn' play ah horse fiddle. But God bless da missy, her-n tried, an' ah tole dat boy ob our-n if he-n eber hurt da poor woman's feel-ns, when her-n war ah tryin' so hard to help, an' tryin' so to show as how hee-n lak he-n singin'. Ah'd plum ring his-n black haid clean off his-n shollers.

Mah Henry loved ta sing, an' ah could sing wat suites me. Mah chillen all em could sing, but Billie da best. Mr. Abe wan-ed sad songs or da church. Spacely da colored folks religion songs. He'n ofen laugh whan Billie would sing 'em though. Cause Billie clap his-n hand, roll oba on da groun' an' act sometime lak he-n war flyin' to heaben.

Mr. Abe ask he-n onst 'Whare did you learn such monkey shines Billie?' Billie ups an' say, 'Day hain't monkey-shines, dat's da way day 'spose ta be sung. Dat's da way day all do in church.' Afta dat Mr. Abe would sometimes jine in wid clap-n an' fly-in jestas. Mr. Abe couldn' sing no more-n da missy could play da spinet. But da missy say, 'I always knows when Mr. Lincoln isn't worrying, if there ever is a time when he isn't, for he goes about singing or whistling.' Sometime he'n play da mouf organ or harp. He'n could do dat betta' than sing.

You-n neva could get mah Billie ta sing low. He-n allays sung loud an' clear, He'n even wake up in da night an' let out such ah blast, all da young-ns would get stirred up. At lass mah Henry lammed he-n a good one an' tole he-n if he-n mus' cut loose ta git out do' doors. Wal Billie hab one hitch at dat, sing'n out at nite. Da white trash 'roun' dat went hog-wild. Day hab Billie rested an' he-n hab ta go up fore Mayor Sutton.

Ah jest 'bout went crazy, 'til Mr. Abe say'd he-n see wat he-ns could do. Mah Henry say eben efn Mr. Abe get he-n off, dem white trash would grab Billie an' string he-ns up.

Wal mr. Abe war right dar dat day ta stan by Billie. Da white trash war dare to. Day done hab hens down fa disturb da peace. Da say hin got out at night an screamed, afta day'd gone a bed a sleep. Brayed lak a jack-ass an hooted lak ah owl. Billie war mad ahs blazes, sayin sich bout hens singin. Hen spoke "an scream, days dam liars. Ah war singin.

Order in da court say mayor Sutton - Billie say, Ah'll show youins ah can sing if youins let me. Still mr. Abe say, "Billie can sing, your honor. Maybe you will favor me by giving Billie a try. I believe you will be a fine judge of his voice, as you have a marvelous voice and are versed in music. That may be a good way to prove right now, whether he sang or hooted. Mr. mayor Sutton said, "Request granted.

Billie broke loose wid all hens heart an soul an wid all hens actin up. Mayor Sutton an Mr. Abe laugh almose as loud as Billie sang. Da white-trash done got out ob dare faster dan lightn an tween mayor Sutton an mr. Abe, day say - "Case dismissed,"

Billie started to run to, but dat mayor Sutton call hens back an say "Not so fast Billie, You an I need to talk this happening out, as man to man." Dat plead Billie ah heap, to call hens a man. Later Billie says to hens Pa an means, Dat mayor Sutton air mose da best man sides mr. Abe. Hens got a good word fa eber one. Hins say dar air no white trash just unfortune an we'ns no worser or no betta dan day. Hens say "Billie you have a fine voice, God has been good to you. You should use it for the glory of God. From no on, dont waste it on anyone who doesn't appreciate it. You really did disturb the peace, but as this is your first offense I'll let you go if you promise me, you'll not get out at night and wake your neighbors up.

Billie you have a wonderful voice, tho' from now on when you want to sing. Come and sing for me, or go to the Lincolns, who love your singing and want only the best for you. You may go now" Billie rush out singin at da top of hih voice Glory Glory Halla Lula Ahs on mah road to glory now. Throw'd his hat in da air an dance an clap ever step until he war gone. Mariah told me the author jas did a number of members of the white churches in Danville, that from the time they moved to Danville, Ills in 1860 until his death in Dec 1900 Billie though not

"The Mariah Vance Story of Mr. Abes' Babtism

De missy (mariah could not say Mrs Linsoln always Lincolinum when she tried) wahs Presteesh (instead of Presbyterian) Al dat woman even say "She war nigh up in Heaven whan she sots in thar pew on de Sabath. Onst when she was carryin on mr. Abe jokenly says, Says he 'mothah caint we find ohplace har, somewhar, for dat are pew, so as youse can sot in it evah da?"

Missy would beg him to jine em (Presbyterian church) She shure says it wood hep hime up in de worl. Mr Abe than and thar says mothah Ahs not wanteng to be hepped erp in de worl, de way youse sees it. Ah wants to live so Ah could hep up, If'n Ah could sot on uh stow box in front Hoffman's row and wid only one uh mah unpolished common stories hep one uh em boys. One uh that common hurd as youse calls em, uh story that wood lead that boy to Christ as Ah knows him. Ah'd give all mah chanses to be President, as youse so much hankers for. (This subject of church affiliation must have extended over a long period.)

Yas mr Abe wood go to meetin sometime wid har. Don't think he done liked that high fleuten airs in that are church. He onst says. It shur woodn't be any hardah to go down on thar knees, than to do all that are bowen an scrapen. Nothah time he says "Ah sometimes wondah if it are uh church or uh circus, thar all decked out in so much trappens and finery und perform so.

He shure knowd of thar onpaid bills. For he says mothah how cain those folks go out und make sich uh show in onpaid finery? And others thar, are robben thar folks uh bread, meat und milk, jest to make uh show."

He allays wanted to be babsized. He done promise his mothah when ah little tike way back thar in Indiane, whan he war old enough to knows de meanings, he wood be babsized. Und dem are Presterahs don't go by bein dunked down undah watah. Und Missy says hats back woods now. 'Sides Mr. Abe had shamed her und de boys 'nuff by hisn old fangled ways.'

Onst he says to me, "Mariah do you thunk it has hepped save youse soul to be babsized. Yas Ah says Mr. Abe. Shur allahs make me knowd Ah done did one ting Christ done did. He let John babsize him in de Rivah Jordan. He shur mus thot dat it war good. So ahs thot good. Yes Mr. Abe says, Its show youse airin earnest bout youse soul. Youse wants youse sins washed ahs clean ahs watah can make youse body—

A few days aftah that he says, Mariah ahs goin to be babsized Do youse thunk it wood be sinful if ahd be babsized und not let on to Missy Lincolnun? Now Ahm not shamed, but she'll raise Ned, und I don't thunk that wood be uh good way to go to youse babsizing. 'Sides ahs not, it likely to start up a misery in mothah haid. Ahs got too big a load now to tackle getten ovah that, und still try to have de ming that war also in Christ Jesus when Ah goes to mah Babsism. Nothah ting that bothahs me a heap Mariah is how gossips und sight seers most likely to come in mobs. Not to reverence but to mock and begile my tenshuns. Ah don't like show of any kind whar it cain be hepped. Ahd like to know hs how to hep it. Mariah youse a good haid for plann Jest how cain Ah be babsized so mothah won't be upsot? Somewhat of a crowd is boun to congrate.

Ah says Mr. Abe Youse cain thunk and thunk but thars onlah jist one way—Youse got a go at night He jist stood thar an stared at me. Ah jist knowd ahd given him a shock He wahs de saddes looken

Wal he says Mariah, Ah done bin babsized. He didn't say more for some bit. Ah says Mr Abe, wants youse to tells me how it all comes off. Wal says he the Rev,— Parson come in the night time and babsized me and went back in the night time. We didn't go the regular cow path jest waded persimmon scrub, hazel brush an wild grapevine. Ah jist know if that parson felt as Ah done did he was as glad to get in that thar rivah as Ah. For de nettles war thicker than dog flees on rover. Now Mariah Ah 'aint meaning Ah, wasn't ponderen and consideren. Ah and that parson had a mighty sacred charge to keep. An deep inside of me Ah was praying. Now Ah really praise mah Lord and mah God Ah took de right step. You know Mariah many weeds has to be trampled to reach de right road. Glory to God Alleluja.

Then he said mah mothah was ah Babtist, Ah had a Babtist parson to say words over her body back in Indeane, an she shur she wood like it if'n Ah had a Babtist parson to babsize me. Yah knows what Mariah I feels free now. Ah knows God will watch ovah me and do all fow de best.

Mrs. Lincolumne thought Ah war with Billie (Herndon) Thats all Ah regrets Ah caint tell her whar Ah was. If Ah tole her she'd shur have worse misery.

Aunt Mariah after she cleaned and prepared dinner she went to the barn for her mule and cart and there was wet shoes, shirts, long underwear and pants hanging up drying — The next time she returned to do washing the clothes were down from nails where they hung in barn and there were 2 shirts and 2 suits of his underwear in the washing — The ones that hung in barn She said she was sure they were ones they used when Mr Lincoln was babtised. And accordeng to Anna Neals account of the babtism told to her by her father, which follows, Mr. Lincoln did supply the minister, clothing, used in Babtism.

are parson 'round har could let me down in the river, but none 'cit be sartan could hoist me up" — und Ah knows its jest got to be a little secret twixt all of us und ah God.

Ah jest say right thar und then to Mr Abe. Yes sah ah says. Ah swan Mr Abe you nevra need be jumpy, Ah wont even tole mah Mistah Henry — He'd look at me an scowl onery like an say, Better mind you own nitten and stop mouthen other folks complaints. An to this are very live long day Ahs nevra onst tole a sole, but you (meaning me the author.)

And I believed her. I've learned since that the minister did tell of the babtism years later after Lincoln death. Possibly after Mrs Lincoln's death. — As stated by Rev. Ankrum and Mr Waggoner — Dill later state the story written to me by Anna Deal daughter of Mr Waggoner.

We uns never talked it over no more 'til one morning, orly one cold morning. Ah always went orly the days was gitten so short. — I was toten my last young-un wid me that morn.

Mr Abe was nevra a one to git up early, but Ah swan thar he was long the plankway in front — Wid his haid down ponderin and considerin. Ah went on to the shed an tucked my young un in. Ah was straighten up the kitchen. It was sich a little cubby hole after Missy changed the whole house around. Things jest git in a fierce pile with the left over dishes to do. Ah was on mah way out to the shed to get some soft soap when Mr Abe cum up. He kind-a sad like says "Mother has a misery agin. Ah gave her some pery gorie. She's most quilt now." Wal I knowd good and well she war in a tantrum. Poor missy she woks a sick, sick woman in her haid. Well sah there was nothing in this liven world to stop that stread in her but perigoric. No sir E.

Ah cleared away all the soil and done fixed Mr Abe some breakfast. I fried some mush cakes. He liked mush cakes and sorgam. He jest didn't wayt more. He ate a lit more and shoved his chair back on the 2 back legs.

nothah thing that bothahs me, would the people come in mobs to cuss and discuss my tensions. Ah don't like show of any kind only whar it cain't be hepped. Ah like to know now how to hep it.

Mariah youse a good head for phanen. First Jest how can Ah babysed and keep mother from being upset? Somewhat of a crowd is bound to congrate Ah say Mistah Abe you can thunk and thunk but thar onlah one way youse got a go at night. He jus stood thar and stared at me. Ah jes knows it gave him a shock He wah the saddes lookem crittah Ah ever did set eyes on in mah life. Ah tht he was gwinin to bust out cryin — Ah jest walked off saying "God help us". I said "Halah Lulyah Mr Abe." In a little while he came to the kitchen an he said, Mariah youse done saved the day for me. Ah's not gwinin to Washington without doin all Ah can to keep Christ commandment, Ah couldn't expect God to hep me lead a nation so full of woes, if I failed him. Ah write to a Rev. Parsons and have him come if he will lets pray he will. He must have been a very large parson because he said. "Any one of these are could let me down in the river but none I'd be parson could light me up. Und Ah knows it has to be a little secret twixt all of us und God."

Ah just say to Mr Abe Yes sah Ah says Ah owan Mr Abe you never need be jumpy Ah even tole my Mista Henry He'd look at me in a covery like Ah say. Better mind you own nittin and stop mouthen other folks complaints. An to this very live long day Ah's never once tole a sole but you. And I believed her. She learned since the minister did tell of the babtism years after Lincoln's death as stated by Rev. Ankrum and Mr Wagoner.

She told me practically the same story of the babtism as told by An na Deal in the article referred to abov but in her own words.

We uns never talked it over no more until one mornin Ah comes early one cold morning, toten my last young un. Mr Abe

From the Maryland and Pennsylvania Historical Sketches
by Rev. Freeman Ankrum A.B. Masontown Pennsylvania
1947. Page 121 Chapter 3 I quote.
" Elder D. P. Saylor was a great admirer of President
Abraham Lincoln, and a frequent visitor at the White
House. He spent many an hour with Lincoln who was
always glad to see him and called him "Bishop Saylor". The
president told him that he considered him capable of
filling any office to which he might be called. When
addressing him earnestly he said "But Brother Saylor,
I ordain you a Dunkard preacher forever"
    And on page 37 Chapter 7.
When Abraham Lincoln viewed the desolation around
the Dunkard church (Antietam, Maryland) he had more
than a passing interest.
    Before taking office as president and while still in
Springfield, Illinois, Lincoln sent for a minister of the
German Baptist Church, commonly called Dunkards,
and was baptized by him in the river. He promised that
after his term of office expired, he would conform to the church.
    From a letter to me by Mrs. Anna Deal of June 30, 1956
I copy the following account.
" My father David E. Wagoner past 76 years of age at this
date Feb, 12, 1935 relates a circumstance told him by
Elder Isaac Billheimer, at one time a resident of
Tennesee and later a resident of Heath, Indiana. An
Elder of the Fairview Church
Isaac Billheimer told father he was acquainted
with the minister who Baptized Lincoln (father doesn't
remember the name)
The minister who baptized Lincoln was a member of
the German Baptist Church (nick-named Dunkard)
Lincoln sent this minister word to come to Springfield
on a certain train, which arrived there after night
(Lincoln had sent him twice as much money as he needed)
Lincoln met him and they went to the river where

Lincoln was baptized yet that night (Lincoln had brought the extra clothes needed for both.) Having changed clothes they went back and waited for the train to arrive. The minister went back home, left soon after midnight. Lincoln promised after his term of office expired he would conform to the church."

"(This is a copy of original account written by Anna Etta Wagoner Deal dictated by her father on Feb., 12, 1935)"

The Story of The Ann Rutledge Likeness

One afternoon not so long after Mr. Lincoln was elected President of the United States. Mr & Mrs Lincoln who had been gathering together articles precious to them, which they wanted to keep, either store or take with them to their new home. From a long list Mrs. Lincoln had made, she said "Perhaps we should look through the pictures while we are in here." They had finished disposing of a few ornaments that had been cracked or broken. Some of which she gave to Mariah saying "You can throw these away." But Mariah treasured them as little keep sakes of her association with the beloved Lincolns.

She said "I think it best not to clear the house of all decorations now. We'll just remove these things that are damaged ar ones, we will not care to keep." At that she had You know we'll have to live here and do some entertaining almost until the last day before we leave." At that, she had Mariah to remove several pictures from the wall and stuck, were grouped to be removed to the shed. A few family pictures were grouped together on the wall. Among them were two photos of Mr and Mrs Lincoln which had always hung together. Had been in the same place on the wall ever since Mariah had worked there. Mrs. Lincoln removed them. Brushed them carefully and caressingly held them to her saying — I'll hang there back, they belong there to the last. They are so precious to me, taken when we were young and so desparately in love." Aren't they lovely? They will grace the walls of the "White House" " Mr. Abe laughed and said "I trust that, that grace never slips a peg and becomes disgrace."

They came to the photograph albums which had always held a place on an attractive marble top table in the parlor. One of these albums belonged to him and one to her. Her album was larger than his. Of fancy brown leather with 2 clasps. It contained family pictures (that is the Todd family) Others were friends, & some southern belles. The album was pulled apart and badly worn.

From her album she removed many pictures, and after remarking about them (Quite a few of which in previous chapters are stories connected from Mariah's colorful and vivid memory) discarded some. Others she put to one side saying "Those I wish to keep I'll buy another album to put them in. No doubt will add new pictures in Washington.

Next she sorted from a stack of photos in cases a number she wished to keep, then handed the remaining ones to Mr Lincoln who also kept a few and discarded others. Always laughing and reminiscing. Each called forth an amusing or strange incident

After they had finished with the ones in cases Mr. Lincoln picked up his own album, a much abused, small brown one with white porcelain buttons, said, "We'll now take a peep in the rogues gallery " Most of the pictures in his album were small tin-types or of card board, many of the slots and pages held name cards, old time campaign badges, cartoons and programmes. The sides bulged with little keep sakes, he has treasured. He said, "By the looks of these I think the boys have decorated them with sticky fingers." "Look here mother the precious little rascals have given me a black eye with licorish candy. They both had a hearty laugh. This one Marie, had washed which damaged it.

He came to his father's picture, he reviewed how and why it had been taken. As if it had been quite a while before he said I remember distinctly riding off the circuit to reach Pa and ma's place in Coles Co. That road would have mired a horse to its belly in rainy weather. It wasn't too good at that time. But the boys had so often asked me about my family, I decided, if I could get them to consent I'd take them somewhere and have their pictures taken. It took some pleading, ma said she didn't want to break the camera. I told her, she just wanted me to tell her how pretty she was. Ma was good and in her face she looked it. I'd have called her a pretty woman even then. Pa said, he didn't have clothes to have a picture taken in. I said "That's right Pa, but I'll fix that, So I took him and got him a new suit." I expect he was buried in it if John didn't wear it out." (John Johnston his step-brother) I hitched up my horse to an old wagon Pa had and while I was doing so Pa bathed. I don't remember Pa ever having shaved but I never knew a cleaner man. Way back in Ky he'd even take soft soap and sheeps wool (perhaps before carded) to the creek, cut the ice and bath. Ma usually cut his hair when it was cut. His hair was black but not stiff and stubborn like mine. And she did a pretty good job. He came out to the wagon with a new wool plaid shirt on. Ma (Sarah Bush Lincoln) had made for him. A white stock and tie. I can still see that look of pride and happiness. Pa hadn't been away from that farm for ages. He said, I wish Sally would go too, but I couldn't coax her to. I got him this suit and by the time the picture was taken it was about 3 o'clock in the afternoon. I had promised the boys to meet them in the circuit, so we couldn't loiter. I'd have liked to have seen and talked with ma more. Seen her expression when she saw Pa in his new suit. I always knew he was a good looking man but clothes made me pretty proud of him and glad for him. At that Mrs. Lincoln took the picture, and looked at it long - Yes, she said, He looks like an aristocrat. If he was just as cultured as he looks (She never wanted Mr. Lincoln's people around) That suit is nicer than any you ever purchased for yourself and fits him better. Lincoln laughed and said "Well Pa was a better clothes horse than I."

3 Another one he discarded was one supposedly - Mr. and Mrs Lincoln and Robert when young. At the time I saw it, I was not familiar enough with these pictures to judge the authenticity. Mariah failed to put them with those I purchased. I've searched for them, this family group of three among her grandchildren and friends but never unearthed them. If not in some Lincoln collection must be lost. Mariah said, Mr. Lincoln said this about the picture. "Dat tographer shure done mixed us up. Gave us this picture of a giraffe, bear and baboon, 'stead of us uns' picture". The three were standing in picture.

The last picture he opened the album to was a tin type a little larger than the others (measured by my eyes about 2½" × 4" or maybe a little over.) A three-quarter figure of a young, beautiful girl, with a lovable, innocent, childlike face. Quite beautiful. Mr. Lincoln looked at it long and intently, but made no remarks, while studying the picture. which Mariah said he had found in a gallery some five years before & brought home. When at that time he showed it to Mrs. Lincoln, she asked who it was. He said, "Well mother you have always wanted to know just how Ann looked to me. This is not her picture, but one so much like her, especially at time I first met her it could be her. Mariah said. During the intervening years she had come across him looking at the picture. It must have always reminded him of their love (and proved his appreciation for her help and happy association.)

In placing picture back which was partly secured in slot The album accidently slipped from his knees and fell to the floor, scattering contents, but staying open to where he has fastened Ann's likeness. He picked it up and replaced it on his lap. Not until then did Mrs. Lincoln say a word. She got up from her chair, stood behind him and looked down at the picture. During the silence they both seemed to sense a benediction. As if to speak would make the silence less hallowed or consecrated. There had been so many hard words from her before that. Called forth by her jealousy. Perhaps though more to be assured of his love (Now perhaps she knew her lifes ambition had been attained a new life was before them that needed all their attention.) But she asked softly. A question which so often before this time had resulted in bitterness on her part. "Mr. Lincoln have you never put her out of your life? As if dazed by his reflections he hesitated quite a while to answer her. She began to twist her hands and show signs of becoming hysterical. Sensing what might happen. He looked her squarely in the face. Put his arm around her and drew her to him. (A demonstration rarely indulged in before his household.) Then said, "Mary perhaps Almighty God reopened this chapter in my life, so we could renew & review it and then close it forever."

No I have not put her out of my life. She was put out years ago. Since the higher power seen fit, we cannot question the ways of such Devine Intellegence." mrs Lincoln (a Presbyterian who believed in predestination) then said, "Then you do believe our ways are planned". His answer No not in the sense, you have in mind, as you are questioning me! (Sometimes I think God should have always been spelled Good: God as an individual mind seems narrowing and hampers the power we should feel is omnipotent. Good is all inclusive, All things if good are relative, hinge, help each other and work to-gether for good for those who love good. Thus to love good is to work out our own destiny, with the help of all good. Regardless of our own plans and often highest desires, our destiny gaged by our own thoughts and actions, often comes to pass far better than we ever hoped for. Love - Good leads the ways."

When I was experiencing hardships in my youth, I never dared hope for the blessings I now enjoy or such priveledges and blessings as my family may now have." My blessed mother and conscientious hardworking, honest father started me in a way, I never forgot. May God help me to always stay in that way.

Above all it has ever brought me in contact and the elements that have made it possible to climb to the hightest place in this Good -Station. Mary among those who helped me climb who instilled ambition in me was Ann. She had her part not because it was planned at my birth, but because I tried to be good and she was good. Like begets like. I attracted her and she attracted me. At that time we needed each other in our lives. Assuredly at that time she was most dear to me and her memory has been so since. A lingering part of my existance. But to-night she seems strangely far away and going out farther and farther. Our associations as I tried to review them while ago when looking at this likeness were blurred. In some cases so blotted, they were as perhaps a partly forgotten beautiful dream which I could only vaguely recapture. Only disconnected parts would return to my memory."

"To you mother, I now owe my love and devotion. You too have helped me climb and are still helping me. Ann is a memory. You are a living reality, not to be put aside an instant for anything or anyone whomsoever. Let us live the Good life not alone for ourselves, but for our precious children we have brought into the world. So that only good will come to them. Let's improve our remaining life, with good, unwarped thoughts and deeds. Let's let the past remain the past and thank God Good it was so. The past has played it part and played it well to make to -day for you and I.

(over)

He waited a moment and then said, Dropping the album to the floor, "Mariah you can take this keep out and burn it"

"All done didn't burn it for her it is"

ALBUM

One afternoon not so long after the ~~Lincoln's~~ Mr Lincoln was elected President of the United States, Mr ~~and~~ Mrs Lincoln ~~who~~ had for several days been gathering to-gether articles precious to them, which they wanted to take with them to their new home. ~~Mrs Lincoln from a long list~~ From a long list which Mrs. Lincoln had made of the necessary and desirable she came to pictures, photographs and albums. She imediatly took from the wall some pictures which she stacked to-gether to be packed. A few family pictures, were grouped to-gether on the wall among them were 2 photos of Mr and Mrs Lincoln which always hung to-gether. Had been in the same place on the wall ever since Mariah had worked there. They were taken when they were young. When Mrs Lincoln took them down she caressingly brushed them and held them to her saying These are my two most precious pictures. They will grace the walls of the White House. She laughed and said "I trust that, that grace never slips ~~by~~ and becomes disgrace."

They came to the ~~te~~ photograph albums which had always held an attractive place in the front parlor on a marble top stand. One of these albums belonged to him and one to her. Hers was a larger album than his of fancy brown leather with two clasps. It contained her family (that is the Todd family) pictures ~~Others of~~ were friends of some Lexington bells, and after ~~From it~~ she removed many pictures, remarking about some, discarded them, others she put to one side saying "Those I wish to keep I'll buy another Album to put them in and no doubt we'll ~~add~~ ~~did~~ new ones in Washington. This album is quite badly worn.

She then sorted from a stack of photos in cases a number she wished to keep. She then handed the remaining ones to Mr. Lincoln who also keep a few and discarded others. Always he laugh and reminiscences. Each one called forth a funny or strange incident. A few of which I have relited in previous chapters of this book.

After they had finished with the ~~those~~ ones in cases, picking up his own album, which was a much ~~unused~~ small brown one with white porcelain buttons, He said. Well now take a peep in the Rogues Gallery." Most of the pictures in his album were small tin-type or of card board. Many of the slots for pictures held name cards, old time campaign badges, cartoons and a few programmes. The sides bulged with little keep sakes he had placed between the pages. He said, "By the looks of these I think the boys have decorated them with sticky fingers" "Look here mother this one of me" given at attack eye with leaguerish comedy why he came to the floor, picture he regretted the story of them. He let it drop to the floor, after a hearty laugh from him. This one mariah had washed which damaged somewhat the picture — Another one he discarded was a group supposedly mr. & mrs. L. and Robert when young. At that time I was not familiar enough with these pictures to judge the authenticity. Since Mariah evidently failed to put them in container I purchased and searching among her grand-children have not unearthed them, I feel sure if not in some Lincoln collection must be lost. As for the Lincoln group of the 3, mariah said. mr. Lincoln said "Dat tographer Shure, done mixed us up save us dis picture of a giraffe a gorilla and a baboon instead of us hens." It was of the 3 standing.

One of the last pictures. One taken on a little larger plate than the others, was the last he stopped look at. He looked at it long and intently It was a three-quarter figure of a very young, beautiful girl with a lovable, innocent face, a childlike face. Mr Lincoln made no remarks while studying the picture Which mariah said he had found in a gallery some five years before and brot. home. When at that time he showed it to Mrs. Lincoln, when she asked who it was he said "Well Mary you have always wanted to know just what Ann looked like, this is not her picture, but one so much like her, especially at time I first met her it could be her. It is her to me. Many times after that mariah said I he had seen him look at that picture.

It must have always reminded him of their love and proved his devotion to both her and her appreciation for her help and happy association.

While he was looking for the last time at this likeness of Ann Rutledge Mrs Lincoln got up from her chair and stood behind him. She too did not speak. But they both looked during the silence as if each sensed a benediction, as if to speak would make the incident less hallowed or consecrated.

Except for that ~~incident~~ once, most of the contents of his album had called forth a remark of a pleasure or ~~experience~~, many resulting in hearty laughter.

He layed the album on his knees but it accidently slipped and fell to the floor. The loose contents left in it, that he had not already discarded, scattered around. But as so many things that happened in Mr. Lincoln's life, as though to settle his course of action. Almost as if a divine hand were taking part. The album fell open exactly where this picture (supposedly exactly like) of Ann Rutledge was partly fastened in. Mr. Lincoln did not stop to pick up the articles strewn on the floor. Nor did Mrs Lincoln pick them up.

Mr Lincoln raised the album to his knees leaving it open ~~to~~ the ~~way~~ place it had fallen open to. Mrs Lincoln was the first to speak. As she had asked so very often before, many time which resulted in bitterness on her part, but which after all under the circumstances was probably only human she asked. "Mr Lincoln has you never put her out of your life?" As if dazed by his thoughts he hesitated quite a while to answer her. She started to twist her hands and show signs of becoming hysterical. ~~He put his arm~~ At last sensing what might happen if he didn't speak. He looked her squarely in the face, Put his arm around her waist and drew her to him. A demonstration rarely indulged in before any of his household. There said "Mary perhaps "Almighty God reopened this chapter in our lifes, so we could renew and review it and then close it forever."

No I have not put her out of my life. She was put out years ago. Since this higher power seen fit we cannot question the ways of such Divine Intelligence. Mrs. Lincoln (a Presbyterian who believes in predestination) then asked. "Then you do believe our ways are planned." His answer. "No not in the sense you have in mind as you are asking me." Sometimes I think God should have always been called Good. God as an individual mind seem narrowing and hampers the power we should feel is omnipotent. Good is all inclusive. All things if Good are relative, huge, help each other and work together for good. Therefore, what is good for those who do their best regardless of their own plans and sometimes highest desires, often comes to pass far better than planned or ever hoped for. God – Love – Good leads the way. "When I was experiencing hardships in my youth, I never dared hope for the Blessings I now enjoy or such priveledges or blessings as my family may now have." My blessed mother and consciensous hardworking thought father started me in a way I never forgot. May God help me to always stay in that way. Then only Good will come to me for that way is Good. Above all it has brought me ever in contact with those and the elements that have made it possible to climb to the highest place in this Good – nation and Mary among those who helped me climb was Ann. She had her part not because it was planned but because I tried to be good and she was good. Like begets like. I attracted her and she attracted me. At that time we needed each other in our lives. Assuredly at that time she was most dear to me. A part of my existence. But to-night she seems strangely far away and going out farther and farther. Our association as I tried to review it awhile ago when looking at this likeness was blurred. And Incidents in some cases so blotted they were as perhaps a partly forgotten beautiful dream I could only vagely recapture. Only disconnected parts would return to my memory. But to you I now owe my love and devotion. You too have helped me climb and are still helping me. Ann is a memory. You are a living reality. Not to be put aside an instant for anything or anyone whomsoever. Let us live the Good which we should not alone for ourselves, but for

our precious children, we have brought into the world
that only good will come to them. Let's improve each
moment with good, unwarped thoughts and deeds.
Let's live to-day. Only one day at a time. Let the
past remain the past and thank God it is so.
The past has played its part and played it well
to make to-day for you and I.   Dropping his album
He waited a moment and then said - Mariah
you can take this heep out and burn it.
I done didn't burn it for here it is.

The Last Time Aunt Mariah Ever Saw Mr. Abe

I asked Mrs. Vance if she ever saw Mr. Lincoln or any of the Lincoln family, after the Vance family moved from Springfield to Danville Illinois

The reason for asking this question was because, a number of people had told me, that Mr Lincoln, had called for her, if in the crowd, who met the presidential train, when it stopped at Danville on the trip to Washington, for Mr Lincoln's first inaugeration. Others told, that Mrs. Vance made a trip to Washington to have her husband released from the army, after the war was declared over, because he was so much needed at home. That at the time she was in Washington, Mrs Lincoln refused to see her.

These were Mariah Vance's answers to these reports, which I am convinced she truthfully answered

Oh yes, Ah seed Mr. Abe onse. You'n see we'ns left Springfield shortly afta Mr Abe war 'lectes president in Novemba in 1860. mah Henry hab got work in de mine outside Danville. He'n an mah Billie hab gone on wid ahload of plunda, Den Billie comb back for us'n an da res of our'n stuff.

You'n see da whole countra war in ah mess. President Buchanan cause he'n war goin out of office. An couse lots in Washington unda he'n war fa slavery; he'n just sot dare an nary tried ta stop dat war what war brewin. So da colored folks war near skeered out of dare hide. au moved fartha north, as we'ns planned afore.

No Mr. Abe nevva call fa me'ns or any ob ah fambly dat ah know of, or hear tell of. when da president train stop at Danville

Mr. Abe, an Mastah Robert hab comb ta Danville 'bout Christmas time in 1860. Day stop at da Etna House if ah rightly recomembers, fa some meetin wid some big men in poltics an some dare friends. One war Dr. Fithian ah recomemba.

But noow on dat day, ah messinga boy bring a to our'n house. Ah tell'n you ah war shur mah Henry hab been kill or hurt in da mine. But da telgram war

2 fromb Mr. Abe. It say on a slip of hotel papa hein hab send by dis messenga "Am at this hotel for a short time to-day. Robert is with me. I would like for you and Bill to come here between the hours of 3 o'clock and 4 o'clock. We will be very, very desappointed if you don't come. Give messenger your answer. With Esteem—A. Lincoln & Robey

Well Billie hab comb in fa dinna. Hein war doin some work fa do Stegler. Dat es a nice rich fambly who hab made money in da Smelta works. All da German folks war good to usin. Seems as how, since I recomemba 'gin, dat war fore do Stegler work. Maybe et war some street work mah Billie war doin.

Work or starve, nothin not a soul ting on dis arth could ah kept mah Billie away fromb goin ta see mastah Robert. When wen's move here mastah Robert war in some school in da east. Maybe Phillips' cademy at Exeter, New Hampshire or Harvard. So Billie f. hab ta comb away widout ah sight of da blessed Bobbie.

We'ns dress en ourin best clothes. Ah comb da braids out ob mah head an made mah har neat, as if it hab beed wax on it. Billie slick up too.

Right at 3 o'clock sharp we'ns reach da steps up ta da door ob dat hotel. Mr. Abe an mastah Robert almost run down da steps ta me usin. Ah thot Bobbie an Billie war goin ta kiss. Dose two Lincolumns war shear pleasured ta see usin 'gin. Jus smilin an laughin an shaken hans. Lak no ones war on dis 'arth, but da Vanses. Just lak no white folks war 'round gapin, lak day hab nevva saw da lak afore

Right dare an den ah know, President or no president, nothin would eba change Mr Abe an Bobbie. Dey would nevva on dis form 'arth evva get da swell head. Ef bein president wouldn couse et nothin would.

Wall Bobbie put hisn dear arm 'roun Billie's shoulda an say. We'll go into the lobby an visit. We would have come to your home, but pa has such a short time to get his business settled here, and see those he must see. Pa thot it best to give you the time it would take going

3, to and from your home.

Mr. Abe took men by da arm lak ah war da Queen of Sheba an hep me up dose steps. Eba ones en dat Hotel Lobby gaps. So Mr. Abe took men to each man an ah few women dare, seated in a kind a circle, an entaduced me, as a very fine colored lady, who hab lives in da Lincoln home fa Two years. Ah notice hen didn' say servant or was woman. Den Bobbie stan up an say. An dis is mah bes frien Billie Vance.

Mr. Abe ask 'bout mah Henry an each one of mah younguns. Said, he'd just love to see them all but didn't have the time to do so. Ah ask hen 'bout Willie, Taddie an da missy. He say, Willie and Taddie coats to come along. But mother, who is the busiest woman this side of Washington, couldn't manage to get them ready and I suspect she needed them for company.

Several men comb up an shook hands wid Mr. Abe Gratslated hen. Hen only say, a few words to each, 'til hen got thro' visitin' wid won. Da men what hen war dare in Danville to see comb in. Sumbob dem hab gone out, den comb back in lak day war anxious fos Mr. Abe to be wid dem. But Mr. Abe war allus a poke-easy. Hen tole dem men ta stay right dare, he'd be wid dem shortly.

Den hen say to Billie. Bill, I have only one desire before I go back to Springfield and that is to hear you sing again. Den hen say to da man hind dat desk. Would you mind, if Bill is willing, for him to sing for us? According to my opinion, Bill has one of the most beautiful voice, God ever gave to anyone. Billie nevva war skeered ta sing. He got out ob dat char in a shake. Billie war allus quick 'bout eba ting. Hen didn' wait ta hear what Mr. Abe want ta hear. He jus up an sang, uh new song hen' larn since combin to Danville. Dat war da Mocking Bird Song. An he whistle too lak da bird, all thro da song when hen' warn't singin da wards. You'n could a hear a pin drop, as day say, all dose folks jus couldn' believe it. Day war spell boun.

4. Den hen knowd Mr. Abe sake- "Ah's on mah road
ta Glory Now." Fore day quit clappin fa da
"Mocking Bird" hen start singin "Ah's on mah Road"
makin all da jesters, as hen larned en church. When
hen war done, hen quick as ahdart sang notha song
Mr. Abe love. Et war a church song ah jist can't
recomemba da name, but day all stop - Somb laugh an
somb cry, Mr. Abe an Bobbie too. Mr. Abe hole up
his hand, wipe hisn eyes an say, kinda jerkin up,
"Am I not right when I said Bill has a most beautiful
God - Given voice. And I know Billie will use it to
glorify God, an set all he meets on the Road to Glory Now -
But maybe were all on our road to glory." "God grant
this scourge will pass away." From dat on Billie war
call ta sing most any what.

Mr. Abe gave Bill somb money Ah done memba
how much. Hen gib men a basket of fruit, and
a bag of candy, an from his grip what he open, hen
hab toys an presents fa all. Hen an Bobbie shook
hans, even held ourn hans an both dem an
wen's cried. Ah jes couldn help cause, ah knowd
deep down, Mr. Abe war goin out into dis wicked
country ta be crucified as Christ was, for da
colored folks ta be free.

Afta dat meetin, from dat on, ah hab all da work
from da rich an fine folk, ah could do - Dat war da
very las time ah saw Mr. Abe.

'Bout goin ta Washengton, ah nevva did go, but mah
Eilen hen go, for to get Mr. Abe ta let her man comb home.
Hen didn want ta see Mrs Lincolumn, my Eilen
war allus skeered ob da messy, so da missy couldn
hab refuse ta see Ellen, or me cause ah warn dare.
But ah bet hern would ah want ta see me hab ah been dar.
As afore, ah's tole you, Robert allus comb ta see
usn when in Danville.

You'n know folks, hab tole da God - awfulles lies
'bout dose poor Lincolumns.

Mariah Meets The Lincolns

After a bad storm in April of 1850, about four o'clock in de afternoon, Henry (date mah man) and ah war sottin out front whar we lived on Washington Street near Jackson. He were war watching the comings and goings of a rainbow, what showed up after de storm in de east sky.

Henry fussed cause he thought it foolish like, for me to tellun de young'uns 'bout Noah an de flood. It did done be a long drawn out tale. Ah war 'bout windin it up, tellin as how de rainbow war to remind us of God's covenant. Dat never again, no sir e, dar would never be a nother flood. Ah's tryin to larn dem dat de flood had to come. It or somepen else had a come, cause folks war so wicked.

My Henry tole me to keep mah clap shut we war goin to hav company. Henry had watched a tall man headed ah way. Comin down Jackson. Ah never onct sot eyes on him until up he stepped an turned squar in our front yard. It war mr Abe Lincoln.

We all knowd him. We all knowd he war a good man. We'd hearn tell stories about him. Dat he war a frien of colored folks, just as how he war a frien of white folks. My Henry spoke to him right friendly. He liked mr Lincoln. But not most white folks. He an his'n folks had been slaves, He never knew his real pappy. He done got the name of Vance, from a slave holder dat owned his mammy when he war born. His'n pappy had been sold off to a nother slave holder. But mah man en his'n mammy got up north thro de unner ground.

Now me ah war never a slave. Mah kin folks lived just cross de Ohio from Kaintucky. We'ns often wandered down to de banks of de ribber to play. Wal now I just don't member rightly how many of us'n der war. Only know dat while we played a big boat sailed up to de bank. Some mean white men, got out of dat boat, an drove de older ones of us'n away. Ah war so young ah don't zackly 'member, so as how ah cain't tell it all. Ah hearn tell ah an a brother ran an hid. It war an older brother Neal what come up in time to save me. Neal war not so big cause as he done run wid me, he letin me fall on a stump. Ah war too heavy for him. See dat white scar on mah shin? Must have struck my shin bone parful lick. You war-e- Ah'll carry dat mark to mah buryin. It are de only white 'bout me. Ah's just flam black coon I hear she laughed showing her pink tongue in her toothless mouth. But Ah's right proud ah's real black. Had a black pappy an black mammy african black with good red blood and white hearts. Laud goodness et mammy grieved a heap over loozin her chil'n. Poor pappy he'd go puttterin aroun war no use tryin to spunk her up.

out of her way. She paid no mind to any ting in dat Godforsaken wilderness, but tryin to do what war needful for mammy. He'd fix a pot full of possum. But de possum war tasteless to mammy. Pappy'd say, Et taint rightful dat you youngns should starve. So I'd me et a gorge of possum.

A travelin parson done come along an set up a camp in dat wilderness. Mammy an pappy goes to de camp meetin, Dey done got de Love of God in der hearts. Ah's shur pappy would hab lust clean out a dat meetin, but he see as how mammy war gettin happy, so he'd got up grit and stayed. He didn't dast go. He'd been ah plumb fool not to see de home war going to be right as not again. You'se can see ah was raised a christian woman.

After de meetin we done went farther narth an west. He wound up in Illinois, somewhar close to Springfield. Dat's whar I met my Henry. Ah war just a skit of ah gal wen we got hitched. Five youngns in eight years war born to us'n by the time we set foot in Springfield in 1850. We didn't have much but youngns an old mule and wagon, a cart and a wee bit a plunder.

We'n hardly got settled in our hut, 'til folks, good folks they be, wanted mah man to haul wood an do chores. Et war so cold in us'ns hut et froze ice in der water becket an outside in der cistern. My Henry said we picked the Lowd awfulist time to move. We just had a go whar we could find work, cold or no cold, or plum starve. Ah got scrubbin and washin from folks. We'n got kitched up on food stuff, an warmer togs. The lop youngns stayed in so didn't need shoes. Rent war only 75 cents a week.

Shat spring et had rained a deal. Specially April. Ah warn't asked to work a heap. De mud in streets war black an sticky an worse'n black whar cows roamed an pigs wallered. Guess folks figered better leave well enough alone, while rain kept up. Rather than have dat muck in dar homes.

Ah war speculatin on gettin most something to do, after the rainbow promises no more floods, an war about to tell my man, when Ah hear'n Mistah Abe say after greetings, I'll come right to the point Mrs Vance, I believe you are the lady who did cleaning in our office a while back. Anyone who could clean those windows so you could see through, Really clean scrub that floor, straighten up, and make that office smell fresh, is the kind of woman we would like to do our washing and other household chores. I'm going an Id like the most way, for you to come in the morning. I'm going an of town on the circuit for a spell. Mrs Lincoln will be alone with our son, Robert. To make a long story short, my wife is not well, We just lost our little boy, our precious Eddie. Mrs Lincoln has lost other relatives. She loved and her heart is grieved. Besides, we think she is with child. She has morning sickness besides bad pains in her head. If you'll say you'll come I's be powerful much obliged. But my man right pertinent spoke up.

Mr. Lincoln, I caint no how find fault wid any yourns doins er how you done treat folks. But I don't want mah woman screamed at an chasted off'n de place, like youse woman hab done did other workin woman folks, so ah's heer dem tell. Now mah Mariah is a mild woman, an ah's got a shield her an take her part. She might talk back a 'bit, but ah's feared she'd nevvah fight a she cat. Ah's not wantin to hurt yourns feelins Mr. Lincoln, but I caint bide by sich, like as day say 'bout dat woman of yourns.

Mistah Abe stood right still, right dar, as if rooted to dat are groun'. Youse could jest see as how dat man had a world of trouble. After a spell he said, Perhaps what you have heard is partly true, but you know when a ball starts rollin in the mud, it gathers more mud.

Now tell me Mrs. Vance, what do you earn? When you wash, do you work by the piece, by the day, the hour or by the week? I know with a very sick woman to work for, it is going to be quite a trial. But if you'll try to understand my wife, I think you'll learn to like her. And I think she'll like you. Sometimes it's all in getting acquainted. I'm not a saint, I know I have ways which sometimes jar on Mrs. Lincoln. Whatever you've been earning I'll be glad to pay you more... because you'll have more trials than at most places due to Mrs. Lincoln's condition.

Wal I says to mistah Abe, Since mah Henry is not working now and won't need the mule and cart, he can stay wid de older chilluns. If'n he says so, ah can take the two wee ones. If'n yourn has a place to tuck 'em in while ah works? Wal says mistah Abe Ah'll be much obliged and I'll find a place for the children, mah youngest Julia war still nursin, an ah had to take her. Ah could put her to nap, but when she done woke up, if'n she had no company, her would cry. Dat's bout the onerist thing for me to put up with when workin. A cryin young'n. So I took Phebe too.

Mah Henry says, Just this onst Mr. Lincoln an no more, if'n your woman bruises my Mariah. Mistah Abe says, Now Henry and Mrs. Vance, I'm ever so grateful to you, I feel relieved to leave my family and home in a good woman's hands. He gave the chillen some stick candy. Tole mah man he'd get him all the work he could. Said I'll have the water pumped and the boiler on early. You wont have to rush too much. Not so much you'll have to neglect your own family. At that he sauntered 'round the corner.

Well, ah got to Mr. Abe's about 7 o'clock the next morning. Shur enough thar war Mr. Abe pokin wood (from a stack he had cut & piled in the yard) under de boiler on a brick contraption in de back yard. De lid of dat ole battered boiler war bouncin up an down like it had a hot foot. De wood wash tub with a new fangled wash board in it war on a stool. An plenty of lye soap. De wash war all in a pile on de floor of a shed.

Ah tucked mah sleepin younguns in de corner of dat shed an asked mistah Abe if he done had hisen breakfast He said, All I care for, but there's a mess in the kitchen I fear I cant tackle. Ah went in dat nice large kitchen. In dat kitchen war a big fire place, a large table, a small work table an a corner cupboard. De dishes, pans and scraps of food war every whar stacked Ah figured while dar war plenty of hot water, ah'd be mighty smart to clean up the soil roun 'bout, fore starting de wash. Ah'd hardly started stackin dishes an brushen up fore I heard some body coming down de stairs & war a boy 'bout seven years old. For de life of me I nevvah sot eyes on sich a sober looking boy, Proud lookin he war too. I felt a little queer roun sich a boy, So differment from mistah Abe's sad patient look. Mastah Robert I discovered later had one crossed eye mistah Abe's eyes war so sunken. But I loved that little man Robert right off. He den done smiled such a friendly smile; dat shure as youens and Ah's sotten har on dis door-step, washed off dat sober proud look right away, He said, aren't I deserving of any breakfast, As says, Land a goodness Honey Chile youse serving of all de breakfast you little fat belly can hold. Ah's cook all day an all night to feed sich a dear sweet little boy man, what he likes best. But don't rub dat smile off. Dats worth heaps of shining gold. Mastah Robert laughed, Really laughed out loud. He war a very very still boy and most awful serious most all de time.

Mistah Abe says, Robert this is our new help Mrs Vance, I'm about to leave now, and I'm going to put you in charge, I want you to help all you can. Be good to your mother. Helpful & comforting. Your mother is not well and when I'm gone you are all she will have. Ah finished with Mastah Roberts breakfast an de kitchen an went out to mah wash, Ah was sorten the clothes in de shed, when what should step right up to dat door but the most prettiest woman ah's ever laid eyes on. I says Howde missy. She paid no heed to mah Howde, Just walked over to de corner whar my younguns war tucked in, and said " It hats this "? and gave a turble jirk on Julia foot, Julia woke wid a loud split en ear yelp. The missy screamed, "Get those dirty yelling niger brats out of here", Get em out of here I say right away. Ah's about to oblige her - when Mr Abe comes in, Quiet like he says, says he, Mother this is Mrs Vance the lady who is going to do the washing and help while I am away.
I dis the missy Well what can she do with them whelps screamin.

my head! Oh my head! Mother, Mother you know full well what you'd do if a cyclone come up, sudden like and jerked you out of bed. You'd do more than yelp. You'd raise the neighborhood and after you got them raised, you swear that the cyclone was possessed of a demon and raised them. Mr Abe had a powerful bad time wid her. He turned to me and says, Mrs Vance please pay no attention to what Mrs Lincoln jus said, she is such a sick woman. Go on with Your work and I'll make mother comfortable. She's a good woman but so sick and troubled, Ah jus thot right thar an then Ah don't see no good only pretty to look at. She's ah she devil an she aught to have 'em troubles for how she troubles Mistah Abe. Even dat poor dear little Robert ran to de barn like he war shot from a flip jack.

I settled Julia wid mah suckin and gave Phebe the other young un, a cracklin Ah'd swept from the table. The washin war big an hard, I shur knowd it warn't jus a weeks wash.

Robert kind a time's like came back bringin kitten an a ball. He played in dat shed with my two uns the rest o dat blessed morning. He war bein helpful like his pappy tole him to be. Ah jest figgered he missed his little brudder who had jest died. He told mah chilluns it war Eddie's kitten an ball.

When mr Abe lead de missy away, Ah heard him say Caint I jist for once leave here with a happy thot o you. Why Oh why do you always send me away to worry. Mebt he seemed to say it to himself." But she spoke up if you were half as smart as I once thot you were, you wouldn't have to go wandering over the country, leavin us to get along the best we can with low life help. You'd stay at home like my people do and make a decent living. He says then, Well Mary maybe we both made a mistake and I declare I don't know which one of us made the worst mistake. But I'll do the best as I see it, I git you something to quiet you and then must be on me way. I don't want to keep the others waiting. He poured something out of a glass jug an handed it to de missy. Since then I knowed it war parigoric. He took her up stairs an put her to bed.

Ah had finshed hanging de wash. Some war dry an ah war foldin them. Mr. Abe had come down stair and says Mrs Vance your work is done right fine. The clothes are so clean my wife is going to be happy with them. I am glad you stayed. You must have an understanding head and heart. Mrs Lincoln is always ashamed after she has one of these spells. I want you to come once a week if you can. I don't think Henry will object when you explain to him. Ah knowd my Henry a heap more'n Mistah Abe knowd him. We uns needed dat money. Mr, Abe paid me 50¢ extra.

He packed the rest of his belongings in de bag. Come out to de clothes basket an sarched out some clean bandanas an socks. Carried in de baskets filled and packed down hard with clean clothes Ah'd taken down from line. Put some papers in his tall hat. Took Robert on his knees, kissed and held him close. I declare I remember as twar yisterday de big tears dat rolled down as, splashed. That man twar a man of God and he war crucified every day of his life. He said, Good Bye and again said thanks God for your help. Then he slumped away to de barn to hitch Buck.

Ah pitched in and finished straightenin de house. Set Mastah Roberts dinna an de kitchen table, sent food up to de missy. When I come back with mule hitched to cart out come Robert carryin Julia and leading Thebe. Sad like he said Good bye an trotted back to de barn carryin the kitten such a lonesome little tike. Ah knowd right dar an den dat Mastah Robert war born to trouble. Wid such an ailing mother. If he didn't die from it, some day he would be a great good man like his father an good to look at like his mother. How my heart plum melted for that poor little lonesome tike.

(over)

-1- After a bad storm in April of 1850 about four o'clock in the afternoon Henry and the kids an I were sitting out front where we lived on Washington street near Jackson. We were watching the coming and going of a rainbow, which appeared after the storm in the eastern sky.

Henry thought it foolish for me to tell the young uns about Noah and the flood. But tho it was a long draw out story I was just winding it up telling the kids about the rainbow. That it was a covenant from God that there would never be another flood and trying to larn them that the flood had to come. It or something else cause people was so wicked, when up stepped Mr. Abe Lincoln from aroun the corner of Jackson.

We all knowed him. We knowed he was a good man. We'd heard tell stories about him. That he was a friend of colored folks as well as white folks and my Henry spoke to him right friendly. my Henry didn't much like white folks. He and his people had been slaves. We never knew his real pappy, but was given the name of Vance from a slave holder who owned his mammy when he was born.

Now me I was never a slave. my kin folks lived just across the Ohio from Ky. We often wandered down to the bank of the river to play. Well now I don't remember how many of us'n there was. I know while we played a big boat sailed up to the bank. Some mean white men got out of dat boat and drove the older ones of us'n away. I was very young, now I caint tell it all. I hear'n tell a brother ran and hid. It was an older brother that U he some how come up in time to save me. He was not so big because as he run with me, he let me fall over a stump. I was too heavy for him. You see that little scar over my shin. Must have struck my shin bone a painful lick. Yes sir. I'll carry that mark to my buryin. Its the only white about me. I'se just plain black one, and she laughed. But I'm proud I'se black real black. I had a black pappy and a black mammy. They were African. Black, black African God red blood and white. I'se mammy grieved a heap over loosen her chile. Lawsy good nus, it war no use tryin to spunk her up. Poor pappy 'ked go puttern around oiten her way. He paid no mind to any ting in dat Gawd forsaken wilderness, but tryin to do what war needful for mammy. He'd fix a pot ful of possum. But de possum war tasteless to mammy and pappy. He say "It haint needful for you young uns to starve." Then mammy an pappy goes to de camp meetin held by a travelin lar of Gawd in der heart. I'se sure pappy would hab bust clean out of dat meeting, but he see as how mammy was gettin happy, so he got up grit. He didn't dast go. He'd be a plumb fool not to see de home war going to be right as not again. Yuise can see I'se raised a Christian woman.

After the meetin he done went farther north and farther west. Wound up somewhar in Illinois. Wait I met my Henry in Illinois. I was just a skit of a gal when we got hitched. Five young uns in eight years was born to usn by the time we set foot in Springfield in 1850. We didn't have much but young uns. A mule an old wagon and cart and a little plunder.

I'se hardly got settled in our hut, until folks, good folks wanted my man to haul wood and do chores for them. It war so cold in that air hut, ice froze in our cistern. He picked about the worst onfuliest time to move my man said, But we just had to go whar my Henry could find work, or plum starve. I got a little scrubbin and washins for folks, He got sacked up an supply of food stuff and warm togs. The lap young uns stayed in so didn't need shoes. Rent was only 75 cents a week.

It had rained much in April and I warn't asked to work much. The mud in street war black and sticky and worsen than black where the cows roamed an pig walled. Guess folks most figgered better leave well enough alone while rains lastet. Ruther than have that muck in thar homes.

I was spectating on getting most something to do, after the rainbow promised no more floods and was about to tell my Henry so. I hearn Mr. Abe say after greetings. I'll come right to the point missus Vance. I believe you are the lady who did cleaning in our office a while back. Anyone who could clean hose windows so you could see through. Clean scrub that floor, straighten up and make that office smell fresh, is the kind of a woman we'd like to do our washin and other household chores.

I'd like most for you to come in the morning. I'm going out

asked me for the story and I copied the one I was sending to Dr. Warren for him. Dale Wilson is now dead. If you can have Dr. Warren to have story in his files.

on the circuit for a "spell". Mrs. Lincoln will be
alone with our boy Robert. Now to make a long story
short. My wife is not well. It i just lost Eddie. Our
precious Eddie. Then too Mrs Lincoln has lost other
relatives she loved and her heart is grieved. Besides we
think she is with child. She has morning sickness. If
you'd just come I'd be powerful much obliged—

But my Henry right pertinent spoke up Mr. Lincoln
I caint no how find fault with any your doins or
how you done treat folks. But I don't want my your
woman screamed at and chasted off the place like your
woman has done did to other folks. So Ise hearin tell
Now my Mariah is a mild woman. And Ise got to
shield her and take her part. She might talk back some
but I feared she'd never fight a she cat. Now Ise
not wantin the hurt youse feelins, but I can't hide by
sich as they say about youse woman.

Mr. Abe stood right still, right thar, as if rooted to
dat are ground. After a spell he said, Pirhaps what you
have heard is partly true. But you know when a ball
starts to rollin in the mud, it gathers more mud.
Now mrs. Vance what do you earn. Do you work by
the piece when you wash or by the hour. Or by
the day. Or by the week. I know with a very sick
woman to work for its going to be a trial— But if you
will try to understand my misses, I think youll learn
to like her. And I think shell like you. Sometimes it
all in getting acquainted. I'm not a saint. I know I
have ways that jar on mrs Lincoln. Whatever you earn
I'l be glad to pay you more. because youll have more
trials than most places at this present time.

Wal I says to mr. Abe since my Henry is not working
now and can stay with the older young un. Ifens he
says so, I can take the two young n. If'n youse has a
place to tuck me in while I work. Well says mr. Abe
I'l be much obliged, and I'll find a place for the chilni
you see my youngest Julia was nursin and I had to take
her. I could put her to nap but when she done woke, if
she had no company would cry. And thats the orneriest
thing for me to put up with when workin.

My Henry said, now for sartin Mr. Lincoln, just this
oust and no more, if your woman mistreats my woman

Mr. Abe says Henry and Mrs. Vance Ise powerful much obliged to you. I feel relieved to leave my home in a good woman's hands. He gave the chil'n some stick candy. I ole Henry he'd get him all the work he could ~~and sauntered around the corner~~, said I'have the water pumped and the boiler on early. But don't rush too much. So much ~~to~~ you'll have to neglect your own family — at that he saundered around the corner

Wal I got to ~~Mr~~ Abe's about 7 oclock the next morning. Shur enough there was Mr. Abe poking wood, (from a stack he had cut, piled in the yard) under the boiler. The lid of that old battered boiler was bouncing up and down. The wooden wash tub was on da stoop in da back yard. The clothes was all in a pile on the floor of the corner shed. I tucked my sleepin young in in a ~~basket~~ of the shed and asked Mr. Abe. Did he done have his breakfast. He said "All I care for, but there's a mess in here I fear, I can't tackle — I went into a nice large kitchen. In that kitchen was a big fire place, a large table, a corner cubberd, a smaller work table, but all pretty well stocked I figured while there was plenty of water hot. It be he mighty smart to clean up the bois around about befor starting washing. Ah'd hardly started stacking dishes and brushing up afore I heard some one coming down the stairs. It was a boy about seven years old. a very sober looking boy, proud looking too. I felt a little queer around seh a boy, So different from Mr. Abe's sad deep eyed patient look. But the boy Robert smiled and said. Arent I serving of no breakfast? I says Land of goodness ~~Honey~~ chile you serving of all the breakfast you little fat belly can hold. It took all day and all night to feed such a dear sweet little man — boy, just what he likes best. But don't rub that smile off. ~~Dilsworth~~ precious gold Robert ~~it~~ laughed, Really laughed out loud. He war a very still and serious boy.

Mrs. Abe says Robert this is our new help Mrs. Vance. I'm bout to leave now as I'e going to put you in charge. I want you to help her as much as you can. Your mother is not well you know

to be helpful, and comforting. I went out I finished with Robert
and do kitchen and went out to my wash. I was
sorten the clothes in the shed, when who should step
in but about the prettiest woman I'se ever seen, I says
Howde Missy. She paid no head to my Howde, just walked
over to corner whar my young'ns war tucked in and
said Whats this. And gave a jerk on Julia foot
Julia woke with a loud splitten ear yelp. The messy
screamed, get those dirty niger brats out of here. Get
them out a here I say right away. I'se about to oblige
her when Mr Abe came in. He says quiet like, mother
this is Mrs Vance the lady who am givin to do the
washings and hep while I am away. Says the missy -
Well what can she do with those young whelps screaming
around. mother, mother you know full well what you'd
do if a cyclone came up, sudden like and jerked you out
shed. You'd do more in yeself. You'd raise the neighbors Lord.
and often you got em raised you'd swear the cyclone did it
Mr Abe had a powerful bad - ung with her. He first turned
to me and says, Says he Mrs. Vance I done tole you Mrs
Lincoln is a sick woman. You pay no heed to what
she has said - Just go on with your work and I'll make
mother comfortable. Mrs Vance she's a good woman but
is sick and troubled. That right there and then Oh dont
she no good only pretty to look at. She's a she devil - She
aught to be trouble cause how she troubles Mr. Abe. Even
that from little Robert ran to the barn, like he was flip jack.
    I settled Julia wid my sucken and gave - the other
young'n a cracklin I'd swept from the table. The washing
was big and hard, but I had it done dry and fold in a basket
Robert kind a timid like came back bringing a kitten and
ball. He played in that shed with my two the rest of that
blessed morning. He was being helpful like his papa had told
him to be. I jest figgured he missed his little brother who
had jest died. He told my chillen it was Eddies kitten & ball.
    When Mr Abe had the missy away I heard him say. Cant
I ever once leave here with a happy thot of you. Why do you
have to send me away to worry, She said to him - If you war
half as smart as I once thot you was. You wouldnt have to
traipse over the country, leavin us to gittalong the best we
can with low life help. You could stay at home like my people do
tend to your home & your business and make a dacint living.

I see him pour from a glass jug a big dose of something & hand it to mrs Lincoln. Since then Ive learned it was perigoric. He took her up stairs put her to bed. Packed his belonging for his trip in a bag. Put some papers in his hat and ~said~ came out to where I had finished hanging the wash. Some clothes were dry ~the~ and I was folding them. He says mrs. Vance Your work is done right fine. The clothes so clean. mother is going to be happy about them. ~I'm glad~ you stayed. You must have and understanding kind & heart. Mrs Lincoln is always shamed after she has one of these spells. I want you to come out a week if you can I don't think Henry will object, when you explain to him. Nel I didn't explain to Henry. I knowed my ~Henry~ a heep more'n Mr. Abe knew him. He needed that money. Mr Abe paid me 50 cts extra.

I pitched in finished straightened up — Sent a plate of food up for the missy. Got Roberts dinner on the ~with~ table in the kitchen for him. ~and~ Brot the dry clothes in folded in basket.

When I came back with mule hitched to cart out came Robert carrying Julia and leading. Sad like he said Good-bye & went back to the barn carrying the kitten. Such a lonesome little tike. I knew right there and then, that Robert was born to trouble having such an ailing mother. But if he lived thro' it some day he would be a great good man like his father.

The week hadn't passed when one afternoon I sees a small boy chasing ~in our~ ~house~ yard. I lashes of lightning and weak thunder war coming out of the sky — But that is another story.

De week hadn't passed when one afternoon about four Ah sees a small boy chasing, all out of wind, right in on our front yard. Flashes of lightning, an week tunder was coming down out of de sky. It was that poor spunky little Robert calling out mrs Vance. mrs Vance come quick my ma is in torment. Ah got him quietin a spell. What air you mean youse ma's in torment. Ah wanted how to say, Hers getting her just whippens, clamped down from Almighty God or hern's. But sheer as dir is dot loof in Heaben, when Ah looked at dot poor skeered baby boy ah says to masef—luit you infernal evil, devil thinkin an gentle down. Ah says Whats ailing you mammy? Oh mrs Vance do come, I've asked everyone I know, an it's no good. No one wants to help her. One woman says to me Lit her die an go to hell. They hate her they hate her and they hate me. She's afraid of this thunder an lightening, She's got her head covered and screaming for help. Pa's gone and I'se all ma has! You heard pa say so my Henry sating that says marster, thinks as how you better go. Ah'll mind the brats a spell. Roberts eyes lit up like one of those new fangled oil lamps. Den he spied our Billy. Billy was about de size of Robert. Dey took to each tother bout as how two monkeys in a cocanut tree. Robert forgot he was in a shake to hep his ma. But I did done no fiddlin I want to get goin an get back fore the storm broke loose. Not a form thing would gentle those boys down. So I says Robert should Ah take Billie along in de cart mid us? He was so pleasured he had a attack of chuckles right off. Right der an den Ah knows mah block Billy and dat blessed little white Robert was going to be fast friends—

We uns loaded ohselves in de cart an away that mule shoved, along with each clap of tunder. De boys yelled & laughed with heeps of spirit. De tunder got louder an de mule got faster. Ah shur believe Robert war more joyful than he'd ever been before in his onhappy little life.

Bout hafe way der We'd gone bout 3 or 4 blocks Out jumped a rascals, to try to stop dat mule. De mule put dat mule head of hisn down. You never know what dat darn fool mule war about to do—til he doed it. But he pushed right smack thro dat heep. An did dey scamper a spell. Then dey putdere heads together an give chase an screamed at poor little abused Robert. Ole rail splitin Abe's boy is a nigger lover. They cotched up wid us and grabbed dat cart in de rear an pulled back hard. Ah pulled as hard

wen dey war et up, her brushes up the crums right quick
Then says, Boys stand up. Billie war a wee bit higher and
Bobbie war heaps fatta. Flea she says. Bobbie go up to your
room and bring me your waists and pantaloons and some
of your waist coats. Billie started to follow but she grabbed
him by the sleeve, what war so dirty I war ashamed. Now the
missy says, You sit right there and be quite, if you can
for a little while, I says, fore Afthot cause ah's larned a
lesson the missy wouldn't bide by cruelty. Ah says, Ill
strap him ifn he done don't. Oh, no you wont she says.
I'un this house and you're going to do as I say, Do you
understand that mariah. Billie yelled loud as tunder
"Harrah for de missy. Gibe it too her missy both barrels."
Dot pleased de missy an as black an dirty as he war
I thot shur she war going to kiss him. From that very Gawd
blessed day on she loved my Billie an he war tooth and
toe nail for hern. Ah still that Ah's strap him when Ah got him
home. Ah jest caint figger how dat woman as sick as she
war when Ah left her wash day an as sick as she war de
day we got der on dat tightning day, could in betwickst de
two done bock loads of works. On wash day ah'd onla washed
and straightened up a spec, but der war narry a speck of
soil on a form ting as big as a fly speck. She war a fine
house kapa. Side de house as clean as de driven snow
She hab planted flowers, onions, lettace, peas an lows Ah
done know as how wha all in groun Mr. Abe hab dug up,
Har pretty dimples hans were all scard and dat dist groun
in whar dat lie soap hab made cracks. Ah tole de missy
she shouldn hen ober in harns conditon. She says - I'd
like to know who else would. Mr Lincoln is too tall to bend
He's bent so much already carrying the boys, bless them,
stradling his neck and playing piggy back he is already
stooped. Then he carries the whole world on his shoulders.
Hall hern tole Billie to put on some of Bobbies cloches
Dat Billie grabbed de bunch an went racing to de shed.
Ah got der wid a wet towl de missy handed me, and
brushed him up a bit. Ah war when youns can see dirt
on a black nigger, days dirty. Ah got oulah de worse offn him.
Ah hab a fight wid him to make him kape on a ruffle
be dubbed waist an fataloons butloned at de neck. But ah led
him in to de missy by de ear. He screemed bloody murder.

(2) on de straps. An dat mule seemed to have lose sense for once. He slow'din up. Ah know'd my Billy and Bobbie were no match fer'n that pizen of rascals. My Billy would have gotten out ofn that cart quicker den a cat could catch ah rat, but ah grabs him by de seat of his'n pants while he war going over de eng an halled his back. He called dem white trash a good condemned awful neme. With a flook ah gave him a lick ober his defiled blasphemen mouth and knowed he's been mixing around wid dem white trash on Jackson street. Ah gave him another lick for good measure and warned him efn I cotched him wid any dem low down heathens again ah'd blister him worsin Shadrack, Meshach an Abednego would gotten ifn God hadnt resced them frow de fiery furnace.

But all dat talk to dem youngens roent plum thro bothe ears. Ah war ah'd hardly got my speech out of my mouth than Billie hollered Mammy, Mammy, hellas pepper black snake, give it to dem. Dem blasted white trash warn crawlin in de back end of mah cart. Jist as Ah grabbed dat God blessed black snake and cracked it at dem, der war a turble streak of lightning and a clap of tunder dat most upsot us when de mule gave another lung. We all screamed and that mess of white trash boys done must have thought they war struck by dat lightning. I sware "War hoss" couldn't have cotched them DEY SURE DIDN'T MOLEST US'UNS NO MOAH.

But Oh mah God in HEABEN when we done got to de Lincolns it war worse than all de messes ah war ever in, in mah whole born days. Thar war de missy laid up on de old black sofy, her feet twitchen & kicken. Hir head covered wid a quilt and spew all ober de floar. Ah says to little Bobbie run for de doctor, run run you scamps run. But den my Billie always snoofin round says, Mammy, Mammy look at her, We haint no need for de doctor, She's peep'n She's playing possum. jist git dat black snake and gih her a good walloping and she'll forgit its gwine to blow dis awful hell hole up. An dad boys ran out. Ah couldn't cotch them. No sir e before ah uncovered hir head or hold her feet from jerking an twitchen back they came, wid de black snake. Billie came busting in de door, wallup dat she debil good manney, an her'll stop skeering folk out of her wits. Robert looked scared. Poor dear sweet little Robert. Dat chile had never been round any sick as mah Billie –

but ah made him march in to de missy. He say Ah 'doue want these sissy ruffleds. At which Robert spoke up an said you see ma that why they call me sissy. Well see about some of the rest. She picked out the plainer stoughest one and put them in the stack on a chair where the clothes for Julia were laying. She thanked Mariah for comen, said Mr Lincoln would pay her when she come to wash again. Now Mariah I believe you need not come only every two weeks since Mr Lincoln is not at home, I can wash out the few things we really need.

I am going to try to get someone to come to stay with us at nights it's so lone. Maybe on of Bobbie friends, or perhaps an irish girl I know of. She can get breakfast and clear the dishes, that will give me a chance to catch up on my sewing, that I have neglected. Since my father died last July we're Father going in January to Lexington to here with our either been dear little down sickness, going away and our grief. I believe Mariah you and Billie have been who I needed all along. I feel I'm once again back home with mammy and all the pickaninnies. At that Bobbie spoke up an said Oh ma can we call Mrs. Vance Mammy Mariah. Ah done know why, but dat jus didn' seem right. Ah's mammy to my youngins, but ah war nebber mammy to no white. Ah asked kinda skeered, How ole beein you Mrs Lincolumn. Harn says, She's 32 Mariah. How old are you? Well ah's 28 she's very next month. Dat bein June. And ah's no ways as how ole enough for youns to call me mammy. All right mariah. Maybe you wouldn't object for Bobbie to call you Aunt Mariah. Woud you like that? Ah war so pleasured to bein called Aunt to a little white boy liken Bobbie Ah says Youse a beautiful good woman Mrs, Lincolumn, an she says I hanks mariah if it's hard for you to say Lincoln you cantrue call me missy as I overheard you calling me to Billie. But Billie you must call me 'missy too, it sounds so sweet of you.

Ah tole her ah'd pay her in works for de youngn duds she'n gibbin me, but her'n jist shew me off. Tole Billie to git in de bottom of cart, and spread all dese cloths ober him, so de white trash could see him on de way home.

③ Oh right der an den gave him a cut wid dat black <ins>MAYBE AH AINT TO DONE IT.</ins>
snake — He gave out a screech, <del>an howl</del> worsn dat wunce — Up
jumped the missy. Hairs dowy, an all tangled like, face
covered wid spew. Ah, say <del>please</del> missy, dont up sot youse
self. Ahs come to protect youse. Dis storm bows to be ober
soon, mah Henry allahs say, De harder de storm de quicker
its ober. But Lowd Gowd she warn't jumpin about
de storm. Her war screeching mad cause I walloped
Billie. She said Haint youse even got niger sense, my
Billie only told the truth. This is a hell hole and I
Ive made it so. If any one need to be beat I need it.
But no one needs cruelty and I wont lay buy, no
matter how I feel and see it practiced in my house.
Bobbie, done ran to his ma and cried — Oh ma. Dont scold
Mrs. Vance. She's a good understanding woman in her
heart and her head I heard Pa tell her so. Yes Oh yes
Bobbie says the missy. It was good of her to come over
in this storm to be here <del>when</del> to protect us. I shouldn't
<del>have called her</del> have had you go for her, but I was so
afraid. Well I just tole her she'd have to get more love
in her ins heart, for mah good book says Love casts out fear.
Well she says, If love cast out fear mariah. Love will
cast out whippings too. Ah didn't want to arguefy wid her
but mah teachins never sayeth any ting about whippens —
De storm just as Henry sayed did'nt last.
Ah got a basin of water for the missy to wash her'n face
Ah ashed her'n if she would want as how Ah should clean
out a clutter of parcels all aroun. Do you ins know
what her'n up an sayed. Why mariah those are your darlins
little dresses Ive made for your baby Julia — from I was so
sorry I disturbed Julias her sleep. I do so many wrong things
when I have these head aches. Wal yes Ah says to her now
youse a very sick woman. But jus shouldn't carry on so
wid dat baby youse got to lab born, en bless youse
pretty heart, youse did'nt owe my black young un any dresses.
We ins didn't see her soon enough but thar stood a
strange woman in de door. De missy spoke right up. Nice
time for you to be coming Liz. Den this Liz spied the
spew on de carpet. She acted all upsot. Went over to de
missy and said — Mary baby why didn't you tell me. Even tho
Ive been swamped with work I must give that party, I would
(over)

CHAPTER TWO, SECOND DRAFT 177

④ have ~~come~~ dropped it all and come right over when Bobbie came. The missy say, well you know well, how afraid I am when it storms and that Mr. Lincoln is away. All you think about is prettying up ~~yourself~~ that big house and cook cook, ~~look for~~ parties. Well Mary ~~this~~ Liz says if you'd think less of serving up all the goods in the county (looking at the material strewn around) and learn more about cooking for your family, they'd be better off.

Mary huffed up right smart about that. Now Lib (when her war mad she called this Liz, Lib.) I'm just making a few little dress for this fine colored woman's child. This Lib up an says. Since when have you become so patronizing to colored folks. Well says the missy. She come to me when you wouldn't and you know Lib I wouldn't send for you or anyone else unless I needed them. Dat missy shur had a world of spunk ~~in~~ She says in de sweetest voice God ever put in a human bein. "This is my sister Elizabeth, ~~Mrs. Edwards~~ Mariah — Mrs. Henry Yance. She came to help us out Monday Lib. She is a good clean honest woman. Rite quick like Elizabeth spoke out. Well Mary you need some one and I hope you don't take any tantrums with this Mariah an run her off — I couldn't bear to hear dat sick woman talk anymore like that, so I says "Lib ~~herinlaw up like a sister~~ a sick, sick woman. I know, I know says Mrs. Edwards. But there isn't anything wrong with her that good common sense won't help some. Mother father and I have humored an spoiled her to death Because she demanded it an now Mr. Lincoln has to take the brunt of all our foolishness. He has to take it or get out — a great many times he gets out, so Mary can have her way. I let servants get out and stay out. I hope once in her life, she has common sense enough to keep a good servant. Dat war all sweet talk to me, but poor missy herin spilled over a bucket of tears crying her heart out, Lib sofened like poppies cotton balls and so shur as Gowd made little apples, she went over to the missy, kissed her wiped her tears with her silk handkerchiff, and cried a little hernself — Lawd a goodness I never onst seen such carrying ont. Blazing mad at one an tuther one minute an nest minute lovin and kissin like 2 turtle doves.

maybe dat's good raisin, For me an my Henry, a little bit
of fight to git to make up seemed powerful good. But two kin
folks ah jist caint see any common sense in it, my pappy
would hab gibben uns a lesson wid his harness strap what
or would be needin for kissn an makin up. He'd dasn't
nebber fuss & fume in wens home. Speck they'd
betta kiss and smooch den der wouldn't be no fumin roun'
But for ten years Ah seen such doins. Dat wid Mr. Abe
Bout time he gotten his tank ful of sich foolishness, he jist
up an walked off. Not dat Ah always could bide by dat
But dat man, war a man, ob God. He jist didn't like fumin
round enough to take his part. If der war, no need to kiss and make up.
Ah, hardly could hep myself, but it war soon over
an Mrs Edwards went home, saying she'd come every day or
send ninnian, dat war her husband.
     When Elizabeth left Mrs. Lincoln said - Elizabeth is very
dear to me and I love her very much, but she has always
tried to direct my life as she wants it. She would
resent it if I meddled into her affairs. Elizabeth has
been so kind through the years, that perhaps I should
look over her few faults. But I have both the Todd
and the Parker southern tempers which I was never
persueaded to try to control. Oh I've so many ways. And
again started to cry. Ah says to her, Missy Yous'e not evil
Yous'e a sick, sick woman, An yous, shouldn't be tiring you
self making dese dresses for my Julia, Is'e weening her
should have a spell back, but she war so puny, and de
chilen needed all de vitals we could get ah hands on, we
war so hard up. Milk sickness was going round and
colrah and ah's feared. Dese dresses is most to flub dub
for poor colored folks. Maybe you could let some you rich
folks have them. Right den an dere I made a horbal
mistake. Ah don't see why I caint leave well enough alone
an keep mah big black mouf clamped. For de missy raily
wan't as how to make up wid me because she'd filled Julia's
les an made her'n howl.
     She says, Oh mariah wont you use them. Maybe I can change
them some and they would be more like play dresses. They
are good strong material and colored that wont show soil
easily. I've so many more. But if you dont feel you want Julia
to wear little angel Eddie close I'll put them back in the chest
                                                            (over)

Der war a lot of stiches of love in das clothes and here
I haid put a lot more in to make up to Julia. So ah
says, why'n bless you good christian heart, ah sees
you had heaps of good sense bout dressing little girl baby
if'n you never had any of youns own. Ah jest plain
black nigger an habent got a heap of sense bott close
no how. Henry guining to hat to change Lisa mind 'bout
you, I clamped my han ober my mouth faster than
cat lightning had been. For shur nuff ah let de cat out of de
bag. But jest den in bounced Billie an Bobbie wid two
little stray baby kittens. Ah saw right den, if I didn't get dat
Billie o mine out of dat house all holler war gain to brake loose
in de Missys clean house. Hern hab it so clean it glistens like
only a wee litta around whar hern hab been stichen, and
de wet spot whar Miss Edwards hab clean up de floor.
  Robert said to Billie you can have the kitten or you can
give them to Phebe and Julia. Ma dont like cats. She say they
make her sick to look at. Now pa he bring all de cats and
dog or other animals in the circuit. One time he brought
us a white rat in one pocket an a turtle in the other—
He put candy in each pocket for them. But the rat ate a
hole in his pocket and was almost out when he got home
the turtle snapped his finger as he took it out of his pocket.
It's the only time I ever heard pa howl. But when he laughed after
he laughed bout as loud as his howl. Which put him in de mun
mins of a story it Parson was gain a toast to the Bealy
good things in life. He said, Parsons are preaching for them,
lawyers are pleading for them, doctors are prescribing for them,
authors are writing for them.— Soldiers are fighting for them.
— but only a few are enjoying them. May we never forget
that nice things us, even in our pleasures; but virtue consoles
us even in our pain. At which one of their congregation replies
may we never feel want, nor want Billie. He makes no
friends who never made a foe. So let the dirty bums sting. In
this case snaps. You see befriended a rat who
chewed up his coat pocket and a turtle that bit him after he
gave them candy. Bobbie shur nuff like de story by my wife Billie back of
I dat woman hab out gain turned back to de pretties angel
woman ah most ever seed. Ah dont know how she did it so quick
like But he took de boys careful like by de arms and sat them
on de floor an tole them to be if they be quite they could hab some
cakes with raisins, But take dat cat out side first— Billie cam
in screeming for cookies— but Bobbie war a gentman. Missy brot de cookies

Mr. Abe Cures Bobbie's Eye

Ah got ovah to da missy aroun six to do a 2 weeks wash. Dar war da fire ready ta light unda da boiler and da boiler filed with water. Ah went in the shed and da clothes war sorted. The tubs were on da bench, the lye soap and board. All ah had to do was wrench de clothes in cold clear water, while the boiler (biler) done got hot, for the hot suds to wash with.

Ah had walked over. Da spring weather war so beautiful. Da flowers war up an some blooming and as I found I was coutched as well as da missy (Afcone weened Julia in the nick of time) just knew ah'd better keep movin, to keep well for da next kid.

About seven as ah war hanging up the white clothes Bobbie rushed out of the house and done took for a neighbors whar a boy frien lived — Like da little gentman he war he called howdy do Aunt Mariah. Dat Aunt Mariah made me right smart happy.

Ah finished da colored ones. Emptied up brown, an taking down the first ones dried, when ah seed a red head gal leave. She war young. Maybe going to school. Hern name war Lauri.

Da missy had done tole me Bobbies eyes war still weak an a little oncertain yet after an opration by on his eye by a German doctor an Doctor Wallace, that she warnt sending Bobbie to school until fall. He war old enough, an smart enough. She had taught him to read an write an some numbers, oh yes an a little French. He didn't like da french, but just guess hern crammed it down him.

Well wen ah carried in da folded clothes ah saw Lauri had stroiten up a bit. Da missy heard me an called "Is dat you Mariah."

Ah axed her how war she. She says "I've been too busy Mariah to think of myself. I've made curtains for the entire house. Made clothes for Bobbie to start in school an clothes for the new baby that will be here a girl I'm sure it will be, for Mr. Lincoln and I would, both love to have a girl. Well ah says well ah hope mine'll be a boy.

at that da missy say, Why Mariah why didn't you tell me before. Wal ah says because ah didn't know ah was cautched, couldn't tell as how, as long as Julia war nursin. But since they are weened it showed up. Ah do hope its a boy, Billie praise the roof if ah notha girl shows up.

Eeelen da oldest he bats aroun, Geeess its jist his way of sayin, he wish she war a boy.

That makes me think mariah why didn't you bring Billie? I've fixed over the clothes he called sissy. You must bring him the next time maybe Bobbie will stay at home awhile if you will bring Billie I never know where he is or what hes doing when his father is away & thats most of the time.

I haven't heard a word from Mr Lincoln. I wouldn't blame him if he never wrote - Even if he never came home the way I cut up.

Wal now ah says - missy you dont just know how his kind should be nursed. Wal she say, "Doggyone" I tried every trick, and at the end of each trick, if it just doesn't work, I get discouraged and blow up. He just doesn't love me, and there's no other way to reach him.

Oh now, ah says, Back up missy, Dat man loves de whole worl. At that she had me stumped when she say, Ah dont want him to love me like he loves the whole world. I want him to love just me, as any man should his wife - Ah could think of only one thing to say after ah pondered an considered, Wal dat mistah Abe be a man of God an God is Love, as mah good preacher say.

Stein sent me home saying take care of yourself, mariah, you're the only one I have to depend upon. Come in two weeks and bring Billie -

Ah went home with a doun cass spirit - Everyone thought she war a bad woman, Stein war oula a badly mixed up woman. Ah woman who'n didn't unerstan her man or her man unerstan her'n.

Wal ah went back in two weeks, it war now June. Ah took mah Billie wid me. Mr Abe war that dis time an such a mr. Abe. He war po poor an holler eyed look as how he had nary a thing to eat all month. He had all ready for mah wash, an a heap of wirin cut - but ah swar ah know ah'n nerah seen the ah call out morin mr. Abe, He spied was Billie an doubelieve he thot it war Billie who say't morin mr. Abe. Hen perked up by littles. Billie's lak his manny nevvah could keep his fly trap shut. Calls "hey there Are you'n deaf. Mars. Bobbie?" Mr Abe say nary a thing but pointed up stairs. Billie knows nonk of dis "hard sign talk," so he took an old sock ball out of his pocket and socked it up on da house war mr. Abe had pointed. Dat shur woke him up some. Hen caitched da ball and throws it to Billie. Billie slammed it back an that got der acquaintance started. They kept moving by littles down closer to da barn. Ah figured mr. Abe waned to get out of mah way an far nough way so dat ball wouldn't strike da house 'gain. Day keep up dat play til I was near done my wash an it war a hard one. Mr. Abe had brot home a heep of dirty clothes. Smelled bad like he'd had a fevor an forgot to take them off when he went a bed.

Finely they got tuckered out thsowin an caitch'n mr. Abe & Billie sout down on da wood pile. Billie squirmed roun awhile, an finely went after the lice he coutched in dat black wool of his'n. Guess he done got dem stirred up playing what mr Abe called a fast game of hand ball. Dat man sure loved to play him ball.

Mr. Lincoln noticed Billie scratching, he said, "mariah what's Billie digging up there after?"

Mr. Abe, Ah aware if he coutched dem agin, playing wid dat bad set next us. Ah'll never know what to do with him Ah allies tell my younguns to stay way from them'n white trash!"

Mr. Lincoln caught Bill and cracked a big louse with his fingers. "Well he said, mariah I know the very fellow who can get rid of these in a hurry, if you'll let me take Bill to him. Aunt mariah consented.

Lincoln took Bill to his barbers and later brought back a shaved-headed bald boy. At first mariah didn't know her own son and said." Who dat ape? When she recognised us Bill, she said "Ah got so affered mad ah nearly left the Lincolumn's then an dare. Ah had no idea mr. Abe would done get hisn head shaved. Eet took a plum year grown hisn wool back, Da colored folks in dose day was proud of der wool, Ah war worried until it began to grow back, straighter but still wool

Well mariah say mr. Abe, I can't say I'm surprized that you love those kinds, after seeing my unruly black wig at least kinks stay where you put them.

Mariah raved again Ah's most about to gib him nother punishment, a little peach oil as you says. Mr Abe. But maybe hen had most enough. Lousy, an a bald pate fer gettin too thick wid dem white trash.

Well said mr. Abe, Ah's white trash, Now Ah says mr Abe Youse done 'bout 'nough awready without tellin me Ah's workin' fer white trash.

Lincoln laughed and laughed

Mariah said Ah war 'bout to pick up mah younguns and leave. But Mr. Lincoln stopped laughing an said

Well Mariah, if mother can stand me you should be able to and if my boy gits lice Ah'l have his head shaved.

But as for white trash, I was called white trash. My people were scoffed at and called white trash, and I must admit some of them were a little trashy. But if they'd all met a Mary Todd, to put up with them and love them. maybe they'd tried to match her, trying as I did.

Now Mariah, when you go home give those white trash neighbors a little kindness, if you cant love them, Wid your big, kind heart I believe you can make them over to be as fine as your own family are. Remember there is only one power. - love. for God is love.

At that he took from his long coat pocket a sack of licorice sticks and passed them around.

Mariah said, Oh Lawd and sure am shamed I cut up so Ah heard steps in time to push Billie sock cap down tight over his bald head- Mr. Abe, Billie and Ah all laughed. The missy got specious and said So you can find pleasure with something or someone outside your family. Dat dat talk took us all by sprize. Ah sobered up. Robert grabbed Billie an rushed fo da barn and Mr. Abe looked black.. Ah never saw such a down cast black look. As hen left wid the missy I heard him say. Now mother, don't get up set again I had to take Billie to the barber to get his wool cut for it was full of lice. Guess Aunt Mariah was ashamed of Billie's bald pate and pushed his cap down so tight it covered his eyes. That's why Billie stumbled and almost fell when Robert grabbed him and rushed away. Is there any harm in laughing at that?

Da missy raised the paregoric bottle and drank from it. Ah know dat bottle was a pleum gallon. Mr. Abe said mother, mother I wish you wouldn't. I suppose this means another day of stupor.. If you'd only try to control yourself for the child coming, if for no other reason.

Da missy says Little you care about me or the one we have. Leaving us month at a time without a word and when you do come with your filthy clothes and hideous appearance, expect me to appreciate your return and fawn over you. Well even the sight of you is repulsive. So get out get out I say

He got out and went to da barn whar da boys whar Ah heard Bobbie say Pa ah want mah head shaved lak Billie's. Not now says Mr Abe. Not now. But if you get lice. Off that beautiful hair comes. Am going to get lice then, Bobbie said. Well Robert if you do I might give you a little peach oil onto before the shave. Ah gee Pa, you never do what I want. You said you'd take me to the woods sometime, but you never have done it. I want to see the flowers and the giant trees life you said you have off. I want to climb one a those trees and do what you used to do when a boy.

I know for sure that's what's made you big and strong and good. I don't like to hear people say mean things about your rail splitting, as if it were mean.. Pa can't we go now, Can't we.

Ah guess that war to mech for Mr Abe. He took Bobbie by da hand, picked up the axe and started off. Ah finished carrying in da wash, straighens up a little aroun. Fixed some eats on table and went back home with Billee.

All da way back ah's war pondering what ah would say when my Henry saw Billies shaved head. Ah tole Billie then sturr mus kepe his cap on in house when we got home. But da firt thing he done did was to sling dat cap across da room. It war no time 'til Henry called come har Bill. When Bill come har my Henry grabbed him and afore ah could even think had dat boy across his knees. Henry were short from his belly to his knees. So all ah could do war to grab Henry by de feet and yank. Down slid Billee to de floor an made a dash for da door. Ah grabbed Billee by da collar. Ah heard da buttons snap, and Billee war out of that door like greased lightning.

Dat nigger man a mine war so mad hisn eyes popped out and his face swowl up as big as a red balloon. Red war that mad. He wood bruk out dat door an after Billie, but ah stood mad my back against that back door. An he knowd ah's taken my stand. Ah says now you big black ignorn coon, youn back right back to dat chair or ah'll dent your ole dum hai with dis poker. Now youins lisin to mah. Ah Bill cotched lice from dees poor white trash hen's been playing around wid. Mr. Abe took him up to hisn barber an had his head shaved. Ah war made to when Ah saw that fine crop of wool gone. But it air gone, so is da lice, an how you going to put dem back ah say. Not by scorching dat poor boys bottom. All my man could say was that long legged jack scare-crow. That ugly lantern jawed scare crow.

Ah waited till he done ran out of abusing Mr. Abe an said Billies had hisn punishment nough. Ah let on it war settled, an went bout getting the vitals on the store. Ah made Billie wash the dum offn his hands he got in mes. Abe's barn. Made him sew de buttons back he popped off. Sore I'd give him any sow belly an beans. That seemed to please my Henry. But he still growled once in awhile, but that tapered off when he flopped up in the warl. Once he says mothers Ise not wanting to be hepped up in the worl as you says. I want to live so I can hep up. If I could sot on a stare box in front of Hoffman's row and tell only wan of the common herd as youse call 'em one of my unpolished common stories that would lead that are boy to the Christ as I know him Id give all my chances to be president, as you so much wants.

Yas mr Abe would go to church with her sometime. I dont think he liked any the high flutin airs in that church. He wont says It wouldnt be any harder to get down on thar knees than to do all that bowing and scraping. And another time he says, I sometimes wonder if it a church or circus thas all dressed in so much trapping and finery and perform so.

He must have had occassion thro' court proceeding against some of the members as he once said much of that finery isnt paid for and ruther had better given their families more bread meat and milk.

He always wanted to be baltized. He promised his mother when a little boy way back in Indiana when he grew old enough to know the meaning, he would be baltized. The Presterahs didnt believe in bein dunked down unda watah. An the missy says Thats backwoodin'or. An mr. Abe's shamed her an the boys enough by his old fangled ways.

So he says to me (mariah) Do you think it has hepped to save you soul to be babsized? Yes I says mr. Abe I allahs made me knowd I done did ary thing Christ doue did He let John babsize him in the riner Jordan. He must thunk it was good. Yes mr Abe says It shows youse in earnest bout you soul. You want your sins washed as clean as watter can make youse body.

A few days after that he says to me. Mariah Ise goan to be babsized. Do you thank it would be a sin if Id be babsized an not let Mrs Lincolun know? Now Im not ashamed, but shed raise shed. and I dont think thats a good way to go to youse babsism. And Ise got too big a load now to tackle getting over that and still have the mind that was also in Christ Jesus. When I go to my babsism. Now mariah

The Missy Gets Confidential

Ah caint quit recommember ef it war de nex two weeks after Mr. Abe ant Billie hes off or not but somewhars near dat time, ah went. De doors war locked. No water out an no clothes in de shed. Ah was plum skeered, Ah thot de missy might had taken too much paregoric, an lee up der dead. Ah was poundin on de door an wringing mah hands an praying God to had mercy on thet are poor critter missy's soul, when Bobbie open up dat very same door ah war pounding on an said Boo Aunt Mariah. I jumped as high as da door knob. Ah almos fell in da door an ah shouted Glory Hel lulah Glory Hel lulah. Bobbie near split his fat little side laughing. Ah gave dat young tease a spank on his'n rump, an says Wars da missy, whats da fault wid her'n now? Nothings wrong Aunt Mariah. She had folks in after church yesterday. The preacher an$g$ his wife, Aunt Lizbeth and Uncle Vinnie, Uncle Wallace and Aunt Francie and some of the children. They ate dinner and supper. Played chess ang some other games in evening. Ma didn't get to bed until late, so she sleeping to make up this morning

Ma said "Go let Aunt Mariah in before she breaks the door down. The neighbors are going to tell I've been beating you and your father to death. Hurry Robert before I have another spell. She tries to scare me, but I'm used to ma's spells. So dont you'll Aunt Mariah git ~~scared at me~~ either used to them to, Pa says she ~~just~~ still just a little girl who has never grown up. But I wish she'd grow up ar I would. I expect if I was grown up I'd put her across my knees like your Henry does Billie —

Now, now I says to that Bobbie. Your mommy ~~air~~ a powaful sick woman. ~~She~~ needs care ~~the da~~ worst ~~of~~ way an love. Don't you neva neva say unkind things ~~about~~ her ar to her.

Aunt Mariah I don't dare say them to her, then he stopped right there on chew 'cause ah pointed my finger at him an sayed shew. Hen skipped out da door dew came back and said — Ma said there would be no washing; she did it Friday and ironed Saturday; But she wants you to clean the kitchen an get dinner — Said use up what you can of the left overs. I almost forgot Aunt Mariah.

I'll swar dat woman war the mostest ~~saving~~ on vitals, Only when ~~she~~ has company.

Ah had da kitchen scrubbed until it war white as sand Ah had to habe a hot fire to heat da water. Dar war stack of dishes. Ah stood of some old hemp sacks in me corner of da kitchen when ah washed da dishes —

Da floor war dried and da dinner of corn dodgers chicken cut in little bitay pieces and ~~cot ove~~ heat wid da left over sop. They call dat some ~~fig~~ name now like fry asee (frickasee) it war just warmed over chicken but da missy who smelled it an can down to eat, said Why Aunt Mariah with the left over vitals, desert an that fine smelling chicken gravy over corn dodgers, it really tastes better to me than our Sunday dinner.

And this drink Aunt Mariah, what can it be, its delicious. Wal I just tole da missy. Ah couldn't find any wine about for you. Da bottles laying around war all empty so ah just parched some corn rolled it down fine wid do rollin pin and then billed it in water. Ah an my man an chillun like it. Bobbie drank two cups full. He said Ma, can't we drink this every day. Maybe I'll get stout like Billie – She missy didn't answer. Ah could see eben if hern did like it. To hern it was black folks or poor white trash food.

Ah had put a tin cup full of wilted wild flowers in the center of da table. The missy spied them an said, I'm glad you didn't throw them away Aunt Mariah – Robert brought them home from the woods last Saturday when his father took him as he had promised so often to, sometime. Robert and Mr. Lincoln must have had a grand trip – neither one could stop talking about it. It brot back so many memories of Mr. Lincoln early life that he always seemed so reluctent to talk to me about, but which he revied in detail to Robert –

Robert on his own initiative gathered the flowers

for me. That is one way Robert is like me - He loves every little tiny blossom. Even weed flowers are beautiful and precious to him. So I'm making these last as long as I can. Its his first full bouquet to me. I'm glad he's like what is best in me, if only a little. *So like the Todds in body but* He's so like his father sensible an honest.

They brot back slippery elm, hea bread and robbed a tree of honey - Robert was honey from his chin down. You should have seen him when he and his father came home. It was a picture I'll never forget. Bobbie was so smeared and bed drabbled but so happy - I believe his father was the happiest I've ever seen him - That trip will bind them closely. Closer than anything else. They've found a common bound that lasts. I pray God that Mr. Lincoln an I could find a mutual tie. I think we've both tried. But our foundation to begin with was so warped and insecure. And our perspective have grown farther an farther apart -

He is the kindest father and husband in the world, and sometimes I think I am the meanest, most exacting and demanding : Ah didn't wan a say anything to much cause ah sees her'n wanted to talk something aet, but I *just* had to tell her what my pappy used to say. He war ignoran but *he'd dot* tole us so often if we could see us, can't you see your onery when we uns says yes, he says well no one eber quit dar oneriness until they can see it.

Well ahé tried so hard da missy says — Ah says ah believe if you'd humble yourself before da Lord, hed help you out of dis hell your in — now Ah don't think your bad, only to you self Just humble you self unto da Lord. No mariah I can't humble myself — Ah jest don't see ah says wha makes folks so gish durn proud. We's all flesh bone and blood an alls born without sense an all will die an den no sense. Ef youns proud of youns poppy money, Whar is et now? So ah specks you'd better settle yourself to Mr. Lincoln way, Yous' just betta try or you'll wind up always drinking that pisen paregoric.

Well mariah I believe youre serious and honest But if paregoric were poison the whole Todd family would have been dead years ago. Some never born. We were raised on it.

Well ah says its like da debil Et does its work slow an sneakin, Jus ya lisen to Mr. Abe an stop dat. Et are worin him most awful. Mr Ab are 'fraid while he are gone you'll kill your self or set you sef or set your sef crazy. Or may be give some to Marster Bobbie yous jus betta quit pendin on dat such like, and pend on God. Dat ole paregorie is da debil, an hes got you hooked.

Robert and Bill Go Fishing

Ah racked da Lincolumns' about same as afore, on time to start da wash at tween 6 & 7—

Ah unhitched maud. Ah cautched Billie spitten out a cood of bakka. Boxed hem good an Lord on da mouf. Hen let out a yelp dat brot. Mr. Abe.

Mr. Abe said, Bill, whats got yu this time a horse fly—no Mr. Abe, Ah boxed Billie fos chewn backa. now now Aunt Mariah. Bill surely had too much licorice candy in his mouth and spet part of it out. No Mr. Abe I see dat cood at young big toe, Ah hadn't notice hen war bare foot ontil them. Dot man hab da most awfules feet aw eba saw. Sides be'en 2 times as big as da auta be. Da hab bumps all oba. He saw us'n lookn

He said, When barefooted I feel more at home Aunt Mariah But what' we going to do about Bill chewing to-bacca that would be bad if he taught Robert that. You know Robert thinks the sun wouldn't rise if Bill weren't on earth Just den Billie heaved up. It war hens fiast chew ob backa. Mr. Abe laughed an laughed—Guess that ends it, he said, Aunt Mariah, He won't ever be afraid he'll teach that to Robert

Da missy hearn, da noises an coma terren', Nat a sight dat poor missy war. Hern hab been doin' da wash, an Mr. Abe war hangin out. Wal Ah swar Ah says. Hair Ah comes oba mid Billie, as you said an youn done need ma. Day missy say, Well Mariah I declare when I told you to come an the 4th of July I thought Monday was the 4th. When I found out yesterday that to-day was only July the first. (The preacher spoke about the celebration being on Thurday yesterday, in his sermon.) I felt sure you would come Thurday the washing isn't done, We've only started. Mr. Lincoln hab hung them to dry as best he could. Yu'd had a seed dose close Et war dd moest mixed up mess, you'd eba seed. De missy wink'd Et an hook'd hern's haid pro in time, so as ah kep mah big mouth shut. Mr. Abe warn't fool, Hen went'd way grinnin.

Ah took mah slat bonnate off'n, Rolled up mah sleevee an had da white ones done in short orda. Ah straitn out dose on da line, what Mr. Abe had hung, Da would'n hab dried in a week. Da missy say Ill go in and clean the house. Then clean myself as Elizabeth is coming to go with me to the picture gallery.

What shall I do about Robert — He was going with us too — When You get through mariah, will you straighten the kitchen and fix our dinners. We have left overs again And do make Corn coffee. Robert has never got thro talking about it. Has Mr Lincoln in the notion for some corn coffee too Said he never had any other drink but it and water when in his father's home. Id burn the corn if I tried to parch it —

Rev. Smith and wife come home with us after the services yesterday. The hired girl so she would get to-day off helped prepare dinner and serve, But after dinner took off with her gentleman friend — If it wasn't for being alone at nights Id dismiss her. Unless I watch every thing She does I have it to do over: I could get Howard Powell — Roberts friend — If we needed help in the night he could go with Robert to get whoever we might need, You couldn't awaken if a cyclone struck — But still she's always here, at least during part of the evening and night, while Howard doesn't always come, His folks are talking now of moving — Well molly you think of everything say Mr Abe. Well theirs one thing I haven't mentioned What made Billie sick out at the barn. Ole aught ta a hab mah big mouth smash'd like Ah smash'd Billie — Ah tole de missy bout Bill chawin backa An dat whal nary heaved Jonah up any worsta. Da missy an Mr Abe cut loose da mos awfa laughs Ah'd eva heard bout dat house. Herin choked laughin an hen's as shure as ah's sitten har on dis door step screamed, while her beat herin on da back to hep her'n stop chokin. Ah thut shur Mr Abe wood break her'n back or her'n wood die choken. Ah raut day war both goin plum crazy, Kase ah couldn see nothing ta laugh 'bout, When day stop laughn ah said Glory Hal Nelluh Praise da God youns hain daid. Dad started dem two up gain. Da mus hab haid sompin powful good for ah come ta make dem so happy. Maybe affa all her'n tole me, She sided dat what ah tole her was gospel truf. Her'n shud get happy an dat wood drive da haid aches 'way."

mr. Abe picks up his'n self an moseies to da front hall prop hen's sef gan a chair bak wid a pilla pulls up his knees, an sittles down a read. Onst in while ah hear a laugh from hen. must hab been notha Artemus he war readin. Da missy got dress an sot down ta sew what Akin waits fa Lisbeth. Ah went ta da barn for ta hitch maud and dar war dat blessed masta Bobbie tach'n mah Billie schooln. Whan we reach home Billie war as proud as a strutin cock. He knew lettas an numbers. How masta Bobbie eva got hen to sot long nough, ah be bless'd if ah ever knowd. mah Henry war proud as da Lucifa as da good book say.

Fore win left mr. Abe comb out an say — Mariah has Mrs Lincoln paid you for these weeks you've worked. Ah says Yes sah Mr. Abe, da Missy has morin pay me. You cain see fa youns sef, Billies nice pantaloons an shirt and she dress mah Julia like hen belong to Pharoah da King. Mariah that isn't pay, that's a gift. An do ya kno wat dat mistah Abe done. Hen took a big ten dolla out ob hen's pants pockat an gib hen et to me. mah eyes watah an spiled ober. Ah war dat boaf sad an happy. Ah nebba hab dat much mona all at onst in mah hole lafe. Ef he hab let me ah'd got down on mah knees an washed dose dirta feet ob hen's wid mah wool. Lake da woman Mara Mg wash Jesus feet.

mistah Abe say I'm leaving mariah for Chicago, mariah, on the Fourth. I have business there. Will attend attend the U. S. District Court meeting. I believe Mrs. Lincoln will be looking for you and Bill then.

Wal we'd hardla got thro eatin ah grub until Billie began ta beg mah maw ta take go fishn. Henry war kinda tuckered from tendew da younguns whil ah and Billie war gone so hen's said no. No ment no whan Henry said it. But he war so all fired proud ob Billie larn lettas an numbers hen's said, maybe to-marrow. Wal Billie said, Dat's jackla wen ah waned to go — To-mor to da ribba. Henry said — Ef youns tink ah bout to walk 6 miles ta hold a string in da wata youns plain dumb. Wal ah spoke up an say wal ef youns don't you's plumb lazy. You shur can do dat much fa youns boy whats quin to get edicated. Billie brows dat back cap an sot down an made

all da lettas an numbas mastah Bobbie had tell'n
hime how. Onst ken said, marrow et eight.

Ah fixed dem a pocket of corn bread an sow meat
my Henry made fish poles and pin hooks for our Billie
an dug some squirma fish'n worms. Ah war glad
day war gone. Henry war aw'ways in mah way
when ah war work'n ta home. Hit'ood be da mos
agervatin man when ah wanted to clean. An Billie
war allas fightn wid da girls, or ah war fear'd whar
he war, ef out of mah sight—

Da come home as da sun war bout to go down, and
does you'n kno hab a string of fish. Dar war 8 or 10
nice fat fish. Da war tired out. But sot rite down
an cleaned dem fish
lak da store fish, not a gut lef in any ob dem.

Ah made a pile ob griddle cakes an fried some ob
does fish right way. Day war so hungry an da fish war
so good we'n lak to busted eatin dem.

Den Billie up an say Ah bet Mr. Abe an his Bob
wish da had some of da fish day gibben to us'n — mah
Henry looked down dat flat nose of his'n — Ah say now
Billie what you been up to. How's come Mr. Abe an Bobbie
war fish'n dar wid you? No wonda you'ns know'd jis
when to start dis mornin — Ah says, Ole man are you gwin
to sat dar lak a bump an a notty log an let him's lead
us'n an da Lincolumns aroun by dg nose. Ah Bet
my best shimmy Mr. Abe saw through Billie's schemes, if
a knot haid lak you couldn. Seems you'n an dat
scare crow, as you'n calls Mr. Abe, musta made up.
Al da good book say, a little chile shall lead them.
Wal, mah Henry say. Ef you'ns stop dat dam preachin, dat
ah get so fernal tired of hearn, ahll let you'n know a
blind man could a saw what does two scamps put da
hooks to us, afore we put da hooks to da fish.

Just whn we'ns got to da ribber. Billie waned to
climb a tree. Ah let hems. Him's clum clean to da top
an look 'roun an roun. Den come down slow all
tuckered. Hen his got his's wind, about five or ten minute
hen put both two fingers in hins mouf an whistled sick a
god awful loud blow. bout scared me stiff. Ah said
Billie, if you'ns dare do dat gin ahll break does fingers oh
you'ns plum off, so you'n caint scare hell out a me gin.
But jis den not so far off was a whistle not so

loud as Billie had blast out. At dat ah knew if et warint a bird, anyxing somethin war up. Ah say "Billie, you'n blow you!" Billie right way blow, an fore dat blow got 2 feet way, you'n nevah heard such a ear splitin noise in you born day. Dat Mr. Abe knew as well as ah what war up an he had answer. Den wen met wen shook hans and laughed. Mr Abe didn't say one word, an ah thot, if he'n can keep his fly trap shut, so can I. We went right down to dat Sangamon an started fishin'. Dar warint any talk. Mr. Abe an his Bobbie got da first fish, an kep gettin more'n wen's. But day sure had a good long fish pole an some cooked bait wid meat in an sweet-oil. Mr. Abe say he hab some portant work, an must go. He wish us luck, an took Bobbie by da han. Bobbie want a stay, but Mr. Abe say, lets give Mr. Vance an Bill (just like ah wer a gentman) da fish. Mr. Abe sure taught me, ah lesson. He'n didn't fus at Bobbie or whip her'n, or scare da fish by not to spoil da day for wen, or scare da fish by rantin an razen. Ah took a nap before wen's come my.

Den mah Henry say "Wal, Ole woman, what you'n goin do 'bout it? De you'n's ole man got brains or hain't he Ah say, "wal de hes thing Mr. Abe taught you is, as he say "Ah still tongue make a wise head. Hal muh Henry say, my Henry's lak an ole womans I hab to have last word. He say "Spose you take some dat larnin' too!"

When Mr Abe comes home from Chicago, hims meets a gets right out on da circuit. Da missy sends Bobbie ober fa meus to come quick. Ah jus couldn go. Mah Henry war out wid da mule. Billie war wid him, an ah war dang head ober heels den at home. Ah hates it ka worse way on count oh Mastah Bobbie. Ah severe dat boy look bout as glum as his pa done did da mose of da time. Hims need da work da worse kind. Times war bad an winta war comen on ta prepare fa. Da fruit weis hab war mosely wild fruit. Mah maw had clean out some attics an lightning cored an brot home a heap of plunda, 'mong it war a pile of lightning jars. Dey war top heavy wid big gobs of glass at da top, but ah cleaned dem up. Mose of dem held plum a haf gallon. Ah canned fruit an some vegabls out ob our garden. Tied on dem pieces of unbleeched muslin, and washed. Den cover ober wid wax ta seal all oh da air out. Den, ah fill da crocks wid cabage kraut an made some cida vingar an cida. Ah figured wid da fish mah Henry an Billie would catch. Da possum, wild turkey, hare, an wild hog we could live. All we need buy war meal, a few duds. We didn't need much duds, cause da missy hab gibben uns stacks of closes. Besides close Henry brot home from attics. Mr Abe hab helped Henry by givin hims a good name to any one dat need work done. Does war sure hard time. Dr war a few ah still work for fore ah went to da Lincolums. Ah couldn quit da Lincolums fust. Den ah didn like da slack dey gave mens on da fourth. Ah lak ta fagive even ta 7 times 70, but, da missy would pile da hurts up ta 70 times 70. Bout 2 clock dat same aftanoon – poor litta Bobbie comes back. Oh Aunt Mariah, hens say, wont you come. Ma needs you so much. She is giving a party – Louie got out of patience and left. Aunt Lisbeth can't come until time for the party. She hab her hands full in her own home. Ma has sent for a dozen almost who say, I wouldn't work for her if she gave me a million. She's too mean or bossy. Let her go down to Kentucky an get a niger she can flog. Wont you come Aunt Mariah? Mah heart war plum broke for dat litta tike, but ah jus couldn go.

After hard work ah sent mah oldest gal Ellen, tho a need her ta run errons an tend Julia – Ellen shur didn want a go –

Ellen war a pretty light colored gal, an whoa slick up war fit ta be a queen's maid. Hern hab spunk an pride. Ah tried ta teach mah chilluns it war a black sin ta be proud. Ah sometimes wonda if some white masta's blood didn run in my chilluns. It mussta been on mah side cause mah Henry war black wid a flat spread nose. An hern wool war so matted ah couldn a comb it out wid Mr. Abe's comb hen use on Buck's tail an mane.

Ellen didn come back 'til war getting dark. Hern still didn lack da missy. Say da missy sher war a slave driva – But rite dare ah tole hern, ah speck fore shen died shen hab to do lot a hard work. Toubla war ah nevva put much on mah chilluns shoulders to carry. Ah'd nevva been a slave, an my pappy an mammy let us putta an play. Weuns were puttan an playn an da Ohio when dat white men drag mommy an pappy chilleen off in dare boat. Ah had a easy chile life. When ah tole Mr. Abe, hern say Mariah yoe had an easier life than I and perhaps were far better cared for than I. Even to-day there are many more colored folks, who have a happier and more care free life, are more learned that a great many white people. Including many slaveholders.

Mariah you can thank God you wasn't a slave, but you can thank God you had kind Christian parents. I shall ever endeavor to give my children all I can, both of this worlds goods and happiness. I'll feel then, that in their later life, with a foundation of love, they can more easily cope with the vicisitude of life.

Ellen say when hern fust went a work fa da missy, da missy put hern ta wipen dishes – Wa fust thing hern did war ta drop a sassa of fine china dat da missy nevva use for common. Hern grab hern bonnet an war bout to run. Da missy say "Ellen that was only an accident. You are just nervous. You didn't do it on purpose. So come right back an finish these dishes. so Ellen stayed, but skird fa feah shen would break more ob dose thin, possied dishes trim in gold. Da missy hab some heavy ones with three pictures on dem, dat hern gave ta men lata at. Ellen dere hab to polish silva. Some war heavy. Too heavy for Ellen, who war not yet seven. Den hern hep lay da table an dis dustin up stairs an down. At las hern come home currying a big basket with something of all da fine salads jelly cakes fruits an a big ham bone for men to cook. Lots of good meat on it yet. Ah knew mah Ellen war tirda dan hern ever been in hern life. Ah say right dare an den ah'd never sen hern agin. Ah go fust ef it kill men.

Several girls worked for da missy fore little Willie war born. Ah declar ef Ah had to depend on some un to do mah work ah wouldn be so fin-a-ky. Ah couldn get mah Ellen to go back even had ah waned hern to. Herin war plum scared of da missy. Willie war born in December, fust part. An da missy warnt so well for nigh a month. Dr Wallace dat war herin broth-a in law, waned her to be quiet. Herin wan-ed to get out an go to da parties goin on, but hen put hisn foot down. Ah don-no know of any one dat could make herin behave but Dr. Wallace. She even named da baby William Wallace for him.

My Billie thot da William was for hein but I stole him to come off hisn high horse an dat hen war gettin too big for hisn breeches. Dat da missy wouldn't name one of her precious litta ones afta a black coon - no sir ee. Even of day done did like him a heep.

At Christmas har come dat blessed Bobbie with present for all ob us, a lot of close. Da dresses fo me war to hih flutin. Some of herin. When da missy got up, hein couldn wear dem wid a baby out of hern. Henry got shirts an bandanas an Ellen a right pretty hood. New toys for da rest da kids. Ah forgit hein sint 2 silva dollas

Bobbie stay ah long time. Hen war shure larnen at Me-Cislaboos school. Hen sot right down at our kitchen table an learned Billie an Ellen what hen had larned. Mah Ellen larned fasta than mah Billie. But Billie put lettas to gither an made words. Bobbie come back afta dad ever few days. Mah youngens learned to read an count. Mah Henry neva catched on, but der an den is wen I got mah larnen

Ever time Bobbie come hen brot fittals an chesnuts an taffy I took da dishes an pans back afta Christmas. Ah wan ed to see dat blessed little baby William Wallace. Day allas call him Willie. Ah neva knew da little angel Eddie. But da say dat Willie war da spitin image of him. I learked why da hat send

Bobbie ober so offen. Day wanted to git him out ob da house so he wouldn' disturb da baby or da missy. Wal ah waned to tell dem day war maken a mistake, but her'n warn't fit to talk to. Cause her mind were set

She run dat poor little Bobbie out eber time he comes neah. He'n tip toed aroun like a little mouse.

Dat missy tole me her'n got coatched while visiting in Kentucky, an when she come home after Mr. Abe had about a month afore. Dr. Wallace said she war so unstrunc lak she haf go to bed. Ah tink dat war about time ah furst wen to da Lincolnmns to work. Day Mr. Abe had been to Lexington, but da missy sayed her'n had stayed longer, an was near worn out.

Wal I put da fan an other things Bobbie had brot our'n presents in away whar da belonged. Ah wash baby Willie for da missy. Straighten around for her'n. Dat gal day now had war not so bad, thet hab her hans ful trying to please da missy. Ah didn't stay only a speck dase. He'n tole me af ah felt able ah could come on regular wash day, for dar would be a little wash she wouldn' trust to day maed. Ah didn' take Billie next time, an ah didn' see da missy or Bobbie 'bout. He fire an all war ready. When she war done an went in der war no dishes or kitchen to clean but Bobbie cotched up with med fore ah retched da barn an said ma wanted me. Ah didn' much wana see her'n. Ah waned to get home. Some way ah didn' feel so good twards dat woman. Ah pray if da good God to take dat awful sin of hate out ob mah heart, but her'n hadn' done cleand mah heart yet, eben wid all da Christmas Bobbie brot.

Ah when up stars to war her'n war. Her'n say, "Mariah I owe you an apology, I knoo I have hurt you deeply, for what I said to you on the fourth of July. I'm deeply sorry for this injustice to you and Billie, an I sense you haven't gotten oer it. Can't you find it in your heart to forgive me?"

Ah wilted plum down lake da little snow man Bobbie hab made.

Dat winta war long, but pass quick lak, it seem. Henry hab
lot a haulen fo stove wood. He-n haul da Lincolnmn 'bout
8 or 10 cords. Da poles Mr. Abe chopped hem self, People nuvva
forgot Mr. Abe war ah wood-choppa. Ah allas wonda wat war
so strange lak 'bout dat. But Bobbie came home one day in da
spring, complainin dat da boys war now makon fun of he-is
pa 'cause he-n war a wood-choppa. Eet use ta be Bobbie's
iyes day made fun of now et his pa wood-choppa. Da missy say
da Estabrook (Estabrooks) school shoul' have better control over their pupils
She tolt Bobbie to tell them his father had had 8 years in the
state legislature, was in congress of the U.S. at Washington for one
term, was a successful lawyer, And someday would be
prehident of the U.S. and if wood-chopping started all that
maybe some of their fathers should go to the woods to see if it
wouldn't make something out of them. Tell you that war
mad. But dat didn stop Bobbie's hurt feelings. He'n jus nevva
got so up things 'bout his pa and ma to him. He-n
hab such a tenda heart, au would nuvva say tings tit for tat
to dem, who-n tormenta he-n. Nevva da worl ovva could you'n
fine a fina man den Bobbie turn out to be. He'n war-a
stuck up. He-n came to mah house when ever in Danville, au he-n
ate corn pone at mah table. Onct he-n brot he'n little girl Mary
Todd Lincolnmn as hem war going ta see his mekker who war a
very sick woman, at aunt Lizbeth in Springfield dat war afta
Mr. Abe was sasinata. He brot me little Abraham picker. It war
that picker book you-n bot ob me-n. He-n cried so
'bout his ma.

    After day tease Bobbie 'bout his pa being a wood-choppa he-is
pa came home, took da poor little hurt boy by da han au say
Son. Im not ashamed of any honest labor I ever did, or am I ashamed
Im a son of a common illiterate, laboring father. They have all been
stepping stones to a better life. Yes son I split rails. Though no
rail is ever going to stop me. So let them rail on. Their railing
only spurs me on, as most all pioneers have been spurred on and have
acheived. Some others just have become honest men,
men with honest thoughts and deeds, that is producing a
progressing America. So son push all that teasing those youngster
are up in the back of your mind, Just feel sorry for them, that they
use this precious time, the power to think, so foolishly. They
are the loosers not you Robert, I can't wish harm for them Robert.
So dont you, But the bread that is cast on the waters comes back. It
may reap the humiliation Someday they are trying to afflect you with.
They may then think. But son never let anyone know you they are
master oder you. If they have started you to worrying they are master

over you in a wrong way and are not good to listen too. I want your child hood and infact your life to be a happy one also. But without a happy child hood. You have a poor foundation for a happy out lok in life, So do like the engineer on the last train I road on to Chicago did. A big hog and a little litter of pig war on the track. He stopped the train, dismounted, and by throwing some food from his lunch pail off the track, in front to the hog, suceeded in getting the hog an most of the little pig off the track. The little straglers he picked up with a little help from the passengers, and quickly hollered all aboard. We scrambled back in. The bell rang and the whistle blew and we were on our way again — Not one of those lot of swine could think of us as anything but friends —

It might be a good idea to shame them, or make friends of them by getting them off the track of ill manners, by helping each one in some way — never say rude things to them, and put yourself on their level. It'll pay off son. You try it.

Pa I just cant see where the engineer getting the hog and the pig off the track has anything to do with what the boys say to me about you. If Id sell them hogs an pigs that would be rude, wouldn't it? Mr. Abe laughed. Son I ment to emphasize the fact that the engineer, didn't rudely plow those swine off the track with the engine cow-catchers. If he had plowed into them he may have derailed the train, thus injuring the travelers on board the train. And otherwise costing a large amount to have the train repaired — By saving the lives of the swine, which he no doubt would have killed, had he plowed into them, the loss would have been quite a little to the farmers who owned them. You see son, tho it delayes the train a little, the engineers gentle thots, level head and kindness paid off. So will it pay you Robert to deal with them and all difficulties by careful thought and kindness. If it cant be done that way, these boys are not worth the effort, so steer clear of them as much as you can. At least if they see it isn't bothering you, they will cease. That has been my experience, most of the time. In other words if you cant cure, you can learn to endure.

You knows wat, Ah belives what Mr. Abe preached into Bobbie head helped a heap, cause right away Bobbie had some boy friens he nevva had afore. He was more cheaful an happy for a spell. Ah wunda wich 'vice he done took. Dat of his pa or his ma. Ah allus that it war good dat dey didn' gin der 'vice, fore each other. Day war bof of dem so diferent. Coud hab end in a rumpus, tween dem.

Et war Esta vacation fo Bobbie, an Mistah Abe war goin out on da circuit. He—n even in, pick little Willie out hom crib in da room off da parlor. Da missy had made a nursey dare. Da still hab ah ole fashien crib. Look lak ah hollow out log, cut wid a hood at da haid an ah set de roskas on da bottom. Da missy hab it all flub-dubed up. Dat Willie war such lak ah pitcha. He—n war dress lak ah dress mah girl babies—maybe da missy wan—it ah girl so bad war why her—n dress it dat way. Her—n dress Bobbie wid flub-dub an ruffles—til Bobbie fo suct got he—ns dauba up—

Mr. Abe walk roun' bout da house carten Willie on his shoulda, as young as he—n was. He kissed Willie an fo da fust time since ah know dem kisses da missy. Bobbie walk to da barn wid him—til he—n hitch Buck. He—n come runnin back fo his—n pa stove pipe hat. He—n carried it to his—n pa, wid da top down so to not spill out Mr. Abe's papas. Dat da only time ah evva did know ob he—n leaven his—n hat. Must ah hab ah heaps ob someting on his—n mind to forgit dat hat, hen didn't act natural.

Da missy war so happy dat morn—n. Ah tink dat blessed Willie war ah blessen. Ah wen ebba two week an war nothan new. Ah did'n heff at parties, cause her—n hab ah Irish maid 'gin. An her—n hab partas all da time. Et shud hab been hard fo her—n. Da missy had eash ah time, had to be en bed after dat blessed Willie Wallice war born, but her—n hab party on her—n brain, an ah knew would be ob no 'count to tell her—n it war not so good fo her—n. Once da missy say "at least my guest won't have to wade through cow an hog track to git to my parties."

Ah thot she should go slow cause she ah hearin Mr. Abe say "et business side of the "Alton & Sangamon Railroad" is slow. He now have this little account wid the Jacks Brung bank but et won't permit any large withdrawals. With a new baby and all expenses relative to his birth its 'made a syable hole in our checking accounts. Please don't dissipate our deposits drawing interest. Try to use some judgement and spend more time at your home." Her—n did'n say ah word, but he—n hardly got way wid Buck til her—n begin to plan fo parties. Mr. Abe did—n come back fo eight or nine weeks. Her—n say she—n would hab to let Irish pay go. Den he—n went to Mr. Abe's office to get Mr. Abe's share of what Mr. Herndon (dat man she hates) hab save fo he—n. Her—n used all dat, den made a big in the party, fo folks who—n say all sort of mean tings bout her—n. Becka as one who—n she always included in her—n "ciety," she mea. She entertains more fine than any ob us who could far better afford sach. An we'n done git a fidla down fo her—n.

When Mr. Abe comp home, her—n war delighted wid da $200 he—n put in her—n lap, but not with he—n. She still amad cause her—n ran out ob money 'cause he stay so long away (People war sayn tings bout dat) an cause she had to go to his—n dirty office an talk to dat Billie Herndon—

4 Afta dat tings seem ta cool down fa 'while. Hen Mr Abe
lift ah thot eber ting war all right 'tween dem.

Hin hardla got way wid Buck 'til her-n gin da flau-n fa
partas. Her-n say ta me-n, "Mariah I just must get out some
from now on, and must make more friends, at least I
must return to my place in society. I've been iselated
too long already. People will forget there is a Lincoln
family in Springfield. The Todd family have always enjoyed
social distinstion and I'm determined the Lincoln family will
not lag behind."

Wal dat missy hab one parta afta anotha. Her'n eben took
a parta ta ah show, an den brot dem home an feed em.
Mr. Abe didn comb home fa eight or nine weeks, wid out
ah word from he-n. Hir'n hab use up da check 'count,
an hab bills run et da grocra, da goods stoas an ebben
say her-n would hab ta let mah Joy go 'til Mr. Abe
comb back.

At last her'n hab ta go ta Mr. Abe's offis ta get Mr. Abe's
share ob wat Mistah Herdon (dat man wat she-n hate) hab
save fa he-n. Her'n would hab use all dat, but Mr. Abe
comb back da nex day. Jus tink use all dat air money
on partas for folks, who-n say all sort ob mean tings bout her.
Sech as one who-n her-n allus include in her'n 'ciety, tole
me-n. She-n entatains more fine dan any ob us-n, ohs could
far betta ford sech. An we'n done gib ah fldlas dam fa her-n.

When Mr. Abe comb home, Her'n war dalighta wid da $200.00 he'n
put in her-n lap, but not wid he-n. She-r'n would-n let he-n
kiss eben her'n foot ef he'n hab wan-a to. Her'n war mad 'cause
he'n stay away so long. I'm arta cause her'n hab ta go ta dat
Billie (Herndon) fa money. Dat filtha man an filtha office
wat kin ah clients would go ah sech ah place. Yet you, her'n say,
would have your wife go to such a place. Would make it
necessary by deliberately staying away from your family
all this time, Robert wonders why you stay away. And
people are gossiping because othe laroyers-n cum come
home. Yet you stay away after all I've endured this last year
of grief and sickness."

"Well Molly, Mr. Abe say, I'm sorry if you ran short of
money. I thought our checking account was sufficient.
I'm truly sorry you had to bother Billie Herndon." At dat
she-n of fairly tore da roof off. She'x and at he-n wid
a butcha knife. Ah got out ob hat house quick, but Mr.
Abe grab her hen an took da knife 'way. Dat war da wors
the cat spell ah eber saw. He-n den sat her-n down in
ah chair. He said "Molly did you run any bills."

s. Her'n lie an say "No". Well he-n say, maybe the money
did run short. I don't feel too surprised now.. I want you
and the, boys to have all the comforts of life. And since
your indisposition for a year, besides your change of
figure, you did need clothes? Dat man git her-n
eber chance to say how she-n had spent so much money.
Her-n onla look black a an black a - But her-n
held outa that air mona her'n got from Mr. Abe's share
at da office an da $200°°. dat man brat home.
Finela he-n left da house. But warn't gone long-
you-n could tell he'n war dread ful distarb. He-n
wen right back in da back room off da parlor, whar da
missy war. Wen he-n got mad he-n talk squeeka an at
times lak he-n war choaked. He say, "Mary little did I
think that my wife is both a liar and a cheat. I can
put up with your tantrum, and that incessant false
front you put on for public agrandizement, but never
can I tolerate a deliberate liar and a cheat. You said you
had run no bills. There are accounts you have run
every place you can, but that is not the worst at the
drug store you took out bottles of perfume opened them
used part of the perfume and then returned, saying
they were poor quality. It's common talks among the
hundreds you entertained while I was gone about this
one act, besides your extravagance. I want that money
molly to go down and settle up - It may not be enough
but I'll make it stretch as far as I can. She threw the
money at him and said, Here you are and your pinch pennys
Get out. I wish I had never laid eyes on you you homely
uncouth brute. I wish I had married in my circle. I wish
I had married Mr. Douglas. Well said, Mr Abe I wish you had
to. But there is only one reason you didn't he was smart
enough an learnt soon enough what has taken me ten
years to learn. You are both a cheat and a liar. Ah didn't
proof of all he-n said. Ah realla felt sorry for da missy fa onct
Ah still believe her-n love him. Et war onla ah mad cat fit
an nothia tantrum. Wen her-n call him names. But her-n
wound up wid da las word. I have grand-mother Parker an
my fathers estate I can draw on. And when they are settled
I'll penny pinch with you no more but will take my sons
and get out! Ah really don't think he heard an onla fa
Robert an Willie Ah dont tink he-n would care. He-n left
da house an wen ta da barn. Dare Robbie wer play'n wid
a bunch ah his-n new friens. Da had ah theta wid boxes fu
seats an war from da house fa stage curtain.

6. Robbie jumpt up an down wen he-n see his-n pa. "Oh pa" he-n say." the told dees boys you-n would take us to the woods and show us how to chop a tree down." Den boys all gatha roun an say. Will you Mr. Lincoln? Bob said you took him once and he climbt trees too. Then he went fishing with you too". Ah wonda if he-n tole dem 'bout mah Billie an mah Henry go an fish-n too? Ah speck he-n did. Robbie war not proud! He nerra mis treat Billie, cause day call him niger lova.

Well, Mr Abe say, Now's as good at time as any to take you boys to the woods. You boys run home and tell your mothers where I'm taking you if they have no objections and Robert you go in an tell your mother.

But God ah mighta. Dey nerra wen to dat wood. Robbie came ah runna ta me an say, "Mas laying on the bed with her head hanging over to the floor, and baby Willie looks jist awful. Ah push he-n out da door an say, "Get you pa quick. Mr Abe mus-a take onla two steps ta da house an tore he-n shirt to get in to war dat missy war. He-n had taken ah big swig ob par-a-goric an den let Willie nurse. Mr. Abe shook her-n an shook her-n but her-n did-n budge. Then he-n pick up baby Willie who-n mite hab jis hab a natura sleep. But Mr. Abe that maybe her-n hab gib him some par a goric to. He-n rush Bobbie off to get Aunt Lisbeth an Uncle Wallace. Tole Bobbie ta not tell any one but dose two.

Dr. Wallace camb in three shakes, as did Aunt Lisbeth. Dr. Wallace knew at once what ta do. He had hab some of da same in he-ns own home. He-n tole Lisbeth ta make some black coffee. Dar war-nt ah form ting in dat house Da coffee an eberting hab been gobled up by her partas. Mr. Abe hurries ta da people who-n wrote da dose. Ah missy Fransis. An hersgave me Abe ah pot ah coll coffee wat we put on da stove an got et hot. Dr. Wallace tasta et. made et weak and gabe ah litta at time wid ah spoon to Willie. Dr Wallace say Ah hate ta gib dis ncfa stuff ta ah baby so young, but its 'bout all ah can do until he-n wakes up an ah see he-n had no paragoric. Mr Abe had shoo Bobbie out afore Dr. Wallace came, so he-n would-n hear Said fo he-n to tell da boys he-ns ma war sick an tha ah go 'notha time.

Dr Wallace say, The child could n't have nursed that from mary. It has been too short a time for it to take affect. She has given him a little perhaps. But I wish she wouldnt.

7. It has been such a fine healthy child. But Mary has been under a heavy mental strain to have done this. He gave her some black thick looking medicine. Then had Mr Lincoln to take one arm and he took the other and walked her. Her head lolled from one side to the other. Mariah said — Her'n was afsleum awful sight, finely she became very sick and up came medicine and paragoric —

Lisbeth began poor baby. Poor baby, you were awful sick. Now you'll be all right." But she wasn't alright nor was Willie for a number of days. Dr Wallace watched them both carefully.

'All dis' cause Mr, Abe cautchher-n in a fie —

Ah nevva did see sech ah fernal mess as dose Linerlumas could git dem self in! Ah war gittin out of dat house as fast as ah cud. Ah make up mah mind ah nevva complane 'bout me or mah folks gin. Ah war on mah way to hitch Maud an git for home, when de Blessed Bobbie comeb terren up from da barn, he say, Aunt Mariah bring da meat cleava an come to da barn quick — He got cauched in da trapeze tryn ta show us'n how te skin da cat. My Aunt Mariah hurry! Ah could'y move ah jist hab ta stan thar still, an held mah sides. Ah 'bout busted laughn, Bobbie rush in get da meat cleava an hust out gin — He'n grab mah han an say, run Aunt Mariah run quick — When ah got aut dar, dare war Mr Abe hang n ba da feet an had all tangla up in da trapshun him hab fix for da boys. They'n hab comb bac te get to da wood but Mr Abe war gittin dem settle 'bout not gavin dat day to da wood. He-n war wan an dem ta sta out da house to. He-n war laughn at da top ob his voice — Ah war split in mah sides, an da boys all but Bobbie yellon an jumpin roun lack wild injuins! Mr Abe got ah little settle an say'n Mariah du ah mighty uncomforable. Ah gana hold on much longer. He-n war high up. He-n say Aunt Mariah jist shop dat rope nex to da plank it ah tied on an let me drop — Ah swor ah was so weak fa laughn ah could hardla raise dat meat cleava to chop. But wen ah gib et a soun whack, down Mr Abe fell. Ah thot he-n would ah break he-n back or neck, but do you know he-n landa on hisfeet, lack de cats he-n love.

 Af for home an Mr Abe put for da office. He-n tole da boys ta not go to da house. To be good boys an he-n take dem to da wood da nex time he-n got back from screwit —

When ah reach home ah nevva tole mah Henry 'bout that air fracus at da Lincolumn. Ah tole he-n 'bout Mr Abes trapesh an ah thot dat belly of his'n would wiggla off he-n laugh so hod. Ah was glad ah did'n take Billie. Billie would'a kilt da niguns hab he heard da fracus. But he-n war mad he-n did'n see da formance

After da fight 'tween da Lincolumns, mr Abe miss hab 'sided ta stay home ah spell. Henry war workin' down to what day war tear'n down old ramshacks, an buildin' new brick buildings. Some—3 stories high or nigh 'bout, Henry am ken' bout eber day. One mornin' mr Abe comb out his'n ken' bout eber day, One mornin' mr Abe comb out his'n as Henry war start'n ta work. mah Henry say, it's da talk he—n do mose anyting ta get way from da missy. Now mr Abe hab heaps on his'n mine. He'n make he'n livin' wid his mine, an he'n hab ta he war he'n can tink sherting out, my say you dum as ah ox, Mariah. It hy dat man air on da street mos' of he'n time when here. Crack—n stories. An ah bet he'n an buonah in he—no office 'til 2 or 3 in da morn'n, just raisin hell an laugh'n, 'til war 'too late to go home. Dat would be tough an so much fun. Afta sach ah dam good time ta go home ta dat piece he—no got fo ah wife.

Ah couldn' git what Henry say, 'bout mistah Abe am da talk ob da town. If al ah know'n people talk, Ah know da talk 'bout da missy to me. But ah's sprized da talk 'bout Mr. Abe. Ah jis' like ah should go ta his'n office an tell he—n. Ah might have enla Henry toll me'n so offen to keep mah nose out of dare business an maybe dare war some truf in Mr Abe have'n hell at home, an maybe no human can hold dare tongue fa eber. But ah swar, mr. Abe did raise some hell. He'n tole he'n all he'n had stick up in his'n head 'bout her'n. An he'n did'n choke on lies, cause da war no lies. Still ah thinks da missy serves ta be fa give. I a hear so mixed up. An ah 'liene her'n do lode da man an war near dyie cause he'n thinks he'n done care fa her'n. But he—n say "I'll out be we—n part". So ah tinks he—n stay wid her'n 'til death. An may be day'll patch it up. Ah tole mah maw to keep his lip button 'bout both deir, cause dey both air ah friends an help us. An Bobbie right den war gibben he—no edicatión to us.

Bobbie come over an say "ma had been sick again with headashe. She dasn't want my friends and I around making noises. She me over to play with Billie. Ah could'n hard la kep from guine right down to mr Abe office an tell he—n should be at home wid dat poor woman an dat blessed Willie Wallace. Ah ask Bobbie how war Willie, he—n say "Oh Willie his fine. Once he had colic. An holds his breath until hes blue in the face. That scares ma. wanted to hold him, but they are afraid I would let him drop. Am almost ten and ma still thinks of me as a baby. Ah say, I told you. causes Bobbie. You—n war born in 1843 an did es onla 1851. Well anyway, he'm say. I'm taking latin an pa studying with me. He—n ask Billie if he'n would lak to study some latin. So sy Billie ahd rath learn how to spell and read. mah kids all gine in an day. Day all want al learn how to count an put lettas 'getha so day could read. He'n da

& Bobbie come et air please da whole bunch "so. Den God bless dare little hearts day all hot on da floor an hab school. Ah war larn'in too to read an' count.

Ah send mah Billie up ta da town to tell he-n poppy to bring home some corn for hominy, an to make parch corn. Ah could go cause mah man hab moud an da cart. Bobbie wen 'ah long. Dey did'n stop wid Henry long. Dey wen on ta town an ran onta Mr. Abe. Day cosy he-n ta take dem fish-n. It war a nice day, but he-n say, "I have some important work to do. Not to-day! Maybe to-morrow. But right way he want a ta know why Bobbie war down town wid Billie. Bobby say "ma sent me over to play with Billie cause she wanted the house quiet. She didn't want it over run with boys all day. She wanted Willie to sleep as he didn't rest last night. Then when I was playing with Billie, Aunt Mariah want Billie to come here to see his poppy and tell him do bring home some corn for hominy and parch corn. I got sum— oh first straight say Mr. Abe— Now here is a nickel spiice. Go, get you some candy. Get off the street it is so torn up, from the building going on. Well say Bobbie, How it come you are on the street instead of in your office. Mistah Abe war allus so willin to explain things, but mah Henry would say "Shut you'n impidence' fore Ah knock yo'n teeth down you' throat.

So he-n say, "You must learn Robert, that men can do a great many things little boys can't. But to get to the point son, I have business on the street." Billie say, wid his big mouf. Stan-n 'roun crackin jokes wid da same. Listen Billie, I don't know where you got such notions, but that crackin' jokes as you call it, or telling stories as the truth of the matter is, I must be friendly with all people. That's my way of being friendly and if I makes friends I may get their business. If they like me they will come to me. There's too many lawyers round these parts to neglect ais you can do to get a share of the law business. Some of these folk you call bums—are mostly poor folks. Their business, too be sure cannot be very profitable. But it gives me experience and sometimes helps these poor souls. I do the same thing on the circuit and in court, I make friends and I like friends. Always remember boys, you can't buy friends. You have to merit them. People will be more apt to be your friends if you make them happy. But as I said, I like friends. Until I came to Illinois I was never in a position to make many friends. The country where our family lived was sparsely inhabited. It was a wooded and desolate country. I often longed for companionship that I could talk with and learn from. Especially discuss the learning one gets from books. Don't misjudge this last statement boys. Always remember you can learn from everyone. Even the lowliest. If not anything else, often good common sense. My father nor mother had no book learning. Even in their way had good common sense, Did the best, their meagre education, permitted, And above all were happy."

Bobbie spoke up an say "Pa then why don't you act happy at home"? Well, say maybe I don't act silly, I feel. Often I must think out how to make as we are, or meet obligations. At home, when away from the rest but

3.   the public I can concentrate and plan. I guess I must have
formed this habit early, of thinking things out, trying first to be
right before going ahead. You see, the habits you form when young
are almost impossible to break.

Maybe I haven't spent enough time with you Robert. We'll go
fishing to-morrow. Bill ask your pappy to go fishing with us."

Bobbie he'n stay fo dinna, den git off home. Went mad mon
comb fo him dinna. Billie lak allas popped off 'bout eber ting,
'ut old Abe Lincolumns can go fishin wid youens, but how da hell
he him think ah can fish an work at da same time. Why can't he
go on Sunday ef he-n want fo mee'n to go 'long. Jus cause he-n know
ah cain't go. Couitch a white lawer gwine any whar wid ah niggar.
Specely one what got hitched to ah white high flutin 'ciety woman
like Mrs. Lincolumns.

Billie say, dat ole' woman did'n wan mammy an me to go wid her
on da Fourth of July. Ah hush he'n up by say'n, Wal we-n did'n wan
ah go. So wee'ns even. But Billie stuck up fo Mr Abe by say'n Wal wen
wee'ns war fishin 'gethe, he'n walk clum home wid us-t. But mah
Henry had hardly got way wan dat blessed Bobbie comb tear'n back
an holla "Billie Oh Billie! what do you think the whole gang is going
fishing with us". Billie look down his'n nose—Who's da gang. Bobbie ups
and say "The bunch of boys I play with now, I told them you could
whistle like all the birds, could get the little wild animals to come
to you, there we could catch them, and that you are a peck of fun.
They all want you. You come over in the morning early. We'll fix
a nice lunch for you too. So don't stop for that, We can go, can't he,
Aunt Mariah?

It an da gang all got to da Lincolumns. Da missy say "That Bobbie
o mine will some day be a diplomat or an embassador", An shur
'nough wat da missy say come true.

Day all wen ta da wood. An Billie done made all dem boys
he'n frien. Some of dose boys war da one wat ah had ta cut wid
ah black snake to get dem ta leave us'n alone dat time in da cart.
Bobbie made frien wid dem, Den he-n fix et so da war Billies frien.
Mr. Abe brot mah Billie home frist. Billie had caught a possum.
Bobbie had da crow. Billie climbed da tree an coax to him. Mr. Abe
left a long string ob nice fish. Billie say if you'd cut da crows tongue
it'll talk. If you'll leave it here pappy will do dat. Mr Abe that
dat a little cruel. But Billie tell 'em pappy know how so it want
hurt a bit. So Bobbie kissed da crow an gave it to Billie—All da
boys wanted to go back da nex day an get a crow fo each ob dem.

Bobbie lak a little gentman, 'duced each frien ta me fore da go home.
Jus lak ah war da grandest lady in da lan. Oh yes, he-n tole me his'n
ma wouldn't want me fo 'while. Ah didn't go back 'til en November.

Da missy done did da wash and house an all hern sewing, sides takin
da best care of Billie, twixt da time ah work for dem las, an time ah

4 went back when Mr. Abe come home from da circuit fa da winta. Herh war makin' up fa da parties hein spend so much money on. An her'n shure 'nough look lak ah work woman.

Ah work fa Tha folks. Sar some dese folks gave da Lincolum fits. Day say wen Mr. Abes pa died, da missy want Mr. Abe ta wear ah band oh crepe' round hein's hat. Da missy say Hein war shown no grief an no respect fa hein's pa. Hein say "Pa war never in Springfield and they'd think ah war mournin' fosome of mah cats." He said "I did all I could for him when he war with us. I left money with ma, when there last. That for jist what might hoffen to either of them And ma promises to keep it for that purpose. I know she didn't spend a penny of it for any thing else. She is so honest. If I had gone back when pa war still alive, brother John and I would have had to fight it out. That would of hurt pa more than what pleasure my visit would have been to him. So I stayed away. John is a shiftless spend thrift — Da missy say to Mr Abe. Hadn't you better write to John now and relieve yahr mind of all your pent up feeling. Maybe then you can take care of business pending. "Perhaps I should mother", he replied" If I don't, he'll shove mother out of her home, and then write me for a Christmas present of a few hundred dollar for relieving her."

Mr. Abe war walkin' da flo whan ah got back dare in Novemba. Hein war talkin to hein sef or praps little Willie. Hein hab Willie in hein's arms. Hein pay no tenshun whan ah say Good-morn mistah Abe. Dreetly da missy comb an took litta Willie fromb hem. Hein woke up a speck an say" Do you know mother, I can remember my little brother somewhat? My father called him Tim Tom 'Tinker'. I believe I've figured out who our baby looks like besides little Eddie. It is my darling little brother buried back near our last home in Kentucky. "Da missy say", that may be fa Willie does favor you." Den as in ah dream he war lookin' fur off hein' say "Mother took sister Sarah and I to his grave, before we moved to Indiana. Pa left us in Kentucky while he went to find a place for a home in Indiana. Mother knelt down at his grave. She had sister and I to kneel too. She told us to bow our heads as she prayed. She asked God to stay near him, so he wouldn't be lonely after we were gone. Pa was religious too, but not the kneeling kind. Da missy say nothin', jut walk' 'way wid tears in her eyes. Willie commence' cryin' fa' titty. Dat woman war so full o' milk I war from her all da time most. Mr. Abe just brot a poor little starved neighbour's baby to her ta feed, to wet nurse, so et could live. Et war a help ta her too. To get rid of some of da rivva o' milk. An dat poor baby got well an' fat.

Et war gettin' 'bout the lass of novemba an Willies birthday war soon in December. Hein wood be one year an da missy war givin' a parta for he-n.

"After mah wash ah roas'n done fa da missy ast me'n ta go up stairs an straighten, den ah got up, dar was Mr. Abe sot right on da floor his knees up mose ta he-n chin, ah read'n, maybe Shakspse, fa he'n war mos'n lack ah act in ah show. He'n allas read out loud. Once say, he'n larned dat in da blab school. Da kids all blab at once, so da teacha know days not fudgin'."

Well ah took my broom an say Mr. Abe ah'll has ta sweep you'n out. He'n sot fa ah spell 'til ah nudge he'n wid da broom. He'n den mosied out ta da stair. He-n sprawled on da three top step. En ah litta ah heard da missy scream. Con't you move. I'll give you until I count three. Then if you aren't up and going down stairs, I'll grab a bunch of that black hair and pull you down the steps. He'n started hern count One, two, Mr. Abe look up an say "That puts me in mind of an experience I had in Indiana.

I was on my way to the home of a man who had lend me a book to read. I was busily reading some lines, I wanted to be sure I had committed to memory correctly. As I walked I paid little attention to where. I was reminded where, by falling head first over a billy-goat eating the long grass in the road. I landed in a mud hole.

I was leaning over to retrieve the book that went in the mud with me, when, Mr. Billie Goat having a vindictive disposition, decided that my posterior was just in the right position to retaliate, for the way I had disturbed him. My second header seemed to strike him as a game he liked. After a few baa baas, he put his head down and made another lunge. This time I was ready for Mr. Goat, I stepped to one side. Grabbed his whiskers. After tussling for awhile. Swung him in the air, I managed to land him head first in the mud hole. He picked himself up. Shook his head as if to say, I've decided this game of leaf frog is not for me." Da missy say— "You wouldn't dare."

He'n say, "Anyone who takes a dare, kills a horse and eats its hair." Et dat he'n got up. Turn 'round. Put one of his big feet on da top step. Lay da missy ovra his'n knee, an spank her-n bottom!

He'n comb'n'ta to whar Ah war workin as please as a grinin kitten. Ah swar you-n nevva could 'side how dose folks would wine up in dare arguefyin. He'n wen down da stair laughin fit ta kill. An her'n smilin an singin' at her'n work. Ah guess da patch et up 'bout da cheatin an lyin business. Altho'da missy tole me lata, dat Mr. Lincoln would nevva temporize with evil. Least of all the lesser evil morals that lead to crime.

He'n wash work war done, ah wen home wid a load of food, clothes big pay of $2.00 for da wash an clean'n and my back pay dat we'uns could make use of. En an invite ta bring Billie da nex time.

Da next time ah war back ta da Lincolnmns ah hab ta take Billie and
da crow. Dat crow was unda mah feet an in mose eber ting in ouc'n shack.
Wa're darin let it lose. When Billie did take it out hei'n habta hold fass
ta et. Et cour cour do, da white-trash could put Billie in da jug ur worse
still string he'n up. But ah' clare those white-trash had simmer down
some, since da foun out Billie now hab high flutin white frien. An
my Henry plum simmad afta he'n saw da respec da Lincolnmns
an dare friens, show Billie an Ah.

Henry boss on da buildin' tearin up, was saying some mighta mean
ting about da Lincolnmns one day. My man knew ta keep his'n job
he'n hab ta keep his mouf shut auf keep his'n fists to he'n sef. Et was
all he'n could do. But he'n comb home meada a danced poked hornet.
Ah tole he'n now he'n knowd how he-n soun'd wen he'n war pop'n off
bout someting dat he'n oula spect an hab no sense in he'n blabbin.

My Henry say when mah younguns git edicaton from Bobbie, dale
know how to help all da poor niggs wats he'n lushed an drivin. Ah
wish Mr. Abe would get back en pulitics, an go ta Washton 'gin. Dis
time maybe he-n could put some sense 'in dem Sedalatus heads, an
hafll see, black an wool is no diffament then Red Head an freckles. Cause
ause is ignorance. An da worse ignorance is ta tink God made any
differance in our-n souls. Ah war happy to heah mah Henry say
God, as he'n didn go on fa dat stuff vera much, he'n allus say.

Et war a litta late dat mornin twixt Billie birthday an Christmas dat
we'n got ober to mah wash. We'n hab ta walk cause pappy war haulin, an
it war cold. Ah wash en da shed. Eber ting war ready. Mr Abe hab
het da watta out doa an carries it in. Ah hab to bile da clothes out
When ah got thro mr Abe build up more fire fa da hog he' war killin.
He'n kill two chickins and pick them afta scoldn. Ah dress dem. He
dinna know does chickis war fa me until ah started home. Ah got ah
lot of dat hog too.

Bobbie an Billie stay in da shed, cause et war too cold in da barn. Da
managy ta keep quite 'til ah wen to da kitchen ta clean da' whiles mah
close dried. Da froze dry. Da missy hab knittes ah pair ob mitten fa me,
an each ob mah chillun. Dat took ah lot of knitten. An da bout a
pair of hose hide gloves fa Henry. Does new wool gawn mitten shure hep
mah hans warm when ah took down da cloth.

Billie didn get much larnin from Bobbie. Dat crow got da larnen
mah Henry done did ah good job fix'n dat crow. Does boys say stop
to each os offen, dat crow finely learn ta say stop. Bobbie laugh
'til he cry, an beg his ma ta let him have da boys comb ta heah. But
he-n ma say notha day.

Ah stir up a batch of fresh cracklin bread with fresh chops an
gravy for dare dinna. Ah wan a put off fa home ta get mah Henry
something hot, so dde could'n coax me ta stay. Bobbie coay mein ta
let Billie stay, but da missy put her-n foot down. He'n say if Billie
stay, da rest of da gang will get here some way, an dit house

will be soon run with boys. Some wottma day wan you'n can all go to da barn. Any way hern say, Bobbie you have to practice your recitation, which you are on the program to give Christmas eve at Church. Bobbie say, Oh shoot ma. But hers got no fatha. Hern send han up stairs.

Mr. Abe say, Since you can't keep the crow an it's about to become a bone of contention here, I've made a cage for it. maybe when it learn this is it's home. When it becomes more tame, it wont go far when let out and will find its way back to it's friends here. I've always loved a parrott. I saw a cockatoo at a circus. It could talk betta than a parrott. But I like this crow, maybe I can talk to it once in awhile instead of talking to myself. It just might be able to prompt me on some of my pleas I practice, when it learn to talk better. Then he laughed. As he was about to go out da door dat Jim crow, right up an flew on his shoulder. Mr. Abe patted it, an brushed down its feathers as it saw cawed. Den Billie hold out han arm an de crow flew ta he-n. Bobbie war a little scared when he'n turn cause dat crow act jus lak et wars goin to fly at he'n. 'Stead it lit on his head. Bobbie laughed so loud an long. You'n can believe oh not, dat crow laugh too.

Mr. Abe say I hate to cage that bird. But these six cats. Especially the black tom will have to be tamed a little more, as well as the crow. The crow may come up missing its wings and tail and the tom may have his eyes picked out. If anything should happen to the little kitten I know Mr. Crow would have to go back to the woods. Mrs. Lincoln doesn't care too much for the noise of the crow since Willie the precious little rascal is here. Since a cat jumped in the crib with Willie. she keeps them out in the shed or barn most of the time. Our little white rat that I brot home once in my pocket that nibbled a hole in my pocket, I had to let loose. You know cats like rat meat and bird meat. Our turtle has hibernated somewhere for the winter. I had it tied in the barn. Part of the rope is still there. Mr turtle may be miles away to the south where the climate is warmer. Turtles know what they want and go after it, slow but sure. I'd love to know their minds. In fact all living creatures minds. maybe they think better thoughts than we. maybe some day who knows, they will rule man instead of man ruling. Take that crow it can talk our talk so we can understand. Can we talk their language. So they wouldn't understand nor would we know how to go about understanding them. The nearest I ever knew anyone coming to talk with them is when Billie answer them or they answer him. Billie will be a fine man, God has given him his greatest talents and Billie is using them. The Bible say, If you don't use your talents they are taken away. Bobbie spoke up an say. What's my talents pa. Well Robert you are a very sincere, kind, lovable boy. You make friends who are worth while, heah a few love friends and you keep them for the same reason. Didn't your ma say, Someday, our Robert is going to be a statesman an ambassador or diplomat, because you smooth out the hurts that might develop into worse hurts among your friends and with them. You caused your friends to be Billie's friends. Just to show you what I mean, Den mah Billie dat awful blab gut spoke up au day. My pappy was mad as heck tord Mr. Abe and you me until he foun youin war not stuck up. He'd fight hell out of anyone wot he could. He'n mad as hell at hen boss for talking bout da Lincolumns. He war 'fraid to fight him cause he'd loose his job. But Ah bet somethin awful will happen to dat boss fur saying dat 'bout you'n. Ah finely grabt Billie by da arm an marched him home. Ah preached to him all da way home 'bout bein ah tattle-tale.

 Us got home fore Henry. Da kids war all hungry, Ah made corn cakes au cooked dat chicken. Wen had ah meal at finealy any one Christmas dinna. Dat chicken wid chicken sop, and some flub dub food from Billie birthday parta was licked up clean by wen's seven

It war in January 1852 fore I went back ta wash. Da Lincolumns war in a funk bout da grandma Parka 'state. Somethin' 'bout ah law suit commenstion wid two colored people, dat had ah high edicate, an den war shipp off to Africa. Da oba war bout missy step motha getin too much. Da step-son war makin trouble. Mr. Abe war in da middle of all dis as he'n was lawin for da missy. Aunt Lisbeth and Aunt Francey. Et war all so mixed Ah couldn get much sense. But Mr. Abe war going to Lexington. But he'n went on da circuit as usual dat spring—An went in da summer

There wasn't too much excitement ah any kind dat I could tell. Only da missy raven fust 'bout one an den 'notha of herapeople. Mr. Abe say its no use crossin a stream fore you'n git to et. Still I hear'n her say. Ef you'n could see 'yond youin nose youd know wen war in da middle of a big puddle now. He'n tried her'n best to keep he'n off da circuit as she said he'd make more ali roun settlin dese states. But dat Mr. Abe knew dare war too many to get dat state money for anyone to get rich off et. Cause her pa owed money dat had to come out first,

Ah didn't know much dat wen on that summer. As da missy 'gain did her-n work.

(He'n war all worke up dat fall) nor maybe it war da next fall in 1853 'bout some money had ta repaid back ta state, cause her pa had giben or lend Mr. Abe money — Da had written to Mr. Abe while he war on da circuit about et. He'n say it war all ah blac(k lie) Such fusing oher ah lotta dat of money bi brothers an sistas who could all get out an make more dan dat wuld get in less time than et took to fuss over et. Day war all smart enough. Ah heard Mr. Abe say, I wouldn't drag out all the family skeletons for people to snicker and gossip about for all any one of you will get. But he'n war da lawya and had ta do as she said. Et war da money hern day her would get out on and take da boys when herb war mad. He'n would come slippen back. 'Cause dat money would keep hern in clothes lak we-n hab, fa long.

not long afta mr. Abe camb back from da circuit. Dare frien Henry Clay died. My but da missy war greived. She tole of what a fine man he-n war. And about his son, who was bitta gin slavery. Hern say, mr. Abe war selected to eulogize mr. Clay in da State House or some other big building in Springfield. Hern had an honor but what a big honor dat war. Henry Clay who felt afta hein fatha next to God. Hern say when youens shy dream an plan to marry Henry Clay; so someday, shen would be da first lady, fa Henry Clay would some day be president. Ah didnt know then that love entered into marriage. Her love for mr. Clay was as one would love a kind, good an intelligent grand-father. She was fin our home so much anymore so often visited his home (Ashland). That same year the death of Webster, another strong Whig supporter as war Clay. Den my Abe talked a lot about dem. Hen got hold fan new book "Uncle Tom Cabin" an he wan I day an hear him read it clear thro'. He read so loud ah could understan it, but ah had to go home. Hin was terrible terrible work up ober dat story an said, maybe some day I can take a crack at slavery an when olds I will make it count, if I can't bust it completely up. He say hin glad for the Underground Railroad. This system has been in peration for at least two years. It has stations at regular intervals. Already many thousand have been took north. The main route is from Richmond to Philadelphia. They are even coming through coffin boxes. But tho he liked Fillmore who was made president after Taylor death he signed the fugitive slave law. He lost prestige because the north didnt want slave owners invading the north, Siege! any fugitives they said was theirs or any negro whether a fugitive from. Without process of law drew them back south into servitude. Many free negroes whom were always free and had always lived in the north for years, were virtually kidnaped. Ah didnt tell mr. Abe, but mah Henry war skeered.

Mr. an Mrs. Lincolnum talked of all da new things that had happened since ah wen to work fa dem in 1850. Ah may not allas get da dates right now since it is gettin hard for me to remember dem. But ah do remember them talking ah lot about a beautiful an fine singa from Sweden. Hern name was Jennie. Hern had traveled in ah private railroad coach. Had meet the White House and da Fillmores. Dare war yacht races. America won da prize from ah bunch of English yachts. Ah bet dat made dem English mad as blazes.

Ever time da would talk about boats or railroad da missy would plan to travel some place. Nen day talk of Transatlantic steamship crossing Atlantic in 10 days. Hern war going to get ready for a trip to France. Ah swear ah nevva saw such a griped up woman. Instead hern got caught again. It war sure gonna be a girl this time hern say. Day Mrs. tole she-n dat Mr. Abe had been sulked or something strange, wouldnt talk to hern or stay home from coming home, from circuit last of June til he caught hern with morning sickness in August. Then he was ashamed and jolly, even more like himself. I tried everywhy to interest hern. I talked to him about the very book he is now reading "Uncle Toms cabin". But he acted when I talked of this book, like he didnt hear me marridly weve had so many fight, I now sometimes doubt my sanity, I reallly threw a stick of wood at him and hit him. Ah that to myself, maybe mr. Abe didnt really love that poor woman. But den how could he be way then carried on. Ef he talked he wrote words and hen didnt talk he-n war wrong. Maybe what day say den war true. Hin had so much hell at home he hates to go home. But he tole Bobbie, he liked to be alone. Alone with his thoughts to think things out. Ah just offen wonda so smart a woman os hern was and as hard os de worked why she didn simmma down. Let hern boss hern house work an tiety an mr. Abe take care of his business. But no, de missy had to boss it all. An mr. Abe war hern score too too, many years to be bossed is what da now call self jont government. My man say when two head strong hosses got to gittden one from da north an one from da south let jus has to be a fight to settle it.

Mr. Abe ran fa da senate against Stephen Douglas or so da missy declared he would in 1855. In da primery da call it. Mr. Lincoln and Julia Jayne husband Lyman Trumbull were both on da ballot. Lincoln war way ahead on da first ballot. At times da legislatur selected da ones ta run for senator. Den on da res of day ballots hen slip an slip til hen tinks hest ta give his votes ta Trumbull who was elected. Da missy wid out any sense at all hated dat girl Julia Jayne from dat on. And hern war so mad at Mr. Lincoln, cause hern thot dat war shur goin to da White House again an' finish Steven Douglas forever. She raved an ranted for a month or more. Took more perjorie. Had headaches an tantrums. Neglected her children until Taddie and Willie took sick. Taddie near die with lung fever. Dr. Wallace work night and day to save them while Mr. Abe war in Chicago on business — Willie war left wid weak lungs. Da missy send word to Mr. Abe. When hen comb home shen blame him. Cause hern hab so much wid de care of dose boys alone. Hern couldn' handle it all. Dat da first time Ah eber felt lak chipin in rite dare an say what ah knew war so. It war jus cause dat woman couldn' go ta Washington 'gin. An maybe Jayne Trumbull would get to go. Ah do believe da woman's jealous thots war da very debil in hern. Har sister Lisbeth for once didn' pet her or wasn't eben disturb cause Mr. Abe warnt chosen. Day Edwards had a big party ready for Mr Lincolumn dat night of the selection. Day Day thot shur hen war to be choose. It didn' botha them at all because da party hab ta be call off.

Mrs Lincolumn didn't give any more parta or go to parlas for weeks. Said she war too humiliate. Mr Abe wen back to da circuet. But said, day an night, he would work an pray for da colored people. He say he knew someday; some God would liberate them. I don' 'lieve his heart war on law or polties afta dat. Dat humans were held in bondage, abused and not permitted to rise about servetude made him miserable. Dat man war so sad hen hardly hab a smile eben for his little boys.

One rainy day wen hern got ober hern huff (dat woman hab sent out invatations a week afore fa a parta fa da boys) hern hab a parta. Da mothas could come ta sew fa da church mishnary. Hern put all da boys play tings in da shed an hab da barn clean an fix as a stage an seats. Afta da sewing da missy serva what hab been 'greed on. Just 2 things cakes & fruit. Of course coffee

2. Herń fix cakes an candy in da shed fa da boys. Emilie habń't gone home yit and herń hep serve.

Et shur war a nasty day an da missy say herń speck most of dem wouldń come. Herń put a piece of carpet out fa dem to wipe dare shoes on. An as herń receive dem, herń put dare wet brellas an wraps on da new hall-tree. Herń got dat from herń pa's estate. Day hab et ordered 'bout a year or so fore et came

Da sewing war ober, as well as da gossip 'bout does who warń't dare, an da 'serving 'gin. Wen in march Willie an dat whole kitten possy oh boys. Each one hab an amal (animal) Willie first let down da white rat on da floor. Da woman gau to put up dare feet an scream. Some shen stood on dare chair. Den a hop-toad, a turtle, some kittens, some chicks, an ol dog an a big bull-frog an jim-crow began to jabber. "Get out ya bums," Da boys hab taught him. At las some one let down da big black Tom cat. Da screamń scared him an ah neba saw such racing aroun in one house in mah born days. Day woman put fa da door, grab dare 'brella an coats, as day 'dasparted. Scream at dare kids ta come or day would beat da day lights out of dem. Emilie laugh until she cried. Ah busted mah sides an da missy war 'gin humilitated. Herń grab Willie an scream why did you do such a thing to me? It war always me. Litta laddie lake it so much herń roll an roll on da floor. Ah bet dat war da best parta does boys eber hab. Da missy kept repeatin. Why did you do it? Finely Willie say, Da boys got tired of all but Jim-Crow. So wen 'cided ta hab a circus parade. Let da animals act. He waned some oh da ladies ta see da show. I was to bring in da chariot driven by the white rat. Each animal was ta have an act. Jim Crow was the clown. He was to say "Get out yee bum" jus as the circus clown said in the circus you took jis to. You remember that dont you ma? Da missy didń't answer. Herń war so mad. Den Willie say. Well fa will laugh; he dont lik a gang of women here all the time anyway. Herń eyes pop fire. William Wallace. Did your father say that? Willie war smart. He grin an say no, Ma, but ah can tell when fa doesn't lik a thing. He's sad an quiet. But I'll bet he'll like our circus. There night when Mr. Abe comb home, an Mrs. Lincoln told about all the fracus dat boys hab raise. Mr. Abe in herń high pick voice scream Good. Den twins all talk at once tellin 'bout, an Emilie bust out an say Brother Abram, you missed the biggest show of your life and they laughed so hard and so long, da missy really scream an pull her hair. An Mr. Abe say little sister I do believe I like you better than ever. Herń paid no attention to da missy's rantin. He was happy again for awhile. Herń say I'll never tell a story that tops that. Herń start for da up stairs. Ah dont tink she war sorry wen Emilie wen home

3. &ardays afta that Mr Abe would bust out laughin and if Willie or Taddie war near Hen would pat an hug them. Afta that as long as Mr Abe war home dese two would hab one of dose animals in the house. If hen sat down on da floor ta read a chick white rat or eben Jim-Crow would be climbing ober him, wid those two boys. Once in awhile hen would jine in da fun wid dem.

Wen Masta Robert came home from school, the boys told him about the circus parade dey had. Bobbie couldn' help but laugh, but hen knew what pests those boys were. They war always tormentin someone. Bobbie couldn' call his life hisn own. And if hen complain, Da missy would scold him. No matta who took sides gainst his ma. Robert would smooth et ober. He war so kind and thotful an good. An so sensitive hen sef. He felt sorry for hisn poor ma. Ah tink all da boys lak dar pa da most. Da nevva stop ta tink. Der pa could presate dem da more, cause hen war not wid dem mush. But dare ma sewed, cooked, sometimes washed. Stressed dem, kept a nice home for dem, kept dem clean. Took dem ta shows an church, an waited on dem when sick. Eben if hen warnt much fun. Hen nevva abuse dem an waned do best in da world fa dem as well as hen sef. Ah tink Bobbie knowd more dan hen let on. Ah tink hen knowd hisn ma war a sick woman in hern mind.

Once wen Masta Robert war on hisn way ta see his ma den sick at Springfield hen come ta see me. Ah don't tink hen eber went through Danville widout stopin at 812 Oak St. Dat war our home close ta the Big Four track as it is now (1902) He talk about heirs pa ta. Say I'll never believe pa ever was any happier than when he signed the Emancipation Proclamation. Robert say, One time was a trip from school to see the folks at the White House. I happen in his room unexpectedly. Pa was kneeling, praying earnestly to be directed aright. The north were beseeging him to free the slaves so they could fight. The officers and Stanton (Sec of War) said he was so slow he was ruining the country. But pa said I trust a mightier guide than these mortal man. The emancipation will be signed. But when it is, God will direct my hand that holds the pen. He suffered for the fallin soldiers in the south as much as for those who fell in the north. He excused the rash abuse that was heaped on him. Once he said Father forgive them. He died many death before Booth killed him. I firmly believe if there is a heaven such as is written that God would choose pa to sit at his left an Christ chosen to sit at his right. Ma was a good woman an did much to smooth away

4 pas primitiveness. ~~But~~ No one could ever influence my
father for one second, if he didn't think it was right. ~~Old~~
That God would act in his own good ~~season~~ He never took
credit for a thing. He never intentionally hurt another feeling.
It was always that. I wish I were like him.

~~was that~~ Robert was always a good boy, so tenda, an easily hurt. He
put ah brave front on afore men, but aha saw him cry his heart out
about the passing to God ob his brothers, his boy Abraham Jr. Isin pa
and da shape hisn mah war in. But ah done think ah eber hear
hen cry when ah work in derin home in Springfield. Et war da
years dat made ~~hen~~ sad. ~~But~~ Hen saw Garfield an McKinley
both kill, an hen cry for both. Maybe da shot back Mr Abe to
both kill, an hen cry for both. But hen war so tenda heart. When a litta boy an eben when
hen war 16 an 17 when Willie or Taddie abuse da birds or anmals
all ober dare home place, masta Robert would pet dose anmals an
then kiss dem. Often when hen's ma war upset hen would go up ta
her, put hen's arm roun her an pet her. Mr Abe nevir courge a
her in hern tantrums. Dose las 2 years ah work right steady
at darin home. Ah hear Mr Abe say Molly, youn make youn
self sick. Or cant youns be mo siderate? Hed mo often leave, but
sometime kiss her good-bye. Du minute Mr Abe war outda house
dat woman would settle down an be hern self, leas hern took ah notin
ta take peri-goric. All da talking Mr Abe, Dr Wallace, Lisbeth
or mens gih her didn da no good. Hern love dat peri-goric. One
wen da missy say Abram youn mouth is black all roun wid
da licorice youns ~~father~~ chewin. Youns mouth is ugly nuff wid
out da. Dat man hah da pretties teeth ah eber saw. But day
did get black when he chaw licorice. Hen say. Well mother I
I like licorice like you like peri-goric. The difference is in the
effects. Licorice if it be a nice, will not injure me or anyone
else ~~but~~ Some day unless you stop, it will destroy you.

Hen Dr Wallace war doctorn da boys ah hear hen say, Now you listen to
me Mary, if you give another drop of that dam stuff to these children, Im thro
Do you want to kill these two also, Ah war plum shook. If I knew wher
you get it Id take the law if I had to, to stop it. Abraham has done the
best he can, curse it if you must, tho I swear by the Eternal God
Ill not stand by an be a part of your ruining your own soul, Day
didn say Peri-Goric, but ah say ta mahsef ~~what~~ else air it?

Hern war so good when eber twig went her way. Ah mean ~~both~~
when ~~hen too~~ get Steven Douglas all tangle up in hisn speech makin.
But war hern make dat first speech an slam dare side dat Douglas
all rumple, wid not a coat or colla, one galles and muddy boots, hen war
humilitate. Den when Mr Abe gave hen's votes ta Trumbol hern war mad
an jealous. Wen hen say nice tings of Ann, da Salem girl, hern war mad an jealous.
Hern got so hern didn wan Mr Abe to praise any one what hern didn lak,
an some of dem hern did lak. Lak litta Emilie.

5. Afta herin fix da house differment, an war busy gitin et all pretty up, ah tink dat woman war happy wid her partes. Ah believe me take really lak his home, betta an war more happy fa a while. Herin never say a word bout wat war spent on et. Herin still hab his spells of deep thit. Herin war ask hear an dare say eber war ta speech make. Some time herin take da missy. Afta herin ansa (answer) Stephan Douglas in Springfiels Herin speech make in Peoria. Urbana Quincy Jacksonvill an eben Chicago. Dees speechin came from herin heart gainst extend of slavery – Da missy war happy herin war back in polities. But Mr. Abe say Ef ets a means ta an end I must go back. But I'll be on the side and with the issue I think are right. The end in question is the recognition of our Constitution. The issue involved here is,—That all men are created equal. That the extension of slavery is wrong. Even as it exists we in this republic are taunted as hypocrites. That for economic reason alone self-interest we would sacrifice human souls and bodies in a dastardly, brutel acts against fundamental principals of civil liberty.

Early one morning wen ah came ta work. Da table war cleared and pappes from Mr. Abes stove pipe hat war piled high on da cente of da table. Herin would take a pappa an write down. Den herin would do da some. Some war tings dey cut from pappas all ober da Unite Stete. Quee herin cuss da newspappa. Cause herin took so much time reading dem. Now she read all dem an cut, cut, cut from dem.

Den Mr. Abe would take da stack herin hab. Some herin would say Hais it is not dis man or dat man's convictions. Its a political manuevour to get votes. I'll jot down the nub of the points I want to make. God will place on my lips the words to speak on each point. If I wrote out a hundred addresses Id never speak them as I wrote them, so that's no go. I heard all I wanted to w that when I was in Congress in 1847-49. Political scoundrels by twisting an issue gained support of older scoundrels. I'll tell you Nelly, there are more scoundrel in politics, especially on the slavery issue, than there are scoundrel in our penitentaries. Oh Abram herin say You are a radical on that one subject. Yes, Im a radical as is Cassius Clay. Dare to do right and be true in the face of ridicul, failure and even death. If that must come

Ah didn't stay only a speck dare, but Kein tole me, if'n ah felt able ah could come on da reglar wash day. For dare would be a little wash Ah didn take Billie next time, an ah didn't see da missy or Bobbie bout, but da fire an all war ready. Wen ah war done an went in dare war no dishes or kitchen to clean, but Bobbie cotched up wid mein fore ah retched da barn, an said ma waned me.

Said ~~Kein~~ owed me an apology, ~~Dat Kein were out a~~ ~~sorta cold,~~ Mrs. Abe decided apology. Mariah I owe you an in my heart for the unjust things I said to you. I'm deeply sorry I was the cause, even indirectly of you losing your child. I know God will punish me. I just can't seem to learn why I be punished ~~in time~~ I was to but art. I wanted to go to Chicago ~~with mr. Lincoln~~ so very much ~~with Mr. Lincoln~~ But at the last minute I had a little upset physical condition and he decided the trip would not be too good for me. But Mariah that isn't all I never receive the least attention from him unless I approach him first. You could see when he left he kissed Robert over an over but didn't even wave good buy to me. Ah laughed an said Wal missy maybe he thot ~~going~~ think it a baboon wavin at youn. Kein really smiled a wee bit. Ah's tried to tell youns Honey couches more flies dan vingar. Den da missy say. Only God knows how this will turn out. All he thinks about is the circuit or some other trip. Anything it seems to keep away from me. I believe if he felt justified in taking Robert he would take him and leave for good. The only hope I have, is that I love him so desparately, that that Love will find a way to keep him and cleanse my heart.

Well dat trip to wash war so much for mems I didn't get back again that fall. I don't know how she an Mr. Abe made out. But she tole my dat ah had spoil her so with my fine wash. Kein would do it afore seeing washed by fus any one

I sadignust have been most fins & Willie geban, Ah
comb ta wash dat morning. Et war pretty cold. mr
Abe war out speech-makin' or on da circuit. Ah just
don't rightly memba. Ah hab ta build ah fire ta heat
mah watah - Dat war sure ah surprize as da wattah
war always hot fa men. Da clothes sorted an eba ting
ready. Ah didn' see a soul 'round. Ah counted mah
fingus ta be shure et war da right week. Ah hab left
narcissa at home, ah only brot mah wee chile Rosa. Her
war such ah litta sleepy head ah nevva had trouble wid her.
'Cause ah made da fire in da kitchen ah hab ta
carry da watta to da shed, whar ah wash. While ah war
busy ah nevva stop until done. Dis marn-n ah
smell smoke. Ah look up an see da smoke coming
from da kitchen doar. Ah says Holy God da Lincolumn
house es burnin' down. Ah dash in da kitchen an
dare stood Taddie an Willie in dare night clothes. each
wid a soap bubble pipe in his mouth. But no soap
bubbles. Day hab torn paper an dried corn silks in dare pipes.
Day hab start da pipes wid mah kitchen fire. Ah scream
at them dat day would sot da house on fire. But day paid
no heed an each spit some black spit in da fire. Dat
scare me, until ah found it war licorice juice da war
spittn out, tending et war bacca juice. Ah say wake young
mah. Willie say Don't you dare wake mah, Aunt Mariah
She was up late with guests and wishes to sleep this
morning. We are the men of the house. Ah say Youns not
men Youns two bums. Smokin' an spittn an skeerin
da day lights out of me wid youns smoke. Youns pa is a
man an he don't smoke an chew bacca. Well say Willie
mah's guests are the cream of Springfield an they smoke
and chew because we saw them last night. Ah up
an say Who-n do youns think are da best man in dd worl.
Buck say pa is. Well ah ask. What would you ratha be
youns pa or one ob dees bacca chewn or smokin men. Taddie
threw his'n pipe and wad of licorice from his mouth in da
stove an scream papa Now get out an leave us alone say Willie

2. Da missy comb tearing in. Hern hab an idea ah were da cause ob da bedlum. But Taddie gave it 'way— Hern grab Willie pipe, what Willie war holdin' kind ob hen and say ef you tell mah ahll hit you Aunt mariah wid Willie's pipe. Tad didin talk as plain as dat cause hen couldin.

Dar missy allays seem ta fava Willie. Hern say, Willie precious, tell mother, what you and Taddie were doing? Willie war smart and hen say meek like. We war only playin. But da missy say. How playing? tell me about the pipe an this smoke. Give me the pipe Taddie. Hen held it back ob hen fa a spell, but finely shove it at her. Da missy look at it. Smell it an say. Come ta mother boys. Taddie step up bold like, but Willie hung hen's head an went slow like.

Now boys hern say. I know you were playing, but this is an order from mother. No more such playing.

But mother Willie say. Those men at your party smoked an chewed an you didn't tell them to stop. Why should they have more privileges in our home than we have? Hern say. Men can choose ar can limit themselves when it comes to vices. But little boys must be guided ar directed by parents who love them. Your father would not do what he would not have his boys do. You know he would not want you to pattern after men who are careless about their habits. Don't you want to please your Dear father. They both of course say day do. No spankin, no scoldin. Dat da way the Abe an da missy manage dose boys. Ah nevva did see da like.

Ta dose boys wen back to dare makin soap bubbles, wid out 'notha word.

As allus afta partas, ah hab stacks ob dishes an da house ta keep clean. Now dat da missy war up, ah knew ahd nevva get 'way 'til da las speck of dirt war out ob dat house. Ah hurried wid mah wash cause it war a big one. Hern must ah strip da beds ob contaf aigns and chars ob tidies ans da windows of sash curtains. Dare war a lot of cleaning rags besedes da regular tings. Hern tell da boys ta play in da yard an not get in Aunt mariahs way. But mercy 'live dose boys wen from one ting ta 'nother so fast, da kept me yelpin at dem ta keep

3 fromb trompin dem down. Day allus skeer me when day clumb da wood pile, Et hab poles at bofe ends but da stock war so high an day clumb ta da top. Willie allus drug Laddie up, Ef dose poles hab busted an start da wood ta role. Dose boys could ah been mashed plumb flat wid dat wood, Comb ob da chunkes make big an heavy. All mah kids seems ab how, nevva got inta so much devilment as does two.

Ah don't know why ah worried so much bout does litta scamps. Dare mah an pa didn.

Ah work warn't oba until time fa dinna. So ah hab to fix moah left-overs, as allus afta partas. Herin let men bring Rosa in— Herin say onse, herin didn lak smelly colored babies— Herin hab given men powda ta put on afta ah diddied Rosa ta keep her from gauddin But ah know'd et made herin smell good too. Da missy gave me a bag af assafidity to hang on a string around her nesk. Herin boys allus wore dem ta keep way 'skasso Rosa war too litta ta eat, but ah gave her nurse from men (Da missy allus say Aunt Mariah don't say vulgar word titty—say nurse) Ah do faget once in now an den, but fore God ah done mean ta be vulga.

Wen hab hardly started eatin when Mr, Abe comb in, by surprige. Ah tink by sare talk hen hab got a wire ta comb ta Chicago on business. Right way herin plan ta go long. Mrs Abe war heaps pledsurable 'bout someting. But ef they had fracuses afore. Et warnit afstaken ta die one fore hen wok home long—

He say mother (dis war, after hen hab eat a bite or two at da table wid dem,) I have something here (He reached in hisn pocket and drew out af pictua) that you've asked me about so often. Now this is not a picture taken of the little girl I knew and who was very dear to me in New Salem. However it couldn't look much more like her if taken of her. I picked it up in a pecture gallery to bring home to show you. Herin take da picha. Ah hope ta die right here on dis spot ef dat woman didn push herin char back stan up an slap dat picha down hard on da table, an say, You'll never make me believe

4. if you tried to convince me before a tribunal, that a girl who looked like that cared an iota about you. The way she is dressed shows she is not a common country girl. "I'll say Mr. Abe - It's the face. The face of a young innocent angel. Boot Boo say da missy - Innocent, then she would go with you, while engaged to marry another. Hern look like tunda and hern look like hern was struck by lightning. Hern grab da picha up an start fa da stove. He'n quicka, quicka dan ah eba see hern move afore, grab her and squeeze da picha out ob her fingas. Dat woman plum aint well, hern scratch at his face. Pick up a fork an ah beleeve hern would a dug his'n eyes out wid it, but dat man grab hern han, an got da fork away. Den he sot hern in a char. Drew one out fromb da table an sat square in front ob her, an look hern right smack in da eyes an say - Woman how long sufferin do you think I am. Had you destroyed that picture, you would have destroyed one of the simple, one of the greatest happiness I've had for a long time. Not only because it is so like a little lady who tried to help me, but because it is also so like my angel mother. Had you destroyed it you would have destroyed a part of me, that can never be replaced. You would have destroyed something that could be encouragement to go on to better things - could help me live through trials, Could help me live over and over the greatest happinesses I've had in my life - I wouldn't lie to you woman. If you continue these fits of insane contemptableness I'll promise you and myself before God, you'll just be a mother of my children and no more - If you try you can stop this silly jeklous disposition you've let yourself go unchecked until it has become an obsession. I thought I was marrying a woman who would be a help meet instead of a hindrance. No man can go on and up shouldering such. You can make up your mind. He started for the door, She screamed. Ran at him - Threw hern arms around his'n neck. Tried ta drag his head down ta kiss hern, or hern kiss him. But Mr. Abe stood like a statue. Before hern let loose wid both han round his neck - Hern drew back one han an slaps dat man a God awful slap in da face. Den hern ran to da door lock it, an tole him if hern left hern would kill hern sek..

CHAPTER SIXTEEN, SECOND DRAFT 227

5ᵗ Den weu heard poundin at da door. Daddie war cryin ta come in; Mr Abe say give me that key or I'll have to take it from you. I ke threw it at him. He opened the door and in rushed the boys. Who had been shewed out when da fracus begun Daddie had a big splinta in his'n foot. Willie hab drug Daddie up on da wood pile gin. Mr Abe pull out da splinta. Put on some turkpantine. Wrop a rag 'round den kiss da boys an start'in out 'gin. But gin da missy trio ta lock him in. He pushes her'n ta one side an goes out, Her'n goes out to. Grabs his coat tail an hangs on. Wal dat woman sure hab him, cause Mr Lincolumms didn want ah public spectal. No one on da outside knew his'n trouble, Cause her'n tole no one. Guess her'n war too shamed. Her'n come back in.

Her'n try an try ta talk ta him but her'n pat wid his char lean back gin da wall wid his'n head down, an his'n arm wrap 'round his'n knees.

Ross war sleep all through dat hella-ballu. Ah hab ta pass Mr Abe ta go out. Her'n pay nary ah word but reach in his pocket. Take out some money an han it ta me. Ah didn know it war five dollas until ah stop at da sto an da sto-keeps hans me da change 4 dollas an ah quarta. Ah war sure her'n didn mean ta give mo dan 2 dollas, so ah walks back ta da Lincolumms. Dore ah got dore ah knew her'n or somebody else war comin cause ah saw a brush limb of ah tree ova da fence wiglin an a long stick stuck thru da bottom ob da fence dat struck da board walk. It war Mr Abe combin wid his'n head down. Dat man nebba would a comb out ob dot sad look if dat brush limb hadn knock his'n hat off an da long stick got tween his'n legs an stop him. Doze litta scamps laugh at da top of dare voices an Mr Abe laugh, reach oba da top ob da fence, put one on one shoulda and one on da otha and dot da way dey

6. war when ah met dem at da corna ob da street.

Mr Abe day wid out ah smile. Ah takin' dees two sacks of corn ta da mill ta have growed into meal. Does two boys began ta wiggle. Saddie say no meal papa da (Way hab teached dare Saddie ta say papa. Da others all say pa an ma. Sometime mostah Robert say fatha an matha) Den Saddie gin ta kick wid both feet. Mr Abe let dem both down kissed dem. Gave dem each ah love pat an send dem back. afta he'n tole them ta be good boys, an not forget ta close da gate.

Nevva once did dat man smile gin afta does boys rund back He'n say Aunt Mariah did you forget something. No ah say, Mr. Abe you'n make a keep big mistake Ah stop at da store for some tings and day gave me dees four dollar an ah quarta back. Now ah know'd you'd done made ah mistake, Cause da five dolla's what you'n gib me warn't da two dollar ah specs it war. Wal mr. Abe say. You'se a very honest woman Aunt Mariah, but I made no mistake. I knew that five dollars was all I had in that pocket. When you first came to work for us, all you was supposed to do was wash. But You've been ready and willing to take time from your family, ta help with all the other work. Have you always been paid for this extra work you've done. Ah says Why mr. Abe. ah'll nevva be able ta pay you'n fa all dd extra you's giben men— you'n an Mr Wallace an da missy Gifts are gifts Aunt mariah. An work is work that is only compensated for, by pay in dollars and cents. I would never forgive myself, or expect to gain if I cheated you out of what you' rightfully earn. No one will eba know, just how really God-like dat man war.

AH WAR SAD FOR DA NEXT TWO WEEKS 'BOUT DOES LINCOLNS. AH COULDN'T DO OR SAY A THING TO HELP DEM. BUT A GUESS SOMETHING MUST AH COME UP TO PARTLY STRAIGHTEN THINGS OUT. AS DE MISSEY GOES TO CHICAGO WITH MR ABE. HER'N TELL ME 'BOUT THE WONDERFUL TIME DAY HAVE AT THE SHOWS, AND HER'N BUYS DRESS GOODS AN MORE CURTAIN STUFF.

Mr. Abe nebba brag about nothin'. Hen whip Steven Douglas
pants clean off ~~him his~~ just by tellin de God truth in hen ~~now idea~~ speech makin. Hen nevva, nevva
took da credit fo bein' smart. Hen say, while he was speech
makin, all hen had were da points. Hen save in hen hat, what
hen want ta touch on. Dat da good Lord God Almighty in some
way ob hen ~~~~ carried hen through. Once hen tell wen da
missy ast if he warnt 'fraid hen would make a bobble if hen
didnt go oba all da points wid her. Mabye she could suggest
something from a politcal angle, os that was her fort. She
had been versed in politics since a small child. Henry Clay
was a mighty politican and he knew the tricks of his trade
So does Steven Douglas. You must hold in mind always that
he is a powerful weapon fo the slavery faction for his ~~~~
~~politics, for himself and~~ against any opponent who get in his path
Abram don't let him slay you.

Says Mr. Abe. Well ~~mother~~ Im well aware of the fact that you
are a real little politican. And I sincerely appreciate your
earnest and abiding faith in politics, youre ambitious also, ~~but~~
I sincerely believe if I am true to my convictions, no matter
~~principals of this Republic, that I can depend to follow the~~
~~what side I am on politically, that is the principals of the party~~
that I can depend upon God to put the right ideas in my
mind and in my voice to speak. For he always has, when I yield

A long time ago I sensed that if I voluntarily chose to let
God fill my mind with the right, he would not forsake me
in any difficult undertaking. Now it's not a question of
whose mightier or righter God or Steven Douglas? Right
is might. And I know if at any time my frail mortal mind
chose to lust for might, if it be not right—God will either set
me on the right track by some demonstration of his might
or that I will fail by failing to recognize his loving care.

Its unexplainable to me as so much has been, especially
since my residence in Illinois. At that time out of a clear sky
came the thought. You are twenty-one. No longer you should
~~defend or on others care or order of~~ I had largely felt that I was
subject to my fathers direction and care. I'll admit I had some
fear of embarking alone, as a new adventurer in a new country
~~But~~ Immediately I found new helpful friends. Every step until
now has been test, and try with many trials I'll admit. But somehow Ive learned there is a mighty power, outside of the physical or
mortal mind, that directs us, if well put our trust in it. Some

2 day I hope to gain mariah's faith; The "faith Bigger Dan de mustad Seed" The faith "that will remove the mountains of trouble for the colored people. Involuntary slavery is so wrong If I can through God's help utter one word that will produce a chain of reaction that will eventually free the black man, I shall never cease to thank God for that one word.

I know now God has put many words in my mouth

I promised God when I've tried many cases to quit the case, if the person or parties I was trying to defend were guilty. Even in unexpected ways that promise has paid off. Take the stories, true stories always I try to use to illustrate a point. The stories seem to suggest themselves. I never know why. Sometimes I seem to be treading on thin ice. But I have never once been let down. The finish of the story seems to finish not out of my own mind, but through my mind and voice. The outcome and the point gained is so new to me. I have to laugh with my hearers, often more heartily than they. You see it is not me or my will only as I submit my will to God. Christ said: "It is the father in me" and "not my will but thine be done. Remember how mariah gave up her little Phebe, How she accepted it and was comforted – Did we do that with Eddie's mother

Da missy, began to get powerful nervous and say, Abram lets not have anymore sermons from You. Once a week at church is the place for that. Its all I can digest. Lets get down to earth and be practical. Sometimes I think you talk like a crazy man. You'n see her'n warn't a God woman, but Mr Abe war a God man.

I'en try to be patient wid dat woman an say. Mother I've tried and tried your plans. You've helped me in so many ways But when it comes to our my planning an address, it just doesn't work out. I've stood for hours reciting what I that I would say in defense of a client or of a conviction It just didn't work. Those words just didn't come out. New words were put in my mouth to speak that were triumphant You know what, the outcome of one of my rehearsals. Mariah got a black eye. And her'n laughed an laughed. Da missy say now I know you are crazy. You'n see jes as Dr William Wallace say Dat aristocracy is Big me an litta you. Eben God is da litta one

Mr. Abe hah all da laugh taken out ob her'n. Dat man as always look sad, put on his tall hat an shawl an put off out doa. It war no use. Eber time her'n open her'n mouth dat woman drove a wedge tween dem father an father – Her'n talk an talk to me afta Mr. Abe war gone. Ah couldn' say nary a word. But ah knew day war as much differrent as day an night. An if ah spouted off, ah get mah foot in it up ta mah neck.

? Herin say, Its a wonder Mr Lincoln didnt mention that common Ann from the backwoods, where he came from to Springfield. He's never directly told me he loved her or that she loved him, but he has mentioned her, and given her the credit for his start in law. I've so often asked him what she looked like. I suppose some straggly, ill cared for farm girl. But he always says, She's too etherial to describe. Has said, The only one who has ever reminded me of my mother, buried back in Indiana. I remember my mother as a gentle, christian. So was Ann. Then he becomes quiet and sad. Won't talk to anyone for a day or two and wonders around, as if in a daze. It leaves one wondering if its his mother or this Ann that occupies his mind so completely.

Wal ah thinks, maybe ah'd feel hurt too as herin does. But ah'd shus try ef ah loved him ta change mah ways an be more luk de ones herin loved, for dare gentle, christian ways. An ah's try ta undastan Mr. Abe. more dan herin. Dat wen herin got on a subjec he's nevva, nevva got off dat subjec until herin had thot et out. Herin should hep dat man by stopin herin blabbin, an scoldin an wild tantrums. How herin could seal dat mind of hisn off gainst herin outburst at da world. Herin didn relize et war causin talk dat maybe warn true. An causin herin thots dat were bad fa herin. Maybe God got dose two strange folks ta getha to make bof of dem stronga. But et war ah tussel fa herin, cause herin war nevva happy less Mr Abe war doin someting big instead of something good. Da common lak circuit ridin an common frens made herin mad. Ah woad wonda, if ah didn know ah remind herin of mammy Sally back in Lefton, how herin could lak men, an he so good ta men, an mah chilluns. But mammy Sally war an ristocrat coon cause herin belong to ristocrats. Now since Mr Abe belong to herin, herin war ristocrat. But none ob his peoples. Shen didn want hisn people round nor any herin frens. Wen herin hab a parta do guest war don christin. But Mr. Abe didn care. He warn thar half da time an when herin war, herin act jus as natrel as ef day warn thar. I herin go ta da table wid no coat or no collar. In herin sock feet if his feet hurt. Maybe eben wid out socks. Slide bones from herin meat on da table cloth. Drink juice left from herin desert out of da sauce dish. Scoot food stuff from da tureens an meat plates to hisn plate an worse of all wip his mouth an hisn sleeve. Da missy would act as if herin didn see an be sweet about it 'til da guest leave, den her would raise tickular hell. Eben mah Henry hab betta table mannas. Dat man just love ta tease herin. Ta when herin stop raven, herin stop doin. Dat man jus couldn be driven. An wen herin settle down

4 fa 'while an stop driven, da man would go higha an higha in law an big jobs.

Does boys ob da Lincolums must hab taken dar teasin from dare pa cause day war da worse teases ah eber saw. Once when da missy hab a big day parta, some ob da lady 'brot dare brats 'long as da missy call them. Kerin say da put heru boys up to mischief. But Williaund Taddie loved mischief bella den dare toys an if dose woman's boys could teach dem two Lincolum boys any new tricks da missy should gib dem one ob da parta prizes.

Mr Lincoln hab just tole dem bout always tying heru step-matha apron strings ta da rounds in a ladda back chair eber time he-n could. 'Til herin finely made heri repair da damage ta da strings an sometime da apron. He tole bout holdin a lита bare foot boy up side down so's he could walk on heri step-mas white wash ceiling wid heris dirty feet. Cause heri step-ma made heri wash hiri feet fore he track on heri clean scrub floor. Hein make a funnel from a leak in da log cabin roof to a wooden stave stub. Whar he caught water good rain water, so's he wouldn have ta go ta da spring to carry da wata. One day heri's pa raved cause dat spring wata taste lake roof rain wata. Heri went ta da spring ta try ta discova da cause. When he comb back heri clumb ta da loft of dare cabin an foun Mr Abe's funnel. Da funnel and da fun end rite dare. Cause heri's pa lammed heri good. Heri's step-ma took dat boys part an laugh bout da tracks on da ceiling an da funnel. But Mr Abe nevva war a ting lak heri's pa only lak ta wandar from one place ta anotha. Heri love ta wanda unda the star at night. Loved da woods an da circuit. An made extra trips to Injiana, to see hiri pa an step ma. Ta see Dennis Hauk an hish step-sista, who war Dennis wife. Any place so he war on da go.

Mr Abe once tell da missy if heri would go on da circuit wise and enjoyed te changes, or would take the boys fishing shed learn to love nature. Da only nature heri loved war heri flowers. Heri say heri got enough of nature from dar country home in Kentucke Heri war always afraid out dare. And I can't see any sense heri say in rambling aroun when dare are so much in dis big world ta see. The great wonders lik niagar falls. Da liberty Bell all the culture of Boston Then London au France. No none of that if you make a long trip its goin ta be ta the wild country of Califoni an Oregon. But the wonders of the world aed

5. what God created still in it's primitive state - untouched
and never decorated by man. Should man by his medling should
change the course of the stars the moon or the sun, then
the end is near. That perhaps, if ever, will be ages from now.
But the bible says there will be no seasons, no time. The
powers of the heavens shall be shaken. This couldn' be by
a God who creates them and is good. It must be by medling
wicked man. man will destroy man by heeding the wrong
instead of the right. I believe as the bible say the jewel & gold
of the great temples will be distroyed. The wealth squandered on
such should have helped to provide for the helpless and poor who
are worthy.

    But in spite of dat man's good ways hen provoked dat woman.
But hen couldn' see ah fault in hern boys.
Does boys at da parta wid does otha boys dare - tied all da
ribbons an sashes does ladies hab strung from dare hats an
dresses, to da back of da chairs. Da war lak little mice at
dare jobs. Da left da streamers loose but tied da knots tight -
When da ladies moved or turned dare heads too far. Off popped
de hat to one side or da otha, or dare bonnets fell on da floor -
And woman had da streamers from dare neck choken dem or
sashes pulled clean off when day got up from dare chairs. Dat
parta ended en does woman screaming at da kids. Da kids
hoopin an laughin. woman blamin da otha womans
Mr Abe fairly roled off his char laughin when tole about it
an hug does little rascals to him, as if day war little angles stead of little
torments. Hen say I couldn' reprimand them for doing what
I so often wanted to do when at church, some of those woman
floing themselves about and wiggled those jew jaws. How they
did love to attract attention to their finery. Da missy laughed
some, but she thought not her boys but the others were to blame.
But said sorry it had to happen in her home. It broke up
the party and reflected on her ability as a perfect hostess.

    mah goodness but dat house war shore purty after da missy
hab it made ober. Hern eben had wall paper from Paris. And
de mose new arnaments on da mantle an what-not. A new
banjo clock. New carpets an curtains an drapery an drapery
tie-backs. A crystal light from da ceiling of da front parla
with lots of bangles of glass and candles. Ah tink maybe a dozen
candles. An candles in hern mantle. When hern hab a parta
and da tables war all set wid hern fine ching an crystal, wid all
da mounds of good eatins. made huns know at what money
an good notions 'bout what partas should be work and money.
    But ah never give up dat good old big kitchen an dat nice long

6. table for all da rest of da house fixins. When hern hab much comp'ny da hab te set da table in da settin room. Even da dinin room hern cut off from da big kitchen wasn' big enuff.

Hern gib usin da nice kitchen chars black painted wid fruit an flowers painted on. Da old bed Mr. Abe say hen out growd and a load of pretty little ornaments. Some blue chiny and almost mah cart full ob pots, pans, old carpets an old clove. Mah Henry help me unload dis plunda in da shed. Said someday maybe we could ad a notha room of plank to da shack. But hen neva did. Most that plunda stay in da shed 'til weins move ta Danville. Mah kids broke up mose da ornaments playn wid dem. Weins wore da carpets and clove out. But da res, ah hab, an ah'll sell fa money ah need. Am old now, an dey are in da way ta clean. Since Julia dead and mah chillun don't care for dem or mah stories about dem. Day got tired years ago lisnin to da Lincolumns talk ah guess. Ah'll get what ah can out of dem. (I bought what she had, ornaments, China, jewelry, furniture, books and pictures).

I asked Aunt Mariah if she knew why Mr. Lincoln left the Whig party.

Wal ah did hearin tell, one time when Mr. Abe war talkin polties. Hen war talking poltics with big folks. Some what comb wanta get artcals ta put in da paypa Udas what wanta jobs wen hen got to Washington as senator.

Wal Mr. Abe say. "It might surprize you to hear that I was once an Andrew Jackson man. All the Lincolns were Democrats. My father, the Hanks and Johnstons were Democrats"

Ah did hearin tell, let's see ah tink it war Mr. Sam Graveses, whose litta boy war Willie's playmate fore Taddie come. Hen say, not one ob Mr Abe's no count relations voted fa hen. But ever last one ob dem would be after dat poor Mr Lincolumn fa money when hen got ta da Whitehouse. Ever los one, of da Lincolumns neighbours voted fa him, an day did gin in 1860 fa president. Cause day all say so. Day war da county sheriff Chas Arnold. Da constable Abner Watson Sam Graveses, ah engineer Wm. Billington and a surveryor who Mr Abe sometimes helped an liked Benj. Moor. Den ah knows the Franceses, the Trumbells and Browning's war hen friends. Some of dar woman folks didn like da missy too much. But when day got in high polties and made lots of money from da railroad an da missy had a fine carriage an went in 'ciete. Day all hover round ta get an invite. An dats jes what da missy did. Hen war forgiven, but hen also had a heep of polties. Hen knows how ta git votes for Mr. Abe. But Mr Abe warn made senator. Da little giant, as Mr Abe call Douglas, beat hen to it. Dat if Stephen Douglas fell in da Sangamon river, day would pull hen out with hen's pockets full of fine fish.

One thing Mr Lincoln didn like about Mr. Douglas was, Mr. Douglases defense, which should be clear an concise, from moral, christian, or politcal angels were nothing more or less than dirty attacks on hes

2, opponents. Always laden with nasty insinuations and quite often smears that were untrue.

I stopped Aunt Mariah because she had failed to tell me why Mr. Lincoln left the Whig party. She said, Ah git so all fired excited, when ah think of how Mr. Abe war abused, by every one, da newspapers wid dare nasty pictures an da democrats, most of dem pig heads at dat time makin fun ob dat poor man. Ah git all rattle up. Now whar war Ah.? I told her, back where you said, that his father, the Hankses and Johnstons were democrats. Oh yes said Aunt Mariah. — Mr. Abe say.

At the time I turned Whig in 1826, (I think date should be 1833) the uncertainty of the currency was the deciding factor. My friends at that time were Wm. Jones and Wm. Woods who were strong Clay men. They gave me Clay speeches written up in newspapers from Cincinnati. I became a fervent supporter of Clay's great principals. I read other papers from Louisville — One called the Journal and another the Telescope, which friends gave me I learned what I read word for word, so I could repeat correctly. They called me their walking news boy. The Whig party has finally petered out from it this new Republican party (named for this our Republic has been born. The Republican principals are not wholly unlike the Whigs. It supports in every way the original constitution of the United States which I feel quite certain will keep us a United States as long as the world stands, Following its precepts and leading this new party, all men everywhere can eventually be free. Those who oppose freedom will become extinct, Men from the beginning were given the free moral rights to choose between right and wrong. Some may choose wrong because they have been mislead But there is where his strength of character and the power of a good mind will seek and find the right road. The lack of mental development causes wrong choice.

3 Hen say, his pa say He'd know right from wrong if hen was raise in a rat hole. Hen allus say his poor pa was a good man, but without a developed mind, was often mislead. His Pa done right as he saw the right. But his pa never had even a good start. As for me, I had an angel mother and step-mother and wonderful good friends. Such help as I received from them that helped to develop my mind, overbalanced those who opposed me.

Pa opposed me but he thot he was right. A great many people here in Springfield think Mrs. Lincoln and I are not bringing our children up right. The first step in blocking anyones development is to not allow them freedom. One should set a good object lesson before their children, then give the children freedom to learn from the object.

Mr. Lincoln oula hab two Sundays ta home during his'n debate wid Stephen Douglas for da Senate job. But does Sundays from Friday 'til Mon' war so full with partas by da missy an odars, an ah heap of peoples comb ta see Mr. Obe. Day war all so sure hen would be 'lected. Wat time Mr. Lincoln war'nt traveling from one speak-makin place to dabada dozen da debate, hen hab no time to take care ob his'n poor feet! Sides is corns an bunion, dare war an ole case ob frozen feet dat botha dose big feet of his'n. Ah don't link dat man wood ore comb home does two Sundays, but it gave hen a chance to soak an docta dose poor feet. When he war home it war a whirl (as da missy say) of partas. Sides moh work, day hab Mary. But da missy keep Mary so busy her'n 'bout fall in her'n tracks. Den one day wan she war goin to fix fa a big parta cause Mr. Abe war home. Dis war a polical parta. Mary got sick an couldn' come.

Mr. Abe wen up stairs. Ah thot maybe he war up dare restin his poor burning, aching feet. Ah habn seed hen take up da foot tub an watta. Ah nebba seed ah man wash his'n feet so much.

Dare war lots of work up stairs ah hab ta do afta mah

H. kitchen work. An dare, war Mr Abe an da two
boys. Day too war tearing around up stairs, in mah
way. When ah wen up dar war Mr, Abe wid hisn
poor feet in da watta an da two kids squatting an
da floor in front of hen, looking at da pictures on
dat ten foot tub. Seems day nebba could get nough
look at dose pictures. Mr. Abe carry da water up
stairs fromb da pump in da back yard. Summa or
winta dat man wash hisn feet in cold wata
When ah first work dare in 1850 Mr, Abe use soft
sopp. But wen hen make lots of money wid town an
da railroad job, day hab costeel stop.
In dis day of da bigges parta. Wen about da whole
Sfringfield would comb in dare carriages an finery
Ah war busy upstairs an da missy down stairs, an
mary sick. Wen war workin like niggers shur nuff.
In da midst of all dis hub-bub. Da missy cleanin
down stairs, rangin' da table fa da parta. Da boys
dose two little rascals up stairs, wid usn Mr Abe an
Ah. Dare comb ah bunch ob men down en front.
Mrs Lincolnma hid. Ah war not fit ta anss da
door. So Mr Abe pull hisn wet feet out ob da tub.
Isave dem a swipe. Put on hisn carpet-slippas, an as
cool as ya please, let dat mob in. Took dare hats.
Lead dem in da parla dat was ula 'bout half done clean
Sat dem down an'gin ta talk.
Dar war da missy caged fa a full half hour in da
kitchen. Mr Abe called hern, then went ta look fa hern
ta intadasce hern ta da gang in da parla. Not findin'
hern hen say. I suppose, shes out mussin up something
so she can have something to straighten up, Day all laugh
hartly.
Ah war doin mah hest ta keep does boys caged up stairs
ah say Do dis an do dat ta help. When ah say. Youn
pa hab leave dat tub right in mah way. Ah started
a hulla-ballo, But ah still didn stop gabbin ta dem boys
Hen allays throw da wata out da upstairs window. Ah
can throw it far nuff, it done didn drip down on da house.

5 Ah tole da boys ah'd make dem johnny cakes (Day lacked johnny cakes wid maple syrup;) if'n day would be quiet an not scatta trash 'bout, fasta dan ah could clean.

When day got too quiet ah hab ta see what war up. Shur nuff dose two, were workin like litta scamps (dat da war) pullin' dat foot tub, so as et would be out ob my way, so ah thot. Day war whisparin' ah thot it war 'cause ah ask dem ta be quiet. Rite dare ah say, Dose two can be litta angels fa johnny cake. In less dan a shake, ah heard dat foot-tub tumblin' down dose stairs. Ah ran ta see. Dose boys war laughin' so loud, wid da noise ob da tumblin' tub; mr Abe an da missy comb tearin'.

Mr. Abe 'scuse hisn sef ta da men, an say, "Ive a little job to take care of for a second." Da missy war ringin' hern hands, Mr. Abe, gentman like say, "mother its nothing much to worry about" But put hisn han oba hern mouth, fa fear hern would rant and scream. Den hern pick up da foot-tub. Put Taddin et, an led da missy wid his arm 'roun hern, Hern knew dat war da way ta quiet hern'f hern made a little love ta her. Dat otha rowdy follow wid hern pa, ma and Taddie out ta da shed whar mr Abe lock da boys in. Kiss da missy an pat her. Den come back laughin'.

Wen hern asked da boys why day did et, day say "Well pa you'n tole us 'bout niaga Falls an da cat racks, so we war hepin Aunt Mariah and makin' dose Niaga Falls an cat racks. Dat tub war jus da boat goin' oba da falls. mr Abe say Well boys You've got the right idea, but in the wrong place. As as allus, Hern laugh split ta kill.

But dat stairs war shur ah big mess ta clean. an dry wid all da pile of oda works. All mr. Abe say war "Well thats one way of cleaning the stairs and carpet in short order". Hern nebba left hisn foot watta standin' gin. Da missy say. Dat war notha zample hern hah ta set fa hisn chilluns ta follow. Dat stairs got clean shur nuff for da parts. But mr Abe hilt.

6. Ah really don't tink, does men really knew what all the runkiss war 'bout. Mr. Abe wen back in da parla, as cool as ah cucumba. Talk, awhile Den comb out ta da hall. Gih dem dare hats from hat rack. Day wish him luck fa his 'lection ta Senate, An da door close afta dat full hour ob citement.

Mr Abe put out ta da shed ta let dose litta rascals out. No whippin, no scoldin, no do dis or do dat. But dose day war perched on he'un shoulders laughin fit ta kill, cause Jim crow war screamin ta dem come back come back. Dat crow missed dem, wen out ob sta sight, lak dey war its lost brothas. He'un kept dose two out ob da house 'til dinna playin han ball, antny oba an lord know what all. Cause dat man knew da missy war fit ta be tied, he'un war so worked up. Et just warn't possible ta leave dose boys out ob youn's sight fa a blessed minute.

When Mr. Abe did leave ta go ta da office for a spell dose boys war in da barn playin wid da little wooden wagon. Dat whole Lincohenn fambly love cats. Day had cats ob all kind. Litta kitty, baby ones nursin dare mammy and big toms. Da missy wouldn hab dem in da house do, Day had ta stay in da shed or da barn. Dis mornin, day oula a speak after Mr Abe left. Day decided ta take da mammy cat and some suckin baby kitty for a trip ta see dare brotha Robert, who war in school. Dose cats need education too. So day put dose cats Day hitch 2 toms te da tongue oh da wagon. Willie hold dem so day couldn't start off til Taddie put da motha cat an babies in. Den Willie start ta lead dose two tom cats. Bout dat time Taddie 'cided day hab betta go fasta or day wouldn't get ta school dat day, so he'un gib dat wagon a shove from da 'hind, by runnin an shoven da wagon. Ah guess dose toms that, da'bsa one hab 'cided ta fight, so day 'gin da god awfullest ruckus you'n eba did hear. Taddie run up ta hold da black

7. tom while Willie hold da strife tiga cat. Dose war big cats. Au in da tussel ta help dem cats from scratch'n each otha eyes out of dare head, dem boys got scratch on dare face au arms. Dose cats hiss au hiss at each otha. An scratch an scratch. But does boys hold au. Finely Faddie say "Willie let's make them make up. I kats what ma au pa make usn do. So they holp does toms snoots right up ta each otha to kiss. But do day kiss. No its more scratch an claw. Dis war just toomuch. So here dose boys come, screemin' to Aunt Mariah ta help. Ah threw up mah hans in plumb horrow at da sight ob dose boys. Blood all oba dare faces au arms, au clothes torn. Screemin Aust Mariah make dose blasted toms make up. Ah took both dose torments by da hans and took fa da barn. Dose cats hab broke loose da strings from da wagon au war in a real cat fight. Kissin, spittin clawin au cryin. Da tiga got da best of da fight, da ole black tom crumb up wid al clawed eyes. Ah hab ta get a buggy wip and seprate dem. Au all thru dat hell a baller dat mammy cat au her kitties layed in dat litta wagon bed as content, as if dare had been no uprloar. But cats are da laziest critters on god's green arth. Au da dumest. All day know is ta lay 'roun in folks way ta stumble oba.

Ah got dose boys back in da house. Wash dare dear litta bloody face au arms. All da missy eba saw war da torn clothes au scratches. And dat war nothin knew fa does two boys. Ah hob she seen dem 'fore ah clean dem. We'd hab ta send fa da undataka. Her'n war ready to drop wid dhot magare, au da partas fa dot day au night. Why dat woman cantsee what et war doin ta her'n is plumb alministry. All her'n tink 'bout es how their con maneuva ta get back ta da White House.

Well Mr. Abe an da missy hab jus comb back ta Springfield, from da las debate at Alton Ills. Da missy war argufyin' 'bout some mistakes mr Lincolnnn hab made, dat gave mr. Douglas da best of him. Well mr. Abe say "Mother you'll see someday, I tricked him into really asserting himself. He may become the senator, but never the President. The South will see he is really at heart not a slave man." But has been maneuvering for notes from both political parties. That Little Giant is a wonderful politicians. But I think I tripped him up this time, another thing maybe Ill be better know throughout the country. an account of the publicity given me. You see this association with Stephen A Douglas, who is already nationally and internationally know as a power, cannot help but give me some prestige as his opponent. Douglas is too smart in everyones estimation to consent to debate with anyone easy to defeat.

Shure nuff every before mr Abe were nominated fa president he war asked to speach make clean thro ta da Atlantic ocean. I just can't recommember where alls or wen. But one war Coopers Institute. An at school war Bobbie war goin in da east I guess that school didn't think day war goin to get much of a speach, wen day first saw Bobbies fatha, but after he'n spoke, dat blessed Bobbie war awfully proud of he'n. Da day wanted Mr. Abe ta speach-make more and more. Da missy got a letta afta dat from Bobbie tellin all about hisn pa' visit and how proud he war of him, and what a difference it made with hisn class mates opin of he'n.

most times da missy go long - Her'n went te Ohio ah think Columbus, Dayton an Cincinnati. Day left da boys ta home. Dare Aunt Lizbeth cook each day

2 Mary an her brotha Georgie stayt at night ah war dare most eba day. Dose boys ware ush all clean thread bare. But weins dasent punish dem

Georgie went ta day school and so did Willie. It war in da fall ob da year. Georgie didn go in Willie's class so war not pestead by Willie durin school. But da two made up fo et at night. Ah know dat Georgie war da glades boy alive when Mr Abe's comd home. Fore hay lef day eben say. No screaming ar scoldin do boys Aunt Mariah. Day say da same ta Mary. But Aunt Lisbeth made Taddie keep clean an spruced up while herin war dare. An when hen got too frisky sent het scamp ta bed or made hen sat on da kitchen chare

I herin would allus use da ketchen chars cause Taddie kicked an squrm so much hen hab all da stuffing pull out ob da betta ones.

Da messy comb back braggin' bout how siety envite dem to dare mansions in all dose Ohio places

Herin kinda got oba da tantrum 'bout Mr. Abe not being lested to Senate. Dat woman nebba got 'naugh 'ciety. Mr. Abe said onst Mother you want ta go to Washington for no other reason than to be in the highest spot in society in our land. Mrs. President. I have pula one desire to go back to Washington and that is to save the Union and do what I can fore the colored people and others who must be given a chance to rise. Dose two folks were as far apart in all thay that an strive for as noth an soth. An da sad an sorful part is day nebba nebba would be any diffarment

Mr. Abe ask da missy afta dare trip effen herin thot herin could settle down fo 'while until herin make some more money. Dat dat debate herin wid Stephin Douglas hab bout strapped hem. Dat war a hard job but herin did try ta save by oula stayin home an sewing togetha all da lace an pieces of goods herin got while away.

3 Mr. Lincolumn hab lots of work - An lots of big men in politics from all oba da country comb ta see him - Ah know dat man nebba want ta be president - Ah teh tole one man dat war dare dat heh really warn fit fa da job. But da missy agged heh on an on - Da oula rest dat man got war when heh clam up an wouldn talk or when da boys demand a rompus. Ob course da war ebba time heh step in da house. Mr. Abe still chop wood, milk da cow, feed an ten ta do horses, go on circuit, joke wid da men down town, an walk da street late at night. Most ta be alone an not be pestared. Dat war afta heh war nommnated fos President. But heh still hab heh trip to Chicago an now speach makin - Da speachin would come out in da pappa, when ah go home at night an my Henry found a pappa in da trash heh hauled ah read ta him what da pappa say bout his speach. Mah Henry near hab ah hemrig bout day slam and awful pitchas of Mr. Abe. It war a shame. Wrah Henry say dose fellows whate moke up such blasfilien pitchas should be strung up lak dy do niggas - If niggas wrote such stuff an drawd such hellish pitchas bout whites, day would be burn an cut up inch by inch - But Mr. Abe would oula laugh - But da missy hab head aches from worn. Den take paragoric - No so much as fust, but too much -

Mr. Robert comb home afta hiz pa war nominate. But da poor boy got no peace from dose two little imps. He tried ta play with them - ta keep dem home an content. Were day boy war played out an ween ta hiz room da follow. Crawl all over him. Write wid hiz pencils oba eba ting. Den scream and fight lak little demons. If dat blessed Bobbie held dare hans, da missy say he war busein dem. Finely dat poor boy hab ta lock hiz self in hiz room ta get any rest. Den dose scamp would pound on hiz door.

Mr. Robert want ta study up to go to another school

4 dat fall. He want ta go to Harvard. Hew try ta get in dare onct, but war'n g'ood 'nough. Now wid some instructin' da gave him at Exeter wid study in da summa hew could succeed. Dat poor boy rarely went anywhere Hiss old friends hew hab play wid, wen a litta like say hew hab da swell head. But war'n so. Hew couldn step out da some one ob does demcrats kids would make fun ob his pa an ma. An tell hew how Douglas hab wallup his lejin pa. An wood wallup hew 'gin fa President.

Day say eben hiss pa couldn speak good english. Dat mrs Lincolumn and hiss pa talk niger talk, mr Robert didn say words jus lak his pa an ma say dem. Hew spoke correc! Hew spent a lot of time tryin' ta get dem ta say tings differment but war no use. Both Mrs Abe and da missy did talk lak Kentuck folks, what day war

Matta Robert spent lots ob hiss time wid my Billie wen Billie war home dat summa. Hiss ma an pa war gone most all dat summa, here an dare Aunt Lisbeth ware ova ay hab the boys oba ta dare house. But Uncle Nin couldn bide dem boys. Hew say "da were ruptin hiss house, an war a bad influence for his boys an gran chillum. Et war imposs ta keep dem fromb devilment."

Once or two time dare ma an pa took one or both wid dem. Dats 'bout all da time dat blessed Bobbie hab any peac Hew try so hard ta entatain dem, but et hab ta be some debilment lak makin tick tack on da windows, or darvin' needle punches on da bottom ob dos chairs, up thro' da seats, ta stick anyones whon sat down on da seat war da darn'n needle war. Day'd pull da string an it would go tit tat on da window. An punch jams up thro' da seat. Ah do believe Mr Robert enjoy some of dat, since hew couldn bide da airs ob some of does folks dat came callin.

On time da missy hab a parta fa does whon comb to 'gratulate Mr. Abe afta hew war nominated. Et war at night an day hab put da boys ta bed. Mary da maid read ta dem until she thot day war 'sleep. But da war playin possum, When da parta got goin. Down day slip in dare red flanne

5 nighties. Out doors day go wid da tick tack on de window. Some day ladies that it war spooks from da otha worl an say et war a shuer sign ob bad luck. Maybe some one dare war goin ta die. Maybe Mr Lincolumn wouldn' be 'lected. Maybe would get 'sassinate. Mr. Abe wen out, carry dose two rascals in, an say hear our spooks. Da ladies all pulled away from dem. But as soon as one big fat gal sat down on da char wid da darnin' needle. Pull went dat string. Hern jump up an scream sayin' debils an hornets war in dat house. Mr. Abe knew but say nothin'. Ah could see him shakin' his hide off mosely, he want ah laugh so bad. Wid da boy Hen march out get a flat roun board, wen use on da clabba crocks, put it on dat char an sat right down on dat board. Da boys didn' knew, so pull da string. No punch, no stickin' from da darnin' needle, so day that da fun war oba, an put up ta bed lookin' sore but as meek as little lambs.

Ah tink Mr Abe an da missy war most awful proud ob masta Robert. Hen war quiet but such a gentman alleus. Den hen pass da examination; an day let him in Harvard. An ah tink Robert war proud of his ma an pa. But netba netba proud, da show off kind. Hen tole me one time wen he comb ta visit, hen want a go as a private in da reglar army. Hen pa want for his ma sake that he should stay out or take some easy lak an officer, unda Grant. Hen war unda Grant, but took dangerous missions. Ah knew pa would be critsiz, but ma war pos problem. Hen war a long time had in hern mind, aus war Robert to be kilt she would hab ta be put away, as Robert hab ta put her away wen she perform so in Chicago. Robert left hisn home an stay wid hern. But wen hen wen halk home ta hisn beaufal wife, da missy ran roun naked in hotel would hab gone out dat way on street if not stop, an spent money so foolish, dat poor little Taddie would be widou, fa an education. Masta Robert cried an cried he war heart broke cause da thoratives say he muss do et. His motha blame hen. But what whar dat poor poor Bobbie to do - Lisbeth eben war mad for awhile, until da missy

6 stay wid hern an hab to put up wid hern dark room. Her heaps an heaps of trunks an eben hern 'cusin' Lisbeth ob stealing hern money — Lisbeth hab ta ask Masta Robert to forgive hern then.

When Mr. Lincolumn war 'lected President, dar war 'notha change in da parade at dare home. Mr. Abe hab ta see so many politics men, an dose who want hen to git dem jobs in Washington, dat he hab to move to da state house. Da missy couldn hab dem trampin in at all hours an his'n office warn't big 'nough. Den too, dat Herndon who turn out ta be a no 'count, lying scalwag, jist as da missy allus say he war, tried eber way to ruin Mr. Abe's lection. 'Cause hen couldn hen wrote mean things 'bout da missy an eben some 'bout Mr. Abe atta da day poor Mr. Robert tried ta make Herndon take back. It hab gone too far, too many want ah balive 'bout da missy. Mr. Robert war plum crush. Eben lots ob da dirt en da office day blame on Mr. Abe war not Mr. Abe fault. Hen took da blame to shield Herndon. Truth is Mr. Lincolumn send me ta office ta clean many times. Ah would go, but ah couldn git in 'cause dat Herndon war lock in dare stone drunk. Onct ah went jist as hen war comin out — Hen say you can't go in, Am lockin up ta leave. So you'se see hen blame dat dirt on Mr. Abe. Hen da truth as shur as God is, was all Herndon dirt — Da missy plead an plead ta git rid ob dat bum an git ah nice boy hen hab come to dare home to eat, sometime. But hen say Herndon war smart an could help him. Mr. Abe done all hen could ta lift dat man out ob da gutta. Den ya see how hen pay da Lincolumns back. Hen tell jus 'nough truth ta make it all sound lak truth, Mr. Robert say. But hen pay fa et, 'cause dat onry man die in da day.

Dar war ah bunch came ta notefy Mr. Lincolumn dat hen war 'lected president — Da boys war all dress up fa da cashun. Da shook hans as these gentlman come thro' da gate. Mr. Abe met dem, an enterduce dem

7 to da missy what war in da parla, all dress up waitin. Herin plan ah litta party fa dose whon could stay dat night. Herin tole da boys ef day stay good an clean what herin woad gib dem, as pay. Day go up stairs to dare room an war as still as litta mice. Ah say da little angels, can be good ef day get what da want all da time fo it.

Well da hab chicken an some fancy fixins. Mary wait on da table. When da boys comb in at last. Dake day war wid ravel aut sock yarn tied all oba dar faces fo whiskers. Dare ma hab call dem litta men so often day 'cided ta look lake dare pa an hab whiskas what he hab grown cause a litta girl done writ him dat ef hein grow dem whiskas hein look betta, an mabe would hep hein git 'lected.

Mr. Abe war allus proud wen hein boys want ah be lak him an et please him. Day missy wouldn' scold dem 'fore company. So dare day sot eatin chicken an soup wid dem black sock yarn whiskas on.

But God in Heaben youin should ah saw doss boys wid da drippen soup an stuff from dare whiskers. Mr. Abe say they held the stage and the attention of the audience. Hen laughed and laughed 'cause they got out of commettin my self to those men. Thanks to Willie an Robbie, but da missy say as she cut off doss whiskers. You don't deserve all I was going to do for you. An until you learn how to behave I'll make you stay at home when parties are giving for your father before we leave for Washington. But ah notice Mr. Abe edged dem in, ebery place hein could whar dare war a part a

1.   <u>The Mariah Vance Story of Mistah Abe's Baptism</u>

De Missy (Mariah could not say Mrs Lincoln
always Lincolinum, when she tried), and wahs
(Prestarch instead of Presbyterian) Wal dat woman
'even says. She wah nigh up in Heaven whan she
sots in thak pew on de Sabath. Onst whan she
wah carryin on so. Mistah Abe says. Says he
'mothah caint we find uh place har, somewhah
for dat are pew, so as youse can sot in it evah da'
   Missy would beg him to jine 'em (Presbyterian church)
She shuks says it wood hep him up in de worl
Mistah Abe than und thar says mothah Ahs not
wantn to be hepped up in de worl, de way youse
sees it. Ah want to live soes Ah cain hep up. If'n
Ah cain sot on uh stow box in front uh Hoffman's
row und wid onla one uh mah unpolished common
storiés hep one uh em boys. One uh dat common
hurd as youse calls em. Uh story dat wood lead
dat boy to Christ as ah knows him. Ah'd give all mah
chances to be President, as youse so much hankers for
(This subject of church affiliation must have extended over a long period
   Yas Mistah Abe wood go to meetn sometime wid har
Don't tink he done like thar high flutin airs in dat
are church. He onst says. Eit shuks woodn't be any
hardah for dem to go down on thar knees, dan to do
all dat bow'n and scrapin, nothah time he says, Ah
sometimes wondah if'n it are uh church or uh circus
thar all decked out in so much trappens und perform so.
   He shuks knowd of thak onpaid bills, For he says
mothah how cain dose folks goes out und make
sich uh show in onpaid finery? Und others thar
are robben thar home folks uh bread, meat und
milk, fust to make a show.

2. He allahs wanted to be babsized. He done promise his mothah, whan uh little tike way back thar in Indiani, whan he was old nuff to knows de meanings, he wood be babsized. Und dem ole Presterahs don't go by bein dunked down undah watah. Und Missy says Dats' back wood now. Sides Mistah Abe has shamed hah und de boys nuff wid hisn old fangled ways.

Onst he says to me Mariah do you thunk et has hepped save youse soul to be babsized. Yas Ah says mistah Abe. Et shure allahs make me knowd Ah done one ting Christ done did. He late John babsize him in de Rivah Jordan. He shuke mus thought dat it was good. So ahs dat good. Yas, Mistah Abe says. Et show youse air in ernes bout youse soul. Youse wants youse sins washed ahs clean ass watah can make youse body

Uhfew days aftah dat he says, mariah Ahs gwinen to be babsized. Do youse tink et wood be sinful if ahd be babsized und not let on to Missy Lincolnmum.

Now Ahm not ashamed, but shell done raise Ned und Und wid dat worry on mah mind ah don't tink dat wood be uh good way to go to youse babsism. Sides like ahs not wood start up in her haid notha misery. Ahs got too big uh load now to tackle gitten ovah dat, und still try to has de mind dat war also in Christ Jesus, whan Ah goes to mah babsism. Nothah ting dat bothahs me uh heap mariah gossipe und sight seers most likely to come in mobs, not to reverence but to mock und begile mah tensions. Ah don't like show of any kind whah et cain be hepped Ah'd liken to knowd jest as how to hep et. mariah youse a good haid for planen. Jes how cain Ah babsize so as mothah won't be upsot. Somewhat of uh crowd is boun to congrate. Ah says, Mistah Abe. Youse can thunk und thunk but thahs onlah jest one way. Youse got to go et night.

He jest stood thar und stared et me. Ah jest knowd Ahd given him uh terbul shock. He wah de saddes looken

3. critter ah most evah sot eyes on in mah life. ah thought he war goin to bust out cryin. He jest walked off mutterin — God Hep Us, Ah says, Hallah Lulya Mr. Abe.

In ah little while, hah he comes to the kitchen und more cheeri like says, mariah you done saved de day faw me. Ahe not gwinnin to Washington widout doin all ah e can to keep this won of Christs' mandments. Ah couldn't spect God to hep me lead de nation so full of woes if ah failes him. Ah'll write to Parson Elkins (I've always thought, espacially since I read somewhere that Elkins was the name of the minister who presided at his mother grave that Mariah got the names mixd. Perhaps he, if still living after 40 years, was around 70 years old. He could have been a very young minister when he came to preach sermon at Lincolns' mother grave In that case it might possibly have been the same minister who come to Springfield to baltize him and have him come if he will — Let's pray he will (He must have had in mind a very large minister because he said) Anyone of dese parsons round har could let me down in de Rivah, but none I'd be sartain could highst me up. Now mariah, it's jest got a be uh little secret twixt all of us'n und ah God.

Ah jest says right thar und then to mistah Abe Yes sah. Ah says. Ah swan mistah Abe youse nevva need be jumpy. Ah wont evah even tell mah Henry — He'd look et me und scowl onery like, an say Better mind youse own nitten und stop mouthen otha folks complaints. Und to dis very live long day Aho nevvah onst tole a sole but youse (meanin me und I believed her) (I've learned since that the minister did tell of the baltism years later — After Lincolns' death, Possibly after Mrs. Lincoln death. Later I will give an Account of the baltism, as told by Rev Ankrum and will write a copy of the letter written to me by Anna Deal in which she relates the story of the baltism as told to her by her father David E Wagoner)

4. We uns nevooh talkes it ovah no more til wan mornin, ~~only wan~~ cold mornen, Ah alleys went orly, ~~de days~~ wah gitten so short. Ah war totew mah last young-un wid me dat morven

Mistah Abe war nevva ~~wh~~ one to git up orly, but ah swan thar he war long de plank way out front. Hid his haid down, ponderin und consederin. Ah went onto ~~the~~ shed und tucked mah young-un in. Ah wahs straiten up ~~de~~ kitchen fust. Et war sich ah teeny cubby hole, aftaa de missy changed de hole house 'roun', things jest got in ah fierce pile wid de left ovah dishes to do. Ah war on mah way out to de shed to git some soft soap whan mistah Abe cum up. He kinda sad like says mothah has de misery agin. Ah gave her some pery goric. She's most quiet now. Wal Ah knowd good und well she war in ah tantrums. Poor missy she war ~~wh~~ sick sick woman in har haid. Wal sah aar wahs nothin in dis liven worl to stop dat streak in her cept peri goric. No sir E.

Ah cleared way all de soil und done fixed mistah Abe some breakfast. Ah fried some mush cakes. He shur liked mush cakes und sargam. He jest didn't want more. He ate ~~ah~~ bit und shoved his chah back on de two back legs.

Wal he says, Mariah Ah done bin babsized. He didn't says more for some bit. Ah says mistah Abe, wants youse to tells me how it all comes off? ~~Wal~~ says he the Rev. Elkins(?) comes in de night time und babsized me und went back in de night time. He ~~wha~~ didn't go the reglar cow path jest waded persismnns, scrub, hazel brush und wild grapevine. Ah jest knew, if dat parson felt as Ah did he wah as glad to git in dat ~~thar~~ hivah as ah. Now Mariah teh aint meannig ah warn't pondering und considerin But I awake

5. de nettles war thicker on us dan dog fleas on Rover.

Ah und dat parson haid a mighty sacred charge to kape, und deep inside of me Ah was praying. Now Ah raily praise mah Lord und mah God Ah took de right step. You knows Mariah many weeds has to be tramped to reach de right path. Ah say to Mistah Abe Glory to God Allileuya

Den he said mah mothah was ah Babtist. Ah haid ah Babtist parson to say words ovah her body back dar in Indiani und ahs shuah she wood like it if'n she knowd Ah haid uh Babtist parson to Babsize me. Yah knows what Mariah I feels free now. Ah knows God will watch ovah me und do all fou de best

Mrs Lincolinum thought Ah war wid Billy (Herdon) I hats all ah regrets. Ah caint tells her wah Ah was.

After ah cleaned and prepared dining ah went to de barn for de mule und cart, und dar war mistah Abe's wet shoes, shirts long underware und pants hang'n up dry. De next time Ah returns to do de washn, de clothes was down fruem de nails war dey hung, in de barn, und der war 1 shirts und 2 suits uv long underwar in de wash to do. De ones dat hung in de barn

Ah knows day war de same he gets babsized in.
And according to Anna Deals account of the Babtism, told to her by her father, which follows, mr Lincoln did supply the minister, clothing, for the Babtism

was never ah one to get up early, but soon thar he was long the plankway in front with his head down ponderen and consideren. Ah went on to the shed and tucked my young un in. Ah was straighten up the kitchen. It was such a little cubby hole after the missy changed the whole house aroun. Sting jist got in a fierce pile with the dirty dishes left over to do. Ah was on mah way out to the shed to get some soft soap when mr. Abe came up. and he knid a sad like says. Mother has a misery agin. Ah gave her some pery goric and she's most quiet. Ah knows good and well she was in a tantrum. Poor missy she wahs a sick, sick woman in her haid. Well ah thear was nothin in this leveen worskd to stop that streak in her but pery goric. No sir e.

Ah cleared away all the soil and fixed mr. Abe some breakfast. I fried some mush cakes. He liked mush cakes and sorgan. He didnt want mare. He ate a bit and shoved his chair back on the 2 back laigs — Wal he said Mariah Ah done hin babsiged. He didnt say more faw some bit, Ah says mr. Abe. Wants you to tell me hown it all comes off? Wal says he the Rev Parson came at night time and babsiged me and went back at night time. We didnt go the regular road cow path but waded, Jeramm hazel brush and wild grape vines — Ah jest know if that parson felt as I done did he was as glad to git in that thar rivah as ah. for the nettles war thicker than coalfles on rover. Now mariah taint meanin warent ponderen and consideren all respects the charge to keep Ah and that are parson had. Ah really praise my Lord and ma God I took the right path. You knows Mariah many weeds have to be trampled in to reach the right path. Mah mothe was a Babtist, I had a Babtist minister to preach over her body back in Indiani and I wah sher she would like it if Ah had a Babtist parson to babsige me. Ya know what Mariah I feel free now. Ah know God will watch ovah me an do all for the best. Mariah Mother that I war with Billie. Thats all I regret I caint tell her whar I was or shed have worse ah misery

Onst he says to me, "Mariah do you thunk it has hepped to save you soul to be babsized." "Yes I says Mr. Abe sure allahs made me know I done did one ting Christ done did. He let John babsize him in the Rivah Jordon. He must sure that it was good." "Yes, Mr Abe says, It shows you ahs in ernest bout you soul. You want you sins washed ahs clean ahs watah can make you body."

A few days after that he says, "Mariah Ahs goin to be babsized. Do you thunk it would be sinin if Ah'd be babsized an not let on to Mrs. Lincolumn(?)? Now Ah'm not shamed, but shell raise Ned, and Ah don't thank that ares a good way to go to youse babsiging. Sides it might like as not start up a misery in mother's laid. Ahs got too big a load now to tackle getten over that are, an still try to have the mind that wares also in Christ Jesus when Ah goes to mak babsism. Brother thing that are bothah me Mariah is how gossips an sight seers would come in mobs, not to reverence but to mock an begile my tentions. Ah don't like show of any kind whar it can be hepped; Ah'd like to know now how to hep it.

"Mariah youse a good laid for planen. Furst, jest how can ah be babsized so mothah won't be upset. Somewhat of a crowd is boun to congrate."

Ah says Mr. Abe — "You can thunk an thunk but thar's oulah jest one way — You ares got a go at night." He jest stood thar an stared at me. Ah jest knows it gave him a shock. He wahs the saddest looken crittah ah most evah did sot eyes on in mah life. Ah that he war goin to bust out cryin. He jest walked off sayin "God Self Us" I said "Hallah Lukya Mr. Abe."

In a little while here he comes to the kitchen an more cherie like says "Mariah you done saved the day for me, Ahs not gwinin to Washington without doin all ah can to keep this one of Christ commandments. Ah couldn't 'spect God to hep me lead a nation so full of woes if I failed him. Ah'll write to (Parson Elkins) here — I supplied Parsons since she had forgotin the names and have him come if he will. Lets pray he will. He must have had in mind a very large Parson because he said, "Anyone of these

The Last Time Aunt Mariah Ever Saw Mr. Abe

I asked Mrs. Vance if see ever saw Mr. Lincoln or any of his family after the Vance family moved from Springfield to Danville. She said Oh yes. The reason I asked, was because a number of people had tole me that Mr Lincoln had called for her, if in the crowd as the presidential train stopped at Danville, on these trip to Washington. Others had said she made a trip to Washington to have her husband released from the army as he was so much needed at home, That at the time she was in Washington Mrs. Lincoln refused to see her. According to Mariah Vances answer to these reports, which I am convinced she truthfully answered, she said, Ok yes, Ah seed Mr. Abe once.

Youin see weuns left Springfild shortly after Mr. Abe war 'lected in November. Mah Henry hab got work in da mine out side Danville. Hen'ry mah Billie, hab gone on wid a load ob plunda. Den Billie came back for us. Youin see da whole countra war in a mess. President Buchanan cause hen war goin out, an 'cause lot in Washington unda hen war fo slavery, he just sot theze on nary try to stop dat war what war brewn. So da colored folks most all moved fatha narth, as we'd planned afore.

No Mr. Abe nevva call fors men or any ob ah fambly as da president train stop here (Danville). He an' maslah Robert hab comb to Danville 'bout Christmas time in 1860. Day stop at da Ætna House if ah rightly member, fo some meetin wid some big men in politics an friends. One war Dr. Fifthian ah memba. 'Bout noon on dat day, ah messnga boy bring a telgram to ourn house. Ah tellin' you ah war shur mah Henry hab ben kill or hurt in da mine. But da telgram war from Mrs. Abe. Sayin (on a slip) ob paper hen hab sent by dis messenger boy. "Am at this hotel fora short time. Robert is with me. I would like for you and Bill to come between 3 o'clock and four. We will be very, very disappointed if you dont come. Give messenger your ans. With Esteem. A Lincoln and Robert

2. Well Billie hab comb in for dinna. Hen war doin somb work fo da Steglers. Dat war a nice rich fambly who hab made money en da smelta works. Da war German folks. All da German folks war good to usn. Seems as how since I recomemba 'gin — Dat war fore da Stegler work. Maybe et war some street work mah Bill war doin. ~~Anyhow~~ Work or starve, nothin, not a soul ling on dis earth, could ah kept Billie away fromb goin ta see mastah Robert. When weins move here, Mr Robert war in some school in da east. Either Phillips "Cadamy" at Exeter ~~N Hampshire~~ or Harvard. So Billie hab ta comb away widout a sight of dat blessed Bobbie.

Weins dressed in our best clothes. Ah comb da braids out ova mah head an made mah hair neat, as if if hab bees way on it. Billie slick up too, Right at 3 'clock sharp we reach da steps up ta da door ob ~~that~~ Hotel. Mr Abe an masta Robert almost run down da step ta meet us. Ah-shot Billie and Bobbie war goin ta kiss, Dose two Lincolumns war sheer pleasured ta see us ~~agin~~. Just smilen an laughin an shaken han. Lik no ones war on dis 'arth but da Vances. An lak no white folks war 'round gapin. Like day hab nevva saw da like afore. Right dare an den ah knew President or no fresdent, nothin would eba change Mr Abe an Bobbie. Dey would neba on dis form 'arth eba get da swell head. Ef fresdent wouldn' carese it, nothin would.

Wall Bobbie put his'n dear arm 'round Billie neck an say Well go into the lobby an visit. We would have come ta your home, but pa has such a short time to get his business settled here, and see those he must see. Pa, thot it best to give you the time it would take going to and from your home.

Mr Abe took me by da arm lak Ah war da Queen of Sheba an hep me up da steps. Eba one en dat Hotel lobby gap. So Mr. Abe took me to each man an a few women dare seated in a king a circle an intaduced me as a very fine colored lady who hab lived in da Lincoln home fa 2 years. Ah notice he didn' say servant or wash woman. Den

3, Bobbie, stan up an say an this is my bes friend Billie Vance. Mr. Abe asked about mah Henry an each one ab da youngins. Said he would love to see them all, but just didn have the time. Ah ask him 'bout Willie an Taddie an da missy. He said Willie and Taddie coaxed to come along. But mother, who is the busiest woman this side of Washington, couldn' manage to get them ready and I suspect she needed them for company.

Several men came up an shook hands with Mr. Abe, 'gratelated hen. Hen only say a few words ta each, until hen got thro visiting wid um. Da men what hen war dare in Danville ta see comb in. Some ob dem lak gone out, den come back in lak da war anxious fa Mr. Abe ta be wid dem. But Mr. Abe war alles a poke easy. He tole dem men ta stay right dare hed he wid dem shortly. Den he say ta Billie - Bill I have only one desire before I go back to Springfield and that is ta hear you sing again. Den hen say ta so many 'hind da desk. Would you mind if we listen ta Bill is willing, for him to sing for us. Bill has according to my opinion one of the most beautiful voices God ever gave to anyone. Billie nevva war skeered ta sing. He got out ob dat char in ah shake. Billie war alles quick 'bout eber ting. Hen didn' wait to hear wat Mr. Lincoln want ta hear. Hen just up an sing da Mocking Bird Song an whistle like dat bird all thro da song when hen warn't speakin da words. Youn could hear a pin drop, dey just stood round, spell boun. Den hen knew Mr. Abe like - "Ah's on my Road ta Glory Now" an say quit clappin fu as Mocking Bird hen start singin "Ah's on mah Road" makin all da jesture. Mr. Abe say when day all quit clappin. Some laughin an some cryin (Mr. Abe an Bobbie too) maybe were all on our way to Glory Bill. But kinda perkin up afta he say dat, hen say Am I not right when I say Bill has a God-given beautiful voice somun dat on Bill war call ta sing most eba whar. Before wen start back home, Mr. Abe gave Bill some money. Ah don' memba how much an git men a basket ob fruit. From dat on ah had all da work

4. from da rich an fine folk, ah could do. Dat war
'Bout goin ta Washington, Ah nevva did go, but
mah Ellen went, for ta get Mr Abe to let her man
comb home. Herin didn want ef see Mrs Lincolumn
my Ellen war allus skeered of da messy, so
da messy couldn hab refused ta see Ellen, not me,
I bet herin would ah want ta see me.

As far seein Robert ahs tole you he comb ta
see usn when in Danville. You know peoples
will tell the God awfullest lies about does poor Lincolumns